The First

28 Years of

MONTY

PYTHON

D0117804

The First
28⅞ Years of

MONTY
PYTHON

Kim "Howard" Johnson

St. Martin's Griffin · New York

Monty Python's royalty from this book will go to the Rainforest Action
Network to contribute toward the replenishment of rain forests cut down
to produce this edition.

All sketches and other original Monty Python material are reproduced by permission of Python Productions Ltd., the owner of all rights in such material, none of
which may be used or reproduced in any manner whatsoever without written
permission.

THOMAS DUNNE BOOKS.
An imprint of St. Martin's Press.

BOOK DESIGN BY CAROL MALCOLM RUSSO/SIGNET M DESIGN, INC.

Library of Congress Cataloging-in-Publication Data

Johnson, Kim, 1955–
    The first 280 years of Monty Python/Kim "Howard" Johnson.—
[rev.ed.]
        p.   cm.
    The number in the title on t.p. is given as 280 with an X through the 0.
    ISBN 0-312-16933-7
    1. Monty Python (Comedy troup)   I.Title.
PN2599.5.T54J64   1999
791.45'028'0922—dc21
[B]   97-23627

FIRST EDITION: MAY 1999

10 9 8 7 6 5 4 3 2 1

This second edition is dedicated

to the next generation of Python fans,

and especially Morgan Edward Johnson,

my own wonderfully fierce creature,

with lots of love.

Contents

Foreword

The *First 28X Years of Monty Python* by Kim "Howard" Johnson has got to be the greatest book ever written. I particularly like the writing in it—it has lots of writing in it, and another thing I like is the color of the outside jacket. It's "really" great. The typeface is particularly good—very good, and I like this book much more than Salman Rushdie's book which had larger type and was not about Monty Python (well not much of it was about Monty Python). A great work by a truly great writer, and "Howie" Johnson will be remembered long after other great writers have been forgotten for his contribution to the fast food industry.

GEORGE HARRISON

Preface

Kim "Howard" Johnson has been pestering us for years, coming round "interviewing" us, asking "questions" and generally writing damn-fool "things" about "Python." Now he is "publishing" it all for "money." Well what else can you expect from a man who sticks quotation marks in the middle of his name? Still, good luck to him, though I don't think Boswell will be turning in his grave. . . . At least now you have a chance to see what we've had to put up with all these years. The patience of saints, I'd call it. Beats me why anybody'd write a book about Python, let alone read it. Have they nothing better to do? Are they all mad? Is this enough words for a Foreword? Is the cheque in the Post?

John Cleese once told me he'd do anything for money: so I offered him a pound to shut up. And he took it. 'Nuff said.

—ERIC IDLE
LONDON, APRIL 1989

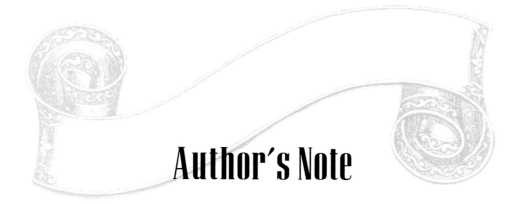

Author's Note

In keeping with the finest American tradition, when I was a kid, I ran away from home to join the circus. This, however, was a flying circus, and it was run by Monty Python. So much for tradition.

Actually, I started watching *Monty Python's Flying Circus* almost from its first American broadcast. I was flipping through the dial when I accidentally came upon a still picture of the larch tree. This segued into a town full of Supermen where the local hero was a bicycle repairman, a children's show host reading the youngsters rather twisted tales, and a very bizarre restaurant. I was hooked. It wasn't *The Ed Sullivan Show*.

Word of mouth was spreading, and the show soon became PBS's top-rated entertainment program. By the time *Monty Python and the Holy Grail* opened in 1975, the group had developed a sizable core of fans, and the team flew into New York to promote the film. During the publicity tour, I met Terry Jones and Graham Chapman very briefly at a Chicago theater appearance, and wrote to the pair of them afterward. Terry invited me to New York early the next year, when the group would be performing at the City Center. He took me backstage before the show, and I had the opportunity to meet the entire group.

Slowly but surely, I began amassing information about the group with clippings, photos, letters, and whatever other materials I came across. In early 1978, I put out the first of a three-volume Python fanzine (highlighted by a phone interview I did with Michael Palin while he was working on *Saturday Night Live*), which was the forerunner of this book. Response from the Pythons themselves was most encouraging and flattering; at the end of his letter, Michael Palin foolishly stated "If you're ever in London, look me up." I left the next month. While in London, I visited nearly all of the group as they were preparing to leave for Tunisia to shoot *Life of Brian*. I eventually ended up going to Africa for the main portion of the filming, living and working with them on location—truly a once-in-a-lifetime experience.

During the subsequent years, I have done numerous interviews with the Pythons for magazines and

radio, attended and participated in the Hollywood Bowl shows, and gotten to know the group members personally and professionally. Thanks to them all, the results are in these pages.

Since my original contacts with the Pythons, I have gone on to various writing and performing projects. Somehow, Monty Python has been responsible, either directly or indirectly, for most of my successes.

We all have gurus in our lives who help us along the way, providing advice, encouragement, or opportunities. Most of the time, however, we aren't able to pay them back for all their help. This book is one small attempt, a twentieth birthday present, to thank the Pythons for all of the guidance, inspiration, and above all, laughs.

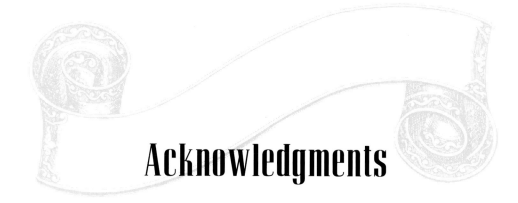

Acknowledgments

This exhaustive (and exhausting) look at the Python television shows would not have been possible without the assistance of many people. First and foremost are John Cleese, Terry Gilliam, Eric Idle, Terry Jones, Michael Palin, and the late Graham Chapman for their support, encouragement, time and friendship. Also essential for her assistance was Anne James and everyone else at Mayday Management past and present, particularly Steve Abbott, Alison Davies, Kath James, Ralph Kamp, Roger Saunders, Kristen Whiting, and Jim Yoakum, as well as Henrietta Fellows and Amanda Montgomerie.

Thanks are also due to Charles Alverson, Rebecca Barrett, Connie Booth, Carol Cleveland, Jeanna Crawford, Alyce Faye Eichelberger, Maggie Gilliam, John Goldstone, George Harrison, Neil Innes, Alison Jones, Tania Kosevich, Charles McKeown, Lorne Michaels, Helen Palin, Hazel Pethig, David "the Widow Chapman" Sherlock, and Barry Took. Gracias to all at Cornerstone Communications, Kenzer & Co., and 7th Level, as well.

A misty-eyed hail and farewell to others who have left us—Harvey Kurtzman, Harry Nilsson, Don Thompson, and John Tomicek.

Special thanks also go to my agent, Dominick Abel, who always believed, and to Tom Dunne and Pete Wolverton at St. Martin's Press, who took what I gave them and made it better. Thanks to the Python fans who kept me on my toes and continue to pass on clippings, news and gossip: Steve Bursten, Roland Coover, Jr., Barbara McCoury, Valerie Miller, Dana Snow, Maggie Thompson, Eric Zorn, and the incredibly reliable Tom Mason. And devout fans looking for more must look to PythOnline, and a wonderful bibliography and electronic newsletter edited by Hans ten Cote (see www.pythonline.com/bibliog and www.pythonline.com/llama. Both are linked to PythOnline, an award-winning Web site that is, quite simply, the best place on the Net!).

And where would I be without the usual suspects—the Baron's Barracudas, Diane Burroughs, Mike Carlin, Del Close, Max Allen Collins, Mark Evanier, Jeff Garlin, Mike and Linda Gold, Bob Greenberger,

Joey Gutierrez, Tim Kazurinsky, Michael McCarthy, David McDonnell and the whole gang at *Starlog*, Bob Odenkirk and David Pasquesi, as well as the Armstrong, Dunavan, Hall, and Stouffer families?

Of course, continued thanks to my mother, Marge Johnson, and my late father, Kenneth Johnson, who probably enjoyed the success of the first edition even more than me, which will always be a source of tremendous pride for me.

And the biggest thanks of all are to my beloved wife, Laurie Bradach, who always seems to know when to help me with my writing and when to leave me alone. Without her, this second edition would have never been finished. And yes, sweetheart, now that I'm finished, I promise to clean out the office . . .

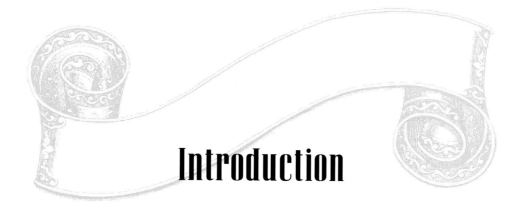

Introduction

It has now been almost thirty years since *Monty Python's Flying Circus* was first broadcast to a small portion of the world. In its original late-night time slot on the BBC, where it was often pre-empted (or not run at all in the provinces), it slowly but surely took hold of an influential segment of the British public, a following that gradually began to grow.

From such humble beginnings (Michael Palin claims their first viewers were insomniacs, intellectuals, and burglars), Python gradually became a phenomenon. Their TV shows were popular around the world, while their films became critical and box-office hits.

Even more important is the way Python shaped and changed comedy for a new generation of viewers. The original shows sideswiped traditional TV conventions—there were no guest stars, very little music, and the sketches did not always have a beginning, middle, or end—at least not in that order.

Even stranger was the form the shows developed—there was very much a stream-of-consciousness approach to each program; any given show was linked by means both obvious and subtle, including Terry Gilliam's animations. Characters from one sketch could turn up much later in a different sketch; performers could step out of character and talk to the camera. And, lest the shows be deemed a triumph of style over substance, it should be noted that the group broke new comedic ground in their use of such less-than-traditional themes as cannibalism, royalty, and dismemberment. They waged a battle with the BBC over their innovative use of sex, violence, and language.

As brilliant as the subsequent films, records, and stage shows are, it is the forty-five TV shows that established Monty Python as one of the most significant comedic forces in decades. These shows are full and rich in their material, and represent a high-water mark in British comedy. *Monty Python's Flying Circus* was to British TV comedy in the '70s what *Beyond the Fringe* was to British stage comedy in the '60s, or *The Goon Show* to British radio comedy in the '50s. Although *All in the Family* and *Sanford and Son* were based on English TV shows, Python was the first British comedy successfully broadcast intact in America. It was

seen and noticed by the creators of such shows as *Saturday Night Live* and *Cheers*, and has had its effect on countless writers and performers in the years since.

Python only ended—or appeared to end—with the death of Graham Chapman on October 4, 1989. Though he did not live to see the first edition, it is a source of great pride that he was able to see the completed manuscript and was very happy with the result. Graham gave very generously of his time while I was preparing the book, and I owe him for that and for so much more.

When my agent, Dominick Abel, and publisher, Tom Dunne, approached me with the idea of doing an updated second edition to *The First 20X Years of Monty Python*, I wasn't sure that I would find enough material to make it worthwhile. After all, Python had ceased functioning as an active entity by 1989, and the only new material would seem to be a final tribute to Graham and some comments on his passing.

But as I again delved into Pythonland, I began turning up facts and information that offered more than a postscript to the first edition. The Pythons were nice enough to submit to additional, often extensive interviews, as did Carol Cleveland, the longest interview I've yet done with her. I added a lengthy, detailed section on the pre-Python days and expanded and updated the entries on the individual Pythons, sometimes cannibalizing from my own *Life (Before and) After Monty Python* material that should probably have been included in these pages originally. The effort is capped with an extensive bibliography of audio, video, and print works by the Pythons. I have attempted to make the result, which you are now holding in your hands, the definitive overall look at the Pythons and their works gathered between two covers.

Of course, just when it seemed that Monty Python was a closed book that could be put on the shelf, the Pythons themselves characteristically threw us a welcomed curve. PythOnline was unveiled, presenting new and rarely seen material by all of the Pythons, including news, games, a shopping channel, and much more. And today, the remaining five members continue to talk about another project together, though what form it could take—film, stage show, or something completely different—is anyone's guess.

In March 1997, Terry Gilliam, Terry Jones, and Michael Palin (with John Cleese and Eric Idle making pre-recorded appearance on tape) were presented with the Empire Inspiration Award by Elton John, "for a lifetime of comedic inspiration to generations of people across the world." The future almost inevitably seems to hold more such tributes to them, as the world acknowledges their comedic importance. There is a strange irony here, life imitating art, as the group that used to spoof British awards shows is feted at just such an event. As uncomfortable as it may make some of the individual Pythons, however, there is every justification for this and future awards.

And in January 1998, Monty Python truly entered the final frontier. When astronaut Andy Thomas

was launched into space for a stay abroad the Russian space station, he carried with him the *Monty Python's Complete Waste of Time* CD-ROM. He called it "the ideal piece of equipment for a flight on Mir."

As in the first edition, this volume is an effort to salute those forty-five classic shows that are still seen daily in America and around the world, as well as the films, books, and records that followed. As much as is possible, the Pythons themselves discuss in their own words the concepts, writing, and performing that went into their series. Although in some cases one recollection may contradict another, each has been recorded as faithfully as possible, in hopes that the individual perceptions will prove enlightening. The interviews and research have continued for over two decades, and ultimately this book would not have been possible without the ongoing support of the group members themselves over the years.

KIM "HOWARD" JOHNSON
FEBRUARY 1998

X i X

Part One

THE GATHERING STORM

Before the Beginning

Growing Up Middle-Middle Class

THE SIX INDIVIDUALS who would become Monty Python grew up in postwar Britain, with the exception of American Terry Gilliam, too young to experience much of the devastation of World War II (although Graham Chapman wrote in his autobiography of seeing "bits of people hanging from trees" following an aircraft explosion when he was three years old).

Times were tight and rationing was relatively common following the war, not unlike the times depicted in Michael Palin's *A Private Function*. Still, the Pythons lived a comfortable lifestyle Palin referred to as "middle-middle class, with aspirations to upper-middle class." Gilliam also enjoyed a middle-class lifestyle during his first years in Minneapolis, moving to California when he was eleven years old.

It was that middle-class existence that may have laid the foundation for their comic attitudes, expos-

Things to come? John Cleese (front row, second from right) sits next to a boy called Andrew Parrot in this Clifton College football team photo. Photo from the Collection of John Cleese, used by permission.

ing them to a widespread respect and a comfortable adherence to conformity that fed their rebellious natures. In other words, it gave them something to rebel against, but not in a meanspirited way. In fact, it was

quite the opposite—for all of the silliness and sometimes shocking sketches in Python, there was still a gentleness to most of the humor that was discarded only during occasional satirical moments.

There were a few indications even during their childhood that the comic potential was there. Palin often tells of his stage debut when he was five years old; while playing Martha Cratchit in *A Christmas Carol,* he fell off the stage. John Cleese theorizes that he began making people laugh as a defense mechanism; he was six feet tall when he was twelve years old and made jokes in order to feel less of an outsider. And Gilliam remembers

being a fanatical reader of *Mad* magazine and hiding it from his parents in their garage.

It was at college, however, that their comedic talents were truly honed. Cleese, Chapman, and Eric Idle gravitated toward Cambridge University. There, the Footlights society, famed for producing David Frost and *Beyond the Fringe,* held a strong attraction for the trio. Palin and Terry Jones likewise wound up at Oxford and became involved with the theatrical world there. On the other side of the ocean, Gilliam continued cartooning when he arrived at Occidental College in California, but none of them could have guessed what was to come.

Cambridge University

Cambridge University held a certain allure for would-be actors, writers, and humorists in the early 1960s. Although the school's Footlights society had been in existence since 1883, the club had just mounted its most successful revue to date.

The 1960 Footlights show, *Beyond the Fringe,* was written and performed by Peter Cook, Dudley Moore, Alan Bennett, and Jonathan Miller; the show ran for years in London's West End and on Broadway, and revitalized satire in Great Britain. Its creators, like the future Pythons, were all fans of Spike Milligan's *The Goon Show,* which was presented during the 1950s on BBC-Radio. Created and performed by Spike Milligan, Harry Secombe, and Peter Sellers, its anarchic, unconventional humor and wordplay provided a heavy influence on the then-teenage Pythons.

Chapman, Cleese, and Idle did not attend Cambridge primarily for the Footlights, however. Chapman was going to study medicine, Cleese was a law student, and Idle planned to study English. Their plans took a detour, this time by way of a circus that was not yet flying.

Graham Chapman was the first of the future Pythons to arrive at Cambridge, where he continued his medical studies at Emmanuel College. Although he didn't make it into the Footlights during his first year (he was turned down by the club's secretary, David Frost, who explained that aspiring members had to be invited to audition), he teamed up with another student and they put on their own smoker.

"There were only twenty-five undergraduate

performers of this club (the Footlights) each year, and in order to join it, you had to be asked to do an audition," explained Chapman many years later. "In other words, you had to be noticed somewhere around the place doing something funny, performing or something. Then you were asked to audition in front of a few members of the committee, and if you were good enough for them you were allowed to audition at a smoking concert.

"Now, a smoking concert is a strange thing. It originated when the gentlemen retired after dinner and were entertained—in various ways, I imagine, but this was not like that," he laughed. "None of that stuff, none of that at all! This was not your nude ladies, this was nothing at all to do with them.

"This was really a group of people trying to be entertaining to their fellow members of the club. If the auditionees at one of these smoking concerts entertained the people sufficiently, they were then allowed to join the club. And that was done on a strict voting basis, so you could really keep out a lot of people! It was possible to keep it down to about six members a year, by which you would ensure yourself a place in the annual revue."

Footlights members who saw their show invited them to audition, and Chapman became a member his second year at Cambridge, inducted at the same time as first-year law student Cleese. For them both—and the other Footlights members—the annual revue was the highlight of the year.

"The annual revue had quite a professional standard of budget, so it was a worthwhile thing

to be in. There were a lot of little extras," noted Chapman. "Because of the smoking concerts—and we had about two of those every term, and we had all these people auditioning—that meant there was a lot of material being produced, a lot of material being written, and a lot of people performing in all sorts of different ways to try to get into this damned revue each year. That meant that the actual revue itself had quite a reasonable standard. It was a semiprofessional sort of thing, and a lot of people went on from that into entertainment. It was like a separate college, in a way."

John Cleese had finished up at Clifton College and then passed the entrance exam for Cambridge's Downing College, but it was two years before he was able to enroll. In a move that calls to mind his Monty Python schoolmaster character, he went back and taught at his old prep school during that period.

"I completed public school at the age of eighteen and then taught for two years without a thought of a career in comedy, except that when I'd done a house entertainment at Clifton in my last year, somebody said 'Oh, when you go to Cambridge, you must join the Footlights.' I said 'Oh, must I? Who are they?' "

In view of this encouragement, Cleese indeed decided to try to join the Footlights, but like Chapman, he was also rejected the first time.

"When I went up to Cambridge over two years later, I did stop at the Footlights desk and ask about the club. They said 'Do you sing?' I was worst singer in Europe, fourteen years in a row. So I said 'No,' and they said 'Oh, never mind. Do you dance?' My jaw dropped and I went red, and said 'No,' They said 'Well, what do you do?' and I said 'I suppose I try to make people laugh.' And I said something else, and just retired in confusion."

Fortunately, a friend of his had been asked to write some pieces for the club, and he asked Cleese to collaborate with him. When the pair presented the sketches to the group, the law student found himself elected to the Footlights.

"Nothing happened at all until Alan Hutchinson—he's my closest friend now, we met my second day at Cambridge—came up to me halfway through the year and said 'I've bumped into an old school friend who helps to run the Footlights. Would you like to do a sketch with me, and we can both get in it?' We wrote something together and performed it, and we were both elected. Subsequently I did some sketches and gradually began to get the hang of it, although it took me several attempts to write—I didn't have the slightest idea what I was doing.

"It was a friendly enough club. By the time I was halfway through my second year, I was beginning to show one or two glimmerings of talent. By the time I got to my third year, I was writing some sketches that were really quite good."

Graham Chapman had been at Cambridge a year before John Cleese enrolled, and the future writing partners met through the Footlights.

"I think the two of us met at the end of my first year, so I suppose I'd been in the Footlights for about a term, and didn't really know anyone yet," recalls Cleese.

"I vaguely remember my first meeting with Graham, and funny enough, my main impression was I didn't like him much! I think we met at some sort of audition, and we went out afterwards and had a cup of coffee and a tea cake together. I didn't feel very comfortable with him, and I didn't find him likable. But I seemed just to forget that, and as we started to see each other on a more regular basis, we were just sort of drawn to write together. I don't ever remember whether he suggested it to me, or I to him, but we became a regular writing partnership to the extent when, if anybody came into my room and saw a pad of paper and a pencil and an open Bible, they would say accusingly, "You've been writing a sketch with Graham again!"

"I suppose all together, we probably wrote a dozen top-drawer sketches while we were at Cambridge. We did start writing in 'sixty-two. We wrote a mountaineering sketch for the *Footlights Revue* of that year, and several other things with other people, with three or four people writing some of those sketches. Then Graham went off, having finished a year earlier than me, and did medicine at Bart's while performing cabaret in the evening with a guy called Tony Hendra.*"

Neither Cleese nor Chapman were cast in the revue their first year, but they appeared together onstage for the first time in mid-1962 in *Double*

*Hendra later became the editor of the *National Lampoon* from 1971 through 1978, and co-created the British TV series *Spitting Image*.

Take, which also featured Tim Brooke-Taylor, Humphrey Barclay, and Tony Hendra. This was also the first year in the Footlights for an English student named Eric Idle, who, like Chapman, was invited to audition after he staged a smoker for the club; he would not appear on stage with Chapman and Cleese for a few more years, however.

Idle began appearing with other actors in Cambridge revues, including an appearance at the 1963 Edinburgh Festival. Ironically, Terry Jones was featured in the Oxford Theatre Group's show there at the same time. One critic, Harold Hobson, writing in the August 22 *Edinburgh Evening News,* called their two shows among the best in the festival:

> *If any section of the official dramatic Festival achieved its aims as completely as the Cambridge University* Footlights '63 *and the Oxford Theatre Group's * * * * achieve theirs, then this Festival would not only be—what it is—good, but unrivalled.*
>
> *Yet these Oxford and Cambridge late night revues are given in makeshift halls, down sinister streets and crooked alleys. Their chairs are uncomfortable, their stages look as if they have been run up by amateurs when they were thinking of something else, and one might almost guess, from the appearance of the Oxford troupe, that they have no running water. . .*
>
> *[The halls] suit the Oxford team, who, apart from a ravishing girl, are, it must be admitted, a shabby lot, supremely well, and to Cambridge, suave, civilized, soigne, brushed and bourgeois, they afford a setting of illustrating contrast.*
>
> *The Cambridge quartet—Richard Eyre, David Gooderson, Eric Idle and Humphrey Barclay—have the stronger personalities. They give pleasure by what they are, by the irresistible efflorescence of their spontaneity. They attract admiration as effortlessly as the sun attracts the flowers. Oxford, on the other hand, compel it. What they do is diabolically clever. Every one of them—Ian Davidson, Jane Brayshaw, Douglas Fisher, Robin Grove-White and Terry Jones—is a first-class mimic; they are superb, all the time, as someone else, whether it be the creator of the tattoo, the Prime Minister, or a pro-hyphen, anti-peerage Labour M.P. Most people here unaccountably describe the Oxford revue as an escape from satire. It*

is, in fact, satirical from beginning to end. What throws people off must be the fact that it is funny.

While Idle was performing *Footlights '63* at the 1963 Edinburgh Festival, Chapman was using his sabbatical from performing after *Double Take* to study at St. Bart's Hospital. Cleese kept at it, though, and appeared in *A Clump of Plinths* during the summer of 1963. The show proved exceedingly popular, and apparently through the efforts of Humphrey Barclay, it was mounted in London's West End after its initial run at the university, and its title was changed to *Cambridge Circus.*

"I had no idea that *Cambridge Circus* was a success at the beginning, until two things happened," notes Cleese. "First of all, two extremely nice men in gray suits, Peter Titheradge and Ted Taylor, came into the Footlights club room one evening and said something like would I ever consider starting a career writing comedy for BBC-Radio, which, after a little bit of thought, and a slight hesitation about not doing something respectable like being a solicitor, which is what I was being lined up to do—with a little bit of thought, I was able to let go of the legal world rather easily. Being the BBC, it had other aspects of the civil service which reassured my parents, because of the apparent stability of working for the BBC.

"The other thing that happened was an impre-

A 24-year-old John Cleese "with my Maurice Chevalier grin" on top of the Aeolian Hall, which housed BBC-Radio Light Entertainment. Cleese says he caused a minor commotion by not wearing a jacket and a tie when he first began working for the BBC. Photo by Jo Kendall.

sario called Michael White arrived in the club room somewhere around the same time as my two friends from the BBC. Michael said he wanted to send us to the West End, which was quite a thrill, and gave us a little bit of a launching pad. He managed to get us into a West End theater and get us Equity cards. There we were, performing in the West End not so long after leaving Cambridge!

"That had two effects. First of all, it was a thrill, because people actually came to see us. I also remember it was incredibly useful for me, because I'd left Cambridge with the dearth of six hundred pounds. This was simply the sum of money that my father was supposed to have made up over and above the state scholarship in science that I'd got from the Bristol council, but he wasn't able to give me any money. As that was exactly what he was supposed to give me, although he guaranteed it at the bank—whatever that means—I was six hundred in the red the day I left Cambridge. The wonderful thing about Cambridge was that after about two months in the West End, maybe a little more, I'd actually paid off the entire debt! So, something that I was expecting to carry around my neck for two and a half years as a solicitor's clerk was gone, and I was back to zero. That was an *incredible* help."

Cleese's BBC career began by contributing sketches to Frost's *That Was the Week That Was* while still in school.

Cleese had become friendly with David Frost during their days together in the Footlights, and when Frost's fortunes started to rise in the BBC after he had left Cambridge, he wisely began to bring up talented friends he had known at the university to work for him (including Bill Oddie, who also contributed to *TW3*).

The show marked Cleese's first important professional work in television. Although his contributions were sporadic, as he was still preoccupied with his studies and the ongoing *Cambridge Circus,* it did provide a foot in the door.

Cleese wrote a sketch called "Regella," which originally appeared in one of the Footlights shows, and submitted it to *TW3*, where Frost bought it.

" 'Regella' is a little solo about the stupid use of statistics in astronomical programs, like 'Regella is so far away from the sun that it would take an ordinary white rhinoceros running at 16 miles an hour over 1,600,000 years to get there,' and 'If the Royal Albert Hall was the size of an orange, then Regella is 139,000,000 times as big as a pomegranate.' It's that kind of stuff," explains Cleese.

"I only wrote about three sketches for *That Was the Week That Was,* and then sent in a couple more, and didn't try after that. A lot of people think I was in it, because that was fronted by David Frost, who was very welcoming toward my attempts to send in material. Frost also fronted *The Frost Report,* so I'm often accused of being in *TW3*. In fact I was only a student at the time."

Cleese's sketches for *TW3* grew into a regular writing position at the BBC. He wrote jokes for *The Dick Emery Show* and other BBC-Radio shows, including a Christmas special called *Yule Be Surprised,* the memory of which still embarrasses him.

"It's quite true—the first script they ever gave me was called *Yule Be Surprised.* It was written by a man called Eddie McGuire. I was given the script and told to take some of the jokes out," Cleese says with a laugh.

"After a short pause, another guy, whose name I have sadly forgotten, was introduced to me. He was going to write most of the sketches. That was my first experience at any sort of regular work in those days—four months out of Cambridge and about a month out of *Cambridge Circus.* There I was, sitting at my desk writing this one sketch a week. I based it on an archetype of a Peter Cook sketch which I had never seen but had always been told about. I remember Trevor Nunn telling me about it when he directed the 'sixty-two revue—it was called 'Interesting Facts.' I subsequently had the very great joy and privilege of performing that sketch with Peter Cook in an Amnesty show."

Cambridge Circus ran for five months at the Lyric Theatre in the West End, beginning August 16, 1963. Chapman was not with the show when it opened, but joined the cast when one of the actors, Tony Buffery, dropped out; the cast also included Tim Brooke-Taylor, Bill Oddie, Jo Kendall, and David Hatch. Cleese was writing for the BBC during the day, while Chapman found himself making hospital rounds at St. Bart's and thrashing around on the Lyric stage every night.

"The success of *Cambridge Circus* meant that I had a job at the BBC, a steady job which I then did

until about June or July of the following year, 1964, when Michael White suddenly suggested we should take the show out of the deep freeze, warm it up and take it to New Zealand, with the possibility of America. We weren't confirmed vis-à-vis New York until we were towards the end of the New Zealand trip. But, the whole point was, it was a jaunt, a little bit of excitement, a bit of money, and a chance to see the world. I don't think any of us thought of it very much in terms

The Custard Pie Sketch (which was eventually seen in Monty Python Live at the Hollywood Bowl*) was actually written by Terry Jones and Michael Palin in the early 1960s; they loaned it to John Cleese, Graham Chapman and the rest of the* Cambridge Circus *cast when they performed their show in London's West End. Left to right: Bill Oddie, Tim Brooke-Taylor and Jonathan Lynn. Photo from the Collection of John Cleese, used by permission.*

of where it would lead, and I think we were very doubtful whether the show would work on Broadway, a doubt which proved to be a very accurate assessment of the situation!" Cleese declares.

So Cleese took leave from the BBC, and Chapman decided to take a year off from his medical studies, but he didn't quite know how to explain it to his parents.

Around this time, a number of medical students were invited to have tea with the Queen Mother, and Chapman was among those selected. While he was speaking to her, he happened to mention that he had the opportunity to tour New Zealand.

"It's a beautiful place," she told him. "You must go."

"I told my parents about it," Chapman later explained, "only I phrased it as though I had been given a royal command which I couldn't refuse."

His parents, properly respectful of the Royals, allowed him to give up his studies for the duration of the tour, and Chapman, Cleese, and the rest of the cast were off to New Zealand for six weeks.

"The tour was mainly chaotic because New Zealand, in those days, was more or less another planet," notes Cleese. "I remember standing on a beach, staring across the sea, thinking 'Only three thousand miles to Chile!' "

One of the stranger moments occurred when Chapman had difficulty ordering a three-egg omelette. He was finally served three fried eggs that were sitting on top of an omelette.

"The New Zealanders, in those days, were a little bit out to lunch and almost nothing in New Zealand worked. The only thing was, because they were New Zealanders, they'd never been anywhere where things *did* work. So, if you criticized them, they thought you were mad!" Cleese says with a laugh.

Still, some of Cleese's favorite moments in the Footlights occurred on the New Zealand tour.

"The man in charge of the show did not realize that he had to not only get the flats* in at the beginning of sketches, but he had to get them *out* at the end. I remember Graham coming on to do a solo towards the end of the first half, and he could hardly get on, because there were so many of these flats that had been flown in, and just left there," explains Cleese.

"I remember him picking his way through these flats eventually, one of them bumping him on the shoulder while he was doing his routine. He never registered the fact that it was bumping him on the shoulder from behind.

"When he got off, I said 'Didn't you realize you were being bumped? The audience could see you were being bumped—why didn't you react to it?' And he said 'Well, I assumed you'd gotten behind me with a broom and was poking me with it!' Which shows what passed for a norm in those days. . . ."

At the conclusion of the tour, the cast traveled to New York, where *Cambridge Circus* opened on Broadway on October 6, 1964. It ran for twenty-

*Large canvas covered wooden frames painted for use as scenery in theatrical productions.

8

three performances (including an appearance on *The Ed Sullivan Show*) and was then transferred off-Broadway, where it ran until early 1965, and an American cast took over. (A soundtrack album was released featuring the original British cast, however.)

"The American show was a bit of a blur, really. We got there and started rehearsing the show, and strange shadowy men sat halfway back in the stalls without us really knowing who they were. Then messages came that material in the show wasn't right. At first, we reacted in a defiant way, and then realized that they probably knew a bit more about American audiences than we did," Cleese recalls.

"We managed to get a couple of extra items and fit them in the show at short notice. One was a number Graham did, a parody of the Marc Antony death speech. He actually carried the body, but found it progressively harder to carry the body satisfactorily. The body started as dead, but then became more alive as it tried to help Graham carry it. I think there was also some Beatles' takeoff based on the music of the 'Hallelujah Chorus.' We did that as a Beatles' number, and it was a great success.

"We got very good reviews, except for one former sportswriter on *The New York Times* called Howard Taubman. He gave us a bad review, and it killed us. Walter Kerr, who was a proper critic and knew what he was talking about, loved the show, and in fact wrote twice about us in an attempt to keep it alive. But we came off before we'd even started. I think we'd been on for three weeks, and we just weren't in a routine. We always knew we were in trouble, so we never sort of settled. It was all a bit strange and temporary."

It was during *Cambridge Circus* in New York that another significant event occurred in the history of Monty Python. John Cleese was selected to appear in a photo-feature for *Help!* magazine, and found himself working with a young assistant editor called Terry Gilliam. It was a meeting that would have unique repercussions.

After *Cambridge Circus,* Cleese opted to stay in the United States, while most of the others re-

John Cleese rests up as the **Cambridge Circus** *cast prepares to tour New Zealand for six weeks. Photo from the Collection of John Cleese, used by permission.*

turned to Britain, Chapman going back to medical studies.

Meanwhile, back at Cambridge, Eric Idle was busy with the Footlights. Following in the footsteps of *A Clump of Plinths* was intimidating, but Idle wrote, directed, and appeared in the 1964 Footlights revue at Edinburgh, where he first met Michael Palin.

For Idle, 1965 proved to be the breakthrough year. He was elected president of the Footlights and was responsible for changing the bylaws to allow women to become full members. One of the first female members of the Footlights was, in fact, feminist author Germaine Greer.

(Strangely enough, America's most famous feminist also has a Python connection. Gloria Steinem served as Harvey Kurtzman's first assistant editor on *Help!* magazine, a job later taken by Terry Gilliam.)

Idle wrote for and appeared in the 1965 Footlights revue *My Girl Herbert.* He claims the show itself was not outstanding, though it toured Britain and ran for three weeks at the Lyric Hammersmith in London. With the end of *Herbert,* Idle had also ended his days at Cambridge, and set out to make his way in cabaret, repertory theater, and the BBC.

Oxford had no equivalent of the Footlights, which was fine with Terry Jones, who had no theatrical ambitions at the time. A native of Colwyn Bay, Wales, he was accepted at both Oxford and Cambridge. Though he actually hoped to attend the latter, he decided to pursue his history studies at Oxford's St. Edmund Hall because that school was the first to accept him.

Jones's classmates and one of his instructors were responsible for his interest in theater, and he began performing with the Experimental Theater Company (or ETC) during his first year. The turning point came during his second year, however, when he encountered a first-year student named Michael Palin, who was studying history at Oxford's Brasenose College.

Palin, a native of Sheffield in Yorkshire, had been writing and performing comedy with Robert Hewison. Jones had seen the pair perform, and he and Palin ended up writing a sketch together for a show called *Loitering Within Tent*.

Amazingly enough, this very first Palin-Jones collaboration was subsequently used in the Monty Python stage shows, and appears in *Monty Python Live at the Hollywood Bowl*. It is the famed "Slapstick/Custard Pie Sketch," in which a professorial type discusses the history and evolution of comedy, while a trio of assistants demonstrate the throwing of custard pies, slipping on banana peels, and hitting each other with boards. It was so admired by their peers at Cambridge that they gave Chapman, Cleese, and company permission to perform it in *Cambridge Circus*.

Jones explains that he never planned any extensive collaboration with Palin.

"It was just for that revue, *Loitering Within Tent*," reveals Jones. "He had started doing cabaret with Robert Hewison. That's where I first saw Michael—he was doing this revue with Robert Hewison, who is now a theater critic. They did these rather existential sketches, like a tape recorder in a bucket. Mike and I then wrote the 'Slapstick Sketch,' we worked on that together."

After *Loitering Within Tent* in late spring, 1963, Palin and Jones went their separate ways. Palin was busy doing plays and cabaret during his first year at Oxford. The theatrical career of upper-

Terry Jones dabbled in straight acting at college before plunging into comedy. Here he stars in the Haymakers' production of Time Remembered *at Oxford. Photo from the Collection of Terry Jones, used by permission.*

classman Jones, however, got a significant boost due to an obscure British pop song.

"The first revue I did for Oxford was in Edinburgh with Doug Fisher, Ian Davidson, and Robin Grove-White," states Jones. "They had done the revue in Edinburgh the year before, and they were going to do the revue again that year, my second year. The fourth member of their team, a guy called Paul McDowell, had just made a hit record with a group called the Temperance Seven. They had just made a record called 'You're Driving Me Crazy' that had become number one, and he was the vocalist, so he couldn't go with the group to Edinburgh.

"I had just done *Loitering Within Tent*, when I got a phone call. Ian Davidson said 'Come and do the revue in Edinburgh,' so I got up and filled in for Paul McDowell. That was really a turning point in my life, that phone call from Ian Davidson, and I got into the revue."

The revue, * * * * was very well received. The August 22, 1963, *Glasgow Herald* reported:

Whether the title is intended as a censored fashionable word or an automobile organisation rating, this Oxonian late-night revue is a scintillating success.

Largesse in talent, wit, and execution is dis-

tributed with infectious offhand abandon. Conversational gamesmanship with tennis scoring, door-to-door sales of 'You, too, can be the life of the party' skit, anarchic Tory women, a modern English civil war documentary, songs, excellent music, and visual knockabout make a memorable hour.

Ian Davidson, Jane Brayshaw, Doug Fisher, Robin Grove-White, and Terry Jones are all quite brilliant in this effervescent nocturnal whoop-up.

After Edinburgh, * * * * transferred to the Phoenix Theatre for a brief run in 1964; Graham Chapman and John Cleese were performing *Cambridge Circus* in London's West End at approximately the same time. *Cambridge Circus* continued to receive positive notices for its production there, although reviews for the London production of * * * * were more mixed. Critic David Nathan wrote "There are one or two, perhaps even three or four, good things in it. . . . One of the young men, Douglas Fisher, shows a great deal of promise, but generally speaking they project an air of bumbling amateurism which ensures that most of the points are lost in a theatre far too large." However, Christopher Driver wrote:

*To judge from * * * *, which has come from Oxford to the Phoenix Theatre via Edinburgh, the Oxbridge joke-engine has changed gear again. * * * *, despite the brashness of the title, is distinguished by a certain economy in humour, a relaxation of the hectic phut-phutting of laughs that has categorised earlier models. Several models are unusually long for revue and until one has accustomed oneself to the cast's demure observance of the speed limit, some of them even appear slow. But by the end of the evening the trick has worked.*

*Is it only coincidence that two of the most successful sketches are not only of several minutes duration but also explore the concept of the meta-joke, the joke about joke-making? In one, a university lecturer expounds with the assistance of three impassive laboratory demonstrators the origin and construction of various simple japes like the banana skin and the custard pie. In another, two joke salesmen fit out a simple fellow with a few appropriate spiels. . . . * * * * goes back to first principles, allowing mime and fancy full rein. Mr. Davidson, ably assisted by the crisp and sly Douglas Fisher, plays it sweet and cool. Vaut le voyage."*

After * * * *, Jones returned for his third year at Oxford with the distinction of having performed in the West End, and was much in demand. He decided to work on a new production for the ETC called *Hang Down Your Head and Die*, set in a circus ring, with capital punishment as its theme. The show, which also featured Michael Palin, ran briefly in the West End as well and was lauded by critics.

Don Chapman, writing about the original production in the February 12, 1964, *Oxford Mail*, cited:

The kaleidoscopic brilliance with which it presents its almost encyclopaedic view of the subject, and the astonishing adroitness with which it rings the changes on it with everything from farce to pathos is unique in my theatrical experience. . . . Left trampled under the feet of the other performers is the white-faced auguste, an exquisite mime in the form of Terry Jones, who is destined to play the part of the victim and to be carried screaming to the gallows as the rest of the company belt breezily down to the footlights to take their final bow. It is this figure . . . which gives the evening its dramatic unity. . . . I don't suppose . . . anyone . . . expected such professional and intelligent entertainment from amateurs.

Other newspapers were just as effusive in their praise, and Terry Jones, playing the condemned man, was singled out by several critics. Writing in the February 19, 1964, *Cherwell, the Oxford University Newspaper*, Rudman calls the show "bloody marvellous," and says "the quiet authority and graceful talent of Terry Jones gives the show a core of sympathy that no audience can fail to dig."

And Daphne Levens, writing in the February 20, 1964, *Oxford Magazine*, calls Jones the star, and says, "Pathos, scorn, sweet-sour foolery, horror, hearty indignation are glancing moods round a bitter hard centre, deftly expressed in stage terms and collated with cool intelligence. . . . Terry Jones is an accomplished actor and a delicate mime—he can even borrow from Marcel Marceau without need for apology."

Perhaps the most prestigious review of *Hang Down Your Head and Die* was written by Harold Hobson and appeared in the February 16, 1964, *Sunday Times:*

11

. . . They offer a programme which is both horrible and beautiful. If the last inexorable progression towards an execution, made the more awful by its grotesque and bitter caricature of a Punch and Judy show, proved too strong for the nerves of some of the audience, it also had in it things which even my theories admit to manifest theatrical value. I am thinking particularly of the pantomime choruses about the hangman which the audience has been cunningly inveigled into singing, and of the heart-shaking and pathetic moment when the condemned man goes on singing alone after everyone else has stopped. His voice falters and he too falls into silence. . . . This moment of appalling discovery is magnificently revealed by Robert Hewison, David Wood, and Terry Jones.

Lay [sic] Down Your Head and Die transcends its purely forensic values. . . . In any case, these are considerable. There is as much curious information here as in 'The Anatomy of Melancholy'. . . . At Oxford, you will find out these things, and others besides. They are imparted with the cold disgust of those who have gone too far to argue any more, and have moved from debate into faith. . . .

When Jones returned to Oxford for his final year, he began working on *The Oxford Revue* with Palin, Doug Fisher, Annabel Leventon, and Nigel Pegram. Although Palin and Jones had been working together on occasional shows, their real collaboration began with this revue. Jones feels the show's nontraditional approach to comedy was instrumental in the development of Monty Python.

Terry Jones and Michael Palin began their long, successful collaboration in 1964 in The Oxford Revue. Photo from the Collection of Terry Jones, used by permission.

Left to right: Douglas Fisher, Terry Jones, and Michael Palin in The Oxford Review. Photo from the Collection of Terry Jones, used by permission.

"It was an escape from satire," explains Jones. "Mike and Doug and I all felt that the show we did was nonsatirical, it was fantasy. In a way, looking back on it, I can see the kind of material we were doing had a Python feel to it."

The Oxford Revue, directed by Doug Fisher, was presented in Edinburgh in the summer of 1964, as Jones was finishing his final year at Oxford. Although the show then moved to London, its venue was less than prestigious.

"We got an offer to perform it in London at a club called The Establishment, which had been started by Peter Cook and that lot," Jones recalls.

"It was started as 'the' satirical club in London, but by this time, around 'sixty-four, it was a bit run-down—I think it had gangster connections," he laughs. "It was pretty sleazy by the time we did our show there. Most of the time we outnumbered the audience. Mike was in that show, but he couldn't come down because he was back at university, so we had to replace him with a guy called David Walsh.

"We did that for about six weeks at The Establishment, usually, as I say, outnumbering the audience. Occasionally the croupier from upstairs—it was really a gambling place by then—would come and sit at the front of the audience and laugh and clap very determinedly, and look around very threateningly at the rest of the audience.

"I did that for about six months, then I did another little thing at another club called the Poor Millionaire with a guy called Noel Carter. We wrote this pantomime takeoff one weekend. I was just getting going a bit then," notes Jones.

While he was trying to survive life after Oxford, Palin was continuing on with his final year at the school. Still collaborating with Robert Hewison—his partnership with Jones was an on-again, off-again situation—Palin co-wrote, produced, and directed *The Oxford Line,* which opened on August 23. He and Hewison were also featured performers in the review, along with Diana Quick, Mick Sadler, and David Wood. Palin's written contributions to the show (many of them co-scripted) included the "Opener," "Vicar," "English," "Getting to Know You," "Jean-Paul Overe," "Restoration Box," "Battle of Wits," "Brassomania," "Bananas," and "How Wintrop Spudes Saved the World from Total Destruction"; "Tinpally" saw Terry Jones share a writing credit with Palin and three others (the cast biography of the then-twenty-two-year-old Palin notes that "Michael aims to take up a career as a scriptwriter"). Graduating in 1965 and with his university days behind him, Palin headed to London to join up with Jones, who had found a home with the BBC.

Occidental College

Strangely enough, Terry Gilliam entered Occidental College in California as a physics major. Not so strangely, he didn't last long in the science department.

"After six weeks in physics, I decided 'It's the arts for me!' I was an arts major for a bit, and couldn't stand the art history professors, so I became a political science major, and that's how I graduated." Gilliam laughs.

The crew-cut Gilliam's interests were not solely in politics, however, and he even joined a fraternity, but he soon became bored with most of the rituals. He had developed an interest in cartooning several years before, and began honing those skills with his work on *Fang,* the school's humor magazine.

"There was a gang of us, and we were always looking for outlets, and I suppose the college humor magazine seemed to have potential as an outlet. So, we took it over and turned it from what was basically a literary poetry-oriented magazine into a humor magazine. We started lowering the tone early, and we continued to do so.

"I was editor of that my senior year," Gilliam recalls. "One of the people we were ripping off was Harvey Kurtzman with *Help!* magazine."

The 19-year-old Terry Gilliam was at Occidental College in southern California, where he edited Fang, *the school humor magazine. Photo from the Collection of Terry Gilliam, used by permission.*

Academics bored him, and despite his abilities, he barely graduated. One of the more important influences on Gilliam in the early 1950s was *Mad* (founded by Harvey Kurtzman), the comic book-turned-magazine. During his last years at Occidental, Gilliam had been sending some of his work from *Fang* to Kurtzman, who at that time was in New York editing *Help!*

"I was hoping for some kind of approval, and he did send a really nice letter back saying he liked what we were doing, so after college, with nothing better to do, I decided to go to New York and meet Harvey. I just walked into this job—it was waiting for me!" reveals Gilliam, even though Kurtzman had tried to frighten him off.

Gilliam says he had always been a cartoonist, though he never had any artistic ambitions.

"I had no ambitions, really," he says with a laugh. "I never knew what I was doing. I always just did what I liked. The only thing I wanted ever to do was to be a film director, although there was one point in college where I thought I was going to be an architect. But I worked at an architect's office one summer, and that was the end of my architectural career. I didn't like all the bullshit that went with it. I really had no ability to work within normal systems, I suppose...."

One of John Cleese's earliest BBC enterprises also proved to be his longest-running. During the West End run of *Cambridge Circus*, Humphrey Barclay, who had gotten a job as a BBC radio producer, assembled the cast members to perform three programs in 1964.

"When we'd done the stage show in the West End for a time, Humphrey Barclay and I were offered jobs with the BBC. 'Writer-producer' they were called, but I only wrote, and Humphrey only produced. I can't remember when David Hatch came into the BBC, but [it was] not long after. So, it was kind of inevitable that the material from the *Cambridge Circus* show would finish up on the radio. We did three half-hour shows based on it, which I quite liked," explains Cleese.

The cast members, who included Cleese, Chapman, Tim Brooke-Taylor, David Hatch, Jo Kendall, and Bill Oddie, had grown up listening to *The Goon Show* during the 1950s and were eager to attempt a similar radio show for the '60s. They called it *I'm Sorry, I'll Read That Again.* The initial three shows were so successful that the performers were soon awarded a regular series.

But there were some changes when the show resumed in October 1965. Graham Chapman had left the group and was replaced by Graeme Garden. (Brooke-Taylor, Garden, and Oddie went on to create *The Goodies* for BBC-TV a few years after.) John Cleese was in the United States at the time; he didn't rejoin the show until the second series in 1966, but appeared throughout the entire run of the show.

"When I got back from America, I found all my *Cambridge Circus* crowd, plus Graeme Garden, who had not been in the original cast were back in England. I was still in America doing *Half a Sixpence* and *Newsweek,* so they did a number of *I'm Sorry, I'll Read That Agains* without me. When I got back, I found that they'd already done one series, and Graeme had, in a sense, filled in for me. They sort of opened up and made a space for me, and I came in," recalls Cleese.

And it became one of the longest-running programs in BBC history. There were eight series that ran from 1965 to 1974—the show began years

prior to and did not end until after the final series of *Monty Python's Flying Circus.*

Barclay produced the first half of the eight-series run, and the program was acclaimed by audiences and critics. The *Sunday Times* called it "Radio scatterdemalion . . . deliberate irreverence . . . and terrific verbal agility."

ISIRTA gave Cleese a chance to grow as a writer and performer, and he developed an appreciation of the medium of radio, even though he eventually tired of the routine and stock characters in the show.

"At the beginning, I enjoyed it a lot, because it was wonderful practice for me to get in front of an audience with that script. I was still learning how to work an audience, still figuring out how to time things, still trying different ways of doing it. I

Tim Brooke-Taylor and Graham Chapman join the self-professed "most un-musical man in Europe" for the recording of "I've Got a Ferret Sticking Up My Nose" for I'm Sorry, I'll Read That Again. *Photos from the Collection of John Cleese, used by permission.*

hadn't acquired that almost automatic, gut understanding of how to do things, which you do when you've been doing it for twenty years. In those days I was still experimenting and learning every day. I also felt that I kept my violin tuned, so to speak, by doing this once a week. It kept me in practice for my television work," reveals Cleese.

"However, by and large, I began very rapidly to tire of *I'm Sorry, I'll Read That Again.* Its material was very much to do with bad puns, which the audience laughed, but mainly groaned at. There was a lot of reliance on catchphrases, and although it was okay, the atmosphere was terrific, the audience was wonderful, people liked the show, and we produced something with an extraordinary individual sound to it, I never ultimately respected the material enough. It worked, but it didn't get the adrenaline going. I didn't very often get sketches which I thought 'Oh, that will be fun to perform.' Whereas on most of the television work I was doing, whether it was *Frost* or the *1948 Show,* I really did love most of the material and was excited about doing it.

"*I'm Sorry, I'll Read That Again* went on and on and on, and in the end I think I did over one hundred shows. In retrospect, I'm not sure why. I think I should have bowed out gracefully earlier on, but in those days, I probably didn't know how to gracefully leave a group. I got better at that later on," Cleese says, laughing.

"And I probably didn't want to be left out. I probably felt I needed the money and the exposure, although at thirty-two pounds an evening, it was hardly highly paid work. And, considering it was radio, it was a bit funny to think I thought of it in terms of useful exposure. But I did. When the show finished, I must say I never missed it, and my enthusiasm for it, which waned rather early, just went on gently waning. It was helped by the fact that I was fond of the people I was working with. I always got on well with Tim, and I was particularly fond of David Hatch, who stayed a good friend. Like Graham, who respected him, he was a wonderful voice man and could do any accent he liked. I always enjoyed performing with Jo, because I thought she had good timing. But it just didn't ever turn me on."

Eric Idle also became involved with *I'm Sorry,* *I'll Read That Again* after leaving Cambridge, and the show was his first writing job after graduation.

"I went to do cabaret after the university revue, which came to London. I did cabaret at the Blue Angel and the Rehearsal Room," relates Idle. "Then I went to rep [repertory theater] at Leicester, did *Oh, What a Lovely War.* Hated rep, hated being rep, and so I started to write backstage for *I'm Sorry, I'll Read That Again.* I was busy writing one day, and another actor came up to me and said 'Going well, is it?' and I said 'Yes.' He said 'Do you mind joining me on stage?' So I realized then that I wasn't actually cut out to be totally an actor!"

The shows were sometimes reminiscent of *The Goon Shows* with their quick wordplay and puns, and there were often recurring characters. The second half of each show would usually feature a longer sketch, often the "Prune Play of the Week." (Angus Prune was one of the recurring characters, and the *I'm Sorry, I'll Read That Again* theme song was called "The Angus Prune Tune.") Cleese's participation in the shows became increasingly sporadic, and he seldom wrote material for the series.

"I did write a little bit of material for it right at the start. Certainly I wrote a lot of those first three, before we went to New Zealand and America. When I got back, I wrote the odd sketch, but I was normally too busy with the TV writing. I really functioned as an actor, but did a few rewrites on the day [of the performance]," recalls Cleese.

Despite his eventual boredom with *ISIRTA,* though, Cleese still retains a fondness for the medium of radio, and he continues to write and perform radio commercials today.

"The tremendous, tremendous advantage of radio is that there are not too many things that can go wrong between the script and the listener," explains Cleese. "It's as though there are fifteen different stages where something can come between a film script and the end product, and in television there are about seven or eight. In radio, there are about two.

"For example, in *Fawlty Towers,* it's frightening to hear how many funny lines are lost by sound. You'd think it was very simple to get the sound on the track, but a lot of lines are partly covered by audience laughter, or the mike isn't in the right place. There are very funny lines that are missed as

a result of that. You'd never get that happening in radio. If you do a good performance on radio, unless the sound controller actually dies, it works. That's the nice thing about radio.

"It's tremendous fun to go into a studio for a day and play with a script. Very simple, and it's not very technical. You don't have to do hundreds of rehearsals over so the cameraman knows where to put his shots and the sound man knows where to put the boom. It's simple."

Cleese is still proud of some of his work on *I'm*

Sorry, I'll Read That Again. At one point, he grew fond of rodents, particularly ferrets. (Several of their publicity photos picture the cast all holding stuffed ferrets.) During the Monty Python stage shows, he always wanted to perform one of this songs from *ISIRTA* but was overruled. Pity. What Python fan could resist John Cleese singing "I've Got a Ferret Sticking Up My Nose"?

Hired by the BBC

After graduating from Oxford in 1964, a less-than-affluent Terry Jones moved to London while Michael Palin was finishing up his last year at the university. The two were friends and had worked together while still in school, but it was by no means a certainty that the team would continue beyond graduation. Jones was looking around for occasional writing assignments, sometimes writing with Miles Kington, when a bigger opportunity arose.

"A guy called Willie Donaldson, who had produced or put up the money for *Beyond the Fringe,* gave me fifty pounds to write this thing called *The Love Show.* He just had the title. Basically, he intended it to be sort of like *Hang Down Your Head and Die* and *Oh, What a Lovely War.* I decided it was going to be about sex. So, I started researching," Jones recalls with a laugh.

As he was working, Jones decided he could use another hand on the project, and contacted Palin at Oxford.

"Terry had been doing some work on a thing called *The Love Show,* which was like a theatrical documentary about sex and attitudes about sex throughout the ages," explains Palin. "This fit in very well with Terry's twin interests, sex and theater. He had got to a certain point and needed someone to bounce ideas off.

"*The Love Show* was really a way of looking at and examining these attitudes, but not in a stuffy way. So, when I came down from Oxford, I really had nothing to do at all. I didn't know what I was going to do, and he said would I help him rewrite it?

"He took me to see a man called Willie Donaldson, who is a very funny, humorous man, but

dodgy as an impresario. He was the man who had financial control over the thing. We went to a pub in Sloane Square, I remember very well. We sat and discussed it, and Willie Donaldson said that he would pay me fifty pounds. That was the first money I ever earned! There and then in that pub in Sloane Square, he sat down and wrote a check for fifty pounds to help Terry write *The Love Show.* Which was my first paycheck ever," notes Palin.

"We worked on it at Terry's home in Esher, and in the end, I don't think it ever got done. It was the first time that Terry and I had collaborated outside of Oxford."

The writing process for *The Love Show* stretched on and on. The script was ultimately never produced, though they continued work on it after

Terry Jones and Michael Palin created a series of short films for Twice a Fortnight as they continued to break into television. "The Door" was a surreal film in which they discovered another world on the other side of the door that they were carrying through the countryside. Photo from the Collection of Terry Jones, used by permission.

Jones had been hired by the BBC and Palin began performing after Oxford.

While Terry Jones was working on *The Love Show* with its £50 paycheck, he also started writing another abortive project.

"Somebody gave me a commission to write a TV thing for 200 pounds. It was called *The Present,* and it was never seen—I wrote it, but we never shot it. But that 250 pounds really kept me going my first year," relates Jones.

His financial problems only contributed to his general discouragement at the end of his first year in London, and he began to consider seriously packing it all in and going back to Oxford. At any rate, Jones was ready for a change.

"I decided I needed to get a job," he recalls, "So, my second year, I canvassed around. I remember I was having trouble with my then-girlfriend, and thinking I was going to go back to Oxford— she was still at Oxford—and I'd just had this terrible phone call. It was really all over with, and I thought 'I've just got to be near her.' I was walking over Lambeth Bridge—I was living in Lambeth at the time—and I suddenly thought 'This is a deciding moment. I either go back to Oxford and mooch around and get visible, or else I go back and get a job. I've got to do one or the other.' So I watched the water going under the bridge for a long time, and decided to go back to London and get a job."

Aware of the symbolism of crossing the bridge, Terry Jones chose to utilize his Oxford experience and try his luck at television writing.

"Eventually I was offered a job as a copywriter for Anglia Television, which I had accepted. Then I was contacted by Frank Muir at the BBC. I went to see him and he offered me a job in a very small office, with two desks and two typewriters and a telephone. I was meant to be a trainee, to have a look around and see what was happening."

His job responsibilities were not well defined, and after a few months, his employment became a bit more tenuous.

"I was there about six months, I suppose, being a script editor and seeing what kind of material came in," he explains. "I was occasionally writing for programs like *The Billy Cotton Bandshow* and *The Kathy Kirby Show,* just being around. I had carte blanche to wander over and watch shows being made. It was very educational. There were several of us that used to sit there writing jokes."

The apprenticeship came to a less-than-triumphant conclusion, though Jones managed to make it through without being fired.

"After about six months in this strange job where I didn't know quite what I was doing, I went on a six-month director's course to train as a director. My friend Ian Davidson, who directed the first revue I did at Edinburgh, was in the same course. Unfortunately, I got peritonitis halfway through and didn't manage to finish it," reveals Jones.

"At the end of the course, I then became a production assistant in the BBC. I was *absolutely* unqualified for this. I'd gone on this course teaching me how to direct, but I didn't know how you went about being an assistant. I was the world's worst. I was shouted at by a director once on the street. So, I did that for about six months, until it looked like I didn't have much of a future at it, and it might not go on much longer!"

While Terry Jones was serving his shaky apprenticeship at the BBC, Michael Palin had graduated from Oxford and gotten his first job in television. It wasn't strictly comedy, however—instead, the fresh-faced, amiable Palin found himself hosting a teenage pop music show in Bristol called *Now!* for the now-defunct Television West Wales.

The show's producers were apparently hoping for the British equivalent of Dick Clark, but wound up with a young Python. Palin remembers that the exclamation mark in *Now!* was a very important part of the show's name.

"*Now!* exclamation mark is what I remember about that program. It was very important—that gave the show the feeling of excitement and immediacy that we all were led to believe was important at that time," he recalls, laughing.

"I have really ambivalent feelings about it. The standards of the shows were not great. What I had to do was fairly humiliating, like walk around Bristol dressed in a long Edwardian swimsuit and huge boots on, miming to Nancy Sinatra's 'These Boots Are Made for Walkin'.' I'd just come out of Oxford with a history degree! I mean, this didn't seem to be the natural logic of things. . . ."

Sophomoric as much of it was, the show provided Palin with valuable on-camera experience and was also financially useful.

"When I did *Now!* from about October of 1965 to May or June of '66, it paid me enough to be able

to write scripts with Terry Jones, which were in the end much more useful to us. That put us on the road to working with the other Pythons. So it was, in its way, just what was needed—a fairly easy way to earn quite good money."

Palin finally developed a method to get him through the madness, a secret he is finally ready to reveal to the public.

"I always did it with two pints of Guinness in me, I'd go down to the local pub and have two pints of Guinness—it was the only way I could tape the show," he laughs.

A Brit in America (and an American in Britain)

Cambridge Circus opened on Broadway in September 1964 and ran for three weeks. During the Broadway run of *Cambridge Circus,* the troupe appeared on *The Ed Sullivan Show,* and Cleese had been selected to appear in the previously mentioned *Help!* magazine photo strip about a man who falls in love with his daughter's Barbie doll (under the direction of then-assistant editor Terry Gilliam).

A negative review in *The New York Times* caused the *Cambridge Circus* to close in less than a month, but the cast rapidly agreed to an offer to appear off-Broadway, where it played until February 1965.

"Some nice people came along, and said 'We've got a little theater off Washington Square. Would you like to do the show there?' We went, and I was happier there," recalls John Cleese. "It was a smaller place, where you didn't have to project, you didn't have to do makeup, and you could roll up ten minutes before the start of the show. I thoroughly enjoyed performing there. I'd rather do small acting than opera acting, and in a small house like that you could do subtler stuff. Maybe that's why I always worked better on television and film than I ever did on stage. Anyway, we stayed there for months, and then they suggested we should do a second show, which we did—some new material and a bit of old stuff polished up."

Graham Chapman returned to London and resumed his medical classes after *Cambridge Circus* ended its run on Broadway. This time around, he completed his studies and became a qualified physician with no further intervention by the Queen Mother. Although his TV work during this time was minimal, he did do some scripting for *The Illustrated Weekly Hudd,* later explaining that he wanted to do some writing on his own, without collaborating with Cleese.

John Cleese, on the other hand, was trying his luck in the United States. While he was performing off-Broadway, Tommy Steele came to the show and liked Cleese.

"The next thing I knew, I was being asked to audition for *Half a Sixpence,*" he recalls.

"I went along as a joke, because I'm the most unmusical man in Europe, and thought it would be very funny to tell my grandchildren I'd once auditioned for a Broadway musical. Of course, they gave me the part.

"Then the director was fired and another director came in, a guy called Gene Sachs, who became very famous. I didn't really know what was coming. Originally, I'd been told I might write a bit of the book, and I did. Some of the people liked it, but it was one of those Hollywood situations. You didn't quite know who was in charge, and the producers were around in twos and threes, with none of them really working together. So, none of my stuff got on. When the director was fired, we went

Left to right: Jonathan Lynn (who would go on to direct Eric Idle in **Nuns on the Run***), John Cleese and David Hatch (who co-starred with Cleese in the long-running radio comedy series* **I'm Sorry, I'll Read That Again***) appear in the* **Oscar Wilde Sketch** *in* **Cambridge Circus***. Photo from the Collection of John Cleese, used by permission.*

back to the original book. But it went reasonably well in Boston and Toronto, and when it got on Broadway, it got very good reviews."

Half a Sixpence was a learning experience for the young John Cleese, in a great many ways.

"I enjoyed doing it—it was amazing!" notes Cleese. "I'd never spent my time with a lot of gay guys before, who were, incidentally, the singers. The dancers were straight—it's usually the other way around. I got very used to it and formed some good friendships. I was extremely fond of a lot of people in the cast, but lost contact with almost all of them, unfortunately."

Opening on Broadway in February 1965, Cleese played a man who embezzles money from Tommy Steele. Evidently, his acting skills were enough to overcome his lack of musical ability, and the director allowed him to stand in the back and mouth the words while the rest of the chorus sang. Still, the production had its problems prior to opening night.

"What I remember about *Half a Sixpence* is a complete sense of bewilderment, not knowing what was going on where. There were lots of different people, singers, actors, dancers, all rehearsing in different rooms—I didn't quite know what was going on, but assumed that it was all normal," relates Cleese.

"Then I ever-so-slowly realized that there was a bit of a panic. Although I loved our little director, called Word Baker, who had directed *The Fantasticks,* I suddenly realized it just wasn't happening. It was just not being pulled together. Then Gene Sachs came in with a short amount of time, very businesslike. The first few days he was almost like a sergeant-major. I think he needed to be that to give us a sense that things were under control and somebody was in charge, somebody knew what direction we were going in.

"The main problem I had with Gene was that I had no idea how loud you had to speak in a musical, and he kept at me, saying 'Louder, John!' Eventually I went on stage in Boston at a dress rehearsal, and I did it so loudly, just to annoy him that he would say 'Not *that* loud!' To my astonishment, he said 'That's it! That's the level you need!'"

"I had never realized that if you go on after a big dance number, you practically have to shout for anybody to even notice you standing there."

Cleese says he admired all of the people in the production, including its star, Tommy Steele.

"I enjoyed the show a lot, liked all the people in it. I only had a small part, a few lines here and there, one scene with Tommy, who would always take my wrist and try and lock it and shove me gently into the orchestra pit—I don't mean he really tried, but I had to be on my toes in order to avoid getting a shove," he laughs. "I enjoyed that, I thought he was very professional. A lot of fun, but he was very tough on anyone who was unprofessional in a way the audience would notice. I admired that, I thought he created a good atmosphere. [There was] a very good team spirit, although there were a lot of cast changes at the beginning—I had three mothers in about eight weeks!"

After spending nearly six months in *Half a Sixpence,* Cleese began a brief tenure at *Newsweek* magazine in July 1965, a job for which he says he was "spectacularly unqualified." Although initially hired by the International Affairs Department, he ended up writing the obituaries for people who were still alive.

"I attempted to get out of show business by becoming an international journalist with *Newsweek,*" he explains. "I failed after a month because my mentor was sent off to cover some upset in the Dominican Republic, and I didn't know how to write *Newsweek* style—or probably any style.

"At *Newsweek,* I just remember going into these meetings where all these very well informed people were having ideas about what we should be writing about. I was given the lighter items to write, and I thought I did one or two of them quite well," he says, but notes that it was difficult to translate some of this humor to the magazine's style.

"The trouble is, a lot of humor which is based in fact has got to use ellipses. They could never dare to allow ellipses to occur, because it meant that one or two of the readers might have to make a mental effort to understand something. So, they did tend to explain my jokes by putting in the one sentence that I'd left out in order to make it funny.

"But they were nice people. If my mentor had not disappeared, I might have picked it up. I certainly thought it was a very good magazine, and I was very respectful of the professionalism that people there showed. Eventually I realized they

were going to let me go, so I wrote a letter of resignation, saying 'Thanks very much but I know I can't do it.' "

John Cleese was not out of work for long, however. Deciding to stay in the States awhile longer, he immediately joined The Establishment (a group founded by Peter Cook), which was then touring the country.

"I got involved in The Establishment because I knew John Morris, who had the rights to the old Establishment show. When I was about to resign from *Newsweek,* he said 'Do you want to be in the show?' I said 'Sure,' I left *Newsweek* on Friday, and on Sunday afternoon I started to rehearse. I was quite proud—I don't think I've ever been out of work for a day in my life. Lucky!"

The Establishment began performing in Chicago in September and a few weeks later traveled to Washington, D.C. Toward the end of the year, Cleese received a phone call from David Frost, who was trying to organize a new TV show to be called *The Frost Report.*

"I was intending to come back to London and perhaps marry Connie, when Frost said 'Would you like to be in a TV show?' He just rang me up from the airport, as he so often did. I said 'Yes, please.' He said 'There are two people, both called Ronnie, who no one's heard of, but they're both very good. When are you going to come over?' I told him and he said 'I'll see you in the New Year.' "

While Terry Gilliam was working with Harvey Kurtzman on *Help!* magazine, he met John Cleese in a well-documented collaboration when Cleese posed for a photo comic strip for the magazine called "Christopher's Punctured Romance." The two promised to keep in touch.

"When *Help!* folded, I went off to Europe for six months of checking out. I decided I'd better come back to the States to decide whether Europe was the place for me or not," explains Gilliam.

"I was back in New York for a bit, where I lived in Harvey's attic for a couple of months. Then I moved back to L.A. and was working as a freelance illustrator, doing comic books and things. I actually did a book called *The Cocktail People* with Joel Siegel."**

**Siegel is now the film critic of ABC-TV's *Good Morning America.*

Gilliam did work for comic magazines, such as *Surftoons,* but found it tough to make ends meet.

"The whole business of freelance illustrating was proving to be pretty rough. I was broke again, and at that point, Joel was working at this advertising agency called Carson Roberts. He got me a job there. The interesting thing was, the guy I went to work for used to be Stan Freeberg's writing partner, and so he had a soft spot for funny folk," he notes.

"I had long hair at the time, and I think the agency thought 'This is really groovy, a guy with long hair.' I was basically hired as both copywriter and art director, so I was able to do everything myself."

Before long, though, Gilliam started tiring of the rat race.

"I was getting disillusioned, but what finally broke the camel's back was that they had the account for Universal Pictures. At the time, Universal was just doing really shitty B movies, and Joel and I had to spend our time doing ads for Universal Pictures. I lasted at the agency for eleven months. I just got fed up with it. I can't remember whether they fired me before I quit or not—it was a neck-and-neck affair," he recalls with a laugh.

The advertising agency marked Gilliam's last brush with corporate America, but the experience proved useful years later.

"Several of the things in *Brazil,* like the offices pulling the desk back and forth—all that came from working in the ad agency, my few months of corporate bureaucratic life. You get a lot of information very quickly in those surroundings," he laughs.

It was time for a change, and Europe beckoned once again.

"The girl I was living with was English, and she was keen to come back to England. I was keen to leave the country, so I came to England!" he recalls, noting that when he arrived in 1967, he began doing more freelance drawing.

"I was doing illustrations for magazines and newspapers, ad agencies, and cartoons for magazines back in the States. She got a job as editor at a magazine called *London Life* and I started working with her as art director on the thing.

"The one connection I really had in London that was my own connection was Cleese, who I'd met in New York when we were doing *Help!* John was very successful in television, and I said 'I've

got to get out of magazines. Can you introduce me to somebody?' " Gilliam reveals.

Cleese introduced Gilliam to Humphrey Barclay, who was producing a new show called *Do Not Adjust Your Set,* and Barclay introduced him to Eric Idle, Michael Palin and Terry Jones.

The Frost Report

The Pythons have endured a love-hate relationship with David Frost over the years, but his influence on their careers was certainly significant.

In many ways, Frost is a modern-day Renaissance man adept in using the media, and the Pythons mercilessly skewered their former boss at several points during *Monty Python's Flying Circus.*

In "Timmy Williams' Coffee Time," a man who is devastated at a number of personal misfortunes, including the death of his wife, goes to have a heart-to-heart talk with his old friend "Timmy" (who more than resembles Frost), but he is constantly interrupted by reporters, a documentary film crew, and numerous fans, all of whom are glad-handed and offered jobs. The closing credits attribute the writing to "Timmy Williams" in large letters, with the "additional writing by" credits containing dozens of names as they whiz past.

Frost is also caricatured as a block of wood on the talk show sendup "It's a Tree," uttering "Super, super" at every inane moment. Even though several of the Pythons' memories of the incident have faded, Frost's home telephone number ended up in the "Mouse Problem" sketch early in the *Flying Circus.* And, a few years later, Eric Idle did a deadly accurate version of Frost in a sendup of the Frost-Nixon interviews for *Saturday Night Live.*

David Frost was a member of the Cambridge Footlights shortly before John Cleese and Graham Chapman. He starred in their revue and immediately afterward went on to do TV and nightclub work. In November of 1962, however, he leaped into the public eye in *That Was the Week That Was,* a live, satiric, political, musical variety program that was a forerunner of shows like *Monty Python's Flying Circus* and *Saturday Night Live.* The series, which came in the wake of *Beyond the Fringe,* received great acclaim and made a star of Frost. An American version of *TW3* was short-lived, but Frost nevertheless established himself in the States as well.

Among the legions of contributing writers for *TW3* was a very young John Cleese. In fact, his occasional sketches and jokes marked Cleese's first professional work in show business, and so when Frost began work for another series in early 1966, he contacted Cleese and other members of the Oxbridge group that had drifted into television writing.

When Cleese returned from the United States, he brought in Graham Chapman to write for the series, and the pair resumed their writing partnership.

"When I got back, it seemed the most natural thing in the world for Graham and I to link up together. So, as I arrived back in England with the invitation from David Frost to do *The Frost Report,* I simply said yes, and more or less without thinking or checking with anyone brought in Graham," explains Cleese.

Scripting *The Frost Report,* under head-writer Marty Feldman, were Barry Cryer, Dick Vosburgh, Peter Vincent, David McKellar, and Cleese, Chapman, Idle, Palin, and Jones. The show brought the future Pythons into closer contact, even though the five of them had known, or at least been aware of, each other as a result of their university work.

"We met Eric at Edinburgh in 1965. He'd been doing the Cambridge revue while I was doing the Oxford revue, so we'd met up," relates Palin, but admits that *The Frost Report* was the first close encounter with the Cleese-Chapman team for Jones and him.

"It was my first contact with Graham and really the first time I spent much time with John. I knew that he was a successful Cambridge writer, brilliantly funny, and had written a piece about a man watching stones. That was the first time we had ever worked together, and we cemented that relationship the following year, in sixty-seven."

Although he usually wrote alone during the Python years, Idle recalls that he sometimes worked with partners during *The Frost Report.*

"I used to write with Tim Brooke-Taylor a bit and with Graham for a little tiny bit. [I was] writing sketches for that for several years, and we won the Golden Rose of Montreux. So that's where

everybody came together—Mike, Terry, Cleese, Chapman, me—all meeting every week at the writers' meeting, discussing ideas. That's where we first became accustomed to working together, just thinking along the same lines.

"It was a very big success—Cleese was a big star," says Idle. "I mean, John is four years older than me—people tend to forget. Now I'm very, very thrilled to find that he is four years older than me!"

Monty Python's Flying Circus was only three years in the future, but at this point, most of its creators were still considered inexperienced rookies when they got the call from Frost.

"Terry and I were contacted while we were working together in 1966," explains Palin. "I think we were working on *The Love Show* at the time at Terry's parents' house in Esher, with their wonderful cat Geronimo, when the phone rang. It was a guy called Jimmy Gilbert asking Terry and me if we could write sketches for this new series starting up, *The Frost Report*.

"We eventually found that we were two of many, many writers, but it was my first introduction to the real comedy-writing world of television. I remember going to a script meeting—we had a meeting every week where ideas would come up, a bit like *Saturday Night Live*—and this meeting was held in a church hall. We'd go along, very junior—very junior, indeed.

"I remember going on one day without Terry and thinking 'Nobody will know who I am now.' I walked into the room sort of timidly, and the two people who came up and introduced themselves to me and made me feel welcome were Marty Feldman and Barry Cryer. I've never forgotten that. They actually bothered to come along and say hello and introduce me to some of the others. That was spring of 1966, when I was also doing *Now!*"

John Cleese was the only future Python who would be a regular performer on the show. Making the adjustment from small American stages to national TV in Britain wasn't difficult in itself, but the prospect of performing on live TV before millions made him very nervous.

"The transition from playing small clubs in Washington to being on prime time in English television was not completely painless. There was a great deal of terror, because it was a live show. I can still remember not being able to sleep the night before. I had this thing called the autocue [electronic cue cards], but I had never used it before. I wanted to try and remember [my lines]," he reveals.

"I just remember lying awake for hours, running lines again and again, occasionally forgetting them, and then increasing my state of panic. So, those first few shows live—I don't imagine that a matador going to the arena could have felt much more nervous, and I remember thinking that once before a show. But anyway, we got through it, and of course they were successful."

Cleese was actually very good at memorizing lines throughout the series, partly due to his cabaret training, but he did have one catastrophic moment on national television.

"There was one sketch I was doing where they kept cutting four lines, and they'd put it back in, they'd cut it again and put it back in—when I actually got to that moment on the taping, live, I suddenly realized I couldn't remember whether the lines were in or not," relates Cleese. "They'd been taken in and out every day that week, and I couldn't remember whether they were in or out!

"During the time it took me to think of that, I realized I didn't know where I was in the sketch anyway. At that point, I was supposed to say to Ronnie Corbett 'You know, you must be one of the smallest men I've ever met,' and I managed to say to him 'You know, I think you must be one of the tallest men I've ever met.' I remember he looked pretty startled at that. I somehow got through it, I don't know who—somebody inside my skin got through it for me.

"At the end, I had a sort of battle fatigue reaction to it. I went home, laid out on the bed, and I just cried for about an hour out of sheer fright. What I'd been frightened about for a series and a half, forgetting my lines badly on the air, had finally happened. Of course, the next day I discovered nobody'd noticed!" he laughs.

"It was a major discovery for me. I also realized that if you did forget your lines, the only thing to do is to look very determined and interestedly at another actor!"

Aside from such terrifying moments, Cleese found *The Frost Report* a very good experience.

"There was a very calm, pleasant, orderly Scot in charge called Jimmy Gilbert, whom I remain very fond of. There was a very, very good panel

of writers who were good judges of material. On the whole, the good stuff was selected and the bad stuff wasn't. There were so many people writing, you were never short of material. In fact, I was instrumental in getting one or two of my sketches cut! We usually found we were overlength on certain days, and when I had a sketch I didn't have much faith in, I used to try and talk it out of the show, usually successfully, partly because I was very scared doing it all live in front of this very big audience—we used to get fourteen million."

Cleese's fellow performers were also very talented; he notes that he learned a great deal from "The Two Ronnies."*

"I was very lucky to learn with Barker and Corbett, because they were very relaxed but hugely professional. You could always rely on them. Ronnie Corbett's timing was extraordinary. I felt he could do some bits of timing that almost nobody I knew could carry off. Whereas Ronnie Barker just played any character that you liked—it didn't matter whether it was an effete, upper-class Englishman or an Albanian peasant, he would play it and it would be believable and funny. It was great to have such a high degree of friendly professionalism around me, and they took the strain from all my nerves."

The Frost Report, which debuted on March 10, 1966, consisted of eight shows in the first series and seven the following year, with a Christmas special at the end of 1967. Each of the programs dealt with a theme; these included love, money, authority, elections, education, and class. One recurring scene featured Cleese, Ronnie Barker, and Ronnie Corbett as representatives of the upper, middle, and lower classes; Cleese, naturally, was the upper-class gentleman, while the lower class was always the butt of the jokes. (Cleese would occasionally appear a few years later to reprise his role on *The Two Ronnies,* where Corbett and Barker revived the sketch.) In between the two series of *Frost Reports* was *The Frost Programme* for the now defunct Rediffusion television company, featuring Cleese; it began appearing October 19, 1966, and ran through the following January 4.

*Ronnie Barker and Ronnie Corbett would star in their own TV comedy series, *The Two Ronnies,* a few years later.

"It was entirely sketch comedy. You either wrote sketches—by and large John and Graham wrote one very funny sketch each week—or you wrote link material, which Frost read off the autocue, jokes and such. I used to write pages of that," reveals Idle.

Palin and Jones also found their own niche on the show.

"We wrote little jokes for David—he had a long monologue at the beginning and little jokes throughout the show, so we'd write little one-liners for him," notes Palin. "We'd try to break into sketch-writing, but that was pretty well sewn up by the likes of Cleese and Chapman, and Barry [Cryer] and Marty [Feldman] and the regulars.

"The ad libs were written by the likes of us. We did actually get to write one or two little sketches, minisketches—quickies, I suppose you'd call them, one of which was in the show that won the Montreux Golden Rose Award in 1966. So, if we weren't writing much and we were getting paid absolutely nothing, we were in a show that was very prestigious."

Graham Chapman explained that despite the prestige attached to *The Frost Report,* it was actually a fairly conventional show, and the frustrations Cleese, Idle, Jones, Palin, and he developed doing shows like *The Frost Report* would eventually lead to *Monty Python's Flying Circus.*

"It *posed* as a satirical show on a weekly basis, but it was really just a compilation of sketches, and those sketches always seemed to follow a similar format. They had to have a beginning to let people know what was going on, a middle, and an end—a tag which was often very artificially introduced, just to let the audience know it's ended," Chapman laughed. "In a way, it was almost infantile in its approach to what we expected the audience's intelligence to be able to take.

"We felt they were a little brighter than that on the whole, and didn't have to be spoon-fed—so much so that I think a lot of comedy then was spoiled because it was overexplained. You could see what was going to happen. If you were even averagely bright, you could see what was going to happen seconds before it did, which in some cases can be satisfying, but a lot of the time in comedy, gets away from the surprise element. Consequently, you lose your audience."

Frost and his producers were aware that their

writers were paid very little. As a result, even though Cleese was the only one of the future Pythons to perform as a part of Frost's stock company, Palin, Jones, and some of the others were allowed to appear in small roles, in order to collect paychecks for acting.

"In the second series we wrote much more. We ended up writing short films, like 'Judges in a Playground,' what judges do after they leave the court—they go out to this playground and muck about, go down slides and on swings and then go back to court. We began to write one or two sketches, and I think that's how our humor really came to the notice of John and Graham, who were writing superb sketches at the time," noted Palin.

As *The Frost Report* was drawing to a close, two of the performers received an offer from Frost himself.

"Frost came to me and Tim Brooke-Taylor individually and said 'How about doing a show each?' We said we'd like to do one *together*. We pulled in Graham; then, after very little thought, Marty [Feldman], and then we of course had *At Last the 1948 Show*," explains Cleese.

At Last the 1948 Show would prove to be another valuable stepping-stone in their collective careers, although *The Frost Report* was the most important program to date for Cleese, Chapman, Idle, Jones, and Palin. While they were also doing some occasional writing and performing for a variety of other TV shows, all five were forming the bonds that would develop into Monty Python.

At Last the 1948 Show

At Last the 1948 Show was, for Graham Chapman and John Cleese, the immediate predecessor to *Monty Python's Flying Circus*. It was the show that allowed them to experiment with comedic ideas and concepts that they later perfected in Python. Certainly, credit must be given to David Frost, who offered his co-workers the opportunity to create their own show. It's safe to say that without the freedom they were given in *The 1948 Show, Monty Python* would have been quite different, and may not have even come into existence at all.

". . . *The 1948 Show* was where, for the first time, we got a little bit of freedom," recalled Graham Chapman. "We were the actors as well as the writers for *The 1948 Show*, and that removed an element of control—no interpretation by the actor of what you write. Also, no egos in the way that 'I'm not going to do that, because that would ruin my reputation with my public.' That was no concern to us, we didn't worry about that. No reputations to lose, I suppose, at that point!" he laughed.

"So, we *were* able to do *sillier* things because we were a little more in control—to do things that were a little more risky, too, that were not so conventional. I think we felt a little bit stifled sometimes, particularly writing for *The Frost Report,* which was a fairly conventional sketch show. We'd take material along to script meetings, and the cast would laugh at it a great deal, but then say we couldn't possibly do it, because it was wrong

for their image, or they felt a little bit too infantile—it might make them look silly."

*(Clockwise from top) Aimi MacDonald, Graham Chapman, Tim Brooke-Taylor, John Cleese and Marty Feldman: the cast of **At Last the 1948 Show**. Photo from the Collection of John Cleese, used by permission.*

One of Cleese's favorite photos from Rediffusion's **At Last the 1948 Show.** *(From left: John Cleese, Marty Feldman, Graham Chapman, and Tim Brooke-Taylor.) Rediffusion photo from the Collection of John Cleese, used by permission.*

Graham said that doing their own shows after *The Frost Report* was very emancipating.

"When we first did our own show, and when we had even more control with Python, it freed us from all those constraints. Half our comedy shows before that used to have songs and dance routines in the middle—it was a hangover from the days of variety," noted Graham.

"It was almost as though they were afraid to have a whole half hour of solid comedy. *We* were, in a way, because it took a lot more writing—harder than 'And now so-and-so sings this song!' We thought it was a little bit lazy, even though we were lazy ourselves. Being lazy ourselves, I suppose that's 'why we were overjoyed when we were joined by Michael Palin, Terry Jones, Eric Idle, and Terry Gilliam—that meant we had much less writing to do.

"We were a little annoyed at how conventional comedy had become, and wanted it to break free of that and change things. If it worked, fine, if it didn't, then no matter—it was a worthwhile experiment. The initial experiment for John and myself was . . . *The 1948 Show.* That seemed to work, but even in that, we often felt obliged to have an end to a sketch, where often it was not necessary,

and to put more structure in than we really needed. But we did take some risks, and we were able to do that more so with Python," related Chapman.

Even Cleese, who is often overly critical of his early work, still enthuses about *At Last the 1948 Show.*

"It was terrific. That was the first chance I ever had, when I was given my head by David Frost," he recalls. "He offered Tim Brooke-Taylor and myself shows. We didn't want shows separately, so we decided we'd do one together. We brought Graham in automatically, because obviously he was going to be the third, and we looked around, and suddenly decided that we would ask Marty [Feldman], who was only known as a writer. So, Marty's first screen appearances were in the '48 Show.

"I can still remember David when we said we wanted Marty to be one of the four performers. Dear David said [sotto voce] 'But won't the audience be a little uncomfortable about the way he looks?' And of course, it's so funny, because the way he looked was his fortune."

First broadcast February 15, 1967, the cast also featured "the lovely Aimi MacDonald." One of the running gags in the series centered on MacDonald's believing that she was the centerpiece of the show; one program featured the "Make the Lovely Aimi MacDonald a Rich Lady Appeal." There were two series of *At Last the 1948 Show* and a total of thirteen shows, which had been thought lost for many years.

"They've mainly been wiped,* but we recently discovered that Swedish television has some in their vaults. They're in black and white, and not of very good quality, but it's fascinating to see Marty's first screen stuff," explains Cleese.

At Last the 1948 Show broke new ground because it was one of the first shows to use the medium of television to send itself up, utilizing state-of-the-art 1967 technology, according to Chapman. They attempted to ignore or flout the conventions of the typical TV variety show, and bend the formats with the same anarchic point of view as their hero, Spike Milligan. The result, though not perfect, was a large step forward.

"It was a very happy show, because we started

*Wiped out or erased.

to do a wilder type of humor than I'd ever been allowed to do before, and that's always marvelous," recalls Cleese. "We were allowed suddenly to do something that we'd been held back from. But it was also a bit of a nightmare, because we weren't very experienced. We did it in a great rush.

"I remember being up at half-past ten at night trying to write sketches that we were going to have to put on tape in three days' time. The pressure on us was pretty tremendous, and I got used to that terrible feeling of panic and slight depression as you're writing late at night, because the other things you've written the previous days aren't working, and you've got to come up with something new. You're feeling tired and depressed, which makes it even harder. A lot of young comedians will recognize that feeling. Well, that's when I went through it."

The show also gave Eric Idle a chance to perform in some small roles. *Do Not Adjust Your Set* had not yet come about, so Idle was the only one of the future Pythons to appear in both of these ground-breaking series.

"I used to play small bits in it," recalls Idle. "I'd come to be the dead body. The first time, I was the defense counselor in a courtroom sketch, and they used to use me every week just to play the odd bits. It was my first real experience doing TV after Cambridge, in a professional sense, with people, and not being nervous. I never had much to do, and yet I was around this comedy show. It was a very funny show!"

At Last the 1948 Show was the first TV project to offer him great personal satisfaction, says Cleese, who remembers it fondly. "There was a kind of terror and excitement at doing . . . *the 1948 Show,* the first time I ever had a really major stake in a television thing. There was terror and excitement at doing TV comedy for the very first time under pressure, not enough time, not enough resources, and I think I shall always remember that as a sort of good young person's experience, an interesting first blooding as to what it was all about."

John Cleese and Graham Chapman became more heavily involved in writing and performing in films than Eric Idle, Terry Jones, and Michael Palin, particularly after they had finished *At Last the 1948 Show.*

The best-known of these films is undoubtedly *The Magic Christian.* A vehicle for Peter Sellers, who starred as the richest man in the world, the film co-starred Ringo Starr and featured a soundtrack by Badfinger that included the top-ten hit "Come and Get It."

John Cleese and Graham Chapman were brought in to write some additional material for **The Magic Christian,** *and were each featured in small roles. Here, Cleese jokes between takes with stars Ringo Starr and Peter Sellers. Photo from the Collection of John Cleese, used by permission.*

Graham Chapman and John Cleese were brought in to rewrite one of the many drafts that had been prepared for the film.

"John and I were writing one day, or wondering what to write, and we got a phone call from Peter Sellers. We didn't know him, but we thought a Peter Sellers movie script would be interesting. He said would we do some rewrites on the script? When he mentioned a figure of five hundred pounds a week, that seemed a lot to us at the time, so we thought yes, we'll have a look at it and see whether we will or not," explained Chapman.

"The Terry Southern script had been through thirteen drafts by the time it got to us. We read one that contained the most elegant and verbose stage directions I have ever come across in my life, but quite hopeless dialogue, I'm afraid," notes Cleese.

"Graham and I managed to put this script into shape in three or four weeks until we got it to the point where they were able to raise money on it, at which point Terry Southern arrived and was laid to rest in a nest of bourbon crates. They went back to a script that was more or less as terrible as the one that Peter had refused to finance in the first place."

John Cleese appeared in one of the best sketches in the entire film, not coincidentally written by Chapman and him, and shot on the first day.

"I was lucky enough to get to play quite a good sketch that Graham and I wrote, which was set in a Sotheby's showroom. It was about Guy Grand buying a portrait and then cutting the noses out because he was only interested in noses. It was what he collected. It was about greed as opposed to aesthetic morality, whether you'd sell a Rembrandt to someone who was only going to cut the noses out. It was a good sketch, and I enjoyed playing it, but basically, the film was a complete mess," relates Cleese. "It was done by a very nice man who had no idea of comedy structure, and it finished up as a series of celebrity walk-ons."

Chapman recalled another interesting aspect of the first day's shooting, which revealed how Ringo's part (as Sellers's son) was diminished due to Sellers; it involved the scene that Cleese appeared in.

"Ringo was still in it, but not very much. One curious thing occurred on the first day of filming. It was characteristic of Peter, although I didn't know it at the time.

"Guy Grand and his son were wandering around Sotheby's, the auction room, collecting valuable articles of art. As soon as they had paid for them, they would throw them into a shopping trolley—really very valuable articles that they then treated as though they were nothing; the whole film really was about money and what you can do with it. That was quite a nice sequence by the end of the day," explained Chapman.

"That was shot again the second day. Peter claimed that he hadn't quite got his character right, but the real reason was that Ringo Starr got a lot of laughs."

American Python fans will note that *The Magic Christian* provides a relatively rare opportunity for them to see Cleese and Chapman performing in their pre-Python days; they both performed in sketches that they wrote, and Chapman can be seen as the leader of a rowing team (although he isn't listed in the closing credits).

Do Not Adjust Your Set

"*Do Not Adjust Your Set* was really the first major, indeed most important thing that I was to do," notes Michael Palin of his early years.

Several of his collaborators on the show could say the same. *Do Not Adjust Your Set* was as vital to the development of *Monty Python's Flying Circus* for Eric Idle, Terry Gilliam, Terry Jones, and Michael Palin as *At Last the 1948 Show* was for John Cleese and Graham Chapman.

Do Not Adjust Your Set actually began as a children's show, but soon developed a cult following with adults. BBC-Radio producer Humphrey Barclay, who had worked on *I'm Sorry, I'll Read That Again,* first approached Eric Idle with an idea for the series.

"Humphrey Barclay came to me and said 'I want to do a kid's show,' and he asked me to write it and be in it," recalls Idle. "I knew him at Cambridge—we'd done Footlights together, shows at Edinburgh. He said 'Will you write for me?' and I said 'Yes, but I want to work with Mike and Terry.' He thought that would be a good idea, so we got Mike and Terry in to write and perform it

too. Then he brought in David Jason and Denise Coffey, and the Bonzo Dog Doo Dah Band."

Michael Palin recalls that he joined the team as part of a Palin-Jones package.

"*Do Not Adjust Your Set* was very important, really, because it was the first time we were given a free hand as writers and performers," relates Palin. "Humphrey Barclay had asked Eric and Terry to do something with him. He hadn't asked me, and Terry said 'Uh, well, I'm not doing this unless my friend Michael comes along,' and he said 'All right.' So they asked me along, and it turned into a very nice team."

As Terry Jones explains, the allure for most of them was the chance to perform their own material on a regular basis.

"Our agent was saying 'What do you want to do a children's show for? Why don't you write a stage show for someone that you can make money out of?' We wanted to do it, obviously, because it was performing," reveals Jones.

The group did two series of thirteen shows each for *Do Not Adjust Your Set* as well as a Christ-

mas special titled *Do Not Adjust Your Stocking.* The first series was for Rediffusion Television, but after they went out of business, the second series was picked up by Thames Television.

"We became a cult hit," notes Idle. "We were the biggest thing on the TV before the *Ten O'Clock News.* It went very well. We won an award early on for children's TV excellence: the Silver Bear of Berlin, or Munich, or somewhere."

Do Not Adjust Your Set was also responsible for yet another addition to Python personnel. Michael Palin says that since it was a children's show, it was broadcast from about five-fifteen till a quarter to six, including five minutes of ads.

"We had to supply about twenty-five minutes of material, but then we also had the Bonzo Dog [Doo Dah] Band, with Viv Stanshall and Neil Innes," relates Palin. "It was the first time we met Neil. They were the resident music act on the show, so that cut our time down to—we could get

(Clockwise from upper left) Eric Idle, Michael Palin, David Jason, Denise Coffey and Terry Jones. Photo from the Collection of Terry Jones, used by permission.

away with about twenty minutes or so of written material."

Neil Innes was an art student and musician, and the band was mostly made up of other art students. Their live performances were highly theatrical, and their approach to music and performing was Pythonesque even before Monty Python existed. The Bonzos released a number of albums in the late 1960s and early '70s, and even had a hit single, "I'm the Urban Spaceman," which was produced by Paul McCartney (under the name Apollo C. Vermouth). The Bonzo Dog (Doo-Dah) Band even appeared in the Beatles' *Magical Mystery Tour,* singing "Death Camp for Cutie" while a stripper performed in the foreground.

After meeting the ensemble on *Do Not Adjust Your Set,* Innes went on to do occasional audience warmups for *Monty Python's Flying Circus* and even performed a bit in the fourth series of shows. But Innes is probably best known among Python fans for his roles in the films and stage shows, beginning with *Monty Python and the Holy Grail.*

During the middle of the first series, the final, significant ingredient was added. Terry Gilliam had returned to London earlier in the year and found himself unemployed. Cleese provided him with an introduction to Humphrey Barclay, who was producing *Do Not Adjust Your Set* at the time, but Gilliam found it difficult to make contact with Barclay.

"I caught him on the phone," explains Gilliam, "For a month I'd been trying to get through to him and I was getting nowhere. One day I called and he picked up the phone, so I got a chance to see him. I had some written material and some cartoons, and it turns out he was an amateur cartoonist. He liked the cartoons a lot, and he liked a couple of the writing things, and bought two, which then got forced on Mike, Terry, and Eric. I can't even remember what they were—they were really more conceptual than dialogue-oriented."

Gilliam recalls that Jones and Palin were not particularly pleased at having this American writer foisted on them at first, though Idle warmed up to him more quickly.

"It was the first time they used something from someone outside the group. They didn't really like it, but fortunately they decided to be nice and give me a break," he recalls. The American joined *Do Not Adjust Your Set* midway through the

first series, though his contributions were minimal at first. He attempted to write sketches, but never quite found his niche. It was not until after the first series that Gilliam found himself doing animation for the very first time.

Glimpses of Python could be seen in *Do Not Adjust Your Set,* and it was certainly not an ordinary children's show.

"We'd do a little sort of cold opening, and then sketches, some of them very quick. There'd be regular features—I played a chef who cooked silly things, and Denise Coffey played Mrs. Black. Then there was a character called Captain Fantastic, who was a little man in a shabby mac who went around, having slightly magical powers, but not quite enough," reveals Palin.

"Other things were very much what became mainstream Python. We'd do a sketch about shop assistants trying to sell a suit which manifestly doesn't fit—I'd do all this spiel, 'The jacket is lovely,' 'But there's a sleeve missing,' 'Ah, that's how they're wearing it this year.' Things like that. There was the man who is called to rescue someone who has fallen off a cliff and is hanging on by his fingernails, and the man who is sent to rescue him recognizes him from television, so he has this long talk about what programs he's been in, and all that, while the man's life is ebbing away. . . . Fairly run-of-the-mill stuff—we had to write them fairly fast."

Each of them was also involved with other projects while working on *Do Not Adjust Your Set.*

Between the first and second series, Eric Idle and Terry Gilliam were involved with a fascinating failure of a show called *We Have Ways of Making You Laugh.* While Terry Jones and Michael Palin were doing the second series of *Do Not Adjust Your Set,* they were also collaborating on *The Complete and Utter History of Britain.* In addition, they were continuing to write sketches for a variety of other programs.

"That was our phase of being script doctors, open all hours, which really continued until just before Python," says Palin of the writing sessions with Jones.

"We had a break suddenly in 1969, when the second series of *Do Not Adjust Your Set* had finished, *The Two Ronnies* had finished. *The Complete and Utter History of Britain* had been done. We'd worked ourselves flat out, and it was just suddenly nice to have a bit of a breather. And then after the breather, Python came along!"

Do Not Adjust Your Set had prepared its writers for *Monty Python* better than they had realized. On January 28, 1968, Michael Palin told the *Sunday Times,* "Every time we write a sketch which we can't use on the programme because it offends one of those taboos, we just file it away. Very thrifty. We should be able to flog the lot to one of those adult comedy shows." Little did he realize at the time that they would soon be using some of that material in "one of those adult comedy shows" called *Monty Python's Flying Circus.*

We Have Ways of Making You Laugh

"We Have Ways of Making You Laugh was very unfunny. We didn't have any ways of making them laugh!" recalls Eric Idle.

After the first series of *Do Not Adjust Your Set,* Humphrey Barclay set about creating a new show for a new network. Perhaps in a mood to experiment, he decided to develop a talk show that would include several comedy sketches, in addition to a house cartoonist who would do funny drawings of the guest panelists. From *Do Not Adjust Your Set,* he brought along Eric Idle to write and perform sketches and Terry Gilliam to do cartoons. "Humphrey went over to London Weekend Television and produced *We Have Ways of Making You*

Laugh, with Frank Muir hosting," explains Gilliam. "Humphrey dragged me along to do cartoon sketches of the guest stars. Everybody would be sitting around making witty comments—the team was Frank Muir, Dick Vosburgh, Dennis Greene, and Eric—and the camera would look over my shoulder as I was drawing a cartoon of the person."

"It was the first show on London Weekend Television. It won the franchise, and it was the first show actually on the air," notes Idle.

When they performed the first show live, Idle says it worked perfectly. "It was very funny, the audience roared out in laughter. Strangely enough,

Humphrey Barclay came back and said 'Well, congratulations, but unfortunately, it didn't go out—the unions pulled the plug.' We'd done this thing, so we said 'Why didn't you tell us?' 'We didn't want you to stop in case they put the plugs back in!' So after that, the show never really went as well again.*

"Gilliam used to sit around drawing sketches. I used to be a performer, and Frank would sit around with some guests—it was sort of a loose half chat, half comedy. People are always trying to combine chat and comedy, which never works," says Idle.

We Have Ways of Making You Laugh may be best remembered for giving the world Terry Gilliam's first animation. He had never done an animated film before, but the opportunity arose one week when the show featured a disc jockey who was notorious for terrible puns.

"He was obsessed with connecting links to records with one pun after another," notes Gilliam. "Dick Vosburgh collected three months' worth of this material, and he didn't know what to do with

it, and I suggested an animated film. I had two weeks and four hundred pounds to do it, and so the only way I could do it was with cutouts. It was in black and white.

"It went out, and people had never seen anything like that. It was just amazing, the effect of going out to millions of people watching television. The immediate effect was all these people going 'Wow, this is incredible,' and they said 'Can you do another one for us?' "

That was the beginning of it all. Gilliam then followed it up with another film called *Beware the Elephant.* One of his earliest creations was visible during the Python stage shows, which featured a short cartoon titled "Christmas Cards." Consisting of figures and symbols from Christmas cards that come to life in typical Gilliam fashion, the film was originally done for *Do Not Adjust Your Stocking,* a holiday version of the series. So, from humble beginnings on *We Have Ways of Making You Laugh,* Terry Gilliam had established a niche for himself as an artist who could produce wonderful little cartoons.

How to Irritate People

After *At Last the 1948 Show,* Graham Chapman and John Cleese were writing and appearing in a number of TV and film projects. Cleese wasn't quite certain what he wanted to do. He knew he wanted to involve Connie Booth, who had recently moved to London from America, and he had also become interested in working with Michael Palin.

It was David Frost who stepped in again and suggested they develop the special that became *How to Irritate People.*

"David asked me to do it," explains Cleese.

"Connie and I got married after our three-and-a-half-year courtship, a lot of which was conducted across the Atlantic, and it was the first thing I did when I got back, because I wanted her to be in it. I wrote some stuff, mainly with Graham Chapman.

"Graham, Connie, and Michael Palin were the main actors, though I think Eric did some of it, and I think Barry Cryer was involved."

The video of *How to Irritate People* was released in Britain in early 1990 by David Frost, who was the executive producer, says Palin. "I had a look, and thought it had strengths and weaknesses, so we made a few cuts here and there and we put it out.

"Frost was quite important to things at that time. He had Cleese and Chapman under contract to write films and all that. He had a contract with Westinghouse Systems in America, and he wanted to break British humor in the States.

"He got Graham and John to write *How to Irritate People* for him, which was a number of sketches about getting into situations where people irritate you, such as waiters in restaurants

*Even though Terry Jones and Michael Palin weren't involved with *We Have Ways of Making You Laugh,* they still managed to get caught up in the disastrous opening days of London Weekend Television.

"I had been signed up as an actor to work with the Two Ronnies on *Frost on Saturday,* which was a variety show with sketches and interviews and all that. I was a sort of fall guy for the Two Ronnies, so although I wasn't on the first night of London Weekend Television, which opened with *We Have Ways of Making You Laugh,* I was there on the second night with *Frost on Saturday,*" reveals Palin.

"There was a strike, as happens when new television companies are on the air. They're a bit vulnerable, so they will call a strike. We carried on and produced this strike-breaking show, with heads of drama working the cameras. I remember Frank Muir, who was head of light entertainment, working as floor manager—it was like troupers carrying on while the shells were exploding above us. And it was just extraordinary that we got this show done!"

being terribly fawning. One of them involved a husband sitting around the home and company coming around for dinner; the wife is getting him to tell a joke, and he doesn't want to tell it, but as soon as he starts, she keeps correcting him. There were lots of nice things in it," relates Palin.

Another sketch was inspired by a real-life incident involving Michael Palin. He had bought a car, but when he started having problems with it, the salesman refused to accept that there was anything wrong. When he complained that the brakes were going out, the salesman told him "Oh, well, it's a new car, bound to happen."

Cleese and Chapman were both so taken by the story that they wrote a sketch around it for *How to Irritate People,* in which Palin played the car salesman. When the group was looking for old material to rewrite for *Monty Python's Flying Circus,* Chapman suggested substituting a dead parrot for a defective car, and it became a classic.

Chapman and Cleese wrote the script themselves. Palin and the rest of the cast were simply brought on as actors, as most of them were involved in other projects.

"The show was done in 1968, but things overlapped. We'd rehearse *Do Not Adjust Your Set* in the morning and do this in the afternoon—we'd just work all the hours God gave," Palin recalls.

"But it was very good. The script was the funniest thing, the most impressive selection of sketches I'd seen in a long while—intelligent and also very silly—all of the hallmarks of Cleese and Chapman's stuff. I was just asked to act in it, and I was very flattered to be asked—myself and Tim Brooke-Taylor and Connie Booth, John and Graham. . . . It was a wonderful thing to work on, but it all fell apart at the recording stage.

"Although we'd gotten the rehearsal done very smoothly, the actual shooting and recording was done very badly. John, who was doing the links, had to come out of character each time—he'd dress up as the linkman, do his one link, go into the next sketch, come out, take his clothes off, get dressed as the linkman, do that, change again. . . . Why they didn't do all the links together, God only knows, but it meant it went on for a very long time and put considerable pressure on all the cast. In the end, the audience was just leaving to catch their last buses home . . ." notes Palin.

"Unfortunately, it was not nearly as successful as I think it should have been, but it has some wonderful things in it, including some of the best work that Graham's ever done—very funny sketches. So it's worth it from that point alone."

How to Irritate People was also worth it in that it allowed Palin to collaborate with Cleese and Chapman to a significant extent. They would be working together again soon.

The Complete and Utter History of Britain

While Terry Jones and Michael Palin were getting the second series of *Do Not Adjust Your Set* underway, they were asked to do *The Complete and Utter History of Britain.* Work on the two projects overlapped, and the sixth and final episode of the latter was broadcast just days before the first episode of the second series of *DNAYS.* Originally, there were seven different *Complete and Utter Histories,* but the seven were eventually edited down to six when they were broadcast.

"Humphrey Barclay was again involved," notes Palin. "He'd been the man behind *Do Not Adjust Your Set,* and he was providing programs for the new London Weekend Television. He asked Terry and I what we'd ideally like to write, so we came up with this idea.

"The show's about history as if there had been television facilities around at that time, so we could have people interviewed on television, in the showers, after the Battle of Hastings. We had Samuel Pepys doing a chat show, and things like that. It was a nice format, but it didn't work nearly as well as it probably should have done."

Although *The Complete and Utter History of Britain* was the last major project that Palin and Jones would embark on before Monty Python, they still had to labor under the usual constraints of television before they could start breaking all the rules.

"*Complete and Utter History* was pre-Python in the sense that we were controlled in some way by the format," Palin explains. "We had to use whatever actors we could get rather than do the roles ourselves. I think the difference shows.

"People say sometimes that we were very self-ish in Python, but at least we did it the way we wanted to, and it was much more indicative of what was really needed then than what we did before, which was to get guest actors in and hope that they would understand our humor, which they did not always do. And that's really what happened on *Complete and Utter History*—we didn't get people who quite knew what we were on about. It had some nice stuff."

Terry Jones agrees with his partner's assessment of the series. "They weren't terribly successful, in my opinion. I think the scripts are really funny. In fact, somebody from Columbia Television was suggesting redoing the scripts, and there's some smashing material. We just didn't have control over it, and the actual casting wasn't very good.

"Mike and I were doing mostly anonymous subsidiary roles, and I personally think the people they had doing some of the other things were a bit heavy. They weren't quite in the spirit of the thing, though they were quite good performers."

The Complete and Utter Histories provided the last important link in the chain that led to *Monty Python*. John Cleese and Graham Chapman had finished *At Last the 1948 Show* and were writing and performing TV and films. Palin, Jones, Idle, and Gilliam had finished *Do Not Adjust Your Set* (and, in the case of Palin and Jones, *The Complete and Utter History of Britain*), and were similarly writing and performing in various projects in 1969.

"I think it was really the *Complete and Utter His-*

Terry Jones in one of his many roles in the six-part **Complete and Utter History of Britain**. *Photo from the Collection of Terry Jones, used by permission.*

tories that got John saying 'Why don't we do something together?' " explains Jones. "John particularly wanted to work with Mike, and Mike said 'I write with Terry, can Terry come along too?' We just came as a package, and John and Graham said Eric and Terry Gilliam can come along as well. So in the end, Python was *At Last the 1948 Show* meets *Do Not Adjust Your Set*."

The Road to Monty Python

By 1969 Graham Chapman, John Cleese, Terry Gilliam, Eric Idle, Terry Jones, and Michael Palin were all in demand.

As a result of their recent successes, the television networks were eager to work with them all, in whatever partnerships or teams they chose. Cleese had a virtual standing offer to do his own BBC series, while Thames Television was eager to continue working with the group from *Do Not Adjust Your Set* when that series ended.

"Thames wanted us to do a grown-up show, and we were talking about that when this BBC opportunity came up," explains Idle.

In fact, Idle says they were very close to creating a new Monty Python–like show for Thames when they were contacted by Cleese and Chapman; that effectively ended talks with the independent network and was the official beginning of *Monty Python's Flying Circus*. Thames has always regretted the loss.

"The controller of Thames, Jeremy Isaacs, who was head of Channel Four till recently, still kicks himself that they didn't get us," according to Idle. "I think we actually had a slot, and then they came back to us and said 'No, we can't put you in that slot, but we do want you to continue to develop

the show.' Meanwhile, Michael had been talking to John, I think, and so that all happened very quickly. Suddenly we were on with thirteen [shows], so we said to Thames 'Sorry.' They still think they missed out on Python!"

Of course, any series the group would have developed for Thames would have been distinctly different from Python. At that stage, Thames was hoping for a grown-up version of *Do Not Adjust Your Set,* and it would not have involved Cleese and Chapman.

"At that point, it was more like David [Jason], Mike, Terry, me, and whatever we could develop as an adult show," reveals Idle. "It was a longer slot—I think three-quarters of an hour was talked about at one stage. And then it suddenly happened very quickly. Mike had been talking to John and done a show with John called *How to Irritate People.* So, John and Graham were a pair, and he was interested in Mike. Mike, Terry, and I were sort of put together, and I guess we dragged along Terry Gilliam for that, too."

Barry Took, a producer and father figure to many of the younger writers and performers at the BBC, felt that combining the Cleese-Chapman team with Palin and Jones would be a worthy experiment. Cleese had always wanted to work with Palin, and a phone call to Palin one evening by Cleese laid the groundwork. They each brought along additional ingredients in the forms of Chapman, Idle, Jones, and, in an inspired touch, Gilliam. At their very first meeting with the BBC (arranged by Took), they were given a commitment for thirteen episodes.

During much of this time, Cleese had been under contract to David Frost; when he began to get interested in Python, Frost excused Cleese from the contract. That was the final obstacle, and *Monty Python's Flying Circus* was at last off the ground.

The BBC was reportedly interested in doing a series with John Cleese, while Cleese had wanted to work with Michael Palin. The two groups got together, and thanks to the efforts of producer Barry Took, they had the opportunity to do an as-yet-undefined comedy show.

"Mike was the connecting element that got our two different groups together," recalls Gilliam. "John had this standing invitation from the BBC to do a program—I don't think they knew who all of us were. They knew we'd all been writers, we'd

worked on stuff for Marty Feldman and David Frost, but John was always the one they liked the most.

"Mike, Terry, and Eric were all intrigued by the animation, and the idea of having this element in the show. I don't know if John and Graham were interested at all," he laughs.

Michael Palin remembers getting a phone call one evening that got it all rolling. "John Cleese asked what we were all doing. He was sort of kicking his heels, and said 'Why don't we try something all together?' We'd also done the animation with Terry Gilliam, and since John had also worked with Terry, we said 'Fine, let's talk about it.'

"At the time, Barry Took was sort of a father figure for us younger writers, and he was working for the BBC as a script editor. He provided our first entrée to the BBC. He got us in to talk with Michael Mills, who was head of comedy at the time, and we just had a meeting. The BBC suddenly said 'Well, you can have thirteen shows for the late night slot.' So saying, they left the room!" Palin laughs.

Took had known all of the group since their early days with the BBC. A number of writers and performers were emerging from the stage revues at Oxford, Cambridge, and elsewhere, and Took was aware of this surge of creativity. In addition to smoothing the way at the BBC, Took also helped throw together the most interesting creative groups he saw at the time.

"It struck me that of the twelve or fifteen very talented men around, I thought the people who had the most influence on each other would be John and Graham on one hand, and Michael and Terry on the other. Fundamentally, it would be the impact of those two different sorts of brainwaves coming together that would make the comedy. They added another couple of ingredients, to become Monty Python," says Took.

"I went to them all and said 'Would you like to do a program with these other people?' and they all said yes. They all had qualms about it, and didn't want to feel trapped by a group show that they could not then get out of, so I said 'If you don't like it, there's nothing to hold you, you can leave.' I wanted to have a very free feeling.

"If one has people with talent, I say 'Go with that,' don't ask what they're going to do—let them do what they feel is absolutely apt. I wanted to im-

pose the antithesis of censorship or control. It sounds a contradiction, but I wanted to say to them 'Look, if you let people run free, they'll produce better work than if they're constrained in old-fashioned formulas.' They say, 'You can't do that because it's never been done before,' but the other side of that is 'We must do that because it's never been done before.' I said [optimistically] that once we gave these young men their head . . . 'They're so bright, how could it not work?' . . . before it ever happened. And every piece of evidence suggests that the initial guess was the right one," Took points out.

The first meeting of the six was encouraging, recalled Graham Chapman, and although they had not all performed together, they tended to be familiar with the others' work. "When Barry Took hit on the idea of putting us all together, it was fine by us—although at that stage, I knew nothing about Terry Gilliam at all. I'd seen him a couple of times on *Do Not Adjust Your Set,* and that was about it—a shadowy figure!

"The first meeting was a convivial affair. We knew of each other and what kind of work the others had put out for such things as *The Frost Report.* There was already a working relationship, even though we'd never actually worked together.

So, after the very first meeting, which was really just saying 'Hello,' and 'Yes, it would be a good idea to work together,' we went away and had a sit-through, and looked at all of the old material we had left over from *The Frost Report,*" Chapman laughed. "Just to see how much material we would have for our first few shows . . . Actually, there was quite a bit, which made us feel safer. We knew we had some bankers, as it were, in the way of sketches that we knew were good and hadn't been used to that point. So we began writing more, meeting together, and reading stuff to each other. That's how the whole process began."

Once the BBC approved the idea of such a show, it was up to the six Pythons to decide just what the show should be. As Michael Palin recalls, they already had a time slot, but they didn't know what shape their program would take. One of the most important influences was Spike Milligan's series *Q5.* Milligan had been an idol of the group ever since his *Goon Shows** aired on BBC radio in the '50s, and the stream-of-consciousness approach of *Q5* was closely noted. In fact, the

Pythons asked for *Q5's* Ian MacNaughton to direct their new show, and MacNaughton ended up handling all but the first four shows (which were directed by BBC staff producer John Howard Davies).

The unique structure was most intentional. After working under the constraints of TV comedy at the time, the group members were chomping at the bit to bite the hand that had been feeding them. And when they were unleashed, they did just that.

The show distinguished itself immediately with its use of animation, used to present short Gilliam bits and to connect sketches that could not be linked in any normal manner. As Michael Palin notes, "For a couple of weeks, Terry Jones and Terry Gilliam were very keen on this stream-of-consciousness approach. Gilliam was very influential in those early days in setting the style of Python."

While Palin, Jones, Gilliam, and Idle—the *Do Not Adjust Your Set* group—emphasized stream of consciousness, Chapman and Cleese had their own thoughts on the shape of the show that complemented the others' ideas.

"Partly because of *At Last the 1948 Show,* John and I already had in mind what it should *not* be, and that was conventional," Chapman said. "We'd gotten further away from most TV sketch shows by ignoring the conventions established over the years—that sketches must have a beginning, middle, and end, and a punch line, above all. They must also be interspersed with songs and dances—that was always the tradition, a holdover from stage variety or stage revue. We protested that—it was laziness on the part of the writers to say 'And now over to a song' when we could conceivably have half-an-hour's worth of television show which was *all* funny. 'You *can* take it,' we thought. It's just that people weren't industrious enough to write it. So, we did want each part of the show to be worthy of its place on the basis of comedy.

"We had gone further and further with the *1948 Show.* We got quite a long way indeed from the conventional formats by sending them up, quite often, by having silly announcers—they were obvious ciphers. A running thread through-

*Other original *Goon Show* members included Michael Bentine, Harry Secombe, and Peter Sellers.

out one show was the 'Make the Lovely Aimi MacDonald a Rich Lady Appeal.' We also added a sort of supernumerary pleasant-looking lady each week . . . and those girls would say even less, some being given [only] the word 'and'—which often proved difficult for them," Chapman laughed. "When you've only got the one word, you'd better get it right. Of course, that creates awful tension!"

"Anyway, we did slightly send up those old formats, to get away from them and mess around with the shapes. Also, no one up to that point, really, had decided to write something for television—forget all that film and stage nonsense— think about television, what one can do with it. And, that's the way we should be doing our comedy.

"Of course, we were influenced by the anarchic school of comedy as represented by *The Goon Show,* and particularly Spike Milligan's *Q5.* So, to an outside observer, some of the strange links and the weirdness, and the bits of obvious television that we left in, like shots of cameras that said quite obviously 'This is television and we don't mind' were quite reminiscent of Spike Milligan. It was nice to find that we were moving in the same direction."

Monty Python:
The Writing

IN A WAY, Monty Python was formed as a writers' collective. As Eric Idle has said, the individual members began performing somewhat out of self-defense to protect their material.

Graham Chapman and John Cleese had written together since their Cambridge days, and tended to do so throughout most of Python. Likewise, the Oxford pair of Michael Palin and Terry Jones wrote together for most of the Python shows. Eric Idle was left to write—and present—material largely on his own, while Terry Gilliam was so independent that the others seldom knew what he was working on until he walked into the studio on taping days with his completed reels.

Still, as the series continued, the writing partnerships would temporarily shift to keep everyone fresh and to stave off boredom. Yet they always managed to revert back to Chapman and Cleese, and Jones and Palin.

"Toward the end of the first series, I tried to break up the writing partnerships, because I thought we'd get more original material by going with the different pairings," explains John Cleese. "Michael and I wrote the 'Hilter' sketch, the 'North Minehead Bye-Election,' Eric and I wrote the 'Sir George Head' mountaineering sketch, and I think Mike and I wrote the sketch about the Army protection racket with Luigi Vercotti.

"Then, for some reason, we drifted back into the original pairings—which I regretted, because I thought it was much more fun to keep breaking them up."

During the Python days, Terry Jones admits it was his own lack of self-assurance that prevented him from writing with different members of the team. "I always felt very unconfident about material that I'd written," he confesses. "It was only when Mike had okayed it that he and I worked it out, and I felt more confident. Mike always used to read our stuff at meetings, and he was certainly much better than I was."

Still other changes would occur in writing partnerships for various reasons.

"It was just for the sake of change sometimes, or if someone was absent for some reason or another,

Rare, never-before-seen photos of the first Python meetings and writing sessions, held at Terry Jones's house in South London. Eric Idle and John Cleese look over a sketch in Jones's garden, with Graham Chapman in the background (above); while Michael Palin soaks up some sun as he looks over some pages (below). Photos copyright Terry Jones, used by permission.

or someone wanted someone else to help work on a particular idea—that would happen, too," Graham Chapman recalled. "I would do little bits with Michael or Eric from time to time, though I never really did anything with Terry Jones or Terry Gilliam."

The teams were useful for a more pragmatic reason, however. When the group met to decide on what material to use in each show, they would vote—which left Idle at a disadvantage.

"Eric's problem was that he always wrote on his own. He always felt that he only had one vote. On the whole, if we read out material that we had written as a pair, we would both vote for it. Eric was always a bit sore, he was a bit outnumbered," says Cleese.

Idle concurs, and figures it was fifty percent harder for him to get his material in the shows. "I didn't have somebody to laugh when I came to the joke bits," Idle smiles. "Michael would read out, and Terry would fall about laughing. But, since everything had to be really auditioned, I don't know how much difference it made.

"It probably didn't matter much on the TV shows, but it always made more difference on the films, because we'd constantly rewrite them. Therefore, I'd have to do it again each time, and I'd have to sell it several times to finally get a piece into the film.

"So, I got whittled away more on films. There was so much more material on TV—where we'd be doing thirteen shows—that if it finally got some kind of laugh, it would be in one of the shows. But I guess I had a higher percentage wipe-out rate."

Idle says that since he was on his own, he couldn't really conspire with a partner to get votes, but the group setting was very useful for them to advise each other. "If it worked and we got laughs, there it was—it was obviously funny. And if it didn't get laughs, or if it only got a few laughs, then we had immediate advice: 'I can help this sketch go here,' or 'What it needs is this.' And we could do it in a rewrite, or someone else could take it on. That happened a few times."

John Cleese says there was a slight contrast in style between the Palin/Jones team and Idle, Chapman, and himself, and he may have picked up votes at times due to a slight Oxford/Cambridge bias. "We always valued the other peoples' styles—it was just that if there was a disagreement as to whether a sketch should go in or not, the voting was often along Oxford/Cambridge lines," Cleese notes.

"The split was *always* between Oxford and Cambridge," emphasizes Terry Jones. "It was always John and Graham and Eric who tended to like something when Mike, Terry Gilliam and I didn't. Terry was sort of 'honorary Oxford.' The split was *always* on those lines. It *never* happened that Graham joined us, for example. It was just a question of taste."

The one Python who usually escaped such politicking was Terry Gilliam. His involvement in planning the main body of the shows was usually peripheral, but he took advantage of his freedom within the group.

"When the others were working on ideas for a program, I always had things I wanted to do as well," Gilliam explains. "Sometimes when we were putting together a program, I'd say 'Well, I've got this idea of doing that,' which would get them to say 'Let's stick that in there, that sounds like it might work.' But, most of the time they would run out of steam, so I had to get them from that point to the next bit.

"I would go away and do what I was doing, and they would see it on the day of the show. I'd arrive with this can of film under my arm, and in it went! They would be confused. I think John was always vaguely intimidated by visual things, and he would never make obvious comments like 'It doesn't work,' or 'It's utterly awful,' because he didn't know whether it was or it wasn't! I escaped a lot of criticism because people just seemed to be too uncertain about these matters to pass judgment!" he laughs.

Gilliam was obviously the most independent member of a very independent group. His role was very different from that of the other five Pythons, and his method of production further encouraged that status. "It was always very difficult to comment about what I was doing until I'd done it, so in most cases it was a fait accompli—there it was.

"Whenever I actually talked to Mike or Terry, who were the most sympathetic to what I was doing, and tried to explain what I was working on that week—well, I would tell it very badly," Gilliam laughs. "I would explain it in the worst possible way, and they would immediately start panicking, thinking 'Oh, oh, he's really done it this time!' And after a while, they really just didn't want to know what I was doing."

Although several Pythons might work on various stages of a sketch, they never attempted to write an entire sketch all together. The only complete group efforts were usually short, linking material.

"When we were assembling sketches into shows, we inevitably needed to rewrite the top, tail, and maybe another part of a sketch, because we wanted an interruption from an earlier or later sketch to come into it," said Graham Chapman. "We didn't usually spend a great deal of time rewriting while we were all actually together. Usually, if a whole sketch needed rewriting, we knew the direction it needed, and those responsible would go off and do that. But we would do the two or three lines in between each sketch when we were there as a team. And at that stage, a lot of the structuring and original ideas for new short sections—or even longer pieces—came up. There was a lot of cross-pollination there."

The principal difference between the two contingents was that between visual (Oxford) and verbal (Cambridge) humor, at least during the early shows, although Jones and Palin (Oxford) were, along with Gilliam, also more concerned with the stream-of-consciousness structure of the series.

"Mike and I tended to write silent film things. My heart was in the visual stuff in those days, and we tended to write more inconsequential stuff," says Jones. "Also, we were interested in the whole shape of the show, whereas John and Graham were always much more interested in verbal humor. They wrote really tight idea sketches."

Working with each other as closely as they needed to often resulted in each influencing the others, a phenomenon that increased with each season. As a result, there is really not a typical Jones/Palin sketch, for both subtle and overt reasons, according to Terry Jones.

"What was a typical Jones/Palin sketch, when we started writing, is now no longer a typical Jones/Palin sketch," Jones says. "In the early days, it was a sketch without many words, and was mostly visual; it was 'Pan over countryside and play music' a lot. Gradually, John and Graham would send us up so much about this, that we tended to stop writing visual sketches, and got more into verbal sketches.

"And at the same time, they did the opposite. They started writing more visual sketches while we got more verbal. I think the real difference is that Mike and I will tend to write things that we can't justify, so far as writing from a gut feeling. There isn't a rationalization of the concept, whereas John is a very rational person.

"John introduces amazing sketches which are terrifically funny to me, but they'll have a very rational base . . . and [you can] say 'That's why it works.' I think John has a need to seem to be ex-

plaining a problem; the actual sketch is the result of a rational process that one [can] analyze," Jones says.

"When John relaxes, he writes some of the most wonderful, absurd things. He loves absurdity, but he likes it to have this rationality behind it. He doesn't like stuff that Mike and I write that can't be explained, like the 'Spam' sketch. I don't think John or Graham ever particularly liked that, because it doesn't have any rationale behind it."

The writing didn't always go easily but, without a doubt, the most worrisome problem that developed was Graham Chapman's dependency on alcohol. His battles with the bottle, and his subsequent recovery, have been well documented elsewhere, especially in his own *A Liar's Autobiography*. His drinking naturally affected his Python teammates.

"Graham went on record as having gone through an alcoholic phase," says writing partner Cleese. "Obviously, that introduced certain difficulties, just because he tended to be a bit vague about what we were writing."

Michael Palin affirms that, of all of them, Chapman changed the most since the television days, and much for the better. "Graham was the first to admit that going off the booze did wonders for him. He was always a very funny man, and a good writer of inspired silly material. But he got his act together.

"If anyone changed, it was Graham, because his whole life did change when he went off the drinking. Basically, he did what he was doing before much more efficiently. He just didn't crawl under tables and bite waiters."

The other major difficulty that evolved during Python writing sessions was a virtual

Michael Palin polishes an early Python sketch in Spartan-like conditions. Photo copyright Terry Jones, used by permission.

polarization within the group, with John Cleese and Terry Jones at opposite extremes. The two had radically different temperaments, and used to lock horns over material, or even the form the shows should take.

"They were real extremes—extreme right-wing and extreme left-wing!" Eric Idle jokes. "They always argued as if the entire world depended on it, and they *are* both extreme characters.

"But it was good, because John could actually stand up to Terry. Terry is very Welsh. When he's very emotional about what he thinks and feels, it's impossible to change his mind. If he says A, you say B; he says A, you say C; he says A, you say D. You're trying to give in, because he's still saying A!" he laughs. "John was good at standing up to that, 'cause he'd always see it as emotional pressure, and analyze it, and not give in to it.

"So work was actually more fun with the others. I think it was easier, but the work, in fact, was not so good after John left, because the balance wasn't there."

Looking back on it now, Cleese admits he and Jones were at the opposite ends of the spectrum. "This came out of the fact that we were *completely* different temperaments, and we didn't, perhaps, have that little greater understanding of ourselves that we have in middle age.

"Jonesey was really the romantic, and I was really the classicist; that's a reasonable way of describing it. We used to lock horns, which neutralized us, and then the others could jump on the scales and make the decision. I heard from one or two of the others that when I left the group Jonesey be-

came a bit too dominant at one point, because he always believed in everything very strongly. I always used to say to him, 'Terry, have you ever believed in something *not* very strongly?' Because I often *didn't* believe in things very strongly, but I'd got fed up with being steamrolled.

"Terry always had such strong emotions backing up his argument. We gradually began to get over that around *Life of Brian,* when I realized that we often disagreed because we didn't quite understand what the other person was saying. It's a temperamental thing. Jung wrote a book about psychological types because he was fascinated with why he and Freud split; there was something in the way they approached the world that was so radically different. With Terry and me, we had differences of opinion that resulted from that. And it was often hard for us to understand exactly what it was the other person wanted. I discovered that I could listen more to Jonesey and then understand more of what he wanted, and then I began to realize that most of the time, we were *not* in disagreement."

Jones says he wasn't really aware of the strong differences with Cleese toward the beginning of the series. "I suppose I felt that John didn't really get on with me as well as he might have. Maybe we were on slightly different wavelengths. We certainly used to have fights, but I only threw a chair at him once!" he says, laughing.

"At the beginning, I was very concerned about the shape of the show, getting this flow. That didn't mean anything at all to John; he used to get a bit irritated by that. But as things went on, he began to realize that it was important to the series. I always had such a respect for John's material—I always thought it was such good stuff!" says Jones.

The years have mellowed them all, though, and the two enjoyed their *Meaning of Life* collaboration immensely. While directing, Jones was encased in a huge costume as Mr. Creosote, which he says was like trying to direct from inside a cage. "Every morning, I'd come in and set up the first few shots, then go and have three hours of makeup while they were setting up for lights, camera, and sound. Then I'd come out and get into my costume, which was about six feet around—the world's fattest man—and I couldn't really move. It

Though their working relationship had suffered some strains during the TV shows, by **Life of Brian,** *Cleese and Jones were back on track. Photo copyright Kim Howard Johnson.*

was quite horrible." Jones laughs, but points out that the only other Python around consistently was Cleese, who helped him enormously.

"I really enjoyed the week working with John on Mr. Creosote," Jones says. "Quite often, John and I are poles apart, but working together was really pleasant. John was in top form, producing very funny stuff and coming up with ideas and suggestions. It was really good fun!"

Whatever creative differences existed between Jones and Cleese, it seems that in the long run they probably helped the show. "I think it was good to have that tension going on, though it had all eased up by *Meaning of Life,*" says Jones. "At the time, I never saw it as being between me and John, but other people have told me that's what the situation was. As long as there was a fight going on, there was a dynamic happening within the group."

4 1

*An early generic group shot, minus Terry Gilliam, and one of the very first publicity shots taken by the BBC to publicize their new comedy show, **Monty Python's Flying Circus** (left to right: Cleese, Chapman, Jones, Idle, and Palin in the foreground). Photo copyright BBC and Python Productions.*

Writing with Cleese and Chapman

Graham Chapman described a typical writing session with him and John Cleese:

"There was very little variation; it either took place at John's or my house. I would be half an hour late, even at my own house. John was usually fairly punctual, but forgetful about everything else.

"John would lose entire sketches with ease, even on his own desktop, and they would never be found again, even if we went through his entire house. It definitely had disappeared. It was probably a shredder or some kind of sketch-like Black Hole that existed somewhere around, but material that John thought needed rewriting somehow magically disappeared . . . We never found it again, so we did have to rewrite it, which often worked out to our benefit. Other than that, John was just forgetful and disordered in dealing with actual physical objects around him, though mentally he kept a fairly tidy mind!

"In the first half hour or so, we would both try to avoid work, really. It's an awkward moment when we actually had to commit ourselves to saying 'Well, what are we going to write today? What is the subject going to be?' And, we're committed to writing down something which is hopefully going to be funny. So, we'd talk about any subject that came into our heads while having loads of coffee. We could be chatting about newspapers, television news, or literally what had happened on the way to work while trying to decide whether what we were working on yesterday was any good or not. Frequently, if there was a glimmer in it, it was a good idea to start out working on that, because at least we'd have a foot in the door, and

 4 2

might actually get something finished before lunchtime.

"That was always the aim, to go off for a satisfied lunch. But quite frequently lunchtime got very close before anything had been achieved at all. In moments of real desperation, when *no* ideas seemed to come, then *Roget's Thesaurus* or the *Bible,* or any sort of reference book, would be taken out and thumbed through, in the hopes that something would spark off an idea—and often, they did!

"Between John and me, he would be the one to do the actual physical writing on paper 99.99999 percent of the time. I was rather inhibited about that, because I was afraid that no one else would be able to read what I had written, and also slightly inhibited because of my scientific, rather than artistic, schooling. I never really worried too much about spelling or grammar. I knew about it perfectly well, but couldn't really bother to think about it and write neatly. Getting the facts down in a rush was the important thing.

"I also found it a bit inhibiting. I'd rather be able to let my mind wander, and not have to concentrate on the actual physical work at all. So, John would write them down and lose them, and we would read out the rewritten sketch at the next meeting. In the end, we probably wrote out three sketches a week, which is not an enormous amount."

Python Meetings

"The basics of a Python creative meeting was to read out what we had just written, separately, to each other," explained Graham Chapman. "Rather like still being at school, we would mark the sketches like essays.

"They would get three ticks if they were very good and made everyone laugh, two if they were very good but could be improved, one if it was good enough to be in a show somewhere but probably needed a bit of work, and then none if it was really a waste of time. I suppose that latter category is not a lot of stuff that we really all regret throwing out, although each of us has his own pet in that batch of material.

"But it was like the marking of essays at school. Whether it made me laugh and observing whether it also made the others laugh is how we arrived at what we regarded as quality material," Chapman explained.

"We would spread it around a little bit, so that we'd had a couple of good ones in each show if we possibly could. We didn't always have that luxury—sometimes they were a bit thin around show nine or ten, I suppose. Then, there was a little bit of a revival toward show thirteen at the end, as we kept a little of the good stuff back, or else just saw the light at the end of the tunnel, and we would start writing very silly stuff again."

No matter how the writing went, though, the group could also switch around sketches and shows—and often did. Individual scenes were changed around from show to show regularly, and shows were not always broadcast in the order they were recorded, for an assortment of reasons.

"Sometimes it would have to do with pure timing—we were over-length, or whatever. We had to be fairly exact about that at the BBC, though less exact than we would have had to be at

Graham Chapman (in what Terry Jones referred to as a typical pose), with a blurred John Cleese in the foreground, at an early Python meeting at Jones's house in south London. Photo from the Collection of Terry Jones, used by permission.

a commercial network," Chapman said.

"The weight of individual shows was another reason. If we'd found we'd got a lot of really good stuff in one show, and another one was a bit thin . . . we'd sometimes mix them around . . . to try and get some good laughs in it.

"It happened for a variety of reasons. Sometimes there had been an objection in the form of 'No, you can't do that' because of something happening in the news, like an airplane crash when we'd just done a sketch about an airline. We'd say 'Well, we can't put that out for a week or two!' That sort of thing happened a little, and some sketches were also removed because of censorship, though I've found it very hard to be specific about that. . . . "

Taking a break from Python writing in the garden of Terry Jones's house are Michael Palin, Graham Chapman, John Cleese and Eric Idle. Photo from the Collection of Terry Jones, used by permission.

An Animated Discussion

The greatest contribution the other Pythons made to Gilliam's creations usually occurred after he had finished the animation. Acknowledging their verbal superiority, he would occasionally recruit his teammates to do voices for his footage.

"A lot of times I would have the stuff, and a vague script with actual lines of the characters. I'd grab John in the hallway or something, and say 'Can you say this?' And he would say that, plus other things. The stuff would grow, and they would invariably improve upon it verbally," says Gilliam.

"Terry had the animation so clearly worked out in accordance with his own ideas for the week, that we didn't even know what the pictures were," says Cleese. "We never saw the animation until we actually got to the studio on the day of recording, where they'd play it about three. We just trusted him. There was no point in making suggestions because we didn't know what the pictures were. Three or four of us would suddenly get called into

some room, and he'd ask us to do screaming, or arguing, or running up stairs. . . ."

Strangely enough, another major source for Gilliam's voices, and virtually *all* of his sound effects, was Gilliam himself. "I did do a lot of voices on the animation myself, because I couldn't always get my hands on the others. I made all the sound effects myself.

"I'd sit in my flat with a microphone and a blanket over my head, making all these terrible noises—getting kitchen utensils and banging, and shrieking, and doing whatever was necessary," Gilliam says. "I also had the advantage of the BBC sound effects library if I wanted . . . It's very crude stuff to listen to. I got away with it on television, because it's coming out a little three-inch speaker, but if one really listens to it in the cinema, it's shit! But because it was crude, it was effective and made an impact—it wasn't subtle. I did everything. I'd edit the stuff, and it was great—I was doing everything myself!"

Performing

THE PYTHONS ALWAYS tried to get each series of thirteen shows written before going into production each season. The bulk of the shows *had* to be scripted beforehand, so that the group could shoot the film segments before going into the BBC studio for thirteen weekly turnarounds. About five to eight weeks before recording the shows in the studio, the Pythons would go off to film. The first season's film was shot in two weeks, nearly four week's shooting for the second series, and then five weeks of filming for the third series.

"We gradually used more and more film as the budget allowed, but we had to write everything well in advance, because we obviously couldn't film show thirteen if we hadn't written it," said Graham Chapman.

"By the time we actually went into the studio to shoot the first one each season, we would have about eight shows absolutely mapped out, four of them written, typed up, and in the office, then gradually attack the others. We would have enough material for almost all of the shows."

Monday would see the group going into the studio to start work on the week's show. "We rehearsed mornings only, then spent the afternoons doing bits of rewriting or, if we were lucky, doing nothing!" Chapman laughed.

"On Saturday, we would go into the studio for rehearsal with cameras. Sometimes we would get a full camera rehearsal, but often not. Then we would do the show in front of a studio audience that night. They allowed us an hour and a half of studio time. We could go up to two hours, but the next half hour would cost us time and a half or double time. They just wouldn't allow us to go over two hours, because by then we would be past the time when the electricians could actually just black out the whole studio—and if it looked like we were going on, they would! It was something of a limitation."

As Python developed a following, fans packed the studio to attend tapings. However, the audiences for the first few shows were not exactly Python followers.

"The BBC ticket unit was responsible for getting people into shows, and most of the BBC audiences were the type of ladies who went to holiday camps," explains Michael Palin. "The audience was not a Python audience in age, education, or whatever—not the audience that one would spring something new on at all! They liked the comfortable, familiar old comedians telling the old jokes, and they liked a bit of music.

"Those were the people we got for the first two or three shows, until they realized what Python was. So, we'd have some moments where there was practically no audience reaction at all—except for Connie Booth (John Cleese's first wife), who we could hear laughing a mile away. She really ought to get a credit! One sees those early shows, one can always hear Connie—great noise . . . In those early shows, we could hear our friends laughing politely. We could hear Terry Jones's brother laugh quite a lot!"

"The studio tapings were always preceded by comics doing rather traditional audience warmups, which pleased the early audiences not as familiar or comfortable with the more unorthodox Python style.

"Python hadn't been assimilated, and hadn't permeated the great British public, and so audiences were quite happy to listen to someone tell a few jokes," says Palin. "Increasingly, we used to make appearances during the warmups, and eventually we ended up almost doing the warmups ourselves. By the second or third season, we realized the people wanted to see us, and we'd go out and do a little bit ourselves. But we had other people. We'd come back with a musician that we'd met on holiday—'Oh, I met this wonderful person in Mykonos and I said he could play the guitar before the show.' 'Oh, did you? All right.' That's what would happened toward the end."

The actual taping of the shows was similar to live theater, according to costumer Hazel Pethig. "The studio was great and exciting, like doing a stage show, with the music, and audiences, and quick changes. It was much more like theater than television, because we had a limited amount of time. There was a wonderful theatrical feeling. The dressers all enjoyed it in terms of the number of quick changes—except for the suit of armor, with the chicken. Getting them in and out of that quickly was always a trial."

Never-before-seen behind-the-scenes photos of the Pythons filming on location. Terry Jones took pictures while highwayman Dennis Moore (John Cleese) holds up a stagecoach. Photos copyright Terry Jones, used by permission.

Michael Palin has some help (above) before being featured as a fop in the Dennis Moore location filming (below). Photos copyright Terry Jones, used by permission.

Terry Jones confirms that they tried to present it all as a real show, while the limited time they had in the studio helped to move things along.

"It seemed very important to keep the audience boiling with us all the time," Jones explains. "The show was usually shot in order; we usually had just the length of the film clips to change into the next sketch, so it was important to get the audience looking at the film inserts. We did stop and start, though, we didn't shoot continuously.

"Mike, Eric, and I had just come out of *Do Not Adjust Your Set,* which was shot on a very low budget. [On that program] they didn't want to cut the tape, so we actually did these as live shows—everything was done to real time. Coming out of that background, we tried to do Python that way and keep it moving. Inevitably there would be moments when we'd have to stop at the end of the sketch. But it was very exciting."

As much as Jones enjoyed the writing process and taping the shows in the studio, he preferred shooting the film segments because of the control they could exercise. "We could have much more of a hand in the filming. Usually Mike or Terry Gilliam and I would go with Ian MacNaughton to scout locations, and we worked closely when we were actually filming it all. Ian and I could discuss it as we were doing it."

There was a great feeling of camaraderie filming on location, recalls costumer Hazel Pethig, and the cast and crew all worked and played together. "They were always very generous, taking us out to supper. They didn't pick and choose who they were going to be nice to—it didn't matter who you were. Whether it was the dresser, or whoever, there was no discretion at all."

Although the budgets were small in the TV days, they all managed to get along. "We were very much the poor relations at the BBC, so I had very few facilities," Pethig says. "I once had a lorry that had literally been used as a cattle truck, and I'd be changing people in that! One minute they'd be in a muddy field, and the next sequence would be in white shirts!

"Terry Jones and Mike used to be suckers, really. They used to do stunts like jumping off a bridge in the middle of winter while wearing a funny costume. They were always willing. All of them were important, but I felt that Terry and Mike, in a physical way, held Python together. All

of them contributed something different, in terms of holding it together. Terry and Mike were like schoolboys full of energy, with their physical ability to keep it going, because it was really trying. And with costumes like the pantomime goose—Graham was often the pantomime goose—they were unspoiled; they coped with it better than they might do now. They were willing to throw themselves into any problem that I had. Even though they had done so much, I felt they shouldn't have to do everything themselves," says Pethig.

The filming was always enjoyable for the group, but the loss of control when they moved into the studio particularly concerned Terry Jones.

"Once we got into the studio, we were totally in Ian's hands as to how to shoot something. We had less input by then, we were really just performers, keeping an eye on the monitors and thinking 'God, that's not quite right,' and sneaking up to the control room and suggesting to Ian, 'Maybe we should do something over there,'" Jones says.

The shows were usually edited later in the week, immediately following the recording. From the beginning, Jones tended to take a strong interest in the process, recognizing the importance of the timing to the laughs. He accompanied director MacNaughton to the editing sessions to provide the input from the Pythons.

"In many ways, I think I enjoyed the editing most of all," Jones says. "It was difficult to begin with, because Ian used to have two hours booked, and wanted to get out of it quickly. He didn't like me going along and sitting there looking over his shoulder while he was editing.

"But the shows were really made in the editing. We could tighten up gaps and pauses, and we could segue into things. Ian began to realize that I wasn't undercutting him when I sat in on the editing—it was just part of the whole creative process. By the second series, and particularly the third series, Ian had really gotten into the editing, and knew to take a day. We'd spend a day in front of the video machines, cutting it down, trimming it, taking out pauses, and making everything work. . . .

One can see that in the shows. The editing in the first series is rougher, whereas by the later shows, it really flows by," says Jones.

There were only two directors throughout the four Python TV series: John Howard Davies was credited with directing only the first four shows, while Ian McNaughton directed the remainder.

"I was always interfering right from the beginning, not on the studio floor but in the filming," says Jones. "I was always sitting on John Howard Davies's or Ian's shoulders, and I always went along to the editing with them from the beginning. My role never changed, really. I was always there, being a pain in the neck for the directors. John Howard Davies directed the first four, but I think Ian had already directed some of the film inserts, because we always shot the film inserts for the whole series before we'd record the shows. I think Ian was much quirkier than John, probably prepared to take more chances. Certainly the relationship with Ian got better as we got on to the second series, and by the third series it was very much a good partnership. At the beginning, Ian very much resented my interference and going along to the editing with him. By the second series it was much better, and by the third series we had a really good relationship going. It was a good collaboration, whereas at the beginning, Ian felt he wanted to edit shows in two hours and then get out of it. He didn't really want to make cuts that I wanted to make, but by the end, Ian was looking for cuts as well, and it was really good."

Undoubtedly, the same part of Jones that drove him to become a director made him look harder at the technical, behind-the-scenes aspect of the Python shows, unlike the rest of the group.

"I don't think the others realized how important it was, to begin with, or else they were more interested in the performing and writing. I'd always felt the editing was crucial. We could write and perform a funny script, but if it wasn't shot right, or if it was shot in the wrong location or something, then it wouldn't work if it wasn't edited properly," says Jones, who still likes to work with the editors on his own films today.

Arthur Megapode's Flying Circus

Choosing a title for the series was a rather lengthy, frustrating process, and Chapman, Cleese, Gilliam, Idle, Jones, and Palin found they could never agree. Each had favorites, including *Owl Stretching Time; A Horse, a Spoon, and a Basin; Sex and Violence;* and *Bunn, Wackett, Buzzard, Stubble, and Boot.*

Python fans are familiar with many of these alternate titles, and the Pythons have spoken of many of them throughout the years. What those fans may not realize is that a lengthy list of titles was made at one point, most of them long forgotten—until now.

Terry Jones was kind enough to open his files to me. As I eagerly perused the various clippings, notes, and scripts, I encountered five pages of lined notebook paper filled with strange titles.

Terry casually explained that when the BBC insisted that they absolutely must decide on a name for the series immediately, they had a meeting (held at three-thirty on Thursday, according to the notes). It was a brainstorming session at which Terry acted as secretary, writing down all the possible suggestions for their new show. Terry favored using the name Arthur Megapode in one form or another, and each of the others had favorites as well. There were also many "Flying Circus" variations listed with the possibilities.

But, enough talk. Listed below are the alternative titles (as listed in Jones's notes) for the series that came to be known as *Monty Python's Flying Circus.*

1 2 3
Megapode's Flying Circus
Arthur Megapode's Flying Circus
Admiral Megapode's Flying
   Circus
The Sparkling Music and Stars
   Interview
The Political Satire Show
Ow! It's Megapode's Flying
   Circus!
Owl Stretching Time
Them
It's Them!
Gwen Dibley's Flying Circus
It's T.H.E.M.
Arthur Megapode's Cheap Show
The Horrible Earnest Megapode
Megapode's Cheap Show
Megapode's Panic Show
The Panic Show
The Plastic Mac Show
The Venus De Milo Panic Show
El Megapode's Flying Circus
Noris Heaven's Flying Circus
The Amazing Flying Circus

The 37 Foot Flying Circus
The Flying Circus
The Fly Circus
Vaseline Review
Vaseline Parade
The Keen Show
B B Circus
El Thompson's Flying Circus
Megapode's Flying Circus
Megapode's Atomic Circus
The Whizzo Easishow! (Guaran-
   teed to last 1/2 hour! Money
   back if not!)
Human Circus
The Zoo Show [crossed out]
Arthur Megapode's Flying Circus
Arthur Buzzard's Flying Circus
Myrtle Buzzard's Flying Circus
The People Zoo [crossed out]
Arthur Megapode's Zoo
Charles IInd's Flying Circus
The Laughing Zoo [crossed out]
The Comedy Zoo [crossed out]
El Trotsky's Flying Circus
The Joke Zoo [crossed out]

El Megapode's Flying Circus
Nigel's Flying Circus [crossed out]
Brian's Flying Circus [crossed out]
Brian Stalin's Flying Circus
The Year of the Stoat
Limb's Flying Circus
The Plastic Mac Show
The Nose Show
El Moist's Flying Circus
Sydney Moist's Flying Circus
Stephen Furry's Flying Circus
Will Strangler's Flying Circus
Cynthia Fellatio's Flying Circus
El Turbot's Flying Circus
Norman Python's Flying Circus
Bob Python's Flying Circus
Ken
Monty Python's Flying Circus
   [the eventual winner]
O
The Down Show
Owl Stretching Time
The Full Moon Show [crossed
   out]
Ow! It's Colin Plint!

Recurring Favorites

As Python developed, certain characters and conventions came along and proved popular—or useful—enough for return appearances. The Pepperpots and the Gumbies, discussed elsewhere at length, certainly fall into this category, as do Graham Chapman's Colonel, Michael Palin's "It's" Man, Terry Gilliam's Knight with the rubber chicken, and Terry Jones's nude organist, along with such less obvious characters as Cleese and Idle's Mr. Praline and Mr. Badger. The more traditional show business convention, however, carried with it some dangers, according to Graham Chapman.

"We were quite conscious of the heritage of the worst aspects of the earlier shows we'd been associated with, particularly the radio show *I'm Sorry, I'll Read That Again.* It was obviously too easy to rely on the same character appearing, and thereby getting an easy laugh, whether a laugh of recognition or whatever. A person could say 'Well' and they could get a laugh. So we wanted to avoid that easy, catch-phrase reaction.

"We did try to keep it to a bare minimum, but there are characters that did crop up more than once. Obviously, the Colonel was a very useful linking figure in that he was able to stop something, and start something else off without there being a logical connection between the two—yet, it seemed reasonable that he should do so. . . . He could also forestall possible complaints by actually complaining about something, or stopping it himself, saying it's gotten too filthy or it's too silly, then stopping it and going on to something else, hopefully disarming a potential Mary Whitehouse,* or BBC censor!" Chapman laughed.

Despite their usefulness, running characters like the Gumbies were not enjoyed by everyone. "They were useful to come back and link, or comment on something we'd done, but they were never great favorites of mine," says Eric Idle. He says he has no favorite characters or sketches because he was too close to the proceedings.

*A one-time self-appointed monitor of British TV

"We weren't really fans—we just did it," Idle says. "I don't really have favorites because I don't sit there and watch my own work: 'Aren't we wonderful here?' . . . By and large, my memories are not of the shows, but of actually doing them—bits of filming where it was raining, and we were stuck in a pub for six hours dressed in strange costumes. It isn't like we sat around watching the show together, going 'Oh, I loved that.' So, favorite bits are not really relevant in this context."

It's

One character that started in the very first show, and appeared in nearly every program following, was the appropriately named "It's" Man, who would run up to the camera and gasp "It's" just before the opening titles rolled. "There was really no reason why we did it," says Michael Palin, who brought the character to life, "but of course, there was a reason why we did things for no reason at all. I'm sure the 'It's' Man must have been born of that."

The "It's" Man wasn't a parody of any other program, however, but a new invention for Python. "We were always quite keen to split up the show in slightly nonsensical ways, like cutting to a Viking saying 'the' in the middle of a sentence. The 'It's' Man was rather like that. Instead of having a smooth presenter saying 'Now it's *Monty Python's Flying Circus*' or 'Welcome to the show,' we started with the antithesis of smoothness. This was a hunted, haunted, ragged, tattered creature, obviously in the terminal stages of fear and exhaustion, coming toward the camera—but we only let him say 'It's,' he never got to say the rest," Palin explains.

"It was rather like this character who, maybe one day many years ago, had been a presenter, and had been allowed to say whole sentences. But he'd fallen on hard times, and was now cut off immediately after he said just the first word. In fact, one of the titles of the show was 'It's,' so he must have been in there fairly early on. On a list of titles I've got scribbled in a notebook was 'It's' and just 'It,' so that's probably where he came from," Palin says.

The "It's" Man segments were shot along with the other filmed portions of Python, generally on locations, and later inserted into the studio part of the show. The "It's" Man was usually filmed wherever the group happened to be at the time.

"The first one I remember was at a place called Cool Harbor in Bournemouth, with very nice, sunny weather," recalls Michael Palin. "Unfortunately, the 'It's' Man had to emerge from the sea. I had to get dressed up in all these rags and tatters, walk into the sea, wait for a cue from the director, get down under the water, count ten, and then come staggering out.

"But we were at a place called Sandy Bay, or something—very aptly named, because it was all sand; there was hardly any sea there at all. I walked out to where I thought I'd be underwater. I'd gone out several hundred yards, and it was still just below my knees! By the time I found enough water to submerge in, I was out of earshot, and everything had to be done with waving hands, and screams, and shrieks. I just felt very silly. I was dressed like this, and there were a few holiday-makers who looked extremely bewildered, as this terrible figure strode out, trying to get lower and lower, occasionally ducking down in the water to find that my back was still showing, so I had to go further . . . That was baptism of water!

"The nastiest 'It's' Man of all, though, was where I had to be hung up on meat hooks. In those days, we couldn't really afford harnesses or anything—I was just hanging. I can understand why they kill things first, because it's extremely painful to be hung on these bloody hooks if you're still alive."

Women's Institute Applause

Another bit that frequently recurred through the entire series was a two- to three-second film sequence showing a group of older ladies applauding, stock footage of a Women's Institute meeting. The bizarre shot was intercut to reveal the ladies clapping at a Python sequence that the real women would probably never have anything to do with.

But, the film was peculiar enough to occur in a great number of shows, often more than once per show.

"We had a researcher in the first series, Sarah Hart Dyke, who probably got these bits of film. There's an awful lot of that stuff in the BBC film library," says Palin. "It was rather good, I must say. It was rather like our own audiences [at the start]."

"The Python Theme Song"

By John Philip Sousa

Yet another Python trademark around since the first show is the use of John Philip Sousa's *Liberty Bell March* as the Python theme song, a curious but somehow appropriate choice to accompany the show's titles and credits.

"We chose that off an album in an office at the BBC," says Palin. "We obviously had to get something that was out of copyright. I think Terry and I chose that because we wanted something that was rather like brass band music, something lively."

Terry Gilliam maintains there was no actual thinking behind the decision to use the Sousa march. "Like most of the stuff, it was all spur of the moment—if we liked it, we did it. We might have been talking about marches, or something martial, while trying to think of music for the opening. I just remember sitting there listening to a lot of music, when suddenly that thing came on, *The Liberty Bell.* I thought 'That's got to be it,' it was wonderful, just exactly right.

"So, we got it and I cut it down to thirty seconds; we rearranged it and cut sections out. It was the bell at the beginning that did it for me. *Bong!* It was a great way to start something. We cheated the bell so it's actually much louder than it is on the original recording," Gilliam says, and smiles as he points out that it is in the public domain.

"It was free; a lot of people just don't know that the song is Sousa, but he deserves full credit—it's a wonderful tune! Before Python, I don't remember hearing that song, but now I hear it all the time. The International Horse Show in London, a big thing every year on TV, inevitably plays *The Liberty Bell,* and they play it at football games. It's always now associated with Python, not with Sousa. To me, that is now Our Song and nobody else's."

The march turns up in many unexpected places, to the delight of Python fans, but Michael Palin has one special memory which may carry even more meaning in retrospect. "A wonderfully Pythonesque moment happened on one of the endless programs during the wedding year of Charles and Diana. There was an in-depth interview in a room overlooking the Horse Garden Parade in London, where they were talking about 'Where will you live?' and 'How will you educate your children?' Suddenly, from down below, one could hear this band practicing, and up came the music! It must have been the Guards practicing. It's just subliminally in there, but it was quite a wonderful moment to anyone who knew Python! They were going on answering these questions, while we heard the music drifting up. It was a real absolute delight!"

The Pythons weren't able to play all of their parts themselves, and were lucky enough to have a very talented stable of supporting players to back them up. But, whether they appeared in one show or dozens, none is as dear to the hearts of Python fans as their Number One Ingenue, Carol Cleveland.

If there was ever a seventh Python, there can only truly be one candidate. Carol Cleveland started out in the very first *Monty Python's Flying Circus,* and appeared in two-thirds of the original forty-five shows, as well as virtually every important Python film and stage show that followed.

Carol brought exactly the right attitude to the shows, and the group always tried to use her whenever a real woman was required. She was actually discovered by the *MPFC* original director, John Howard Davies, and hired to appear in the first few shows only.

"We didn't know who she was when we started the series," says John Cleese. "John Howard Davies cast her and we all liked her, so from then on, we used her for all but the more upper-class roles. We simply liked what she did; she was very easy to get along with, she could be very silly when required and she didn't have an excessive sense of dignity. I thought she was absolutely ex-

Helping out with the Montgolfier Brothers, Carol Cleveland found herself hanging from an airbag by the fourth season of Python. Photo copyright BBC and Python Productions.

cellent. She was very solid, very professional, very likeable and easy to have around."

"Carol just had a real inspiration for fitting in. She was absolutely right for what we wanted," says Terry Jones. "She would play these parts, the bosomy, sexy girl, larger than life, and make it funny—she was acting in tune with the rest of us. When Ian MacNaughton took over, he kept trying to bring other girls into the shows, and they were always hopeless. Because it's very difficult to come in and try to hit the same key—but Carol did. We'd insist on Carol if it was a big sketch, but when it was a small bit, especially in the first season, we'd allow Ian to choose other girls. But they never worked the same as Carol did. They would have all been much better if we'd always just had Carol."

"Carol, of course, was excellent. She was the unsung heroine because she was so spot on," says Michael Palin. "We never had to tell her how to play a scene, she just had a Python way of thinking about it. She instinctively knew how to get all those laughs out, which is not necessarily by going over the top or mugging. It's all teamwork, sharing the laughs with the others. She was so very good when she was in love with the pantomime horse! 'Oh, pantomime horse, I do love you so!' Things like that, she did very well indeed—she was never, ever, upstaged."

Carol Cleveland was born in England and raised in America, she explains.

"I'm half and half," says Carol. "I was born in England, my mother and father are both English, and my mother remarried an American who was in the air force. When I was five years old, we went back to America where my mother married him. We stayed in the States but moved around a bit. We spent a year in Philadelphia, then went on to San Antonio, Texas, for about six and a half years. Then we moved to Pasadena, California for another seven years. I went to Pasadena High School and John Marshall Junior High in Pasadena, so I was born in England but bred in America. That's why I have a dual nationality."

"My mother wasn't a pushy, theatrical mom, but I think she was delighted that I went in that direction," Carol says.

She began taking ballet lessons at about five, but in her early teens decided she would rather be an actress. "I was the leading dancer in an amateur production, and played Cinderella at the last minute when the girl that was supposed to do the part broke her leg. That was a great turning point for me, and I decided acting was a lot of fun. From that moment on, I've never really wanted to do anything else."

"I came back to England in 1960 because my grandparents were both quite ill," she says. "I had decided by then to be an actress, and we decided I would finish my high school education and I would go to drama school in England, which I did. I actually got a scholarship to RADA [Royal Academy of the Dramatic Arts]. We went back occasionally for visits, but there was never any question after that of returning to live in America. We settled in England."

Being an American actress in Britain had its drawbacks, but Carol soon discovered there were advantages that led to acting roles.

"I had a very broad American accent, and at RADA they tried very hard to get rid of my terrible, terrible nasal American accent with no success," she says. "I remember thinking I would never work in this country, but I was very wrong. At the time, there was a lot of American stuff going on here where they used a lot of Americans and Canadians, things like *The Saint* and *The Avengers,* and all the series I did at that time, like *The Persuaders* and *Man in a Suitcase.* And in various films as well—they tended to use a lot of Americans and Canadians. Of course, being American but having no problem working in England, I was in! I did one theater job out of RADA, and then I went straight into television. Within a few months of leaving RADA, I was introduced in a leading part, playing a Texas millionairess. For the best part of the next two years, I played just Americans. That was my 'in' into the business, having this American accent. I was very grateful for it!"

During this period, Carol briefly found herself working for the most famous film comedian of all in *A Countess from Hong Kong,* directed by Charlie Chaplin.

"I did a little bit in that film," says Cleveland. "Sophia Loren was the star—I didn't have a scene with her but I wish I had because I've always been a great admirer of hers. I was playing a nurse in a little cameo role, but I was directed by Charlie Chaplin, which was very interesting. Marlon Brando and Sophia Loren were obviously in awe of

him, and anything that he would suggest, they did. I remember being fascinated by the fact that, although he had changed physically and obviously looked much older, he directed everybody, including Marlon Brando, in this Charlie Chaplin manner, having them do these rather silly walks! They had everything but a cane and a mustache! They were all doing these sort of Charlie Chaplin impersonations—it was just the way he directed them. It was a very strange little film, but I had very little to do. Still, it was a joy to work for someone like that."

Cleveland had worked with many other British TV and film comedians in the mid-'60s, but none of the Pythons-to-be.

"I knew who several of them were, obviously having seen a lot of their previous work, but I'd never met any of them," says Cleveland. "I had been doing a lot of work at the BBC with other comics, working with people like Charlie Drake, Ronnie Corbett, Ronnie Barker, Spike Milligan, Roy Hudd, doing very much what I've always referred to myself as, a 'glamour stooge.' That's what I was, a tall, glamorous creature with a few funny lines, looking good and being funny. I somehow got into that mode. I never started off like that—prior to that, as I say, I had been doing these *Avengers* and *Persuaders* things, playing absolutely straight parts. When I got to the Beeb, one thing led to another and I began this glamour thing.

"I'd been doing a lot of that, and obviously someone—they'd been looking for a female for Python, and at that stage they'd only written five episodes. They were looking for a female to be in four of those five episodes. They didn't know what was going to happen after that. Someone, I don't know who, suggested me, and John Howard Davies asked to see me. We chatted, and he cast me."

Cleveland admits she had no idea what the new show was going to be like, and was given no indication as to how completely different this new series would be.

"I didn't know anything about it when I got the first few scripts—I just knew it was a new comedy show," says Cleveland. "It was a series of sketches. I remember reading through them and thinking some of it was very funny, some of it was very bizarre and some of it went right over my head! I thought 'Well, we'll see what this is about when we get there . . .' On the first day's rehearsal,

I was sitting there with a frown on my face, not quite understanding what was going on. I couldn't piece together what it was all about. I thought they were all absolutely mad! I thought 'Well, I'll just have to throw myself in there and do what they ask me to do, and hope for the best!' Which is what I did."

Cleveland was expecting it to be somewhat similar to some of the other comedy shows she had been appearing on around that time, but soon found out how Python was different from all of those series. "The rest of them I could make sense of!" she laughs. "They all seemed pretty bland and straightforward, boring, actually, compared to Python. They were just very *normal.*"

Her performances in the first shows impressed the Pythons and they insisted that Carol be kept on the shows.

"I was only meant to be in those four, and it was because of the Pythons—no one else—that I stayed on as their regular female," says Cleveland. "By the time we got to episode three, they decided that I fitted the bill nicely. I looked right and sounded right, and they were very happy with my contribution, and decided they wanted me to stay on. There was a little bit of a hoohah about it, because by then, Ian MacNaughton had taken over the direction from John Howard Davies. Ian had his own ideas about this, and I think there were various ladies he had already had in mind to cast in bits. So there was a bit of a disagreement between Ian and the fellows, but they very firmly put their corporate foot down and said 'No, we want Carol!' And I'm eternally grateful."

Despite their unorthodox use of women, costumer Hazel Pethig confirms that Carol was gradually accepted and embraced by the group. "I remember always having to strap women's boobs up to make them look big. It wasn't a very emancipated show," she laughs. "But Carol was gradually given character roles. In the beginning, she wasn't very comfortable, but she got used to it. It was great being able to dress her up as a character, and forget the fact that she was young and glamorous. She fitted in very well."

Though she was actively involved with the shows, she explains that she never went to any of the script meetings, where the material was first presented by the Pythons . . . and the subject of sometimes lively discussions.

"I wish I had been there, so I could have seen Terry chucking chairs at John! That came later . . . I would have loved to have sat in, because that's when they had their disagreements, which I was never a party to," says Cleveland. "Any friction at any stage, I never saw, because they kept that away from the public gaze. It didn't happen on the set or even in rehearsals—I think it mainly went on in the office and production room, and when they were writing. I knew that John and Terry Jones would often be butting heads and disagreeing about the way sketches were to be done, but I didn't know to what extent until later on, actually, when I started reading *The First 20X Years of Monty Python*! I didn't know about the chair-throwing, but I can certainly imagine it!"

While she appeared often throughout the first three series, it was during the six shows of the fourth series, filmed without John Cleese, that saw Cleveland take on bigger and more frequent roles.

"That was probably due in part to the lack of John—they used me more because they had to use the people they had," says Cleveland. "That was certainly one reason. I think they started to appreciate me a bit more by then, and felt like they should really give me more interesting roles to play, rather than bits that required me to shed bits of clothing. Of course, it was a great shame that we didn't have John. There's no doubt that it didn't work as well without him. We were all very aware of that at the time and it wasn't as much fun to do that fourth series without John. I *did* have more interesting parts to do by then. I don't remember ever appearing in a bikini at all in that fourth series, I'm happy to say. There were things like the Montgolfier brothers that were great fun—I loved hanging around from the balloons. I did have more to do by then, and I think I was appreciated more in that series."

Fans all have their favorite sketches featuring Carol Cleveland, she notes. "The Marriage Guidance Counselor sketch is one they seem to remember," she says. "Attila the Hun, they don't remember until I mention it, and then they say 'Oh, yes, yes.' Scott of the Sahara they remember, the Spanish Inquisition, Travel Agent . . ."

Michael Palin notes that Carol Cleveland's contribution to Python was very important, because she did precisely what was needed.

"We used to do most of the women ourselves, but we couldn't really do the young, dishy women," says Palin. "So we had real women in to do the young dishy women. There were a number of them in the first series, but Carol was head and shoulders and—if you'll excuse the expression—chest above the rest! She was a good actress, and I think that's why Carol stayed. She also had a marvelous temperament. Maybe it was because she was American, but she could cope with the Python madness. She thought we were all crazed, but she really enjoyed doing anything she could do. She loved any part that was put her way, and gradually she got bigger parts and more to do.

"She had a great appetite for acting, she's got a natural talent for comedy, but I think the great thing about Carol was her temperament. She was able to cope with anything that was thrown at her. She didn't particularly want to become a Python, she didn't want to write, she didn't seem to hold any grudge against us for not writing better parts for women. She enjoyed doing what she did, and she knew she did it well, and there was a feeling of confidence when we'd give a part to Carol. You knew exactly how it was going to be done, and it was done right."

After Python ceased to be an active entity, Carol continued her distinguished stage and TV career with a variety of roles. Today, she retains her stunning looks and figure while making the transition from glamour girl to character actress. Carol Cleveland continues to appear occasionally on stage and TV, her most recent notable screen part in *Annie II: Miss Hannigan's Revenge*; and she often performs pantomime around the holiday season. She is also weighing offers for a series of college lecture tours on her Python days, not unlike those presented by Graham Chapman.

Carol says she is obviously best known in America for her Python work. "I come across Python fans in America who keep talking about sketches which I have long since forgotten. I think 'Oh my goodness, yes, that was a funny one, I'd nearly forgotten about that one.' For me, the favorite one that I did was the very funny send-up of 'Scott of the Antarctic.' That was one of the few long sketches that worked, because on the whole, the long sketches in Python have been the least funny. But this was very funny, and we all played these very definite, extremely funny characters. I played a film starlet à la Marilyn Monroe, all blonde and kooky. I had to stand in a trench when the film director comes up to me and says, 'We think we'd like for you to play this scene out of the trench today,' " Carol says, and goes into her character voice.

" 'You want me to play the scene out of the trench? But I've never acted out of a trench before! It's dangerous, I might fall over!' Lovely things like 'I'm terribly sorry, I just can't remember my lines, my doggie's not well.' For me personally, that was the one that I enjoyed doing most of all.

"Monty Python was one of the happiest experiences I've ever had. Little did anyone know at the time what a great fantastic success it was going to be. I just thought 'Well, this is fun.' But, I've never loved anything quite so much."

Neil Innes

Neil Innes was involved with the members of Python before Monty Python actually existed, and then became reinvolved when the series was underway. He eventually did music for the records, all of the stage shows, and the films as well. Innes, however, was rather well known before his Python career began.

While at Goldsmiths College in London around 1965, Innes became involved with a group of other art students that formed the now-legendary Bonzo Dog (Doo Dah) Band. They began playing in pubs around London, doing '20s dance tunes and rock and roll, with instruments that included banjos, saxophones, tubas, and spoons, in addition to guitar, piano, and drums. Their high-energy, fast-paced playing was accented by their costumes, stunts, gags, and explosions by the time of *Gorilla,* their first album in 1967. They played concerts with Cream and the Bee Gees, and appeared with the Beatles in *Magical Mystery Tour.*

The Bonzos also began performing on *Do Not Adjust Your Set,* the children's series that also featured Terry Jones, Michael Palin, Eric Idle, and Terry Gilliam, shortly before Python came into being. They all became friends, but wound up being pulled in other directions.

Innes and the Bonzos had become quite popular in England, but seemed to lack the business acumen to become financially successful. In 1969, they

Neil Innes, 1997. Photo copyright Neil Innes, used by permission.

did two tours of the United States, and played the Fillmore West with the Byrds and Joe Cocker. Although they always went over well in the States, nobody on the industry side seemed to appreciate them, with management apparently deciding there was no market for them. During this final period (their last performance was in January 1970), they had become more committed to rock. Innes began to come into his own as a musician and songwriter, talents he would carry over into his post-Bonzo work. He joined the short-lived group The World in 1970, followed that by working with Grimms in 1971, and the Bonzos reunited in 1972 for one last album.

Increasingly on his own, Innes became more drawn to his Python friends. "When they all formed Python, the Bonzos sort of packed up," Innes explains. "I met up with them later, when Eric rang me up and asked if I'd like to come along and do a warmup at the BBC. I said 'I don't do warmups,' and he said 'It's twenty-five quid,' and I said 'Done!' Their regular man was ill. I've never done a warmup since," he says, laughing.

Innes worked with the group during their stage shows, and during the fourth series he wrote some musical material and cowrote two sketches for the shows. He then did the music for *Monty Python and the Holy Grail,* where he also performed onscreen, chiefly as the minstrel who sings "The

Ballad of Sir Robin"; he acted in *Life of Brian* as well, most memorably as the scrawny Samaritan who battles the gladiator.

Innes actually became a Python regular earlier with his appearances in all of the stage shows. He performed songs like "How Sweet to Be an Idiot," "The Old Grey Whistle Test,"* and the old Bonzo favorite "I'm the Urban Spaceman" in costumes which suggested the Bonzo days. Although the Bonzo albums are hard to find, Innes can be heard performing solo on the *Drury Lane* import and the *City Center* live albums, as well as *Monty Python Live at the Hollywood Bowl.*

Neil Innes relaxes in a casual moment offstage. Photo copyright KHJ.

John Belushi, George Harrison, Mick Jagger, Bill Murray, Michael Palin, Gilda Radner, and Paul Simon, with Idle, Innes, Rikki Fataar, and John Halsey as the Pre-Fab Four. The album was nominated for a Grammy for Best Comedy Recording of 1978.

Innes also starred in his own comedy/music series in 1979, *The Innes Book of Record,* which included an appearance by Michael Palin. A soundtrack album of the series was released in Britain on Polydor Records.

Innes spent much of the next decade doing music for several children's TV shows, achieving no small measure of renown in the field.

After the breakup of the Bonzos, Innes says it was fortunate to have another funny, talented group to collaborate with. "I much prefer working with a group of people," he explains. "It was very good for me after the band ended, to meet up with another group of people who were just as silly and clever in their own way, a very good thing to move on to from the Bonzos. There was the same sort of anarchy. Whereas the Bonzos were completely anarchic, though, the Pythons knew how to get things done in front of the camera."

Innes and Idle continued collaborating, particularly on Idle's *Rutland Weekend Television* series in 1974 and the soundtrack album released at the same time.

The greatest Idle-Innes collaboration, however, is undoubtedly "The Rutles," their Beatles parody that developed out of a film done for *RWT.* Idle conceived the group, and Innes wrote and helped record all of the Rutles music for the Warner Brothers soundtrack album *The Rutles.* Idle had turned the concept into a full-length "docudrama," *All You Need Is Cash,* which aired on NBC March 22, 1978, and also featured Dan Ackroyd,

In 1994, Innes put together a new group to perform a one-night stand at the Troubadour in Los Angeles, coinciding with the twenty-fifth anniversary salute to Python at the Director's Guild. Billing themselves as "The New Rutles," the elaborate show (which even included a string quartet) played before a standing-room-only crowd, and a second show was added two days later. Following this success, a new Rutles CD was eventually released at a time when the *Beatles Anthology* was reviving interest in the original Fab Four.

Eric Idle chose not to participate in the resurrection of the Rutles, feeling that the original film and record were near-perfect on their own. Still, he agreed to allow Innes to use the Rutles name, and 1996 saw the release of *The Rutles Archaeology* CD, with sixteen "new" Rutles songs (Idle is credited as the Rutles' creator, but has no involvement with the project otherwise). The Idle-less Rutles even performed live in concert for the first time in the late '90s, and in addition to his many other projects, Neil Innes still appears occasionally at Beatlefest conventions, both alone and with the New Rutles.

---

*"The Old Grey Whistle Test" was a late '60s–early '70s TV rock show.

And a Cast of Many

The Pythons generally drew their supporting cast from a pool of friends and colleagues, and even wives—Connie Booth made several appearances in sketches, along with the then Mrs. Idle. Booth and Cleese were married just before Python began, and she began appearing early in the first series.

"I don't remember my first sketch, but I think it was a Canadian scene, with the Mounties, and me singing. I had to learn an English accent for one thing, but I mostly did little tiny bits," says Booth, who is a native of Indianapolis. She says her appearances were rather sporadic, due to the nature of the show.

"I didn't think I was that suited for much of the stuff, but if something came up that they thought I was right for, I did it. Carol Cleveland was hired to be their steady lady, while I was only in for little bits. Carol was also very good at different voices, and I usually only did American parts.

"I never really felt that Python wrote for women. They wrote for men to do women, and they played women much better than women did," she explains.

"I was very flattered to be amongst Python, because I admired what they were doing, but I always felt I was never particularly funny. They were the funny ones, and I was always the fall guy, the dumb blonde, and they were the ones being eccentric or interesting."

Of the supporting men, probably no one made more appearances on the TV show than Ian Davidson.

"Ian was a friend of Terry and myself from the same Oxford University Revue. Now he writes for the BBC, and in fact does a lot of work with Barry Humphries," Michael Palin says.

"It was generally friends that we used back then. There was a guy named David Ballantyne who appeared in a number of sketches. He was a very nice, presentable-looking lad, more presentable than any of us, with a nice haircut. He was a very good, straightish guy found by Ian MacNaughton.

"There was a chap named John Hughman who was immensely tall, and used to appear in things like 'Spot the Looney.' Terry and I had used him in *The Complete and Utter History of Britain* for his enormous size. Generally, people we liked were invited back a second time. They had to be people who were just prepared to go along with it and not complain—they had to like it or lump it!"

Connie Booth with former husband Cleese in Tunisia, writing the second series of **Fawlty Towers.** *Photo copyright KHJ.*

Help!

IN EARLY 1965, Terry Gilliam was working as associate editor for Harvey Kurtzman's *Help!* magazine in New York City. John Cleese was in the same city, where he appeared in Broadway for several weeks in *Cambridge Circus*.

The magazine regularly ran a fumetti feature—essentially a comic book using photos, rather than illustrations. For an upcoming feature, Cleese was tapped to portray Christopher Barrel, a young executive who falls in love with his daughter's doll. One of Gilliam's duties was to supervise the shooting of the feature, and for the first time Cleese and Gilliam worked together on a comedy project.

The meeting proved to be significant for the both of them, and for comedy lovers everywhere. It was that meeting which led to Gilliam's eventual collaboration with the five Englishmen. Without Gilliam's animation and contributions to the structure of the show, *Monty Python's Flying Circus* would have looked quite different—if it had even come about at all.

Gilliam kept in touch with Cleese, and when he journeyed to England, after a series of jobs, he looked up Cleese in hopes of working in television. Cleese referred him to a BBC producer, and Gilliam's persistance resulted in TV work. This eventually led to work on *Do Not Adjust Your Set,* and meetings with Eric Idle, Terry Jones, and Michael Palin—and the rest is history.

But that history began in the May 1965 issue of *Help!* magazine, and "Christopher's Punctured Romance." Although brief portions of it have been presented in the past, this significant piece of Python history has never been reprinted in its entirety, until now. It holds up very well indeed, and Cleese's expressions are a wonder to behold. One can almost hear that familiar voice mouthing the lines.

But now one can judge for oneself. For the first time since 1965, "Christopher's Punctured Romance."

Behold Christopher Barrel, returning dutifully home to his wife, Wilma Barrel — with a case of ennui. Look at him. This sort of thing happens to a man. Too much sameness, too much tedium, too much everything everyday, and then the ennui sets in. Some survive, some never get out of it and some never notice; but to some there is An Occurrence . . .

CHRISTOPHER'S PUNCTURED ROMANCE

BY DAVE CROSSLEY
JOHN CLEESE AS CHRISTOPHER BARREL
CINDY YOUNG AS WILMA BARREL
MARTIN IGER, PHOTOGRAPHER

"Christopher's Punctured Romance." Photos copyright Harvey Kurtzman.

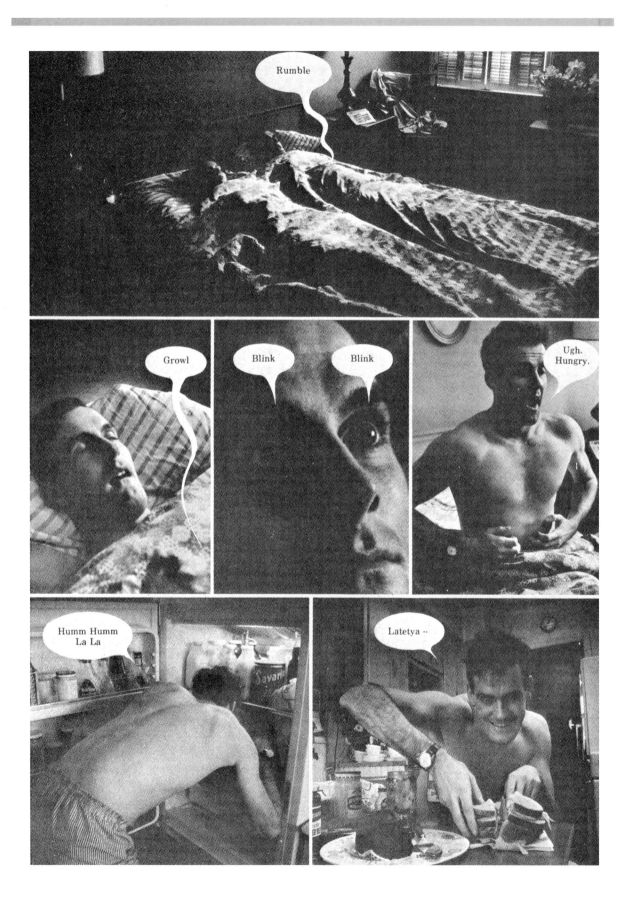

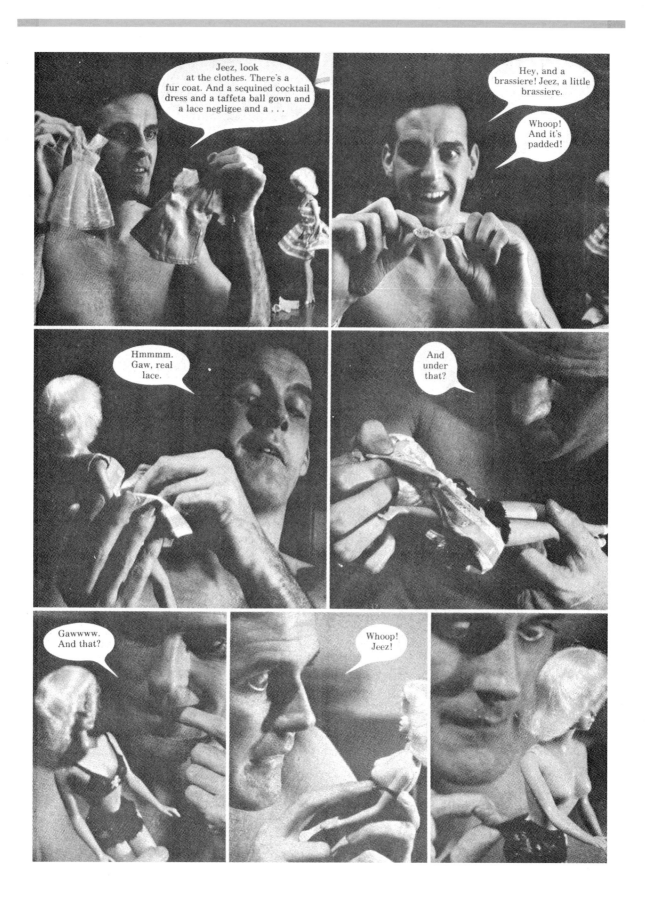

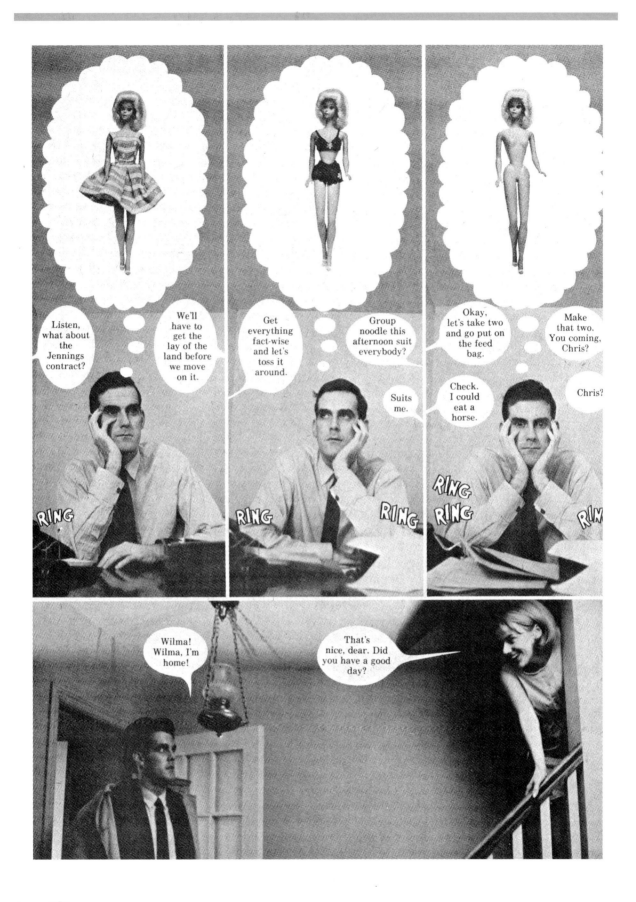

Good, yeah, good.

How's your *ennui*?

Ennui? What *ennui*?

The *ennui* that you . . .

Well, well, here's little Barbee, eh? Say that's quite a little bathing suit ol' Barbee's got there. Yes sir, well what do you think of that? Ol' Barbee's quite the little cutie, isn't she?

Oh yes, Little Nellie's just in love with her. Even little brother Marvin is in love with her.

He's *what*? In *love* with her? Listen, I don't want Marvin getting mixed up with that little hussy!

With that little what? What did you say, dear?

Oh, I just meant, you know, that kids shouldn't become too attached to *playthings*.

Well, it's only a doll, after all.

I'll go get dinner on the table, okay?

Yeah, a doll. Heh heh, just a little doll.

Right. Right you are. Listen, Barbee baby, what say we get you dressed for dinner, eh? Something classy. Bra, lace panties, slip, no girdle? Right, no girdle. And some classy shoes. Let's see what's in the closet, eh? Nice evening gown, okay?

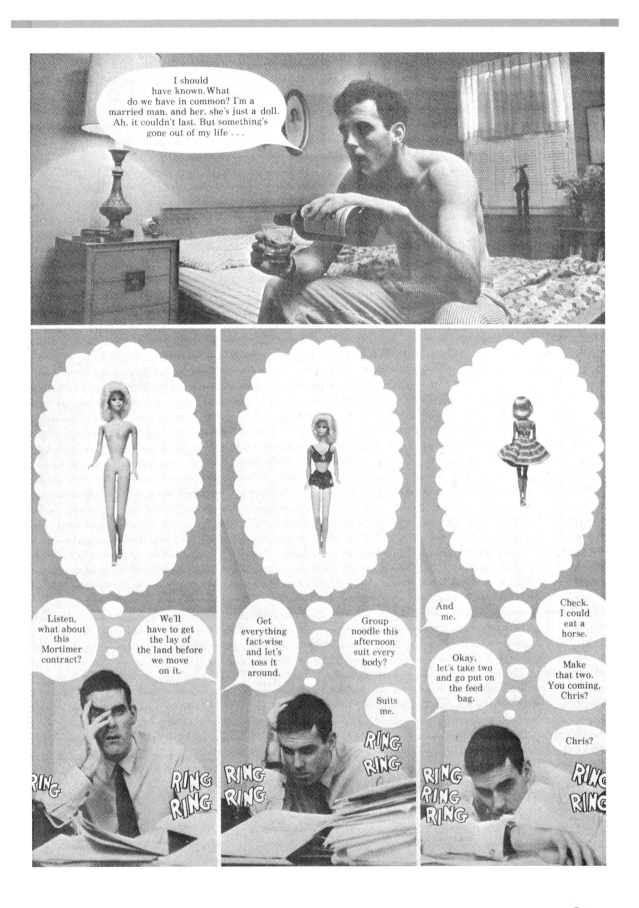

Part Two

THE CLASSIC FORTY-FIVE SHOWS AND MORE

The First Series

Aired Oct. 5–Oct. 26, 1969, and Nov. 23, 1969–Jan. 11, 1970

 WHEN ALL OF the groundwork had been laid, and all of the advance filming completed, it was time to go into the BBC studios and record the first show. Although Michael Palin had remembered it as being less than successful, when he checked his 1969 journal, he discovered that everyone was actually quite optimistic about it all. Palin writes:

> *Barry Took won the audience over with his warmup . . . At 8:10,* Monty Python's Flying Circus *was first launched on a small slice of the public in Studio 6, Television Centre. The reception from the start was very good indeed, and everybody rose to it, the performance being the best ever. The stream-of-consciousness links worked well, and when, at the end, John and I had to redo a small section of two Frenchmen talking rubbish, it went even better—the audience really seemed to enjoy it!*
>
> *It went better than we'd ever hoped, but have yet to see a playback. Afterwards, there was the usual stifling crush in the bar, with genuine congratulations, polite congratulations, and significant silences. Our agent, Kenneth Ewing, did not appear to like it, and he's probably waiting to hear what other people think. About sixteen of us finished the evening in a festive mood, a pool of relief. This evening I felt very, very happy.*

Palin writes that on September 1, 1969, he went to the BBC in the afternoon to watch a playback of the show:

It looked very good. Sagging in a few places, but these can be edited out because we overran by about four or five minutes. It looked very relaxed, it was well directed by John Howard Davies, whose reputation now seems totally restored.

NOTE: The following show synopses are based on the rehearsal scripts as well as repeated viewings of each of the programs; any dubious-looking spellings can be attributed to those scripts. When the Pythons published all of the scripts in two-volume form (and later as a single volume), they are based on those scripts, but there are some discrepancies between those scripts and the final versions of the shows. Whenever possible, I have noted those discrepancies in the notes following each synopsis.

There may also be some discrepancies in the background or incidental music as noted here; as music licenses expire, it sometimes becomes necessary to replace more unimportant tunes in the broadcast episodes or videocassettes.

Shows are presented in the order in which they were originally broadcast, rather than the order in which they were recorded. Sharp-eyed readers may note that the order of episodes has been revised slightly from the first edition of this book; this was done to synchronize them with the scripts in the aforementioned *Monty Python: All the Words* (known as *Monty Python: Just the Words* in the U.K.).

Whenever possible, the initials of the actors appear next to their characters, though in some cases they could not be determined. This is particularly true in the case of various extras, mostly without speaking parts, whose names are buried in the bowels of the BBC.

Various discrepancies also appear throughout the shows (i.e., Supt. Harry "Snapper" Organs of "Q" Division changes his rank and his division during his several appearances). Consistency was not highly valued by the Pythons, and will be viewed with similar disdain within these pages.

And now, the classic forty-five shows. Pay attention—there may be a quiz!

Show 1—Whither Canada

Recorded as Series 1, Show 2—Prod. #53346

The "It's" Man (MP) runs out of the sea, and says "It's" . . .

Titles

An announcer (GC) walks onto a set and sits on a pig; a picture of a pig is crossed off a blackboard.

"It's Wolfgang Amadeus Mozart" features Mozart (JC) presenting the deaths of historical characters, complete with judges and a sidekick, Eddie (EI), to recap the scores. Deaths include Genghis Khan (MP) and Mr. Bruce Foster (GC), by request, and the finale is the demise of Admiral Nelson, who is hurled off a building. A pig is heard squealing as he hits the pavement, and a teacher (TJ) in an Italian language class crosses another pig off the blackboard.

The teacher attempts to instruct his students, but all of them are Italian and speak it fluently, except for a German student (GC) wearing lederhosen, who is in the wrong class. The teacher then sits on a pig. A pig on the blackboard becomes animated, and runs away before it can be crossed off, leading into a commercial where Pepperpots claim

they cannot tell the difference between Whizzo Butter and a dead crab.

"It's the Arts," hosted by a Linkman (MP), begins with an interviewer, Tim (JC), conducting an interview with celebrated film director Sir Edward Ross (GC). After calling him Eddie Baby, Sweetie, and other too-familiar terms, he walks off the set. The Linkman promises an upcoming film of Picasso painting live on a bicycle, and then shoots a pig.

Another Interviewer, Michael (EI), talks with composer Arthur "Two Sheds" Jackson (TJ) about his nickname, ignoring his music. The first Interviewer then joins Michael after Two Sheds protests, and they throw him out. The Linkman introduces an Eddie Baxter type (MP), who stands in front of a map of Picasso's route describing his plans. On the Guilford Bypass, Reg Moss (EI) talks with British cycling champion Ron Geppo (GC) on Picasso's strategy, as there is no sign of the painter yet. Sam Trench (JC) reports live from another location, where several cycling painters go by, but Pi-

casso has apparently fallen off his bicycle and failed in his first bid for international cycling fame, ending "It's the Arts" as the closing credits roll.

The closing credits are interrupted by Victorian animation ("Sit up!"), with heads flying off bodies, dancing soldiers, and a pig falling on a man.

Ernest Scribbler (MP) writes the funniest joke in the world and dies laughing. His mother (EI) discovers it and also falls over dead. A man from Scotland Yard (GC) tells an Interviewer (TJ) that he will enter the house, aided by somber music and laments by men of Q Division, in case he accidentally looks at the joke. The army becomes interested during World War II, and the joke is tested and carefully translated into German. On July 8, 1944, the joke is first used in combat with fantastic success, while a German joke is unsuccessful against the Allies. A Gestapo Officer (JC) and his assistant Otto (GC) interrogate a Prisoner (MP) to discover the joke, Otto providing the sound effects of slapping. His captors fall victim to the joke, as does a German Guard (TG), who bursts into the room to stop him. The Germans were found to be working on their own joke as the war ended, when joke warfare was outlawed and a monument was erected to the Unknown Joke.

At "The End" the "It's" Man is poked with a stick and rises from the beach into the water, as the credits roll.

ALSO APPEARING: Carol Cleveland
Terry Gilliam

Pigs 9 British Bipeds 4

📹 Some sequences here were trimmed, and several other bits were scheduled to be in this show. Taken out and used in other shows were the "Lingerie Shop Robbery," The "Holiday Camp MC," "Donkey Rides," and the "Restaurant" sketch, set to follow "It's the Arts," as well as Johann Gambolputty de von Ausfernschpledenschlittcrasscrenbonfriediggerdingledangledongleburstinvonknackerthrasherapplebangerhorowitzticolensicgranderknottyspelltinklegrandlichgrumbelmeyerspellerwasserkurstlichhimbleeisenbahnwagengutenabend-

bitteeinnurnburgerbratwurstlegerspurtenmitzweimacheluberhundsfutgumberaberschonendankerkalbsfleischmittleraucher Von Hauptkopf of Ulm.

📹 The "Italian Lesson" featured a longer sequence in which a fight breaks out in the class over which city is better, Milano or Napoli; the "Killer Joke" originally had a Churchill speech, as well as a modern-day BBC interview on German jokes coming through Britain.

📹 The Scribblers' house is located on Dibley Road, Dibley coming from Gwen Dibley; Michael Palin originally wanted to name Python *Gwen Dibley's Flying Circus* (see Dibley Notes).

History Comes Alive

"I always liked the famous deaths, which I introduced as Wolfgang Amadeus Mozart. I was particularly fond of the death of Nelson at the Battle of Trafalgar. We'd gotten this enormous model of Nelson and threw him out of the top window of this modern bloc, and as he sails through the air, he shouts "Kiss me, Haaardyyyy . . .' " says Cleese, and slaps his hands to indicate a splat.

The Deadliest Joke in the World—Revealed!

"It was actually German gibberish," Eric Idle explains. "It's written-down gibberish, because we all had to learn the same thing, yeah, but it's gibberish! It doesn't mean a thing at all. At least, I don't *think* it does . . ."

But, for the souls brave enough to withstand it, here is the Deadliest Joke in the World, revealed for the first time in print: Venn ist das nurnstuck git und Slotermeyer? Ya! Beigerhund das oder die Flipperwaldt gersput!

Show 2—Sex and Violence

Recorded as Series 1, Show 1—Prod. #53440

The "It's" Man (MP) dashes through a field laden with trap doors, running up to the camera and announcing "It's"

Titles

Part Two Sheep

A City Gentleman (TJ) talks with a Farmer (GC) about his sheep, which are up in the trees under the misapprehension that they're birds. This leads into a pair of Frenchmen (MP and JC) who lecture in pseudo-French on the commercial possibilities of aviation by sheep, and several Pepperpots (Python old ladies) on film discuss the French and their philosophers.

An animation sequence follows involving "The Thinker," and "I think, therefore I am."

Eric introduces the next sketch with "And now for something completely different." It is an interview with Arthur Frampton (TJ), a man with three buttocks. The Questioner (JC) attempts to get him to drop his pants ("Our viewers need proof!"), with no success, even after switching back to him several times. Eric introduces several other people, including a man with three noses (GC), who blows his stomach, and there is the familiar stock film of the Women's Institute group applauding.

An unctuous MC (MP) introduces Arthur Ewing and his musical mice, consisting of twenty-three highly trained white mice that each squeak out a different tone when Ewing strikes them with a large mallet. He attempts a song, but is dragged offstage before the indignant crowd.

The Marriage Guidance Counselor (EI) is vis-

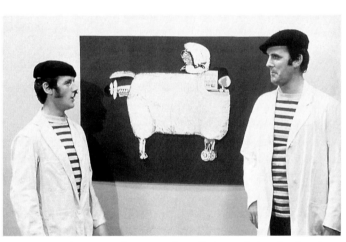

Two Frenchmen (Cleese and Palin) explain the intricacies of flying sheep, while trying to maintain their composure. Photo copyright BBC and Python Productions.

ited by Arthur and Deidre Putey (MP and CC). The Counselor and Deidre hit it off, and they send the mild-mannered Arthur out of the room as they step behind a screen, removing their clothing. Outside, Arthur is met by a man in black cowboy garb (JC), who tells him to be a man and go back in for his wife. Determined, Arthur goes back inside, but when ordered away, he meekly complies. The caption reads "So much for pathos!"

In the north country, Ken (EI) goes home to visit his parents (GC and TJ). Ken ran off to work in the coal mines, instead of laboring in the theater like his parents, who "fill their heads with novels and prose" and are worn out with "meeting film stars, attending premieres, and giving gala luncheons." His father is afflicted with writer's cramp, and finally throws his son out.

The downstairs Neighbor (MP) pounds on the ceiling with a broom handle, and introduces a Scotsman on a horse (JC), who is applauded by the stock Women's Institute film. The man with three noses (GC) blows his elbow, and an animated sequence features Harold, the flying sheep.

"The Epilogue" (introduced by JC) features Monsignor Edward Gay and Dr. Tom Jack, Humanist (author of *Hello, Sailor!*), wrestling to determine the existence of God. Arthur Waring (EI) is master of ceremonies for the bout, and while it continues, the Host (JC) begins a gun battle with an animated cowboy.

The animation continues with a political speech being closed down, a baby coach that de-

vours old ladies, and "The Lovers" statue that becomes musical.

"The World Around Us" (hosted by MP) focuses on the "Mouse Problem"—men who dress as mice, eat cheese, and squeak. Harold Voice (TJ) interviews Arthur Jackson (JC), who describes how he came to terms with his own mousehood, while clips are shown of historical figures who were also mice. There are hostile opinions by the man in the street, and secret film of a mouse party, climaxed by a farmer's wife cutting off their tails. The Host (MP) shoots Harold the sheep, who lands on his desk.

The "It's" Man (MP) runs away as the credits roll, and a voice-over announces the existence of God by two falls.

ALSO APPEARING: Carol Cleveland

The BBC script is actually titled "Owl Stretching Time," but the title is crossed out on the inside page, where "Bunn, Wackett, Buzzard, Stubble, and Boot" is handwritten in its place.

Further Pepperpot dialogue on the French philosophers (vs. German philosophers—"Would you swap Descartes for, say, Hegel and Heidegger?") is cut from this show.

The "Musical Mice" sketch was not in the original script, but inserted by hand; Arthur Putey is variously referred to in the script as Arthur Posture and Arthur Pewtie; and a panel of nuns was cut from the final version of "The Epilogue."

A Linkman (MP) interviews "The Amazing Kargol and Janet" (TJ and CC), a psychiatrist/conjurer act, in a scene that followed the Jackson "Mouse Problem" interview; it was also cut from the final show.

A filmed sketch called "The Wacky Queen" was intended for this show, just before "Working Class Playwright." Silent with voice-over by Alfred Lord Tennyson, it featured Queen Victoria (TJ) and Gladstone (GC) walking along the lawn at Osborne. The slapstick bit begins with the Queen pushing the gardener into a manure-filled wheelbarrow, and squirting Gladstone with a hose, whereupon Gladstone dumps whitewash on the Queen. The

cake-throwing climax ends in a freeze-frame that turns into the photo on the mantle in the "Working Class Playwright."

The Mouse Problem and Peter Sellers's Milkman

The "Mouse Problem" sketch had been written earlier by Graham Chapman and John Cleese; they had held onto it, knowing it could be used at some point in the future.

"We'd always been rather fond of it," Chapman explained, "and it cropped up in Python. I was always quite fond of mice, or little rodents of any kind.

"In actual fact, we had written the sketch for the Peter Sellers movie *The Magic Christian*. He had liked the item very much indeed, but he went off it the very next day, when his milkman didn't like it."

Carol's First Time

Carol Cleveland was in the first episode of *Monty Python's Flying Circus* ever recorded, and her first full sketch, the Marriage Guidance Counselor, is still one of the better known. Most fans are not aware, however, that she actually appeared in the very first sketch—though "appeared" may not be the correct term.

"They changed the order when the shows came out, but the first episode included the Marriage Guidance Counselor sketch," says Cleveland. "That was in the first episode taped. But the very first utterance I made—and one can say it was an utterance—was in the sketch about the flying sheep. I believe that was the very first sketch in the very first episode. These two farmers were discussing flying sheep, and you hear everybody else being sheep in the background. You hear a little baby sheep every now and then in between these 'BAAAAAs!' Every now and then you hear a little 'Baa!' and that was me! That was my first utterance—a baby sheep plummeting to the ground!"

The Marriage Guidance Counselor sketch was

her first big opportunity in the Python shows. She notes: "I didn't have a lot to do in that one except giggle," says Cleveland. "That's when my famous Cleveland giggle was introduced. The fellows loved it and used it quite often after that, because they thought it was wonderful. John, particularly, always liked giggly girls. Quite often they would say 'Okay, giggle now, Carol, giggle!' That's what I remember about that, my giggle."

Show 3—How to Recognize Different Types of Trees From Quite a Long Way Away

Recorded as Series 1, Show 3—Prod. #53376

The "It's" Man (MP) runs through a forest, says "It's"
Titles
Episode 12B—How to Recognize Different Types of Trees from Quite a Long Way Away
Number One: the Larch.

Harold Larch (EI) is in court, giving a long, impassioned speech about freedom, but the Judge (TJ) points out that it's only a bloody parking offense. Mr. Bartlett (JC), a barrister arriving late, tries to question Mrs. Fiona Lewis, who delivers rambling, gossipy testimony before being led out of the courtroom. A coffin containing the late Arthur Aldridge is brought in and questioned, but the Judge accuses the barrister of dumping bodies in his courtroom. Bartlett calls in Cardinal Richelieu (MP) as a character witness, but Inspector Dim of the Yard (GC) gets the Cardinal to confess that he is actually Ron Higgins, a professional Cardinal Richelieu impersonator. Dim sings "If I were not in the CID,* something else I'd like to be . . . ," but when Bartlett starts to sing, he is hit with a rubber chicken by a Knight in armor (TG).

Number One: the Larch.

Mr. F.G. Superman (MP) lives in a town inhabited entirely by Supermen. But when the need arises, he becomes their greatest hero, Bicycle Repairman.

The Commentator (JC), wearing a jacket and tie, and sitting at a table in a garden, goes into a tirade against Communists, and eventually flails about, as the Knight (TG) follows him offscreen.

In "Storytime," the Host (MP) begins reading several stories for children, but stops as they all contain sexual assault, transvestism, contraceptives, discipline, and nudity. The childish animation at the end turns violent, and an animated priest hammers a parishioner into the ground with his forehead.

"Donkey Rides" at the beach is featured briefly, while the unctuous Host (MP) introduces the "Restaurant" sketch.

A couple of (GC and CC) dining at a three-star restaurant point out a dirty fork at their table. Gaston the waiter (TJ), Gilberto the headwaiter (MP), and the Manager (EI), all apologize and beg forgiveness (Gilberto orders the entire washing-up staff fired). Mungo the cook (JC) storms out of the kitchen and tries to attack the customers, when the punch line "Lucky we didn't say anything about the dirty knife," is delivered.

Back at the beach, the unctuous Host (MP) is hit with a chicken by the restaurant Customer (GC), who returns the chicken to the Knight.

An animated commercial is shown for "Purchase a Past"—for fifteen shillings one can purchase bits of other peoples' more interesting lives (including photos) and pretend they're your own. The plan falls apart when numerous animated relatives arrive and start filling up the house, and the animation is crumpled up.

A happy, whistling Milkman (MP) is led into the house of an attractive customer in a negligee (CC). She leads him upstairs, into a locked room where there are numerous other milkmen, some with long beards, others dead.

Newsreader Michael Queen (JC) is reading the evening news, when a shootout erupts around him. He continues reading, oblivious, as he, his

*Criminal Investigation Division.

The cast of "The Dirty Fork Sketch," another early generic group shot, though not as early as the previous generic group shot. (Left to right: Idle, Chapman, Palin, Cleese, Jones, and Gilliam, who wasn't involved in the sketch, and very rarely appeared on camera toward the beginning of the series.) Photo copyright BBC and Python Productions.

desk, and his chair are wheeled out of the BBC Television Centre by the gunmen. He is loaded onto a truck, driven through town, and finally pushed from a dock, all while he keeps reading.

And now—Number One: the Larch. Number Three: the Larch. And now—the Horse Chestnut.

A man (JC) interviews three children (EI, MP, and TJ) in a "Vox Pops" film segment about trees, but they request Eric's "Nudge, Nudge" sketch.

Norm (EI) sits in a pub, making insinuations about another man (TJ) and his wife, asking about their personal lives, nudge, nudge, grin, grin, wink, wink.

The "It's" Man (MP) runs away from the camera as the credits roll.

ALSO APPEARING: Ian Davidson

This show was originally called "Bunn, Wackett, Buzzard, Stubble, and Boot" in the BBC rehearsal script.

In the original BBC rehearsal script, the "Larch" was not included, and the Harold Larch character was originally named Harold Millet; "Storytime" was to lead into the "Vocational Guidance Counsellor," rather than the "Restaurant" sketch; "Irving C. Saltzberg" originally followed the "Milkmen," with Saltzberg calling for the newsreader for the hijacking sketch.

Graham was originally supposed to be one of four children in the "Vox Pops" scene just before "Nudge, Nudge."

 **Faster than a Speeding Lawyer**

"Bicycle Repairman" came about from the Jones/Palin tendency to think visually. "That sketch came from Mike and me thinking about re-

hearsals," Terry Jones recalls, "though it also came from thinking about what would look funny. And it *did* look funny seeing a lot of Supermen all walking around."

Although the "F.G. Superman/Bicycle Repairman" sketch involved groups of people in (what else?) Superman costumes, the group apparently met with no legal repercussions from DC Comics for the use of their character. Michael Palin explains that they had very little trouble from legal sources, especially in their first season. "When we used Spam, I don't think we ever got permission from them—we just used it. In the end they were very keen, and promised

they would send us several tins of free Spam. We said 'No, that's all right, thanks anyway . . .' And, we had no repercussions that I can remember from the comics.

"We were not well known at all then, and there was no export potential to other countries. We were just a silly little late-night Saturday show, not even aired in all of Britain. The first series wasn't even seen in the Midlands—they got farming programs. Eventually, people in Birmingham got angry and felt they were missing something. But by the second series, the comedy lovers got the upper hand over the farmers."

Performing "Nudge, Nudge" live onstage had its problems—in this case, Jones and (standing), Idle are halted by the Colonel (Chapman). Photo copyright KHJ.

Show 4 — Owl-stretching Time

Recorded as Series 1, Show 4—Prod. #53485

The "It's" Man (MP) is hurled off a cliff. He crawls along the ground toward the camera and gasps "It's"

Titles

Episode Arthur   Part 7   Teeth

A Guitarist (EI) strums and sings "Jerusalem" live from the Cardiff Rooms, Libya, while he introduces the next sketch.

In "Art Gallery," Marge and her friend Janet (GC and JC) are trying to keep track of their children, who are running around the museum vandalizing great works of art. They discipline the kids just off-camera, and finally start to eat some of the masterpieces themselves. An Art Critic (MP) in the next scene starts nibbling at pictures himself, along with a girl assisting him in the discussion.

The Guitarist is seduced by a girl while trying to sing, and the slogan "It's a Man's Life in the

Cardiff Rooms, Libya" is criticized by the Colonel (GC). He says it's too similar to the "It's a Man's Life in the Modern Army" slogan, and warns them against using it again. On his orders, the cameras cut away.

In "Changing on the Beach," a man (TJ) tries to change his clothes at the beach, in the under-cranked style of an old-time silent comedy. He tries to change behind trucks, stacks of chairs, etc., until he accidentally ends up onstage, where he takes the opportunity to do a striptease. The Colonel objects to the caption "It's a Man's Life Taking Your Clothes Off in Public," and orders the next sketch to begin.

In a gymnasium, a Sergeant-Major (JC) teaches a group of recruits (TJ, MP, GC, EI) self-defense against an assailant armed with various kinds of fresh fruit, and asks them to help demonstrate. He

shoots Harrison (GC), who was armed with a banana, and Thompson (TJ), armed with raspberries, is struck with a sixteen-ton weight.

An animated operation sees spare body parts become two flunkys, who carry a sedan chair to the beach. The eighteenth-century Gentleman (EI) inside the chair exits, undresses, gets back inside, and is carried into the sea.

The post-coital Guitarist sings, introducing a man (JC) walking through the hills with "It's a Man's Life in England's Mountains Green," but the Colonel stops him before he can deliver his rustic monologue. The Colonel wants to see something about teeth.

A Tobacconist (EI) enters a bookstore, but the Bookseller (JC) says they are all out of books and tries to get rid of him, until the Tobacconist explains he was told to come there. The Bookseller gives the sign and countersign to no avail, and the Tobacconist says he was told to come there by a little old lady in a sweet shop. The Tobacconist starts to become suspicious, and asks for "An Illustrated History of False Teeth." He is accused of being a dentist, and Stapleton, the bookseller, pulls a gun on him. Another secret agent, LaFarge (MP), bursts into the shop, immediately followed by another couple dressed as a dentist and his nurse, all looking for the secret fillings. They all assure the Tobacconist that nothing is going on. Brian (TJ) then bursts in with a bazooka, getting the drop on them all, until the Big Cheese (GC) rolls his wheelchair in, shooting his pet bunny Flopsy. He threatens them all with death, but they break for lunch.

The Tobacconist reveals himself as Arthur Lemming of the British Dental Association. When a chorus sings a refrain about him, with the caption "It's a Man's Life in the British Dental Association," the Colonel stops the show. The "It's" Man is nudged with a stick and runs away as the credits roll, and is thrown off the cliff again.

ALSO APPEARING: Dick Vosburgh
     Carol Cleveland
     Katya Wyeth

The original order and contents of the show were quite different in the BBC rehearsal script. It was to have led off with the "Bookseller/Dentist/Spy" sketch, followed by "Changing at the Beach," the "Art Gallery" and "Art Critic and Wife" link.

The show then went to "Buying a Bed," used in Show 8, then the "Sedan Chair," into the "Hermits," also used in Show 8, to "Soft-Fruit Defense."

Haute Cuisine

"Those picture frames that we ate were apparently some kind of pastry, made with flour and water paste," Graham Chapman recalled. "They weren't sweet, and they were rather dry . . ."

To Laugh or Not to Laugh

Since the makeup of the early studio audiences was somewhat less than that of the typical Python fan, the sketches didn't always elicit the desired reactions. In fact, some of them played to a bewildered silence.

The group didn't let the reaction (or lack of such) distract them unduly, as a number of technical considerations were involved as well, and the Pythons simply had to rely on their gut instincts to judge their timing.

"We just had to watch it and say 'Is it funny or not?'" says John Cleese. "There is some stuff that doesn't work with a studio audience, yet I still feel is intrinsically funny. They're not the only criteria, not least because there's a certain way of presenting a sketch to a studio audience that they will laugh at, but there are other ways of doing it.

"For example, when they have to look up to monitors when we've cut from studio to film—those pieces always play to dead silence. The audience is always looking at the wrong place at the wrong time. But those sketches can still be very funny at home."

Changing on the Beach

The Jones/Palin team had, by the time of Python, developed a visual style that was most apparent in their short silent film done for this show. Although it was funny and mostly successful, it was a far cry from the type of material usually in-

cluded in Python, and Jones says it didn't really work.

"'Changing on the Beach' doesn't seem like Python, really," he says. "There were certain bits that were never done quite right. I was wary of the part where they take the deck chairs away—it's just too slow, and we didn't undercrank it enough. I always liked silent film stuff, though. That was the kind of thing we'd been doing for *The Frost Report*—it was 'our' style of filming. But it didn't go down well with the others."

Jones (who is a big fan of Buster Keaton) also performs the first of the two stripteases that he does during the series. Both are hilariously convincing, despite his claims of inexperience. "One of the first days of filming was the striptease in this large theater . . . It was quite nerve-wracking, and I was frightened," says Jones. "I hadn't worked out at all what I was going to do. I don't think I'd even *seen* a striptease back then!"

Show 5—Man's Crisis of Identity in the Latter Half of the Twentieth Century

Recorded as Series 1, Show 5—Prod. #53947

The "It's" Man (MP) rows a boat toward the camera and says "It's"
   Titles
   A Suburban Lounge Near Esher
   A middle-aged Couple (MP and TJ) call the vet for their cat, who is suffering from boredom—it just sits out there on the lawn. The vet tells them that their cat is in a rut, and badly needs to be confused.

   They send for Confuse-a-Cat Ltd. The Sergeant (MP) drills the group, and the General (JC) orders the "funny things" out of their van. They build a stage in front of the cat, and put on an amazing show, one using locked cameras, undercranking, jerky motion, jump cuts, etc.; it includes Long John Silver, prizefighters that keep changing their identities, Napoleon, a traffic cop, and a penguin on a pogo stick. At the end of the show, the cat gets up and walks away. Credits are shown over a picture of the General, whose animated moustache grows, turning into yarn for knitting needles.

   A Customs Official (JC) stops a suspicious-looking man (MP) who appears to be smuggling watches. The Official won't believe him, however, even when he confesses and shows him the watches. He makes the man go on through, but the next person, a Vicar (EI), is ordered to undergo a strip search in the next room.

   "Vox Pops" one-liners follow on customs procedures, and the Chairman (TJ) of a TV discussion group on customs enforcement measures inter-

views a duck, a cat, and a lizard. Man-in-the-street interviews follow, including one by Mr. Gumby (JC) on law enforcement measures. Gumby is then hit with a chicken by a Knight (TG).

   Police Constable Henry Thatcher (GC), with police dog Josephine waiting outside, raids the apartment of actor Sandy Camp (EI), looking for illicit substances. He drops a paper bag on the floor, but it is found to contain sandwiches, causing him to wonder what he gave his wife. Two more letters are read, and man-in-the-street interviews continue.

   A BBC Newsreader (EI) reads an item about a man wanted for robbery, and the picture of the suspect shown on the Eidaphor screen behind him reveals it to be the Newsreader.

   "Edited Highlights of Tonight's Romantic Movie" are seen by Bevis (TJ) and his girlfriend Donna (CC) while in bed; the film includes tall, soaring trees, waves crashing, a fountain, fireworks, a volcano, and other such symbolism. Finally, a caber is tossed, a plane falls, a tree crashes to the ground, and the tower at the beginning of the film collapses.

   An animated commercial is shown for "Charles Fatless."

   David Thomas (GC) applies at a Management Training Course where the interviewer (JC) terrorizes him. He makes noises and faces, has him stand up and sit down several times, making him generally nervous and upset, and a team of judges score him. The Head of the Careers Advisory Board (MP)

then begins talking about how he originally wanted to be a doctor or lawyer, etc.

A Burglar (EI) knocks on a door, but the Housewife (JC) doesn't want to let him in because she's afraid he's an encyclopedia salesman. Film of an unsuccessful encyclopedia salesman is shown, and he is thrown off a tall building.

The "It's" Man rows away, as the credits roll.
ALSO APPEARING: Carol Cleveland

🎬 The cover of the script reads "Beware, Poison, Not to be Taken Internally."

🎬 The BBC rehearsal script has the "It's" Man hurled off a cliff at the beginning of the show; David Thomas's original name was Stig; and the "Ron Obvious" scene was to appear at the end of this show (it is now in Show 10), with the film of the "It's" Man shown at the beginning run backwards, while Vercotti sits on the beach.

The War against Animal Complacency

Their working environment often had a major influence on Python writing, explained Graham Chapman. When John Cleese came over to his penthouse apartment to write one day, an idea was sparked off that became a classic sketch.

"I had noticed a neighbor's lawn for the last two weeks. It was very carefully tended—she even brushed it—but there was a cat on it, which was *always* in the exact same position. No matter what happened, it didn't move. It didn't even move in moderate rainstorms. It would just sit.

"So, I discussed this with John, and wondered what the problem was with the cat. We decided that it was complacent, and had seen it all, and therefore needed shaking out of its complacency. So Confuse-a-Cat, Ltd., were the guys for the job! That sketch came about purely from what was around."

Chapman said that when desperate, they often relied on reference books to spark ideas. "Whether from the news, from a book like *Roget's Thesaurus,* or from what was happening around us, all ideas have to come about through some sort of observation. It sparks an attitude, and some object or emotion causes a reaction in the other person. They think 'That's an interesting way of looking at it,' and then build a sketch out of it."

Show 6—The BBC Entry for the Zinc Stoat of Budapest

Recorded as Series 1, Show 7—Prod. #54772

A phone rings on a tree stump in the forest, and is answered by the "It's" Man (MP).

Titles

Next Week—How to Fling an Otter

This Week—The BBC Entry for the Zinc Stoat of Budapest (Current Affairs)

The price of the preceding captions is shown and added up, as several more costly captions are displayed.

Arthur Figgis (GC) (first shown riding a bicycle with Arthur "Three Buttocks" Frampton in an earlier show) signs an autograph for a fan (MP), and the ink lines become animated as the scribble wriggles away, to eventually be shot from an animated cannon, whereupon it becomes Michelangelo's *David,* and the introduction to "It's the Arts."

Arthur Figgis introduces the program, which discusses the German baroque composer Johann Gambolputty de von Ausfernschpledenschlittcrasscrenbonfriediggerdingledangledonglebursteinvonknackerthrasherapplebangerhorowitzticolensicgranderknottyspelltinklegrandlichgrumbelmeyerspellerwasserkurstlichhimbleeisenbahnwagengutenabendbitteeinnurnburgerbratwurstlegerspurtenmitzwem-

A gang of vicious thugs hatch a brilliant, elaborate plot to buy a watch. Photo copyright BBC and Python Productions.

acheluberhundsfutgumberaberschonendankerkalbsfleschmittleraucher Von Hauptkopf of Ulm.

An Interviewer (JC) questions his oldest living relative, Karl (TJ), who dies while attempting to say his name; the Interviewer, disgusted, throws away his microphone and begins digging. There are "Vox Pops" of different characters saying Johann's name, and the close of "It's the Arts" sees an animated hand reaching for the leaf covering *David;* a blue-nosed censor is underneath.

A gang of desperate-looking robbers (JC, GC, TJ, EI) listen to their boss (MP) devise an elaborate plot to buy a watch. One of them, Larry (TJ), complains that they aren't doing anything illegal. Several short "Vox Pops" follow, with bank robbers, judges, and a police inspector (JC), who announces that he'll be appearing in the next sketch.

Sure enough, Inspector Praline and Supt. Parrot (JC and GC) visit the office of Arthur Hilton (TJ), the head of the Whizzo Chocolate Company, to question him about the Whizzo Quality Assortment, which contains such items as Crunchy Frog, Anthrax Ripple, and Cockroach Cluster. He is taken into the station, while Parrot becomes ill trying to warn the public.

The "Dull Life of a City Stockbroker" (MP) is next. As the Stockbroker leaves his house in the morning, his wife has an affair with two men, a Zulu tribesman throws his spear at his next-door neighbor (narrowly missing him), he buys a newspaper from a nude woman, is nearly killed by Frankenstein's monster while waiting for a bus, and is caught in the middle of an army battle before arriving at his office, where a number of violent deaths have taken place. He remains oblivious to it all, and begins reading a comic book, which becomes animated as a super-hero tries to break out of a panel. The curtain closes on the panel to begin the "Theater" sketch.

An American Indian (EI) in full warrior dress takes a seat (next to GC) in the theater. The Indian says he is a big fan of Cicely Courtneidge, explaining that the Redfoot tribe are mighty hunters and actors. When a theater spokesman (MP) announces that Cicely Courtneidge won't be appearing that evening, he is pierced with arrows.

The next morning, Mrs. Emma Hamilton (TJ) and Edgar (ID) read about the Indian massacre at the theater the previous evening. A Policeman (JC) enters, and does an advertisement for people seeking policemen as friends, and has Emma draw the next sketch from his hat. She chooses a Scotsman on a Horse.

Young Lochinvar (JC) rides through the countryside to a small church, where a wedding is going on. He arrives just in time, and carries away

One of Cicely Courtneidge's fans (Idle), complete with bow and arrows, waits impatiently for her appearance, to the uncertainty of other theatergoers. Photo copyright BBC and Python Productions.

the groom (MP); there is stock film of Women's Institute applause.

Another animated sequence follows, with a vicious baby carriage that chases people, leading up to "20th Century Vole Presents."

Producer Irving C. Saltzberg (GC) talks to six writers (JC, EI, TG, MP, TD, ID) about his next movie. The terrified writers quickly praise his every suggestion, but he begins throwing them out for the slightest hint of disloyalty, until the room is empty. He picks up the phone, and the phone on the tree stump rings.

The phone is answered by the "It's" Man, who runs away as the credits—all involving Irving C. Saltzberg—roll.

ALSO APPEARING: Ian Davidson

 The first sketch was originally three men in a pub (MP, JC, EI) trying to recognize a fourth (TJ), who looks very ordinary, with plastered-down hair and pinched spectacles. They ask him to repeat phrases to jot their memories, but he turns out to be Arthur Figgis, an accountant, rather than Jimmy Stewart, Eddie Waring, Anthony Newley, David Frost or their other guesses, and leads into Johann Gambolputty . . .

 The "Dull Life of a City Stockbroker" is not in the BBC rehearsal script, while "Young Lochinvar" and "Irving C. Saltzberg" were written for earlier shows.

Bon Appetit!

When the "Whizzo Chocolate" sketch was performed in the stage shows, Terry Gilliam usually took the Superintendent's role, but had no lines. The reason for this was evident at the conclusion of the scene, where TG vomited into his police helmet, to the delight or disgust of the audience. He then placed the helmet back on his head.

Backstage at the Hollywood Bowl, he was

During a live performance of the Whizzo Chocolate Sketch, Gilliam (right) stands quietly, his mouth full of cold beef stew. Photo copyright KHJ.

asked how he could stand to have the fake vomit in his mouth throughout the scene. "I don't know why everybody gets so grossed out by it," he said straight-faced. "It's only cold beef stew."

Hi-Yo, Silver!

The shots of Young Lochinvar on horseback were not actually done by Cleese; he didn't learn to ride a horse until fifteen years later, while making *Silverado* in New Mexico, for which he took several weeks worth of riding lessons.

"I actually did have some rather good riding shots in *Silverado*—I looked remarkably good on a horse—but they didn't fit in the film. They've actually got a shot of me leading a posse that I'm really proud of. My daughter Cynthia was obsessed by horses at the time, and I thought I could finally win a little respect from her! In fact, all of the wider shots in the film are stuntmen with crepe beards," Cleese says.

"In 'Lochinvar' there were closeups of me riding, but I wasn't on a horse; the long shots were done by a stuntman. I'm actually on a horse for all the closeups in *Silverado,* at least. In 'Lochinvar,' I think I was sitting on a bicycle."

A Day in the Life of an Ordinary BBC Comedy Writer

"The whole 'Dull Life of a City Stockbroker' sequence was an interesting piece of writing," said Graham Chapman. "It obviously wasn't an ordinary day in the life, except—well, such extraordinary things happened around him, but he clearly never noticed, which is why he had such an extraordinary life. Quite a nice point to make, but a fairly straightforward one.

"That was actually written by Eric Idle and myself as a sendup of a Terry Jones/Michael Palin script. They wrote a lot of sketches for Marty Feldman with a Day in the Life of a Golfer theme—it was almost a genre with them. So we thought, 'Well, that's pretty easy, let's write one of those and see if they notice,' Chapman laughed. "But

they didn't say anything about it at the time, and when we finished up filming it, Eric and I just kept quiet about it."

I Remember the Face, but the Name . . .

When they presented the rest of the group with the "Johann Gambolputty . . ." sketch, Michael Palin says there was surprisingly little grumbling over the frighteningly long name they would have to remember. "It was our University Revue background that made us take great pride in being able to cope with difficult things like that, difficult names and long speeches without cue cards.

"That was the stuff of University Revue. It was verbal dexterity, memorizing long speeches, talking without a break. So there it was, and we just had to learn it. There was never a question of anyone saying 'Well, it's got to be easier.' It was just 'That's it, that's what it is, and we'll learn it.' "

Only one of the troupe got lucky.

"I never had to do all of it," Eric Idle says, smiling. "I played an old man who died halfway through it, so I only had to memorize the first bit."

An Irving C. Saltzberg Production

"That was an early sketch, a holdover from old material that hadn't been used before. John Cleese and I had written it for *At Last, the 1948 Show.* People generally liked it, though we'd just read it through and hadn't actually cast it," said Graham Chapman.

"Suddenly, Marty Feldman wanted to play Irving C. Saltzberg, which was okay. I suppose I'd seen either John or I playing him, but we would, of course—we wrote it. Anyway, that was fair enough. But when we came to rehearse it, suddenly Marty wanted to pull out—he got nervous for some reason. I don't know quite why, but there it was. So, we used it later.

"I did enjoy it. The Colonel was fairly dominating, but Saltzberg was *overdominating.* We did feel a slight resentment toward the Hollywood

moguls, who clearly couldn't tell Whizzo margarine from a dead crab, no way. That was largely due to our experience with *The Magic Christian,* although in the years after the . . . *1948 Show,* John and I spent a couple of years writing for movies. We wrote for *The Magic Christian,* and quite a chunk of *The Rise and Rise of Michael Rimmer* in that period, as well, and filmed it just pre-Python."

Show 7—Oh, You're No Fun Anymore

Recorded as Series 1, Show 6—Prod. #54006

The "It's" Man (MP) runs down a mountain and through brush, and he is prompted off-camera to say "It's . . . It's . . . It's . . ."
Titles

An interviewer, Peter (JC), quizzes Mr. Subways (EI), an unsuccessful camel spotter who used to be a yeti spotter. In seven years, he's spotted nearly one camel. He is actually discovered to be a train spotter, so Peter tells him "You're no fun anymore." Animation follows which includes an old band and more.

"You're no fun anymore" blackouts follow, including ones with Dracula (GC) whose fangs fall out, a man being lashed to the yardarm (EI), and Mr. Subways.

In "The Audit," Wilkins (MP), a very new chartered accountant, gives a financial report to the Board of Directors of the Multi-Million Pound Corporation and its chairman (GC). A sign on the wall reads "There is No Place for Sentiment in Big Business." The company has grossed a shilling, but Wilkins has embezzled a penny. When one of the board members (TJ) says "You're no fun anymore," Mr. Subways ties him to the railroad tracks for using his phrase.

Viewers are invited to complain to Mr. Albert Spim at a given address (the voice-over and caption don't match), and one-liners follow.

The "Science Fiction" sketch is introduced by an unctuous, red-jacketed Host (MP) in a near-empty theater, and begins with shots of galaxies and a voice-over. Mr. and Mrs. Samuel Brainsample (GC and EI) of New Pudsey are overlooked because they are so boring, and instead Harold Potter (MP), a gardener and tax official, becomes the first Earthling to be turned into a Scotsman by a flying saucer. Other victims include a Detective Inspector (TJ), a man at a bus queue, a policeman, mother and baby, a black jazz saxophonist, and a company of Welsh Guards; all are transformed into plaid clothes with kilts.

A scientist named Charles (GC) searches for a cure when his girlfriend (DR)'s father, Mr. Llewellyn, becomes a Scotsman. England is deserted, while an animated map of Scotland shows the crowding, with three men to a caber.

A tailor, Angus Podgorny (MP), and his wife, Mary (TJ), receive an order for forty-eight million kilts from the planet Skyron in the Andromeda Galaxy. Mary is eaten by what is found to be a Blancmange* impersonator and cannibal named Jack Riley.

Charles discovers that since the worst tennis players in the world are Scotsmen, and several tennis players are eaten, the Blancmange means to win at Wimbledon. And Podgorny is the last human being left to challenge the Blancmange.

Angus is losing to the Blancmange at Wimbledon when Mr. and Mrs. Brainsample run onto the court and eat the Blancmange. Angus practices, and fifteen years later becomes the first Scotsman to win at Wimbledon, playing himself, as the credits roll.

ALSO APPEARING: Donna Reading

What's My Motivation?

Critics have often cited Terry Gilliam's Python acting debut for its subtle nuances and understatement, and for good reason. During his first appearances, Gilliam was forced to emote through a medieval knight's helmet, with no more than a rubber chicken to react with. Still, with a success-

---

*A kind of custardy pudding.

ful career in animation assured, why did Gilliam decide on the additional career?

In his own words: "I wouldn't even rate the knight with the chicken as performing." Gilliam chuckles. "I was just filling up holes that nobody else wanted to step into. I had done all of my work, and was sitting around all day when everyone else was up there doing things. It was very tedious, and so it was better to keep busy doing something. I would just wear costumes and do the things nobody else would touch. It was really more out of boredom."

indeed. Getting enough costumes was a common problem for the Pythons, and they often had to improvise. "I used to throw spare things onto this big van, and try to imagine what they might ask for, or what range of costume types I might need. I might need to outfit five Scotsmen in kilts, but if I found more, I'd throw on as many spares as I could, and anything that might relate to that kind of sketch.

"I can remember the whole crew dressing up as Scotsmen, and running onto the hillside. It was totally unethical and against union rules, but the crew was so happy on the show that they were quite happy to do it."

Lots of Scots

If not for the foresight of costumer Hazel Pethig, the Blancmange's prey would have been very few

---

Show 8—Full Frontal Nudity

Recorded as Series 1, Show 8—Prod. #54698

The "It's" Man (MP) sits in a lawn chair and is served a drink by a blonde in a bikini, who then hands him a bomb as he says "It's"
> Titles
> Episode
>> 12B
> Full Frontal
>> Nudity

Several "Vox Pops" on nudity and the permissive society introduce World War II footage from 1943, which leads into "Unoccupied Britain, 1970."

Private Watkins (EI) tells his Colonel (GC) that he wants to leave the Army because it's too dangerous. He was shocked to find out that they use real guns and bullets, and is afraid someone will be hurt. He says he only joined for the water skiing and travel. A Sergeant (JC) introduces Dino and Luigi Vercotti (TJ and MP), who try to sell him protection for his Army and intimidate him. They say it would be a shame if someone set fire to his paratroops, and make other insinuations. The Colonel finally stops them, saying

Palin and Cleese, in drag, are two members of Hell's Grannies, geriatric delinquents terrorizing the younger generation. Such film segments were actually shot in the streets of London, to the astonishment, curiosity, or disinterest of the British public who happened by. Photo copyright BBC and Python Productions.

The Hell's Grannies in action, terrorizing the townspeople. Photo copyright BBC and Python Productions.

the whole premise is silly and badly written, and orders the director to cut to the next scene.

An animated Dirty Old Man goes to the theater to see full frontal nudity, but at the crucial moments, people stand up in front of him, and cars and trains pass by in front of the women. More "Vox Pops" follow on full frontal nudity.

An Art Critic (MP) discusses the place of the nude, and film is shown of the Art Critic strangling his wife (KW) in a field.

Running through the same field are a bride and groom (TJ and CC), who run into a department store to buy a bed, and are waited on by Mr. Lambert (GC) and Mr. Verity (EI). Lambert divides every measurement by three, and Verity multiplies them all by ten. They are then warned not to say "mattress" to Mr. Lambert, and instead say "dog kennel." When they say "mattress," he puts a paper bag over his head, and they all have to sing "Jerusalem" to get him to remove it. When they

say "mattress" a second time, they have to get a large crowd to stand on a tea chest and sing, and there is stock film of a huge group singing. The bride says "mattress" a third time, but she begins crying and says it's her only line. The Colonel interrupts the show again, saying the show is getting too silly, and calls for a good, clean, healthy outdoor sketch.

Frank, a hermit (EI), talks with another hermit (MP) who lives in the cave just up the goat track. They discuss caves and moss, and the second hermit recommends birds' nests, moss, and oak leaves for insulation. The mountain where they are living is populated with several other hermits. Frank says he enjoys his lifestyle, and would never go back to public relations. The Colonel walks on and stops the sketch for being too silly, and chases the actors and camera crew off the mountain.

An animated broom sweeps the cast and crew figures into a meat grinder, where they emerge as

Cleese, with his pacamac fully buttoned, studies the ex-parrot. Photo copyright BBC and Python Productions.

the hair of *Venus Rising from the Sea,* who does a dance and falls into a fish tank at a pet shop.

In the pet shop, Mr. Praline (JC) tries to return a parrot which he claims is dead; the Shopkeeper (MP) disagrees. Say no more.

The Shopkeeper sends the man to his brother's pet shop in Bolton, which he thinks is Ipswich, but actually turns out to be Bolton. He complains to a Railway Clerk (TJ), but the Colonel stops the sketch.

A Newsreader (EI) introduces frontal nudity in a film featuring a Flasher (TJ), and then introduces a report on Hell's Grannies, a gang of old ladies who trip young girls, terrorize young people, and ride motorcycles through shops; their favorite targets are telephone kiosks. This is followed by vicious gangs of baby-snatchers and Keep Left signs, until the Colonel stops the show.

The "It's" Man's bomb explodes as the credits roll.

ALSO APPEARING: Katya Wyeth
                  Rita Davis
                  Carol Cleveland

"Buying a Bed," originally intended for an earlier show, was much longer in its previous version, and involved substitutions of several other words, such as "pesos" for "lettuce."

In the original rehearsal script, following "Hell's Grannies," the Colonel presents a sketch he's written called "Interesting People," which is used in Show 11.

Death of a Parrot

With the possible exception of the "Lumberjack Song," the "Dead Parrot" sketch is probably the single best-known Python bit. It has been performed in all of the stage shows, and included on numerous Python albums. Although it was chiefly written by Graham Chapman and John Cleese, Michael Palin says the origins of the expired Norwegian Blue actually go back further than that.

"I did a show with John Cleese, purely as an actor, called *How to Irritate People,*" Palin explains. "It was written by John and Graham in 1968. There were some very funny sketches in there.

In a slightly different costume for the Hollywood Bowl performance of "Dead Parrot" (actually, Palin and Cleese are hurrying through a dress rehearsal). Photo copyright KHJ.

9 6

"I had told John about my experiences with the local garage guy who had sold me my car. He was one of those people who could never accept that anything had gone wrong. I was telling John that the brakes seemed to be gone, but when I told the mechanic this, he said 'Oh, well, it's a new car, bound to happen.' He had an answer for everything. He would never, ever accept any blame for anything at all. I'd say 'Well, the door came off while I was doing 50 mph,' and he'd say 'Well, they do, don't they?'

"John liked this character very much, and worked him into *How to Irritate People*. I played a guy selling a car, almost literally line-for-line verbatim what the garage man said.

"So when John and Graham were looking around for stuff to write for the first season of Python, they plundered that show. They felt they couldn't do a garage man again, though. I think Graham had the idea for the parrot, which was marvelous. Bringing back a parrot which is dead, to complain about it, is just a marvelous idea," Palin says.

The costume worn by Cleese was the finishing touch, recalls Hazel Pethig. "I thought John could wear a pacamac, a folded plastic raincoat, and it worked very well. It was a really odd costume. He buttoned it right up to the neck, and that made him look really odd—a creepy English character."

"Very good with animals, they were, John and Graham, good animal writers," says Palin. "They had a feel for animals—fish, parrots, strange animals like that. They did *awful* things to them!"

Show 9 — The Ant — An Introduction

Recorded as Series 1, Show 10—Prod. #55307

The "It's" Man (MP) runs through the woods followed by explosions, as he announces "It's"

Titles

Part 2   The Llama Live From Golders Green

A pair of South Americans (EI and TJ) sing a song in Spanish about the llama, while another man (JC) describes colorful facts about the animal. English subtitles are shown, and a Señorita (GC) wheels in a motorbike to end the scene.

A man (JC) in a dinner jacket sits at a desk behind Ada's Snack Bar, and announces "And now for something completely different." A man with a tape recorder up his nose (MP) plays *La Marseillaise*.

Arthur Wilson (EI) applies for a job on a mountain-climbing expedition with Sir George Head (JC), who unfortunately sees double of every-

Led by Cleese, the Spanish quartet sings the praises of the llama. Photo copyright KHJ.

thing and assumes Arthur is twins. The expedition plans to search for traces of the previous year's expedition (led by Head's brother), which had hoped to build a bridge between the two peaks of Mount Kilimanjaro. The leader of the current expedition, Jimmy Blankenshoff (GC), tries to reassure the young mountaineer, but he climbs over the furniture in the room, knocking everything down and inspiring little confidence.

Twins at two desks (JC) introduce a man with a tape recorder up his brother's nose (MP and GC), which is played normally and again in stereo.

An animated Clergyman sells encyclopedias, and is then awarded a kewpie doll.

A Businessman (TJ) visits a shop where the Barber, Bevis (MP), is afraid to cut hair for fear of

Meanwhile, backstage a lovely senorita (Chapman) prepares to ride a motorcycle into the midst of the Spaniards. Photo copyright KHJ.

slaughtering his customers. He tries several subterfuges, including playing a tape of haircutting sounds. The Barber explains that he hates cutting hair, and actually always wanted to be a lumberjack. He then sings a song about lumberjacks, backed up by an increasingly disgusted chorus of Mounties (six Fred Tomlinson Singers, along with GC and JC) as the song takes a transvestigial turn. This is followed by letters of complaint.

Prof. R. J. Gumby (GC) sings while hitting himself on the head with a pair of bricks.

Compère Henry Lust (EI) gives an elaborate, sniveling introduction for "someone whose boots I would gladly lick until holes wore through my tongue," Harry Fink—who isn't there. Instead he introduces Ken Buddha and his Inflatable Knees (TJ), followed quickly by the animated Brian Islam and Lucy, a pair of eccentric dancers.

Meanwhile, the Barber tells his customer about outdoor life, which leads into a hunting expedition where the hunters shoot at everything in sight. In driving game from the brush, they also flush out lovers, and fight a duel, and find a parachutist and an Indian.

The Knight (TG) with the rubber chicken is told that he isn't needed this week, and walks away disappointed, passing the man at the desk (JC) in a chicken coop, who announces "And now for something completely different."

Victor and Iris (GC and CC) are timid lovers suddenly interrupted by the arrival of Arthur Name (EI), a strange man Victor met in a pub about three years ago. He changes their music, insults Iris, and tells an off-color joke. He has also invited the next visitors, Brian and Audrey Equatol (JC and TJ), who sit on the cat. More unwelcome visitors include a poof* (TG), a disgusting Old Man (MP) and his sick goat, and a group of miners who gather around the piano and start singing "Ding Dong." When Victor orders them all to leave, Brian shoots him.

The "It's" Man runs back into the woods and is blown up, as the credits roll.

ALSO APPEARING: Carol Cleveland
Connie Booth
The Fred Tomlinson Singers

 In the original BBC rehearsal script, the show leads off with the "Barber," a version in which the entire cassette is allowed to play out through the end of the haircut without the customer wising up. This is followed by letters and Ken Buddha, and an earlier, rather different version of the "Visitors" sketch, in which a couple arrives seven hours late for dinner, and the pajama-clad, sleepy host tries to act as though nothing is wrong, remaining polite as long as possible.

The Lumberjack Cometh

Without a doubt, the "Lumberjack Song" is the most popular Python song and, along with the "Dead Parrot," is probably the most famous Python sketch. It has been included in all of the stage shows, with either Eric Idle or Michael Palin singing the lead role, and the rest of the group as the Mountie Chorus. The group has been joined in past shows by such celebrity Mounties as George Harrison and Harry Nilsson. It was even performed in German as the "Holzfeller Song," with a chorus of Austrian border police. When Harrison toured America in late '74, the "Lumberjack Song"

*Slang for gay.

Sir George Head (Cleese) interviews a prospective member (Idle) of his mountaineering expedition. Afflicted with double vision, he hopes to find traces of last year's expedition, which tried to build a bridge between the twin peaks of Mt. Kilimanjaro. Photo copyright BBC and Python Productions.

The hunting party, which claims heavy casualties among its members (left to right: Chapman, Idle, Cleese, Jones, and Palin). Photo copyright BBC and Python Productions.

was the last music played over the PA system before Harrison and his group began performing.

Michael Palin says he doesn't remember much about writing many of his sketches, but he does recall the day when he and Terry Jones wrote the "Lumberjack Song."

"We'd just had this very long work day trying to finish off the 'Barber' sketch. We were quite pleased with it—it had a nice manic feel, but we were stuck for an ending, or a link, or anything to take us out of it. It was such a looney sketch in itself, so surreal and strange, and it's always more difficult to link something that elusive in itself, rather than something more straight.

"It was about a quarter to seven in the evening, and we'd worked on a lot longer than we normally would. We were just about to give up, and someone shouted 'Supper in half an hour!' We were just ad-libbing, and had the barber say 'Oh, to hell with it! I don't want to be a barber anyway, I wanted to be a lumberjack!' And this huge spiel just came! Terry said 'Quick, we'll write it down!' And not only did the spiel come, it just seemed natural to go into a silly song, because, lumberjacks sing songs.

"I think the whole 'Lumberjack Song' was written by a quarter past seven . . . and we even had the tune for it, which we thought we'd written. It's just an amalgam of various of those sort of jolly musicals-cum-stirring march-type songs. And that's really how it happened. It was just one of those nice little flashes of inspiration. We just roared with laughter when we wrote it, so we

knew we had something good there. How wrong we were . . ."

The original Mountie Chorus was made up of the Fred Tomlinson Singers, along with John Cleese and Graham Chapman.

"I wonder how we did get stuck there," Chapman mused. "I had no particular *wish* to be there, but I suppose it was quite jolly. And it was the end of the show, so I didn't really mind. I suppose John and I were tallish, and so the Mountie costumes fit."

Outrageous

"The Visitors" sketch is one of Carol Cleveland's favorites.

"I loved it, it was tremendously outrageous. I think it was one of the very first over-the-top, really outrageous sketches," says Cleveland. "I remember it was one of the first sketches where we all just went for it, and we didn't care what anybody thought. It was a chance for them to be really disgusting. I think my favorite character in it was Michael as this dirty old tramp who appears with his goat; and coming in and saying 'Well, the goat's got poohs,' and the goat actually pooping all over the place, and John sitting on the cat. A wonderful sketch, I enjoyed doing it immensely. Whenever they asked me to do anything outrageous, that's what I enjoyed the most. I wish they'd asked me to do more outrageous things!"

The "It's" Man (MP) is hanging among pig carcasses,

Show 10—Untitled

Recorded as Series 1, Show 9—Prod. #55176

and gasps "It's"

Titles

A Bandit (JC) and a Clerk (EI) wait impatiently on a store set, looking at their watches.

Frank, a Plumber (MP), sits in his kitchen reading a letter from the BBC, asking him to appear in a sketch. His wife (TJ) encourages him, and as he leaves to do the walk-on, she tunes in the sketch on her TV. Frank arrives at the BBC, and walks off

the store set just before the Bandit walks in, and the sketch begins.

The Bandit is confused because he thought he was in a bank. When it turns out to be a lingerie shop, he leaves with just a pair of knickers.

David Unction (GC) laughs and welcomes everyone to the show, and introduces the glittering world of show business with Arthur Tree. "It's a Tree" is a talk show hosted by Arthur Tree, a talking tree, with several tree guests, including Scott

Pine and the Conifers; the audience is a forest. Tree (who speaks like David Frost) welcomes his first guest, a block of wood. He also features an animated Chippendale writing desk which does impressions, including Long John Silver, Edwood Heath, and a play by Harold Splinter.

Several animated curtains open to reveal the "Vocational Guidance Counselor" sketch, with the title sung in harmony. The Vocational Guidance Counselor himself (JC) joins in, as the scene begins in his office. He is visited by Mr. Anchovy (MP), a chartered accountant who says his job is too dull, tedious, stuffy, and boring. He wants to be a lion tamer, but when the Counselor shows him a picture of a lion, he screams and faints. The Counselor calls for a piece of wood and the larch tree is shown briefly. Anchovy continues to snivel. The Counselor asks people to send money to the League for Fighting Chartered Accountancy, 55 Lincoln House, Basil Street, London SW3.

David Unction is caught reading *Physique,* a body-building magazine, which he tries to hide; he argues with a Viking (TJ) over how butch they were.

The sea begins the story of Neaps End, who hopes to be the first man to jump the English Channel. He is interviewed (by JC) and explains that he plans to jump into the center of Calais, even though his furthest previous jump is only eleven feet six inches. He is being sponsored by a British firm, and so is carrying fifty pounds of their bricks.

After failing that jump, his manager, Luigi Vercotti (MP), has him attempt other stunts, such as eating Chichester Cathedral, tunneling to Java, splitting a railway carriage with his nose, and running to Mercury. After he is killed, Vercotti says he is having Ron Obvious attempt to break the world's record for remaining underground.

A Customer (JC) wants to buy a cat at a pet shop somewhere near Melton Mowray. The Shopkeeper (MP) wants to make a terrier into a cat, but the man refuses. He then offers to do a parrot or fish job on the terrier.

A Vicar (TJ), another Man (GC) and a Lady conduct interviews in the town hall for a librarian. They question a gorilla for the job, but it turns out to be Mr. Phipps (EI), a man in a gorilla suit. The next applicant is a dog.

Several letters lead into "Strangers in the Night." Vera Jackson (TJ) and her Husband (MP) are in bed when a Frenchman, Maurice Zatapatique (EI), enters through the bedroom window looking for her. Roger Thompson (JC) then enters and confronts the two of them, while her husband sleeps on. Biggles (GC) and Algy enter also, to see Vera, as does a Mexican Rhythm Combo, which asks her husband for directions. He goes for a tinkle, and turns out to have a blonde stashed in the bathroom. Since he is gone, the rest of the characters in the bedroom see no point in continuing the sketch, and decide to end it.

Several animated animals devour each other, and the "It's" Man is carried away to the slaughter, as the credits roll.

ALSO APPEARING: Barry Cryer
                     Carolae Donoghue
                     Ian Davidson

🎬 The "Vocational Guidance Counselor" sketch had originally been planned for Show 3, the "Lingerie Shop" was intended for Show 1, and "Ron Obvious" was set for Show 5.

🎬 The "Accidents/Self-Destructing Room" sketch, in Show 18, was originally intended for this program, between "Ron Obvious" and the "Librarian" sketch.

Animals, Animals, Animals

"Mutant animals are very much the Cleese and Chapman area," says Michael Palin. "They like stretching animals out, fitting things to cats and converting them to fish. The animal humor section of Python is quite strong and extensive—converting parrots to emus, and all that."

John Cleese and Graham Chapman both admit to a strange fascination with animals. "I've always thought that animals were funny, and I can't quite put a finger on why," says Cleese. "But *all* comics think animals are funny. One can never believe that God bothered to make them all. The very fact that they sometimes seem to behave with emotions that are connected with human emotions make them doubly funny.

"There are dogs that can't make up their minds whether to fight or not, and scratch themselves

with a puzzled look on their faces before either running away or attacking the other dog. One sees that kind of behavior in people, in ways like tie-straightening. It's very funny to watch."

Strange animals pervade Python humor, some of them taken from real life. "A couple of items involving cats came in as a direct result of my trying to get a message over to John Cleese without saying so directly—that maybe the cats in his apartment were having parts taken away from them on rather too regular a basis," said Graham Chapman.

"They were almost becoming mechanical cats. Claws were going, and wombs. All right, we expect wombs, and perhaps [loss of] claws in a flat one can understand, but then the voice box? Taken one step further, what's next? So I suppose 'Convert-a-Pet' came out of that.

"I was particularly fond of penguins and little furry animals. John's favorite at one stage was ferrets. On the radio series *I'm Sorry, I'll Read That Again,* we even wrote a ferret song for that: *I've Got a Ferret Sticking Up My Nose.* It's a nice song. It was one of the closing numbers in . . . *the 1948 Show,* done on a grand scale, with cannons exploding, a fleet sailing by and all that, while John sang this rather weedy song about some man with a ferret up his nose."

Show 11—The Royal Philharmonic Orchestra Goes to the Bathroom

Recorded as Series 1, Show 11—Prod. #55375

The "It's" Man (MP) runs through traffic before gasping "It's"

Titles

Episode Two   The Royal Philharmonic Orchestra Goes to the Bathroom

A Man (MP) knocks on the door impatiently, as the Warsaw Concerto by Rachmaninov is heard inside. A series of angry letters of objection follow; there is film of the orchestra playing as they flush, and a sequence of toilet-oriented animation follows as people leave the concert hall.

Prof. R. J. Canning (GC) hosts "The World of History," discussing the Black Death, but he is interrupted once too often by film of undertakers, including one scene where two hearses drag race past other undertakers having tea.

Meanwhile Inspector Tiger (JC) enters an English drawing room to investigate an apparent murder, but has trouble announcing to Colonel Pickering (GC) and his Wife (CC) that no one is to leave the room. After Tiger is taken away by nurses and receives a lobotomy, he returns to the scene, where the lights go out suddenly. When they come back on, Tiger is found with an arrow through his neck, a bullet through his forehead, and a bottle of poison beside him. Lookout of the Yard (EI), accompanied by a Constable (MP), arrives to investigate the murder of Tiger, but is himself shot when the lights go out. The next investigation is conducted by Assistant Chief Constable There's a Man Behind You (TJ), followed by Constable Fire (ID).

More film of the undertakers carrying a coffin down a road shows them dumping the corpse and dancing away with the empty box.

Intellectual sports analyst Brian (EI) interviews the extremely stupid footballer Jimmy Buzzard (JC), who is only capable of three sentences. Another clip of undertakers follows, then a return to the murder scene (where the bodies are piling up), and more undertakers, as they become animated. The animation continues with two rather bitchy ladies, and escalates into warfare.

The host of "Interesting People" begins the show by interviewing Mr. Howard Stools, who is half an inch tall. This is followed by Ali Bayan of Egypt (TJ), who is stark raving mad; the Rachel Toovey Bicycle Bell Choir playing "Men of Harlech"; a man (JC) giving a cat influenza; Mr. Thomas Walters (EI), who becomes virtually invisible before our eyes; and a cricket match is held in a boxing ring. The show continues with Ken Dove (JC), who is interested in shouting, Don Savage (GC) and his cat, who is flung through the air into a bucket of water, and Keith Maniac of Guatemala (TJ), who puts bricks to sleep by hypnosis.

Back at the interview (after we see four tired undertakers), Jimmy Buzzard falls off his chair. The coffin then drives itself to the cemetery, as miners, surfers, and Orientals climb from the hole; there is animation of the coffins below ground.

This leads into a series of nude women, who introduce "The World of History," discussing eighteenth-century social legislation. A.J.P. Taylor (cc, with voice dubbed by jc) rolls around in bed wearing a negligee as she lectures, interrupted by a "bit of fun" (a quick striptease). Next is Professor Gert Van der Whoops (mp), of the Rejksmuseum in the Hague, trying to lecture in bed while being caressed by a blonde. A man wearing wings (tj) is lowered to the ground to introduce R. J. Canning again, who discusses the Battle of Trafalgar. He introduces Professor R. J. Gumby (mp) and his friend (tj), who claim the battle was fought on dry land near Cudworth in Yorkshire.

Short links follow with the Gumbys, then "The World of History" shifts to Mrs. Rita Fairbanks (ei) and her Townswomen's Guild, who reenact the Battle of Pearl Harbor in a muddy field. Canning is interrupted again by film of the undertakers, and a funeral in which the Vicar (jc) shoots into the grave after dirt is thrown back at his face. The undertakers all drive off in a brightly painted hearse. Canning begins a letter to Lord Hill, as the "It's" Man runs back across the street.

ALSO APPEARING: Carol Cleveland
Ian Davidson
Flanagan

"Interesting People" was originally written for Show 8, presented as a sketch written by the Colonel. Cut from the scene is a bit with Herbert Arkwright, who eats herds of buffalo.

Another sketch (originally following the "Agatha Christie" sketch) was apparently never used. It featured a punch-drunk interviewer talking with new British light-heavyweight prospect Henry Pratt, who combines a lack of ability with extreme physical cowardice.

Fun on Location

"The attack on Pearl Harbor was the most painful thing we ever shot. Very unpleasant!" recalls Michael Palin. "It was a cold day, and we were filming up in North Yorkshire. It was really awful—we were just covered with filth, and there was nowhere to wash off, except for a little outhouse at a farm with cold water. It was very bizarre. We had all these people, soaked and covered with mud, peeling their stockings off and removing these mud-stained bras . . ."

Show 12 — The Naked Ant

Recorded as Series 1, Show 12—Prod. #55628

The "It's" Man (mp) runs through a forest, bouncing off trees like a pinball, gasping "It's"
Titles
Episodes 17–26   The Naked Ant
A Signal Box Somewhere Near Hove. A Train Engineer (tj) struggles with a polar bear (wrestling it for 3.48 seconds, according to the script).

But in an office off the Goswell Road:

Two executives (ei and jc) sit near a window working, as several men fall past their window. They argue about their identities and place bets on who will be next, realizing there is a board meeting in progress.

A letter of complaint is begun, but the author falls while writing. In the office, more people fall, then animated people fall sideways and bounce off the stomach of a woman. An animated magician conjures flowers, and eventually a globe, which begins:

"Spectrum," in which the Presenter (mp) talks about what it all means, why, and what the solution is. Alexander Hardacre (gc), of the Economic

Affairs Bureau, speaks intensely and with great authority as he shows charts and graphs, while Professor Tiddles of Leeds University (JC) and a pro cricketer (EI) are interviewed, and the Presenter begins talking increasingly rapidly.

There is more train film, and the Engineer is still fighting the polar bear.

At a small boarding house in Minehead, Somerset, a holidaying couple, Mr. (EI) and Mrs. Johnson visit a landlady (TJ), describing their journey and saying they are ready for tea. They are then introduced to Mr. and Mrs. Phillips (TG and CB), and Mr. Hilter (JC), Mr. Bimmler (MP), and Ron Viventroff (GC). Hilter gets a phone call from Mr. McGoering. He is a Bocialist candidate in the Minehead election. Film of their campaign rallies in Britain shows them riding through the streets, and Hilter gives a speech from a balcony to a Farmer (TJ) and some children, while the sounds of a crowd are played on a phonograph. Mr. Gumby and a conservative businessman give their views on Hilter.

"Spectrum" sums up.

A Man (TJ) tries to report a burglary to a Police Sergeant (JC), who asks him to speak in a high, squeaky voice. Another Sergeant, Charlie (GC) replaces the first one and has him talk in a lower voice, followed by a Detective Sergeant (EI), and the policemen try to talk to each other.

"Vox Pops" follow, with an Upper-Class Twit saying "Some people talk in the most extraordinary way" leading to:

The 127th "Upper-Class Twit of the Year Contest" at Hurlingham Park, which includes such events as Walking a Straight Line, Jumping Three

The group lines up in a display of upper-class fashion sensibilities. They enjoyed deflating such upper-class twits, though never with such pinpoint accuracy as in "The Twit of the Year" contest. Photo copyright BBC and Python Productions.

Rows of Matchboxes, Kicking the Beggar, Insulting the Waiter, Taking the Bras off the Debutantes, Waking the Neighbors, and eventually Shooting Themselves. Their coffins are decorated with ribbons, and a letter is read that tells how wonderful it is to be able to get rid of these people this way.

Animation sees a soldier fall apart, and then become stuffed in a pipe by Terry Jones. A balloon, a flea, and a humpback whale then escape from the bowl of the pipe.

Ken Shabby (MP), a filthy, disgusting man who cleans out public lavatories, asks a Father (GC) for permission to marry his lovely daughter (CB). The story so far is summed up, with a voice-over and peculiar pictures.

A corner of a bedsitter watches a party political broadcast by the Wood Party. In the middle of his speech, the Minister, the Rt. Hon. Lambert Warbeck (GC), falls, apparently through the earth's crust, according to a studio technician (EI). Another man, Tex (TG), throws him a rope; the Minister tries to continue his speech while dangling from the rope. He slips, but the picture is turned upside-down. Three Linkmen (TJ, EI and JC), all named Robert, discuss various aspects of the incident. One talks about the structure and heat of the layers of the earth, another analyzes distances fallen by politicians, while the third becomes so excited that he is set on fire.

Everyone on the show agrees that they don't have anything more to add, and a sixteen-ton weight is dropped on the Host of "Spectrum."

The "It's" Man runs back through the woods, as the credits roll.

ALSO APPEARING: Connie Booth
Flanagan

The BBC rehearsal script reads "MONTY PYTHON'S FLYING CIRCUS STARRING ERIC IDLE with Graham Chapman, John Cleese, Terry Jones, Michael Palin and Terry Gilliam."

The original script for this show did not include the Upper-Class Twit contest, which was an insert written in by hand; Ken Shabby was also not in the original script.

The script for the Rt. Hon. Lambert Warbeck's speech reads as follows:

Good evening. We in the Wood Party feel very strongly about the weak drafting in the present Local Government Bill. And we intend to fight— (He thumps on his desk and he falls through the floor. Yes, Mr. Director, you did read that right. He fell through the floor and added a fortune to the budget.)

Comedy with a Vengeance

The "Upper-Class Twit of the Year Contest" was another sketch that was suggested by environment, according to Graham Chapman.

"John Cleese had an apartment on a street just behind Harrod's, not far from Sloane Square," he said. "There were a lot of Sloane Rangers* wandering around at night in the wine bars. As I remember, there was a wine bar just over the road from John's called "The Loose Box," where there were a lot of these chinless wonders with names like Nigel. They would indeed make braying noises, and generally behave like the twits in the sketch. They would, in fact, keep John awake quite late at night by banging car doors and so on. So that was our revenge on them!"

*British yuppies.

Four undertakers carry a coffin; the "It's" Man (MP) emerges to say "It's"

A slide announcing a short intermission

Titles

Another slide announcing a medium-sized intermission

Animation in which a man in a bird's nest is fed the word "intermission"

Douglas (JC) and his wife Shirley (EI), who never stops talking, are seated in a restaurant by Hopkins, the maître d' (TJ), who then leaves to commit suicide. Thompson (MP), the Head Waiter, tells them that it's a vegetarian restaurant, of which they are not only proud but smug. They speak to the Headmaster (GC), and the now-nude Hopkins is wheeled by on a cart. He says he's the day's special, Hopkins au gratin à la chef, and advises them against eating the Vicar (EI), who has been there for two weeks.

Another intermission slide promises a whopping great intermission.

Pearls for Swine Presents: an ad for Soho Motors (on the second floor), and an ad for the La Gondola Restaurant, managed by Luigi Vercotti (MP), featuring a variety of Sicilian delicacies.

A salesgirl (JC) in the theater tries to sell an albatross to a customer (TJ).

A very short intermission follows, as does an announcement that there will be no feature film presented that evening, as it cuts into the profits.

The customer with the albatross introduces a Man (MP) reporting a stolen wallet to a Policeman (JC), with the Man eventually propositioning the Policeman. This is followed by the stock film of the Women's Institute applause.

Mr. Burtenshaw (TJ) visits a doctor (EI) and nurses (CC and JC), and go through the "Me, doctor, she, nurse, he, Mr. Burtenshaw" confusion, again followed by stock film of Women's Institute applause.

Mr. Gumby asks to see John the Baptist's impersonation of Graham Hill, which leads into "Historical Impersonations," featuring host Wally Wiggins (MP). Cardinal Richelieu (MP) does his impression of Petula Clark, Julius Caesar (EI) imper-

sonates Eddie Waring, followed by Florence Nightingale (GC) as Brian London, Ivan the Terrible (JC) as a shoe salesman, and W. G. Grace (animated) as a music box. Mr. Gumby makes his request again, with more Women's Institute applause. Napoleon (TJ) impersonates the R-101 disaster, and Marcel Marceau (GC) mimes a man walking into the wind, as well as a man being struck by a sixteen-ton weight.

A Man (JC) interviews two small Children (EI and MP) who would like to have Raquel Welch dropped on top of them. He then interviews two businessmen in the same condescending manner, including Trevor Atkinson (GC) of the Empire General Insurance Company and his Friend (MP). Trevor requests more police fairy stories.

Another Policeman (TJ) pumps up an inflatable robber (EI), and a group of policemen give chase. An Officer in a tutu (MP) uses a magic wand on them.

"Probearound" looks at the Special Crimes Squad, with a Host (EI) who has just shot the First Host (JC). Inspector Harry "Snapper" Organs of H Division (MP) uses a voodoo doll, several policemen use an Ouija board, and other policemen use wands on illegally parked cars.

Attila the Hun (MP), the son of Mr. and Mrs. Norman Hun, wearing horn-rimmed glasses and a suit, turns himself in to police (TJ and JC) for looting, pillaging, and sacking a major city. The Sergeant (JC) brings in a breathalizer, which shows he is actually Alexander the Great. Objecting letters are read, and there is animation featuring a police car.

Dr. Larch (JC), who wants it made clear that he is a psychiatrist, has his first patient (TJ, dressed as Napoleon) leave before he can give his first line. The next patient, Mr. Notlob (MP), hears guitars and people singing "We're All Going to the Zoo," and visits a Doctor Friend of Larch (GC) who operates on him. A Hippie (EI) and a Nude Woman (CC) are found living inside him as squatters. The Police (JC and MP) get a court order to go inside and drag them out.

Animation highlights the end of the series, and

the "It's" Man runs from the undertakers as the credits roll.

ALSO APPEARING: David Ballantyne
Carol Cleveland

A final intermission slide appears, noting that when the series returns, it will be put out on Monday mornings as a test card, and will be described by *The Radio Times* as a *History of Irish Agriculture.*

📽 Several sketches here were not in the BBC rehearsal script for the show, including "Police/Come Back to my Place," "Historical Impersonations," "Children's/Stockbroker's Interviews," and "Magic Police."

📽 A one-page bit was cut from the "A.t. Hun" sketch, with the Police Constable solving crimes sent in by viewers.

History Comes Alive

Of all the historical characters in Python, John Cleese has his own favorite. "I love the impersonation I do of Ivan the Terrible as a shoe salesman. I've got that funny bent board that they use to put the foot on. So, when the guy sets his foot on it, I draw this *enormous* sword and *completely* bisect him! I loved that one . . ."

Police Friends

Of all the politicians and public figures that the Pythons took aim at, very few of their targets ap-

parently responded to the group. Reginald Maudling, a frequent target, died not long after the Pythons featured him, though most of the other politicians are still around. Michael Palin is proud to point out that they were sending up Margaret Thatcher years before she became Prime Minister, but admits that Thatcher doesn't speak to them much.

"On the whole, our targets haven't mixed with us that much—except for the police," Palin says. "We always used to get on about police corruption, and how thick the police were. Various police used to come and see the show, and they absolutely loved it.

"We could do the most obvious attacks on the police, suggesting bribery and corruption and all sorts of venality, and they thought it was absolutely wonderful! It just shows that satire doesn't really change people at all. They never believe they're the target, they always think it's somebody else. For some reason, John Cleese is very friendly with the police—we're not sure why. He used to invite them along," Palin laughs.

Cleese admits to the police charges leveled by Palin. "I've always been fascinated by the police. I think they do an extremely difficult job. Because I'm an introvert and a coward, I'm fascinated to know people who are extroverts and brave.

"I've always been intrigued by those guys. But of course, the Pythons, being basically left-wing, have the usual paranoid attitude that all policemen are bad persons, and that one should not associate with them for fear of becoming morally contaminated," Cleese smiles. "This is an argument which I do not accept, as can be seen from the curdling of my lip."

Test Your
Python Quotient

1. *How did Mrs. G. Pinnet have to sign for her new gas cooker?*
2. *Why does the Minister of Silly Walks arrive at his office late?*
3. *What is the annual budget for the Ministry of Silly Walks?*
4. *What was the Piranha Brothers' prison sentence?*
5. *What was the occupation of Arthur Piranha, Doug and Dinsdale's father?*
6. *What happened the week Dinsdale did not nail Vince Snetterton Lewis's head to the floor?*
7. *For which surveillance role was Harry "Snapper" Organs of "Q" Division panned by critics?*
8. *What was the name of the giant hedgehog that followed the Piranha Brothers?*
9. *How large was the hedgehog?*
10. *What is pneumoconiosis?*
11. *In the Disgusting Objects International at Wembley, how did England defeat Spain?*
12. *What did the Chairman of the Board of Irresponsible People feed to his goldfish?*
13. *True or false: Goldfish are quite happy eating breadcrumbs, ants, eggs, and the occasional pheasant.*
14. *"Still no sign of land. How long is it?"*
15. *What three ways does the undertaker initially recommend to deal with stiffs?*
16. *What is the name of the man who has a "fifty-percent bonus in the region of what you said"?*
17. *What is the song attempted by Arthur Ewing and His Musical Mice?*
18. *What would members of the stock exchange do about the "Mouse Problem"?*
19. *What is the name of that most dangerous of animals, the clever sheep?*
20. *What are the only four phrases spoken by Jimmy Buzzard?*
21. *Why is Mr. Howard Stools particularly interesting?*
22. *What is the name of the flying cat that lands in a bucket of water (when she is flung)?*
23. *Don't you ever take the bones out?*
24. *What play did Leatherhead Rep do with the Redfoot Indian tribe?*

25. *Which two stars did Irving C. Saltzberg plan to star in his next film?*
26. *Why does the llama have a beak?*
27. *What does R. J. Gumby croon while hitting himself in the head with bricks?*
28. *What does the barber drink before cutting Terry Jones's hair?*
29. *Which Python is featured in the Stop the Film segment on "Blackmail"?*
30. *How many things did the Australasian branch of the Society for Putting Things on Top of Other Things put on top of things last year?*
31. *Name two methods for waking Ken Clean-Air System.*
32. *Which of his films does director Ellis Dibley call a "real failure"?*
33. *How many votes did Kevin Phillips Bong (the Slightly Silly candidate at Luton) receive?*
34. *"Do like all smart motorists—choose _____."*
35. *What is Archbishop Shabby doing for peace?*
36. *What is the first lesson in not being seen? The second?*
37. *Coventry City last won the F.A. Cup in what year?*
38. *The other works of art voted unanimously to support the strike by the paintings in the National Gallery. Which work abstained from voting?*
39. *What tool does Mr. Gumby use in flower arranging?*
40. *The "Black Eagle" was based on what novel?*
41. *What was the official slogan of the British Army?*
42. *What does the smuggler claim his watches are?*
43. *What is in the brown paper bag planted by Police Constable Henry Thatcher?*
44. *What is the secret of Charles Fatless?*
45. *What are the five chief weapons of the Spanish Inquisition?*
46. *What does the Gumby Brain Specialist want done to his patient?*
47. *What joke did Hitler come up with to challenge the Allied Killer Joke?*
48. *Who is high scorer in "Mozart's Famous Deaths"?*
49. *What is Whizzo Butter compared to in a TV commercial?*
50. *Who serves as a character witness for Harold Larch? How does Inspector Dim trip him up?*
51. *What would Dim like to be (if he were not in the CID)? And Bartlett?*
52. *Where are the numbers on a camel?*
53. *Why would men turn into Scotsmen?*
54. *In separate shows, which members of the group played Dracula and Frankenstein's monster?*
55. *Why was the Norwegian Blue sitting on its perch in the first place?*
56. *What does the bandit steal from the lingerie shop?*
57. *What program follows "It's a Tree" at 9:30?*
58. *What is the ideal job for Mr. Anchovy?*
59. *What are Mr. Anchovy's qualifications for lion taming?*
60. *What does Cardinal Richelieu perform on "Historical Impersonations"?*
61. *What message do the police get on their Ouija board?*
62. *What does the courteous hijacker call out as he is pushed from the jet?*
63. *What kind of car insurance policy does the Vicar have?*
64. *What is the main food that penguins eat?*
65. *Who sings a Jimmy Durante song?*
66. *What is the name of Rev. Arthur Belling's church?*
67. *How did Roy Spim lose his left arm?*
68. *What did Kemal Atatürk name his entire menagerie?*
69. *What was the first scene shot in "Scott of the Antarctic"?*
70. *What did the crew of "Scott of the Antarctic" use for snow?*
71. *What is Michael Norman Randall's sentence for the murder of twenty people?*
72. *How do you put budgies down, according to the book?*

73. *What do Mrs. Premise and Mrs. Conclusion sing while phoning Jean Paul Sartre?*
74. *Who is featured on "Farming Club"?*
75. *What was Brian Norris's first book?*
76. *What was the result of treating athlete's foot with explosives?*
77. *What is the jugged fish?*
78. *The Church Police conclude their arrest with what hymn?*
79. *What is Anne Elk's theory of the brontosaurus?*
80. *What does the Fire Brigade request to drink (in unison)?*
81. *What was Biggles writing thank-you notes to royalty for?*
82. *What do the men from the lifeboat order with their tea?*
83. *What is the name of the man who owns the Cheese Shop?*
84. *Why did Reg Pither crash his bicycle?*
85. *What does Eartha Kitt sing to the Central Committee?*
86. *The poster for the Moscow Praesidium advertises Eartha Kitt, Burgess and Maclean, Marshall Bulganin and "Charlie," and who else?*
87. *Where is the bomb (for a pound)?*
88. *Which two countries are in the finale of the Olympic Hide and Seek?*
89. *Where does Don Roberts hide?*
90. *Who is the author of "Gay Boys in Bondage"?*
91. *What is Dennis Moore's horse's name?*
92. *Which two shows feature animation that parodies 2001?*

Answers

1. *Since the invoice was made out to Mrs. G. Crump, she was requested to sign it "Mrs. Crump-Pinnet."*
2. *"My walk has become rather sillier recently."*
3. *Three hundred and forty-eight million pounds a year.*
4. *Four hundred years' imprisonment for crimes of violence.*
5. *He was a scrap metal dealer and TV quizmaster (he married Kitty Malone, an up-and-coming East End boxer).*
6. *Dinsdale screwed his pelvis to a cake stand instead.*
7. *Sancho Panza in* Man of La Mancha.
8. *Spiny Norman plagued Dinsdale.*
9. *He ranged anywhere from twelve feet to eight hundred yards.*
10. *A disease miners get.*
11. *A plate of braised pus bested a putrid herring.*
12. *Cold consummé, sausages, greens, potatoes, bread, gravy, etc.*
13. *True (according to the Board of Irresponsible People).*
14. *Thirty-three days (a rather personal question).*
15. *Burning, burying, or dumping (in the Thames).*
16. *Arthur ("Is that chair comfortable?") Frampton.*
17. *The twenty-three white mice played "The Bells of St. Mary's."*
18. *Suck their brains out with a straw, sell the widows and orphans, and go into South American zinc.*
19. *Harold.*
20. *(1) Good evening, Brian; (2) I'm opening a boutique; (3) I hit the ball first time, and there it was in the back of the net; (4) I've fallen off my chair, Brian.*
21. *He is only half an inch tall.*
22. *Tibbles.*
23. *If we took the bones out, it [the frog] wouldn't be crunchy.*

24. Dial "M" for Murder.
25. *Doris Day and Rock Hudson.*
26. *For eating honey.*
27. *"It's Only Make Believe."*
28. *Red Eye.*
29. *Terry Jones.*
30. *Twenty-two.*
31. *Drive a steel peg into his skull with a mallet, or (when in a deep sleep), saw his head off.*
32. Finian's Rainbow *("Ten seconds of solid boredom").*
33. *None.*
34. Crelm Toothpaste.
35. *Raising polecats.*
36. *(1) Not to stand up; (2) Not to choose a very obvious piece of cover.*
37. *This is a trick question. Coventry City have never won the F.A. Cup.*
38. Venus de Milo *(she didn't raise her hands).*
39. *A large wooden mallet.*
40. The Blue Eagle.
41. *"It's a Man's (Dog's) (Pig's) Life in the Modern Army."*
42. *Vests.*
43. *Sandwiches.*
44. *Dynamo Tension!*
45. *Fear, surprise, ruthless efficiency, an almost fanatical devotion to the Pope, and nice red uniforms.*
46. *He wants bits of Mr. Gumby's brain taken out.*
47. *"My dog's got no nose." "How does he smell?" "Awful!"*
48. *St. Stephen.*
49. *A dead crab.*
50. *Cardinal Richelieu; he reveals that the Cardinal died in 1642, and that he is actually Ron Higgins, an impersonator.*
51. *A window cleaner; an engine driver.*
52. *On the side of the engine, above the piston box.*
53. *Only because they have no control over their own destinies.*
54. *Graham Chapman played Dracula in "Oh, You're No Fun Anymore," and John Cleese played Frankenstein's monster in "The Dull Life of a City Stockbroker."*
55. *It had been nailed there.*
56. *A pair of knickers.*
57. *"Yes, It's the Sewage Farm Attendant," in which Dan falls into a vat of human dung, with hilarious consequences.*
58. *Chartered accountancy.*
59. *He has a lion-taming hat.*
60. *Petula Clark's "Don't Sleep in the Subway."*
61. *Up yours.*
62. *Thank you . . .*
63. *A "never-pay" policy.*
64. *Reginald Maudling is close enough; pork lunch and meat, Spam, themselves, horses, armchairs, pepperoni, lasagna, lobster thermidor, Brian Close, Henri Bergson, and a buffalo with an aqualung are all wrong.*
65. *Beethoven's mynah bird sings "I'm the Guy Who Found the Lost Chord."*
66. *St. Looney Up the Cream Bun and Jam.*
67. *In a battle with an ant.*
68. *Abdul.*
69. *Scene 1.*

70. *Twenty-eight thousand feet of Wintrex, a new, white foam rubber, plus sixteen thousand cubic U.S. furlongs of white paint with a special snow finish.*

71. *Six months, suspended.*

72. *Either hit them with the book, or shoot them just above the beak (although Mrs. Essence flushed hers down the loo).*

73. *"The Girl From Ipanema."*

74. *Tchaikovsky.*

75. A Short History of Motor Traffic Between Esher and Purley.

76. *Eighty-four dead, sixty-five severely wounded, twelve missing and believed cured.*

77. *Halibut.*

78. *"Jerusalem."*

79. *All brontosauruses are thin at one end, much, much thicker in the middle, and then thin again at the far end.*

80. *A drop of sherry.*

81. *Eels.*

82. *Two dozen fruitcakes and ten macaroons.*

83. *Henry Wensleydale.*

84. *His pump got caught in his trouser leg (badly crushing his sandwiches).*

85. *"Old-Fashioned Girl."*

86. *Peter Cook and Dudley Moore (Leningrad has never laughed so much).*

87. *The luggage compartment.*

88. *Paraguay and Britain.*

89. *A castle in Sardinia.*

90. *Shakespeare.*

91. *Concorde.*

92. *"A Book at Bedtime" (in which a bone becomes a space station, and falls on a caveman), and "Spam" (the titles to World Forum/Communist Quiz).*

A Look from the Inside

Of all the production and crew members that worked on *Monty Python's Flying Circus,* few served longer than Hazel Pethig, who was in charge of designing and procuring the costumes worn on the shows. In addition to working on the first thirty-nine shows—three seasons' worth—she also served on *Holy Grail* and *Life of Brian,* as well as such individual Python projects as *Jabberwocky.* As an insider, Pethig had a unique opportunity to work with and observe Python from its beginnings, and agreed to share her thoughts twenty years after the first show.

"I was initially told it was called *Owl-Stretching Time,"* she recalls, "So I thought that was a hint as to its approach. I hadn't done a lot of work before, which was quite good, as I had to be extremely flexible. I can remember Eric asking me at 7:00 a.m., when we were about to set off filming, if he could dress up as a fairy in a tutu. I managed to do it, but I think a lot of people that were established wouldn't have enjoyed that. Not being a traditional costume lady, I was much more suitable for that kind of work—I enjoyed making something out of nothing."

Rounding all of them up for costume fittings proved to be more difficult than she had expected. "I could hardly ever get them for fittings because the shows happened very fast, and they weren't keen on fittings. I managed to get them all in one day for fittings in the stockroom, and they went riot! They were running around like schoolboys, playing around," she says.

The most uncooperative of an uncooperative group was John Cleese, but Pethig says she learned how to handle him. "Sqeezing John into costume was difficult for me. He didn't like wearing costumes, and he didn't like wearing beards and moustaches. He used to puff himself up like a bullfrog so his costumes wouldn't fit. He'd say 'Look, I can't wear it, it doesn't fit.' I had to pummel him until he fit into the costume."

Perhaps the most interesting aspect of her job was observing the interaction of the Pythons in their own environment, a vantage point available to few others.

"As a group, they're quite riotous. Individually, they were different people. John, in particular—he was the rebel of the group. Terry Jones and Mike were like old school buddies, Eric used to bury himself in a book, and Graham was just absolutely zany and adorable. The others were mainly verbal, [but] Terry Gilliam was the opposite. I felt a rapport with Terry, because he used to work alone, late at night, and had to be physically creative, which is what I had to do.

"They used to get into some nice little scraps. I used to enjoy it—they used to criticize one another without upsetting each other, so it was exciting to watch, to

The group never hesitated to take on historical roles, as Eric Idle demonstrates here. Photo copyright BBC and Python Productions.

see a group that could all be honest to one another. I've always found it inspirational to see people having a go at one another, and still seem to care for each other. There were times when I thought they would fall apart, the group wouldn't survive it, but they have all stayed very close, especially Mike and Terry Jones.

"It's taken a long time, in a way, for those two to go and do their own thing, especially Terry. Mike is a very popular guy, he's the most amiable and least cutting of the group, and that's very hard for Terry Jones. When Terry went to do his Chaucer book and Mike had *Ripping Yarns,* that was a very tricky time—the gradual separation of Terry and Michael was taking place. It was tricky because they were very close. And the same was true for Graham and John, because they used to be very close.

"They were all supportive of one another, but at the same time—being intelligent university people—they were taught that one had to be critical, to improve everybody," Pethig says.

"John was dominant and always easily recognizable on the street. He didn't wear costumes and wigs so much, so he was *always* recognizable. Terry J and Mike were always scurrying around, doing all of the dirty work, in a way. Eric was always more caustic, and Terry G worked a lot in isolation. It wasn't just the costumes that were interesting, it was the people."

In the early days, Pethig says she also had to contend with tiny budgets, and make the best of what she had. She often found herself scrounging things at the last minute, or taking extra costumes to be on the safe side. She became an expert on seeking out old clothing shops, and notes that few of them are still around today. "I was always trying to persuade people to let me have things at the last minute," she recalls. One incident in particular involved the "New Cooker" sketch, in which a long, long line of gas men wait in a street outside a house. "I had to find lots and lots of raincoats and spectacles for the queue of gas men. I managed to get hold of all these joke glasses, but I couldn't have gotten them nowadays."

She also worked with the special effects (SFX) people to achieve more elaborate costumes, rising to the challenges the group often presented. "I remember one odd little costume, in which Terry Jones had to be half a Frenchman and half an English businessman," for the Anglo-French Silly Walk. "On one side of the camera is an Englishman in a bowler hat; when he turns around, he's a Frenchman with a stupid shirt. That all had to work quite well—it was tricky! There would be all sorts of costumes that had to fall apart, like the

nude organist who lost all his clothes, which meant working with the SFX guy. I once had to make a carrot costume for Graham that he wore to some university debates—the problem was mainly with the shoulders and the makeup."

The TV series gradually became more and more successful, but Pethig says their success didn't affect them adversely. "The changes came much later—they were pretty consistent throughout. Now that I've worked with other groups, I think Python got along terribly well. John got disenchanted and separated from the rest, and Eric became a little more isolated, and they sometimes found Terry Jones and Michael Palin a little overenthusiastic, but I didn't really see them change.

Cleese's aversion to costumes is seen in this **Life of Brian** *rehearsal shot; he preferred to work in his tunic as much as possible before donning armor for the actual takes. Photo copyright KHJ.*

"When they went to Canada to do the stage show, they could have changed and they didn't. I saw a little wave of it in North America, because they were engulfed with publicity, and parties, and women waiting outside the stage doors—their heads could have been turned, but they weren't. They survived that as well."

As time went on, Cleese in particular became tired of Python. When members of the public would shout at him to "Do the Silly Walk, John!", he found it increasingly irritating. "John *hates* being linked up with that, and sometimes with Python. He's never realized how brilliant 'Silly Walks' is. But there was never any strong resentment, or they wouldn't have kept together," says Pethig.

The tendency, particularly in Britain, to consider Cleese the "star" of Monty Python is inaccurate and unfair, says Pethig. "Sometimes I thought it was unfair the way the populace set John off so much. They all contributed a lot to Python. When I went to the script meetings, they *all* put as much into the script. John *wasn't* Monty Python—Monty Python was the *team*. John was a strong voice, extremely intelligent, but the others put in just as much.

"We see rock groups that never manage to keep together. I remember making friends with some people in Dire Straits, and comparing them to Python—they had similar problems. They can go through a rough patch where they say it's the end, they get through it, and adjust accordingly for the future.

"I can understand the group members not wanting to get stuck with [the Python] identity as well. They have to progress. The public would love for them to do more Monty Python shows, but they've passed that stage—they don't need to do that anymore."

As strong as her admiration is for the Pythons and their work, the group feels the same about her, both personally and professionally.

"John used to say that they could phone me from fifteen hundred miles away, on a crackling line, and tell me what they wanted, and I'd come back with what they were trying to describe. I suppose that did happen."

Pethig was always a great admirer of the Python humor as well, and its legacy. "Python was always breaking down barriers that now people are benefiting from—not just in show business, either. They stood up for their ideas, and their vaguely anarchic, but still responsible attitudes.

"And it was great fun!"

The Second Series

Aired Sept. 15 – 29, 1970, and Oct. 20 – Dec. 22, 1970

THERE WAS LITTLE doubt that *Monty Python's Flying Circus* would return for a second season. The show received a groundswell of support that built slowly but surely, so that the group was certain they would be renewed.

"By the time we'd gotten two-thirds of the way through the first series, there was a definite swell of opinion in our favor coming from all the newspapers, although for the first six shows, nobody could make head or tail of it," says John Cleese.

"All the critics did what they do when they're cowardly and don't know which way to jump, which is to describe in detail what was in the shows, without saying whether they were good, bad, or indifferent. Ever so slowly, about Show 6, there was very clearly opinion that began to form in favor of the show, which gathered strength a great deal."

The second series experienced both the advantages and disadvantages of familiarity. Most of the usable material the group had saved up going into the first series had been dealt with, and so there was not as comfortable a cushion of backlogged sketches to fall back on. But in other ways they were hitting their stride, realizing the freedom of the format they had developed and attempting to take full advantage of it.

There were few changes in the look of the show itself. In fact, they only way to distinguish shows in the second series is by the lead-in to the opening titles. While the first series used a (sometimes lengthy) sequence with the "It's" Man, his part was considerably shortened in the buildups to the titles in the second series. After his initial "It's," he would be followed by John Cleese, in a dinner jacket and usually at a desk, in some peculiar location saying "And now for something completely different," which by now had become the group's catchphrase.

As usual, Cleese's man in the dinner jacket sits at a desk located in the most incongruous locations available. Photo copyright BBC and Python Productions.

"I think we realized it maybe five or six shows in," Michael Palin recalls. "There was very little press coverage about Python to start with—it wasn't reviewed by the normal television critics. The *Washington Post* had one of the earliest articles about Python, by a journalist called Fred Friendly, who said 'This is an absolutely wonderful, amazing show, and it should come to America.' And everyone said no, of course it won't. He was really ahead of the day—that was 1969!

"But a lot of the newspaper articles would have the headline 'And Now For Something Completely Different,' which I think was John and Graham's catchphrase," says Palin. "The great thing was, it was said so often anyway, normally, on television, that we just found ourselves saying it. By that time, we'd identified it as a silly catchphrase, and now no one can say it without really being aware of Python.

The Silly Walk, in profile; Cleese excelled in his portrayals of mad authority figures. According to costumer Hazel Pethig, Cleese hated dressing up in strange and uncomfortable costumes, and would have been perfectly happy to perform all of his Python scenes in a coat and tie. Photo copyright BBC and Python Productions.

Show 14—Dinsdale

Recorded as Series 2, Show 4—Prod. #60530

"The Newsreader (JC) is in a cage at the zoo as he says "And now for something completely different"; the "It's" Man (MP) is in an adjacent cage as he announces "It's"

Titles

"Face the Press" features the Minister for Home Affairs (GC), whose pink tulle dress and accessories are described by the Interviewer (EI). The Minister is to debate a small patch of brown liquid (possibly creosote), and opts to answer his first question in both his real voice, and a silly high-pitched whine. The Interviewer talks on a TV monitor with Air Chief Marshall Sir Vincent "Kill the Japs" Forster, who is attired in outrageous drag.

The program is being watched at home by Mrs. G. Pinnet (TJ); she answers her front door to begin the "New Cooker" sketch. Two Gas Men (GC and MP), in caps and brown trenchcoats, have confused her with a Mrs. G. Crump. She signs the receipt, at their insistence, as Mrs. Crump-Pinnet; after signing more invoices and installation forms, they find the connection order is also for a Mrs. Crump. She decides to submit to the gas fumes for faster service, and the crowd of Gas Men (all with caps and brown trenchcoats) form a long line

After the Gas Men inform her that she is in the wrong house, Mrs. G. Pinnet (Jones) is quick to oblige them.
Photo copyright BBC and Python Productions.

down the street. They are all turning and muttering incomprehensible technicalities to each other, as the group eventually fades into animation.

More animation features vintage model European monarchs in flight, and an old man shaves his neck.

A lascivious, winking Customer with an evil eye (EI) tries to rent a small white pussycat, some chest of drawers, and a bit of pram, but is discouraged when the Shop Owner (TJ) shows him the less-than-naughty items. Meanwhile, a gentleman buying a newspaper in the shop turns out to be Mr. Teabags of the Ministry of Silly Walks (JC) on his way to work (where he passes the long line of gas men).

At the office, Mr. Putey (MP) demonstrates his own rather lame silly walk, and explains that he was hoping for a government grant to make it much sillier. His secretary, Miss Twolumps, makes a futile attempt to bring them coffee, and they screen footage of some vintage silly walks. Putey is offered a position to help develop the Anglo-French Silly Walk (La Marche Futile), unveiled by two Frenchmen (JC and MP) and demonstrated by their Anglo-French subject (TJ).

A BBC 1 announcer introduces "Ethel the

The Piranha's atom-bombing of Luton Airport has finally caused the police to sit up and take notice. Supt. Harry "Snapper" Organs follows them disguised as various theatrical characters, though some critics have chided him for his abusive ad libs and unscheduled appearances onstage.

As the closing credits roll, an animated Spiny Norman cries "Dinsdale!" as it peers over the city skyline. The Newsreader (JC) is still in his cage, while the adjacent cage is occupied by a skeleton looking like the "It's" Man.

ALSO APPEARING: David Ballantyne
John Hughman
Stanley Mason

🎬 The title page of the script credits GC, JC, EI, TJ, and MP, "with prize-winning animations by Terry Gilliam." The unofficial title of the show is "Give Us Money, Not Awards."

🎬 The group had hoped to open the show with a match featuring the Chelsea Football Team. The players would have kicked the ball down the field, running past John Cleese in dinner jacket at his usual desk. The original ending would then have

The Silly Walk in action: one of the public's most-loved Python sketches, and one of Cleese's least favorites. Photo copyright BBC and Python Productions.

Although one report claims this sequence with Michael Palin is part of the "Wacky Queen" sketch, it finally surfaced in the TV series as a segment in the "Vintage Silly Walk" film shown at the close of that sketch. Either way, it is extremely silly. Photo copyright BBC and Python Productions.

Frog," which the Host (JC) explains will be looking at the violence of the Piranha Brothers, Doug and Dinsdale. Interviews with a neighbor, April Simnel (MP), one of their teachers, Anthony Viney (GC), and Police Inspector Harry "Snapper" Organs (TJ) trace the careers of this violent, sarcastic pair.

Stig O'Tracy (EI) has had his head nailed to the floor, but doesn't have an unkind word for the brothers; neither does his wife (GC), whose head is still nailed to the coffee table. A Female Impersonator, Gloria (JC), tells of Dinsdale's fear of a giant, imaginary hedgehog called Spiny Norman. Luigi Vercotti (MP), who runs an escort service, talks about Doug's dreaded use of sarcasm.

The live performance of "Silly Walks," including a silly walk-on by Carol Cleveland, sees Cleese giving his all. Photos copyright KHJ.

occurred in the footballers' changing room. The script notes that Eric claimed he could get the entire team for the pre-credit sequence. Apparently, he couldn't.

The "Timmy Williams Show" sketch had originally been intended for this show, to follow the "Ministry of Silly Walks"; it is now in Show 19.

Michael's Mr. Putey character, introduced in the "Silly Walks" sketch, was originally named Mr. Standford.

Walking Silly

"John Cleese and I were writing together one day, and John had been thinking of doing something about anger. He's very good at it, and he likes that emotion very much indeed. I'd been noticing that there were all sorts of ministries for strange things that were likely to distract people from the main issues of the day, and make it look like the government was doing something. A lot of attention would either go to a drought or flood that probably didn't exist anyway, and there seemed to be lots of useless ministries. I thought, why not a Ministry of Anger?" explained Graham Chapman.

"It's difficult to remember whether it was John's or my idea, but I do know that the next stage was Silly Walks, which was more ludicrous and petty than an emotion like anger. My house was on a very steep hill, and we saw a man walk past, uphill, stooped very sharply backward, defying the laws of gravity! Well, we thought Silly Walks was a good idea, but we couldn't quite think how to develop it.

"As usual, we were supposed to be writing something else when this idea occurred—anything to prevent us from getting to that work! But we thought we'd better get on to writing what we were supposed to be writing. So we rang up Mike (Palin) and Terry (Jones)—to interrupt them from whatever they were supposed to be doing—and made them write the sketch."

"Silly Walks" is one of Cleese's most dreaded sketches today, largely because of the fan reaction that has plagued him ever since. So he politely rebuffs any and all requests to perform it, up through his appearance on *Donahue* with the cast of *A Fish Called Wanda* in August 1988. Featured on a live video link to the N.Y. studio, with Jamie Lee Curtis in L.A., Cleese was badgered by virtually everyone to perform the walk, and appeared to relent. So he stood up, walked off-camera for a few moments, during which he claimed to do the Silly Walks, and returned to an enthusiastic ovation.

Show 15 — The Spanish Inquisition

Recorded as Series 2, Show 3—Prod. #60440

A man (JC) runs across a field, cranking a pair of mechanical wings. He appears to fly, but the camera tilts to show he is actually falling down a cliff, and crashes into the ground. At a nearby desk, the man in the dinner jacket (JC) says "And now for something completely different," and the "It's" Man (MP) says "It's"

Titles

Jarrow, New Year's Eve, 1911, is followed by Jarrow, 1912. Lady Mountback (CC) sits in a drawing room, when Reg (GC) bursts in to announce trouble at the mill, saying "One on't cross beams gone owt askew in treddle!"* When she questions him, he says he didn't expect a kind of Spanish Inquisition.

A trio of red-robed men from the Spanish Inquisition rush in, led by Cardinal Ximinez (MP). He triumphantly announces "No one escapes the Spanish Inquisition!" Unfortunately he keeps blowing his lines, and Cardinal Biggles (TJ) tries to help. They have to make several entrances before Biggles and Cardinal Fang (TG) apply the rack, which turns out to be a rack for dishwashing. They try to get Lady Mountback to confess to heresy. Captions describe their diabolical laughter, and their diabolical acting.

Reg sits calmly in the back, puffing on his pipe, when a BBC Man (JC) arrives, asking if he would answer a door in a sketch. He is driven across town to the house, and obligingly answers the door.

Johnson, a joke salesman (EI), describes his products for the BBC Man (a comedy hernia kit, a Wicked Willie with a life-sized winkle, guaranteed to break the ice at parties), but he is unable to give the punch line for the salesman. When Johnson protests that he wasn't told, the BBC man borrows his head for a bit of animation.

His now-animated head is wheeled in with an animated baby carriage; a can-can dancer passes through his eyes, and a pupil is shot out of a Civil War cannon, which rolls into photos of nude women covered by binoculars, faucets, etc.

The Head of a government commission (JC) on the fiscal deficit tries to find new methods of taxation. Reasoning that everything else pleasurable is taxed, one of the three civil servants (TJ) suggests they place a tax on . . . thingy. A series of "Vox Pops" on taxation follow, including a suggestion from Mr. Gumby.

A Dear Old Lady (MW) is showing some holiday snaps (to CC, who tears them up as she goes), when the Spanish Inquisition, complete with a lengthy historical introduction, bursts in. They pathetically attempt to torture her with the Soft Cushions, then resort to the Comfy Chair. An animated policeman confesses, followed by several other bits of "I confess" animation.

This leads into the beginning of 20th Century

Outside his home office, Palin poses with a Mr. Gumby doll made by a fan. Photo copyright KHJ.

*One of the crossbeams has gone out of skew on the treadle.

1 2 4

Vole's "Semaphore Version of Wuthering Heights," with CC as Catherine, EI as her husband and TJ as Heathcliff. The maid stutters, saying "Your fffather! He's fffallen ill with fffever!" Also shown are clips from "Julius Caesar on an Addis Lamp" (with GC as Caesar), "Gunfight at the OK Corral in Morse Code," and the "Smokesignal Version of Gentlemen Prefer Blondes."

In Central Criminal Court, the Jury Foreman (MP) gives the verdict in charades, and the Judge (GC) finds him not guilty. He acts out "Call the next defendant," who is Judge Kilb (TJ). The first Judge announces that he is leaving for South Africa, where they still have the cat o' nine tails, four death sentences a week, cheap drinks, slave labor, and a booming stock market. His parting shot is sentencing the defendant to be burned at the stake. The defendant says he didn't expect a kind of Spanish Inquisition, and the Inquisition trio tries to rush over as fast as possible before the show ends.

The Spanish Inquisition is on a bus as the credits roll, but just as they burst into the courtroom, it's The End.

ALSO APPEARING: Carol Cleveland
Marjorie Wilde

"The Smokesignal Version of Gentlemen Prefer Blondes" was originally followed by "the all-talking version of the 'Chemist Shop' sketch ('Who's got the pox?')." This version of "Chemist Shop," which is in Show 17, here uses "biscuit barrel" as the naughty words for toilet, instead of "Semprini." "Chemist Shop" is then supposed to be followed by a different courtroom scene, which still ends with the Spanish Inquisition rushing to the courtroom as the credits roll. The courtroom scene in this show was actually intended to run after the final credits.

Taken by Surprise

When Michael Palin is asked how he gets his ideas, he explains that he sits with a piece of paper, and lets something come into his head. "There's nothing odd about that. Sometimes in the morning, when I'm half awake, or just when I'm about to go to sleep, all sorts of strange thoughts will come into my mind," Palin says, laughing.

"There are moments when the mind drifts, and that's what happened with the Spanish Inquisition. There was all this stuff about 'trouble at t'mill,' and Carol saying she doesn't understand. Graham breaks out of his accent, still talking Northern, and says 'gone owt askew on treddle.' 'No, I still don't understand.' He says 'All I came in here was to tell you there was trouble at t'mill, I didn't expect a kind of Spanish Inquisition.'

"I wrote that line, just as it was, and I thought 'Great! What we must do here is bring the Spanish Inquisition into it!' So, the door opens, and in come these people saying 'Nobody expects the Spanish Inquisition!' That's really how it was written—it was just stream of consciousness."

Meet Mr. Gumby

The gum-booted, suspendered, handkerchief-hatted Gumbies were created gradually, but soon became favorites of the group and viewers. Though Michael Palin perfected the characters, it was John Cleese who made the initial appearance in Gumby uniform; he assembled the costume while the group was filming their "Vox Pops" (Voice of the People, man-in-the-street one-liners).

"Recording the 'Vox Pops' was as near as Python ever came to improvising," Palin explains, "because all the studio stuff and the longer film bits were clearly worked out. Many of these little 'Vox Pops' were just people putting on these silly costumes, and saying silly things like 'My brain hurts,' or 'Don't believe a word of it,' or 'It's not really changed my life.'

"John had to say something particularly imbecilic and said 'What should I wear? I've got to go stand in the middle of a stream.' He put on these gumboots and rolled up his trousers, and said 'I'd tax people who stand in water,' while he was standing in a stream.

"So that costume was sort of around, and the next time I did something where he became more of a character whose brain hurt. John had already gotten the costume and the complete mindlessness of the character."

A woman begins undressing in the window of a high-rise, when the Man in the Dinner Jacket (JC) is pulled up on a window-washing platform. He says "And now for something completely different," and an elk explodes. Back on the window ledge, he says "And now for something more completely different," and the "It's" Man (MP) says "It's"

Titles

Another animal explodes in the woods, where Mr. Chigger (TJ) approaches a Cardinal (MP), who is rehearsing his lines for Show 8. Chigger asks him about flying lessons, but the Cardinal says he isn't in the present show. A Secretary (CC) leads him through the woods, wading in a stream past other business executives, through a field, in a cave, under a road, and they finally end

Always equipped with a delightfully absurd logic, Gilliam's animations retained the ability to surprise and sometimes shock. Photo copyright Python Productions Ltd.

up in an office, where a man is suspended in the air. Mr. Anemone (GC) tells him to fly by flapping his arms, but Chigger protests, pointing out that he is hanging from wires, which Anemone goes to great lengths to disprove.

Two years later (actually six years later, after a Balfour Airlines correction), Chigger and his Copilot (JC) are commercial pilots interrupted by a Spokesman (EI) for Balfour Airlines, who points out some mistakes in the previous sketch, as well as last week's "High Chapparal," and begins to wander as he discusses other mistakes. The pilots are interrupted by a pounding on the cockpit door. A

Man (GC) enters who has mistaken the cabin for a bathroom. He apologizes, then steps out of the plane to land on a bale of hay just outside of a bathroom. A Stewardess (CC) enters the cabin followed by a Hijacker (MP) on the scheduled flight to Cuba, but he wants to go to Luton. They throw him out on a bale of hay and he catches a bus to Luton, which is suddenly hijacked to Cuba.

The works of Scottish poet Ewan McTeagle (TJ) are studied, including his poem *Will You Lend Us a Quid?* Lassie O'Shea (EI) reads a personal poem written for her by McTeagle. St. John Limbo, a poetry expert (JC), discusses how McTeagle widened his scope by asking for ever-increasing amounts, and a Shakespearean Actor (EI) reads his masterpiece, *Can I Have Fifty Pounds to Mend the Shed?* A Very Good Playwright (MP) analyzes his work, and McTeagle walks past an exploding animal. A Highland Spokesman (JC) in a kilt stands up to deliver corrections, and has a man under his kilt (MP) examining him.

Animation features dismemberment and other violence, including a garden of hands, and cowboy riding a severed hand. His lasso is attached to knitting being done by Mrs. Ratbag (GC).

Mrs. Ratbag is examined by a Psychiatrist Milkman (EI). As he takes her to a dairy, they pass

an exploding cat and the Gynecologist (MP) who was just examining the Scotsman. They are interrupted by another man who claims they are just making a pat diagnosis without knowing the complete medical history of the patient. This is followed by a complaint about the previous complaint, and still more complaints. Dr. Cream (TJ), another psychiatrist milkman, talks to a cow lying on his couch, and Mrs. Ratbag is led through the field by a milkmaid, following the same route as the walk taken by Chigger at the beginning of the show, but in reverse order.

"It's the Mind," hosted by Mr. Boniface (MP), says the program will look at "The strange phenomenon of déjà vu, that strange feeling we sometimes get that we've lived through something before." Déjà vu strikes him, and he goes through the opening of the show several times. Panicking, he catches a psychiatrist dairy bus and runs back into Dr. Cream's office, only to find himself back on the bus and running to the office again, etc., and the credits roll.

ALSO APPEARING: Carol Cleveland
Jeannette Wild

 "Election Night Special" was originally set to follow "It's the Mind," with a very brief déjà vu ending; it was moved to Show 19.

 In the middle of "Psychiatrist Diaries/Déjà Vu," Mrs. Ratbag's name mysteriously changes to Mrs. Pim.

Auditions

There was a general method followed in distributing roles in Python sketches, according to Eric Idle,

and casting within the group was usually rather easy.

"We'd never cast until the end, because everything had to be written. Once we'd established what the show was, and what was going to be said and done, then we'd sit down and cast it. For TV, we'd cast several shows at once, so if somebody was light in one show, we could make it up in the next," Idle says.

"Basically, it was all done by consent. Clearly, if it was a John sketch, it would be insane not to cast John as the authoritarian figure. As I think about it now, we were pretty good at casting, because people were very British. They didn't say 'Oh, I want to play that!'," Idle says in a sharp American accent. "They'd say 'Oh, I wouldn't mind . . .' People might have their eye on a little piece, and the rest of it was done very quickly. 'Eric, Mike, Terry, you want to do that?' 'I'll do that.'

"There were never any big arguments. As a matter of fact, we operated in reverse—people actually got better and better at giving their stuff away! I remember Terry Jones in *Meaning of Life*, for example, give me a little old lady part in the condoms sketch. He thought I should do it, which was very nice of him!

"I think we very rarely miscast," Idle continues. "By and large, a lot of parts were Eric or Mike. It was clear which parts were Terry Jones parts— the little ratbag ladies; Graham Chapman was always the Colonel, and John, the authoritarian figures. In the middle were a range of characters that could always be Eric or Mike, and they were often written down that way."

Show 17—The Buzz Aldrin Show

Recorded as Series 2, Show 9—Prod #61964

An animated caterpillar/man crawls into a house, and turns into a butterfly/poof. The Man in the Dinner Jacket (JC), with propellers on his desk, flies up to say "And now for something completely different," and the "It's" Man says "It's"

Titles
The BBC apologizes for the next announcement, which is five Gumbies introducing "The Architect" sketch, pointing to an office above them.

In the office, Mr. Tid (GC) throws down water

to silence the Gumbies below, who are shouting "Up there!" He introduces the designers of a residential block of flats. Mr. Wiggin (JC) has designed an abattoir* with which to slaughter the tenants, but he is rejected. His chief regret is that he could never join the Masons, and he begs them for a chance. The next architect is Mr. Wymiss (EI), whose model catches fire and falls apart. He does give the Masonic handshake, however. Several ways of recognizing Masons are shown, including their handshakes, hats with antlers, etc.

An animated Mason (GC) undergoes anti-Masonic therapy.

Another apology is issued as the Gumbies introduce the "Insurance" sketch. Mr. Devious (MP) tries to sell the Straight Man (GC) a policy that includes a nude lady. The Reverend Morrison (EI) enters as the Straight Man leaves, as the script shows he has no more lines. The Vicar's car was hit while parked in his garage, but he is found to have a "never-pay" policy; his policy mentions filling his mouth in with cement. He finally leaves with his nude lady, as a Bishop (TJ) steps into Devious's office.

"The Bishop" titles, complete with secret-agent music, follow the Bishop as he tries to stop an explosion at a baptism and other incidents, but arrives too late. As he walks down a street with his entourage, the Reverend Morrison shouts from the office, and they rush upstairs to get Devious, as "The Bishop" titles roll again. In a theater, Mr. and Mrs. Potter (MP and GC) note that this was where they came in.

The Potters are living in the street, and a Man (EI) wants to feature them in a documentary on Britain's housing program. Mrs. Potter chases them off to do a documentary on the drug problem, and the Potters are revealed as having Alfred Lord Tennyson in the bath. The Sales Manager of the East Midlands Poet Board (JC) does a promo, including an animated jingle, for the Poet Board. Wombat Harness (MP), who goes door to door reading poets, is seduced by a Housewife (TJ) when he tries to read her Wordsworth (EI).

Derek Hart (JC) is the moderator of a panel on nudity, featuring a Nude Man (GC). The music and titles start to roll again for "The Bishop."

*Slaughterhouse.

Animation features men bouncing on a nude woman, with Gumby and the Beanstalk. Animated frogs turn into live Gumbies, and introduce "The Chemist" sketch.

A Chemist (JC) dispenses drugs by asking customers who has the pox, a boil on the botty, and a chest rash. An apology is then issued for using such words as knockers, wee-wee, and semprini; the chemist is arrested (by GC) for a "boil on his semprini."

A Customer (EI) at a less-naughty Chemist (TJ) is taken away for his after-shave joke. A not-at-all naughty Chemist (MP) is visited by a Customer (EI) who wants halibut after-shave. The Chemist pretends to go off to the basement to look for some, and finally pretends to go to Kensington. A "Vox Pops" segment has other people tell what they use for after-shave.

Police Constable Pan Am (GC) runs into the Chemists, and as a fat man shoplifts, the innocent Customer is arrested. The Constable cracks up and calls to Buzz Aldrin; another apology is issued as the credits follow for "The Buzz Aldrin Show," with Buzz Aldrin in most of the credits.

ALSO APPEARING: Sandra Richards
Stanley Mason

The five Gumbies announce "And now for something completely different," as they change into women.

🎬 The "Chemist" sketch was originally intended for Show 15.

🎬 In the original script, when the Bishop and his crew try to break into Devious's office, the whole set shakes and starts to fall.

Improvising Animations

As he would eventually do when he became a film director, Terry Gilliam looked for opportunities to improvise while creating his animations, changing direction when an interesting opportunity presented itself.

"My approach has always been to keep an eye open for lucky accidents or mistakes. That's the

advantage of cutouts. I had all this material sitting around the place, so it could fall into any number of patterns and suggest ideas," Gilliam explains.

"Paper and I had a very good relationship, and inspired each other. Sometimes they would write things like 'Titles for "The Bishop," ' or something like that—a title sequence—okay, so I do a title sequence. I had a very clear idea of what I wanted; I would storyboard what I was doing, and spend a lot of time trying to find the bits of artwork or photos that I wanted. Because of time limitations, I wouldn't quite find what I was looking for, but find something else that was slightly different. Okay, so it was a bit different from what I planned . . . "

Show 18—Live from the Grillomat

Recorded as Series 2, Show 7—Prod. #61851

A BBC 1 world symbol slide announces that the show will be presented live from the Grillomat Snack Bar in Paignton. The host in the Dinner Jacket (JC) is sitting at a table in the Grillomat calling for the Titles, which are preceded by the "It's" Man (MP).

The Host, still at a table, calls for the opening sketch, or the "hors d'oeuvres," which is the Blackmail quiz show, hosted by the cheery Wally Wiggins (MP). He demands fifteen pounds from Mrs. Betty Teal to stop him from revealing the name of her lover in Bolton. He promises to show more of a revealing photo, and introduces a Stop the Film segment, where the amount increases as the film continues. A Nude Organist (TG) plays a fanfare as they attempt to extort the various sums.

A Member (TJ) of the Society for Putting Things on Top of Other Things is late for their dinner meeting, as he has just phoned the Blackmail show. The Society's chairman, Sir William Gore Fisk (GC), gives an annual overview of the previous year's progress, and Cutler, the delegate from the Staffordshire branch (JC), is chastised. The meeting is adjourned, however, when everyone agrees that it's all very silly.

The chairman walks out the door to leave, but is startled to find that he's on film. He tries to escape through the other doors and windows, but when the group sees it is surrounded by film, the room becomes a POW camp, and they decide to tunnel their way out.

In an animated sequence, five of them exit into a stomach, and are expelled through the bowels.

Mr. Praline (JC), the host of a new half-hour chat show, tries to discuss the population explosion, but his guest, Brookie (EI), only attempts to tell jokes. When the Director (TJ) tells them their bit has been cut from the show, they hear noises under their feet, and decide they may still make it into the show as a link.

Below the floorboards (Praline says it's due to color separation), the five animated men travel through pipes beneath them, until they are belched out. One of them lands in a painting of *The Last Supper,* and is taken up to a cloud with the other four; the crowd on the cloud below them urges them not to jump.

Back at the Grillomat, the Waitress (GC) is talking too loudly for the "main course" to be introduced, which is Prawn Salad Ltd., or "The Accident" sketch.

A Man (EI) is ushered into a drawing room by a Butler (GC). He waits alone for a Mr. Thompson, when a mirror suddenly falls. The Butler is skeptical, and after he leaves again, a china cabinet falls completely by itself, though the butler assumes the Man did it. A Maid (CC) enters the room and falls on the Brazilian dagger she has asked him to hold, and an Older Man (TJ) and a Police Officer (MP) both die when they are left alone with the innocent Man. The ceiling suddenly falls on the Butler, and as the Man leaves, the mansion falls apart behind him and explodes.

The five formerly animated men walk past a Bishop (MP), who is rehearsing for next week's show (the man at the Grillomat sees no need to interrupt), and enter the school hall at the Dibley School for Boys, where they are presenting *Seven Brides for Seven Brothers.* Praline and Brookie sit at the piano as four boys (TJ, EI, TG, and JC) represent

the seven brothers, while two girls are the seven brides. The Headmaster (GC) calls in the Padre (MP) to perform the ceremony.

The sheet music becomes animated, and turns into a piggy bank hunting sequence with Neddy and Teddy, ending up as a chart in a butcher shop.

The Butcher (EI) is alternately polite and insulting to a City Gent (MP), attitudes changing with each sentence.

Back at the Grillomat, the Host and Waitress get into a dispute over whether he has offered coffee or tea, which leads into the story of an almost totally stupid boxer.

Ken Clean-Air System (JC) rubs gravel in his hair every day for lunch, according to his manager, Englebert Humperdinck (GC). Interviews with his wife Mrs. Nellie Air-Vent (EI), his mother (TJ), and his Trainer (MP) show a typical day training for a big fight: He arrives at a hospital, thinking it is a gymnasium. His opponent is teen-aged Petulia Wilcox (CB), shown knitting in her bedroom at home; in the ring, he is shown giving her a senseless beating.

At the Grillomat, the Waitress reads a note from the now-departed Host, who is shown leaving the show on a bus. He apologizes and says he won't be back the next week, as some of the jokes weren't as funny as they might have been. As the credits roll, he explains that he's really more of a visual performer, and wishes that he had been able to do his funny walk.

ALSO APPEARING: Carol Cleveland
      Ian Davidson
      Connie Booth
      Mrs. Idle

The title page of the script credits Terry Palin, Eric Jones, Michael Cleese, Graham Gilliam, Terry Chapman, and John Idle.

A lengthy sequence was cut from the final show involving Praline and Brookie rambling on about phone service, while Brookie interjects homely Yorkshire aphorisms, just before the animations appear under the floor.

Following the "Butcher Shop" sketch, a sequence was cut which featured the 1958 Cup Final discussing the implications of the previous sketch on a TV chat show.

The "Dibley" name surfaces again here, as the name of the Boys' School.

Gwen Dibley's Flying Circus: Dibley Notes

When the group was deciding on a name for the original TV series, among the bizarre suggestions—many of which were eventually used as titles for individual shows ("Owl-Stretching Time," "Bunn, Wackett, Buzzard, Stubble, and Boot," etc.)—Michael Palin favored naming the show after Gwen Dibley.

Who?

"There actually was a Gwen Dibley," Palin explains. "She seemed the sort of person who would be miles away from anyone who would ever watch a Python show. It was in one of my wife's mother's magazines, one of these Women's Institute's monthly gatherings, where someone talked about flower display. At the end it said 'And Gwen Dibley accompanied on the piano.'

"I just thought it was a nice idea to give someone their own show, even though they didn't know it. The satisfaction of someone getting their copy of *The Radio Times,* and the children of Gwen Dibley discovering it first—the sheer, stunned surprise that their mother had been given her own show without her knowing it, appealed to us greatly. We also liked the name 'Gwen Dibley.'

"But like a lot of our titles, they worked one afternoon, and the next morning people weren't quite so sure. I think we also thought we might get sued, quite rightly, by the Dibley family, if they didn't like it. It wasn't really fair to drag her into something that no one knew what it was going to be like. And so she lost her chance to be associated with one of the great comedy shows."

Actually, though, the group managed to work the Dibley name into several of the shows, sometimes in the most unlikely places. Among the various namesakes are the Dibley School for Boys, seen in this show as the place where *Seven Brides for Seven Brothers* is staged, director L. F. Dibley, and Dibley Road, the address of Ernest Scribbler, author of the funniest joke in the world.

As it turned out, the group's inability to decide

on a title for the show actually forced the BBC's hand, according to producer Barry Took. "They couldn't think of a title. At one stage, they wanted to call it 'Whither Canada?' and all sorts of things like that. The BBC finally told them 'It doesn't matter what you call it as long as the words "flying circus" are in it,' because all the notes and memos going around internally at the BBC called it 'The Circus.' It would confuse the BBC if they called it anything else, so they went away and invented Monty Python."

Actually, some of the BBC personnel had a further nickname for it as well, but somehow, "Baron Von Took's Flying Circus" never seemed to catch on.

Show 19 — School Prizes

Recorded as Series 2, Show 8—Prod. #61852

The Compère (EI) of "It's a Living" explains the game, the rules and fees received, thanks his guests, and promises to come back next week.

A BBC 1 world symbol announces the time, but the animation following can't find the lights in time for the opening

Titles

The Man in the Dinner Jacket (JC) sits at a desk in a blacksmith's shop, explaining that he didn't say "And now for something completely different" because he isn't in this week's show.

A Man (TJ) looks into the camera, complaining about his toothache, and a Nabarro figure (GC) interrupts to introduce the School Prize Awards. The Bishop of East Anglia (MP) is dragged under the table and is attacked by Another Man (EI), who emerges and claims to be the Bishop of East Anglia. He declines to give out any of the silver trophies, and puts them all in his sack, until an Oriental Man (GC) says he is the Bishop of East Anglia, and claims the school prizes for the People's Republic of China. Inspector Elizabeth Bradshaw (TJ) and the Leader of a commando squad (JC) also try to claim the trophies, as gunshots erupt.

This is all being viewed on television as the latest film by director L. F. Dibley (TJ). An Interviewer (GC) talks with the director, who has made lesser-known versions of If..., 2001: A Space Odyssey, Midnight Cowboy, as well as ten-second versions of Rear Window and Finian's Rainbow, which are shown.

The Interviewer introduces the Foreign Secretary (just returned from the bitter fighting in the Gulf of Amman) on canoeing, and his craft is thrown into a lake by two Arabs as he sits in it. Three other politicians form a human pyramid before each of them is thrown in the lake, and the president of the Board of Trade is placed in a hamper and then thrown in the lake. Leaving the discussion of problems of Britain's industrial reorganization, other public figures are thrown into the lake, concluding with Dame Irene Stoat (MP) reading one of her poems before being shoved in by a samurai warrior.

Two couples at a dinner party are interrupted by a Man (JC) delivering their free dung from the Book of the Month Club. Host Mr. Forbes (MP) tries to refuse it, and another deliveryman (GC) brings them a free dead Indian, and the couple wins the M-4 Motorway. The couple then find they are the prizes in a police raffle, and a Policeman (TJ) describes some of the other prizes.

An animated sequence follows, with a samurai slicing everything—including himself—in two, and the parts are used in a cooking demonstration.

Nigel Watt (TJ), whose wife has just died, is joined at a restaurant by the wonderfully David Frost-ish Timmy Williams (EI). His attempts at a heart-to-heart chat are futile, as Timmy's writers, photographers, and hangers-on are everywhere. Nigel finally shoots himself, and the "Timmy Williams' Coffee Time" credits roll, crediting Timmy for everything.

An Interviewer (MP) talks to one of the country's leading skin specialists, Raymond Luxury-Yacht (GC), whose name is actually pronounced "throat-wobbler mangrove"; his extraordinarily large nose proves to be false, and he is thrown off the show.

Animation of sexual athletes follows, with a nude woman and a topless Mona Lisa.

At a marriage-license bureau, a Man (TJ) tells

Henry, the registrar (EI), that he wants to get married. He is joined by two other men with the same request (MP and GC), but the registrar agrees to marry all of them, until his wife (JC) finds him out.

Animation of a woman applying lipstick becomes the story of an enchanted prince who discovers a spot on his face, and dies three years later, although the spot flourishes.

"Election Night Special" features the entire group with the results of the Silly Party, the Slightly Silly Party, the Sensible Party, and the independent Very Silly candidates. The politicians include Jethroe Q. Walrustitty, Arthur J. Smith, and Tarquin Fintimlinbinwhinbimlimbus-stop F'Tang-F'Tang-Ole-Biscuit-Barrel. Analyses follow, as do the credits, then "Monty Python has held the critics!"

ALSO APPEARING: Rita Davies
Ian Davidson

 "Timmy Williams" had originally been intended for Show 14, "Election Night Special" was intended for Show 16.

 The group uses the name of Ray Millichope, film editor of the first three series, as one of the politicians who forms a human pyramid by the lake ("Ray Millichope, leader of Allied Technician's Union").

The animated Prince first discovers the Black Spot that will kill him and drive the censors insane. Photo copyright Python Productions Ltd.

The Black Spot

Even Terry Gilliam's animations were not immune to the BBC censors, though the inanity of one instance still irritates Gilliam. In the original version of "The Prince and the Black Spot" (and the version still shown in the feature-length *And Now For Something Completely Different*), the Prince ignores the black spot and dies of cancer. However, in all subsequent repeats, another voice is dubbed over the word "cancer," and the word "gangrene" inserted.

"That's the most bizarre, silly, stupid thing, because it went out, millions of people watched it, and the world didn't change—so, I don't know why one changes it on the repeats," says a still-irritated Gilliam.

"It's just crazy. Who's protecting who from what? I don't know. I didn't think it was dangerous to mention the word 'cancer,' but it obviously touched a fear that a lot of people didn't want to deal with."

Chinese Chapman

The individual members of Python tended to specialize in their own characterizations as the show developed. For no apparent reason, Graham Chapman seemed to end up playing Chinese and other Oriental characters. "There is no known reason for that. I had a lot of Chinese friends at the time, so perhaps that's why I tended to get Chinese parts handed to me on a plate. Maybe the lads thought I would like them. I didn't mind."

Cleese and Cleveland as Mr. And Mrs. Attila the Hun, stars of their own sitcom. Photo copyright BBC and Python Productions.

The Wonderful David Frost

At various times, the individual Pythons have all been involved with the ubiquitous David Frost, ei-ther writing or performing for him early in their careers. Although they all enjoyed taking a few jabs at their one-time mentor, it was usually Eric Idle who ended up portraying the various incarnations of Frost, whether as a straightforward interviewer or as Arthur Tree, a tree hosting his own talk show.

According to Idle, however, his impersonation of Frost got no feedback from the target himself until long after the Python TV shows. "Actually, I talked to him after I did the Nixon interviews on *Saturday Night Live*—Danny Ackroyd played Nixon, and I played him.

"I saw Frost about two weeks later when I came back to London. He came up to me and said 'I loved your Frost'—as though it wasn't him, but somebody else that I was doing!" Idle laughs. " 'Loved your Frost' . . . But we all used to work for him, writing ad libs for him in the '60s. He gave us our big breaks, though we would never admit that in public."

The most obvious assault on Frost was "Timmy Williams's Coffee Time." Idle and the Pythons got back at him in numerous ways, including closing credits that include dozens of writers' names.

"That used to be David. His shows would say 'Written by David Frost, Contributions by—' and then three hundred names would roll by, the names of the people who actually wrote the show," Idle says. "He always took a nice big script credit, and I don't think he ever wrote a joke."

Show 20—The Attila the Hun Show

Recorded as Series 2, Show 11—Prod. #62572

A filmed introduction of the Romans fighting ancient barbarians leads into "The Attila the Hun Show," a cute situation comedy with Attila (JC), Mrs. Hun (CC), Robin and Jennie (MP and GC), his children, and Uncle Tom (EI), their black butler. The theme song and opening credits closely copy *The Debbie Reynolds Show,* and the laugh track blares loudly.

The Man in the Dinner Jacket says "And now for something completely different," the "It's" Man (MP) says "It's"

Titles

Attila the Nun is in a hospital room; at the other end, Miss Norris (CC) is going to be examined by Charles Crompton, the stripping doctor (GC), in a room with mood lighting and music, while several shabby men in filthy macs (students) look on.

The Compère (EI) at the Peephole Club applauds, and introduces the Secretary of State for Commonwealth Affairs (TJ), who does a striptease as he delivers a speech on agricultural subsidies and their effects on commonwealth relationships.

Next is the Minister of Pensions and Social Securities (GC), who does a belly dance.

"Vox Pops" follows with political groupies.

Mr. And Mrs. Concrete (TJ and MP) are visited by Leslie Ames (GC), the Council Ratcatcher. He finds that they have sheep instead of mice. He enters a large hole in the wainscoting, but the sheep have guns; killer sheep terrorize the countryside. A Professor (EI) and his assistant, Miss Garter Oil (CC), attempt to handle the problem; they investigate the wolf's clothing worn by the killer sheep. They are interrupted by cricketers looking for the third test match,

Shooting the filmed opening to "The Attila the Hun Show" on location, as Chapman gets into his costume as teenaged Jennie Hun. Photo copyright Terry Jones, used by permission.

and are attacked by some animated sheep, who later rob the Westminster Bank, riding off in cars and on horseback, accompanied by "Foggy Mountain Breakdown"* as they head into the hills.

A Newsreader (MP) gives the news for parrots, and Part 3 of *A Tale of Two Cities,* adapted by Joey Boy, is featured (starring GC). This is followed by the news for gibbons, with "Today in Parliament" (read by EI) after that. Seven hours later, news for wombats leads into the animated Attila the Bun.

Arthur Figgis (JC), village idiot, explains why the idiot is necessary to rural society (in between spasms and drooling). He is shown working out on training equipment designed to keep him silly, and works on his personal appearance. Bank president Marlon Brando (GC) tells how idioting is profitable, and graduation from the University of East Anglia Idioting School is shown. The Urban Idiots Head-

quarters is shown at St. John's Wood, at Lord's Cricket Ground.

Three Cricket Announcers (JC, GC, and EI) on the second day of the first test against Iceland, all drinking heavily, see a green Chesterfield sofa batting, while a spin dryer bowls against it; various pieces of furniture play the outfield. Following that is the Epsom furniture race.

A Bishop (MP) and some priests are seen in the audience of "Spot the Brain Cell," hosted by a Michael Miles grinning-type monster (JC). Mrs. Scum (TJ) is the contestant who tries for a blow on the head.

License fees* for January 1969 are shown, as the credits roll.

ALSO APPEARING: Carol Cleveland
Ian Davidson

Spot the Brain Cell

" 'Spot the Brain Cell' was a sketch that I originally did with Marty Feldman for *At Last, the 1948 Show,* which I'm sure has been wiped out, lost to posterity. It was based on a man called Michael Miles, who had a terrible quiz show in which he treated the contestants—who were almost all brain-damaged old ladies—with a contempt that had to be *seen* to be *believed!"* says John Cleese, laughing. "It was appropriate, but it was still over the top!

"I brought this sketch up again, played it for

---

*Flatt and Scruggs's *Bonnie and Clyde* theme.

*The annual British tax on TV sets.

Terry Jones, and rewrote it completely. It got much, much madder, but I was almost enormously fond of it. It always struck me as being genuinely funny."

When Cleese and Jones were involved in one of the Secret Policeman's Amnesty International Shows, the sketch was rewritten again to add another dimension, and to allow for celebrity guests.

"I incorporated into it an idea that was sent to me by this famous, very straight Scottish singer, Kenneth McKellar. He suggested we have a television show in which a well-known television celebrity turned up and beat up a blindfolded guest, who, while being beaten up, had to identify the celebrity," Cleese says.

"I always thought it was a great idea, and very funny, and I asked Kenneth if he'd come on the show and be the celebrity. I think he felt a little un-

comfortable about it. We used it anyway, and incorporated that into the end of this sketch from the . . . *1948 Show*. It's a very funny piece."

A Cleveland Favorite

"That was one of my favorites, I loved Attila the Hun!" says Cleveland. "We were filming for that in Jersey. I remember that sketch particularly. Everyone was in a very good humor then, I remember John was in top form. Everyone was in top form and very happy, there was no friction, there were no disagreements. Those early days were wonderful."

Show 21 — Archeology Today

Recorded as Series 2, Show 12—Prod. #62576

BBC 1 previews its new fall shows, including *Rain Stopped Play*, the Classic Series presents *Snooker My Way, Owzat*, and of course there's sport; the Voice-over Man (EI) adds "And now for something completely different: sport."

Titles

At the end of the animated title sequence, the foot crumbles. A town springs up and falls, and as luxury flats are constructed, the toe is found and an elephant is reconstructed; this serves as an opening for

Eggs Diamond and his gang, courtesy of Terry Gilliam. Photo copyright Python Productions Ltd.

"Archeology Today," in which the Interviewer (MP) quizzes his guests, the 5 foot 10 inch Professor Lucien Kastner of Oslo (TJ) and the 6 foot 5 inch Sir

Robert Eversley (JC), about their respective heights; he is very impressed by tall persons. Kastner leaves angrily, and Eversley strikes the Interviewer, who swears revenge.

1 5 5

"Flaming Star," with western-style titles, is the story of one man's search for vengeance in the raw and violent world of international archeology. At a dig in Egypt, 1920, Eversley discovers Hittite baking dishes from the Fifth Dynasty, and sings his happiness with Danielle (CC), his assistant. He is tracked down by the Interviewer (MP) and challenges him. Kastner leaps onto his shoulders, and Danielle leaps onto Eversley's shoulders; when several people are stacked up, they battle fiercely, to end "Archeology Today."

Rev. Arthur Belling (GC) delivers an appeal for sanity, wearing a hatchet in his head; he demonstrates what can be done about it.

An appeal on behalf of the National Truss is delivered by a Woman (EI) who can't remember her correct name; when she is eventually knocked down by a Prizefighter (TG), there is stock film of Women's Institute applause.

A Man (EI) visits a Marriage Registrar (TJ) to trade in his wife for a different woman, until an Official (JC) blows a whistle to stop and resume the action. Dr. Watson (GC) begins a sketch with another Doctor (MP), but that one is also abandoned when the Official blows his whistle.

An animated soccer match begins the day for Eggs Diamond, leader of the notorious chicken gang, and an appearance by Spiny Norman. An animated book ad for Raising Gangsters for Fun and Profit leads into a party.

John Stokes (MP) is introduced to Snivelling Little Rat-Faced Git (TJ) and his wife, Mrs. Dreary Fat Boring Old Git (JC). Nora Stokes (CC) is aghast, and Mrs. Git vomits in her purse.

A nice version of the same sketch follows, and a nun who liked the dirty version is knocked out by the Prizefighter, to the stock film of Women's Institute applause.

Roy and Hank Spim (EI and GC) are Australians who go hunting mosquito with bazookas, machine guns, and tanks. They later hunt moth with air-to-air missiles, and go fishing with dynamite.

Two Judges (EI and MP) coming from court discuss their day as they undress, and reveal themselves to be transvestites.

Mrs. Thing (GC) and Mrs. Entity (EI) complain about their day, and discuss the wives of government officials and Beethoven; a flashback follows.

Beethoven (JC) is bothered by a mynah bird taunting him about his upcoming deafness, and his Wife (GC) annoys him as she looks for a sugar bowl and jam spoon, and runs the sweeper while he tries to compose his Fifth Symphony. Shakespeare (EI) and Michelangelo (TJ) discuss their similar problems; Mozart (MP) wants his son to be a ratcatcher. Colin "Chopper" Mozart (MP) is seen calling on the Beethovens, where rats are everywhere; he machine-guns all the rodents.

The two camp Judges are heard again, as the credits roll.

ALSO APPEARING: Carol Cleveland

The Judges say they like the butch voices of BBC announcers who talk after programs are over.

Family Affair

"One of the lovely things about Python was that it was very much a family thing, and bits of peoples' families were dragged into it," notes Carol Cleveland. "Connie Booth did several episodes, Eric's first wife did several episodes in the early days. My mother appeared in several episodes, because my mother did television and film extra work. She was in one of the courtroom sketches, she's sitting with an ax through her head! My mother is in the background of the 'Git' sketch. I remember watching that and going 'There you are, Mom, there you are!' She was one of the guests in the house. I roped her in on Python around six times . . ."

The Music Man

John Cleese has always taken a certain glee in referring to himself as "the most unmusical man in Europe," and his Python musical appearances have been almost nonexistent (except for his performance of "Eric the Half a Bee" on *Monty Python's Previous Record* and "Oliver Cromwell" on *Monty Python Sings.*) In fact, when Cleese's archeologist character is required to sing in this show, a bit of trickery was used.

"Terry Jones actually dubbed me in 'Archeology Today.' I can't remember singing on any other occasions," Cleese says. "I'm appalling. I can't sing at all! I can *just* sing badly. On . . . *the 1948 Show,* I

sang 'The Rhubarb Tart Song,' and someday, in an Amnesty show, I want very much to sing 'I've Got a Ferret Sticking Up My Nose.' "

Shouldering the Challenge

One of the more challenging moments in the course of the TV shows for Carol Cleveland came during the filming of "Archeology Today."

"I supposedly had to jump up on top of Terry's shoulders, but because Terry was standing on John's shoulders, I was supposed to jump on top of Terry's shoulders so we were three tiers high!"

says Cleveland. "Michael and two other fellows did the same thing, and we all came together and have this little fight and knock each other off. Of course this was physically impossible, there was no way I could leap up on his shoulders, so we had to do it in reverse. I actually was standing on top of Terry's shoulders, who was standing on top of John's shoulders. Then, I had to jump backwards so they could show the shot in reverse. Though not impossible, that was far more frightening, to jump backwards off not one set of shoulders, but two! I remember being very nervous about that one. I could have broken my ankles, but it turned out all right."

Show 22—How to Recognize Different Parts of the Body

Recorded as Series 2, Show 10—Prod. #62027

Several bikini-clad women pose sexily, as does the man (JC) at the desk, posing in a bikini on top of his desk as he says "And now for something completely different," and the "It's" Man, also in bikini, says "It's"

Titles

"How to Recognize Different Parts of the Body" begins with 1. The Foot, which is the animated foot from the titles. It is followed by 2. The Shoulder, 3. The Other Foot, 4. The Bridge of the Nose, 5. Naughty Bits, 6. Just Above the Elbow, 7. Two Inches to the Right of a Very Naughty Bit, Indeed.

Eight. The Kneecap leads into the Australian

Before there was Crocodile Dundee, there were the Bruces. In the stage show, Idle, Innes, and Palin (with animated cutouts in the background) slug down Fosters and pelt the audience with their beer cans, before leading the crowd in "The Bruces' Philosophers' Song." Photo copyright KHJ.

University of Woolamaloo, in which all of the faculty wear khaki shorts, bush shirts, and Aussie hats. They drink heavily and are all named Bruce. They are introduced to a new instructor, Michael Baldwin (TJ), a chap from Pommie Land new to the Philosophy Department. They explain their rules, emphasizing "No pooftahs," and tell him they don't like stuck-up sticky beaks there.

Nine. The Ear, 10. The Big Toe, 11. More Naughty Bits, 12. The Naughty Bits of a Lady, 13. Naughty Bits of a Horse, 14. Naughty Bits of an Ant, 15. Naughty Bits of Reginald Maudling.

Sixteen. The Hand, which is pulled off to start the next sketch. An Interviewer (MP) talks to Norman St. John Polevaulter (TJ), who contradicts people. The Man in the Dinner Jacket (JC) is at his desk holding a pig, as more parts of the body are featured: 17. The Top of the Head (the Pope is shown), 18. The Feather (rare).

Nineteen. The Nose starts with Raymond Luxury-Yacht (GC), who still wants his name pronounced "throat-wobbler mangrove." He enters an office in which the nameplate extends throughout the room. He wants Professor Sir Adrian Furrows (JC), a specialist, to perform surgery on his huge nose, even after Furrows pulls it off and tells him it is polystyrene. Furrows agrees to do it if he will come on a camping holiday with him.

The men of the Second Battalion of the Derbyshire Light Infantry put on a precision display of bad temper, followed by close order swanning about when their Leader (MP) orders "Squad! Camp it . . . up!"

Animated military leaders perform the Dance of the Sugar Plum Fairies, and an animated eyeball leads into the Menace of the Killer Cars, which are disposed of by the gigantic Killer Cats. The huge felines prove to be an even greater threat, however, as they gobble down skyscrapers.

Mr. And Mrs. Irrelevant (GC and CC) visit the office of the Verri-fast Plaine Company, Ltd., which seems to use a rubber band–operated plane and a Kamikaze pilot.

At the beach, a Man (JC) introduces Mrs. Rita Fairbanks (EI) of the Batley Townswomen's Guild, and she introduces their reenactment of the first heart transplant. Also shown are the underwater versions of *Measure for Measure, Hello, Dolly!* and animated Formula 2 car racing.

More parts of the body are shown, up to 22. The Nipple, shown as a radio dial. Two Pepperpots (JC and GC) listen to the Death of Mary, Queen of Scots, until the radio explodes. They notice a penguin on top of the television set, and then a television announcer tells them the penguin is going to explode—which it does.

Twenty-six is Margaret Thatcher's Brain (an arrow points to her knee), and 29. is the Interior of a Country House. Two men (JC and GC) and a woman are questioned by an amateur investigator, Inspector Muffin, the Mule (MP), who is not sure whether a burglary or murder was committed.

Sergeant Duckie (TJ) arrives with more policemen, and he sings his entry in the Eurovision Song Contest.* It is announced as the final entry of the contest (by EI in drag), and Chief Inspector Zatapatique (GC) sings the winning entry, "Bing Tiddle Tiddle Bong," as the credits roll.

ALSO APPEARING: Carol Cleveland
The Fred Tomlinson Singers
Vincent Wong
Roy Gunson
Alexander Curry
Ralph Wood
John Clement

 The animated titles were to have included the "little chicken man who drags across a banner reading 'How to Recognize Different Parts of the Body.'"

The film of the first heart transplant is actually the same film used for the battle of Pearl Harbor in the first series.

Take 14

The film portions of the TV shows were usually shot far in advance of broadcast, but the group had a rather limited amount of time for shooting the live action in the BBC studio. Though they managed to make it through, there were few opportunities for retakes—which was often a problem.

"Most of the retakes were little bits, just going back to pick up something because the camera hadn't been on the right person, or somebody had forgotten something minor; but, they usually went through fairly smoothly," explained Graham Chapman.

"Some retakes were for other reasons. The worst occasion was a complete lack of responsibility on the part of John and myself, when we were playing the Pepperpots discussing the penguins on top of the television set. That took us about fourteen takes because of our very naughty laughing at each other. Eventually, we did come to our senses,

*A real, annual, pan-European popular-song contest.

and got through it all right. But it took us a *long* time, because it got so irresponsible. We took no notice of the screaming producer, and that made it worse!"

Say G'day, Bruce!

The Pythons' tribute to the Land Down Under was based on their own personal observations, and the Australian image in Britain at the time, long before Crocodile Dundee. Still, the group's portrait of Aussies is the one most fondly remembered by Python fans.

"It's really a traditional English view of Australians, and one of the few sketches John Cleese and I wrote together," says Eric Idle. "Barry Humphries was always claiming that we nicked it off him. I don't think we actually did. He used to have a comic strip with a hero called Bruce, but I knew some Australians in the early '60s—they were always called Bruce, and they were always in films.

In fact, I based it on a now-famous film director called Bruce, who's done a lot of American films— he always seemed to be around. We just based it on my Australian friends who always seemed to be called Bruce . . . "

The Killer Animation

The Invasion of the Killer Cars, followed by the Killer Cats, is the stuff of grade-B monster movies, which is exactly what Terry Gilliam intended for the animated sequence.

"It's 1950s science fiction, like *The Worm That Ate New York,* a lot of silly things like *Them,*" Gilliam explains. "There's a lot of *2001* influence in the cartoons. It's just taking something monumental and quite serious, and making jokes about it. It's easy to make jokes out of something that serious and on that scale. It's easy pickings—but it's also some wonderful stuff."

Show 23—Scott of the Antarctic

Recorded as Series 2, Show 2—Prod. #60439

A clip is shown from "La Fromage Grande," which takes place on a rubbish dump. Brianette Jatabatique (CC) sits alone, holding a cabbage, and Brian Distel (TJ) comes up and talks with her (their French is translated with English subtitles). Phil (EI), a snobbish, sniffing film critic, explains the subtext of the previous scene. Another clip is shown, with the two of them again on the rubbish dump, intercut with stock shots of war and violence. She is holding a Webb's Wonder lettuce this time, which explodes to end the film, and the critic analyzes the film before a special report on the filming of "Scott of the Antarctic."

Chris Conger (GC) reports from the film set, where Paignton Pier has been transformed into the South Pole. He interviews producer Gerry Schlick (EI), who explains that they are using twenty-eight thousand cubic feet of Wintrex, a new white foam rubber, as a substitute for real snow, along with sixteen thousand cubic U.S. furlongs of white paint with a special snow finish.

Director James McRettin (JC), drinking heavily, has trouble remembering which scene is being shot first; Kirk Vilb (MP) is starring as Lieutenant Scott, Terence Lemming (TJ) plays Ensign Oates, and Bowers is Scott's other assistant. Vanilla Hoare (CC) plays Miss Evans, but has trouble remembering her lines; she plays a scene in a trench while Vilb acts on boxes. She quits when they ask her to act out of the trench, and the director passes out drunk.

Vilb wants to fight a lion, even though there are no lions in the Antarctic, so the film becomes "Scott of the Sahara," and he is pulled across the sand on a dogsled.

Coming attractions show Vilb fighting a "lion," a fight between Oates and a twenty-foot-high electric penguin with tentacles, and Vanilla's clothes are torn off as she runs from a giant set of teeth pursuing her across the sand. She passes the Man with the Dinner Jacket (JC) at his desk, who says "And now for something completely different," and the "It's" Man says "It's"

Titles

Animation shows the foot stepping on several figures, leading up to Conrad Poohs and his Dancing Teeth. Conrad later opens a letter which travels backward to its sender (TJ).

As he leaves the post office, Eric Praline (JC) walks in to buy a fish license for his pet fish Eric from Mr. Last (MP). When he is turned down, he demands a statement from the Lord Mayor that he needs no such license, and the impossibly tall Mayor enters for the traditional signing of the exemption from the fish license.

The Mayor and his retinue then run onto a soccer field to play against a pro team. A Linkman (MP) interviews Cliff (GC) on sports, and the talk turns to China. This is followed by a match between the Bournemouth Gynecologists and the Watford Long John Silver Impersonators. The Linkman is struck by a sixteen-ton weight, and scenes of destruction are seen as the credits roll.

ALSO APPEARING: Carol Cleveland
Mrs. Idle

📽 Several changes were made in "Scott of the Antarctic"; a lunchtime interview with Gerry Schlick, in which he discusses making Evans a girl, was cut, and Lemming discusses Oates. Evans was originally to be pursued by a roll-top writing desk, rather than the set of teeth. Also cut was a scene where Bowers fights a dreaded Congolese ringing tarantula in the desert. From twenty feet away, it rings like a telephone and leaps up to his face. Bowers shoots it and it stops ringing.

📽 The twenty-foot penguin with tentacles was actually a model, about one foot high, that would light up and look electric. It was kept close to the camera in the foreground to appear huge; it was intercut with a lot of phony reverses.

📽 The football match originally involved the Bournemouth Automobile Association (with breeches, boots, and yellow crash helmets), rather than the Gynecologists.

Take That Lion Down

Shooting "Scott of the Sahara" had its share of good times, according to costumer Hazel Pethig, who had to help stage the fight with the lion. "We had footage of a real lion, we had somebody dressed up as a lion, and we had a stuffed lion. Getting a lion's costume wasn't too easy—I remember being totally dismayed! Very often, the costumes that they wore had to be ruined, by going into the sea or whatever, so I had to talk them into letting me use stuff, or find a way around it."

Carol Bares All

The only time Carol Cleveland ever balked at a Python request was when she was asked to appear topless in "Scott of the Sahara," but she was able to negotiate a compromise with the group.

"Only once did they ask me to do something I didn't want to do, and it wasn't for fear of doing it," says Cleveland. "They did ask me to appear topless in the 'Scott of the Sahara' sketch, when I run toward the camera and my clothes are ripped off by the cacti one bit at a time. First my coat comes off, the next cacti rips my dress off, leaving me in my underwear. Then, my bra comes off, which it did do, but the idea was that I continue running toward the camera as it comes off, and that is what I balked at.

"I said 'All right, it can come off, but I'm not running toward the camera.' So in fact, you see me running away from the camera. That was in the early days and I was a little bit shy, I suppose, compared to what I am now. We were on a beach that was choc-a-block with people, tourists! It was in the height of the summer, and this beach was choc-a-block with all these people gawking. I thought, 'There is no way I'm going to do this!' If they'd made that request later on, in the second or third series—I was much braver by then and I might have done it. But not at the beginning. That was the only time I refused any request."

" 'Scott of the Sahara' was wonderful to do," recalls Hazel Pethig. "I remember Carol losing her coat and bra on the cactus; I rushed in to cover her up and ruined the shot! Everybody shrieked with laughter and found it very funny—partly because they had to redo it. So, they got to see Carol losing her clothes all over again!"

Carol confirms that the well-meaning Python costumer actually caused her to do it twice.

"Yes, Hazel rushed into the shot and screwed it up!" says Cleveland. "She knew I was so nervous about this, and she was so sweet. She was there to cover my blushes, but she dashed off so quickly that we were still doing the shot! I was away toward the sea and John's in the foreground sitting at this desk. He looks at the camera and says 'And now for something completely different,' you see me running behind him and suddenly there's Hazel running after me! 'Cut, cut!' And we had to do it all over again! And there was me, thinking 'I'll do this once, but that's it!' Thanks to Hazel, I had to do it all over again!"

To Bee or Not to Bee

The "Fish License" sketch also has a song that was not performed in the TV show, involving the philosophical implications of half a bee. It is heard on *Monty Python's Previous Record,* and is the only solo John Cleese musical performance in all of the Python TV shows. Cleese says he is actually quite proud of the song.

"I started to sing 'Eric the Half a Bee' in the stage show, when we did our British tour, because I was bored stiff with the stupid 'Silly Walk' sketch. They made me do that, and I lost 'Eric the Half a Bee,' which I love doing!" Cleese enthuses.

"It's a funny little sad song with Eric, about this bee that had been bisected. It was a little philosophical song about whether half a bee can be, or philosophically can not be.

"Eric and I had a couple of characters we liked—mine was called Praline. He was the guy who went into the Whizzo Chocolate Company. We got fascinated by Praline when we did the parrot sketch—it was the same character. Eric had a strange man called Badger. We had an interminable sketch we did. I can never remember if it got in one of the shows or not. We thought it was funny, but we didn't think the audience was very interested," he laughs.

Inside Sports

Filming sketches on location always drew interesting reactions—or lack of reactions—sparked by costumes or props.

"The great one was when we were doing the Long John Silver Impersonators football match against the Gynecologists," Michael Palin recalls. "In those days, of course, the BBC had no buses, let alone limousines, to take us to the filming—we just got there any way we could. John and Graham never had a car, so I was always giving lifts to Graham, and sometimes to John.

"I had a Mini, which is about the smallest car made, and John and Graham are two of the largest people made. So, there were four of us squashed in there, complete with Long John Silver outfits, because we'd been to Television Centre and gotten dressed for the filming.

"As we passed a bank, I thought I should go in and cash a check—when I'm filming, I never have any time for mundane things like that. So I went to the bank, and they came along as well.

"So, these four Long John Silvers came up to the girl at the counter, and she looked up. I said 'Can I cash a check?' She said 'Yes, if you've got a credit card.' Not a single mention of the fact that we all had parrots on our shoulders and one leg!"

FX

His solo films have given Terry Gilliam more than a nodding acquaintance with special effects; work on *12 Monkeys, Baron Munchausen, Brazil,* and *Time Bandits* have all involved some rather heavy FX sequences. Although the Python TV shows seldom required much in the way of FX, occasional elements like a twenty-foot electric penguin with tentacles gave Gilliam a taste of what he would eventually be contending with, keeping an eye on the budget while being creative.

"It's all in the *way* the effects are done," Gilliam explains. "Whatever we're doing, I always try to decide whether we can afford it. If we can't, I try to think of a way to avoid the problem. When we write the effects, we have to be naïve enough to think it's all quite easy.

"It's odd, but the effects that are usually the most difficult to do tend to look the most ordinary, while the ones that look the most spectacular are often the easiest. Depending on what the special effect is, sometimes we can achieve it with just the right sound effect, as opposed to an elaborate visual.

"The easiest thing in *Time Bandits* was the giant, because there was nothing special about it," Gilliam says, explaining that they just placed a camera on the ground and aimed it upwards at the normal-sized actor. "We just had to choose the right angle and lens, and shoot it at the right speed. Other shots, like Kevin jumping into the time holes, were extremely complicated shots that look quite ordinary."

Gilliam found the scenes with the giant among the easiest to shoot in his own **Time Bandits,** *using a normal-sized actor and filming from very low camera angles. Photo copyright Handmade Films/Time Bandits.*

Show 24 — How Not to Be Seen

Recorded as Series 2, Show 6—Prod. #60528

An Advertising Director (JC) is reading *Chinese for Advertising Men* as Mr. S. Frog (EI) enters his office through a window. The Director is disturbed about his new campaign for Conquistador Coffee; he has used the word "leprosy" instead of "coffee" as part of a joke/sales campaign. He has come up with "Conquistador Coffee brings a new meaning to the word 'vomit,'" and the introductory offer of a free dead dog with every jar. Although sales have plummeted, people remember the name.

A seaside scene is shown while lush music plays, but a phonograph record playing the music sticks. The Man in the Dinner Jacket (JC) also becomes stuck on "And now for something completely—pletely—pletely different"; the "It's" Man (MP) says "It's" as the Titles roll, though they become stuck as well.

Nineteen twenty-nine. British Prime Minister Ramsey MacDonald (MP) enters his office, exclaiming, "My, it's hot in here," and takes off his clothes, under which he wears a bra and panties.

Exchange and Mart editor Mr. Glans (JC) is visited by Mr. Bee (TJ), who is applying for a job as assistant editor. Glans tries to bargain for his briefcase, umbrella, and chair in exchange for the job, though Bee initially resists, to Glans's bewilderment ("Not for sale? What does that mean?"). He finally trades everything, and bargains with his animated secretary, Miss Johnson, for two coffees and a biscuit.

Unfortunately, the animated secretary falls victim to the International Chinese Communist Conspiracy. The Red hordes fill her office, but she is saved by Uncle Sam, who does a commercial for American defense. Animated commercials follow for Crelm Toothpaste, using two cars, and another ad for Shrill petrol.

John and Jasmina (JC and CC) enter a room to discover her father, Sir Horace Partridge, dead. They discuss repercussions of the local train schedules on the crime, and Lady Partridge (GC) arrives, equally concerned about the murder and the trains. Police Inspector Davis (TJ) and young Tony (MP) both enter, discussing train schedules. Tony is tripped up by his confusion over the details of the schedules, and is forced to confess to the murder

 142

for the old man's seat reservations. It is all revealed as an exerpt from a West End play. "It All Happened on the 11:20 from Hainault" by railroad playwright Neville Shunt (TJ); his play expresses the human condition in terms of British Rail. His works are analyzed by Gavin Millarrrrrrrr (JC): "The point is frozen, the beast is dead . . ."

An Interviewer (MP) then discusses the works of and introduces a chat with writer/dentist Martin Curry (GC), conducted by Matthew Padget (TJ). He tries not to mention Curry's enormous incisors, for all of Curry's actors have foot-long front teeth, as shown in clips from his productions of *The Twelve Caesars* and *Trafalgar*. Curry tries futilely to drink a glass of water.

Arthur Crackpot (EI) is President and God of Crackpot Religions, Ltd., the first religion with free gifts, such as tea trolleys, a three-piece lounge suite, and a luxury caravan; a Nude Organist (TG) plays a fanfare.

A Priest (JC) oversees Mrs. Collins (MP) choose the correct hymn number, and she wins the entire Norwich City Council. Modern methods of conversion are shown. Archbishop Gumby (MP) bashes bricks together, while Archbishop Shabby raises polecats. Also shown are Archbishop Nudge (EI), Naughty Religions, Ltd. (JC), the Popular Religions, Ltd. (GC), the No Questions Asked Religion (MP), the Lunatic Religion (TJ), and Cartoon Religions, Ltd. Religious animation follows.

Next is H.M. Government Public Service Film 42, Para 6: "How Not to Be Seen." Although the participants are usually hidden, most of them are found through a liberal use of explosives. Back in a studio, a Presenter (MP) talks with Ludovic Grayson (TJ), who is inside a filing cabinet so that he cannot be seen. He is eventually blown up as well.

Jackie Charleton and the Tonettes sing "Yummy, Yummy, Yummy, I've Got Love in My Tummy" from inside crates and boxes, though the lights and camerawork continue normally, as in *Top of the Pops,** and the credits roll.

Following the credits, a BBC 1 slide is shown, and an announcer says that for those persons who have just missed Monty Python, here it is again— and the entire show is recapped with scores of clips shown in about thirty seconds.

*A British version of *American Bandstand*.

ALSO APPEARING: Carol Cleveland

The show was originally to start with a strip by Stanley Baldwin (instead of Ramsay MacDonald) immediately following the titles.

The rehearsal script lists the song to be performed by Jackie Charleton and the Tonettes as "Don't Treat Me Like a Child."

The quick reprise of the entire show was in the script of Show 19.

Cut from the show was the Arthur Crackpot handbook, with such entries as "Blessed are the wealthy, for they have the earth," "It is as easy for a rich man to enter heaven as anybody—if not easier," and "Sell all you have and give it to the rich."

More Frost Revenge

Although none of them claim responsibility for it, the Pythons admit to an interesting stunt that apparently actually happened. Due to a still-unexplained mixup, David Frost's home telephone number was used in a sketch, and Frost was soon troubled by numerous phone calls from Python viewers.

"We did it because, when we started, Frost had John under contract to do a TV show, as he had Ronnie Corbett and Ronnie Barker, because they were all on *The Frost Report*," says Eric Idle. "Because he had John under contract, there had to be some sort of agreement to allow him to do Python. I don't know what they agreed, but obviously a contract like that isn't worth very much if somebody doesn't want to appear—it can't be enforced. I think Frost just took a wider view, that John was in his own area now."

Michael Palin claims he doesn't actually remember the circumstances behind the Frost phone number, but doesn't deny that it happened. "I think it was outside a church, when we did Crackpot Religions. 'If you're tired of life, come in here, if you're not, ring ***-****.' It was a Frost joke, he used to use that a lot on his show: 'I was passing a

church the other day, had a wonderful sign, "If you're tired of sin, come in here." Somebody had written underneath "If you're not, ring Blackman 4271." ' There it is. Somebody put his number there when we did it, but I didn't know it was his. I'm certain. I promise I didn't."

Strangely enough, there was an effort to in-clude Frost as a seventh Python—an effort insti-gated by Frost that went no further. "Frost seriously tried to get himself into Python. We'd started writ-ing, and he rang up and said 'Can I be in it?' We said 'No, piss off!' " Idle laughs. " 'No, seriously, I could just do jokes, I could link it, it'd be wonder-ful!' 'No, no, piss off David, you're not in this.' "

Show 25 — Spam

Recorded as Series 2, Show 1—Prod. #60129

Opening titles and credits are shown for *The Black Eagle,* a swashbuckling pirate adventure that begins with "In 1742, the Spanish Empire lay in ruins . . ." As pirates pull their lifeboat onto the beach, they drag it past the Man in the Dinner Jacket (JC) at his desk as he says "And now for something com-pletely different." The "It's" Man adds "It's"

Titles

Beginning with the caption "In 1970, the British Empire lay in ruins," a Hungarian Gentle-man (JC) visits a Tobacconist (TJ), and attempts to use a phrasebook in which phrases asking for ciga-rettes and matches come out as "I will not buy this record, it is scratched," and "My hovercraft is full of eels," as well as several naughtier phrases. The Tobacconist tries out a phrase on the Hungarian, and is punched out. When a Policeman (GC) runs through town to the shop, the Hungarian tells him "You have beautiful thighs," "Drop your panties, Sir William, I cannot wait until lunchtime," and "My nipples explode with delight."

Alexander Yahlt (MP), publisher of the English-Hungarian phrasebook, is put on trial. The Prosecu-tor (EI) explains that the phrase "Can you direct me to the station?" is translated as "Please fondle my bum." Yahlt pleads incompetence, and a Police Con-stable (GC) asks for an adjournment, followed by stock film of Women's Institute applause. Testi-mony is heard from a Page Three girl* cutout, Abigail Tesler, along with newspaper photo blow-ups of Judge Maltravers (TJ) and Q.C.† Nelson Bedowes (JC).

Animation follows in which a protest against the Judge turns into a student demonstration, and a large police helmet turns into a planet for a *2001* parody. The planet turns into a soccer ball for the next sketch.

"World Forum" sees the unctuous Presenter (EI) greet guests Karl Marx (TJ), Che Guevara, Lenin, and Mao Tse-tung; they are all questioned on En-glish football. Karl Marx plays in the final round for a lounge suite.

Ypres, 1914. "In 1914, the Balance of Power lay in ruins . . ." leads to a World War I trench, where Jenkins (EI) talks to Sergeant Jackson (MP) about his family, but the floor manager (TJ) has to clear the set of unnecessary actors, which include a Viking, male mermaid, Greek Orthodox priest, a sheikh, milkman, and a nun. The next caption reads "Knickers 1914," and the director also re-moves an astronaut from the set before restarting the sketch.

In a museum, a sign identifies "Italian Masters of the Renaissance." As two Art Critics (EI and MP) wan-der through the gallery, the Bumpkin (TJ) from Con-stable's *Hay Wain* talks to the figures in a six foot by ten foot Titian canvas, including a Cherub (TG) and Solomon (GC), who reports a walkout by the Impres-sionists. The animated characters from various works go out on strike and picket, while an Auction-eer from Sotheby's (JC) auctions off the works with-out their famous figures, including Vermeer's *Lady Who Used to Be at a Window* and *Nothing at Bay* by Landseer.

The "Ypres" sketch resumes as a Major (GC) in-terrupts Jenkins, the Sarge, Kipper (TG), and the armless Padre (JC). He says there are only provi-sions for four, and they must choose the one who is to die. After drawing straws, doing "dip, dip, dip, my little ship," and scissors-paper-stone and

---

*A photo of a scantily clad or topless girl that appears on page three of London's tabloid newspapers.
†Queen's counsel.

144

The Pythons themselves played all the parts in "World Forum/Communist Quiz" when it was presented live onstage. From the left: Gilliam as Mao Tse-tung, Palin as Che Guevara, Idle as the presenter, Cleese as Lenin, and Jones as Karl Marx, the lucky contestant. In the background of this dress rehearsal, a portion of the lyrics to the "Bruces' Philosophers' Song" can be seen. Photo copyright KHJ.

The title page of the script credits the show to "Alfie Bass, Lew Hoard, and Deidre Sinclair."

The rehearsal script shows very different material intended for the show. "Gumby Flower Arranging" was to lead into "Herbert Mental/Birdwatchers Eggs" and "Pigeon Fancier Racing" (from Show 26), then "Page Three Newspaper Photo Blowups" (Show 24), then into a much longer Sergeant Duckie and "Bing Tiddle Tiddle Bong" (Show 22). "Spam" was not originally intended for this show.

choosing the Major each time, the Padre is forced to volunteer. He gives a long, patriotic speech before he is rushed to the Royal Hospital for Overacting. A Doctor (GC) tours the hospital, where there are several King Rats in Casualty Pantomime, and the crowded Richard the Third Ward, along with several animated Hamlets.

Animated bombs and flowers lead into "Flower Arrangement" with D. P. Gumby (MP), who suggests arranging begonias, tulips, irises, and freesias.

As a Man and his Wife (EI and GC) are lowered by wires into a café, the Waitress (TJ) reads a menu that consists almost entirely of Spam dishes. Groups of Vikings scattered around the café sing about Spam and the Hungarian enters, but is quickly thrown out.

In a studio, a Historian (MP) discusses Vikings, and back in the café they are singing about Spam. The closing caption reads "In 1970, *Monty Python's Flying Circus* lay in ruins, and then the words on the screen said: The End."

The closing credits all involve Spam and/or other breakfast foods, and a quick shot is seen of Marx and Lenin in bed together.

ALSO APPEARING: The Fred Tomlinson Singers

Notes: Instructions for Terry Gilliam's Animations

Terry was given a rather free hand, with the script often just noting which bits were to be linked. Below is an example of the script directions given to him to link the "Overacting" sketch to "Gumby Flower Arranging":

> *He opens door; from here Gilliam's fevered, not to say feverish, imagination leads us into the whacky world of award-winning graphic humor, where comedy is king in a no-holds-barred joke jamboree that'll have you throwing yourself into the Thames.*
>
> *But even this jolly jokesmith from Oriental (sic) College must control himself and provide us with a link into "Flower Arrangement."*
>
> *Delicate music. Studio set. Flowers in vases, etc. Super caption "Flower Arrangement" then another caption "Introduced by D. P. Gumby."*

The Black Eagle

Starting the show with a fictitious historical film, *The Black Eagle,* the Pythons apparently managed to fool audiences who had tuned in expecting to see *Monty Python's Flying Circus*—which was, of course, the idea. As the series continued, the opening titles were often shown later and later (and in at least one show, they weren't included at all).

"Anything to confuse and mislead, really, with the eventual notion that it made things more interesting, and that we weren't starting in the same old way," Chapman recalled. "To actually do almost an entire program where nothing had been announced—that would have been an aim, I suppose.

"Certainly, we took it quite a long way with the smuggling sequence. I even had one or two writing friends changing channels, just to see whether they were on the right channel—that was nice! Of course, it was obvious when they saw John at the desk."

Show 26—Royal Episode 13

Recorded as Series 2, Show 13—Prod. #67550

The Man in the Dinner Jacket (JC) stands, announcing that he won't be saying "And now for something completely different" this week because the Queen would be tuning in sometime during the show. However, he emphasizes that everything else will remain the same.

A new set of regal Titles are used, and "God Save the Queen" is substituted for the usual theme.

Royal Episode Thirteen. First Spoof: A coal mine in Llandarog Carmarthen sees Welsh coal miners argue violently and brawl over such historical trivia as the date of the Treaty of Utrecht (ratified in 1713), Greek architecture, and the Treaty of Westphalia. The arrival of a Frightfully Important Person (JC) is of no help, while a Newsreader (MP) reports on other miners' disputes across the nation, as well as the Disgusting Objects International at Wembley.

The "Toad Elevating Moment" features the Host (TJ) interviewing Mr. Pudifoot (GC), who says things in a very roundabout way. After he leaves indignantly, the next three guests include Mr. . . . Ohn. . . Ith (EI), who speaks only the endings of words, Mr. J . . . Sm . . . (JC), who speaks only the beginnings of words, and . . . Oh . . . . . . I . . . (MP), who speaks only the middles of words. Together the three of them say "Good evening."

Commercials feature two animated dragons demonstrating the maiden-attracting power of Crelm toothpaste; Fibro-Val detergent is used on furniture in a washing machine (by EI); and a young couple romp through a beautiful, animated, Disney-like forest while wearing surgical garments, and it becomes a truss commercial.

"Fish Club" begins, with its Host (MP) demonstrating how to feed a goldfish, based on the recommendations of the Board of Irresponsible People. As sausages, soup, and such are dropped into the fishbowl, he is dragged offstage, and a disclaimer is read.

As sounds of young lovers are heard in the woods, a Birdwatcher (MP) has his eggs stolen by Herbert Mental (TJ), who collects birdwatchers' eggs. Interviewing himself in front of his collection, he explains that he also collects butterfly hunters, and likes to race pigeon fanciers. He is shown racing the latter through a field, while a whole flock of pigeon fanciers (all in trenchcoats and caps) wander through Trafalgar Square.

A series of brief animations follow, including Spiny Norman, plus elaborate titles for the "Insurance" sketch. Martin (EI), a man interested in buying life insurance, has collected twelve gallons of urine to conform with their requirements, but Feldman (JC), the insurance agent, is less than impressed.

Suddenly the Queen tunes in and the actors and audience stand, but before they can deliver the first royal joke, she quickly switches over to the *News at Ten,* where the actual newsreader, Reg Bosanquet,* stands.

At St. Pooves Hospital, the heavily bandaged, crippled patients are called into formation by a

*A newscaster on the *News at Ten.*

Drill Instructor/Doctor (JC) and given a rigorous workout. Another Doctor (EI) explains their system of A.R.T., or Active Recuperation Techniques, in which the patients are there to serve the doctors— although the seriously ill do sport. Brief looks at other hospitals where doctors' conditions are improving follow, including St. Nathan's Hospital for Young Attractive Girls Who Aren't Particularly Ill, and a Hospital for Linkmen that introduces a very brief mountaineering sketch.

Next is the "Exploding Version of the Blue Danube."

In the darkness of a dormitory at a girls' public school, a man searches for Agnes, though the

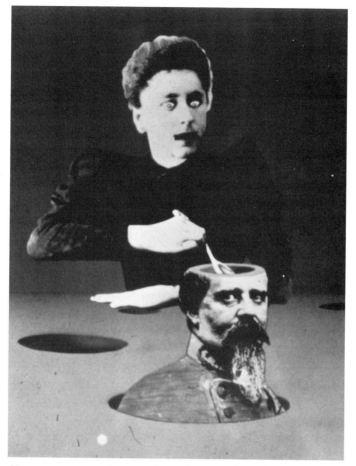

Everyone wanted to get into the act when the Pythons set their sights on cannibalism; Terry Gilliam was quite happy to tackle the subject with accompanying animation. Copyright Python Productions Ltd.

dorm is entirely occupied by men. A still follows promoting "The Naughtiest Girl in the School," starring the men of the 14th Marine Command.

Via stock World War II footage, the girls of Oakdean High School reenact the Battle of Normandy. Then, inside a modern-day submarine, a group of Pepperpots, including Capt. Mrs. Spimm (GC) and Mrs. Lt. Edale (JC), give orders to put the kettle on, feed the cat, and fire Mrs. Midshipman Nesbit. An animated Nesbit is fired through the torpedo tube. A link shows a Man (TG) with a stoat through his head, stock footage of Women's Institute applause, and a Newsreader (MP).

The "Lifeboat" sketch features five men (GC, JC, EI, TJ, and MP) adrift, reverting to cannibalism, and

giving their dinner orders to a passing Waitress (CC). Animated cannibals follow, along with a letter of complaint from Captain B. J. Smethwick in a white wine sauce, with shallots, mushrooms, and garlic, before the action shifts to a mortuary.

A Man (JC) whose mother has just died visits an Undertaker (GC), who convinces the Man they should eat her as his Assistant (EI) lights the oven. The disgusted audience boos, hisses, and rushes the stage to attack them. They are saved when the credits roll to "God Save the Queen," and everyone stands at attention.

ALSO APPEARING:
Carol Cleveland
Ian Davidson

📋 "International Chess" and "Life-Saving" was to follow the "Exploding Blue Danube," which then turns into a "Critic" sketch before returning to the "Girls Dormitory."

📋 This is the only one of the forty-five programs that was never rerun in its entirety in England, though not entirely because of the rampant cannibalism toward the end of the show. In fact, it was reportedly the royalty theme that influenced the BBC's decision.

📋 The cannibalism material, particularly the "Undertaker" sketch, caused its share of contro-

versy at the BBC, however. In fact, as Graham Chapman recalled, the only way they were permitted to perform the sketch was if they allowed the audience to charge onstage and attack them at the end—which they did.

Explosive Humor

One of the trademarks of Python seems to combine comedy and explosions. The group has blown up all sorts of animals, buildings, and people, but one bit of blasting stands out for Eric Idle.

"The best was the 'Exploding Version of the Blue Danube'—I liked that a lot. They absolutely had to do it live. It was spot on, and brilliant! We did it in one take, which was great, because we couldn't afford another one," Idle says, laughing.

Censored

An entire book could be devoted to Monty Python's battles with the censors—and indeed, one has, the excellent *Monty Python: The Case Against,* by Robert Hewison.

During the first part of the first series, the group escaped detection by the BBC, for the most part. In fact, the only BBC reaction to the first shows came from Tom Sloane, then head of light entertainment.

"His first comments to me, after seeing the first two shows, were 'Does John Cleese have to say "bastard" twice?'" recalls BBC producer Barry Took. "I said 'Well, yes, if he chooses to. That's the whole nature of this program. He's such an intelligent man, he would not have said it had he not thought it artistically correct.' He said 'Oh, that's fine,' and that was the only true criticism I'd had at the beginning.

"They were much, much enjoyed by the very top people at the BBC, they thought it was a terrific show. Even though it wasn't immediately popular, particularly amongst the lower ranks of the hierarchy, they persisted with it and booked a new series, because they thought it was really enchanting comedy, just the sort of thing they thought the BBC should be doing around that time."

In general, however, by the second season of Python, things were heating up, because the group was taking more chances, and because the BBC was starting to pay attention to them.

"By the second or third season, the BBC had seen much more, and were a little vigilant," says Michael Palin. "But at the start, we could virtually do almost anything. We were on late Saturdays, and also things were fairly easygoing then. Television had not been taken by the scruff of the neck and made to perform like it is at the moment. Hugh Carlton-Greene was the director-general of the BBC, and had a very artistic view of things—creative people were always right. So, it was very good!"

The Pythonic
Verses

Monty Python's Guide to Life

Accounting

"Well, it'd certainly make chartered accountancy a much more interesting job."

Government spokesman, on a proposal to tax sex (EI)

Ambition

"He was such a pretty baby, always so kind and gentle . . . really considerate to his mother. Not at all the kind of person you'd expect to pulverize their opponent into a bloody mess of flesh and raw bone, spitting teeth and fragments of gum into a ring which had become one man's hell and Ken's glory."

Mrs. Nellie Air-Vent (TJ), mother of boxer Ken Clean-Air System

Analysis (political)

"This is largely as I predicted, except that the Silly Party won. I think this is mainly due to the number of votes cast."

Norman, TV Commentator (MP)

Aptitude

"Our experts describe you as an appallingly dull fellow, unimaginative, timid, lacking in initiative, spineless, easily dominated, no sense of humor, tedious company, and irrepressibly drab and awful; and whereas in most professions, these would be considerable drawbacks, in chartered accountancy, they're a positive boon!"

Vocational Guidance Counselor (JC)

Attitudes (societal)

"What a lot of people don't realize is that a mouse, once accepted, can fulfill a useful role in society. Indeed, there are examples throughout history of famous men known to have been mice."

Linkman (MP), "The World Around Us"

Attitudes (sociological)

"The whole problem of these senile delinquents lies in their complete rejection of the values of contemporary society. They've seen their children grow up to become accountants, stockbrokers, and sociologists, and they begin to wonder—is it really AAAGGHH . . ."

Sociologist as he falls through a manhole (EI)

BBC

"I'm mainly in comedy. I'd like to be in program planning, but unfortunately, I've got a degree."

BBC employee (JC)

Belief

"I believe in peace and bashing two bricks together."

Archbishop Gumby (MP)

Brains (size):

"If we increase the size of the penguin until it is the same height as the man, and then compare the relative brain sizes, we now find that the penguin's brain is still smaller. But—and this is the point—it is larger than it was!"

Prof. Ken Rosewall (GC)

Breath

"I use a body rub called halitosis. It makes my breath seem sweet."

Mr. Gumby (MP)

British Naval Encounters

"They was too clever for the German fleet."
Prof. R. J. Gumby (MP), on why he thinks the Battle of Trafalgar was fought near Yorkshire

British Navy

"There is no cannibalism in the British Navy, absolutely none, and when I say none, I mean there is a certain amount."

Sir John Cunningham (GC)

Bullfighting

"A bull is heavy, violent, abusive, and aggressive, with four legs and great sharp teeth—whereas a bullfighter is only a small greasy Spaniard."

Narrator of "Probe" (EI)

Business Practices (sound)

"If that idea of yours isn't worth a pound, I'd like to know what is! The only trouble is, you gave me the idea before I'd given you the pound, and that's not good business!"

Merchant Banker (JC)

Camel-Spotting

"The dromedary has one hump, and a camel has a refreshment car, buffet, and ticket collector."

A Camel/Train-Spotter (EI)

Celebrity

"Why is it the world never remembers the name of Johann Gambolputty de von Ausfernschpledenschlittcrasscrenbonfriediggerdingledangledonglebursteinvonknackerthrasherapplebangerhorowitzticolensicgranderknottyspelltinklegrandlichgrumbelmeyerspellerwasserkurstlichhimbleeisenbahnwagen-

gutenabenabendbitteeinnurnburgebratwurstlegers-
purtenmitzweimacheluberhundsfutgumberaber-
schonendankerkalbsfleischmittleraucher Von Haupt-
kopt of Ulm?."

Arthur Figgis (GC)

Cement

"I think cement is more interesting than people think."

Prof. Enid Gumby (JC)

Choices

"Your life or your lupines!"

Dennis Moore (JC)

Citizens (senior)

"We have a lot of trouble with these oldies. Pension day's the worst—they go mad! As soon as they get their hands on their money, they blow it all on milk, bread, tea, a tin of meat for the cat . . ."

Policeman (GC)

Class Struggle

"They should attack the lower classes, first with bombs and rockets to destroy their homes, and then when they run helpless into the street, mow them down with machine guns. And then, of course, release the vultures. I know these views aren't popular, but I have never thought of popularity."

Stockbroker (JC)

Communist Subversion

"Using this diagram of a tooth to represent any small country, we can see how international communism works, by eroding away from the inside. When one country or tooth falls victim to international communism, the others soon follow. In dentistry, this is known as the Domino Theory."

Uncle Sam (ANIMATED)

Consumer Education

"If only the general public would take more care

when buying sweeties, it would reduce the number of man-hours lost to the nation, and they would spend less time having their stomachs pumped and sitting around in public lavatories."

Police Supt. Parrot (GC)

Convalescence

"I know some hospitals where you get the patients lying around in bed, sleeping, resting, recuperating, convalescing. Well, that's not the way we do things here! If you fracture your tibia here, you keep quiet about it!"

Sgt. Doctor, St. Pooves (JC)

Crime (statistics)

"If there were fewer robbers, there wouldn't be so many of them."

Anonymous Vicar (JC)

Crimonology

"It's easy for us to judge Dinsdale Piranha too harshly. After all, he only did what most of us simply dream of doing. A murderer is only an extroverted suicide."

Criminologist (GC)

Culinary Experiences

"When people place a nice choc-y in their mouth, they don't want their cheeks pierced."

Police Inspector (JC)

Culture

"One day you'll realize there's more to life than culture! There's dirt, and smoke, and good honest sweat!"

Ken (EI) to his playwright/father

Danger

"There's nothing more dangerous than a wounded mosquito."

Roy Spim (EI)

Definitions

"Your cat is suffering from what we vets haven't found a word for yet."

Veterinarian (GC)

Diagnosis

"There's nothing wrong with you that an expensive operation can't prolong."

Surgeon (GC) to Mr. Notlob

Explosions

"Exploding is a perfectly normal medical phenomenon. In many fields of medicine nowadays, a dose of dynamite can do a world of good."

Doctor (GC)

Flutes

"You blow there, and move your fingers up and down here."

Alan (GC), on how to play the flute

Heroes (identification of)

"Is it a stockbroker?" "Is it a quantity surveyor?" "Is it a churchwarden?" "No! It's Bicycle Repair Man!"

Three Passersby (TJ, GC, JC)

Household Hints

"Now here is a reminder about leaving your radio on during the night: leave your radio on during the night."

Voiceover Announcer (EI)

Ichthyology

"Contrary to what most people think, the goldfish has a ravenous appetite... So, once a week, give your goldfish a really good meal. Here's one specially recommended by the Board of Irresponsible People. First, some cold consommé or gazpacho, then some sausages, greens, potatoes, bread, gravy..."

Chairman, Board of Irresponsible People (MP)

Image (political)

"I don't want you to think of the Wood Party as a lot of middle-aged men who like hanging around on ropes."

Rt. Hon. Lambert Warbeck (GC)

Ingratitude

"When you're walking home tonight and some homicidal maniac comes after you with a bunch of loganberries, don't come crying to me."

Sgt. Major (JC)

Insurance

"We can guarantee you that not a single armored division will get done over for, say, fifteen bob a week."

Vercotti Bros. (TJ and MP) to the Colonel

Intelligence

"Would Albert Einstein ever have hit on the theory of relativity if he hadn't of been clever?"

Host (JC), "Frontiers of Medicine"

Interruptions

"We interrupt this program to annoy you and generally irritate you."

Adrian Voiceover, BBC Announcer

Investments

"I would bring back hanging, and go into rope."

Merchant Banker (JC)

Irony

"It's funny, isn't it, how I can go through life, as I have, disliking bananas and being indifferent to cheese, but still be able to eat and enjoy a banana and cheese sandwich like that?"

Mr. Pither (MP)

Isolation

"That's the trouble with living halfway up a cliff—you feel so cut off . . ."

Frank, a Hermit (EI)

Justice (dental)

"Funny, isn't it, how naughty dentists always make that one fatal mistake?"

Arthur Lemming, British Dental Assoc. (EI)

Justice (traffic)

"Parking offense, schmarking offense—we must leave no stone unturned!"

Mr. Bartlett, Solicitor (JC)

Law and Order

"Customs men should be armed, so they can kill people carrying more than two hundred cigarettes."

Housewife (EI)

Lobbying

"We're in it for the lobbying, you know . . . We love lobbying."

Political Groupie (EI)

Logic

"The point is frozen, the beast is dead, what is the difference?"

Gavin Millarrrrrrrr (JC)

Machismo

"A man can run and run for year after year, till he realizes that what he's runnin' from is hisself. A man's gotta do what a man's gotta do, and there ain't no sense in runnin'. Now, you gotta turn, and you gotta fight, and you gotta hold your head up high. Now you go back in there, son, and be a man. Walk tall."

Cowboy in Black (JC) to Arthur Putey

Marksmanship

"An entirely new strain of sheep! Killer sheep, that can not only hold a rifle, but is also a first-class shot!"

Professor (EI)

Media

"I object to all this sex on the television. I mean, I keep falling off!"

Anonymous Woman (GC)

Medicine (preventive)

"Flu? Perhaps they've eaten too much fresh fruit."

Sgt. Major (JC)

Mime

"When Beethoven went deaf, the mynah bird just used to mime."

Mrs. Thing (GC)

Mollusks

"The randiest of the gastropods is the limpet. This hot-blooded little beast, with its tent-like shell, is always on the job. Its extramarital activities are something startling. Frankly, I don't see how the female limpet finds time to adhere to the rock face."

Mollusk Documentary Producer (JC)

Monty Python

"It's all a bit zany, a bid madcap . . . Frankly, I don't fully understand it myself. The kids seem to like it . . ."

BBC Employee (JC)

Morale

"I abhor the implication that the Royal Navy is a haven for cannibalism. It is well known that we now have the problem relatively under control, and that it is the RAF who now suffer the most casualties in this area."

Letter from Capt. B. J. Smethicke in a white wine sauce, with shallots, mushrooms, and garlic

Mountaineering

"Kilimanjaro is a pretty tricky climb. Most of it's up, until you reach the very, very top, and then it tends to slope away rather sharply."

Sir George Head, OBE (JC)

Nature

"I always preferred the outdoor life . . . hunting . . . shooting . . . fishing . . . getting out there with a gun and slaughtering a few of God's creatures."

Bevis the Barber (MP)

Nostalgia

"Kids were very different then. They didn't have their heads filled with all this Cartesian Dualism . . ."

April Simnel, Piranha Bros. Neighbor (MP)

Opportunity

"Nowadays, the really blithering idiot can make anything up to ten thousand pounds a year if he's the head of some big industrial combine."

M. Brando, Bank Manager (GC)

Peripateia

"The thing about saying the wrong words is that A, I don't notice it, and B, sometimes orange water gibbon bucket and plastic."

Mr. Burrows (MP)

Pilotage

"I wouldn't fancy flying one of these sitting on the toilet. I mean, it'd take all the glamour out of being a pilot, wouldn't it? Flying around the world sitting on the toilet?"

Man in cockpit of Balpa Jet (GC)

Poetry

"A poet is essential for complete home comfort and all-year-round reliability at low cost."

Sales Manager, East Midlands Poet Board (JC)

Policy (culinary)

"Never kill a customer."

Head Waiter (MP) to the Cook

Principle

"I would only perform a scene in which there was full frontal nudity."

Vicar (JC)

Professionalism

"I thought it better to consult a man of some professional qualifications rather than rely on the possibly confused testimony of some passerby."

Reg Pither (MP), asking doctor for directions

Proust

"I don't think any of our contestants this evening have succeeded in encapsulating the intricacies of Proust's masterwork, so I'm going to award the first prize this evening to the girl with the biggest tits."

Arthur Me (TJ)

Punctuality

"I met my second wife at a second-wife swapping party. Trust me to arrive late."

Thompson (MP), Headwaiter

Purpose

"We must never forget that, if there was not one thing that was not on top of another thing, our society would be nothing more than a meaningless body of men gathered together for no good purpose."

President, Society for Putting Things on Top of Other Things (GC)

Responsibility (fiscal)

"Last year the government spent less on the Ministry of Silly Walks than it did on National Defense!"

Mr. Teabags (JC), Minister of Silly Walks

 154

Responsibility (of News Media)

"It's perfectly easy for someone just to come along here to the BBC and simply claim they have a bit to spare in the botty department. The point is, our viewers need proof!"

Interviewer (JC) to Arthur Frampton

Rhymes

"He seeks them here, he seeks them there,
He seeks those lupines everywhere."

Lord of Buckingham (TJ) on Dennis Moore

Romance

"Please excuse my wife. She may not be very beautiful, and she may have no money, and she may be talentless, boring, and dull, but on the other hand . . . Sorry, I can't think of anything."

Douglas (JC), Restaurant Patron

Sanitation

"To me, it's like a mountain—a vast bowl of pus!"

Restaurant Manager (EI), on a dirty fork received by a customer

Sanity

"There are a great many people in the country today who, through no fault of their own, are sane."

Rev. Arthur Belling (GC)

Sartre (Jean Paul)

"I personally think that Jean Paul's masterwork, *Rues à Liberté,* is an allegory of our search for commitment."

Mrs. Premise (JC)

Science (library)

"I don't believe that libraries should be drab places, where people sit in silence, and that's been the main reason for our policy of employing wild animals as librarians."

Library Board Member (GC)

Self-improvement

"Are you nervous? Irritable? Depressed? Tired of life? Keep it up!"

Enterprising Undertaker (TJ)

Shakespeare (William)

"*Toledo Tit Parade?* What sort of play is that?"

Sir Phillip Sydney (MP)

Slogans

"Adopt, adapt, and improve—motto of the Round Table."

Bandit at lingerie shop (JC)

Tactics (police)

"We at the Special Crimes Squad have been using wands for almost a year. You can make yourself invisible, you can defy time and space, and you can turn violent criminals into frogs—things you could never do with the old truncheons."

Policeman (MP)

Taxation

"I would tax Raquel Welch . . . and I've a feeling she'd tax me."

The "It's" Man (MP)

Tchaikovsky

"His head was about the same size as that of an extremely large dog, that is to say, two very small dogs, or four very large hamsters, or one medium-sized rabbit, if you count the whole of the body and not just the head."

Tchaikovsky Expert (GC)

Television

"It's not your bleeding high-browed plays that pull in the viewers, you know."

Mr. Birchenhall, BBC Spokesman (GC)

Tenacity

"Sheep are very dim. Once they get an idea into their head, there's no shifting it!"

Farmer (GC) to city neighbor

Toasts

"Buttocks up!"

Mr. Atkinson (GC)

Tracking

"A mosquito is a clever little bastard. You can track him for days and days, until you really get to know him like a friend."

Roy Spim (EI)

Unemployment

"Here we see a pantomime horse. It is engaged in a life-or-death struggle for a job at the merchant bank."

Voiceover for Nature Documentary (JC)

Unrest (labor)

"There's been a walkout in the Impressionists . . . Gainesborough's *Blue Boy* has brought out the eighteenth-century English portraits, the Flemish School is solid, and German woodcuts are at a meeting now."

Farmer (TJ) from Constable's *Hay Wain*

Urine

"No, you may not give urine instead of blood . . . We have quite enough of it without volunteers coming in donating it."

Doctor (JC)

Wit (failed)

"What's brown and sounds like a bell? Dung!"

Arthur Name (EI)

The Third Series

Aired Oct. 19 – Dec. 21, 1972, and Jan. 4 – Jan. 18, 1973

"I ALWAYS SAY GRAHAM and I really only wrote two totally original things in the whole third series. One was the 'Cleese Shop,' and the other was 'Dennis Moore,' " says John Cleese.

Easily bored, Cleese was already tiring of the TV show, and his enthusiasm was rapidly diminishing by the time of the third series.

"I wasn't even that keen to do the second half of the second season," he admits. "I felt we were repeating ourselves. But in retrospect, I think the others rather felt I was a troublemaker, that I wasn't a good member of the team. But I always said I wanted to do shows with 'em, I didn't want to marry 'em! I felt we were repeating our material, and had lost most of our originality. I slightly resisted the second half of the second series, I resisted the third series a bit, I resisted the second half of the third series even more, but I felt a bit steam-rollered by the others. I suppose they wanted to do it, and they felt it was five to one."

Regardless, some of the finest moments in Python are in the third series, with their experience making up for any lack of initial enthusiasm. Terry Gilliam created a new set of opening titles, and the bits leading into the openings were also altered.

"The titles always got a bit longer in each series," notes Terry Jones, who was noted for playing an organ fanfare, while completely nude, in unlikely locations. "In the first one, it was just Mike as the 'It's' Man; in the second series, we had John saying 'And now for something completely different,' followed by 'It's.' Then, only in the third series, we had the nude organist."

The nude man at the organ was originally seen in earlier shows—notably "Blackmail"—usually played by Terry Gilliam. It was Jones, complete with fright wig, that claimed the role for his own, however.

"We lost a lot of our inhibitions by dressing up and being silly in the street. But Terry Jones had very few inhibitions to start with," says Michael Palin. "When he played the nude organist, he was stark naked in these nice, decorous little country towns—places like Norwich, which is very nice and smart. And there was Terry, sitting on top of the hill by the castle, stark naked, playing his organ. It does wonders for the inhibitions."

Show 27 — Whicker's World

Recorded as Series 3, Show 5—Prod. #75749

"Njorl's Saga" (Iceland 1126) begins over an organ fanfare by a nude organist (TJ); the Man in the Dinner Jacket (JC) says "And now," the "It's" Man (MP) says "It's"

Titles

Michael Norman Randall (EI), a defendant in a murder trial accused of killing twenty different people on or about the morning of December 19, 1971, apologizes to the Judge (TJ), Prosecuting Attorney (JC), and Foreman of the Jury (MP) for dragging them in day after day to hear the private details of his petty atrocities. Several bandaged-up policemen sit by; they all cheer when the polite multiple murderer is given a suspended sentence, and all sing "For he's a jolly good felon."

An animated man in a cell sings ". . . Which nobody can deny," and vibrates until he falls apart. Animated detectives enter his body, travel throughout it, checking the spleen, trying to get out through the neck until food starts falling in on them.

"Njorl's Saga," Part II, is followed by a long introduction, and the exciting Icelandic Saga can't get started. Erik Njorl (TJ) rides twelve days to modern North Malden, which turns into a promotional film for the North Malden Icelandic Saga Society, as explained by the Mayor (MP). The next voiceover promises to conform more closely to twelfth-century Iceland. Njorl battles knights with letters on their chest spelling "Malden," while subliminal and overt messages advise "Invest in Malden," until the film is stopped.

"Njorl's Saga," Part III: In the earlier courtroom, everyone begins reading the "Call Erik Njorl" intro at the same time after a brief tirade about comedy shows by a BBC entertainment spokesman, Mr. Birchenall (GC). The defendant is brought in wearing a body cast, and Supt. Lufthansa (GC) reads the charges against him. Police Constable Pan Am (MP) testifies that Njorl assaulted him (MP's billy club breaks as he testifies); Njorl's head is taken off, and the animated detectives are still inside.

This turns into the "Stock Market Report." The Host (EI) slips into gibberish and non sequiturs until he is doused with water by the animated Mrs. Cutout.

Mrs. Cutout enters a launderette, where Beulah Premise (JC) and Mrs. Conclusion (GC) discuss burying the cat and putting budgies down. They discuss the Sartres and decide to phone them, looking up their number in the phone book and traveling to North Malden by raft (a sign reads "North Malden Welcomes Careful Coastal Craft"), and Whicker (EI) talks about North Malden.

"Njorl's Saga," Part IV: Mrs. Premise and Mrs. Conclusion search for Paris and meet Mrs. Betty-Muriel Sartre (MP) to ask the meaning of *Rues à Liberté;* a goat is there to eat his papers and keep the place straightened up.

"Whicker's World" features an island inhabited entirely by ex–international interviewers in pursuit of the impossible dream. They compete for the camera as the credits roll, with all of the names including the word "Whicker."

ALSO APPEARING: Mrs. Idle
Connie Booth
Rita Davies
Nigel Jones
Frank Williams

The title page reads "Starring Victor A. Lowndes and Alan A. Dale and introducing MIES VAN DER ROHE, the whacky architect who can't keep his hands off prestressed concrete."

The original script includes trailers for upcoming BBC shows used in Show 38 intended to follow the Whicker credits. The show was to end

with a brief "Njorl's Saga" in which Njorl throws a pie in his horse's face.

Ride 'em, Njorl!

Playing Erik Njorl proved to be less than fun, as Terry Jones discovered while filming the sequences on location. The trickiest part of the role involved the horseback riding. Although he had ridden once before in *The Complete and Utter History of Britain,* he hadn't considered the costume he would be wearing.

Jones notes that he did ride his own horse for the show, "and I fell off it, too! The bloody thing kept on bolting every time I'd get on it! I couldn't bend my legs in my boots and I was wearing an incredible amount of fur, so I was top-heavy!

"At the time I volunteered to do the part, I didn't think what it meant, that I was going to have all these furs on with this horse. And, I was allergic to horses as well. It was a *very* unpleasant day of filming."

A Pretty Girl is like a Pepperpot

Drag humor has long been a staple in British comedy, dating back before Shakespearean days, and the Pythons were quick to climb into dresses and wigs when the occasion demanded it. Depending on the types of women necessary, the group would recruit Carol Cleveland, Connie Booth, or other female supporting players ". . . when we wanted *real* tits! I suppose I could put it as bluntly as that," Michael Palin laughs.

"There were certain times when, if we wanted a grotesque woman, we'd use a Python. And if we wanted a real woman, we'd use one of the real women that we knew. And sometimes, I'm afraid it would be because they looked sexy, blonde, nice and curvy . . . Other times, we couldn't actually get the same humor out of it by having one of us play the woman.

"Similarly, if we tried to use a middle-aged housewife to play the kind of parts Terry Jones played, it would just never work. People say 'Oohh, you were really nasty about women then,' except it

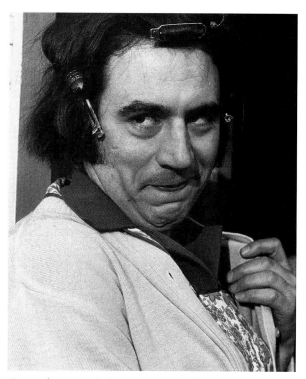

In a characteristic pose, Jones here takes on the attributes of a middle-aged Pepperpot. Copyright BBC and Python Productions.

was actually a caricature of a certain type of woman, a caricature that had to be done with great gusto and panache. It couldn't be done halfway.

"Women become defeminized when we're doing terrible women in a supermarket," Palin says, and demonstrates with the typical screechy voice of a Python in drag. "We just used to screech at each other. Well, we can do that much better, really, for our purposes, than women ever could."

The Pythons referred to their old ladies as Pepperpots, named by Graham Chapman by their perceived resemblance to real pepperpots. And, Chapman said, most of the group enjoyed playing the absurd roles.

"The Pepperpots were favorite recurring characters—favorites to write for, because they had their own idiot logic, or lack of it, and also because of the effect it had on a person. Such a complete transformation of personality by means of costume and makeup meant that we could really behave like something else, instead of worrying about ourselves at all, which was quite liberating. There's something about being in that weird, elderly makeup that was so far removed from my

own persona that it freed the mind quite a lot. I'd be able to ad lib as a Pepperpot more easily than anything else.

"They were also great fun to do because there was another person with a similarly outrageous costume and makeup, who frequently would have gone just a little too far, so that when I turned to look at him, I would be thrown. In working with Terry Jones on the stage show, his lipstick eventually took over half his face! It was really very, very, very gross! Wonderful, in that it just looked absolutely awful and slovenly to begin with, but then it really did get rather over the top," Chapman laughed.

Jones, a veteran at drag, is able to break down and analyze the female roles in which each of them specialized. "I quite liked the middle-aged, suburban, mumsy figures—I looked like my mum when I was doing it!" Jones laughs. "It seemed to be a character I could easily fit into.

"Eric made a wonderful woman as well. He used to do these slightly racier, younger women. Mike's got a great woman. I think his best one was in *Meaning of Life,* as the American lady who says 'I didn't even eat the salmon mousse!' It seems like everybody's got a female character that fits their personality. The middle-aged suburban woman suited me best."

Show 28—Mr. and Mrs. Brian Norris's Ford Popular*

Recorded as Series 3, Show 7—Prod. #76672

In the tradition of "The Kon-Tiki," "Ra 1," and "Ra 2" is "Mr. And Mrs. Brian Norris' Ford Popular," in which Norris (MP) tries to prove that the people living in Hounslow may have originally emigrated from Surbiton. His evidence includes identical houses, costumes, and most important of all, the lawn mower. Norris and wife Betty (GC) attempt to motor between Hounslow and Surbiton to prove it could have been done. They are held up by the Thames, but end up taking the railway. Ultimately, "Wrong-Way" Norris accidently discovers that the inhabitants of Hounslow had actually made the trek to Surbiton, and not vice versa.

A fanfare by the Nude Organist (TJ), the Man (JC) saying "And now," and the "It's" Man (MP) lead into the

Titles

A Headmaster (MP) calls in some students, Tidwell (TJ), Stebbins (EI), and Balderston (TG), to admonish them for running a unit trust-linked insurance scheme. He insists that such massive stock exchange deals must not happen in big schools. He's actually called them in to have Tidwell examine his wife, until he sees Stebbins is a gynecologist.

"How to Do It" features Alan (JC), Jackie (EI)

and Noel (GC) as hosts of a children's show. They teach viewers how to cure all diseases, how to play the flute ("just blow in this end and move your fingers along here"), etc.

Mrs. Nigger-Baiter (MP) tells Mrs. Shazam (TJ) about her Son (JC), talking to him in baby talk even though he's Minister of Overseas Development. They shake a rattle at him, until Mrs. Nigger-Baiter explodes. A Vicar (EI) comes to the door and tries to sell them souvenirs, badges, and little naughty dogs for the backs of cars. A Doctor (GC) appears, discussing the use of explosives to cure such ills as athlete's foot, and the Vicar tries selling to him. An animated man from his anatomy chart falls out of the chart, and out of the edge of the cartoon frame.

In "Farming Club," the Presenter (EI) introduces the life of Tchaikovsky. An Expert (JC) appears, along with a famous Music Critic and Hairdresser (MP) and two Sports Commentators (GC and TJ). They have a three-stage model of Tchaikovsky's body, where they discuss the relative size of his body parts. Sviato Slav Richter (TJ) plays the First Piano Concerto in B-Flat Minor on piano while escaping from a large canvas sack.

Jean Wennerstrom (GC) and two Assistants (EI and MP) discuss weight loss through slenderizing suits and theater. Trim-Jeans Theater Presents shows a before-and-after Kevin Francis (TJ) as Trig-

*The cheapest Ford in Britain.

Middle-period generic group shot (left to right: Gilliam, Jones, Cleese, Idle, Chapman, and Palin). Photo copyright Python Productions, Ltd.

orin in *The Seagull,* where he lost over thirty-three inches. A season of classic plays and rapid slenderizing is promoted, including the Trim-Jeans version of *The Great Escape,* with a cast of thousands losing over fifteen hundred inches.

An animated compère follows, but he keeps losing his mouth before he can introduce the next sketch.

The "Fish-Slapping Dance" sees a Man (MP) dancing around Another Man (JC) and slapping him on the cheeks with two tiny fish, before he is knocked into the water himself. Underwater animation follows with a Nazi fish, and a British fish and Red Chinese fish swallowing him and each other.

Film of the *Titanic* sinking is shown, while the Ship's Captain (TJ) cries "Women and children first." The crew begins changing into drag, children's costumes, Indians, period clothing, etc. The

shout is changed to "Women, children, Red Indians, and spacemen first," while crew members argue over whether one costume is the idealized version of the complete Renaissance man, or a Flemish merchant.

In a barren room, a BBC Spokesman (EI) denies that the BBC is going broke, as he shivers in a blanket.

The British Naval Officers have escaped from the ship, and the Police Chief of Venezuela (JC) interrogates them. The interrogation room becomes a pantomime, as Puss in Boots enters. The Captain explains that they are from the SS *Mother Goose,* but an attempt at a flashback fails. Scene shifters start removing the set, and an Old Lady (MP) chases them from her kitchen so she can use it for BBC 2. The closing credits appear written on real scraps of paper, and a real Foot (MP) steps down on them at the end.

ALSO APPEARING: Julia Breck

A talk show follows featuring Lulu and Ringo, and the "It's" Man (MP) comes onstage as the host. However, as he says "It's" the opening titles start to roll over the picture. The guests start to fight with him and leave.

The title page lists the show as "DO NOT ADJUST YOUR SET (WHAT SORT OF TALK IS THAT?)" instead of MPFC.

The script calls for "four extraordinarily famous guests (John and Yoko)" for the "It's" Man chat show.

Meet the Beatle

The "It's" Man chat show had intended to use, as the script reads, "four extraordinarily famous guests." The script actually suggests John Lennon and Yoko Ono. The group ended up with Lulu and Ringo, for reasons unclear to Michael Palin.

"Ringo was the most extroverted of the Beatles, other than Lennon—he's just that sort of guy. He'll do anything that's a bit silly and mad. He's very nice and uncomplicated and easygoing. We wanted someone incredibly famous, and to get a Beatle at that time—we couldn't get much higher than that. The others were all going through various sorts of withdrawals after the Beatles split up, and had their own particular egos, whereas Ringo just used to knock about. Graham got to know him, and asked him along," Palin says.

"God knows where we got Lulu."

Fish-Slapping

One of the shortest, silliest Python bits is Michael Palin's personal favorite. The "Fish-Slapping Dance"

is twenty seconds of absurdity, which sees Palin slapping Cleese with tiny fish, until Cleese knocks him into the canal with a larger fish.

"It's my favorite of all time," Palin says. "One can analyze things until one is blue in the face, although in comedy, I don't think that one really should, as there's so little to analyze in that!

"There's a very spontaneous, instinctive reaction, the purest sort of laugh one can get, because there's a lot of silliness, and a real pratfall at the end when I get knocked into the canal. I'm just really glad it looked as good as it did, because it was quite painful to do! I got to the canal side, and there was much less water in it than I had imagined, so it was quite a long drop! There really was no question of jumping off feet-first—I just had to do a free fall, just had to go. I must say, I did a rather good fall. I was quite pleased. I just went flat down and into the water. It was very unpleasant and cold. Luckily, it worked as well as it did.

"Of all the Python stuff, that is something I would show people to determine whether they have any detectable sense of humor at all. That's something one could show to a person who is devoid of a sense of humor, and they might just begin to smile. And if they didn't, there would be no hope for them at all."

Palin says the brief sketch seems to crystalize Python attitudes in just twenty seconds. "There is a little bit of absurdity in the costumes we're wearing, and the fact that I'm slapping John with very little pilchards. I quite like that. I think John was breaking up at the time—John is the easiest person in the world to make laugh in a sketch. Well, me, too. I go terribly easy, and have since school . . ."

Show 29—The Money Programme

Recorded as Series 3, Show 1—Prod. #75516

The "Money Programme" features a money-loving Host (EI) who gets carried away talking about it. He bursts into a song about money and is joined by a chorus for a production number.

The fanfare by the Nude Organist (TJ), the Man in the Dinner Jacket (JC), and the "It's" Man (MP) lead into

Titles

Erisabeth L Episode Thlee The Almada

A messenger (MP) brings a dispatch "flom Sil Flancis Dlake" in the New World to the Queen (GC); he and most of the court are riding mopeds, and everyone speaks with a Chinese accent. The Director (TJ), interrupts them and claims to be Visconti. He is arrested for his impersonation by Inspector Leopard (JC, with TG) of Scotland Yard's Special Fraud Film Director's Squad, who is actually Japanese director Yakamoto. Leopard encapsulates Visconti's career and summarizes his films as he reads the charges.

Animated police look for the false Visconti, and a holdup man goes into action.

A radio program asks the panel what they would do if they were Hitler, while an Old Lady (TJ) fixes her Husband (EI) a dead unjugged rabbit fish for supper; all of her desserts have rat in them. Their Son (GC) reports a dead bishop on the landing, so they call the Church Police. An Official (MP) arrives to investigate and a large hand accuses the

Palin, Cleese, and Innes watch from backstage at the Hollywood Bowl, preparing to walk onstage and disrupt the proceedings as the "Church Fuzz." Photo copyright KHJ.

Husband, followed by heavenly animation that evolves into women bouncing through a jungle.

Explorers Arthur and Betty Bailey (JC and CC), Charles Faquarsen (GC), and Mr. Spare-Buttons-Supplied-With-the-Shirt (EI) are led to a restaurant in the middle of the jungle. The guests are sometimes attacked by wild animals, and the owner, Mr. Akwekwe (MP) battles with a gorilla trying to do just that. A BBC slide appears over the next attack, describing it in detail and saying it's unsuitable for audiences, so it is replaced by a scene from *Ken Russell's Garden Club—1958,* in which a crowd of people rush into flower beds, including a Gumby, a nude woman, and a pantomime goose.

Back in the jungle, they are still trying to escape, as they spot the Sacred Volcano of Andu and the Forbidden Plateau of Roirama. A Black Native (TJ) has to borrow their script to carry on.

At the British Explorer's Club in London, Our Hero (TJ) and Hargreaves (MP) discuss the fate of the expedition and also have trouble with their scripts, and check their lines, but the hero resolves to go after them. In the jungle, the expedition realizes it can't be lost, because there is a camera crew filming them. They join the crew and realize they're being filmed by a second crew, etc. Before they sort it out, Inspector Baboon of Scotland Yard (EI) arrests one of the first crew (TJ) as an Antonioni impersonator; he

is actually Ngumba Kwego Akarumba. As the Inspector starts to review Antonioni's career, the credits roll.

ALSO APPEARING: Rita Davies
Carol Cleveland
The Fred Tomlinson Singers

A BBC slide announces another six minutes of *MPFC*.

The Argument Clinic begins as Mr. Print (MP) asks a secretary, Miss Cyst (RD), for an argument. She directs him initially to Prescriber (GC), who is in charge of abuse, and then he goes on to Mr. Barnard-Vibrator (JC) for an unsatisfying, costly argument. He goes to Monday (EI) to complain, but instead, Monday does all the complaining. He is hit on the head by Spreaders (TJ), who gives lessons on the art before both of them are hit by Inspector Fox of the Light Entertainment Police, Comedy Division, Spec. Flying Squad (GC), who arrests and charges them under the Strange Sketch Act. Another policeman, Inspector Thompson's Gazelle of the Yard (EI), arrests them, and another policeman (JC) enters at
"The End"
A BBC 1 slide promises one more minute of *MPFC*.

🎬 "Salvation Fuzz" is not in the original script for this show, though it is noted in its correct position.

🎬 The original "Money" song is as follows:

Money! Wonderful money,
Money Money Money Money!
Wonderful money! Give me
Money-money-money-money Money!
It's money money money money money! etc.

Losing It

"One of the most enjoyable, but by *no* means one of the better sketches, is the 'Church Fuzz,' which we did at the Hollywood Bowl," recalled Graham Chapman. "I don't think we *ever* did the whole sketch completely properly, even then. On the stage, and in the studio, I remember I felt a certain irresponsibility about it. For one thing, all of us

were in it, and when all of us are in something, it's always nice to be a bit naughty, and make one of the others laugh, or be a bit irresponsible, and do something one wasn't expected to do. It's nice to see that look of alarm on the faces of the others."

"There's a certain group naughtiness, when one knows the others are in a similar frame of mind. It always occurred in that particular sketch whenever it was performed. Because it wasn't particularly consequential, each of us had no great problems. It wasn't a difficult thing to perform in any way, so we could let ourselves go."

No, It Isn't

"Argument Clinic" is a favorite of the group, though Michael Palin says it isn't the sort of sketch he and Terry Jones could have ever written. "It's a lovely thing, really marvelous, and very well worked out. John Cleese was much more assiduous and concentrated in his writing, more than Terry or myself. He'd work things out. I think Terry and my minds would have gone on to something else too quickly, but John was very good—he saw that one all the way through, and worked it out very thoroughly."

Carol the Cross-Dresser

To the best of her recollection, Carol Cleveland never stepped into a role that was originally intended for one of the Pythons, but she did enjoy her most out-of-character part enormously.

"I don't know if it was intended for one of them, but my most enjoyable roles were when I didn't have to appear in bikinis or underwear, which is most peoples' image of me," says Cleveland. "On one occasion, there was a jungle episode and they needed another fellow. They decided that rather than bringing in another actor, they would use me, which was great fun. I was most decidedly feminine—they didn't disguise the fact that I was a woman, because I had full makeup and full eyelashes, which I always wore in those days. My concession to being a man was a mustache! And of course, I spoke with this very deep

voice. I enjoyed that enormously. It was great, but of course people don't remember me as this ex- plorer, they don't remember me as a nun or as an old lady. They just remember the garter belts!"

Show 30—Blood, Devastation, Death, War, and Horror

Recorded as Series, 3, Show 2—Prod. #75517

The stock film at the beginning of "Blood, Devastation, Death, War, and Horror" features the Interviewer (MP) and his guest Graham (EI), who speaks only in anagrams. He is working on an anagram version of Shakespeare, but walks off, irate, when the interviewer catches him in a Spoonerism.

The fanfare by the Nude Organist (TJ), the Man in the Dinner Jacket (JC) and the "It's" Man (MP) lead into the

Titles, featuring "Tony M. Nyphot's Flying Risccu"

"Beat the Clock" features Mrs. Scum (TJ) trying to unscramble letters to spell out "merchant bank." When she succeeds, she is bludgeoned by a huge hammer.

A Merchant Banker (JC) is on the telephone setting the terms for a loan (a relative's house, children, etc.) when Mr. Ford tries to collect money for the Orphan's Home. The Banker can't understand the meaning of "gift," however. He decides to try to collect money himself, and drops Ford through a trap door. Two pantomime horses, Champion and Trigger, are then sent in. The Banker must fire one of them, so he orders the pair to fight to the death.

Nature films show sea lions fighting to the death, as well as limpets, an ant fighting a wolf, two men in a life-and-death struggle (joined by an enraged Jacques Cousteau), and a pantomime horse getting a sixteen-ton weight dropped on him. A pantomime goose engages in a life-and-death struggle with Terence Rattigan (JC), and an enraged pantomime Princess Margaret is in a life-and-death struggle with her breakfast.

An animated man and woman feed themselves to rooms in their house. The "Househunters" features men who destroy houses too dangerous to live in; they are hired by NCP Carparks. They hang a "condemned" sign on their prey, and the house becomes a car park.

At a "Mary Recruitment Office," a RSM (GC) hangs up a sign noting that an actor is wanted for a sketch that is just starting. A Man (EI) enters who wants to join either the Women's Army, or else a more effeminate regiment, so the recruiter suggests a particular infantry. The man is angry because he has had no funny lines, so they become a Bus Conductor (GC) and a Funny Passenger (EI), but the man still has no funny lines.

Mr. Horton (TJ), a dull, boring businessman, finds that people laugh at everything he says. His Boss (MP) has to sack him for disrupting his coworkers, and can't help laughing as Horton gives him a sob story.

Meanwhile, the Man (EI) is still unhappy that the RSM, now wearing a silly costume, still has all the funny lines. The RSM puts a fish down his trousers, splashes whitewash over him, and throws a pie in his face, to stock film of Women's Institute applause.

The "Bols Story" (about Holland's most famous aperitif) is a talk show in which Mr. Orbiter-5 (MP) gestures while talking to let people know whether he is pausing or finished. A BBC 1 slide interrupts to annoy viewers, and Orbiter-5 continues. Another BBC interruption explains that they are also supplying work for one of their announcers.

The announcer in question, Jack (JC), says he is grateful and starts talking about his troubles; his wife and an announcer friend, Dick (MP), support him as he introduces the news. BBC Newsreader Richard Baker* is seen reading the news, though the announcers are heard. Strange visuals, including Nixon, breasts, and a man with a stoat through his head are seen, and the Newsreader uses the same gestures used by Orbiter-5.

A James Bond-ish opening for "The Pan-

*The genuine article.

Author Kim "Howard" Johnson backstage at the Hollywood Bowl in Pantomime Goose uniform. Photo copyright KHJ.

tomime Horse is a Secret Agent" features a Bond parody with credits, etc. The Horse is with a Woman (CC) in a rowboat when he is attacked by a Russian pantomime horse. A chase scene involves cars, bicycles, and rickshaws. The chase passes the "Mary Recruiting Office," where the nuns outside are being solicited by the Merchant Banker.

The credits are all in anagrams.

ALSO APPEARING: Carol Cleveland

 The opening caption reads "Loretta Returns to Whitemead College" by Some People and their Brains, then "Blood, Devastation," etc.

Anagrams

Most of the Pythons seem to enjoy word games. In Tunisia, the group would often sit around the *Life*

of Brian set passing the time with various brain-teasers, and Graham Chapman was devoted to *The Times* crossword puzzle. Eric Idle is a big fan of anagrams, which he was able to use in his Python writing.

"I have one of those creative dyslexic brains which tends to look at a word, and break it up, and look at it backwards," Idle says. "I look at 'lager' and see 'regal,' I look at 'Evian' and see 'naive.' It's one of those minds that looks for hidden messages. I guess it comes from English literature. Most people in England start the day by doing the crossword puzzle in the paper—it's part of commuting and goes with the train ride. People do *The Times* crossword puzzle in eighteen minutes. It's very English . . ."

Animated Amnesia

Terry Gilliam tends to dismiss much of his Python animation, claiming he has never been particularly interested in watching his footage; he is reluctant to name any of his favorite bits, in part for that reason.

"I don't remember anything," Gilliam jokes. "The easy answer to that is, my most favorite bit is the one that (director) Ian MacNaughton cut out when Terry Jones's back was turned. I can't remember what the point of the sequence was, but it involved trees that started growing. They somehow grew beyond the stratosphere, and eventually bumped into some invisible barrier in the middle of space, where they started growing sideways. When Terry wasn't looking and when I wasn't there, Ian, in one of his less-inspired moments, cut out this bit, and chopped out the whole interesting part of the sequence. We ended up with things starting and ending, but without things in the middle. That was one of my big irritations . . .

"There was always a lot I liked about the 'Househunters,' but I never watch the stuff. I just *never* look at the stuff. I don't know why—if it doesn't interest me, or if it frightens me . . . We'd watch it when it came out, and all I could see were the mistakes. I couldn't see any of the good stuff. It was the nature of being supercritical—which has its uses, but is terribly frustrating, so I actually can't enjoy the stuff. My theory was always to stay away from it, and then watch it years later, as an outsider. I've done that at different points, and thought it was rather good," Gilliam says, laughing.

Pantomime Critters

Several strange pantomime creatures made their appearance in Python. Graham Chapman said he has to take his share of the blame for many of them. "I don't know quite how, but the pantomime Princess Margaret fell into my consciousness one day . . . There were several pantomimatic items, really, the pantomime goose, Princess Margaret; there was the flag-seller who goes in to see the merchant banker, who has to have the meaning of the word 'gift' explained to him, and then in came the pantomime horses. That led into the pantomime horse as a secret agent," Chapman said.

"In pantomime, there is usually a pantomime horse or cow or cat, something fairly run of the mill. The idea of having a pantomime Princess Margaret—a huge dummy inside of which would ideally be two other people—would have been nice, but we had to make do with just the one. Still, quite a formidable spectacle."

Show 31—"The All-England Summarize Proust Competition"

Recorded as Series 3, Show 9—Prod. #78491

A fanfare by a Nude Organist (TJ), the Man in the Dinner Jacket (JC), and the "It's" Man (MP) lead into the

Titles

The "All England Summarize Proust Competition" includes evening gown and swimsuit competitions. Host Arthur Mee (TJ) requires contestants to give a brief summary of *A La Recherche Du Temps Perdu,* and the judges are all cardboard cutout figures of the Surrey Cricket Club. First contestant is Harry Bagot (GC), who must summarize his first book in fifteen seconds. Failing that, the second contestant, Ronald Rutherford (MP), does even worse. The third contestant, the Bolton Choral Society, led by Supt. McGough (the Fred Tomlinson Singers), tries to summarize his books as a madrigal. Since no one has done well enough, the prize is given to the girl with the biggest tits; she is brought out and congratulated over the closing credits.

ALSO APPEARING: Carol Cleveland
The Fred Tomlinson Singers

Stock film of Mt. Everest (the mountain with the biggest tits in the world) begins the story of the International Hairdresser's Expedition on Everest. Leader of the expedition is Col. Sir John Teasy Weasy Butler (GC), who describes the assault.

Patrice (EI) explains that they couldn't go outside during monsoons because he and Ricky had just had a blow dry and rinse. They receive competition from a team of French chiropodists and thirteen other expeditions. They decide to open their own salon on the side of the mountain, "Ricky Pule's Hairdressing Salon."

There is a cinema ad for "Ricky's" on a mountainside, plus coming attractions for *A Magnificent Festering* (an animated short in which Beatrice makes a fool of herself for James in three different scenes).

Mrs. Little (TJ) calls the fire brigade (led by MP), but they are too busy doing needlepoint and cooking to answer the phone. Son Mervyn (JC) calls them for their hamster, telling his mother to go play her cello. He eventually takes off his shoe and tells them his size after answering "Yes . . . yes . . . yes . . ." while Mrs. Little takes the call after the hamster dies. She tells them her shoe size. Her son Eamonn (GC), carrying a spear and shield and dressed as a headhunter, arrives home from Dublin. The fire brigade eventually comes around on Friday night and she has a party for them, as Mrs. Little talks about her favorite TV show.

"Party Hints by Veronica Smalls" follows, in which Veronica (EI) tells how to deal with an armed communist uprising during a party.

Animated communists hide under a woman's bed, and they go door to door selling communist revolutions. LBJ laughs at communist revolutions, until he falls victim to the Puking Peter doll.

Mr. Tick (JC) is taken through a language lab (by GC), where students are studying tapes on bigotry, politics, effeminate tapes, etc. Tick wants to be likeable, and asks for the "Life and Soul of the Party" tape; the students go into a '30s routine, wearing earphones and kicking their legs to Sandy Wilson's version of "The Devils," but the Proust choral madrigal cuts off their song.

Another shot of Mt. Everest becomes a poster in a travel agency, where Mr. Smoketoomuch (EI),

Idle as Mr. Smoketoomuch is led offstage by Cleese as he continues his oration against travel agents and package tours, to continue it throughout the audience. Photo copyright KHJ.

who is fed up with packaged tours, begins a long tirade on them before the travel agent, Mr. Bounder (MP) and his Secretary (CC). The travel agent can't shut him up and calls the fire brigade, but they don't answer. He tries the police but begins answering "Yes . . . yes . . . yes . . ." The Secretary leads viewers to another room.

"Thrust" sees the host, Chris (GC) speak with Anne Elk (JC) on her theory of the brontosaurus. At the end of the interview the phone rings, and Chris answers "Yes . . . yes . . . yes . . ." They leave through the travel agency as the fire brigade arrives, and the Proust madrigal begins.

The script has the show opening with a boy and girl meeting the Rev. Arthur Belling, the looney Vicar (now in Show 36), and then the titles.

Anne Elk's second theory is: The Fire Brigade Chorus never sings songs about Monsieur Marcel Proust.

Proust Hobbies

One of the better-known cases of censorship of the Python TV show involved Graham Chapman's character in "The All-England Summarize Proust Competition"; he gives his hobbies as golf, strangling animals, and masturbation. The BBC cut the audio track from the final word, although it has been broadcast with "masturbation" intact in America. The BBC version showed audiences breaking up with laughter at "strangling animals," and only lip-readers were able to get the real joke.

Chapman was unhappy that his line was lost: "Golf isn't very popular around here. And, 'masturbation' was cut or changed—we weren't allowed to say that. Ridiculous, isn't it—some safe pastime like that?

"The whole Summarize Proust sketch was actually the product of Michael Palin and Terry Jones," said Chapman. "How they got that into their heads, I don't know. Of course, if one is thinking of having a 'summarize' something, that *would* be pretty tricky."

Going Places

The "Travel Agent" sketch, in which Eric Idle delivers a lengthy diatribe against package tours, is one of the highlights of the stage shows. As Mr. Smoketoomuch, Idle is led offstage (usually escorted by John Cleese) as he rants, only to reappear, breaking away from his captor and continuing his spiel as he walks through the delighted

audience, often more than once. The live version of the speech runs several minutes longer than the original TV version, thanks to Idle.

"That sketch was actually written by John and Graham," Idle explains, "and it was funny enough when we were rehearsing it. But, it wasn't long enough. So, at some point, I took it over and wrote more, in that style; I wrote a couple of extra pages for the stage show. It's basically their sketch, but nobody else wanted to learn it!"

Show 32 — The War against Pornography

Recorded as Series 3, Show 6—Prod. #76570

Newsreel footage is shown of Pepperpots with gray hair and Mary Whitehouse glasses attacking the permissive society. They assault striking workers on picket lines, cover nude statues and attack smut (including Desdemona onstage with Othello), burn books, and wage war against porn.

A fanfare by the Nude Organist (TJ), the Man in the Dinner Jacket (JC), and the "It's" Man (MP) lead into the

Titles

"Harley Street." Mr. T. F. Gumby (MP) enters a doctor's office calling for the doctor, trashing the room in the process, and a Gumby Brain Specialist (JC) decides to take out his brain. The Chief Surgeon (GC) calls for his glasses, moustache, and handkerchief as he leads the Gumby surgical team.

An animated man attempting to study art finds the lights keep going out. The frame adjustment is also off, so he is upside down, sideways, etc.

On TV, the *Nine O'Clock News* is cancelled for the finals of the All-Essex Badminton championships, so Georges Jalin (TJ) and Gladys Jalin (GC) let a man at the door, Mr. Zorba (JC), do a live TV special on mollusks in their living room, with a cardboard TV screen all around him. They are about to switch it off because it's too dull, until he starts talking about the sexual perversions of various mollusks; he is followed by a Newsreader (TG) and other "Vox Pops."

During animation of people tickling a baby, a man becomes part of "Today in Parliament." The Newsreader (MP) talks about developments in strange government departments, until the show transforms into a classic serial, and then into "The Tuesday Documentary" (with EI). It becomes a children's story with animation, briefly returns to "The Tuesday Documentary," turns into a party

political broadcast (with TJ), then changes into "Religion Today" before settling on "Match of the Day." The soccer players, in slow motion, all hug each other and dance about the field, as romantic music plays.

"Politicians—an Apology" asks forgiveness for the way the show depicts politicians as crabby, ulcerous, self-seeking little vermin.

An Interviewer (JC) reports on a British Naval expedition to explore Lake Pahoe, and talks with Rear Admiral Sir Jane Russell (MP) and Lt. Commander Dorothy Lamour (EI) (all the officers have the names of female film stars of the '40s). The Interviewer slowly transforms into Long John Silver, and an animated, psychedelic Royal Navy recruiting film is shown. Another Interviewer (TJ) apologizes for the first one, and talks to Vice Admiral Sir John Cunningham (GC), who maintains that there is absolutely no cannibalism in the Royal Navy. Their expedition is intended to cover up cannibalism and necrophilia, though they claim to be going to Lake Pahoe, which is located in a residential home at 22A Runcorn Avenue. They ask the Woman living there (EI) and her Husband (MP) where the lake is at, and are told to look in the basement flat, where they find a couple (MP and TJ) living in scuba gear, complaining about the dampness.

The host of a focus on the Magna Carta talks with Mr. Badger (EI) on his theories, and is answered in mime. They agree to have dinner together; later, Badger orders whiskeys and a bottle of wine as his dinner from the Waiter (MP). They all decide this is the silliest sketch they've ever been in, and decide to stop, and the closing credits roll.
ALSO APPEARING: Mrs. Idle

🎬 In the original script, "Gumby Surgery" ends

with the doctor pounding on his stomach with a mallet, shouting "Get better, brain!" while GC does not get into his gear.

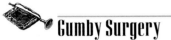

Gumby Surgery

The Gumbies were favorites of most of the Pythons, and Michael Palin is quick to cite his most memorable Gumby appearance. "The Gumby brain surgeon is still one of my favorite things to watch. I love that!

"It's got one of my favorite Python lines, when I say 'My brain, my brain hurts.' John, also a Gumby, comes up to me and starts loosening my trousers. I say 'No, no, my brain in my head!' I think that might have been an ad lib at the time. I just love 'My brain in my head!', suggesting there might be two."

Lake Pahoe

During the expedition to Lake Pahoe, a subur-

ban couple, played by Terry Jones and Michael Palin, were found to be living underwater, in a lake beneath someone's house. Devoted to the cause, Graham Chapman said they used no doubles for the sketch, in which they had to wear aqualungs.

"Mike and Terry actually did go down in all the apparatus. It was very brave of them, I thought," said Chapman. "They spent quite a bit of time learning to breathe underwater. And they seemed to enjoy it, too. Jolly good!

"I did like the idea of a house with a huge lake underneath—not just a lake of the sort that one could accommodate inside a house, but something that was obviously far too big for most countries."

A set was built at the deep end of a swimming pool, according to Jones, and he and Palin were given brief, perfunctory lessons just prior to the filming.

"Some instructor showed up. He gave us these horror stories about 'You have to breathe out when you come to the surface, otherwise you'll be dead.' We were a bit worried about it," Jones laughs. "That was the first time I'd actually used an aqualung—the *only* time I've ever used an aqua-lung, come to think of it."

Show 33—Salad Days

Recorded as Series 3, Show 4—Prod. #75606

The clothes fly off the Organist (TJ) as he plays a fanfare, there is a nude string quartet, the Man in the Dinner Jacket (JC), and the "It's" Man (MP) lead into the
Titles
The "Adventures of Biggles," Part One: Biggles Dictates a Letter is seen over stock film of World War I planes dogfighting. Biggles (GC) dictates letters to King Haakon of Norway and the real Princess Margaret; he wears antlers whenever he's not dictating to Miss Bladder (NH), his secretary. Algy is called in, and when he says he's gay, Biggles shoots him. A pantomime Princess Margaret walks out of the cupboard, and the closing is shown over film of World War I dogfights.
Animated planes lead into a flying sheep being

shot down, which knocks a nude woman out of a nest. When she lands, she causes traffic accidents, and buildings topple over like dominoes.
Not far away, on the Uxbridge Road, a Man (JC) interviews Bert Tagg (GC), leader of a mountain-climbing expedition that is scaling the north face of the Uxbridge Road. Another Man (MP) dressed in furs asks "Lemon curry?" and the climbers all fall down the road.
At Newhaven Lifeboat on 24 Parker Street, Mrs. Neves (TJ) is stuffing a turkey when a Man (MP) enters the house and tells her it's a lifeboat. Other men, also in raingear, find it's not a lifeboat, and go below for tea. In a neighboring house, Gladys (JC) and Enid (EI) stand in the midst of naval equipment, scopes, monitors, and tapes, spying on

"Sam Peckinpah's Salad Says," just before the carnage and blood begin; the crew began filming the idyllic day in the country during the daytime, but finally had to finish in complete darkness with the aid of huge lights. By that time, the cast was covered with artificial blood. Photo copyright BBC and Python Productions.

their neighbors. Gladys leaves her flat and finds herself on a lifeboat, where she tries to get ingredients for a fruitcake from Mrs. Edwards (GC).

The Host (EI) of "Storage Jars" presents a news report on those items. Reporter Ronald Rodgers (TJ) reports from La Paz, Bolivia, on the use of storage jars there, dodging bullets and bombs.

An animated TV viewer, Henry, has his eyeballs taken out, cleaned, and polished by a machine that comes out of his TV. A Good Fairy from Program Control releases Henry from the evil spell he's been under, and becomes a frog.

On "The Show So Far," Mr. Tussaud (TJ) does a recap of the show up to the point where he is hit on the head by a large hammer—and he is.

Mr. Mousebender (JC) enters a cheese shop, where he eventually finds out from the proprietor, Mr. Wensleydale (MP), that they have no cheese at all, so he shoots Wensleydale through the head. He

is revealed as Rogue Cheddar, and "The End" appears.

Phillip Jenkinson (EI), a sniffing critic, discusses cheese westerns, and a clip is shown from *Sam Peckinpah's Salad Days,* in which arms and legs fall off freely in a bloodbath shot in slow motion. Blood spurts everywhere, and it is replayed several times. Jenkinson is shot in slow motion as are the credits, and there is stock film of Women's Institute applause.

ALSO APPEARING: Nicki Howorth

An apology is read to everyone in the world for the last scene, admitting it was in poor taste, and asking viewers not to write in as the BBC is going through an unhappy time now.

The BBC denies the previous apology, claiming that it is actually very happy.

A real newsreader reports that several storage jars were destroyed in a local explosion.

"Interlude" features shots of a seascape, and a man in a conquistador costume (JC) says that the show is shorter than usual this week. He leaves, then returns, saying there aren't any more jokes or anything, and then walks off as the scene eventually fades out.

🎬 The newsreader part at the end of the show is not in the BBC rehearsal script, nor is the final "Interlude."

Biggles

"Biggles is very much the archetypal Englishman, an aviator in the First World War, and the star of a lot of books primarily for boys—they were quite sexist about it," explained Graham Chapman about the character, created by Capt. W. E. Johns, who is unknown to most Americans.

"They were about airplanes and fighting one another, all very brave and stiff upper lips and no dirty tricks—one had to fight fair. Very character forming! It was rather nice to use that in a more familiar way—have Biggles be worried about whether his friends Algy and Ginger might, in fact, be gay. I think he discovered that Ginger was—I'm not sure. He probably shot him, because he was very English. He wouldn't understand anything about anything at all, but knows when he's being fair."

On the Road Again

The British public proved to be unflappable when the Pythons walked among them. The group didn't always travel very far, however. "A lot of it was done in Acton, which was just around behind the BBC—the cheapest place to film, around those little two-story working-class houses from Edwardian times. We used those streets quite a lot," says Michael Palin.

"It's amazing what one can do without people noticing. I remember when we were climbing the Uxbridge Road; that required us to actually lie flat on the road, dressed in mountaineering gear, and pull ourselves along. People just walked past us. One or two stopped and asked what was going on, but most people just carried on with their normal business."

Ship Ahoy

Although there may have been more unpleasant filming days, Graham Chapman and Terry Jones say the queasiest day of Python shooting was undoubtedly the sequence shot on a real lifeboat.

"It was quite rough to do. They didn't take us out into the very high seas for long—they did a bit—but it wasn't too calm in the mouth of the harbor where we did most of the filming. Poor John Cleese had to be underneath the front hatch, the worst place to be, bouncing around in the dark like that. He just had one line to say, which he bravely did. Of course, there were times when we'd just get ready to shoot, say 'Action!', and John would come up and just go 'Ooooaagghh!', I'm afraid. It was just one of those things," Chapman laughed.

"Poor man—he really went through it! Almost everyone was sick on that afternoon's filming. I was relatively unscathed, largely as a result of a bottle of Glenfiddich . . . I was glad to get off the thing, too, but it wasn't quite so bad for me."

As Terry Jones remembers it, about half the group escaped seasickness; unfortunately, he was in the unlucky half, along with Cleese.

"John and I got *incredibly* seasick!" Jones recalls. "It was the first time in my life that I just didn't care *at all* what we were filming. I just wanted to get back on shore.

"The rushes were funny. We saw the cameras roll, and then we saw me throwing up over the side. We hear 'Action!', and then I get up and wipe my face, and stagger through the shot. When I get to the other end, I puke again," he laughs. "At that stage, I was *not* giving a performance."

Cheese Shop

"Any sketch that involved a lot of shouting was always quite good fun, but I also liked playing most of the shop assistants that I'd be doing with John, because they were usually class sketches, and John was great to play against," says Michael Palin.

"John and I could never, ever play the 'Cheese Shop' in rehearsal without laughing at some point. It just got to both of us, and so there was this pitch of tension, this excruciating fear that we were going to laugh at any moment, which really helped us along. I don't think we've ever done it, *ever,* without laughing at some point, sometimes for quite long periods . . ."

Salad Days

The most bloodletting in a Python show probably occurred in "Sam Peckinpah's *Salad Days,*" an affair which required tubes for blood, dismembered limbs, and other bits of gross, exaggerated violence. The shooting proved to be a more ambitious project than the group had realized, and they had trouble wrapping it all up in time. Of course, the scene all started benignly enough, with an innocent little party in the country.

"We really made a mess of this nice little bit of heartland. There were huge cylinders of blood, enormous great things! And it all had to be shot in one day," says Michael Palin. "In fact, if one looks at *Salad Days,* it suddenly gets very dark at one point; we were shooting with artificial light by the end. It started as a nice concert party on the lawn, and ended up being shot in the middle of the night."

Self-Inflation

As Hazel Pethig says, John Cleese hated wearing costumes, and did what he could to get out of them. Fortunately, Pethig knew how to deal with him, as when they were shooting the "Interlude" sequence.

"In Jersey, he didn't want to dress up as a Spaniard," says Pethig. "He didn't want to put on the helmet and tunic and codpiece. He was *determined* not to get into it. So I punched him into it! He literally puffed himself up so that he'd be too big for the costume—'Look, I'm too big, I'm too big!' Anyone who wasn't used to him or was frightened of him would have thought 'Oh, what am I going to do? How am I going to get him into costume?' I had to pummel him into it! John loves to abuse people to see how they react, and if they answer back, he loves it. He would have loved to have been able to get me all flustered with a costume."

Show 34 — The Cycling Tour

Recorded as Series 3, Show 10—Prod. #78642

Reg Pither (MP) rides through the countryside on his bicycle. He crashes his bicycle when the pump gets caught in his trouser leg, and his sandwiches are smashed; he goes to a diner for a banana and cheese sandwich and explains his difficulties (to EI), before resuming his cycling tour of North Cornwall.

Pither falls off again—an animated monster peers from beyond a hill—and he explains his troubles to an indifferent Woman (JC) who does her gardening and ignores him completely. Resuming his cycling tour, he falls off several more times, due to his too-large pump. A Woman (EI) gives him directions to a Bicycle Pump Center, which specializes in shorter bicycle pumps. Pither then visits a Doctor (EI) to ask him for directions to Iddesley. He is uninjured, but wants the advice of a professional man. The doctor gives him a note to take to the chemist.

Pither interrupts a very personal discussion between James (JC) and Lucille (CC), who is urging him to leave his wife. Pither's interruptions cause her to leave him, and James throws him out of the pub.

Pither is picked up by Mr. Gulliver (TJ) in his car. They discuss damaged lunches and safer foods, then Gulliver's car crashes. Pither gives him a ride to the hospital on his bicycle when he loses his memory and believes he is Clodagh Rogers.* Pither proves to be a jinx at the hospital's Casualty Department; the Nurse (GC) takes the particulars, and Gulliver is examined by Dr. Chang (JC) as the hospital collapses around them, and begins another personality change.

When Pither and Gulliver pitch camp that night, they are questioned by a French couple, M. Brun (JC) and Mme. Brun (EI). Gulliver signs autographs for their children as "Trotsky," and there is a quick clip of Lenin singing "If I Ruled the World."

Pither and Gulliver team up again at Smolensk and register with the Desk Clerk (TG) at the Young Men's Anti-Christian Association. Pither then visits the British Consulate in Smolensk, which is decorated in Oriental furnishings. The British consul, Mr. Atkinson (GC), is Chinese, and offers Pither a drink or a game of bingo. His Chinese assistant, Mr. Lovington (JC), leads groups of Orientals that burst out of closets to shout "Bingo!

The Desk Clerk tells Pither that Trotsky has gone to Moscow (to reunite with the Central Committee). Three secret policemen, Grip (EI), Bag (JC), and Wallet (GC), take him to Moscow.

At the U.S.S.R. 42nd International Clambake, a Soviet Official (JC), in gibberish Russian, introduces Trotsky. Gulliver begins to address the crowd as Trotsky, but changes to Eartha Kitt, complete with feather boa, and removes his facial hair as he sings "Old-Fashioned Girl."

Pither is thrown in a Russian cell and faces a firing squad. An Officer (GC) runs up to the squad with a note, which reads "Carry on with the execution." The firing squad misses. They throw him back against the wall, and they miss a second time. Back in his cell, he dissolves back home, where his Mother (EI) tells him he is in a dream, and is actually back in the cell.

At the Committee Meeting, Marshal Bulganin and "Charlie" finish their ventriloquism act, as the Russian compère (EI) tells a few jokes, and introduces Eartha Kitt. Unfortunately, Gulliver has now become Edward Heath, and he delivers a speech to

*A late-'60s pop star.

trade union leaders. He is hit by a tomato and becomes Mr. Gulliver again, the audience riots and chases him through the streets. He finds Pither by the firing squad, and they escape with the help of a "scene missing" card. They finally part company as Pither resumes his cycling tour, and the credits roll.
ALSO APPEARING: Carol Cleveland

Maurice and Kevin, the animated monsters from the beginning, sing the Clodagh Rogers song "Jack in the Box."

🎬 Cut from the final show was a Gilliam animation of a record ad for "Lenin's Chartbusters, Volume III—twenty-six solid gold tracks, including 'If I Ruled the World,' 'Maybe It's Because I'm a Londoner,' 'Chirpy Chirpy Cheep Cheep,' and many others. Out now on the Bolshevik Label."

A Mike and Terry Extravaganza

"If it's long, it's usually by Mike and Terry.

" 'Cycling Tour' was a complete half hour; it was actually complete and put up. What happened—and it was the only time we ever did it— we rewrote it," explains Eric Idle. "It was taken on as a sort of script dare: it had a beginning, middle, and end. We didn't like the ending, so we altered it, and added some input. So it's really a Mike and Terry thing, rewritten by the rest of us."

In fact, "Cycling Tour" was presented as a show of its own, rather than as *Monty Python's Flying Circus*—the opening titles never appeared in the show at all. In addition, it is the only Python TV show that tells one complete story from start to finish, although the "Michael Ellis" and "Mr. Neutron" shows in the fourth season are also quite linear.

Interestingly, this was one show that failed miserably when the group performed it in the studio, according to Jones. "It was strange what shows worked on the recording. The 'Cycling Tour' was very disappointing when we recorded it; people came out saying they didn't like it. Ian MacNaughton and I had a *really* heavy editing session on that, and the show was really made in the editing room. We really cut it around *hugely*. It was a lot longer to begin with, and things weren't working.

"It was shot in a very fragmented way, it wasn't in order; it was different from most shows because it was telling a story. For example, in the scene where Mr. Pither goes into the hospital casualty ward, the casualty ward sign falls down, the board falls on John's fingers, and so on—they had all been shot separately and didn't flow together. It was only in the editing, when we put them all together, that we could get the rhythm going. It was bang. Bang. Bang! And then suddenly we could see what it was meant to be. It was something that we *had* to do in the editing."

Show 35—The Nude Man

Recorded as Series 3, Show 11—Prod. #78735

Captain MacPherson (MP) of East Scottish Airways and his Copilot (JC) are flying when Scottish Mr. Badger (EI) enters the cockpit and demands one thousand pounds to reveal where he has hidden a bomb, though he eventually lowers his demands. The Director (GC) evicts Badger from the sketch.

The Man at the Organ (TJ) is surrounded by paparazzi as he discusses the symbolism of "The Nude Man," the Man in the Dinner Jacket (JC) discusses the Bergsonian theory of laughter as a social sanction against inflexible behavior, when he must say "And now," and the "It's" Man says "It's"

Titles

Ten seconds of sex, accompanied by a blank screen, is interrupted by a Man (GC) who links it to "New Housing Developments."

A housing project built entirely by characters from nineteenth-century English literature is shown by a Commentator (MP). Little Nell from Dickens's *Old Curiosity Shop* and Arthur Hunting-

A television panel with Chapman and Palin, with a nameplate inexplicably reading "The Amazing Kargol and Janet." Terry Jones and Carol Cleveland were supposed to portray Kargol and Janet, a psychiatrist/conjuring act, in Series 1, Show #1, but the sketch did not appear; it was Series 3, Show #9 that saw the pair appear in very similar roles as "The Amazing Mystico and Janet," who erect buildings by hypnosis. Photo copyright BBC and Python Productions.

don (EI) of Anne Bronte's *The Tenant of Wildfell Hall* work on the ducts and electrical system. A crowd of farmhands from *Tess of the D'Urbervilles* is supervised by Mrs. Jupp (GC), the genial landlady from Samuel Butler's *Way of All Flesh*. Meanwhile, character's from Milton's *Paradise Lost* are working on a motorway interchange.

The Amazing Mystico (TJ) and Janet put up buildings by hypnosis. Ken Very Big Liar (MP) explains the advantages of the system, and Clement Onan (GC), architect to the council, claims they're safe as long as people believe in them. A tenant couple (EI and GC) is interviewed, and cease believing for a moment. A biography of Janet follows, and Supt. Harry "Boot In" Swalk (TJ) discusses the recent outbreak of hangings, as the police radio broadcasts conversations and policemen singing "Jack in the Box."

Two mortuary workers (TG and TJ) eat lunch and listen to the *Mortuary Hour* on the radio. Their supervisor, Mr. Wong (JC), comes in to warn them, and a Senile Old Lord (MP) is wheeled in by the

Lord Mayor (GC) and given a tour, but his brain becomes dislodged. The Scotsman (EI) appears again, and says he won't interrupt the sketch for a pound.

The Animator (TG) is caught explaining how he does his cartoons, followed by an animation which sees flying saucers become soldiers.

The Olympic Finals of the Men's Hide and Seek features a Commentator (EI) describing the match between Paraguayan Francisco Huron (TJ), the seeker, and Don Roberts of Britain (GC). Roberts takes a taxi to the airport and hides in a castle in Sardinia. Another Commentator (MP) interrupts for updated results six years later, and the field reporter (EI) is on the scene when he is found in eleven years, two months, twenty-six days, nine hours, three minutes, and twenty-seven point four seconds. A tie is declared, and they must begin the replay the next day.

An Unctuous, Red-jacketed Compère (MP) stands at the seaside, as donkey rides go on behind him. He tries to introduce a sitting-room sketch when he is hit with a rubber chicken by a Man (JC), who then gives it back to the knight. The Scotsman then volunteers a totally free interruption.

The man, Roger Robinson (JC), then arrives home, where his wife Beatrice (CC) has prepared dinner, and she tells him the Cheap Laughs from next door (TJ and GC) will be dropping in. One Evening with the Cheap Laughs Later, their house has been trashed. His wife asks why they have to buy everything just because the Cheap Laughs have one (whoopee cushions, hand buzzers, etc.). A sixteen-ton weight falls on Roger, and later that night when they're sitting in bed, the bed folds up to show "Probe."

The Narrator (EI) discusses the unfairness of bullfighting, and Brigadier Arthur Farquhar-Smith (JC) gives his advice on how to make bullfighting safer, until he starts mincing and is hit by a hammer. The Scotsman turns out the lights and demands to be paid to switch them back on.

Animation features the turning on of the lights, and increasingly cosmic trees that lead to the planet Algon (the instrumental music is to the "Yangtse Song," though it was originally accompanied by a German radio commercial), and Hitler makes an appearance.

A focus on Algon, with a satellite probe, reveals that an ordinary cup of drinking chocolate costs four million pounds, and everything else is extremely expensive. James M. Burke (MP) shows live film from the planet, and reveals that the price of split-crotch panties makes them virtually unattainable. Prof. Herman Khan (EI), Director of the Institute of Split-Crotch Panties, talks about naughty underwear. They locate a girl on the planet but lose contact with the Algon 1 probe.

The closing credits are then read by the Scotsman, who is being paid by the BBC to do so.
ALSO APPEARING: Carol Cleveland
Marie Anderson
Mrs. Idle

A sixteen-ton weight drops on top of the Scotsman.

Live from Algon

The "Algon" sketch was something "slightly wild" written by Michael Palin and Terry Jones, taking aim at news reports, according to Palin. "That was a parody of the instant communication linkups in various areas, and the television presentation of an extraordinary event. The contrast was the discovery of this amazing, wonderful planet, with everyday worries like price inflation, which preoccupies the minds of those that study this planet far more than anything else.

"The American moon landings were wonderful feats, but I'm sure people were more interested in how they got on in their spaceships—wherever did they put their leftovers? The technology is going off into the future, but it's basically operated by humans. And as long as there are humans, there are human trivialities.

"It's wonderment reduced to the banality of humans, bringing this wonderful planet down to everyday life. It's like going to the sun and saying 'Where do we sit?' "

Sixteen-Ton Weight

The Pythons had a number of recurring characters and props; one of the most difficult to ignore was the huge sixteen-ton weight. "That came out of the mind somewhere or another," said Graham Chap-

Various construction crews erect housing projects. Clockwise from upper left: Jones as the Amazing Mystico puts up buildings by hypnosis, while Idle as Arthur Huntingdom from The Tenant of Wildfell Hall, *Chapman as Mrs. Jupp from* The Way of All Flesh, *and Palin as Heathcliffe from* Wuthering Heights *toil at a construction project built by characters from nineteenth-century English literature. Photo copyright BBC and Python Productions.*

man. "I believe it came from not knowing how to end a revue. We were thinking that this enormous boot must come down and crush everyone—and I suppose that's how the sixteen-ton weight came into the picture . . ."

The weight, the knight with the chicken, the giant foot (used in the opening titles), and the frequent Python explosions were all useful ways to get rid of characters.

"They were convenient ways of getting rid of characters, and they livened up the shows a bit. It was the slightly destructive side of Python, get-ting rid of characters as they would in a cartoon, but doing it live," says Michael Palin. "Having a sixteen-ton weight coming down on people: Splosh!

"Television has so many people going on and on, and all we wanted to do was shoot them—nicely, obviously, but just shut them up. The explosions, the sixteen-ton weight, and the man in the suit of armor hitting people with the chicken are our little protests against the way people go on and on."

Show 36—E. Henry Thripshaw's Disease

Recorded as Series 3, Show 13—Prod. #78968

The Proprietor of the Tudor Job Agency (TJ), wearing a Tudor costume, is approached by a customer (GC) who wants a part-time job. All they offer are Tudor jobs: the Proprietor tries to interest him in sailing to Virginia with Walter Raleigh, but the Customer is more interested in dirty books, and is led to the back room, which is the interior of a Soho dirty book shop.

Another Customer (JC) asks the other Tudor Proprietor in the back (EI) for specific titles, but is shown *Bridgette, Queen of the Whip, Naughty Nora,* and *Sister Theresa, the Spanking Nun.* The Customer wants *Devonshire County Churches,* while the Proprietor suggests *Bum Biters.* The Customer is looking for general surveys of English church architecture, but settles for *The Lord Lieutenant in Nylons.*

Suddenly Supt. Inspector Henry Gaskell (MP), in Tudor costume, tries to raid the place. He goes out the back door to a Tudor estate with a woman and becomes Sir Phillip Sydney.

In "The Life of Sir Phillip Sydney," he is summoned from a pub to the coast, to stop Spanish porn merchants who are burying porn books. A swordfight follows, and he stems the tide of Spanish porn, stopping six thousand copies of *Tits and Bums* from entering the country. Sydney returns home to his wife in 1583 London, who is reading Shakespeare's *Gay Boys in Bondage.* He has her start reading it to him, but they are arrested by Sgt. Maddox, a modern-day policeman (GC).

Animation features Shakespeare's "Gay Boys in Bondage," a man falls through a pipe into an organ, and there is a fanfare played by the Nude Organist (TJ).

A Couple (JC and CC) are talking when a Vicar (MP) asks to join them if he won't be disturbing them. He proceeds to break plates, play with rubber animals, spray shaving cream on himself, etc. The Rev. Arthur Belling changes their life, and the entire congregation at St. Looney Up the Cream Bun and Jam acts like Belling.

The organ fanfare (by TJ) is followed by the Man in the Dinner Jacket (JC), and the "It's" Man (MP) says "It's"

Titles

An animated shooting gallery features men and animals, with dead animals dropped into a meat grinder.

"The Free Repetition of Doubtful Words, Skits, Spoofs, Japes, and Vignettes by a Very Underrated Writer" has Mr. Peepee (EI) visit a shop to ask the Telegram Inquiry Man (TJ) about a telegram from his wife. An animated telegram is unrolled to begin

"Is There?" in which Roger Last (JC) introduces a discussion on life after death, with three dead bodies.

In the "Peripeteia" sketch, Mr. Burrows (MP) visits Dr. E. Henry Thripshaw (JC) about his problems with word order; the Doctor decides to name the condition Thripshaw's Disease. The Broadway version and film version (a Hollywood costume drama by David O. Seltzer) includes a film clip

from *E. Henry Thripshaw's Disease*. The Doctor is interviewed about the film, and tells of working on a new disease that he hopes to turn into a musical.

Silly noises follow.

A Man (GC) visits a Vicar (MP) who is only interested in drinking his sherry. Mr. Husband of the British Sherry Corp. (EI) calls on him to deliver more, and a group of Spanish dancers and singers (led by TJ and CC) sing about Amontillado and request dirty books.

Closing credits all contain suggestive phrases: Michael "Bulky" Palin; Terry Jones, "King of the Lash"; John Cleese, "A Smile, a Song, and a Refill"; Terry Gilliam, "An American in Plaster"; Graham "A Dozen Wholesale" Chapman; and Eric Idle, "Actual Size—Batteries Extra."

ALSO APPEARING: Carol "Four Revealing Poses" Cleveland
The Fred Tomlinson Singers
Rosalind Bailey

An announcer says that E. Henry Thripshaw T-shirts are now available.

The title page of the script reads "*MPFC* with Very Few Naughty Words. 'At last, a real work of art,' Don Revie; 'I laughed till I dried,' I. MacKellen; 'Much better than a poke in the eye,' Connie Francis."

The Rev. Arthur Belling was intended for Show 30, and was not included in this script. E. Henry Thripshaw was not intended for this show, either, but for Show 38.

This script contains several lengthy sketches that never ended up in any of the TV shows. These include a big-nosed sculptor bit, an early, extended part of "Eric the Half a Bee" (the end of which was used on *Monty Python's Previous Record*), "Cocktails" (which was performed in part during the early stage shows), and a "Wine-Tasting/Wee Wee" sketch that was filmed, but got into trouble with the BBC censors.

Wee-Wee

Although the "Wee-Wee" sketch was shot, it was never broadcast as part of the Python TV show, according to Graham Chapman. The scene involved a man showing a sophisticated guest through his wine cellar, allowing him to taste vintages that he confesses are actually wee-wee.

The sketch apparently fell victim to censorship from both without and within the group. "I had always imagined that the 'Wee-Wee' sketch had been broadcast, but I know it was controversial at the time," said Chapman.

"Lamentably, John was on the side of the authorities on that one, and in fact, almost alerted them to this 'Wee-Wee' sketch, which had, I think—partly subconsciously—been written with the idea of annoying John!" Chapman laughed. "Mike and Terry knew there was a raw nerve there in John Cleese, who just *couldn't* stand *anything at all* about early toilet training. Anything that had a reference in it to a childish word relating to that area would bring John out in a cold sweat or a rage, or both at the same time—had something to do with his mother, I imagine . . ."

Show 37—Dennis Moore

Recorded as Series 3, Show 8—Prod. #78413

"Boxing Tonight" sees British heavyweight champion Jack Bodell take on the tweed-suited Sir Kenneth Clarke in the boxing ring; Clarke (GC) discusses the height of the English Renaissance before he is knocked out, and Bodell becomes the new Oxford Professor of Fine Arts.

In the corner, the Man in the Dinner Jacket (JC), without his desk, announces "And now" through a ring mike, a fanfare is played by the Nude Organist (TJ) in another corner, while the "It's" Man stands in a third corner and says "It's"

Titles

Highwayman Dennis Moore (JC), with an impressive introduction and theme song (to the tune

Cleese as Dennis Moore makes another visit to rob from the formerly rich, including Palin and Jones. Photo copyright BBC and Python Productions.

robs him; the loot is eaten by a frog with a man's head.

The "Great Debate" Number 31: TV4 or Not TV4? Ludovic Ludovic (EI) introduces the group (JC, GC, MP, TJ), they all respond with a yes or a no, and the credits roll.

Coming Attractions show "Victoria Regina," "George I, Episode Three—the Gathering Storm." A party is attended by several fops in elaborate dress and powdered wigs, including the Lord of Buckingham (TJ) and Grantley (MP). Dennis Moore swings into the ballroom on a rope, as they are all discussing history. He steals all of their lupins and

of "Robin Hood"), stops a carriage with a Vicar (EI), a couple (TJ and CC), and the driver (MP), and brags about his sharp-shooting. They all discuss the trees he claims he can hit, then he robs them all of their lupins, as it is the Lupin Express. He rides off as his theme plays, gives the lupins to a peasant couple, Mr. And Mrs. Jenkins (MP and TJ), and "The End" is shown.

Mrs. Once Off (GC) and Irene Trepidacius (EI) discuss astrology, and predicting the future; Mrs. Once Off's horoscope (her star sign is Basil) describes her as a huge lizard. Irene goes through a list of synonyms for precognition, and a sign listing several is lowered from the ceiling, as the audience is invited to read along with "foretoken, presage, portend . . ." A Doctor (TJ) is lowered on a rope; he smashes furniture in his struggle to open his bag. Once opened, the bag is full of money. He takes Mrs. Once Off's money at gunpoint, as well as money from a hand in her wall, and says "See you next week."

A Doctor (MP) making his hospital rounds takes money from the heavily bandaged Mr. Hanson (TG), and other equally afflicted patients (including Mr. Millichope).

An animated Securicor Ambulance/Armored Car burgles a house, then hits a pedestrian and

Mrs. Once Off (Chapman) studies her horoscope, as she and Mrs. Trepidacius prepare to embark on a Palin/Jones sketch that parodies the Cleese/Chapman writing style. Photo copyright BBC and Python Productions.

takes them to the peasant Jenkins and his dying wife (TJ), his theme playing as he rides. Jenkins asks him to steal them medicine, food, blankets, clothes, and wood. He rides back, theme playing, to the ballroom and steals everything, taking a large bag of swag to the peasants. "The End."

The Fifteenth Annual Ideal Loon Exhibition includes: Kevin Bruce of Australia, ranked fourteenth in the World Silly Positions League; Norman Kirby of New Zealand, who stands behind a screen with a naked lady; the Friends of the Free French Osteopaths performing rather silly behavior; Brian Brumas (GC), who for two weeks has been suspended over a tin of condemned veal; Italian priests in custard; and the Royal Canadian Mounted Geese. The highlight is the judging, and Justice Burke (EI) is pronounced the winner.

Animated plan 38A is put into effect by the police, and a huge hole is set up to trap victims.

In an off license, Mr. McGough (EI) is a solicitor who has caught poetry, and asks for a bottle of sherry from the sales clerk, Mr. Bones (JC). Bones then lapses into the story of Dennis Moore.

Though the rich have become poor, Moore robs them again and rides back (with his theme) to the former peasants' house. They are now living in luxury, and he realizes that redistribution of wealth is trickier than he'd thought, and there is stock film of Women's Institute applause.

The applause continues into "Prejudice," hosted by Russell Bradon (MP), in which they insult all races, creeds, and colors. He helps a viewer find something wrong with the Syrians, and the winning entries of a contest to find derogatory terms for Belgians are read (the winner is "miserable fat Belgian bastards"), and they end with a "Shoot the Poof" segment.

Dennis Moore robs a coach and tries to distribute the wealth evenly among all the occupants as the credits roll.

The man in the off license catches poetry (Idle), while the sales clerk (Cleese) begins the tale of Dennis Moore. Photo copyright BBC and Python Productions.

ALSO APPEARING: Carol Cleveland
Nosher Powell

Losing judges comfort each other on a bus after the contest.

The judges on the bus originally followed the animation after the Ideal Loon, before the man in the off license.

Prognostications of Parody

"We kept on parodying each others' sketches and styles," says Terry Jones, explaining how he and Palin took off on the Chapman/Cleese use of *Roget's Thesaurus*. "We wrote a sketch that we didn't really mean seriously—it was a parody of one of John and Graham's sketches."

It involved two old ladies discussing astrology, just before a doctor is lowered to rob them. "They're going on about star signs and prognostications, and we go to all these other names for prognostication, pulling down a sheet, and getting the audience to do them.

"When we actually wrote it, we didn't intend it as a serious sketch—we were just ribbing John

and Graham," Jones laughs. "We were surprised when it got into the show!"

Learning Lines

Partially due to their training in university revues, the group generally didn't have much trouble learning their lines in the shows.

"I was always good at that," recalls John Cleese. "When I was studying law, I learned to start memorizing something early, and just repeat it a lot, and not try to do it two nights before. When I do the learning at the beginning of the week, by the time I get to the show, it's almost automatic. But I have to start early. If I leave it until late, panic sets in. The great thing about remembering lines is confidence—if I feel confident, I'll remember them."

Cleese says there is a great advantage in writing the material to be memorized (although not on such nonsense things as Johann Gambolputty). "If I've written it, I have a very clear memory of exactly why I wrote each line, from a writer's point of view. Therefore, I have the underlying logic in my head, which makes it easier to learn dialogue."

Show 38—A Book at Bedtime

Recorded as Series 3, Show 3—Prod. #75554

A caption reads that the show will start immediately with the opening titles. We then see the Nude Organist (TJ), the Man in the Dinner Jacket (JC), and the "It's" Man (MP), then the

Titles

"A Book at Bedtime" features Sir Jeremy Toogood (MP), a dyslexic, trying to read *The Red Gauntlet* by Sir Walter Scott. He has difficulty with most of the words, and is joined by stage managers, the director, and others (JC, EI, GC) trying to help.

The Lone Piper on the Battlements of Edinburgh Castle is hurled off, and the Queen's Own McKamikaze Highlanders are trained to leap from the castle. Their Sergeant Major (TJ) and Commander (JC) train them, until only one man, MacDonald

(GC) is left. In an office, a Man (MP) visits a Kamikaze Advice Centre, and steps out the wrong door.

At the castle, the Commander wants to send the regiment on a mission, but MacDonald, the last surviving member, keeps trying to kill himself. The Commander says "No time to lose," a phrase the Sergeant Major has never heard before.

At a No Time to Lose Advice Centre, a Man (MP) tries to learn how to use the phrase correctly, and the Consultant (EI) tries to sell him the phrase.

The animation of "No Time Toulouse, the Story of the Wild and Lawless Days of the Post-Impressionists," is told as he fights a showdown.

Back at the castle, the last survivor continues to attempt suicide, and is sent on a mission with

182

the Sgt. Major. MacDonald tries to jump from a truck, strangle himself, and is repeatedly run over. "A Book at Bedtime" continues briefly, and more people are trying to read.

An animated parody of *2001* sees a bone become a space station, and fall down onto a caveman.

"Frontiers of Medicine," Part II, presents The Gathering Storm, over films of penguins. The Host (JC) discusses accidental discoveries, and introduces Prof. Ken Rosewall (GC). He explains their theories, aided by charts, which claim the penguin is smarter than humans: if penguins were as big as men, their brains would still be smaller, but would be much larger than they were before. Dr. Peaches Bartkowicz (MP) stands under a sixty-six-foot-tall penguin and penguins are shown to be smarter than BBC program planners. Dr. Lewis Hoad (EI) explains that they are actually equal in intelligence to non-English-speaking people. Penguins are then seen taking over such important jobs as working the checkpoint on the Russo-Polish border, along with other animated jobs.

At the Kremlin, Russian officers (EI and JC) are attacked by MacDonald, the Scottish Kamikaze. They call the Unexploded Scotsman Disposal Squad (MP and TJ). A phone in a tree is seen ringing, the camera pans over and shows the Squad in a field, taking MacDonald's head off and putting it in a bucket of vodka.

"Spot the Looney," which includes a whole panel of loonies, features the Presenter (EI) displaying a variety of loonies in films and photos. The Spot the Looney Historical Adaptation presents a looney version of *Ivanhoe,* and buzzers go off whenever a looney is spotted.

An Introducer of Documentaries (JC) walks through the woods and begins a talk on Sir Walter Scott, and another Documentary Man (MP) grabs his microphone and begins to discuss replanting forests. The first Introducer grabs it back, and a fight breaks out over the mike. Angus Tinker (GC) begins his segment on Scott, but a Forestry Reporter (TJ) then grabs his microphone, and a car chase follows.

A slide reads "The End."

The closing credits show film of politicians, with the looney buzzer going off.

A BBC slide announces next week's "A Book at Bedtime," but the announcer can't pronounce *Black Beauty.*

The BBC also announces new comedy programs, including "Dad's Doctor" (with TJ and a nude woman), "Dad's Pooves," "On the Dad's Liver Bachelors at Large," "The Ratings Game," "Up the Palace," and "Limestone, Dear Limestone."

The set is then shut off.

The sketch with Mrs. Zambesi 1 and Mrs. Zambesi 2, in which they order a new brain, was to follow the battle over the microphone. It wound up in Show 39.

The show was to begin with a party political broadcast on behalf of the Conservative and Unionist Party, in which a Politician (JC) tries to dance while delivering his speech, and a Choreographer (EI) interrupts to help him. He is joined by six male dancers in a kick line, and gives a wave and cheesecake smile at the end. Two Labor MPs in leotards and leg warmers are rehearsing their upcoming speech, and an animated Wilson and Heath dance, as well. The initial PBS broadcasts reportedly included this sketch, but disappeared in subsequent versions.

Still More Penguins

There is no real reason for the Python obsession with penguins, admits Michael Palin, except that he considers them to be wonderful birds. "We all love penguins. There's something slightly silly about them, the fact that they can't fly very well, yet they've got these rather stubby little wings.

"The way they move is wonderful, very like Python characters. A group of penguins looks like a group of old ladies in supermarkets," Palin says, screeching "Wellll!" in a Pepperpot voice, "waggling their little flippers and looking self-important. We all rather like penguins, the same way we like haddock, or halibut—fish used to come in a lot as well . . ."

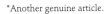

McKamikaze Python

Graham Chapman's alcoholism had become quite a problem by the third series of Python, and had started interfering with his work. While playing the McKamikaze Scotsman he was required to lie in a road, while a truck ran over him several times.

"That was a very simple, straightforward thing to do," Chapman explained in 1988. "In that partic-

ular show, I remember the difficult thing for me—because my romance with alcohol was very much in its heyday—was keeping my limbs stiff while pretending to be dead, lying flat on my back with my knees in the air. I had incredible difficulty, because of tremor. It's absolutely easy now, I just couldn't then. Big problem! Any sharp medical practitioner watching the show would say 'Ah!' Anyway, it's nice to feel better watching it now than I did back then."

Show 39 — Grandstand

Recorded as Series 3, Show 12—Prod. #78817

A Thames TV announcer (David Hamilton*) introduces the evening's lineup on that channel, but first, "a rotten old BBC program!"

A fanfare by the Nude Organist (TJ), the Man in the Dinner Jacket (JC), and the "It's" Man (MP) precede

Titles for the British Show Biz Awards, presented by Her Royal Highness, the Dummy Princess Margaret.

Dickie (EI), the Attenborough-like presenter of the British Show Biz Awards, gives an elaborate introduction for the remains of the late Sir Alan Waddle (TG brings in an urn, which is in black tie), who reads the first nominations. They include Edward Heath for the "Edward Heath" sketch, Richard Baker for "Lemon Curry," and the winner, the "Oscar Wilde" sketch.

"London 1895, at Wilde's residence." Wilde (GC) exchanges epigrams with James MacNeil Whistler (JC), George Bernard Shaw (MP), and the Prince of Wales, the future Edward VII (TJ), who is compared to a jelly donut and a stream of bat's piss.

Animation of a society party has a woman go to the bathroom and loudly "powder her nose." Charwoman sweeps away the last remnants of male chauvinism, she pounds on her chest and her breasts explode.

Back at the show, Dickie puts glycerine drops in his eyes and has the next nomination read by David Niven's refrigerator: the refrigerator, in black tie, is delivered (by TG). Pasolini's *The Third Test Match* (complete with credits), has come in

sixth; it is a Bergmanesque cricket film dripping with sexual imagery. Pier Paolo Pasolini talks with a cricket team, and is seen on television by Mrs. Zambesi 1 and Mrs. Zambesi 2 (GC and TJ). They discuss giving blood. They decide to order a new brain—Curry's Own Brains, for thirteen shillings and sixpence. They call to place the order and answer "Yes . . . yes . . . yes . . ." and give their shoe size, then a Man (JC) arrives with a receipt. A

Nearly all of the Pythons played newsreaders at one point or another (including Eric Idle), in addition to the real British newsreaders. Photo copyright BBC and Python Productions.

*Another genuine article.

dummy salesman, Mr. Rutherford, is thrown into the room, and a Second Salesman (MP) arrives and straps on the new brain, which malfunctions when they go to give blood. On their way there, they pass a Kamikaze Scotsman.

At the blood bank, Mr. Grimshaw (EI) asks the Doctor (JC) if he can give urine instead of blood. After the Doctor refuses, he steals some of the Doctor's blood so that he'll be allowed to donate urine.

"Wife-Swapping" stars Rickman (MP), the host of International Wife-Swapping from Redcar. Wives race from house to house, and Jack Casey (TJ), whose wife wins, is interviewed. Next is the team event: Northwest vs. the Southeast, swapping to the mambo. On "Grandstand," the Host (MP) spotlights a rugby match with a wife as the center of play. "Grandstand" features titles with various wife-swapping scenes, as the credits roll. The credits are shown over "Grandstand," with all the names matched up with various spouses.

ALSO APPEARING: Carol Cleveland
                     Caron Gardner

At the awards ceremony, Dickie cries with the aid of a stirrup pump that sprays tears, as he awards the Mountbatten Trophy to the cast of the "Dirty Vicar" sketch. The sketch is shown, in which the butler, Chivers (GC), introduces the new Vicar, Rev. Ronald Simms (TJ), who starts assaulting the women in the drawing room. Dickie interrupts the sketch to end it.

🎬 E. H. Thripshaw was to follow the Wilde scene and its animation according to the original script; buying a brain was also in the previous show.

🎬 The title page of the script credits "Thomas and William Palin; additional material by Cynthia Cleese" (their real-life children).

The Newsreaders' Ball

The Pythons managed to get several real TV newsreaders to appear on some of their shows in various roles; strangely enough, some of them were fans who were happy to join in. "That was a major sign that we were doing all right, when people like that would do it. We were very fond of newsreaders," explains Michael Palin.

"BBC newsreaders weren't too keen on joining in the fun, though on ITV*, the Thames newsreaders were very happy. In fact, we had a launch party for the first Python book, so we made it a Newsreaders Ball. The newsreaders were invited along, and we had a band. Suddenly people who had only seen these newsreaders from the waist up, saw all these full-length newsreaders there. There had never been a gathering all together of newsreaders, so it was rather nice."

*The privately owned TV stations.

Monty Python's
Lost Episodes

The German Shows

MANY PYTHON FANATICS have virtually memorized the classic forty-five half-hour TV shows, but until recent years, few of them were able to see the two original fifty-minute shows shot in the early '70s for German TV. The second show was broadcast in England on BBC 2, but the first program was only seen in what was then West Germany, largely because it was shot entirely in German. Though the two shows slowly made themselves known in a few retrospective screenings over the years, their first appearances on television were on Comedy Central, although they were shown edited for commercial breaks.

Throughout the years, the group has cannibalized a few of the sketches for use primarily in the stage shows, including the *Little Red Riding Hood* film, the "Silly Olympics," and the "Philosophers' Football Match." In addition, some of the other original bits have turned up on Python albums, such as "Stake Your Claim" and a somewhat different version of the "Fairy Tale" sketch.

All of the material was created especially for the show, however, except for a Bavarian version of the "Lumberjack Song," sung in German, and the sketch in which Colin "Bomber" Harris wrestles himself. Graham Chapman performed the latter in virtually all of the stage shows, and originated it long before.*

The shows actually came about through German initiative in 1972.

"There was great enthusiasm from a producer at Bavarian TV," Chapman recalled. "He had seen some of our work somewhere, and decided that we were amazing, and we ought to do a show for him. The idea

---

*"It's been with me off and on for most of my life," he recalled. The scene requires Chapman to put his body through rigorous physical contortions; backstage on the last night of the Hollywood Bowl show, he happily noted that "This is the last time I'll ever have to do this scene" (as it turned out later, he performed it for some of his lecture tours in the '80s).

of doing fifty minutes totally on film—at that point we were only doing studio stuff with a little bit of film—was something we wanted to have done.

"We went over there to have a look around, to see what might spark off ideas, and spent a couple of months writing each one. The first one was in German, the second one in English, which was later dubbed."

Language problems slowed them down a bit, although John Cleese says he speaks some German. "I spoke a little, and Michael can understand a little, but the others didn't at first. We worked with Germans who translated it. We would say 'What does this actually mean?' and they explained the translation to us.

"Occasionally, we were able to say 'Well, that's not really quite the sense we wanted. Do you have a word that's softer, a word that a schoolmaster would use to a schoolboy?'" Cleese explains. "We managed to get the flavor as a result of that, though none of us speak German well enough to know whether we got it exactly. But we got it pretty much right, and parroted it off. I can still remember great chunks of it," he says, and demonstrates. "I know what it means, but I can't speak the language, as such."

Though the shows were filmed totally in Germany, and written specifically for German viewers, the Pythons didn't hold back. It was quite the opposite, as Graham Chapman recalled.

"They were kind of way-out; we didn't pull any punches. It was probably a stage farther on than any of the TV shows we'd done in England up to that point, in terms of absurdity and peculiar starts, and they lacked any sort of thread to keep the audience sane. Indeed, it was deliberately annoying for the audience, as we often were. It was quite a stupidly courageous thing to have done, I suppose," Chapman smiled.

"The first program was actually screened opposite an England-German football match that night, so I don't think anyone in Germany watched the TV show—except the critics. But they liked it. I suppose that's why we got asked back to do another one the next year."

NOTE: These show synopses are based on the original shooting scripts, and some relatively minor discrepancies may exist. Terry Jones says that a few of the minor links may not have been filmed, but noted his memory may not be reliable more than a quarter of a century later!

Monty Python in Deutschland

A German lady announcer describes the background of the show and the performers. A flat behind her falls down, and she is revealed to be sitting in the open air, near a castle and lake. As she talks, two frogmen emerge and try to drag her in the water. She keeps talking, until they finally drag her underwater.

Animation leads into the opening titles.

"Live from Athens." An Olympic torch runner is run over.

An inaccurate documentary begins on Albrecht Dürer, when a program-planner type interrupts and apologizes for the inaccuracies in the show. They speak to an Australian in the outback drinking Fosters, but his appraisal of Dürer is heavily censored. An Anita Ekberg cutout sings "Albrecht Dürer" to the tune of "Dennis Moore/Robin Hood." An appreciation of Dürer is abandoned for Part 4 of *The Merchant of Venice*, performed by the Bad Toltz Dairy Herd, with the aid

of subtitles. Stock film of Women's Institute applause follows.

The Olympic torch runner becomes a cigarette commercial.

Next is a word from a Frenchman who has only been to the toilet once in the last five years. People who know him confirm this, including Willy Brandt, Nixon, the Pope, and a famous Berlin Specialist who describes their idyllic years together, while lush romantic music plays. A Farmer breeding doctors interrupts their romp in the country.

"The Life and Times of Albrecht Dürer" resumes with animation; the planner runs in, out of breath, and there is much cutting between the Farmer and Dürer.

Act I of *The Merchant of Venice* ends with the cows leaving the hospital. A Critic analyzes Shakespearean productions by animals, and the Doctors' version of *The Merchant of Venice* is

shown, complete with a commercial for the "Victor" Surgical Truss.

The "Little Red Riding Hood" story is shown, with a less-than-demure Hood (JC) and a less-than-intimidating wolf.

L.R.R. Hood becomes manageress of a Holiday Inn in the United Arab Republic. On an Egyptian side street, an Arab tries to proffer dirty photos, dirty socks, dirty woodcuts, and a picture of Dürer, with animated woodcuts and engravings.

A Camper on the Olympic torch runner's shoulders fries an egg on the torch, and a tent is set up at the Pagodemburg, in the Nymphenberg Gardens, followed by ten seconds of sex.

Five Pepperpots arrive in Munich to get shopping accepted as an Olympic Sport, and the team is profiled. They practice counter approach, packing speed, complaining, and bargain spotting, but they specialize in arguing and gossiping. The "International Shopping Contest—Germany v. England" is held at the Marianplatz, with replays and slow motion effects. The winner, Mrs. Elsie Schweiz of Germany, acquires the lease and buys an entire shop.

Scenes are shown from the three-thousand-meter steeplechase for people who think they're chickens, as well as a marathon for incontinents, as they hop, step, and write a novel. A hammer throw leads into

A Wild West town, where Dürer enters a saloon. The program planner stops it, and calls for a panel game.

"Stake Your Claim" features Norman Vowles of Gravesend, who claims he wrote all of the works attributed to William Shakespeare. Mrs. M

of Dundee is thrown off Salzburg Castle and buried as part of her claim. Vowles returns, claiming he wanted to be a holzfeller (lumberjack), and the "Lumberjack Song" is performed in German, with a chorus made up of Austrian border police.

A letter of complaint leads into animation.

A wrestling match sees Colin "Bomber" Harris (GC) grappling with himself.

Film of the Free World's fight against fresh fruit and International Socialism follows.

Two flunkies carry a sedan chair. A nobleman enters, a flushing noise is heard, and they all leave.

Animated titles begin the "Bavarian Restaurant" sketch, in which the food, drink, and service is traditional beyond the point of being sensible, with more traditions than anywhere else in Germany. Coats are taken with musical accompaniment, as are sitting down, bringing menus, etc. The Maître d' recommends appallingly violent food, in the name of tradition.

Historical footage is shown to discover the history of the joke, including cavemen, Egyptians, Greeks (the trip and fall), Romans (the chair pulled out), and medieval times (the plank). Also included are Columbus and the banana peel, the Renaissance, leading up to Baroque comedy and modern-day jokes, with footage of Lenin telling a joke, and robots tripping each other.

The End

Animation features the castle.

The lady announcer emerges from the lake, still talking.

Show Zwei

The second German show was shot the next year, in October 1973. Also entirely on film, this one was later run as a special on BBC 2. It was performed in English, and dubbed for its original German broadcast. By this time, the writing partnerships were as loose as they had ever been, and John Cleese found himself writing with his then-wife, Connie Booth.

". . . In the second German show, we did a prolonged sendup of a medieval fairy tale, which Connie and I wrote. It was actually well liked at

the time, and we used it in the stage show at Drury Lane, though I don't think it was frightfully well directed," Cleese recalls.

"But it was a script that everybody liked, and Terry Jones actually wanted to base a feature on it. That was the first thing that Connie and I ever wrote together."

An abridged version of the "Fairy Tale" sketch appears on *Monty Python's Previous Album,* and the Cleese/Booth team went on to create *Fawlty Towers.*

A William Tell blackout begins, followed by

Arthur Schmidt, stockbroker and international financier, who becomes Superbutcher! He is followed by Norbert Schultze, an economic theoretician who becomes Wilf, the Furry Tiger; and finally Gustav Pedersen, who changes into Mrs. Edith Griffiths. The Presenter becomes Linkman! He flies in animation to the

Titles

Mr. Zurk hosts a show on sycophancy, with Mr. Norman Thrombie and Mr. Twall, who just tries to be polite.

There is a profile of Frank Tutankhamun, who has dedicated his life to preserving mice (and has also opened a National Fish Park). Cowboys ride the four-thousand-acre Big Squeak Ranch, where eight white mice roam freely, and they rope and brand the mice. The Pied Piper of Hamelin is interviewed; he has had to diversify. Outside the "Little Furry Creature Saloon," mice are tethered, but there is a stampede. Elsewhere, a Prospector pans for chickens, and there is footage of the Great Chicken Rush of '49, with animation. Forged chickens are discovered (a cleverly reconstructed rabbit).

An animated opening for "International Philosophy" features German vs. Greek philosophers playing football.

"Learning to Swim" with Arthur Lustgarten, features Part 27, Entering the Pool; the Cowardly Announcer is afraid of the water.

Back in "International Philosophy," no one has moved, and Nietzsche is thrown out of the game for arguing with the referee, Confucius.

More animation leads to a Customer trying to buy a hearing aid from Rogers, a shop assistant. They get Dr. Waring to fit him for contact lenses. Another Customer enters who wants to complain about his contact lenses, and a fight breaks out.

In Happy Valley, King Otto and his daughter, Princess Mitzi Gaynor (CB) live in happiness, for sadness is punishable by death. Mitzi finds the Queen in a clinch with a black man, Mr. Erasmus, whom she claims is her new algebra teacher. Mitzi herself is engaged to Prince Walther; King Otto en-

tertains himself by playing his organ and singing "Ya de buckety rum ting ptoo."

Prince Charming arrives and promises to slay a dragon for Mitzi. At the stadium the next day, he shoots a tiny dragon with his revolver, then starts jumping up and down on it. Walther vows revenge. A witch interrupts Mitzi and Charming's wedding, and changes Charming into a toad, a lampstand, a turkey, and several other objects. She finally changes the entire congregation into chickens, and the prospectors head toward the church as the credits roll.

The Linkman says "The moral is, if you don't have a good way of ending a fairy story, have a moral."

In the spring of 1978, the filming of *Life of Brian* was anything but certain, especially after EMI pulled their money out. Whether *Brian* was filmed or not, the group still planned to do a movie that year.

"Our 'Plan B' is to use the two tapes that we made in Munich in '72 and '73," Michael Palin said in April '78. "They contain a lot of very funny material, like the Silly Olympics, the philosophers playing football, and John as Little Red Riding Hood . . .

"We could probably get together fifty or sixty minutes of material which would form the basis of a sketch show. We would then write and re-record other sketches to go around it in September and October. For a really modest outlay and total control, we'd have ourselves a little Python film to push around as a stopgap.

"It's not as attractive as *Brian,* which would stretch Python far more than doing old material again. On the other hand, the German stuff is good material, and we wouldn't have to bother with any sort of backers and people getting cold feet at the last minute. We'd be doing all that stuff ourselves."

Of course, the money came through from George Harrison, and the need for using the German shows once again ended. The two German shows were eventually screened publicly in America—apparently for the first time—on the after-

noons of February 17 and 24 as part of the 1989 Python retrospective at New York's Museum of Broadcasting. They were also shown as part of the Director's Guild salute to Python in 1994. But, most Python fans got to watch them first as part of a Monty Python New Year's Day Marathon on Comedy Central. Videocassette release began in 1998.

The Fourth Series

Aired October 31 – December 5, 1974

I<small>T CAME AS</small> no great shock to any of the others when John Cleese decided against doing another series of Python. He had been restless to move on to something different, which turned out to be *Fawlty Towers*. Reaction from the rest of the group ranged from regret to anger, but they decided to carry on with six more shows, though they felt mixed emotions at doing so. Cleese had left behind some unused material developed during writing sessions for *Monty Python and the Holy Grail,* and he allowed them to use it in the new series of shows. Much of what he wrote turned up in the "Michael Ellis" show, and can be seen in the script reproduced in the *Grail* book.

"*Holy Grail* meandered about in early writing stages, and it wasn't until Mike and Terry came up with the coconuts scene that we all began to fall for the idea of it being set in medieval times," Cleese explains. "But there was a lot of material in the first draft, which probably wasn't even called *Holy Grail* at that point, and something like ninety percent of the first draft was thrown out. It's in the book, and a lot of it is very funny.

"That was the stuff which I said I was very happy for them to use in the six shows. But apart from the 'Toupee' sketch in the 'Michael Ellis' piece, I can't remember what the other material was. I've only ever seen three of those shows, one of which was excellent, one was pretty good, and one wasn't so good. Everybody said they weren't quite as good as the ones done with me, and the three I saw seemed to be playing with the same kind of average."

For the remaining five, the decision to move ahead on their own was a difficult one, and the final six shows were almost never made. "For a long time, the rest of us were caught between two schools—whether to just give up, or to try and do Python without John," says Michael Palin.

"Every time we thought 'Oh, we can't do Python without John, Python's got to have six people,' we would then get together and say 'Well, all of us want to do some more—we've got some great ideas.' Some of us felt that Python was just beginning to work, while others thought it had passed its peak. But just seeing all that material around and the will to do it together, it would be a shame not to. So we eventually did it. John was happy enough for us to use the 'Michael Ellis' stuff, but the other shows were written without John, which was a pity, in retrospect. It shouldn't have happened like that. Although I did enjoy making most of those shows, they weren't really Python."

The last six shows did away with most of the conventions and recurring characters from the previous three seasons, and a new set of animated titles was created. The name of the show was also shortened to *Monty Python* in Cleese's absence. Terry Gilliam took a stronger hand in the acting, while Neil Innes and others became more involved with the group.

Most important, the programs show a heavier Palin/Jones influence, with half of them involving a more linear storyline from beginning to end, a movement in the direction that would eventually bring forth *Ripping Yarns*. "The Golden Age of Ballooning" featured the Montgolfier Brothers as a continuing thread throughout the first show; "Michael Ellis" is the rather straightforward story of the title character and his attempts to buy a pet ant; and "Mr. Neutron" tells the story of the search for the most deadly and dangerous man in the world. Interestingly, "Ellis" is the only show-length Chapman/Cleese sketch, which can be attributed to its origins as a first draft of *Holy Grail*.

Nevertheless, if the fourth series didn't quite measure up to its predecessors, it can in part be blamed on the fact that the earlier shows set such a high standard for laughter and innovation. In any case, there are still plenty of gems left in the final TV shows.

Incidentally, it was the fourth series of shows that caused the Pythons' biggest legal battle in America. ABC bought the rights to the six programs to air as part of their "Wide World of Entertainment" late-night specials. Unbeknownst to the group, ABC cut, edited, and censored three half-hour shows down to sixty-six minutes and broadcast the results on October 3, 1975.

The Pythons then filed suit to prevent the network from cutting up the second three shows. Although they were unable to prevent the second special from airing on December 26, there was a brief disclaimer at the beginning of the show. The group continued their court battle with ABC, finally winning six months later, establishing a precedent regarding copyright laws, and eventually obtaining ownership of the Python shows.

Show 40 — The Golden Age of Ballooning

Recorded as Series 4, Show 1—Prod. #95141

Animation opens "The Golden Age of Ballooning," introduced by a Plumber (MP) as he fixes a toilet.

Jacques and Joseph Montgolfier (EI and TJ) discuss bathing on the eve of their first flight, while the Butler (GC) tries to introduce Mr. Bartlett. The two animated brothers wash each other, before The End.

An advertisement appears for next week's "Golden Age of Ballooning"; other GAOB books and items are plugged. Part Two Follows, which features "The Montgolfier Brothers in Love." The GAOB titles are run on a home-movie screen in their workshop, where Joseph (TJ) works as his fiancée, Antoinette (CC), is floating like the bottom half of an airship; she complains that he is obsessed with balloons.

The Butler introduces Louis XIV (MP), complete with Glaswegian accent, and two advisors, who want to see plans of their proposed airship. Jacques and the King can't think of anything to say to each other, and he instructs the Butler to search for the claret, and shows their balloon plans to the King. Joseph bursts in with a shower cap and towels to prevent them from taking the plans to the Royal Archives, and points out that Louis XIV died in 1717, and it's 1783.

Part Three of "The Golden Age of Ballooning." The Great Day for France finds Sir Charles Divi-

 1 9 4

dends (GC) on a chat show, *Decision,* with Lord Interest (EI) and a Linkman (MP), who changes the current affairs show into the court of George III, 1781, and tips viewers off on the Montgolfier Brothers' plans.

King George III (GC) is read to (by EI), when they are interrupted by Louis XVI (MP) (after trying Louis XVIII), who sells them the plans and promises to disengage their troops in America. They want their money immediately, but Joseph rushes in wearing a towel, and exposes the phony Louis the XVI. Another Butler (TG) announces the Ronettes, a trio of black women who come in singing "King George the Third."

Joseph Montgolfier and his fiancée Antoinette (Jones and Cleveland) continue their experiments with lighter-than-air craft. Photo copyright BBC and Python Productions.

Back in France, Antoinette paces as Jacques wonders about Joseph, and the Butler still can't find the claret. He announces that Mr. Bartlett is gone, to audience laughter, applause, pandemonium, and shouts of "More!" while being congratulated by the entire cast, as the credits roll.

ALSO APPEARING: Carol Cleveland
Peter Brett
Frank Lester
Bob E. Raymond
Stenson Falke

A voiceover credits Neil Innes for writing "King George the Third."

A BBC slide announces more "Golden Age of Ballooning" items, and introduces a party political broadcast for the Norwegian Party (EI), involving Norwegian gibberish with subtitles explaining the advantages of the Norwegian economy and Norwegian women.

"The Golden Age of Ballooning." Episode Six—Ferdinand Von Zeppelin: Pioneer of the Airship has one of the Zeppelin brothers, Benny (TJ), inflate himself.

Ferdinand Von Zeppelin (GC) hosts a party in his airship, but when his guests refer to it as a balloon, he throws them out. They all land in a small house and disturb a German couple, Helmut (MP) and Hollweg (TJ), as he reads to her. She finds the chancellor and Prince Von Bülow, along with the bodies of ten other military and political leaders in their drawing room. More film and slides of zeppelins are shown, and the director of GAOB, Mike Henderson, is revealed to be a descendant of one of the balloonists.

"The Golden Years of Colonic Irrigation" is next, followed by more ballooning as two *Mill on the Floss* characters float away.

Cut from the final show was an animated sequence showing America becoming New Scotland, with a bagpipe version of the Stars and Stripes.

Also cut was a montage of Benny Zeppelin's life, including a scene at the "Royal Institute For Less-Talented Younger Brothers" with Harpo Nietzsche.

Timeless Comedy

One of the reasons the Python shows hold up as well as they do, decades later, is that they avoided using topical humor. This was a deliberate decision on their part, made for several reasons.

"Since we came along fairly closely after *Beyond the Fringe*, and the social consciousness and satirical label that they'd gotten—somewhat unfairly—we wanted to avoid being bracketed as being another offshoot of their methods," explained Graham Chapman.

"More importantly, however, a very practical reason was repeats. We'd written in TV for a few years, so we'd obviously realized at this stage that if we wrote something in a show that got repeated, then we would get another fee for it without having to do any extra work! Now, that looked like a good idea, and as the BBC didn't pay us very much in the first place, it was almost essential to have the thing repeated. Obviously, topical things were not favored, because they wouldn't work in a couple of years' time, so we did tend to avoid them."

Cleveland over All

Some of Carol Cleveland's most challenging Python moments occurred in the fourth series.

"I had to hold a bazooka or flame-thrower—it wasn't a real one, it was a mock-up, but it was pretty much like the real thing—a real flame shot out of this thing, and that frightened the hell out of me," says Cleveland. "What you don't see in the camera shot is me falling backwards out of shot when this thing went off! That was terrifying!

"There was another occasion where I had to be lifted into the air. This crane lifted Michael and myself, dressed in Edwardian costumes, and these uncomfortable harnesses—they were yanking me up in the air and floating me about. But I would have done anything they asked me, aside from appearing topless—I was game for anything!"

Show 41—Michael Ellis

Recorded as Series 4, Show 2—Prog. #91562

The Titles roll, immediately followed by the closing credits (with a writing credit for JC).
ALSO APPEARING: Carol Cleveland
John Hughman

A Doorman lets in customers at a Harrod's type store; he is kneed in the groin by an Old Lady, and parks the bicycle of Chris Quinn (EI), another customer. Chris walks in, and studies the directory.

At one of the counters, a Woman (CC) complains to an Assistant (TG) about a flamethrower, and one customer is burned. Chris walks by them, and approaches Another Assistant (GC), who mistakes him for a Michael Ellis. Chris demands a Third Assistant (MP), and then calls for the Real Manager (TJ). He tries to explain everything, and is told it's the store's Rag Week.* He is finally waited

*When high school and university students indulge in harmless pranks, ostensibly for charity.

on (by MP), and explains that he wants to buy an ant. He picks one out that he names Marcus, buys him a cage, ant toys, and a book, but as he leaves, he is called Mr. Ellis.

Chris takes the ant home, where his Mother (TJ) complains about all of his other pets that he's lost interest in, including a tiger and sperm whale. She says Michael Ellis has been looking for him all day. He and Marcus watch University of the Air (hosted by MP) on animal communications; it features "Let's Talk Ant," a restaurant scene with an ant-speaking Waiter and Customer (GC and TJ). They begin discussing Michael Ellis when his mother turns the set off. When Chris turns the TV on again, an animated ant is being dissected. He learns that Marcus has two legs missing, and decides to take him back. An elevator lady gives him directions for ant complaints, and he is directed to the Toupee Hall.

Chris enters to find an Old Lady (GC) at a Vic-

torian poetry reading, where Wordsworth reads *I wandered lonely as an ant,* and Shelley reads an ant version of *Ozymandias.* Keats (EI) begins reading his *Ode to an Anteater,* but is pulled out of the hall. Queen Victoria (MP) enters, accompanied by her late husband Albert in his coffin. As she denounces ant poetry and begins to lapse into a German accent, Chris slips away.

Chris is pulled into the Toupee Hall (by TJ) and finds two other Men (MP and GC), all wearing shoddy toupees. He escapes from them and rushes into the complaint room. A Customer (CC) complains to the Clerk (MP) about the lack of a safety on her flamethrower, and sets his desk on fire. Another Man (GC) goes to complain, and they all become surrounded by flames. An announcement over the intercom says it's the end of Michael Ellis Week, and that it is now Chris Quinn Week.

Chris is at the End of the Show Department, and a Salesman (TJ) demonstrates their offerings, including the pullout, the chase, walking into the sunset, the happy ending, a summing up from the panel, a slow fade, and the sudden ending.

Queen Victoria (Palin) with husband Albert (in the coffin) at a poetry reading devoted to ants (Gilliam is seen over Palin's shoulder). Photo copyright BBC and Python Productions.

Much of the "Michael Ellis" show is made up of material discarded from *Monty Python and the Holy Grail,* particularly the parts taking place in the Harrod's-like department store, which is why John Cleese received a writing credit here. Originally, portions of *Grail* were to take place in modern-day Britain, with the knights finding the object of their quest in the Grail Hall. Much of the original version of the script is reprinted in the *Monty Python and the Holy Grail Book* (see the comments at the beginning of the Fourth Series by Cleese and Palin).

A scene between Chris Quinn and an Icelandic Honey Salesman was cut, as well as a scene at the Paisley Counter. Also, the Icelandic Honey Week Man was to be in the line at the Complaint Department.

Fire and Tigers

Although the Pythons seldom took unnecessary chances while filming, the number of potentially dangerous elements somehow seemed to peak in the "Michael Ellis" show. Carol Cleveland played a woman who tries to return a defective flamethrower, while another bit involved a live tiger in a cage. As Graham Chapman recalled, having such props around was fun, and invigorating.

"They obviously took a great deal of care, so there was very little actual danger, but I think we were all quite excited about the smoke and the flames. The guy [was supposed] to catch fire while having a conversation about being up north—some piece of madness—and [really] got set on fire, as well. But he didn't mind.

"I looked forward to the day when we had the tiger on the set, in front of the live studio audience. Terry was complaining about the tiger being on Mandies, how it shouldn't be getting more drugs because they only made it more stroppy. But unfortunately, the thing went to sleep," Chapman laughed. "It needed to be poked with a stick in order to move at all! They'd given it too much sedative before the show in order to keep it quiet, but played far too safe. It was nice having a tiger around, even if it was in a cage. Animals, in general, were always fun."

Show 42—The Light Entertainment War

Recorded as Series 4, Show 3—Prod. #95279

Two Tramps (MP and TJ) walk jauntily along, rooting through a garbage can and pulling out champagne and two glasses, while *Steptoe and Son* banjo music plays. They are run over by Alex Diamond (GC), as James Bond-like music plays. Diamond suffers from lumbago, which leads into Dr. Emile Koning, who battles lumbago (and Dr. Kildare-like music plays). Koning's doorbell is near Rear Admiral Humphrey De Vere (EI) as naval music plays. It all becomes the story of his daughter, a nurse, but evolves into Len Hanky, henteaser (TJ). Following him are the Chairman of Fiat (EI), and several more men, rapidly named, ending with a chaplain, Charlie Cooper (TJ), in a fighter plane, and the story of the men who flew with him.

In 1944 England, a Squadron Leader (EI) reports to his superiors, Squiffy Bovril (TJ) and Wingco (GC), speaking in banter which they don't understand. A Pilot (MP) enters, and no one can understand him; he reports that London is being bombed by cabbage crates.

A Private (EI) reports to Gen. Shirley (GC) that they are being attacked by troops with halos and wands, and the enemy is accused of not taking the war seriously. They are accused of trivializing the war by dropping cabbages and such.

A 1940s courtmartial sees Sapper Walters (EI) accused of taking out an enemy outpost with wet towels. He is charged with carrying on the war by other-than-warlike means. Col. Fawcett (MP), the

Survivors of the Light Entertainment War—and the survivors of the Python TV show, in their last season. (Left to right: Jones, Palin, Gilliam, Idle, and Chapman.) Photo copyright BBC and Python Productions.

 198

prosecutor, says the incident happened at Basingstoke in Westphalia, and the Head of the Review Board (TJ) tries to find the location on a map written by Cole Porter. Col. Fawcett insists it was compiled by a different Cole Porter, and sings a new version of "Anything Goes."

Walters is accused of having a pair of gaiters worth sixty-eight pounds, ten shillings, a present from the Regiment for the ways he used to oblige them. Walters then attacks the entire military system. The Head of the Review Board orders everyone to put on pixie hats, and they all sing "Anything Goes."

War film showing troops in halos and tutus serves as a trailer for a film about a soldier's love for another man in drag, *Coming Soon,* followed by
Titles

Mrs. Elizabeth III (TJ) and Mrs. Mock Tudor (GC) watch the beginning of "Up Your Pavement," and administer a shock to an Arab Boy (TG) near the TV, and he turns the set off. Mrs. Elizabeth III says the programming is for idiots, and goes about proving to her friend that she's an idiot.

Programmers for TV decide viewers are such idiots that viewers would watch a film of the M4 Motorway, which they broadcast successfully. Programmers discuss televising more motorways, and try to decide on new titles for their repeats. A Man from Security (TG) enters and reports that no one is taking the World War series seriously.

Animation of the Television Centre follows as bombs are dropped, and new weather is constructed for a man.

"England 1942." At the manor of Mansfield Vermin-Jones (GC), he, his wife (EI), and his daughter Rebecca (CC) all discuss pleasant, woodysounding words; his daughter is frightened by tinny-sounding words. Mansfield begins pronouncing sexual words, and is joined by the Pilot from the beginning of the show.

Elizabeth III and Mock Tudor shock their remote controller to change channels to the M2 Show, then to themselves watching TV, then to show jumping.

A woman on a horse jumps over the cast of *The Sound of Music,* followed by jumps over a minstrel show and the cast of *Ben-Hur.* They are interrupted by an announcement that World War II has reached the sentimental stage; the Germans started spooning at dawn and the British Army responded

by gazing into their eyes, so the Germans have gone all coy. There is film of a soldier singing "Where Does a Dream Begin" (written by Neil Innes), while the credits roll.

ALSO APPEARING: Carol Cleveland
Bob E. Raymond
Marion Mould

John Cleese and Neil Innes both have writing credits for the show.

Show Jumping

The casts of *Ben-Hur, The Sound of Music,* and the minstrel show, which were jumped by horses, provided some of the strangest visuals in all of Python, but strangely, none of them can remember much about the shooting. Graham Chapman believed there were one or two real people mixed in, but Terry Jones says in the end, they were all dummies.

"Originally, we intended them to be people," says Jones, "but the horses were a bit nervous going over actual people . . ."

Terry Gilliam's Cheap Thrills

It was the fourth series that saw Terry Gilliam really come into his own as an actor, and he appeared in nearly every show toward the end. Although his animations took up much of his time, he enjoyed performing, though he admits it was for less than noble reasons. "It's nice to see one's face up there, and to be recognized, but it's also the cheapest of possible thrills. It's not for the actual joy of performing, it's for the fact that I'm identified and recognized. If I sit and work up in a little room pushing pieces of paper, it's very nice *occasionally* for people to say 'Oh, that's the guy that did it!' That's why I don't think I'm an actor—I don't think I'm doing it for the right reasons.

"Sometimes I enjoyed performing very much," Gilliam says. "I enjoyed *Holy Grail,* being the bridgekeeper, and being Patsy. There are a lot of things along the way that I was genuinely doing for the right reasons. What I don't like about doing

199

them is that I don't like being second rate. I'm afraid that within the group, I am very second rate as a performer. They're very brilliant, so I desperately try to protect my ego, but it's tough going!

Whatever I did, I always felt it was small potatoes compared to what they were doing. I would really go for cheap shots, because that's about all *I* could do—they're great performers!"

Show 43—Hamlet

Recorded as Series 4, Show 4—Prod #95474

Titles roll for "Hamlet," Act I, opening with a car, driven by Hamlet (TJ), speeding down the street. He goes in to his Psychiatrist (GC), and tells him he really wants to be a private dick. The Psychiatrist repeats his "To be or not to be," traces his problem to sex. Another Psychiatrist (EI) claims the first was a bogus doctor, and he is chased out by a third (MP), who has papers to attempt to prove he is a psychiatrist. He then changes into a police costume and a Fourth Psychiatrist (TG) enters. All of them ask about his sexual problems ("So you've got the girl down on the bed and her legs up on the mantelpiece"). The Second Psychiatrist comes in again, claiming that it has all been part of a disorientation test, but he is soon chased out.

Dr. Bruce Genuine (TJ) of the Psychiatric Association gives assurances against bogus psychiatrists and discusses computer psychiatry.

"Nationwide" and its Host (EI) ignore World War III, and study sitting in a comfortable chair. A Reporter (GC) in a chair on a London bridge is then approached by a Policeman (MP) who tells him that his chair has been stolen from a Mrs. Edgeworth, who is standing across the street. He proves he is a policeman and then steals a chair from Mrs. Edgeworth so he can sit and talk to the reporter. As he discusses helmets, he steals lunch and beer from the passersby.

A couple necking on the other side of the bridge (TJ and CC) are to be married, but she tells him that her Father (GC) will have to live with and sleep in the same bed as them. The Father reads in bed with them, and when they turn out the lights, he tries to build a model in the dark.

Titles are followed by a Man (TG) pounding on the wall to stop the noise. He then climbs into a crowded bed and they watch *Hamlet.*

Animation exposes parachutists trying to enter a castle.

On "Boxing Tonight," a Fighter is carried into a locker room following a match in which his head and arms were knocked off. His manager, Mario Gabriello (MP), and Boy (EI) talk about what a great fight they have witnessed while they try to re-attach his head. The press enters to question him; his head has come off in his last six fights.

The next week, doctors and patients in a hospital are listening to the fight on the radio, and heads and arms come off again. It is followed by a soap opera, "The Robinsons," which is also heard by Mrs. Gorilla (MP) and Mrs. Non-Gorilla (GC) as they sit in a park discussing piston engines. Mrs. Smoker (GC) throws cans and bottles at ducks, and is joined by Mrs. Non-Smoker (TJ), who has just purchased a piston engine, and they begin quoting Shakespeare.

Act Two: A Room in Polonius's House (introduced by MP) features live reports from a Dentist (TJ), a Housewife (GC), and a Real Estate Agent (MP), all of whom discuss Epsom and development. At the Epsom race track where the Queen Victoria Handicap is to be run, Brian McNult (EI) interviews several jockeys, of which only their caps can be seen. The race features eight Queen Victorias, and all of the announcers are dressed like Queen Victoria, as are Brian and Hamlet.

An animated Queen Victoria flies, as does a boy holding a bunch of grapes like balloons.

Act Five: A Ham in the Castle sees all of the Queen Victorias take their curtain calls, and bow to the audience as the credits (by William Shakespeare) roll.

ALSO APPEARING   Carol Cleveland
Jimmy Hill
Bob E. Raymond
Connie Booth
K. Joseph

 2 0 0

"Additional blank verse" is credited to John Cleese.

"And then . . ." (MP)

What's in a Name?

In almost every show, there may be characters called either Arthur or Ken, names that seemed to pop up with no particular reason. "That was be-cause of Arthur Lowe, the comedian in *Dad's Army* and all that. I would frequently just say 'Arthur Lowe' for no reason at all. I suppose that's why it crops up a bit, but I was never really conscious of it at the time," said Graham Chapman.

"Jones and Palin were very fond of the name 'Ken' at one stage, I remember . . . It was 'Ken' everything at one point—'Ken, could you pass Ken that piece of Ken paper?' Which got a bit annoying after a time, but Ken was quite popular with them . . ."

Show 44—Mr. Neutron

Recorded as Series 4, Show 5—Prog. #95563

Titles

Housewives deposit missiles and bazookas on a cart driven by a scrap-man (TJ). A Royal Mail van drives past and unloads a dais, microphones, bunting, chairs, guests, and officials for a ceremony to open a new post box, accompanied by a GPO Official (MP) speaking in several languages.

Mr. Neutron (GC), the most dangerous and deadly man in the world, steps off a train in a quiet English suburb, with an impressive animated introduction. He has tea with Mr. And Mrs. Entrail (TJ and MP), and she entertains him with stories about her children and their spouses. Her sour-looking husband Gordon hates everything and everybody.

At the headquarters of F.E.A.R. in Washington, D.C. (the Federal Egg Answering Room, a front name for the Free World Extra-Earthly Bodies Location and Extermination Center), Captain Carpenter (EI) contacts the Supreme Commander of Land, Sea, and Air Forces (MP) to report that Mr. Neutron is missing; all their forces in the world are alerted.

Mr. Neutron is meanwhile helping with gardening and chatting with a housewife (EI), Mrs. Smailes. Though there is no sign of Neutron in Washington, the Supreme Commander (who sniffs and examines himself) is assured that everybody is afraid of the armed forces. He orders Carpenter to search the Yukon for Teddy Salad, the most brilliant man in the world, to save them from Neutron. Salad is retired and breeding rabbits in the Yukon.

In the Yukon, Carpenter tells a Lumberjack (GC) in a cabin that he's from the U.S. Government Ballet, and asks how to find Salad. Meanwhile, Neutron is putting up wallpaper for Frank Smailes (MP) and cooking for him.

In a Yukon restaurant, the Italian Chef (MP), thinks Carpenter is ordering salad, and complains that all that the (British) Eskimos ever eat is fish, so he was happy to fix the salad. The Eskimos give Carpenter directions to find Salad; he spots a Trapper (TJ) with a dogsled, and the Trapper says one of the dogs in his team is actually Salad in disguise. Carpenter gives him a bone and takes him for walkies.

At 10 Downing Street, the Prime Minister (EI) hears a request from the American Secretary of State for a full-scale red alert, but Giuseppe (TJ), a gypsy violinist, plays so loudly that he thinks the Americans are bombing them.

Meanwhile, Carpenter has taken Salad out chasing reindeer, and then has to take him for walkies again.

The Supreme Commander, now nude, orders bombings as the only way to stop Neutron, with animation of the bombs landing in all the wrong places, including Cairo, Bangkok, Cape Town, Buenos Aires, Harrow, Hammersmith, etc.

In a suburban sitting room, Mr. Neutron has fallen in love with a housewife, Mrs. S.C.U.M. (TJ). He has won five thousand pounds in a Kelloggs Corn Flakes competition, and wants her to be his helpmate in his plan to dominate the world.

Around a campfire, Salad talks about his other experiences, but is blown up before he can tell Car-

penter where to find Neutron. The Supreme Commander is told that everything in the world has been bombed except for Ruislip, the Gobi Desert, and his office.

Meanwhile, Neutron makes Mrs. S.C.U.M. the most beautiful woman in the world, but as they are running away together, a bomb is dropped.

A Man from the Radio Times (EI) reveals that Mr. Neutron has escaped and what will happen next, and describes "the most lavish and expensive scenes ever filmed by the BBC," but the credits roll before they can be shown.

ALSO APPEARING: Carol Cleveland
                      Bob E. Raymond
                      Sloopy

"Conjuring Today" features a Magician (MP) about to saw a lady into three bits, but he is chased off by the police.

World Domination T-shirts are advertised.

Neil Innes's "Protest Song" (performed at the stage shows) was to be performed at the very end of the show.

Mr. Neutron

As usual, Terry Jones and Michael Palin tended to write the longest sketches—something the other Pythons didn't discourage. "I liked the idea of bringing some creature from outer space into a mundane English suburban setting, and then being almost ignored, and absorbed into everyday English life," says Palin.

"Bits and pieces were snipped and added by the rest, but that was predominantly Mike and Terry," said Graham Chapman. "There was a great relief when they read off this enormously long sketch. We thought, 'Well that's next week done! Jolly good—we can get off early this afternoon.'"

Show 45—Party Political Broadcast

Recorded as Series 4, Show 6—Prod. #95623

A party political broadcast on behalf of the Liberal Party features the finals of the "Worst Family in Britain" contest and the Garibaldi family. Mr. Garibaldi (TJ) is at the table eating Ano-Weets, saying they unclog him much better than Recto-Puffs. Mrs. Garibaldi (EI) irons clothing and a transistor radio. Kevin Garibaldi (TJ) is at the table eating, son Ralph (TG) lies on the couch stuffing himself with beans, and Valeria (GC), with huge beehive hairdo, applies makeup. They discuss Rhodesia, and are visited by the Liberal Party candidate at the door.

The Compère (MP) explains that the Garibaldis in Droitwich in Worcestershire are the third-place winners in the "Worst Family in Britain" contest, while the Fanshawe-Cholmleighs of Berkshire, upper-class twits, won second place. The winners are the Joddrell family of Durham, but they cannot be shown due to obscenity laws.

Another awful family (EI and TJ) watching the show complains about favoritism, and is interrupted by an Icelandic Honey Seller (GC). He explains that there is actually no such thing as honey in Iceland and they have to import every drop—there is only fish to eat. He is there because it gives him an excuse to get out of Iceland.

Titles

A Doctor (GC) about to perform surgery blackmails a patient, Mr. Cotton (TG) with a naughty complaint. Another patient, Mr. Williams (TJ) enters. He has just been stabbed by a nurse and is bleeding profusely, but he has to fill in a form before he can be treated. Although he fails the questions on the form, the Doctor agrees to give him morphine if he can improve his answers on the history section.

Brigadier N. F. Marwood-Git, Ret. (EI), wearing a tutu, dictates a letter to a bishop, Brian (MP), pondering about the permissible.

An animated opera singer is shot by a very slow cannon.

This is followed by an appeal on behalf of Extremely Rich People who have absolutely nothing wrong with them (delivered by GC).

Mrs. Long-Name (TJ) gets instructions on how to finish her sentences (from EI), and then walks to Stonehenge to find a Linkman (MP) to introduce a Richard Attenborough program.

There is a quest to find the legendary Walking Trees of Dahomey, but they walk too fast for the camera crew. They discover a Turkish Little Rude Plant, an African Puking Tree, and the legendary Batsmen of the Kalahari, who sit in front of a pavilion, and at intervals bring their hands together for no apparent reason. The young men of the tribe offer themselves as human sacrifices when the sun goes down by pouring harmful liquids into their stomachs. They are shown to be fierce warriors, however, and there is footage of them against Warwickshire at Edgbaston. Warwickshire's first man is killed outright and the last is seriously hurt. Everyone else tries to run away as the results are given, and the compère ends the show.

Closing credits roll, and the music is Neil's version of the Python theme, as played by one learning guitar.

ALSO APPEARING: Carol Cleveland
Bob E. Raymond
Peter Brett

Additional material is credited to Douglas Adams and Neil Innes.

As an office party proceeds in the background, the Nine o'Clock News is read (by EI), and leads into a series of silly cuts.

Several references to Michael Ellis were in the original script, but were taken out; the Icelandic Honey Sketch was intended for Show 41. Also intended was a series on Ursula Hitler, a Surrey housewife who revolutionized British beekeeping in the 1930s. Though born with one of the most famous British Liberal names (Lloyd George), she had to keep changing it to avoid publicity. She was very puzzled in 1939 when a Mr. Chamberlain sent her an ultimatum on Poland.

More Writers

In all of Python, only two other persons besides the six group members received writing credits on the show. Neil Innes received a writing credit, in addition to two musical credits in the fourth season; and Douglas (Hitchhikers' Guide to the Galaxy) Adams was credited with coauthoring a sketch with Graham (though there were other contributions by non-Pythons: Connie Booth co-wrote some material with John Cleese for the German shows).

"I didn't work very much on the television side of things at all, but I wrote some things with Graham during that time," Innes recalls. "I don't know how it came about, really—it just happened that way. It was 'All right, you write something with Graham,' and I said 'Okay.'

"I cowrote the 'Awful Family' and their baked beans, and I seem to remember having something to do with the 'Appeal on Behalf of the Very Rich.' I didn't plan to write—I just got dragged into it, gradually, screaming . . . I've always maintained I could have had a decent individual career if it hadn't been for Python," he laughs.

Adams cowrote (with Chapman) a scene in which Graham played a doctor, and Terry Jones was a patient bleeding to death in his waiting room.

"Terry literally had a lot of additional plumbing put around his person, with plastic tubes—for some reason, they often use condoms in devices like that—but there was lots of plastic tubing wrapped around his person, so that he would gush blood," Chapman said.

"That is the one contribution of Douglas Adams to the whole of Python, writing that one with me. John had left, and I had been working with Douglas anyway, so we wrote something for the show."

More Beans

Though the fourth season is generally considered uneven by many of the Pythons, some of the material there ranks with the best of any Python sketches. A highlight is certainly the "Most Awful Family in Britain" competition, according to Michael Palin, with Terry Gilliam's acting particularly delighting him.

"One of my favorite Python characters is Terry G eating the beans," Palin smiles. "*Most* of the characters Terry G played I do enjoy greatly—he's just wonderful. He really threw himself into these awful roles—talk about grossness—he really had an absolute market to himself!

"But that sketch where he was eating beans, just sitting there with a primitive, primeval grunt coming out of him—'More beans, I gotta have beans!'—I like that. John Cleese was never totally comfortable letting himself go like that. That's why I quite enjoy seeing someone like Terry G, or Terry J, *really* throw themselves into things. They didn't mind looking like idiots."

Palin says that Gilliam actually had to be coaxed into acting at first. "He was a bit shy about it. He'd done a little bit of acting school. We'd found out that he was really a bit better than the parts he got. He was given awful parts to do. He was always encased in something like a suit of armor.

"Even during *The Meaning of Life,* many years later, when he was a major film director with a major career behind him, he was still putting on that rubber African outfit—which got stuck and wouldn't open at the right moment in the film. He got his cue, and couldn't open it. All we heard was "Uhh, uhh, can't get out. . . ." Palin laughs.

Credits Where Credits Are Due

A great many talented people worked behind the scenes in a variety of roles. Most but not all of them received their recognition in the shows' credits. So here are the valiant crew members whose efforts helped bring us *Monty Python's Flying Circus* (the series each worked on is listed in parentheses). Note: every series was produced by John Howard Davies, while all the shows were directed by Ian MacNaughton (excepting the first four shows, which were directed by Davies); the only non-Python writing credits went to Neil Innes (4) and Douglas Adams (4).

RESEARCH: Sarah Hart Dyke (1); Patricia Houlihan (3); Suzan Davis (3)

MAKEUP: Joan Barrett (1, 2); Penny Norton (2); (Madeline Gaffney (2, 3); Maggie Weston (4)

MAKEUP AND HAIRDRESSING: Jo Grimmond (4)

COSTUMES: Hazel Pethig (1, 2, 3); Andrew Rose (4)

FILM CAMERAMAN: James Balfour (1, 2, 3); Max Semmett (1); Alan Featherstone (1, 3); Terry Hunt (2); Stan Speel (4)

FILM EDITOR: Ray Millichope (1, 2, 3); Bob Dearberg (4)

SOUND: John Delany (1, 3); Jack Sudic (1); Peter Rose (2); Richard Chubb (3); Mike Jones (4)

LIGHTING: Otis Eddy (1, 2); Ken Sharp (2); James Perdie (2, 3, 4); E. C. Bailey (3); Bill Bailey (3)

DESIGN: Roger Limington (1); Geoffrey Patterson (1); Christopher Thompson (1, 3); Jeremy Davies (1); Robert Berk (2, 3, 4); Ken Sharp (2); Richard Hunt (2); Ian Watson (3); Valerie Warrender (4)

VIDEOTAPE EDITOR: Howard Dell (1, 2, 3)

PRODUCTION ASSISTANT: Brian Jones (4)

GRAPHICS: Bob Blagden (2, 3)

VISUAL EFFECTS: Bernard Wilkie (3)

PHOTOGRAPHY: Joan Williams (2)

SOUND RECORDIST: Ron Blight (4)

DUBBING MIXER: Ron Guest (4)

CHOREOGRAPHY: Jean Clarke (4)

ROSTRUM CAMERA MOUNTED BY: Peter Willis (3, 4)

SILLY EXTRA MUSIC BY: John Gould (3)

DOG TRAINED BY: John and Mary Holmes (4)

The End of
the Beginning

By THE END of the fourth series, enthusiasm for continuing with Python had diminished considerably. Although some of the group would have happily continued, others were anxious to spread their wings in other directions. The success of *Monty Python and the Holy Grail* had whetted the appetite of some to expand into film (Terry Gilliam's *Jabberwocky* in 1977 was followed by Graham Chapman's *The Odd Job* the following year), while others had their eyes on new television projects after John Cleese's success with *Fawlty Towers* (Eric Idle's *Rutland Weekend Television* and Michael Palin and Terry Jones's *Ripping Yarns* followed not long after).

At any rate, the fourth series made it abundantly clear to some that continuing the Python TV series would be a mistake. According to Michael Palin, the departure of John Cleese threw off the balance of the show; he says the group conceded that all six members were necessary for a Monty Python project.

"Everybody contributed something, although I don't think it was obvious until it was taken away," Palin says. "What John took away was a really good authority figure. That was John's great strength—he could play authority figures extremely convincingly, which was absolutely marvelous. One could never say 'Oh, it's a lot of little, resentful people having a go at some of the decent types of this country,' because John looked absolutely the personification of the decent, tall, stiff-upper-lip Englishman. He sent up that sort of character, and it was much, much stronger than if any of the rest of us would have done it.

"And, it also gave Terry and myself, the smaller Pythons, someone to play against. Irritating John's character onscreen was wonderful. Of course, he went on to do *Fawlty Towers,* which is all about being irritated by everything. Really, we lacked John's presence, although I think we were writing some quite good stuff in the fourth series. I thought the last of the six shows, which included the 'Most Awful Families of Britain,' had some very nice stuff," says Palin.

Just as Cleese had left after the third season, others were ready to call it quits after series four, even

though the BBC wanted the show to go on. "They wanted us to continue, and I said 'No'—I was the one who said no at that stage," says Eric Idle.

"The BBC said 'Come and do six more.' I remember having a long walk around the common with Michael, and he said 'Come on, let's do it.' I felt that, whereas before we had this balance between Terry and John, and the others fell down the middle, without John we didn't have that balance to Terry's enthusiasm, which tended to carry provided an embarrassment of riches, comedic or otherwise, in virtually all media.

Even while Graham Chapman was still alive, another movie to follow *Meaning of Life* looked doubtful.

"The idea of another Python film doesn't set the adrenaline running," Cleese explained in early 1989. "It might in another five years, but it has nothing to do with what I want to do at the moment, nothing at all."

Late-period generic group shot, actually shot on the sands of Tunisia while the Pythons were beginning to shoot **Life of Brian** *(left to right: Cleese, Gilliam, Jones, Chapman, Palin, Idle). Photo copyright Python Productions Ltd.*

things into an area just slightly more loaded. John's input had always countered that. If we'd gone on, we would have gotten worse and worse as a TV show, and we wouldn't have done anything else."

The end of the TV series only marked the passing of one aspect of the Pythons' careers. The group would continue with record albums, books, stage shows, and of course, films. In addition, the six individual careers that subsequently emerged have

Graham Chapman said there would be another film when one of them came up with an idea so good that it would virtually write itself, and Cleese agreed there was some truth in that.

"I always used to say that in the time it took us to write *Meaning of Life,* any pair of us could have written at least two movies, probably two and a half. So, I would have reckoned that if we'd split into three groups, we could probably have written

five or six movies during the time we took to write that one!" Cleese said.

The classic forty-five shows still stand as a benchmark of TV comedy, to be watched, studied, and enjoyed by generations to come. But frighteningly enough, the world nearly never saw *Monty Python's Flying Circus* after its initial run. *Python* started around the beginning of the video age, and was one of the first entertainment-oriented shows kept by the BBC. Many of the best BBC shows created just before Python were erased or thrown out, including BBC shows with Peter Cook and Dudley Moore, and Spike Milligan—including *Q5*. Only a few *Do Not Adjust Your Set* shows still exist, while *The Complete and Utter History of Britain* has only recently been rediscovered.

The influence of Python has not always been easy to determine, although wherever anarchic, innovative comedy springs up, an admiration for—or at least an awareness of—Python is seldom far behind. Lorne Michaels was a great fan of the show when he started *Saturday Night Live,* and in fact the creators of *Cheers* had *Fawlty Towers* in the front of their minds when they were developing that program.

Still, it would seem the Python attitudes in humor skip a generation, or at least a decade, according to John Cleese. He says that although he enjoyed some of the British sitcoms in the years that followed Python, there was nothing particularly startling or innovative about them.

"In retrospect, the most remarkable thing is that I remember constantly looking around for whatever good, young comedy group was coming up behind us, and never seeing anyone within miles," Cleese says. "There have been a huge number of first-rate young comics with completely different styles since *Not the Nine O'Clock News,* but there was an incredibly barren period in the ten years following the beginning of Python where there was nothing that interesting going on, in my arrogant opinion . . ."

According to Terry Jones, *Monty Python's Flying Circus* was a product of its times, and would probably never have come about under different societal attitudes.

"I think Python started something in the late '60s and early '70s, and it came out of a period that was very optimistic," said Jones in 1989. "There was a great feel of optimism at that time, a feeling that anything was possible and the world was on the verge of improving. Perhaps that optimism is there in Python as well; Python's got a joie de vivre about it which is very difficult to encapture in the '80s, where everything seems to have turned sour . . ."

Graham Chapman looked back on Python as anarchic, surreal humor that followed in the footsteps of *The Goon Show* and *Beyond the Fringe,* but noted that one of its most important contributions involved its use of television.

"In some ways, I suppose we became a television equivalent to the Goons," said Chapman. "We were one of the few television comedy programs to actually use the medium of television, and use some of the tricks of the trade for comedic effect. Obviously, there are certain things we could do that we couldn't do with film. We made progress in that direction, and also in pushing back the barriers of what is considered 'good taste.'

"There were things the BBC thought one couldn't do before we started doing them; we were often able to do them purely because the BBC didn't really like us very much, and didn't pay much attention to us to begin with. We were able to get away with quite a lot before they even thought us serious enough to read the scripts at an executive level.

"When executives did begin to read the scripts, a few little disputes did break out, but by then, we usually had a precedent to point at. For instance, we could say that we said 'shit' in program two, and they would then have to go back and check and find out that we had in fact said 'shit' in program two, and that no one had written in to complain. Therefore, they would allow us to say it *once* in this program, but not the three times that we wanted." He laughs. "That's the sort of petty bargaining that went on . . .

"We felt it rather strange that comedy should be dealt with differently than drama, that because one was ostensibly serious, it could therefore have rude words in it, whereas something comedic couldn't. It was just bizarre, really. Perhaps the higher the status, the more rude words one can say. I suppose we did push back the barriers a bit more in terms of sex and violence, but in a very minor way . . ."

After looking through his diaries and old notebooks, Michael Palin balks at trying to summarize the Python years.

"One tries to pigeonhole Python and make neat little epigrams about what it was like and what it did," says Palin. In fact, he remembers the show as a phenomenon that could not be repeated, and says they were all in the right place at the right time.

"I realize now that I was in some tremendous, uncontrolled mass of outpourings of material by six people who were ripe at just that particular time. Everybody wanted to write and play these extraordinary characters; each show gave us tremendous pleasure, with a huge amount of energy coming out . . . A lot of it was wasted, a lot was crossed out and never got on, a lot was completely unplanned, but somehow, we held it all together.

"Right from the start, I always felt Python was a centrifugal thing; it wasn't six people who wanted to work together for the rest of their lives. It was six people getting together as a stroke of genius on somebody's part. Yet, from the day we did that discussion about the first show, the seeds of the breakup were there, because people were going off in their various different directions.

"But for a while, for maybe thirty-nine shows—some people say only twenty shows—we actually held it together so well that we got the combined fire of six people working on all cylinders. That's what was so good about Python, but we just couldn't keep that up.

"I think the shows still stand up today because they're so *rich*. Not because they're so good—there's a lot of tedious stuff in there sometimes. Some things go on too long, some don't really work, and they certainly can be improved technically. But they're so rich! I always found that twenty minutes into a Python show, I'd think

'This must be the end,' yet there's more and more! So it's like a thick, well-filled comic book. People are always finding new things in Python. It was layer after layer, because one person would write the basics, someone else would have an idea, someone else would say 'While you're doing that sketch, let's have something on the wall that looks good.' So, we'd have a sketch where people have bits of raw meat on the wall, which one doesn't really see because the sketch is going on. But if one sees it forty-five times, like some people in America have, they get around to noticing the things on the wall. So there's always something new.

"It's that feeling of vivacity which really made Python work, and still makes it work. It wasn't such controlled, polite, carefully programmed, well-worked-out television; the BBC barely kept control over it—that's what was so good. Most television now, they're prepared for everything. When they do something surreal and strange, one can bet they'll have good advertisers to back it, and it's all been worked out. The risk and the danger are not there. They were in those Python shows."

The Python phenomenon is one that can't be re-created, noted Palin in 1988. "When people ask 'Are there going to be any more Python television shows?' I tell them there really couldn't be. There are certain things right for certain times, like Elvis. All of Elvis's best stuff was really before he went into the Army. He did some nice stuff after that, but the really good *Blue Suede Shoes* Elvis that I remember did it all in a period of two or three years.

"That sort of burst of creativity is like a sunspot. It flares up, very intensely and brilliantly, for a very short period. If it lasted any longer, it would never have been as brilliant in the first place."

208

Part Three

BEYOND THE BEEB

Captured Live

CAPTURING THE SPIRIT of the TV shows onstage before a nightly audience would seem to be difficult, if not impossible. Yet somehow, the Pythons managed to transfer much of their television work to the stage most effectively.

The surreal animations that were so vital to the stream-of-consciousness flow of the shows were presented on huge screens, either lowered onto or placed adjacent to the stage, where the occasional film segments were shown as well. Other real-life cartoon gags were actually reproduced with life-sized props, including a giant hammer wielded against Carol Cleveland and Neil Innes, and the Hand of God, a gigantic cardboard cutout used to finger the guilty suspect in the "Salvation Fuzz/Church Police" sketch. If there was some loss in the expansiveness or mobility of the scenes, it was more than made up for by the excitement and energy of the performances before the delighted crowds.

The Pythons were not averse to taking the scenes directly to their fans. The "Bruces" sketch performed live always involved Eric Idle leading the audience in the "Philosophers' Song," while the words are projected on the screens; in addition, the first few rows are sprayed with Fosters' Lager, while additional cans are pitched into the usually appreciative audience.

The "Albatross" sketch generally involved Cleese, in ludicrous drag, walking through the rows trying to sell his bird, when he is approached by Terry Jones. The "Travel Agent" sketch usually ended with Eric Idle being pursued through the audience, still spouting complaints about package tours as he is pursued by Cleese.

Now used to working in TV, the group had to adjust to performing the same show regularly, recalls costumer Hazel Pethig, who accompanied them on the Canadian tour. "For the first few shows, they found it very difficult doing the same thing every night. They weren't used to stage work. But they kept up, and eventually it got better and better. The 'Parrot' sketch got so good that it was exciting. They'd walk onstage to do a certain sketch, and there would be great roars of recognition, like a football crowd—

and *nobody* got bored! They adapted very quickly to the stage."

The Pythons generally managed to fit in all of their most popular sketches that could be transferred to the stage, and Neil Innes, performing solo versions of several of his songs, became a staple of the live shows.

Of course, the "Dead Parrot" is included, with a stuffed bird standing in to suffer the prolonged, choreographed beating delivered by Cleese to prove the bird is definitely deceased. To his inevitable irritation, Silly Walks is always included, and always well received, even though he has long since tired of it. Even more rigorous is the "Colin 'Bomber' Harris" sketch, in which Graham Chapman plays a wrestler who grapples with himself, throwing himself around the ring rigorously.

Of course, the shows always conclude with the "Lumberjack Song," performed by either Idle or Palin, with fans joining the Mounties in the chorus. This is where a few ringers have been slipped in. On separate occasions at the City Center, a rather inebriated Harry Nilsson and a virtually unrecognized George Harrison both took their turns singing.

Despite the reliance on "Greatest Hits" sketches, there is usually some new material mixed in with the old favorites. Film from the German shows has included the "Philosophers' Football Match," the Cleese/Booth "Little Red Riding Hood," and the "Silly Olympics." The "Secret Service/Cocktail" sketch was performed in some of the earlier stage shows, and can be found on the *Monty Python Live at Drury Lane* album.

That sketch, which is almost forgotten today, was apparently deemed too disgusting to repeat in later years. The Secret Service/Cocktail sketch was also performed on the Canadian tour, but it was mostly a visual piece, recalls Carol Cleveland.

"We did a sketch in that stage show that was cut—I don't think it was ever seen after that," says Cleveland. "It was a disgusting sketch and the audience hated it! It takes place in a bar where several gentlemen come in to order drinks. Terry Gilliam pops up from behind the counter and is used as a human cocktail shaker. His head is popped back, and all of these dreadful drinks go

Jones takes a trip on a banana peel as Chapman (behind podium) lectures on the history of humor. Although Palin and Gilliam are there to help demonstrate, Jones always gets it when the pies start flying. Photo copyright KHJ.

into his mouth, and then his head is shaken around, tipped forward into a glass, and then somebody drinks it.

"It was disgusting! The audience was throwing up all over the place. And then I had to come out after the curtain had come down and apologize to the audience. The apology went something like this: 'I've been sent out here by the fellows because they're a little too nervous to come out themselves. They've asked me to come out because they really feel very badly about that last sketch, because you clearly were offended, and they didn't have any intent to offend, and they're feeling very badly. They just asked me to say that they're very truly, truly fucking sorry.' Which I think is probably the most outrageous thing they've ever asked me to do!"

Terry Gilliam's film *The History of Flight* has been included, along with some other animation, while Neil Innes's songs have never been done in the Python TV shows. Some of the original sketches have been expanded as well, including the aforementioned "Bruces' Philosophers' Song" and a longer "Travel Agent" sketch.

The most notable "new" scenes, however, are the "Custard Pies" and "Four Yorkshiremen," both actually predating Python and never performed on the Python TV show. The former sees Graham Chapman as a college professor lecturing on the history of humor, with Palin, Jones, and Gilliam

demonstrating his examples of slapstick (and Jones always getting the worst of it). It was generally so messy that it was performed just before intermission, to allow the three assistants time to clean off the pie and take off their padding. The latter involves four men sitting around playing "Can You Top This?" with stories of their deprived youth. It has also been seen and performed in film and the Amnesty International benefits.

The Python stage show has been rather effectively captured on film in *Monty Python Live at the Hollywood Bowl.* Although some sketches have been removed and the running order completely changed, the performances are typical of the feel of the show, and capture the playfulness as the group performs onstage together for the first time in four years.

The shows are also captured on two different record albums, *Monty Python Live at Drury Lane* and *Monty Python Live at The City Center.* The former is available in America only as an import, and contains some sketches, like "Secret Service" and "Cocktail Bar," that have seldom been seen or heard in any form in the U.S. The contents of *City Center* differ somewhat, and the sound quality is far inferior—Arista Records insisted that the soundtrack album be released before the group finished their three-week run in New York. This was accomplished by recording the first shows, when such sound problems as microphone placement had not been resolved.

Monty Python's First Farewell Tour was actually a three-week series of one-nighters throughout Britain, beginning in Southampton. By the time they ended, on May 24, 1973, they had played a

After receiving his lumps, Jones takes off his padding and cleans off the excess pies, during intermission. Photo copyright KHJ.

Idle plays Michelangelo to Cleese's Pope as he describes his first draft of the Sistine Chapel ceiling. Photo copyright KHJ.

peculiar variety of venues before tiny audiences and groups of thousands. One night proved particularly memorable for Neil Innes, however.

"We were in Birmingham on Michael's birthday, and so we got Eric's mother, who looks *exactly* like Mary Whitehouse, the self-appointed guardian of television standards. At the end of the 'Parrot' sketch, instead of saying 'Do you want to come back to my place?' and Cleese saying 'Yeah, all right,' and then going offstage, Cleese suddenly said 'No,' and grabbed Mike in a viselike grip.

"On came Eric in his horrible emcee's gold jacket, saying how it was a very special evening, and it was Michael's birthday, and they'd gotten Mary Whitehouse to present him with a cake. And brought on Eric's mother. We had the whole audience *totally* convinced it was Mary Whitehouse!" says Innes.

"Michael, with great presence of mind, realized who it was. He took some flowers and said 'Well, I'd just like to say this to the old shit,' and

adopted his Gumby voice, and said 'We take the flowers, and put them in the cake.' The audience was convinced that we'd perpetrated this massive insult on Mary Whitehouse! That's one of my favorite Python memories . . ."

Later that year, they embarked on an extensive, sometimes grueling tour of Canada. Upon finishing, John Cleese—who had informed the others at the beginning of the tour that he wanted out of the TV series—went back to England, while the others headed for Hollywood. In a notorious episode, the Pythons made their first—and only—group appearance on the *Tonight Show*.

Joey Bishop, guest-hosting for Johnny Carson that evening, introduced the group by saying "Now here are five lads from England. *I'm told* they're very funny."

"Can you imagine being introduced like that?" Terry Gilliam laughs. "Anyway, we all came on, and they showed a couple of tapes of us. It was a disaster! The audience just sat there with these wonderful blank looks on their faces—they didn't know what to make of us. They just sat there staring with their mouths hanging open. It was great! A total disaster—complete silence.

"We shouldn't have expected much, though. The first sketch they showed was something with Eric in drag, and the audience had no conception at all of what was going on," he chuckles. "We all had a good laugh about it later."

Python humor may never appeal to a mainstream American audience, particularly *Tonight Show* viewers. That evening, any Python dreams of succeeding in America were completely and utterly crushed. They returned to England, and the following February did a stint at the Theatre Royal, Drury Lane.

It was just over two years later that the Pythons returned to America in triumph, following the success of the TV shows and *Monty Python and the Holy Grail* (actually, they had all spent quite a bit of time in the States in 1975 to promote *Holy Grail*). Warming up by performing at the *Pleasure at Her Majesty's* Amnesty International benefit in London on April 1, 2, and 3, the group then did a three-week run at New York's City Center from April 14 through May 2, 1976, which was a major success, and endeared themselves to their American fans even more. Reviews were good as well, with *Time* magazine noting that "No matter how

high the brow or how low, *Monty Python Live!* creases it with jet-propelled mirth," even though a picture of Michael Palin as a camp judge was incorrectly identified as Neil Innes. The group itself enjoyed working before the live audience, though

***Backstage at the Bowl:** Palin waits in Gumby sweater, Jones is in formal attire prior to exploding during "Never Be Rude to an Arab," and Chapman carries off a box of Whizzo Chocolates. A wireless radio mike is visibly strapped onto Chapman. Photo copyright KHJ.*

***The Pythons'** farewell message to their audience is flashed on the screen at the Hollywood Bowl. Photo copyright KHJ.*

they began to tire of doing the same material night after night. In fact, the three weeks at the City Center was the last time they would perform the show for such an extended period.

"City Center was a lot of fun," recalls Neil Innes. "I took my family to New York that time, and we had an apartment over at West 74th Street. It was quite a phenomenon, because everybody knew the material. . . . There was a great feeling of everybody sharing something, no matter how silly it was."

By the time they finally returned to the stage in 1980, the Pythons only performed for four nights. They took the stage at the Hollywood Bowl September 26–29, with an open dress rehearsal prior to opening night. This was the most elaborate presentation of the live show yet. A large screen for the backstage projection of films and animation was hung over the stage, while two larger screens were hung on either side. These two were also used to project closeups of the Pythons, so that even the last rows could see the smallest details onstage. As the Hollywood Bowl was not designed for the type of show presented by the Pythons, each had to be wired for sound. Individual wireless microphones were painfully taped to each of them, which caused sound-quality problems up until opening night.

The show was also recorded for possible presentation on a premium cable system, or as a theatrical film, with Terry Hughes (who directed *Ripping Yarns*) at the helm. The end result, *Monty Python Live at the Hollywood Bowl,* saw a limited theatrical release and eventually came out on videocassette and cable. *Hollywood Bowl* is representative of the Pythons live onstage, though the show contains new material taken from *Monty Python's Contractual Obligation Album,* which had been released

A constant stream of celebrities was swarming around the backstage area at the Bowl; Cleese poses with Saturday Night Live's *Laraine Newman. Photo copyright KHJ.*

earlier in the year. Terry Jones makes several attempts to sing "Never Be Rude to an Arab," while a barbershop quartet moons the audience after performing "Sit on My Face."

The group actually decided to do the *Hollywood Bowl* shows out of frustration, when they were getting nowhere attempting to write what would eventually become *The Meaning of Life.*

"After about thirteen weeks, I said 'Let's just leave it for a few months,' " says John Cleese. "At the time, we thought 'Well, we spent thirteen weeks not doing anything, and we need a bit of cash. What about the Hollywood Bowl?' We'd been invited to California, and we'd said no because we thought we'd be writing the final draft of the movie. There's very little money to be made out of the show itself—there's only four nights, and one can imagine what it costs. But, out we came!"

Cleese says that, although the show is not that difficult to prepare for, the Hollywood Bowl posed some special problems. "When we're in the Hollywood Bowl, we can very easily lose control of the whole thing, because if the mike dies on us, we are dead," he commented backstage midway through the run. "There's nothing we can do about it. We didn't get enough rehearsal, because it was a very complicated thing to put up, and it was distinctly rough for the first couple of nights."

He is interrupted by Palin, who notes that "The real dress rehearsal was on opening night. I wonder if the Beatles had these problems . . ."

Some of the funniest parts of the stage show were the result of unplanned moments or near-disasters. Palin and Cleese broke each other up fairly regularly during "Silly Walks" and "Dead Parrot," with Palin claiming that he found it so

easy to break up Cleese, that he felt almost guilty about it. The "Church Police" always contained shaky moments; the "Hand of God" fingered the wrong suspect; and Terry Jones's Pepperpot kept losing his wig on one memorable night, resulting in the rest of the group cracking up considerably.

Reflecting on the success of Python, Cleese says they had no idea when they were first writing that they would be performing more than a decade later before thousands of people in America.

"The funny thing about all this is that it was just written in two or three peoples' little houses," says Cleese. "Then we suddenly find it's successful with the BBC, we hear they like it in Australia, and then they're selling it in Germany and Denmark.

The next thing we hear, it's beginning to catch on in America. If it all happened at once, it might drive us crazy, but when it happens very gradually, we sort of accept it.

"These little things were all so private when we wrote them—just two people in a room in London. When we finish up doing them to eight thousand people in California, there's something slightly strange about it."

The running order for the various stage shows varied, but the major sketches generally remained in all the incarnations. The *City Center* shows contained most of the elements of the early shows, as well as some that were only included in the later shows. The running order is as follows:

The Program

The "Llama"
Animation—Nini Nana
"Gumby Flower Arranging" (with Michael Palin)
Animation—Conrad Poohs and his Dancing Teeth
"Link to Secret Service" (with John Cleese as a recruiter)
"Wrestling" (Graham Chapman wrestles himself)
"Silly Olympics" (from the German TV shows)
Neil Innes—"Short Blues"
Animation—*2001* leads to "World Forum/Communist Quiz"
Neil Innes—"I'm the Urban Spaceman"
"Silly Walks" leads to *Silly Walks* film
"Mary, Queen of Scots on the Radio"
"Salvation Fuzz/Church Police"
"Bruces' Philosopher's Song" plus the Song Sheet
"Crunchy Frog"
Neil Innes—"Protest Song"
Animation—Charles Fatless
"Travel Agent"
"Custard Pies"
"Dead Parrot" (with John Cleese)
"Two Camp Judges"
Animation—Flasher Love Story
"Blackmail"
Neil Innes—"Stoop Solo"
The History of Flight film
"Albatross and the Colonel Stopping It"

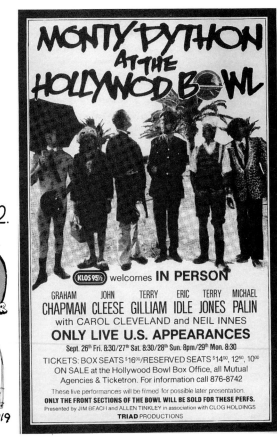

Handbills promoting the City Center and the Hollywood Bowl shows. Photo copyright Python Productions Ltd.

"Nudge, Nudge"
"Idiotting" (demonstration of idiocy under strobe
   lights)
Neil Innes—"How Sweet to Be an Idiot"
Philosophers' Football film – Part 1
"Four Yorkshiremen"
Philosophers' Football film – Part 2

"Argument"
Terry Gilliam's Song on a Wire
Little Red Riding Hood film
"Courtroom"
The "Lumberjack Song"
Opening Titles film
"Pet Shop" (with the Parrot)

The Amnesty International Benefits

The members of Monty Python have taken part in several of the annual Amnesty International benefit shows held in London, performing with members of *Beyond the Fringe,* the Goodies, *Not the Nine O'Clock News,* and numerous other British comedy stars. Contents ranged from old Python sketches to completely new material, with various groups mixing up personnel. John Cleese, in particular, became a powerful force behind the shows, serving as director for several of them.

The first Amnesty International benefit was actually a reunion of the Oxbridge regulars who had carved out some success in TV and films, and by all accounts, it was a delight for the participants. The members of Python and *Beyond the Fringe* had worked together in the past and become friends, and the performers were playful and relaxed for the first benefits. The shows were relaxed, and

Cast members from the very first Amnesty International benefit included (back row, from left) Alan Bennett, John Cleese, Jonathan Lynn, Michael Palin, Bill Oddie, Graham Chapman, John Fortune, Jonathan Miller, Des Jones, and Graeme Garden, with (front row) Carol Cleveland, Terry Jones, Neil Innes, Peter Cook, Eleanor Bron, and John Bird. Photo from the Collection of John Cleese, used by permission.

managed to garner money and publicity for Amnesty International.

Cleese recalls the first shows as "great. They were quick in-and-outs, three or four nights performing. You didn't have to do immense amounts of preparation because it was a charity show done late at night," he says.

"Everybody knew that it was going to be a little bit rough. That was almost the point of it, that was part of the deal. That just meant it could be fun, and it could just be about doing the material as well as you could for three or four nights, and then forget it. That was a good experience."

Pleasure at Her Majesty's, presented April 1–3, 1976, involved all the Pythons (except Eric Idle), along with Carol Cleveland, the Goodies, and most of *Beyond the Fringe.* The show has been preserved as a TV documentary, *Pleasure at Her Majesty's* (shown in America on PBS), a record album, *A Poke in the Eye With a Sharp Stick,* and even an unauthorized film called *Monty Python Meets Beyond the Fringe,* which consists of nothing more than the TV documentary with the backstage scenes edited out (an unscrupulous impresario in Washington tried to pass it off as a new Monty Python film).

The Pythons' contributions include the "Dead Parrot," a courtroom sketch with Peter Cook filling in for Idle as the defendant, and Graham Chapman lecturing on the history of practical jokes, while Jones, Palin, and Gilliam assist him. Cleese and Jonathan Lynn portray the Pope and Michelangelo in a scene recorded for *Monty Python Live at the Hollywood Bowl.* And Terry Jones appears with the *Fringe* in their Shakespearean sketch "So That's the Way You Like It." The show ends with Palin and the entire cast singing the "Lumberjack Song"; in the documentary, he forgets some of the words and is assaulted by the cast members.

Cricketer Mike Brearley prepares to assault Mrs. Yettie Goose-Creature (Terry Jones) while the Presenter (John Cleese) looks on in "The Name's the Game," from **The Secret Policeman's Ball.** *Paul Cox/LFI Photo from the Collection of John Cleese, used by permission.*

An Evening Without Sir Bernard Miles, presented on May 8, 1977, featured John Cleese and Connie Booth, as well as Terry Jones. The rest of the cast included Peter Cook and Dudley Moore, Jonathan Miller, and Peter Ustinov. Directed by Jones and Miller, a record album of the show was released entitled *The Mermaid Frolics.*

By 1979 Amnesty International became more ambitious, and when it asked John Cleese to organize a show that year, pop stars such as Pete Townshend were included. Although Townshend performed acoustically, the shows were beginning to draw rock-and-roll audiences, and the mixture of rock and comedy sketches was becoming more difficult.

The Secret Policeman's Ball, presented in June 1979, and its followup, *The Secret Policeman's Other Ball,* were the largest and most successful Amnesty shows, with resulting books and record albums. The two shows were combined and released in America as *The Secret Policeman's Other Ball,* and again contain contributions from all the Pythons except Idle. A subsequent Amnesty benefit, *The Secret Policeman's Third Ball,* contained only a brief appearance by John Cleese in which he appeared in a sketch to accept an award, which spoofed his refusal to participate in that show.

The Secret Policeman's Other Ball in 1981 saw a flood of pop stars, such as Phil Collins, Sting, and Eric Clapton, join the cast of comedy performers. As a result, John Cleese lost his interest in the Amnesty shows, citing the pop stars and their entourages as a contributing factor; Cleese was much more comfortable getting together with the cream of Britain's comedy crop than organizing rock concerts.

"That one wasn't so much fun, just from a selfish point of view. The first few shows consisted of old friends and acquaintances getting together and doing bits. It was a very cooperative and friendly feeling. That show, pop people arrived in large numbers, all of them traveling with entourages, like Elizabeth Taylor and Richard Burton used to do. So, instead of being surrounded backstage by people whom you knew, and whom you could josh, there were hundreds of strangers standing around, and you didn't know who they were or who they were with," says Cleese.

"Some of the younger comics were using their elbows unacceptably to get more time on stage, and they started using it for self-publicity. What was so nice about the first shows was that you'd say to someone like John Fortune 'Would you mind cutting your sketch on Tuesday and I'll cut mine on Wednesday?' and everybody would say 'Yeah, sure.' I remember one particular guy on the first night, Alexei Sayle, who ran overtime. I asked him if he'd take a few minutes out, and on the second night he did longer than he did on the first night, quite obviously deliberately."

After his experiences during *The Secret Policeman's Other Ball,* Cleese said he wouldn't get involved with any more of the Amnesty shows unless the focus changed.

"I would only do another one under certain conditions," he said. "I would say to them 'Look, you want to do a show with all the pop people, that's terrific. Good luck, I hope you make a fortune. But that's not the one that I want to be in. If you'd like me to organize one for you next year, well, I'll do that, but it'll be the sort of show that I want to enjoy doing.'"

As a result, his participation with the third *Secret Policeman* show several years later was minimal, and none of the other Pythons participated at all. By the time of the fourth *Secret Policeman* in 1989, however, the emphasis was again on comedy, and Cleese and many of the original performers were back.

Python on Film

 THE SUCCESS OF the TV series caught the attention of numerous entrepreneurs, including Victor Lownes of the London Playboy Club. A great fan of the group, Lownes apparently felt that Python would go over well in the States, and the best way to introduce Monty Python to America would be with a feature film.

Lownes approached the group with the idea of refilming some of the best television material for the big screen. He convinced them that the project would make them a great deal of money, and break them into the American market. In fact, with a budget of only eighty thousand pounds, the movie quickly regained its costs, though the Pythons themselves earned very little from it.

So, for five weeks in October and November 1970, the Pythons shot at a former dairy in north London, repairing to the country for some location footage. The group had assembled sketches from the first and second series, and, except for some new linking material, the scenes were nearly the same as their TV originals.

Directed by Ian MacNaughton (who was also at the helm of their TV shows) the group found themselves under the close scrutiny of Lownes. He made suggestions about the design and contents of the film, and probably tried to exert more control over the group than the BBC had at that point. He strongly objected to a sketch featuring Michael Palin as Ken Shabby, and subsequently, Shabby did not appear in the film. Palin has characterized the film as consisting of a lot of men behind desks, and removing Shabby for no logical reason left more sketches behind desks.

Lownes was not content with the removal of Shabby, however. Terry Gilliam designed many of the titles in the typical grandiose *Ben Hur* blocks of stone, and Lownes wanted him to redesign the titles to include his name in such a fashion. Gilliam refused, and yet another battle broke out.

Not surprisingly, the Pythons are not particularly fond of their first screen effort. Although the material is good and the performances tend to be up to par, the feature isn't appreciably better than the TV shows. In fact, *And Now for Something Completely Different* looks much like the TV sketches blown up for the big screen, despite their refilming.

The feature opened in Britain in December 1971, and received mostly good reviews, but due in part to poor publicity and distribution, it failed when it was released in the States in late spring 1972, confirming the opinion of some of the group members that the show would never work in America. It was only when the TV series began to catch on in America in 1974–75 that *ANFSCD* surfaced again, and is now a perennial favorite on campuses and cable, and in revival houses.

And Now for Something Completely Different

Kettledrum/Python Productions

Film, Distributed by Columbia (UK), 1971 88 min.

And Now . . . contains the following sketches from the first and second series of *Monty Python's Flying Circus*.

"How to Avoid Being Seen," followed by the Man in the Dinner Jacket (JC) and the animated Titles. A Theater Compère (TJ) introduces a man with a tape recorder up his nose. A Hungarian (JC) visits a tobacconist but uses a faulty phrase book, and the author is taken to court.

An animated sequence features a garden of hands, and a careless shaver cuts off his head.

Arthur Putey (MP) and his Wife (CC) visit a marriage counselor (EI), who takes a special interest in Mrs. Putey.

Animation involves a hungry baby carriage, and Michelangelo's *David*.

A City Gent (TJ) is annoyed by Another Man (EI) and his innuendoes in a pub in "Nudge, Nudge," followed by a Drill Instructor (JC) trying to teach his men self-defense against fresh fruit. The Colonel (GC) warns the show about getting too silly, after which a group of old ladies, Hell's Grannies, goes around attacking young people. This is followed by a group of military fairies swishing and drilling.

An animated fairy tale features a Prince who notices a black spot on his face. It soon kills the Prince and goes off on its own.

A Young Man (EI) tries to join a mountain-climbing expedition led by Sir George Head (JC), whose double vision has inspired him to build a bridge across the twin peaks of Mt. Kilimanjaro. A link follows with several women in bikinis and the Man Without his Dinner Jacket (JC), leading into "Police Fairy Story" (MP and JC); and a Flasher (TJ) who walks along the street frightening women.

Animated Communist Chinese attack, but are stopped by Uncle Sam, followed by commercials for Crelm Toothpaste and Shrill Oil, 20th Century Frog, and Conrad Poohs and his Dancing Teeth.

"Ken Ewing (TJ) and his Musical Mice" involves a nightclub performer who tries to play "The Bells of St. Mary's" with a mallet and a group of specially tuned white mice, but is chased off by disgruntled patrons.

"It's the Arts" features an interview with director Sir Edward Ross (GC, by JC), followed by a Milkman (MP) who is led into a trap.

"Joke Warfare" follows, in which the funniest joke in the world is written, and anyone who hears it dies laughing; it is quickly put into use by the military.

Animation sees "The Killer Cars," and a dancing Venus, which leads into the "Dead Parrot": Mr. Praline (JC) tries to return a dead parrot to the pet shop from which he has just bought it. The Proprietor (MP) of the shop reveals his desire to be a lumberjack, and launches into the "Lumberjack Song," accompanied by a chorus of Mounties.

A link by the Man in the Dinner Jacket (JC) as he is roasting on a spit, leads into the "Restaurant" sketch, which sees a Couple (GC and CC) in an elegant restaurant given a dirty fork, and the place is eventually turned into a shambles with subsequent apologies.

Animation sees Rodin's "The Lovers" become a musical instrument.

A Masked Bandit (JC) tries to hold up a lingerie shop, under the mistaken impression that it's a bank. Two coworkers (EI and JC) in an office high-rise watch falling stockbrokers and accountants fall past their windows, followed by a letter of complaint. An animated sequence sees a caterpillar undergo a metamorphosis.

The "Vocational Guidance Counselor" sketch features the dull, boring, timid Arthur Putey (MP) visiting the Counselor (JC) in hopes of becoming a lion tamer. "Blackmail," hosted by Wally Wiggins (MP), is a quiz show that attempts to extort money from viewers. In a link, the Colonel (GC) is caught in an embarrassing position before introducing the Batley Townswomen's Guild, which reenacts the Battle of Pearl Harbor in a field of mud. After this, a Couple (TJ and CC) in bed watch suggestive films.

Finally, the "Upper-Class Twit of the Year Contest" sees the Pythons compete in such events as the "matchbox jump" and "waking up the neighbors" before the winners are announced, and the credits roll.

Monty Python and the Holy Grail

The true turning point for Python was the success of *Holy Grail* in 1975. By that time, the TV series had ended for good, and the members of the group were preparing to go their separate ways. Had *Holy Grail* been a failure, they would have likely drifted apart permanently, despite the return of John Cleese for the filming and the success of the TV shows in America.

But for the first time, the Pythons were about to make some significant profits for their work, and discover just how widespread their popularity had become.

The group had toyed with the idea of writing a full-length feature since the beginning of the third series of shows, and they had all begun writing with an eye in that direction.

"I was very keen to do a movie," recalls Terry Jones, "and John really wasn't at that time. John had been very keen on *And Now for Something Completely Different,* and Victor Lownes had been very close to John about that. I think John thought we were going to make a lot of money out of that movie, and we didn't. So, he wasn't that interested when we were setting up *Holy Grail,* but everybody else seemed to be keen on the idea.

"With the first script, *Holy Grail* was just going to be another Python mish-mash again, half in modern-day, half medieval. We had some time off, and during that time I thought to myself 'I'd much rather do it all medieval'—I was in my Chaucer period at that time. When we all met again, I said 'Let's make it all medieval.' I thought everybody was going to object. I was surprised when everybody went along with that."

The Palin/Jones team in particular was turning out material dealing with the Middle Ages, although many of the sketches were set in modern-day Britain, as well. The original idea had been for the knights to buy a grail in the Grail Hall at Harrod's in London, because Harrod's had everything. The Pythons had to watch their budget carefully, which also restricted their possibilities.

The lack of money, however, didn't restrain their creativity during the writing process. "We've never really restricted ourselves in writing, even in *Holy Grail,*" Michael Palin observed years later. "We never said 'We can't do this.' We wrote it, then pared it down if someone said we couldn't do it. We'd been very heavily financially controlled in the TV series, and after that, Python has always been spreading our wings to come out into films. Rather than make economics that ruin sketches or scenes, we write the scenes first, then find a way of doing them."

In fact, it was the idea for the coconuts (knights accompanied by squires clapping coconut shells together, making a sound like horses' hooves) that marked a turning point. They were able to perform without real horses, and decided to set the entire film in the Middle Ages, which Terry Jones had been studying extensively anyway (in preparation for his *Chaucer's Knight* book).

As the creative aspects were being assembled, the business side was hammered out as well. The-

atrical producer Michael (*Rocky Horror Show*) White put together a group of investors for the low-budget project that included members of Led Zeppelin, Pink Floyd, and three record companies. The result was a movie made for the astonishingly low cost of 229,000 pounds. The Pythons performed virtually for free in return for the (hoped-for) profits.

While on the set of *Meaning of Life,* Michael Palin reflected on the changes in less than ten years of Python films. "With *Grail,* we had to do everything ourselves. We only had a budget of 500,000 dollars, and here, we have about eight million, so it makes things a bit easier. I get driven to the studio in the morning, instead of having to drive myself and three other Knights of the Round Table in a pickup truck."

The writing proved first rate and very funny, with all of the group turning out some of their best material. Although the Cleese/Chapman team usually wrote most of the verbal material, one of the funniest visual jokes was written by them as well, involving the killer bunny rabbit attacking the knights.

"John and Graham wrote that very early on," says Terry Jones. "They got more visual while Mike and I got less visual, and that's one of the best examples, actually. . . . It was one of those things that we were dying to do—it sounded like such a funny idea, and it looked so good."

The team wanted to retain as much control as possible, and opted to direct their first original feature themselves; Terry Jones and Terry Gilliam shared the duties. "From the beginning, I was very involved in the shape of the shows when we did the TV series, and I was always involved in the

The group, in good spirits, during the Grail filming. Left to right: Chapman is King Arthur, Idle is Sir Robin the Brave, Palin is Galahad the Chaste, Jones is Bedevere the Wise, and Cleese is Lancelot the Brave; in the front is Gilliam as the brave and loyal Patsy. Photo copyright Python Productions Ltd.

editing of them. I felt a very strong commitment to the finished product, and actually seeing the thing right through to the final edit," explains Terry Jones, who says they really were only concerned with protecting what they had written.

"I don't think there was any desire to direct in the first place. It was just a result of seeing things get screwed up that we knew should be done a better way."

Still, it proved difficult for the group to have the two Terrys calling the shots. In fact, it actually created divisions within the group.

"We really weren't working as happily as we normally did, and there was more friction," Gilliam explained a few years later. "Where Ian MacNaughton got all the shit before, suddenly there was Terry and me to be picked on, because we were the ones who'd been doing it wrong, even though we knew we were doing it better than they could have.

"The group actually started splitting internally. I mean, we'd always argued, but suddenly there were almost two groups. There was the group of four that were just acting, and the other two who were running around doing ten million jobs. Working on a film is a reasonably boring job if we're just acting, because we sit around all day waiting for the directors and the cameraman and everyone else to get their jobs together. Then we go out and do our bit, which only seems to take about a minute, whereas it seems to take about forty-five minutes to set up the shot.

"Everybody gets bored waiting, and I thought tempers went off a lot. And, I think Terry and I

Dressed as King Arthur, Chapman contemplates his greatest real-life battle, as he resolves to quit drinking. Photo copyright Python Productions Ltd.

were trying to prove that we could direct. Actually, it was the first thing we had ever done, so we were very tense," says Gilliam.

"There were great moments, it was a great hoot a lot of times, but I still thought directing *Holy Grail* was very rough. I think directing is a really shitty job, unless it's my own project. Doing a group film, and having to shout at people to get something done that they wrote, gets a bit irritating. I was actually shouting, and got fed up with the whole thing."

The Pythons' first original film actually ran into problems even before they began shooting, recalls Terry Gilliam.

"On *Holy Grail,* just before we started shooting, we were refused admission to all the castles in Scotland that we had already chosen, because the National Trust of Scotland said we wouldn't respect the dignity of the fabric of the buildings, that we'd be making jokes about these places where people were tortured to death and having their eyes put out," says Gilliam. "So, we didn't have any castles. What you see in *Holy Grail* is a lot of painted cutout castles stuck on hills. And they work, they're pretty effective. Most people don't know they're cutouts."

They did find one suitable location, however, and the greatest portion of *Holy Grail* was shot at a castle in the Scottish countryside, and conditions were far from good. The weather wouldn't cooperate—it seemed to rain nearly every day, the crew was dissatisfied, and morale plummeted.

Carol Cleveland recalls a great many problems early in the production when she first arrived to shoot her scenes.

"When I arrived on the set a few weeks into the filming, totally oblivious to the problems they were having, the crew was near to mutiny," says Cleveland. "I arrived to hear talk of them walking off the set. There were various problems with having two directors, which is going to create problems anyway, but especially if neither director has ever directed before—which they hadn't—and especially if those two directors happen to be two loonies!

"They had a routine in which they took turns in filming various scenes on various days. The first scene I was in, Terry Jones was going to be there in the morning and Terry Gilliam was coming along later in the day. Terry Jones spent the whole morning setting up this shot, and we were all set to roll when the other Terry appeared and said 'No, no, no, it's all wrong . . .' And this would go on all the time! So the film crew was tearing their hair out by the roots, trying to get on with their job and find-

Crossing the Bridge of Death over the Gorge of Eternal Peril proved to be dangerous for the cast, and Cleese confesses that a professional mountaineer actually performed the stunt dressed as Sir Lancelot. Copyright Python Productions Ltd.

ing it extremely difficult because they kept changing their minds.

"Apart from that, the weather conditions were appalling. It was Scotland in the middle of winter, and it was extremely cold, so everyone was very uncomfortable. The fellows had to wear these chainmail outfits which apparently were very itchy and horrid to wear, full of fleas and things, so there was a lot of moaning, especially from John, who disliked any sort of discomfort. I remember a lot of grumbling from John."

In addition, Graham Chapman's drinking was worse than ever. As he tells it, he made the decision to stop drinking on the morning of the first day of filming. As King Arthur, he was preparing to cross the Bridge of Death, over the Gorge of Eternal Peril. Early in the morning, out in the countryside, Chapman was disturbed to find that neither he nor any of the crew had brought any alcohol along, and he began shaking. It was then that he admitted to himself that his work was suffering because of his drinking, and decided he was going to quit (which he did, successfully, in December 1977).

Costumer Hazel Pethig also recalls that his drinking had, by this point, started to cause problems. "We were all loving Graham, he wasn't short of love, but when he was forgetting his line—well, we all cared about him so much, but it meant that getting his gloves off was a job, because his hand was shaking so bad."

"Other things I remember during that time—Graham was making a big effort to dry out. It was also the following days, after my first day of filming, that Graham was in a very bad state because he had forgotten to bring anything along to drink, and nobody on the set had anything," says Cleveland. "That was the first time I'd ever witnessed him going through the DTs, which was pretty uncomfortable for him. I remember Graham just during that period making a very determined effort to change his ways, which he eventually did."

Ironically, it was Chapman who came through when tensions were at their peak. According to David Sherlock, a Chapman collaborator, morale was dragging during the first two weeks. "The cast and crew were really being worked very hard, and they had lost a lot of feeling about what they were doing a week and a half into the filming. They still hadn't seen any rushes, so they really didn't get an

idea of what they were doing. Terry J and Terry G were pushing them awfully hard. I don't think they realized at the time just how the crew felt."

Sherlock says that the crew had almost reached the point where they were ready to mutiny—actually walk out.

"Somehow, Graham seemed to sense it. That night, he had the whole cast and crew meet in the bar, and started buying drinks for everyone. Graham had started up a singalong, and I don't think he let anyone else buy a drink all night. Graham is really quite shy, so the whole evening was hard for him at first. But that night, the whole unit seemed to develop the unity that had been lacking; they developed the strong bond that made them keep going.

"The next night, the rushes finally came in, so everybody got a chance to see what they were working on. They saw they had a winner, so they went all out for the film from that point on," Sherlock says.

Carol Cleveland confirms Sherlock's memories and recalls the evening very well many years later.

"I sensed this friction as soon as I walked in on the set the day I arrived," says Cleveland. "That evening, Graham was in the bar before dinner, and said, 'Right, drinks are on me. Drinks on the house!' He just opened the bar up and got everybody plastered, and everybody just cooled down. By the end of the evening, we'd all had a lovely, merry evening, everyone was laughing and joking. The next day, everybody got on with it and it was fine. Graham really did save the day, because the difference between the morning I arrived and that evening was considerable. It really was down to Graham."

Neil Innes, who composed and performed the music, also acted in a variety of roles, notably as the minstrel singing "The Ballad of Sir Robin" ("To call it acting is a bit generous," Innes laughs. "Just say I appeared onscreen."). He recalls that they had to keep each other's spirits up.

"It was pretty miserable, up on the Scottish mountainside in string chain mail, with wet feet, but we did have a bit of fun once in the car, dressed as these silly k-nigets.

Filming is a very lengthy process, and when one runs out of crosswords halfway up a Scottish mountain, one tended to think of other silly games to play," Innes says.

"I said it would be fun to decline the verb 'to sheep-worry.' John came up with the future pluperfect 'I am about to have been sheep-worried.' It was the sort of thing we did to pass the time."

Even though morale improved, the filming still ranged from unpleasant and uncomfortable to grueling. The tiny budget forced them to cut corners and take chances that they would rather have avoided. John Cleese recalls that many of his most uncomfortable, dangerous moments in all of Python occurred during the *Holy Grail* filming.

"The toughest shot for me was swinging backwards and forwards on a rope, because I was getting tired after five or six takes," Cleese explains, describing the scene where Sir Lancelot disrupts a wedding party by slaughtering several of the bridal party and their guests.

"The other dangerous one was playing Tim

Although all the group met in New York City to promote the American opening of Holy Grail, they split up after the initial publicity push to concentrate on regional screenings. Eric Idle and Terry Gilliam traveled to the West Coast, while Graham Chapman and Terry Jones flew in to Chicago, appearing at the theater for its Midwestern premiere, answering questions from the audience, and handing out free coconuts to the first 500 people. Photos copyright KHJ.

the Enchanter, up on a very high mountain peak. Every time I stood up to do a take, the wind would catch my clothes, and I'd get blown backwards slightly. There was actually a drop behind me that would have killed me if I'd fallen, and I was only operating in an area of about three by six feet. That was a bit hairy, particularly as the explosives kept going wrong, and I was up there over an hour."

The only Python stunt Cleese ever backed out of was in *Holy Grail,* as well, and involved running across the Bridge of Death. "I had tried crossing it the previous day," Cleese says. "I walked across, to try to work myself up to running across it. I came back and said 'There's no way I can run across there!' It was slippery, and we were in those strange, knitted-string chain-mail outfits. On the soles of our feet was just a plain bit of leather, nothing on them at all—no rubber, no indentations—so, they got a mountaineer to do it. He ran

across it as though it were a road. Quite extraordinary! That's the only bit I ever chickened out of."

Pethig confirms the problem. *"Holy Grail* was very difficult for them, wearing all that string-net armor, with wet ground underfoot, and helmets. They weren't very pleasant costumes at all. And the things they had to do—Michael had to look as though he was eating mud. It was very uncomfortable for him, lying around in the mud, cold and wet . . .

"Because it was their first feature, there was very little money. I worked as a wardrobe mistress, the wardrobe van driver, the costume designer, and a dresser; we didn't have any facilities. I remember dragging bags of costumes up mountainsides with no one to help us. It was never the Pythons' fault," says Pethig, noting that they suffered more than anybody. "It was their first feature, and they hadn't been backed properly . . . It

During their quest for the Holy Grail, Arthur and Bedevere encounter the fearsome Knights Who Say Ni. Copyright Python Productions Ltd.

was challenging to manage with so little money, and it was terribly hard work. I was happy to just get through and finish it without having a nervous breakdown."

Despite all the trials and tribulations of the filming, however, the final result was most impressive. Audiences and critics alike praised it, but it meant even more than that to the Pythons. It was the group's first major success away from the BBC, so it built their confidence, and proved to them that they could contend with longer forms of comedy.

And it proved as much of a joy to watch as it was an ordeal to film. It was an immediate hit, and they all seemed to realize that the real future of Monty Python would be in movies.

Monty Python and the Holy Grail Released April 1975 by Cinema 5/ Columbia (US) and EMI (UK) 90 min.

The film begins with King Arthur (GC) and his servant Patsy (TG) approaching a castle, Patsy banging coconut halves together to simulate hooves of a nonexistent horse. Arthur is unsuccessful attempting to recruit knights for his court at Camelot, as the residents of the castle are more interested in where he obtained the coconuts.

A Man (EI), collecting dead bodies of plague victims, has trouble with an Overeager Customer (JC), and they identify the King as he passes.

King Arthur encounters a pair of Peasants (TJ and MP) who refuse to acknowledge his authority, citing constitutional theory.

The King encounters a fearsome Black Knight, who tries to prevent him from passing. A fierce and bloody battle leaves the Knight the worse for wear, but still belligerent.

An angry mob captures a Witch (CB), but Sir Bedevere (TJ) questions their judgment, and helps them apply logic and scientific method.

Arthur and Bedevere are joined in their quest by Lancelot (JC), Galahad (MP), and Robin (EI), and they approach Camelot, where an elaborate song and dance fest is in full swing. They see an animated vision telling them to seek the Holy Grail, and they begin their quest at a French castle, where

they are taunted by a Frenchman (JC). A plan by Bedevere to attack the fortress with a giant Trojan rabbit fails. A modern-day historian lectures until he is slaughtered by a medieval knight, and the adventure of Sir Robin begins.

Accompanied by a band of minstrels (led by NI) who sing of his courage, Robin encounters a giant three-headed knight, and bravely runs away.

Sir Galahad the Chaste tries to track down the Grail at the Castle Anthrax, where 160 young, beautiful girls are living by themselves. They try to tend to his every need, but he is rescued by Lancelot, who tries to launch an attack on the girls.

Arthur and Bedevere encounter an Old Man (TG), who gives them a vital clue to the Grail, and the two of them meet the Knights Who Say Ni, and are sent on a mission to find them shrubbery.

An animated sequence finds a monk disturbed by the "bloody weather," and at Swamp Castle, an Angry Father (MP) holds his son, Prince Herbert (TJ), captive before his wedding. His two dim-witted guards (EI and GC) are instructed to keep him in the room, but Lancelot arrives to rescue the Prince, slaughtering several guests and the bride's father.

Meanwhile, Arthur and Bedevere encounter Roger the Shrubber (EI), and complete their mission. They rejoin Robin and the others, and time passes during an animated sequence.

The knights meet Tim the Enchanter (JC), and he leads them to the Cave of Caerbannog, where they have a fierce, bloody battle with the creature guarding the cave. They defeat the small, white rabbit, but do battle inside the cave with the animated Black Beast of Aarrgghhh.

The group finally makes it to the Bridge of Death over the Gorge of Eternal Peril, and have to correctly answer three questions or they will be hurled to their deaths. Some of them make it across during an intermission, and once again encounter the French Taunters, before the final climactic battle.

The film was promoted rather extensively in America; the entire group flew in to New York for the U.S. premiere, which proved extremely successful. A subsequent *Variety* ad showed fans lining up outside the theater beginning at 5:30 a.m. Following the New York premiere, Eric Idle and Terry Gilliam flew out to the West Coast for the L.A. premiere, while Terry Jones and Graham Chapman attended the Midwest opening in Chicago, in

which coconuts were given out to the first five hundred patrons. In addition, several cities featured men hired as knights, who walked around in armor passing out handbills, and carrying huge *Monty Python and the Holy Grail* banners.

It was subsequently sold to CBS in the States by accident, and turned up as the Late Night Movie on two occasions in early 1977, cutting it to remove suggestive words and situations, and excess blood. The group subsequently regained the rights to the film, and it was later shown uncut on PBS in America. It is now available on videocassette, and on laserdisc with a running commentary by Jones and Gilliam.

The Life of Brian

Released August 1979 by Handmade Films for Orion Pictures and Warner Brothers, 90 min.

The Pythons had been talking about a followup to *Holy Grail* even before they had finished filming it. Toward the end of the shoot, Eric Idle came up with the joke title *Jesus Christ: Lust for Glory*. The title went no further, but the idea of a Python Bible story remained. A rough draft was ready as early as Christmas 1976, and work progressed slowly but surely. The Pythons had pretty well drifted off on their own, but as the writing continued they regrouped for such projects as the City Center stage shows.

The concept of a Python life of Christ evolved into the story of Brian, the thirteenth apostle. The group found that there was nothing about the life of Christ that invited ridicule, and so diverted the film into an attack on religions that pervert the teachings of Christ, and those that blindly follow—all years before the televangelist scandals.

"The Gospel According to St. Brian" was to be the story of the least-known disciple, the one who

A rather bored-looking Chapman and Palin relax in Pilate's audience chamber; this is the costume Palin had contemplated wearing on his Saturday Night Live appearance. Photo copyright KHJ.

looked after the business side of things while none of the others were making any money. Cleese explains that Brian always missed the most significant events, such as arriving late for the Last Supper because his wife had friends over that evening.

The group discovered yet another problem in hammering out the storyline: every time Christ would make an appearance, the laughter stopped. More rewrites were called for, and the film turned into the story of a man whose life paralleled Christ's, now titled "Brian of Nazareth." The group decided to go off together on a working holiday in Barbados for two weeks in January of 1978 to finalize the script and the concepts. It paid off, giving them a much clearer idea of the final story. As Cleese wrote shortly after the session, "It is now called *The Life of Brian*. Brian is no longer a disciple, just a bloke in Judea in 33 A.D. . . ."

"That was the first time, really, that all the Pythons had been together for such a prolonged period of time in years, and it was very productive," explained Michael Palin a few months later. "Ideas got thrashed out and worked through very fully, and the script is very much tighter as a result. So we're all very pleased with the script, very committed to the movie, and every single member of Python is raring to go on it."

Arranging the finances proved to be more difficult than they had anticipated, and they suffered a major financial setback. Originally planning to shoot in Tunisia in April 1978, the project was delayed for six months, during which time the script was revised and polished. The result was a very different film than would have originally been shot.

A representative of EMI had encountered the Pythons in Barbados during their writing session, and the company had agreed to give the group two million pounds to make the film. A month later, however, the head of EMI read a copy of the script, and backed out of the deal, leaving the Pythons high and dry. So in April, instead of shooting *Brian,* Michael Palin found himself in New York hosting *Saturday Night Live,* where he discussed the situation.

"Lord Bernard Delfont and EMI, the British company that had given us the money, got cold feet for some reason—partly money and partly taste. I think mostly taste," explained Palin. "He was worried that he might get involved in a film that had imaginative content, and that he might possibly be called upon to justify his support for in the next life. He was unwilling to take this risk with immortality.

"The offer of money was so firm that we had actually started on the film, and we're attempting to recover the money by legal methods. At the moment, we've put the film off until September. Our producer, John Goldstone, is in America at the moment talking to various people, and we hope to get the money together soon. So we have the script, we have done quite a bit of preliminary work on locations, we have costumes being made. I was trying on Pontius Pilate's costume the other day—I thought I might wear it on *Saturday Night Live,* but no . . ."

Palin explains that if the money hadn't come through, they would still have turned out a Python movie that year. If necessary, they would have combined the two German TV shows into a sketch film.

Of course, *Brian* was by far the most attractive option, and the financing finally came through from a rather unexpected source. George Harrison had long been a fan of the group, and met Eric Idle during the Los Angeles opening of *Holy Grail.* When Idle explained their money problems, Harrison told him that he would give the group the two million pounds. Proving as good as his word, Harrison and business manager Denis O'Brien formed Handmade Films, and became the executive producers of the film, simply because Harrison, a Python fan, wanted to see the movie.

Construction crews were sent to Tunisia during the summer to prepare sets and locations under the watchful eyes of Terry Gilliam. After a week's worth of rehearsals, shooting began on Saturday, September 16, in the city of Monastir. The first scene shot was the stoning, in which Cleese plays an official in charge of a prisoner to be stoned to death for saying the word "Jehovah." Since, in biblical days, women were not allowed at stonings,

Chapman and Cleese consult with director Jones inside the Tunisian ribat. Photos copyright KHJ.

the Pythons portrayed women who were disguised as men by wearing false beards.

"We've got a very complicated convention going there," Cleese noted shortly after shooting the scene. "It starts out simple, in that women aren't allowed to go to stonings, so they have to put on beards to go there as men to be allowed to go at all. The complicated thing was, two of the women were being played by Eric and Michael.

Also, Charles McKeown and Terry Baylor were playing two of the other women, so we had a picture in which four out of the nine faces were men pretending to be women pretending to be men. I suspect that's too difficult for an audience, and I hope we're able to reshoot it with at least three more obvious girls between Mike and Eric, just to help the clarity of it.

"There was an odd atmosphere about that first day, and I couldn't work out what it was. Then I suddenly realized that there was absolutely *no* sense of occasion. If anybody had walked on the set, they could have thought it was the fifth week. It was a lovely feeling, everybody knew just what they were doing, and went about their tasks in a very efficient, unhurried way," Cleese observed.

In fact, the filming was as easy and comfortable as *Holy Grail* had been difficult and unpleasant. As Michael Palin noted on the set, "Compared to *Grail,* working on *Brian* has almost been a holiday. The weather has been beautiful, whereas it was almost constantly raining at the locations in Scotland, and everything is going as smoothly as can be. If this keeps up, I'll almost feel guilty about taking the money."

The group views *Brian* as a comedy epic, given the large scale on which the comedy could be played out. In fact, the "Latin Lesson," which was shot on the second day, took on a different tone than most comedies. Upon joining a revolutionary group, Brian is sent to write "Romans, Go Home" on the palace walls, where he is caught by a sentry.

"When I saw the rushes, I was very struck that here we were, shooting the scene in the Roman Forum at midnight, in very real colors, just as though it were a proper adventure story, and the audience would be on the edge of their seat," notes John Cleese. "I'd never seen a comedy scene played in this slightly forbidding, cool blue light. It's much more like something out of a drama film. Although we may lose a laugh or two because it is shot at night, I think the overall effect is to enhance its quality. It's rather interesting."

Most of the shooting took place at the Ribat (Arabic for "castle") in Monastir, an ancient Moslem landmark, and a building next to it that was built a few years earlier for Franco Zeffirelli's *Jesus of Nazareth.* Filming in that area lasted about five weeks, including four days' filming in Sousse, a few miles north of Monastir (where the unit uti-

Before setting out on a commando raid, Palin is fitted with a battery pack for his electric lantern. "All of this electricity forces one to be rather careful when having a pee," he noted. Photo copyright KHJ.

lized the ancient city wall on the same spot "where Robert Powell was crucified for Lew Grade," Eric Idle joked). Zeffirelli had shot in many of the same locations as the Pythons did later, and the two stoning sequences were filmed on the same spot.

Terry Jones served as lone director on *Life of Brian,* with Terry Gilliam stepping back and designing the production instead. Still, as he commented halfway through the shoot, he was kept busy enough with his chores. "This is bigger than any of the films we've done before, so there's plenty of pressure to get the stuff ready in time," Gilliam says. "The scale of the amount of things we've built here—it's huge, it's a real epic! I haven't been able to stop the whole time down here."

Except for the spaceship sequence and the opening credits, the film is devoid of animation, so Gilliam was able to devote all his time to design. "The closer we come to doing real stories in Python, like this one is, the less room there is for

Inside a dungeon, Palin confers with a cheerful crucifee (Idle), as the stammering jailor (Gilliam) looks on. Photos copyright KHJ.

As a nude Graham Chapman throws the shutters open to face the crowd—many of whom were forbidden by their religion to view a naked man—he says he heard shrieks and screams from the local women, which somewhat undermined his confidence.

"Those two big crowd scenes could have been real buggers," notes Cleese, "but we got them under our belts, and they all worked."

The interiors of the bedroom scene, shot the next week, saw Brian's mother (played by Terry Jones) discover Judith in her son's bedroom. While Jones was in front of the camera acting, Cleese stood by to help with the performances. "I know how, as an actor, I need two things from a director. Helpful suggestions and criticisms are fine, but what I really need is faster or slower, and bigger or smaller. If I get that, I basically get it right. Graham was a little bit too big at the start, so I brought his performance down, and he really performed beautifully after that. It took Terry a long time to loosen up in the first half, as we need that loose expansiveness to make a comedy scene work at its best. It was not helped this morning by the fact that Terry's entrance was through an extremely small door; in his second entrance, he caught his foot and skinned his instep. All of this builds up pressure, and makes it difficult to build up the really good flowing timing that makes it funny. But we

animation. The animation was really a linking device, and now that the thing has such a solid story flow to it, there's no need to link."

Two of the most challenging scenes in the film were tackled early in the production; both involved large crowds that had to react in specific ways to the actors. As Pilate, complete with speech impediment, addresses the crowd, the mob below must react with gales of uproarious laughter. And when Brian, totally nude, throws open his windows after spending the night with Judith, the huge group of followers must react to him and his mother.

With the forum jammed with Tunisian extras, a professional Tunisian comedian was hired to entertain the crowd, in order to get the people laughing properly for the reaction shots to Pilate's speech. However, the mob proved adept at taking Terry Jones's direction, through an interpreter, and the comedian wasn't really needed.

"The 450 Tunisian extras were sensational," enthuses John Cleese. "When they first fell to the ground laughing...it was one of the funniest sights I had ever seen. They fell in waves, like something out of a land-based Esther Williams movie."

Although a group of English tourists were recruited for the scene outside Brian's bedroom, most of that group (nearly 750) were also Tunisians, and devout Moslems.

A little rain delays the shooting of the crucifixion party, as Jones, Gilliam (out of his jailor makeup), and Palin confer. The rain bonnet on Palin is to protect the curly-haired wig. Photo copyright KHJ.

The crucifixion party sets out, with Idle and Chapman (as Brian) in the lead. Photo copyright KHJ.

"We decided to take that out in the next draft in Barbados. Judith disappears from the story from about the time Brian goes on the raid. We wanted to get her right back in there just as soon as we could, and this was the first time we could put her back in the story. The scene went through about three different stages."

Like much of Python, Carol Cleveland notes that *Life of Brian* was a family affair for her.

"I went out to Tunisia a couple of times and had great fun," says Cleveland. "I had my husband along on *Life of Brian,* and he was one of the followers. He was out there for a couple of weeks. It was very nice, they paid his way out as a sort of working holiday. They were very good about using friends and relatives and things."

While shooting in Sousse, where most of the commando scenes in tunnels were filmed, *Goon Show* chief Spike Milligan stopped by while on holiday to visit with the Pythons. The comedic hero and inspiration of the group while they were growing up, Milligan agreed to appear in a scene

got a really good take just at the end, and we're there now."

The original bedroom scene was written by Cleese and Chapman, and was considerably different from the finished version. "When Brian woke up, he had two girls in bed with him called Cheryl and Karen, and when his mother Mandy knocked on the door, he hid them behind a curtain," Cleese says. "Eventually they giggled, because they didn't think this was quite the behavior of a man who was likely to lead them out of captivity. Mandy found them and asked Brian who they were, and he said 'They're two of my disciples, Mum.' And she said 'Disciples? They haven't got a thing on! What are they doing here?' And Brian said 'We were discussing eternal life, and it got a bit late, so they stayed.'

Camping it up for the camera, with Cleese (center), Kim "Howard" Johnson (right), and Bernard McKenna (far right) with Tunisian extras. Photo copyright KHJ.

Looking uncharacteristically less than stylish, Palin, in costume as Ben (who has been hanging in manacles for years), sips his tea as makeup girl Elaine Carew prepares another assault on him. Photo copyright KHJ.

the next day outside the city wall in Sousse, when the mob following Brian divides itself into shoe, sandal, and gourd factions (which the Pythons refer to as the "entire history of religion" in two minutes).

A couple of weeks later, their financial angel, George Harrison, took a break from mixing his next album to fly down for an overnight visit. He agreed to make a cameo appearance as Mr. Papadopoulis, the man who rents Brian's group the mount for next weekend (his only line is "Hello").

Two weeks of shooting followed near the desert at Matmata near Gabes (where the *Star Wars* desert sequences were filmed). Most of the large outdoor sequences were done there, including the opening sermon and the Wise Men scene. A scene involving a group of shepherds singing the praises of their sheep was also shot there; although it was originally intended as the opening sequence of the movie, it was eventually cut to speed the flow of the story. A few final days were spent filming the coliseum scene in Carthage, with Neil Innes joining them as the Christian who battles the gladiator. The post-production was all done in London over the next few months.

One scene had to be completely filmed in the studio, however. When Brian falls off a tower, he is rescued by a spaceship, occupied by two strange-looking aliens. Pursued by an enemy craft, the ship zips off into outer space for a brief battle,

After falling from a balcony, Brian (Chapman) lands on a very boring prophet (Palin), with the help of some of the crew. Palin's boring prophet entertained the crew by improvising long stretches of extremely boring, mundane matters while shots were prepared. Photo copyright KHJ.

Chapman poses with a dummy double, who will fall from a tower and land on a flying saucer in his place. Photo copyright KHJ.

which damages both ships. Brian's flying saucer crashes to earth at the exact same place he just left, and a band of Roman soldiers resume their pursuit.

"We were all saying 'We need some animation,' and Graham said 'Why isn't Brian rescued by a flying saucer at this point?' We all thought it was a good idea, though it turned into Terry Gilliam's creation when we did it," explains Terry Jones.

The sequence inside the spaceship was actually the last to be shot, and had to be done two months later in London. At the time, Chapman was living in America, and for tax purposes, he was only allowed twenty-four hours in England.

"I arrived in the morning from Los Angeles, and was driven straight to the studio," Chapman said. "I was put into the box made up to resemble a spaceship, with lights and wires. I was dressed as Brian, shaken around a lot, then taxied back home for a few hours sleep before being put on another plane to L.A. I wasn't in England for more than twenty-four hours, and eight of those were spent in a box. Rather the reverse of one of those relaxation booths—sort of a 'tenser booth.' And it worked, too! I didn't know where I was in the world, or the time, space, anything, for a week after that."

The filmed script ran about two and a quarter hours, and the group had to then edit that down to about ninety minutes. There was some talk of running the entire film, as written, with an intermission. At one point there was even talk of turning it into a two-part film. Finally, it was simply edited down. The shepherd scene was removed, as was an extended subplot to raid the castle and kidnap Pilate's wife (played by six-foot nine-inch John Case in drag), who demolishes her attackers. Perhaps the most controversial scene removed involved Eric Idle as King Otto, leader of a suicide squad. The fascistic, rather Teutonic King told Brian of his plans to "establish a Jewish state that will last a thousand years!" Only a brief appearance at the end, while Brian is on the cross, suggests the vanished scene.

Still, the film proved controversial enough

The life-size model of the flying saucer after it crashes to earth was constructed in a courtyard of the Tunisian castle. It was actually carved from polystyrene of a large statue of Caesar used earlier in the shooting. Photos copyright KHJ.

without it. Fundamentalists, most of whom had never seen the film, picketed and protested to have it banned. Life followed art, as thousands wrote angry letters and made angry calls at the suggestion of their religious leaders, attempting to suppress a film whose chief message was "Think for yourselves." One of John Cleese's favorite moments in all of Python is during Brian's address from his bedroom window to his crowd of followers. He says "You've all got to work it out for yourselves," and the crowd of 750 shout "Yes, yes! We've got to work it out for ourselves." Brian says "Exactly," and there is a pause. Then, the entire group shouts in unison, "Tell us more!" Cleese notes that it seldom ever gets a laugh, but it says all that needs to be said about the protesters.

The film was banned in some southern states in America, and a number of countries as well, but it is still as funny and powerful as when it was first released. Several of the Pythons consider it their best work, and it remains the longest narrative produced by the group.

"It's more natural for six people to produce short spurts," says Terry Jones. "I was always in-

A protest outside the Warner Communications building by another religious group made up largely of people who haven't seen the film— and have yet to learn how to work it out for themselves. Photo copyright KHJ.

Cut from the final print of the film, six-foot, nine-inch British actor John Case played Pilate's wife in the kidnapping attempt. His only remaining role in the film is as Eric Idle's helper in the haggling scene. Photo copyright KHJ.

terested in the progression from *Holy Grail* to *Life of Brian,* the fact that in *Life of Brian,* we were actually able to make a story. In retrospect, the failing of that film is that we didn't have enough confidence in the concept of story. We speeded it up so much, in the way that we've always done for sketches, that it actually is too fast now. I would love to recut *Brian* to make it slower. I think it would work better."

Most of the significant material that was cut from the final version of *Life of Brian* turned up in late 1997 on Voyager's Criterion Collection *Life of Brian* laserdisc. This deluxe version also includes two voice tracks with running commentary by John Cleese, Terry Gilliam, Eric Idle, Terry Jones and Michael Palin, trailers and ads for the original

film, as well as the 1979 documentary *The Pythons,* which was shot on location in Tunisia during the filming. It is the most complete record of the film available for Python fans, and like all Voyager releases, highly recommended.

After *Life of Brian,* and with the nurturing of Handmade Films, Cleese, Palin, and Gilliam made, respectively, *Privates on Parade, The Missionary,* and *Time Bandits* for the company (plans for Handmade to handle *Yellowbeard* did not pan out). Python began drifting even farther apart, but would still reunite for a stage show and a big-budget studio film.

Monty Python Live at the Hollywood Bowl

Released 1982, The Monty Python Begging Bowl Partnership, Thorn EMI Video, 78 min.

The four nights Monty Python performed at the Hollywood Bowl in 1980 were recorded at the time with an eye on packaging the show for HBO or Showtime. While the show was being presented live, cameras captured the action. It was shown on large screens so that even the back rows could see the closeup expressions on the performers' faces. The shows were edited and eventually released to theaters, though the final film received rather limited promotion and release; it was released on video not long afterward.

The film version differed from the stage show in running order and length. Sketches were rearranged in an effort to improve the flow. In addition, the film runs only seventy-eight minutes—considerably shorter than the live performance. The film does include several shots of the crowd, and the rabid Python fanatics dressed in various silly costumes. Although most of the material is available elsewhere, the film does include special performances of songs from the *Contractual Obligation Album,* as well as contributions by Carol Cleveland and Neil Innes.

The Meaning of Life

Universal, 1983, The Monty Python Partnership, 103 min.

After *Life of Brian,* the Pythons had hoped to turn out a followup film not long afterward. In fact, *The Meaning of Life* took much longer than any of them had anticipated, and almost didn't happen at all.

Although the group had come up with a great deal of material, they hadn't managed to agree on a storyline, and the project stalled. At one time, they were considering "Monty Python's World War III," which was little more than an umbrella title for a series of sketches. During the hiatus in which they were unable to decide on a theme, they ended up doing the stage show at the Hollywood Bowl.

An early version began with a warning that a picture of a huge male penis would be flashed upon the screen soon, and the implications of this were discussed at length. The "middle of the film" section was written to include unbilled cameos by

such celebrities as Clint Eastwood and Barbra Streisand. The search for the missing leg also took up a much larger portion of the story than was eventually used.

The possibility of another Python film appeared more and more doubtful, but based on the success of the sojourn to Barbados to polish *Brian,* a writing trip to Jamaica was proposed, possibly out of desperation.

"We decided we'd actually force ourselves to finalize the script," explains Michael Palin. "We actually went to Jamaica with less confidence than we had with *Brian* at that stage. We seemed to be going downhill after three or four days, and nothing new happened."

"There was one point in the writing where we all thought 'This is it, we'll never do anything else again,'" says Terry Jones. "We had a format and

256

The group relaxes during their successful four nights at the Hollywood Bowl. Copyright 1982 Monty Python Begging Bowl Partnership.

that I had a script with the timings on it. I hadn't thought it would be any use, but I brought it along just in case. When I read it, I realized that we'd practically gotten a film. We had sixty or seventy minutes, so all we were talking about was another twenty minutes!

"I came down to breakfast feeling cheerier and more positive. Mike suggested that we all go home and turn it into a TV series, but I said that all we needed was the last twenty minutes. I'd always gone on about it being a life story, only nobody

sixty percent of the material, and couldn't get it into shape. On the way there, we all read the script and thought it was disastrous. When we got there, instead of putting the finishing touches to a script that we already had, we were suddenly back to square one trying to decide on a format. After a couple of bad days, I remember waking up with a sinking feeling in the pit of my stomach, feeling this was just not working out.

"Then, I think it was Wednesday morning, I woke up and thought 'I've *got* to do *something,* this is terrible!' I realized

Michael Palin works on a sketch for the Meaning of Life *script during the group's Jamaican sessions. Photo copyright Terry Jones, used by permission.*

could agree about whose life story it was going to be. At this point, I thought everybody was going to go 'Ooohh, Terry's going on about it,' because that's what I'd been saying for the last two years. But suddenly Eric or John—I can't remember who—said 'It could be *anybody's* life story.' And Eric came up with 'It's the meaning of life!' Over that breakfast, it just returned from the brink of disaster."

The "meaning of life" idea seemed to spark everyone, and the Pythons began creating more material almost immediately. "We clicked onto a very rich vein, and started writing again," says Michael Palin. "In particular, John and Graham went off and wrote a very good opening sketch about a hospital, the birth sequence, which was right up to the very best Python standards. That gave us all confidence, and we came back from Jamaica with the film virtually a definite starter."

The result was a movie that resembled a sketch film, but had a strong connecting thread running through it with the Python version of the Seven Ages of Man.

"Actually, it doesn't feel like a sketch film," says Jones. "It has this weird feeling, this momentum that keeps one hoping it's all about the same thing. It's not like *And Now For Something Completely Different* or *Hollywood Bowl,* which *are* sketch films. It has a continuity of progress in it. While it's not a conventional type of story, it *is* a story.

"Although the structure is much looser than *Brian,* there is a theme, a certain unity to it," says Palin. "I think 'sketch film' sounds dangerously as though we'd put together bits of our old material. I've been saying to people that it's more of a sketch film, but that's wrong. It has a unity and theme."

The Meaning of Life takes aim at a greater variety of targets than *Life of Brian.* "Every Sperm is Sacred," a Palin/Jones song attacking the Vatican's stance on birth control, succeeds on virtually every level, from comedy sketch to social satire to song-and-dance number. Cleese is a headmaster who, with the aid of his wife, demonstrates sexual techniques to a terribly bored and distracted group of schoolboys. Terry Jones as Mr. Creosote forces regurgitation to new highs (or lows) in a gross-out scene so expertly staged and performed that it becomes a triumph of excess.

Other scenes range from a modern-day hospital birth which sees the mother as unqualified to assist the doctors, to the Zulu Wars; from a World War I trench, to a Bergmanesque sequence with the Grim Reaper interrupting a dinner party. The film actually begins with the "Crimson Permanent Assurance," a short subject conceived and directed by Terry Gilliam, which sees elderly accountants sailing their building off for corporate raids.

There is music here, as well, including the title song, the Noël Coward-like "Penis Song," the show number "Christmas in Heaven," and Eric Idle's wonderful "Galaxy Song." *The Meaning of Life* is rich in its variety, and while some sketches misfire and others run long, the winners outnumber the losers, and a few, like "Every Sperm" and "Mr. Creosote," are worth the price of admission in themselves.

Once again, Jones served as sole director of the film, with Gilliam working on his own short subject parallel to the main body of the movie. The majority of the film was shot at EMI-Elstree studios outside of London, although there was a bit of location work.

"The problem really only occurred when we left the studio," says Palin. "There were one or two dangerous moments, where we had shellfire, rockets, and bombs going off, that we filmed just after the IRA had bombed Hyde Park. There were old ladies complaining that they were seeing mushroom clouds in the sky about Elstree, in the middle of the London suburbs . . ."

The "Zulu Charge," shot near Glasgow, Scotland, was the scene of a minor uprising. The black extras apparently claimed they were never told that they were going to be natives charging up a very cold Scottish hillside, and refused to wear loincloths. They claimed it was typecasting, and all went home.

"Actually, it was an absolute blessing in disguise," says Jones. "Because it was a gray day, and the one thing we wanted was a blue sky, because it was supposed to be Africa. Scotland with a gray sky looks like Scotland. I was biting my lip, hoping something would happen that we couldn't do it, and it was amazing—they had this revolt!"

"We had to shoot the next day, with white people blacked up," says Palin. "It was very sad. We deliberately tried very hard to get authentic black people in Glasgow, which is in itself quite difficult, so we ended up with three hundred unemployed shipyard workers. We could only black

up the fronts of them, because we didn't have enough blacking to do their whole bodies—just their fronts were seen as they charged. If we'd filmed the retreat, we'd have had to spend a lot more money."

Python seldom improvised. As writers, they tended to have a great respect for the written word and generally followed their scripts with great care, although they occasionally improvised one-liners during the "Vox Pops" bits during filming sessions. One of the few true improvised lines in Python occurred in *The Meaning of Life.*

"One of my favorite lines in *Meaning of Life* was something Mike suddenly threw in when we were actually shooting it," says Terry Jones, laughing. "When Death visits the dinner party, the ghosts all get up to go. Mike was going, and they were all going on about the salmon that poisoned them all. Just as the ghosts were suddenly going out the door, Mike's character suddenly says 'Hey, I didn't even eat the salmon!' He just threw it in on that take."

Working with their biggest budget yet, the Pythons labored in comparative luxury. For Palin, his most difficult costume was as the American Nancy Reagan-like socialite (wife of Terry Gilliam) in the Grim Reaper scene. "I was very expensively dressed, with blonde, coiffured hair. By the time I got my makeup on—my eyelashes, punitively painful earrings, and a long red cocktail dress—I looked quite extraordinary, like a real old banger!*

"But it was fairly uncomfortable, and it was one of those sketches that just went on and on. It was fairly simple in terms of lines, but technically quite difficult. It involved location work on a very windy, rainy moorland in North Yorkshire, which I think is the single wettest spot in the British Isles," says Palin.

"One day we didn't film anything at all, but had to be dressed, up there, and waiting. While John went out and was filmed doing his bit, I was still dressed as this socialite on the top of this moorland in this hostel. It was really a hostel for walkers, people who go hiking, men with hairy hands who carry backpacks and all that. The look on their faces when they saw me coming down the stairs in the morning to get my cup of coffee had to be seen to be believed.

*Jalopy. Or sausage.

"That was quite humorous for a bit, but this went on. We must have spent almost a week on this scene, and having to get up and into this gear every day really put me off transvestism as a career!"

Carol Cleveland says her favorite sketch in *Meaning of Life* ended up on the cutting room floor.

"It was in the Dungeon Room restaurant," she explains. "Terry Jones was very, very apologetic the day he called up to say that this scene was going to be cut. I was devastated, because I had told everyone about it. I said 'We're going to make cinema history with this sketch.' He was so apologetic, he said 'The scene is fine, it worked very well, you're wonderful in it, it's very funny.' The problem was that at that particular episode, the film was too long. My bit was followed by another bit with John, and it made the whole episode too long. He said 'Something's got to go, and it's either got to be your bit or John's bit. I truly think that your part is funnier, but John's piece is more in keeping with the meaning of life, so we decided, reluctantly, that your piece has to go.'

"I did eventually get an outtake of it. I was a very over-the-top waitress, gum-chewing with a Bronx accent. It's an outrageous little scene with Michael and Eric as an American couple who are ordering all these various things that I bring to the table. It ends up with me plunking a condom on the table and instead of saying 'Have a nice day,' it's 'Have a nice fuck.' And I walk off. But it was cut! I was so disappointed . . . Once the film came out, Terry said, 'Carol, we made a mistake.' He admitted it was a mistake, because the scene they kept in just didn't work. He said 'We should have kept yours in, it was much funnier, and it would have gone over much better . . .'"

Carol notes that her most prominent sketches in the film were very outrageous, both the one that was cut and the other that stayed in.

"In the Mr. Creosote scene, I'm a lady who leaves the restaurant," says Cleveland. "I come up with the line about, 'We have to leave, we have a train to catch, and I'm having a rather heavy period and I don't want to bleed all over the seats.' I can remember a stunned silence in the room when we were filming with all of the extras sitting around. They were sickened to death by what they had already seen. It was the most revolting sketch. The first day—it took three days to do that scene, and

we had this puke, this vegetable soup—there were several bathtubs of it in a back room. As the days went on and under the hot lights, it started to go off a little bit, so this awful stench was coming through this lovely big ballroom we were using. And of course, just watching Terry drinking this sick and then throwing it up, take after take after take.

"The other thing is about film extras. Now as a rule, a film extra will do anything to get an extra day's work on a film. They'll do anything. But these people were leaving in droves! They had to be paid a fortune to stay, and come back the next day. There were saying 'No way! No way! I don't care how much you pay me, I'm not coming back!' They were dropping like flies. They were being sick! At lunchtime, half a dozen people went off and never returned because they were ill! Everyone was very jolly at the beginning, all laughing, cracking jokes, happy to be there, part of a Python film, what have you. A silence came over the room as the day progressed. Finally the second day, they got around to my little bits, when John moves away from that table and comes over to our table. You could see the relief on peoples' faces, 'Oh, finally we're getting away from that, here's this nice pretty lady and we're going to have a bit of nice conversation here.' Terry said 'Okay, we're going to do a little rehearsal here Carol,' and I come out with this 'I've got my heavy period and I don't want to bleed all over the seats.' And there was silence! The whole room fell silent. And then this voice came from a far-off corner, and this fellow said 'Who the hell *wrote* this?!' It *was* revolting, but well worth it."

Terry Gilliam was busy with his own project, as well. The "Crimson Permanent Assurance" was originally intended as a three-minute segment in the middle of *Meaning of Life*. Eventually, however, it grew to occupy over fifteen minutes of screen time, and as much time to shoot as the rest of the film put together. The story of the elderly accountants who become pirates intrigued Gilliam, who had finished *Time Bandits* not long before.

"I had always liked the idea of buildings that sail, so I thought I'd write something around that," Gilliam explains. "Piracy was in the air, Graham was working on *Yellowbeard,* and I always fancied doing piratical-type films. It all started tying to-gether, and so the piratical accountants came to the fore."

Gilliam says it was an interesting attempt to do more and different special effects than he'd done before, but it proved much more complicated than he had first thought. "When I approached it, I thought it would be a piece of cake, but it was more complicated—there was a major panic from a production point of view, because nobody took it seriously until it was too late. Then they realized they had something as complicated as the entire rest of the film.

"This thing just grew. What I thought was going to be a five- or six-minute section done with animation, suddenly became seventeen minutes long, because with live action, everything spreads. That's the joke now, it's one-fifth of the film. It's one thing to draw it as a storyboard for animation, but real people take longer to do physically. I can't just go 'Zip!' across the screen—somebody actually has to walk . . . I really just designed it as a cartoon, and we're trying to do it for real," says Gilliam.

Despite the complications with his pirate short, the most difficult part of *Meaning of Life* for Gilliam may have been the bits of animation. "I don't actually 'think animation' very well anymore. I'm much more interested in live action," he says. "The shortcuts one does in cutout animation, all these quantum leaps every two seconds—my mind doesn't work that way now, and it's proven to be extremely difficult. I have to rethink what I was doing, because I don't do it anymore. I think I'm washed up."

Although he does do some acting in the main film, Gilliam says his main interest is actually doing his own movies. Although he still feels a strong bond to Python, he says working on *Meaning of Life* was rather frustrating for him.

"All of the group have such different styles of working now, it makes it harder and harder to keep together. The film was done very luxuriously, and the money that was spent doesn't seem to be on the film. It's spent on creature comforts and more relaxing working, which is all very pleasant. It's more enjoyable, as a group, working on this film than anything we've ever done before—but I find it hard to work that way. It's too pleasant!"

The socializing came a lot easier than the **Meaning of Life** *writing during the first days of the Pythons' Jamaican holiday/writing sessions. It was Terry Jones' suggestion of the "Meaning of Life" structure that got the group unstuck and moved the film forward. Photo copyright Terry Jones, used by permission.*

The final result puzzled the group. As brilliant as it was, it was simply too long to fit in its place in the middle of *The Meaning of Life.* Though they contemplated releasing it as a separate short subject, it ended up as the first reel of the film, although the pirates do show up briefly in an attack on a boardroom.

The Meaning of Life was quite well received at the box office, easily earning back its eighteen-million-dollar initial budget. Feelings within the group were mixed, however. Cleese was not delighted with the final result, while at the opposite end of the spectrum—as usual—was Jones, who felt it was the funniest thing they had ever done. While Cleese says he didn't enjoy shooting it, Jones calls directing *The Meaning of Life* "quite enjoyable."

As much as he liked making *Brian,* Jones says that he enjoyed *Meaning of Life* even more. "When we were away in Tunisia, there was more of a group feeling, because we were all away at the same time, and saw each other every day," says Jones.

"I sometimes felt I was making *Meaning of Life* on my own, in that it was always me there. It would be either me and John for a week, or me and Graham for a week, or me and Mike for a week. There weren't many times when it was everybody together. It was great fun to do, but it was slightly more analytical, because we were working in the studio, and coming home to our families."

Palin concurs that the "location feel" was missing from *Meaning of Life,* even though it wasn't a difficult film to make for him. "The schedule was reasonable, and we were based at home most of the time. But it lacked the 'location friendli-

ness' that we had with *Brian* and *Holy Grail*. We were all away together, and there was a great feeling of the cast and crew being involved on a project, being friendly and mixing much more."

The question of another Python film is raised less often than it used to be, largely due to the many successes of all of the group members. Still, even those members of the group less anxious to reunite will never rule it out.

Despite his many and varied solo successes, Palin says he hopes to include Python with his own future works.

"I regard Python as something I can only do with the five other Pythons. It brings something out in me as a writer/performer, a satisfaction I can't get in the same way from doing my own stuff. For me, it's terrific if Python keeps going. However successful anything I do, I would love to have the fact that I can go back to Python," says Palin.

"In a way, Python is funnier than anything any individual does. For example, *Fawlty Towers* is unquestionably brilliant, but it isn't as unique and special as Python. I have a suspicion that John knows that, too. I'm not belittling any individual projects, but Python is the one really unique feature of all our acting and writing lives."

Individual Profiles

Graham Chapman

THE TALL, BLOND Graham Chapman was born in Leicester on January 8, 1941. A policeman's son, one of his earliest memories was being taken around by his father to the site of a wartime air raid, and encountering parts of bodies scattered around the area. This may have influenced his decision to seek a career in medicine, as it had his older brother.

It was, however, his love of comedy and his admiration of the Cambridge Footlights Society that led him to study medicine at Emmanuel College, Cambridge. After mounting his own cabaret show, he was invited to join the Footlights at the same time as first-year law student John Cleese, with Eric Idle joining the following year (David Frost was serving as secretary at the time).

Keeping up his medical studies while appearing in the Footlights' production of *Double Take,* he qualified as a doctor at St. Bartholomew's Hospital in London. At approximately the same time, he was invited to tour New Zealand with the Footlights. To obtain his parents' permission, he parlayed an off-the-cuff comment by the Queen Mother, whom he met at a school function, into a Royal Command to tour Australia, which sufficiently impressed his mother. Putting his medical career on hold, he joined John Cleese on tour with *A Clump of Plinths,* which was retitled *Cambridge Circus,* when it ran on Broadway in October 1964 for twenty-three performances.

Returning to England, his medical career proved useful when he started writing for the "Doctor" series, with both Bernard McKenna and John Cleese, including *Doctor at Large, Doctor in Charge, Doctor at Sea,* and *Doctor on the Go,* serving as medical consultant for the series.

Resting before another Python stage show, Chapman contemplates having to wrestle himself once again. Photo copyright KHJ.

Writing for *The Frost Report* followed, where he met and became familiar with Michael Palin and Terry Jones. Chapman began doing more writing with Cleese, who was also performing on Frost's show during this time. With Cleese, Chapman wrote for Marty Feldman's *Marty, The Illustrated Weekly Hudd,* and of course *At Last, the 1948 Show* just prior to beginning Python. The pair also wrote several screenplays during this pre-Python period, including part of *The Magic Christian,* in which they both appeared with Peter Sellers and Ringo Starr, Chapman playing the head of a rowing team. The two also collaborated on *The Rise and Rise of Michael Rimmer,* and another screenplay that was eventually released under the unfortunate title of *Rentadick* in 1972.

As a writing partner, Graham proved to be enormously valuable, recalls John Cleese.

"Graham was a bit lazy, but he was a wonderful sounding board," says Cleese. "The greatest thing in the world for a comedy writer is a partner who knows whether something's funny or not, because first of all, it's encouraging if he thinks it is, and if he doesn't, you're not wasting time and backing up some unprofitable avenue. That was

his great strength to me, he had extraordinarily good taste. He seemed to know what was funny and what was not funny. I remember when we were writing the Cheese Shop sketch, I kept stopping him and saying, 'Graham, is this funny?' and he would just mutter, 'It's funny,' and nod to me as though he expected me to get on with it!

"Now and again, he used to come up with really good suggestions that were completely out of left field, but he didn't have the capacity to be in the engine room. During *The 1948 Show,* we used to say some of the writers were engine room writers and some of them were embroiderers. The engine room people made sure that the script actually got done on time. The embroiderers weren't very good at that, but they were awfully good at coming up with little unexpected ideas, either to start sketches off or to finish them or to give them an interesting twist in the middle. That was very much what Graham did. He used to appear to do a great deal of writing. He would go from one writing meeting during the day to another to another, but I don't think he was ever in the engine room. But provided he had people in the engine room, then he was a really wonderful addition to a team."

Chapman and Cleese also collaborated on a script for Peter Sellers that was never filmed. Chapman later rewrote the script (titled *Ditto*) with David Sherlock. He also helped to write, along with Eric Idle and Barry Cryer, two series for Ronnie Corbett,* *No, That's Me Over Here,* and *Look Here Now.* In fact, Chapman recalled one period while he was simultaneously writing Python, a Corbett series, and a "Doctor" series, doing one in the morning, another in the afternoon, and the third at night.

Of course, Chapman appeared in all of the Python TV shows and films, playing King Arthur in *Holy Grail* and the title role in *Life of Brian.* The Chapman/Cleese writing partnership began drifting apart, and so Chapman began doing some writing with Douglas (*Hitchhikers' Guide to the Galaxy*) Adams; in early 1976, they collaborated on a BBC special titled *Out of the Trees.*

It was during the period following *Holy Grail* that Chapman fought his most difficult personal battle, and stopped drinking. At his peak, he was consuming two quarts of gin a day. Unfortunately,

*Well-known British TV comic, and half of the Two Ronnies.

On the **Life of Brian** *set, Chapman, assisted by rep company member Andrew McLachlan, indulges in one of his regular passions, even in the wilds of Tunisia—The* Times *crossword puzzle. Photo copyright KHJ.*

one of his best friends, Who drummer Keith Moon, fell victim to alcohol and died just before he was to join the Pythons' rep company in *Life of Brian.*

The alcohol-free Chapman turned to his own project before filming *Brian.* He produced, cowrote, and starred in *The Odd Job,* released in England in October 1978. Costarring David Jason, Simon Williams, and Diana Quick, and directed by Peter Medak, the low-budget production was well received, though never distributed in America (the title role, played by Jason, had been written for Moon).

The Odd Job also marked the first time Graham Chapman had produced his own project, which he was surprised to find he enjoyed.

"It was a very interesting experience, actually, and quite fun. I didn't really expect it to be so much fun," he noted shortly after its completion. "I've enjoyed being involved with every stage of the film, right from the choice of script to performers, except I wasn't involved with my own choices! Originally, I wasn't going to be in it, I was going to be producer. That was my idea—I just wanted to have the script developed and written, and then produce it. But if we had someone like me [perform in it]—who was prepared to do it for

practically nothing—we could make it on a low budget. So that's the way it turned out in the end, with me in it.

"After the writing period and after performing the thing, I still had a lot of decisions to make as a producer that I wouldn't normally have as a writer or performer—except, of course, with the Python group, which is rather different. We have much more influence, because we act corporately as producers as well.

"Normally, as soon as the thing's finished, an actual writer has very little influence on whatever the company that produced it decides to do with it. And so, this not being a Python venture, the interesting thing to do was produce it. I quite enjoyed all the politics, the silly games that people play in order to try and get their way. It's kind of fun if you nearly win, anyway—I didn't exactly win, because I really wanted Keith Moon to play the Odd Job Man, and I still think that would have been right.

"There's always compromise, and nothing is ever as you'd quite intended. It's about the same for a producer as a writer and a performer. It's never quite exactly what you wanted and hoped for, but it's near enough. And I think we've produced a good film, so I'm quite happy."

Of course, his largest post-Python project was the pirate spoof *Yellowbeard,* on a scale so large that Chapman later felt that he simply lost control over

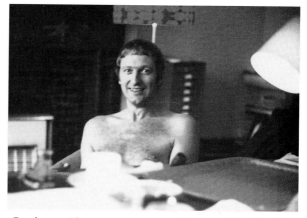

Graham Chapman at one of the earliest Python writing sessions. Photo copyright Terry Jones, used by permission.

2 4 5

it. With a cast consisting of Marty Feldman, John Cleese, Peter Cook, Cheech and Chong, Peter Boyle, Madeline Kahn, Eric Idle, Kenneth Mars (and many others) its Mexican locales, and filming on MGM's *The Bounty,* all the elements were there. When asked to describe *Yellowbeard,* Graham turned to his friend and co-star, Feldman.

"Marty summed it up as 'a rollicking comic yarn for the young in head.' It is quite a fair summary. Don't go expecting anything too deep, but you do need to think a little bit," he explained.

Many members of his cast were people he'd originally hoped for, he noted. "I was kind of amazed in the end that we'd finally got a lot of them. I'd always thought of John, Eric, and Marty, though I didn't actually think of Marty for the part he played. Nevertheless, I very much wanted to use Marty, at first in one of the mad Spaniard parts, but after reading it himself, he chose to be Peter Boyle's henchman. He is actually much more suited to that, really, and Cheech and Chong were more suited to playing the mad Spaniards, so that worked out very well. I didn't think of Cheech and Chong originally, they were suggested by Orion. I didn't know their work very well at that time, but after I'd seen more of it, I thought 'Yes, that's a good idea too.'

"Very early on I wanted Peter Boyle to play the evil pirate, the ex-henchman of Yellowbeard. Madeline Kahn was a suggestion from quite early on too, as Betty. Initially we were thinking of English character actresses for that part, but when Madeline Kahn was suggested and I went back and saw *Young Frankenstein* and *Blazing Saddles,* I thought she was just superb, and was a very happy choice," noted Chapman.

Another friend, Keith Moon, actually provided the initial inspiration for *Yellowbeard,* according to Chapman.

"Keith approached me with the idea of an adventure-comedy, combining the two elements of comedy and adventure—an interesting sort of topic. I suppose with *Holy Grail,* we'd been in that area, and I liked that—it was fun to do the swordfighting, with a lot of stunts and physical acting, and so that attracted me to it. Also, the escapist element attracted me to it. Especially in times of depression throughout the world, one really owes it to people to try and cheer them up a bit, to transcend all the gray times."

Graham Chapman, mid-'70s. Photographed by John Sims for Python Productions, used by permission.

Despite Chapman's presence and writing, as well as John Cleese and Eric Idle being along, Chapman pointed out that much of the humor in *Yellowbeard* was different from Monty Python humor.

"Obviously, it's inevitable that there are quirky little sections that could be slightly reminiscent of Python, but if any of it is comparable to Python, then I suppose you need to think of *Holy Grail,* really. It's not in the Python style—there's more of a story to it," he explained.

Even though he was kept busy with his behind-the-camera workload, Chapman enjoyed many of his acting scenes.

"Although they terrified me before I did them, I liked the fight scenes a lot," he revealed. "They were a challenge and an enjoyable experience when you'd actually finished them, but terrible to wait around for, not being experienced in that direction. I found it quite exhilarating.

"I really did enjoy doing my scenes with Madeline. I found that playing a scene with her, I got so much from her, that it was a joy to push it back at her," he recalls, laughing.

The different comedic styles of the actors—the

group had worked with Mel Brooks, the Pythons, and Cheech and Chong—seemed to be very disparate, but Chapman said they meshed together very well.

"Just to talk to one of them, for example, Kenneth Mars is a wonderfully loopy man who was the rather strange German writer in *The Producers*, and was also excellent in *Young Frankenstein* as the mad burgomeister. He plays a couple of parts in *Yellowbeard* and is really superb, totally mad.

"There are people blending in from different comedy schools, really—Cheech and Chong on one hand, people from Mel Brooks, like Marty, Madeline, Peter Boyle, and Kenneth Mars, and then three Pythons in it as well—three quite different schools—but there are similarities among these schools, and that's what I was hoping to use. There's also quite a lot of mutual admiration among the three schools, as well as envy," he joked.

"I was very pleased with the atmosphere that we had going during the shooting. It was an optimistic movie to shoot, despite the fact that we were in a constant battle with finance in terms of not really having enough money to give ourselves anything resembling a comfortable time, or enough in the way of facilities, such as toilets near the set. That had to fall along the wayside—and so did we—particularly in Mexico. But that led to a group spirit, it was almost as though we were all fighting a war and we were determined to win," explained Chapman.

There was almost a revolving door for the cast throughout the shooting, as different actors would come and go while shooting continued.

"We had a sort of constant cast running throughout, with myself, Peter Cook, Martin Hewitt, Michael Hordern, and Marty and Peter Boyle, and other people coming in at various stages to do their sections. The first part of the movie, it was John Cleese and Eric, but Eric overlapped—he then came out and did his part at sea, and for the last part of the movie, there was a whole section with Eric, and James Mason to blend in as well. Then the next big surprise that I had waited for was to find out what Cheech and Chong were really going to be like.

"There were really sort of three major stages, I suppose—Cleese, Mason, Cheech and Chong. I was wondering how they would fit it, because

they're really the most disparate, in a way. Eric just blended in splendidly, I think he had a good time and enjoyed playing his part, and had a tremendously good sidekick played by Nigel Planer, who was quite a find. He made a convincing foil for Eric—it was in danger of becoming the Clement and Mansell show at one stage, they were being so funny. John had a great time, largely because Blind Pew is such an outrageous, way over-the-top character—he had a wonderful time, and threw in a couple of little extra jokes for us, which was rather nice, one of which he didn't tell me about, and I didn't see it until they did it, and I about fell out of my chair at it!" he laughed, referring to the scene where Clement pays Blind Pew with a coin on a string.

"James Mason was absolutely splendid as the English sea captain, and Cheech and Chong blended in too without leaving any noticeable scars—I enjoyed having them around. And then, because of different people coming in all the time, it also helped to keep us fresh."

Doing a period film like *Yellowbeard* wasn't as difficult as he had expected. "I was anticipating, without ever having worn them, that the costumes would be a bit awkward to wear and move in, but they're not. You feel very free in them—I was quite surprised about that!"

The biggest problem with filming in Mexico, however, was the heat.

"Because a lot of the film takes place on boats, we wanted to make sure we had good weather if possible," explained Chapman. "Inevitably that meant sunshine, which meant it was very hot. It was up around a hundred degrees most of the time in the middle of the day. Particularly from my own point of view, I found that because I was wearing all that facial hair, and having to look bedraggled in it, I was dampened down occasionally—which sounds kind of refreshing until you try it! You get straggly hair flapping into your eyes, which isn't too nice, blowing around on the beach, the false eyebrows and the largest beard I've ever seen, and the frizziest, most fly-away wig I've ever worn too. So it didn't make for a lot of comfort."

One of the more annoying problems on the set in Mexico involved the lack of toilets.

"That was a problem when we were shooting some of the jungle sequences, and a lot of the stuff early on in Zihuatanejo. We had no trailers at that

point, and so no toilets—just tents in jungles, and that was it. We had a few tents with fans in them, but that was all.

"We did the captain's cabin in—well, it's hard to call it a sound stage. It was a corrugated iron warehouse, although 'warehouse' makes it sound a bit luxurious. It was a shack, and the cabin was built in that. Just to make it slightly more bearable, so at least some kind of an attempt had been made at air conditioning, we had fans blowing over blocks of ice trying to keep it cool. That was appalling," he laughed. "It was kind of a closed-off set too, with lights inside it and a temperature outside of a hundred degrees or so. It was really unpleasant!"

Graham classified the shooting schedule as "very tight."

"*Yellowbeard*'s quite a big film, in that there are a lot of sights in it, and a big cast, and most of all, it involves ships. They were notoriously difficult to shoot on, but I don't think we lost a day due to the ship—it was absolutely splendid. That boat must have liked us, for some reason—we certainly liked it. That was one of the greatest experiences, just working on that boat. The only person who was really seasick was the Spanish doctor.

"Most of the film was shot two or three miles offshore, far enough out so that we had a good sweep of the sea to be able to use. We would go out about seven in the morning and come back when it got dark, so we were out there most of the day. It was a rather strange experience to find that, after a while, the hotel rocked as much as it did. Very odd to have that sensation, it didn't seem

Graham Chapman is very much in character in the title role of Yellowbeard. *Photo copyright Orion Pictures.*

right—the boat was perfectly all right, but the land was rocking a lot!

"The captain and the crew were tremendous, just great at getting it heading just the right way for sunlight and wind as well as swells, so that we had some measure of continuity. That's one problem we had, to try to keep the sun in the same direction at the same time, the sails flapping the same way, those kind of complicated things—plus, it's all going up and down at the same time. It's a *miracle* we got it done, really."

Yellowbeard involved its share of swashbuckling stunts, according to Chapman, though some were more dangerous than others.

"This is the first time I've ever worked with real, pro stuntmen, and that was an enjoyable experience. We used them a lot for the fights, obviously, and shipboard, of course—people had to fall from riggings," revealed Chapman. "There was one very difficult stunt, which was Marty Feldman's on-screen death. He was supposedly tripped by a chair and had to fall into a vat of acid about twenty-five or thirty feet down. The vat of acid really wasn't that big, because there was a little island in the middle of the vat of acid where we had the torture chair, so he didn't have a great deal of width to fall into from that height. I shouldn't think it was more than six feet from the edge of the pool to the island in the middle, which isn't very much from that height. It was no distance at all. So, he really had to run up to the edge of the parapet blind and fall into the six-foot width of water—which was only about four feet deep. He had to run off the edge and then fall vertically

while doing a turn in midair. It was tricky, but it was a splendid stunt."

Graham said he had a few tricky moments during the shooting himself.

"The nastiest moment I had, the only point where I thought I might have a big problem, was swimming toward the boat at the beginning, because I had to appear to climb up a rope to climb onto the ship at the end of it. I had to swim fully clothed, and with piratical boots on. They were huge, thigh-length boots, and when you're moving in the water with those, they just fill up, like swimming with huge pools on your legs, and it drags you back. That was really very energetic. Partway toward the boat, I really thought I was going to go under," he said, noting that they were actually out in the sea. "If it hadn't been for our stunt coordinator yelling instructions at me from behind—he was swimming, dressed as a pirate too—telling me how to breathe properly in that kind of situation of terror, I don't think I would have made it! It was a very nasty moment, and I'm not a particularly strong swimmer, so that obviously didn't help me psychologically at all.

"It was quite a good experience just to be able to mess around in a childhood dream, that was the great thing about it," he said, noting it was his most ambitious personal project. "I think it is, obviously, just from the scale of it and the sort of people involved."

Shooting *Yellowbeard* was very similar to shooting a Python film, Chapman noted. "I suppose because John and Eric were around, it was extremely similar. I think it was more comfortable for me than *Brian* on location, obviously much more tropical and luxurious in a way than a barren, harsh Tunisia."

One change he said he would have liked would have been to have more time. "It would have been nice to have had a lot more time to shoot it, because we were really on quite a low budget for that size a movie and cast—it didn't leave us much for luxuries, hence the lack of toilet facilities. It was very, very tight, a lot of work, and I think it did give us a group unity, because we all did feel we were fighting some kind of battle to get the film made."

One of the brighter aspects for the cast and crew involved the cooperative sun.

"The thing that really sticks out in my mind is the incredible luck with the weather—it rained most of the time we were in England, which is just what we wanted, really, to make England look slightly drab. The sun was continuous in Mexico, except for a couple of days—one of those was while we were doing interiors, and the other was a day off. We were incredibly lucky—the rest of the time, it was clear skies!"

Other aspects of the filming were more meticulously planned, even though they proved unpleasant for the actors. Studying history books revealed some devices that Chapman and partner David Sherlock decided to incorporate into the script. Their research showed that historical pirates used to burn fuses in their hair and beards.

"The most famous pirate to do that was Blackbeard. He used to cut lengths of gunners' matches—they were called gunners' matches, but what they were effectively were fuses—lengths of rope dipped in a saltpeter solution and allowed to dry. Then, if you lit them, they glowed sufficiently for you to be able to light a trail of gunpowder or a cannon, but also billowed out smoke, which, if tied into a beard, does look rather effective and unusual," explained Chapman.

"It was all very well. The ones in the hair were fine, except one had to have someone standing by with a bucket of water or spray to put me out after each take. I hadn't really taken into account the ones in the beard, because that means you have smoke coming up your nose all the time, which is rather unpleasant. But I suppose it did look rather fierce-ish.

Chapman said he tried to focus on the over-the-top aspect of Yellowbeard when creating the character. "That was one facet of him that really attracted me, and also made me slightly afraid of playing him to begin with, because he was such an outrageous character, throwing everything into it all the time, with no time to relax—he was always running around the place doing something. So for me, that made him the other end of the spectrum from Brian, really. Brian was someone who was good and running away from things, and Yellowbeard was bad and running straight at them. It was quite the reverse!

"He was a weird one, I don't quite know where he came from. I think he's an amalgam of lots of pirates, bits of Newton, and *lots* of Keith Moon's spirit."

Chapman was himself disappointed with the final result and unhappy with the cut turned in by the director, who was primarily known for his work in television; he noted that the completed film didn't have the sweep and majesty it was capable of having and tended to look more like a TV movie. Graham was also not allowed in on the editing process, which didn't help the final result. Despite its problems and drawbacks, *Yellowbeard* still has a great many highlights, chief of which may be Graham's rousing, over-the-top portrayal of the lead character.

He then developed a script based on his experiences with the real-life "Dangerous Sports Club," a group of Englishmen who hang-glide over active volcanos and launch themselves from catapults.

He remains the only member of Python to write his life story, titled *A Liar's Autobiography, Volume VI.* The highly entertaining, mostly truthful book is alternately witty and startlingly frank as he discusses his alcoholism, homosexuality (including an hilarious account of his "Coming-out Party" and the reactions of his guests), and his various misadventures. He actually began writing a sequel on his word processor, but tragically, the nearly completed work was lost during a burglary at his home, when the computer discs were taken.

Following *Brian,* Chapman lived in Los Angeles for a period, where he made numerous TV appearances. Perhaps the most unusual was a week on the *Hollywood Squares,* Nov. 5–9, 1979, and two evening shows. While promoting *The Secret Policeman's Other Ball,* he made a cameo appearance on *Saturday Night Live* wearing a tutu, and was a regular on NBC's short-lived *The Big Show,* a weekly variety hour in which he performed both new and older material (including a version of the "Bookshop" sketch found on the *Contractual Obligation Album*).

It was during an American tour to promote his book that the seeds were planted for an entirely new activity. Attending a screening at Facets Multimedia in Chicago on March 2, 1981, he discovered on his arrival that he was supposed to address the overflowing crowd. He turned the ordeal into a question-and-answer session, and after reviewing tapes of his performance, decided to hit the road with a series of lecture tours. He performed at scores of American colleges during the mid-'80s, delighting the students who had always wanted to

see a Python in the flesh. "An Evening with Graham Chapman" evolved into a full-fledged lecture, with clips of Python and the Dangerous Sports Club. Chapman became quite polished and confi-

Speaking to a packed house at Drury College in Springfield, Missouri, on one of his U.S. lecture tours. Photo copyright KHJ.

A live concert recording of one of Graham Chapman's lectures was released in 1997 by Magnum Music as "A Six Pack of Lies" (catalog #CDBV-001, phone 011-1491-882858 for information).

dent, in marked contrast to his shyer, more insecure persona.

The revival of the TV series saw Chapman take a major role (as a policeman) in CBS's two-hour *Still Crazy Like a Fox,* featuring Jack Warden and airing on April 5, 1987. Later that year, he found himself hosting a collection of short films and videos for Cinemax. Titled *The Dangerous Film Club,* he played a variety of characters to link the strange bits of film sent in by viewers, though only four episodes were shot.

He also began work on an American TV series, *Jake's Journey,* a comedy/fantasy planned for the Disney Channel. *Jake's Journey* was to be the first TV series created by any of the Pythons for American television. CBS-TV was initially interested in the time-traveling comedy, and the pilot was written, shot, and filmed. Due to the vagaries of television networks, however, CBS changed its mind several times, and the pilot remains the only completed episode of what would have been a London-based sitcom.

Graham received a telephone call in late 1987 from Wits End Productions, which started him thinking about the project.

"They wondered if I was interested in writing something to be shot in England for American television, based on Mark Twain's *A Connecticut Yankee in King Arthur's Court.* At the time, I wasn't really sure—I knew a little bit about the book, but not enough, so I thought I'd read it and see," Chapman revealed.

"I read through quite a bit and skimmed through more, and thought 'That's a nice area there—how clever of him to have done that,' but couldn't see how that was going to shape into a series without being too much in one vein. I wanted more flexibility, and therefore introduced the element of time travel. I grafted onto it the Mark Twain stuff, and a few notions from *The Once and Future King,* where Merlin the Wizard was a tutor to Arthur.

"That relationship had always fascinated me in the book, because Merlin took him into all kinds of worlds which were impossible for human beings to go into—Arthur finds out what it's like to be a fish, for example. That was attractive as a possibility, quite apart from just being able to go into other worlds populated by humans. It seemed fitting

with those times, because of the elements of mysticism," Chapman explained.

"That was the genesis of it, plus a bit of *Alice in Wonderland.* Everything is not necessarily in order when one looks at it, but it has its own internal logic, everything behaving as though it has every right to be that way. In the end, it's a blend of all that—but unfortunately, written by David Sherlock and myself," he laughed. "So, it turns into something that's a slightly different animal than any of them. I suppose it's best described as a fantasy-comedy, or a comedy-fantasy . . . a fantacom. . . ."

The pilot includes a brief moment where they encounter a giant lobster on a cycling tour. Another Pythonesque moment that remains, though heavily edited for time in the pilot, is a verbal encounter with a witch. ("Come in!" "I am in!" "Then I must be out. . . .") Another battle, won by Chapman and Sherlock, was over the network's desire for a time machine—instead, the traveling is accomplished but not explained.

The pilot—with an unusually high budget (for 1988) of $1.2 million—was shot in Britain with Hal Ashby directing. The cast included Chris (*Max Headroom*) Young as Jake and Peter (*Princess Bride*) Cook as the king. Chapman wrote for himself a small role as the queen who never spoke, because she was so stingy she didn't want to give away her words—but he ended up becoming more involved than he had planned.

"I had only been interested in writing it and maybe taking a character role here and there, and I didn't want to give up the character role in the pilot even when I did take the bigger part.

"That came about when they had gotten two weeks into the shooting, and still hadn't come to a decision about casting George. They did want the person in the pilot to do the series—and I must say that since writing this stuff, I secretly cherished the notion of playing that role, but didn't want to because of several other considerations.

"But at this point, I did actually say that I wouldn't mind. They seemed to like that thought, and so did I! I quite enjoyed it, despite the fact it meant going back into armor, albeit even worse, because it was a full set of armor, and rusting," Chapman said, and explained that the figure of George actually is similar to that of Merlin.

"He's a tutor figure, but is also a retired

knight—or should have been, with a scraggly gray beard and rusty armor, but in reality, he could be looked on as a tutor figure, but one wouldn't necessarily know that from the first episode. This tutor-pupil relationship is not actually teaching him anything one could put one's finger on, but George is stopping Jake from learning things wrongly, and stopping Jake from getting fixed ideas about things, keeping him open-minded—probably one of the best lessons we could learn."

According to his original conception, Chapman said that Jake would be drawn to George in whatever time period he happens to be occupying, though their relationship and purpose would not necessarily be apparent.

"Jake—who has no control over it at all—is rather inconveniently brought back to wherever George happens to be. George pulls Jake into his world to help him out, really, to do jobs and errands for him, things that he can't be bothered to do, or is too lazy or too old to do. It can be quite inconvenient for Jake, though it often does happen when Jake himself is at personal moments of crisis—so it can also be convenient. It loses Jake no time at all—he goes away in a bubble, I suppose, and comes back to the same spot precisely, and carries on as usual. And he may or may not have learned something in the process, which may or may not help in current life."

Sadly, Graham never had the chance to film future episodes of *Jake's Journey,* but the show was coming together when he became ill in late 1988. CBS initially passed on the series, but ordered several episodes written during the U.S. Writers Guild strike, and planned to go into production with it. Apparently every CBS executive was very excited about the series, except for one person—network president Lawrence Tisch. When he ultimately rejected it, the Disney Channel decided to pick it up, but time ran out. Graham never gave up hope, but *Jake's Journey* was one project he was not able to see to its fruition.

Cancer was first detected on Graham's tonsil in November 1988, beginning his long battle with the disease. He was in and out of the hospital for the next year. The cancer spread to his spine, but his determination to beat the disease never wavered. It even looked as if he had succeeded by the following September, when he was discharged from the hospital and began making plans to re-

Graham Chapman, early 1980s. Photo copyright KHJ.

sume his career as he was undergoing physical therapy. After he had been home a short time, however, he was rushed to the hospital, wracked with pain, and doctors discovered the cancer had spread too far for hope of recovery.

For three days Graham held on, with friends and family, including his fellow Pythons, at his side. During that time his son, John Tomiczek, was able to fly in from America in time to visit with him. Terry Jones kept a bedside vigil and left early on the morning of October 4; Michael Palin and John Cleese were at his side when he died a few hours later.

"I just talked to him—and then he died!" Palin said later.

"We were always getting on to Michael for talking too much," quipped Eric Idle. "When we talked later about Graham's death, we were able to have a laugh and a weep."

Dying on the eve of the twentieth anniversary of the first *Monty Python's Flying Circus* broadcast prompted Terry Jones to call it "The worst case of party-pooping I have ever come across."

A small funeral service was held for the family a few days later, the Rolling Stones sent flowers, and the other Pythons were responsible for a floral arrangement in the shape of a huge foot.

Two months later a celebration of Graham's life was held in London, followed that evening by the delayed Python anniversary party.

In late January 1990 another memorial was held for Graham in Los Angeles, hosted by the British Academy of Film and Television Arts L.A. chapter. Guests included David Sherlock and Harry Nilsson.

A variety of Graham's friends spoke at the London celebration, including Douglas Adams, Tim Brooke-Taylor, John Cleese, and Michael Palin. Neil Innes performed (wearing his duck hat), and the Fred Tomlinson Singers led the crowd in singing a Chinese version of "Jerusalem." The festivities wrapped up with Eric Idle leading the group in "Always Look on the Bright Side of Life," and sherry was passed around at the conclusion so that everyone could toast to Graham's memory.

John Cleese and Michael Palin addressed the crowd in a manner that Graham certainly would have loved.

Cleese's comments exemplified the spirit of the occasion—and of Graham: "Graham Chapman, co-author of 'The Parrot Sketch,' is no more. He has ceased to be. Bereft of life, he rests in peace. He's shuffled off this mortal coil, turned up his toes, and joined the choir invisible. He's kicked the bucket, dropped off the twig, bitten the dust, snuffed it, breathed his last, and gone to meet the Great Head of Light Entertainment in the sky.

"And I guess that we're all thinking how sad it is that a man of such talent, of such capability for kindness, for such unusual intelligence, a man who could overcome his alcoholism with such truly admirable single-mindedness, should now so suddenly be spirited away at the age of only forty- eight before he'd achieved many of the things in which he was capable, and before he'd had enough fun.

"Well, I feel that I should say, 'Nonsense! Good riddance to him, the freeloading bastard. I hope he fries.' And the reason I feel I should say this is he would never forgive me if I didn't. If I threw away this glorious opportunity to shock you

all on his behalf. It's not a funeral, I grant you, but a memorial service is still pretty good.

"And at this, his very own memorial service, can you imagine how enraged he would be with me if on this, of all occasions, I failed to behave badly? [Laughter] And I could hear him whispering in my ear last night as I was writing this. 'All right, Cleese,' he was saying, 'you are very proud of being the very first person ever to say "shit" on British television. If this service is really for me, just for starters, I want you to become the first person ever at a British memorial service to say "fuck." [Laughter] You see, the trouble is, I can't. [Laughter] If he were with me here now, I would probably have the courage, because he always emboldened me. But the truth is, I lack his balls, his splendid defiance. And so I'll have to content myself instead with saying 'Betty Marsden . . .' [Laughter]

"But bolder and less inhibited spirits than me follow today. Jones and Idle, Gilliam and Palin. Heaven knows what the next hour will bring in Graham's name. Trousers dropping, blasphemers on pogo sticks, spectacular displays of high-speed farting, synchronized incest. [Laughter] One of the four, is planning to stuff a dead ocelot and a 1922 Remington typewriter up his own ass to the sound

of the second movement of Elgar's cello concerto. [Laughter] And that's in the first half.

"Because, you see, Gray would have wanted it this way. Really. Anything for him but mindless good taste. And that's what I'll always remember about him—apart, of course, from his Olympian extravagance. He was the prince of bad taste. He loved to shock. In fact, Gray, more than anyone I knew, embodied and symbolized all that was most offensive and juvenile in Monty Python. And his delight in shocking people led him on to greater and greater feats. I like to think of him as the pioneering beacon that beat the path along which fainter spirits could follow.

"Some memories. I remember writing the undertaker speech with him, and him suggesting the punch line, 'All right, we'll eat her, but if you feel bad about it afterwards, we'll dig a grave and you can throw up in it.' [Laughter] I remember discovering in 1969, when we wrote every day at the flat where Connie Booth and I lived, that he'd recently discovered the game of printing four-letter words on neat little squares of paper, and then quietly placing them at strategic points around our flat, forcing Connie and me into frantic last minute paper chases whenever we were expecting important guests.

"I remember him at BBC parties crawling around on all fours, rubbing himself affectionately against the legs of gray-suited executives, and delicately nibbling the more appetizing female calves. Mrs. Eric Morecambe remembers that too. [Laughter]

"I remember his being invited to speak at the Oxford Union, and entering the chamber dressed as a carrot—a full-length orange tapering costume with a large, bright green sprig as a hat—and then, when his turn came to speak, refusing to do so. [Laughter] He just stood there, literally speechless, for twenty minutes, smiling beatifically. The only time in world history that a totally silent man has succeeded in inciting a riot. [Laughter]

"I remember Graham receiving a *Sun* newspaper TV award from Reggie Maudling. Who else! And taking the trophy falling to the ground and crawling all the way back to his table, screaming loudly, as loudly as he could. And if you remember Gray, that was very loud indeed.

"It is magnificent, isn't it? You see, the thing about shock . . . is not that it upsets some people, I think; I think that it gives others a momentary joy of liberation, as we realized in that instant that the social rules that constrict our lives so terribly are not actually very important.

"Well, Gray can't do that for us anymore. He's gone. He is an ex-Chapman. All we have of him now is our memories. But it will be some time before they fade." [Applause]

John Cleese

Born October 27, 1939, at Weston-Super-Mare, John Marwood Cleese (he once went through a period of using "Otto" as his middle name; and his family name was originally "Cheese" until his grandfather changed it) was tall even as a child, and claims he developed his sense of humor to fend off any teasing by his classmates. He spent five years, from 1953–58, at Clifton College, getting A levels* in physics, math, and chemistry. He then taught at his old prep school for two years while waiting to go to Cambridge's Downing College.

Cleese began studying law, but was invited to join the Footlights his very first year there through three sketches he had written with Alan Hutchinson. In the Footlights he met future writing partner Graham Chapman. He appeared in the 1962 and 1963 Footlights Revues, the latter of which (*Cambridge Circus*) played for five months at the Lyric in the West End. He then took a job at BBC Radio, for fifteen hundred pounds a year, writing jokes for the *Dick Emery Show*. He wrote a Christmas show called *Yule Be Surprised,* with Brian Rix and Terry Scott, a program Cleese claims people still mention to him whenever they want to embarrass him.

Rejoining *Cambridge Circus* in 1964, he toured New Zealand in July, then played on Broadway for three weeks that October (as well as an appearance on *The Ed Sullivan Show*), and continued off-Broadway until the following February (in what is now the Bottom Line).

*Qualifying exams taken around age fourteen that allow a student entry to courses leading to college.

A very young John Cleese with father Reg and mother Muriel. Photo from the Collection of John Cleese, used by permission.

The teenaged Cleese participates in Sports Day at St. Peter's School, Weston-super-mare, on May 30, 1953. Photo from the Collection of John Cleese, used by permission.

During this period, Cleese was recruited to appear in a fumetti feature for *Help!* magazine. The assistant editor was a young American named Terry Gilliam.

After *Cambridge Circus* folded that February, Cleese stayed on in New York to appear in the U.S. production of *Half a Sixpence* for six months,

as the man who embezzles Tommy Steele's money. During his tenure with the show, he claims that his spectacular lack of musical ability caused the director to insist that he never sing, but stand in the back and mouth the words to the songs.

After an unsuccessful two-month stint writing on international politics for *Newsweek,* he then joined the *American Establishment Review* to perform in Chicago and Washington, before returning to London at Christmas time.

Cleese had written some sketches for David Frost's *That Was the Week That Was,* so when Frost asked him to join *The Frost Report,* he resumed his writing partnership with Graham Chapman. Eric Idle, Terry Jones, and Michael Palin were all writing for the show at the time as well, while Marty Feldman, the Goodies, and the Two Ronnies also did some writing or performing for Frost. Cleese performed as well; particularly notable are sketches done with Ronnie Corbett and Ronnie Barker which featured them as upper-, middle-, and lower-class characters. Cleese repeated his role as the upper-class gentleman years later on several of *The Two Ronnies* shows.

During the same time, Cleese was also writing and performing in *I'm Sorry, I'll Read That Again* for BBC Radio, with a cast that consisted largely of the *Cambridge Circus* crew, as well as performing on *I'm Sorry, I Haven't a Clue.* Most notably, he began

In barbership costume and apron, ready to perform "Sit on My Face." Photo copyright KHJ.

2 5 5

At Last, the 1948 Show in January 1967, with Chapman, Feldman, and Tim Brooke-Taylor. Of course, the latter led into Python.

Cleese began 1968 by marrying American actress Connie Booth, and he and Chapman worked on screenplays and TV scripts during the period from February 1968 through August 1969. They collaborated on *The Magic Christian* screenplay, and Cleese appeared onscreen as a Sotheby's auctioneer; the pair also cowrote *The Rise and Rise of Michael Rimmer,* and *Rentadick.* Cleese performed in several films around that time, including *The Bliss*

lowing summer. Despite leaving the TV series, Cleese did appear in the subsequent stage shows, and shot *Holy Grail* in April and May of 1974. Later that year, he and Connie Booth cowrote and starred in *Romance With a Double Bass,* a forty-five-minute film adapted from a Chekhov short story.

The most celebrated Cleese/Booth collaboration soon followed. The couple shot the pilot for *Fawlty Towers* in December, while the first series was done in August and September of 1975. The pair cowrote and performed the six-part series in which Cleese plays Basil Fawlty, the henpecked owner of a small English hotel who is constantly frustrated in his attempts to deal with his wife, employees, and guests. The show proved extraordinarily popular everywhere it was shown, in some places surpassing the popularity of Monty Python. Even though Cleese and Booth were divorced in August 1978, they went on to create another series of six *Fawlty Towers* early the following year. He married American actress Barbara Trentham, whom he met at the *Hollywood Bowl* shows, and the two had a daughter, Camilla, before later divorcing.

A family shot on the set of Time Bandits, *with the six Bandits in the front row; in the back are Terry Gilliam and daughter Amy, film executive George Harrison and son Dhani, a costumed David Warner, and John Cleese with daughter Cynthia. Handmade Films/Time Bandits.*

of Mrs. Blossom, Interlude, The Best House in London, The Love Ban, and *The Statue.*

Becoming restless after the second series of Monty Python, Cleese did not leave the group until after the third series. During that time, his daughter Cynthia was born, and he had founded Video Arts, his industrial training film company, in December 1971, shooting their first film the fol-

Cleese found happiness with American Alyce Faye Eichelberger; after marrying the Texas native, they set up housekeeping in New York and California, in addition to London. His happiness was increased when his daughter Cynthia made him the first Python grandfather in 1997.

His comedic talents were expanded into areas beyond films and TV shows. He has achieved con-

*Cleese resting and relaxing on the **Brian** set. Photos copyright KHJ.*

siderable success writing and performing a long string of TV and radio commercials. Most of the Pythons have done some TV commercials, if only for their own films, but only John Cleese turned commercials into a gold mine.

John Cleese began making commercials around 1973, and discovered an extremely lucrative new career for himself in Britain, America, and around the world, including Australia, Denmark, Norway, Sweden, and Holland. He writes most, though not all, of them. He explains that he applies the same general principles to his ads as he does his training films, emphasizing the key points, whether the commercial is British, American, or Norwegian.

"If the people briefing me are quite clear on what they want to get across, then I will think and come back to them with certain questions. If they clarify those questions, I will then usually do some rough recordings, and hand the tapes over to them. They will then come back and say what they think works," explains Cleese.

"Then we have a stage of cutting, changing, re-shaping, and then another stage of fine-polishing. So, it goes through a few backwards and forwards, but basically, I'm writing them.

"In America, though, I don't pretend to know the sensitivities, so I listen very carefully to what the people say. If somebody says 'You can't say that' in England, I would say 'Don't be so bloody silly, of course it's all right.' But if somebody says that in America, I don't feel I'm in any position to argue."

Several of his American commercials make fun of the relationship of Britain and the U.S., including the Callard & Bowser radio ads. One of the commercials is as follows:

Look, all you American persons, it's been suggested that I urge you to go out and buy Callard & Bowser's extremely fine, rather sophisticated British candy . . . a sort of call to action. Well, frankly, the last thing you Americans need is a call to action. I've never seen such an active bunch in my life, if you're not making millions or defending the free world or putting men on the moon, you're out jogging. I mean, if ever there was a nation of get-up-and-go, let's-get-this-show-on-the-road, it's you U.S. persons, isn't it? You don't need a call to action. You need a call to keep still for a couple of minutes. Put your feet up, open a packet of Callard & Bowser's superior candy, and wallow in the sensual pleasure of a bit of toffee or butterscotch or even juicy jellies. Trouble is, two minutes of that sort of pleasure you'd all feel guilty and have to rush back to work and start slaving away again—the old American work ethic. So to help you, we've made Callard & Bowser candy jolly tricky for you to find. You may have to comb the streets to find a shop that stocks it. And then it may be jolly tough discovering where it's hidden. But when you do find it, you'll have experienced enough blood, sweat and toil to be able to really enjoy it. . . . clever bit of marketing, really, isn't it?

(Co-written by John Cleese and Lynn Stiles)

John Cleese, mid-'70s. Photographed by John Sims for Python Productions, used by permission.

to stop working. Something like the television commercials for Sony in England enabled me to commission six different friends to write scripts—not for me, just friends who wanted or needed to write. I was able to commission them to do it. You can only do that if you've got a considerable source of funds, and that's where the commercials come in," explains Cleese.

"*Families and How to Survive Them* cost me something over twenty thousand pounds from the time I paid for Robin Skynner's time, paid for one or two flights—but that's fine. That meant I was able to make sure that book happened. In fact, I was able to provide the circumstances under which it could happen from the money from commercials. It's the way the world's constructed. You earn these ridiculous sums of money from commercials, and you can spread it around and make all these other things happen!"

John Cleese even filled in for Eric Idle on one of his commercials; Cleese has easily done more commercials himself than the rest of the Pythons put together.

Cleese proved just as successful with Video Arts, the company he co-founded to produce and market management training films.

Video Arts' success surprised even Cleese.

"For five years, it ticked along predictably," relates Cleese. "The product was very good, better than the product of the competitors. We organized it efficiently and marketed it intelligently, so I suppose it was all predictable, all foreseeable. Then suddenly the curve just started to go up and up and up in a way that none of us had anticipated at all.

"Our films, without any question at all, were much better than anything else on the market. Our main rival had to buck up a lot, and they started hiring a couple of top people in British comedy and started making better films. The fact was, the whole standard of industrial training films went up so sharply that I suspect more and more people started using them, because they began to say

Although a few big stars in America still shun U.S. commercials, Cleese says negative aspects of commercials were never a consideration for him.

"First of all, I didn't want to come to America and be a big star, because it just isn't what my life is about. It's never occurred to me to do that. It's suited Dudley [Moore] fine, for example, he's done marvelously well, but it's never occurred to me as being a possibility, and it would never happen. It's just not what I want to do with my life. I've been enormously happy working in England because of the freedom I've got."

Of all the commercials he's ever written, the one he may be the proudest of was actually performed by his mother. When *Life of Brian* was opening, each of the Pythons had their mothers record a radio ad for the film. John's eighty-year-old mother Muriel read an appeal to the radio audience, stating that she is 102 years old and kept in a retirement home by her son; unless enough people see his new film and make him richer, he will throw her into the streets, where she will die. As a result, Mrs. Cleese actually won an award for best radio entertainment commercial of 1979.

"Commercials have been all-important, because they've given me a real financial base, which you just don't get from working in English television. I could do a series every year for English television for the rest of my life, and I'd never be able

'Well, if they're this good, we'll use them.' Whereas, the old market used to be a few not frightfully good films coming from two or three British companies, and a lot of American films that weren't awfully inspired. I think we increased the market by increasing the quality of the product."

About 90 percent of the films are humorous, says Cleese, and the comedy makes them more effective.

"We've discovered that, on the whole, you want about five major points in each film that need to be explored and explained, and the audience needs to be persuaded that

The co-founder of Video Arts. Photo copyright Video Arts.

they are right. We don't tell them, we put in scenes which will persuade them that this is the way to handle a particular situation, and which demonstrate what happens in that situation when you don't handle it properly. So, we have about five very serious and important lessons which are recapitulated, not only when they've just been taught, but also at the end," Cleese explains.

"And we probably have an almost innumerable number of other, smaller lessons which may be absolutely nonverbal. In the 'Interview' film, the guy who's being interviewed has a clock on the wall behind him, so the man who's interviewing him can look at the time without making it apparent to the interviewee that he's checking how much longer he's got. Now that's a point that doesn't appear in the script—it's just there for the people who spot it. There's lots of small points like that, the nonverbals, but five key points are spelled out at great length and then recapitulated in caption form at the end."

Cleese says the comedy is integrated into each film.

"The jokes, on the whole, go all the way through. They're very easy in the scenes where we show people doing it wrong, particularly because the audience watching it is very specialized and immediately knows—I mean, if you spent your time sitting behind the reception desk of a hotel, and you start watching a scene set behind the re-

ception desk of a hotel, you immediately know when a guy isn't getting it right," says Cleese.

"So, the scenes where the man gets it wrong are always funny. The hard thing is making the scenes where he gets it right funny. Sometimes those scenes have quite a bit less humor, but then they're usually pretty short. I would be very surprised in our films if a minute passed without some humor. And a lot of the time, it's almost throughout."

Although many of the films are rather straightforward, some of the others involve seemingly silly moments, such as Cleese (with mustache intact) portraying Queen Elizabeth I.

"That didn't strike me as silly, actually," says Cleese, straightfaced. "In Python, we had some things that were just sheer silliness, like the 'Fish-Slapping Dance'—just joie de vivre absurdity. You never have that in the training films, because everything is in there for a point.

"I think the most absurd scene—which I wasn't in—was a girl playing a sales assistant who couldn't stop a character called Mrs. Rabbit from talking. So she produced a megaphone from behind the counter and shouted at her over the megaphone. That was the most bizarre image I can remember, because most of the comedy in the training films is set very strongly in reality. It's comedy of observation."

The lessons learned by his Video Arts research

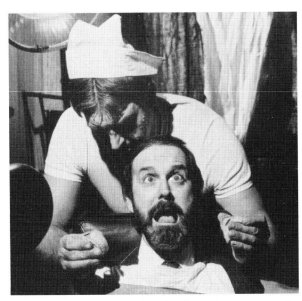

Video Arts' More Bloody Meetings *sees the* Nurse *(David Prowse, who was also Darth Vader in* Star Wars*) treating the Meeting Chairman. Photo copyright Video Arts.*

even profited Monty Python. According to Cleese, the group's meetings used to be long, rambling, unorganized, and inefficient, but after his work on such films as *Meetings, Bloody Meetings,* they were able to accomplish their goals in a fraction of their previous time.

Cleese appears in many, but not all, of the company's films, and says he almost invariably portrays the person who gets things wrong, with a few exceptions.

"We did a film on time management and delegation where I play St. Peter up in Heaven, who actually told the guy who was getting it wrong how to do it right, which was quite fun. It was all in a Heaven set, with the gates and the mist—a little like *Heaven Can Wait.*"

Although none of the other Pythons have been involved in the films, Cleese has featured some of his *Fawlty Towers* colleagues (including Connie Booth, Prunella Scales, and Andrew Sachs) and other English comedians, such as Jonathan Lynn, John Bird, Alan Bennett (of *Beyond the Fringe*), Tim Brooke-Taylor, Graeme Garden, and Rowan Atkinson; several films were even directed by Charles Crichton, who of course collaborated with Cleese on *A Fish Called Wanda.*

Having sold his interest in the company, his in-

volvement with Video Arts today is minimal, though he still appears in new films for them on occasion, particularly when they began updating and reshooting early films (information on the films is available in America by phoning 1-800-553-0091).

"I do a very small number of days of acting with them each year because I'm extremely fond of them," says Cleese. "We remade a lot of films; that was hard work but good fun. But my connection with it is very tenuous now, other than having a great deal of good will toward it."

Having had a good experience with Video Arts, Cleese also helped another doctor/comedian friend form another company to produce health videos.

"It's a company I founded around 1993 with a couple of old friends, including Graeme Garden [of *I'm Sorry, I'll Read That Again* and *The Goodies*]—I

Julian Carruthers (Cleese) meets with Ron Scroggs (John Bird) in Budgeting. *Photo copyright Video Arts.*

did 100 radio shows with him back in the '60s," says Cleese. "He's a medical doctor, very smart and level-headed. I've got him directing, and I've got them being written and primarily performed by this very clever fellow named Rob Buckman. Rob was a Footlight and a very clever doctor, he's been running a major oncology department in a Toronto hospital, and he's tremendously good at putting information across. He coordinates the information from the consultants, writes the scripts, checks them all out with the consultant, and then he and I do a little top and tail. We explain that when most people are told they've got something wrong with them, they get anxious, so that's the worst possible time for them to take in information. Of course, that is exactly when the doctor tells them, and then they have to come back three days later because they haven't heard anything he said, which is a bit of a waste of time for them and for the doctor. The

John Cleese enlisted many of his friends for Video Arts films like **Control of Working Capital,** *including Ronnie Corbett (who appeared with Cleese in the 1960s in* **The Frost Report** *and in 1997's* **Fierce Creatures**). *Photo copyright Video Arts.*

Meetings Bloody Meetings *remains one of the most successful of Video Arts films. Photo copyright Video Arts.*

whole idea here is that the doctor says 'You've got a bit of arthritis in your knee, take this tape home and have a cup of tea and watch it a couple of times, make a note of anything you don't understand, and come back and see me next week and we'll talk about it.' It's intended to save time, and make much more efficient communication between patient and doctor."

Cleese has done an extensive variety of film and TV work in his post-Python days. He has done countless walk-ons and cameo appearances that include *Dr. Who, The Goodies,* the aforementioned *Two Ronnies, Not the Nine O'Clock News,* and *The Avengers.* More extended roles include a 1978 appearance hosting *The Muppet Show,* a 1977 film for London Weekend Television called *The Strange Case of the End of Civilisation (As We Know It)* in which he played Arthur Sherlock Holmes, as well as several roles in *Whoops Apocalypse.* One of his most unusual, and acclaimed, TV roles was that of Petruchio in the 1980 BBC production of *Taming of the Shrew,* in which he was directed by Jonathan Miller.

In addition, Cleese won an American Emmy award for best performance in a comedy for his appearance in *Cheers* on March 5, 1987. In "Simon Says" he portrays a celebrated marriage counselor who advises Sam and Diane. He says he did it because he was a fan of the show, and because he was curious about working on an American situation comedy. Although he enjoyed the people and the experience, he found the pace more frantic than he was used to, with script changes coming throughout the week. A *Cheers* scheduled for April 13, 1989 was to feature him reprising the Simon role (he was to return to collect the money owed him by Frasier Crane from his first appearance), but scheduling conflicts could not be worked out. His next appearance on an American sitcom would not come until the spring of 1998, when he was featured on NBC's *Third Rock from the Sun.*

Another of his non-show business interests turned into a successful publishing venture. When his first marriage was breaking up, Cleese became involved in psychoanalysis and wrote a book with his therapist. John Cleese reluctantly began group therapy with Robin Skynner as a result of problems in his first marriage and to treat a probable psychosomatic illness. After his experiences in therapy, Cleese was so impressed that he wanted to share his knowledge with others. Since their therapist-patient relationship had concluded, they decided to collaborate on a book designed for laypeople who would probably never participate in group therapy on their own.

"Professionally, it was a huge departure for me," notes Cleese. "It wasn't a departure from

John Cleese and friend on The Muppet Show. Collection of John Cleese, used by permission.

what I was interested in. When I was fifteen, what I really wanted to do was study biology, and go into the psychology department somewhere in a university, and do all those tests that B. F. Skinner used to do on pigeons and rats.

"It's not surprising that twenty years later, I got back to it—my principal readings over the years being psychiatry or psychology. When I'd had this experience in the group which Robin Skynner ran, with his wife as co-therapist back in 1974, '75, '76, and '77—three and a half years I was into it—I was going back. Apart from the fact that I needed therapy at the time to get me through a difficult time in my life when my first marriage broke up, I was also going back to what fascinated me. What did Samuel Johnson say? The proper study of man is man."

Cleese says that at first, he found it difficult to open up in his first sessions with the group.

"I was more apprehensive at the beginning," he admits. "For a number of years, I had a fear of the press, not least because there are sections of the British press which are so dishonest and so untrustworthy and so treacherous that one is completely vulnerable. There is nothing that you can say to someone that cannot be distorted.

"At one stage, that worried me a lot. Now, it doesn't really worry me very much, and I don't quite know what the difference is, but something in me's changed. And I think it is well known in England how awful most of the press are, and therefore there's a great deal of skepticism about almost everything they print."

Families is presented in a very user-friendly format, which Cleese says was intentional.

"It's light, hopefully, with a certain amount of humor with a serious purpose. It's not just to keep people amused or to keep people reading, although that's obviously a function of something that's light and amusing and entertaining—it's easy for people to keep reading. The real purpose of a lot of the humor is to relax people. Things that might make them slightly anxious if they were handed forward in a very solid and confrontative way can be absorbed and chewed over because they're put across in a relaxed, playful way."

His work with Robin Skynner was even helpful in his comedy, he says. "When you begin to see a little bit more of what's the healthy way, it's easier to see what is unhealthy and make fun of that."

Families and How to Survive Them established a new reputation for Cleese and turned into a bestseller that has sold consistently in Britain. Cleese says he was happy with the follow-up to the *Families* book, *Life and How to Survive It,* but was disappointed with the general reaction to it.

"I thought some of Robin's ideas were so interesting and so original that I was looking forward to hearing what people had to say about them, even if it was critical," says Cleese. "The reviews that we got finally convinced me that the British press is, for all practical purposes, a waste of space. Some of these ideas were the most revealing and useful ideas I have ever come across, but the reviews consisted of attacks on me, not on the book and not on Robin. The reviews concentrated on the fact that there were a few weak jokes which would be easily taken out for the paperback. There was no serious interest taken at all by the majority of the critics."

He notes that the ideas put forth in *Life and How to Survive It* probably make it a more challenging book for most people than *Families.*

"Sales were pretty good, but that was largely because it was serialized and got a lot of newspaper coverage. It was number one on the bestseller list for three weeks, then it was number two for two or three weeks more—it was in the top ten for thirteen weeks. But whereas people are constantly talking about the *Families* book, I've only had a few people discuss the *Life* book with me. I think it's a much harder book. *Families* is terribly useful; it's more of a self-help book in a sense. People can use it as a self-help book very efficiently, and it is well spoken of by the mental health professionals in the U.K. If you go to train for Relate, which used to be the marriage guidance counsel, *Families* is on more lists than any other single book they recommend to trainees. But *Life* is more about businesses and institutions, society and nations, value systems and religion. It has a much less direct bearing on peoples' everyday lives. I think that's the problem with it."

For the big screen, he went on to write and performed in the award-winning short subject *To Norway: Home of Giants,* and played smaller roles in a wide variety of films, from *The Great Muppet Caper* and *The Jungle Book* to *Frankenstein* and *Silverado.*

John Cleese proved to be a curious yet effective addition to Lawrence Kasdan's epic Western. He was clearly excited about this role, as he ex-

The offer to co-star in a Western enticed John Cleese to Silverado. *Photo from the Collection of John Cleese, used by permission.*

plained that he had never dreamed of doing a Western.

"It's so ridiculous, such an absurd notion, that it has to be attractive," he explained shortly before he left for New Mexico to begin filming. "It's very nice to have the chance of doing one or two things that are slightly straight, because I'm best at comedy and I expect to get paid well at comedy. I don't expect to get paid well for straight parts because it's not a skill of mine. It may turn out I have the skill, but everybody who does it is taking a slight risk. I have a couple of funny lines in it, but it's not a comedy at all, but a straight, exciting Western, beautifully constructed, as you would expect from Mr. Kasdan. To my delight, he's written a small part about a tall, English sheriff. It's very short, but it's wonderful, so I go to Sante Fe and have riding lessons in a Western saddle."

Silverado *director Lawrence Kasdan stays warm in New Mexico with Kevin Kline and John Cleese. It was there that Cleese and Kline became acquainted, eventually leading to Kline's involvement with* A Fish Called Wanda. *Photo from the Collection of John Cleese, used by permission.*

After the film's release, Cleese noted that although he appears only in the first half hour of the film, the whole experience was wonderful.

"*Silverado* was a joy, to suddenly disappear to New Mexico at the invitation of dear Larry Kasdan for the two and a half weeks of riding lessons, and some of the finest scenery I've ever seen, and the chance to get to know a delightful, lovely group of people," Cleese relates.

"It was very interesting to be on a film as big as that—three times as big as the biggest Python film. I think *Silverado*'s budget was more than $20 million. I came to realize that the amount of planning and logistics that went into every single day of shooting—the amount of food that had to be provided, the number of tents that had to be put up so that people could stay warm—was most impressive. It was like being part of an army!

"Filming was very enjoyable. My single complaint was that as New Mexico is at seven thousand feet, it was a damn sight colder than I had guessed. The hours of daylight were quite restricting because it was winter, so we were all getting up at five-fifteen A.M. so as to be available to be shot at first light. Apart from the temperature and the hour at which we had to get up, it was ideal.

"I have the most considerable respect for Larry Kasdan, and I found it very interesting trying to see why he is so good. I realized it was because he visualized so precisely—more than anyone I've ever worked with before—exactly what was going up on the screen at the moment he was writing it on the paper."

One of the added benefits to *Silverado* was that Cleese learned how to ride a horse. He was particularly proud of this ability because he wanted to impress his daughter Cynthia, and was rather annoyed that most of his horseback riding was in long shots. There were other problems as well.

"Every time I got really comfortable on a horse, they gave me a bigger one. I was too tall! They didn't want me to look silly, so the one I finished up on was pretty big, but I adored the riding. Altogether, I went through four or five horses—I don't think they all had to be destroyed after I had ridden them, but every time I got one that I *really* liked, there was another, *bigger* one waiting for me the next day," Cleese recalls with a laugh.

"It was strange, and I got a little lonely. I went out and quite consciously bought a couple of nov-

2 6 4

els by P. G. Wodehouse and Somerset Maugham at one point, because I needed an injection of Englishness. It was nothing to do with unfriendliness, I just felt a little strange after I'd been there a couple of months. A wonderful experience, though, and I was very sad to leave them all."

Cleese found himself appearing in Kenneth Branagh's production of *Frankenstein* because he wanted to work with Branagh.

"It wasn't the Frankenstein aspect that appealed to me," says Cleese. "I have never been much interested in the horror genre. I had met Ken Branagh just before that. I had, to some extent, missed out on the Ken Branagh phenomenon, and then I went to see his *Hamlet*. I met him afterward and liked him enormously—he was very entertaining on the subject of *Hamlet* as a play, because he had this wonderful, practical attitude that I think the best artists have toward their work, remarkably free of bullshit and critical language. I enjoyed him a great deal. I got this offer not long after that and I thought, 'How intriguing.' I read the script just as far as my character's death, because I felt that was all I needed to do at that point, and I was intrigued with the idea of playing a role in which I had to get absolutely no laughs at all. This was the first time somebody offered me a part that was devoid of comedy. In fact, if I got a laugh, I failed. I was very intrigued by that and wanting to know Ken a bit better."

In his makeup, he was nearly unrecognizable, which was part of his plan.

"That was very much the aim, because so many people have said to me that they only need to see me and they start smiling," says Cleese. "I don't know whether they're being flattering, whether they say that because they feel they ought, or whether it's because there's some truth in it. But I thought if there is any truth in it, if I can be on screen for a few seconds and establish the character without people realizing that it's me, then maybe we will have gotten through that type of knee-jerk response. And if they then recognize me, the character will have already established itself as a non-funny character, and maybe we can avoid that reflex smile or laugh. And that's what we seem to have managed to do.

"I did that largely, not through the facial hair, but through changing my mouth, which is one of my most characteristic things, by using dental prosthetic, false teeth. When I change that section of my mouth between my nose and my chin, it disguises me better than anything else I do. I discovered that by accident. A few years ago, I was sitting in a dressing room in Thames Television waiting to do a bit of acting in *Whoops Apocalypse,* I found some funny teeth that had been made by Peter Cook to impersonate a famous English anchorwoman with famously protruding teeth. I put them in and I could not believe how much my appearance had changed. It was absolutely astonishing. So I used that bit of information for the Frankenstein makeup."

After a holiday to Hong Kong proved disappointing, Cleese decided to accept a role in the live-action *Jungle Book* to take advantage of the warm weather on location in India.

"Suddenly I got this offer to go and work in India, earn a bit of useful money, and avoid going back to England for a bit," says Cleese. "I adored the director, Steve Sommers, the part seemed to be something I could do perfectly capably, so it got fixed up very easily, and we buzzed off duly to Rajastan and did a bit of the shooting there. I got to know Sam Neill, whose acting I'd always enjoyed, and Sam said, 'We've met.' I looked at him and I couldn't remember. And he said 'When you visited New Zealand in 1964.' Sam and a friend of his from school—because they were both still in school—came to the show and then came to the stage door, and apparently we invited them in and were very nice to them.

"We decided to give my character a Rudyard Kipling mustache, which sticks forward in an extraordinary way. It was one of the stupidest decisions I have ever made, having to stick this false hair onto my own mustache each morning was okay, taking it off at night was agony! I dreaded it. It was like having every bit of the mustache individually pulled out!"

He took on lead roles in films that he hadn't written, including *Privates on Parade* and *Clockwise.* Although it was based on the successful play of the same name, *Privates on Parade* was not nearly as successful as a film. Co-executive producer Denis O'Brien bought the play's film rights when he took over management of Monty Python, and reportedly wanted all of the Pythons to star in the film, strictly as actors.

"I thought *Privates on Parade,* being sort of anti-

war not so many years after Vietnam, might have a chance in America, and it shows how wildly unrealistic it was. I don't think it was very good. I think I learned a great deal about why scripts work and don't work from that—that didn't even work well in Australia, the only thing I've ever done that didn't really work in Australia," notes Cleese.

After some early screenings, O'Brien reportedly suggested some additional scenes to make the movie more commercial, and more footage was added in which Cleese— as Major Flack— does a silly walk on the parade grounds. The extraneous material was tacked onto the end of the film and is seen as the credits roll. It was used in the trailers for the film, which misled some audiences into thinking they were going to see a movie in which John Cleese does silly walks. This didn't help matters, but Cleese thinks the root of the problem was more basic.

"I think the trouble was that every single person working on it didn't really know anything about film," Cleese observes. "We're talking about Peter Nichols, Michael Blakemore, who is a great director and writer, and myself—I don't think any one of the three of us really knew what we were doing vis-à-vis film. An important learning experience—a shame, because it was a great stage play."

In the autumn of 1984, John Cleese was enthusiastic about making *Clockwise,* calling it "The only really funny script I've ever received through my letterbox—it was written by Michael Frayn of *Noises Off* fame. He's a top-class playwright who's written two or three of the best plays that I've seen in the past ten years; he's written a wonderfully funny script about a headmaster, so I'm going to do that next summer."

He emphasized that he hadn't planned to do any film at that time until he read the *Clockwise* screenplay.

"If Michael Frayn's screenplay had not been so funny, I wouldn't be running around looking for a movie next year," he explained. "It's just that when you see something that's just so joyfully funny that it actually causes your wife to shout in and say 'Are you all right?' because you're emitting these strange, whimpering animal noises, because you've gotten past the point where you can laugh loudly at a thing. When you see a script like that, you just always want to do it. It simply gets the adrenaline going because it's so wonderful."

Originally titled *Man of the Moment, Clockwise* did very well in the U.K. and very poorly in the U.S. Although part of the reason was the lack of promotion, Cleese maintains that it failed to make concessions to an American audience. Some jokes, such as the lack of a working pay phone, were very familiar to British audiences, but Americans didn't have the same sort of experiences and so the

Starring as Brian Stimpson in **Clockwise. Universal-Cannon-Thorn-EMI Screen Entertainment. Photo from the Collection of John Cleese, used by permission.**

scene wouldn't get the laughs of recognition in the U.S.

Despite its drawbacks and lukewarm reviews in America, *Clockwise* has many wonderful moments and plenty to entertain Cleese fans; it marked his last major film role prior to *A Fish Called Wanda*. In fact, Cleese says much of the success of *Wanda* is the result of the failure of *Clockwise*.

"*Clockwise* was a huge learning experience," reflects Cleese. "I look back to it in amazement at the thought that I really believed at the time that *Clockwise* might be successful in America.

"I just wish that other British filmmakers could see how completely unrealistic their illusions are about their films working in the States. The fact that *Clockwise* never even opened in Chicago is still something that astounds me, but I think I needed to be thrown in the deep end, to be shocked by the coldness of the water, to snap me out of the vague, wildly overoptimistic feeling that certain films made in England might work in America. You've got me right up against the reality of it, as a result of which I was able to make *Wanda*.

"*Wanda* wouldn't have worked anything like it did if I hadn't failed with *Clockwise*."

He was also attracted to voiceover roles in such films as *An American Tail 2: Fievel Goes West,* and *The Swan Princess.*

Voiceover acting of the kind he did in portraying a French frog in the animated *Swan Princess* appeals to Cleese's radio roots.

"I started in radio, and every time I go into a sound-recording studio I'm a very happy little bunny," says Cleese. "If I ever did a late-night talk show, it would be on radio, not on television. I love it. They simply approached me about doing this little frog, and I loved the idea of doing him in a French accent, because I like doing outrageous French accents. It required only two fairly long sessions of three or four hours each in a studio in London, followed up by a session later on. In the old days you used to have to fit the voices to the animation. Of course, now they fit the animation to the voices. It was great fun and as far as I can make out, rather successful, particularly on video."

His other children's projects include a video and audio tape reading of a Dr. Seuss book, *Did I Ever Tell You How Lucky You Are.* "Apart from the fact that I'd read several Dr. Seuss books to my youngest daughter, I had no reason for doing it other than the pleasure of doing so. I did it for a small but perfectly decent fee, and I like going into sound-recording studios," says Cleese.

Cleese says it takes no great change of mindset to alternate between adult and children's projects. "The best children's projects are comparable to the more relaxed, fun adult projects," he says. "Anyone asks me to do *Wind in the Willows,* I regard that as a mild classic—it's not *War and Peace,* but it's still a classic of its kind. So, the invitation to do something like that is always very attractive."

A Fish Called Wanda saw Cleese take over both scripting and lead acting duties, but it paid off. Cleese had long hoped to collaborate with director Charles Crichton, and had become friends with Kevin Kline during the shooting of *Silverado.* He had always wanted to work with Jamie Lee Curtis, and the addition of Michael Palin to the group seemed natural. In addition, his real-life daughter Cynthia plays the same role in the film.

A Fish Called Wanda turned out to be the most successful non-Python project John Cleese had done since *Fawlty Towers* many years before. The project literally took years for him to put together, from constructing the story with veteran director Charles Crichton to the eventual promotion of the movie. As early as 1984, Cleese explained that he and Crichton had begun their collaboration, even though they hadn't determined a title at that point.

"Dear Charlie Crichton is working on it, referring to it with a gleam in his eyes as *Corruption.* I think he likes that [title], and I quite like that," explained Cleese. "I always wanted to call a movie *The Last Prawn.* I don't know why. I don't think it would quite work for this one—I may have to write another one."

Over the years, the prawn became a fish, and after its release, Cleese says it was worth it all.

"I couldn't have been more pleased, because it was the first time I've really done a film of my own," he reveals. "Well, I couldn't say it was of my own, because the number of people that contributed to it was huge, but nevertheless, as Charlie Crichton said, it was basically my project. It was my impetus that got it going, I chose the team, and that's what I really take the credit for, and I basically did the dialogue. Everything else was

tremendously a team effort. And because of that, because I put more of myself and more time into it than any other project, I was very touched indeed by how well liked it was."

The plot of *A Fish Called Wanda* is as elaborate and complicated as those of the old Ealing comedies that Charles Crichton used to direct. Cleese had long been an admirer of Crichton and his films, including *The Lavender Hill Mob,* and even worked with him on some of his Video Arts films. When he began *Wanda,* Cleese developed the story alongside Crichton, and at various points in the production, Cleese and Crichton were sharing directing and writing credits as they pieced together their story.

"It is intricate, and I believe it works," says Cleese. "I believe it's almost watertight. I think what anyone does at any time is totally justified—even things like what people are doing when they're off the screen is either implied or is there. It was just a question of working on it a very, very long time, and going through the story again and again and again, and being prepared to rewrite the story every time you had a new idea that you wanted to fit into the movie that would require more rewrites.

"We were juggling scenes, so that the nude scene went from me and Jamie being in the state of undress, to just me being undressed, on a suggestion of Jamie's, which was quite correct because it was funnier. The farce scene, when Wendy arrives home early and catches them all in the house, originally had Wendy's father in it as well as Michael Palin.

"I went through at least three completely different plots before we got anywhere *near* what we finished up with, which probably then took another six or eight drafts, plus a lot of rehearsal. Almost every scene in there was reshaped and done in different ways. In the courtroom, I was originally going to blow George's alibi, to get rid of him so that I could be with Wanda; that was in the script for some time. Then it became obvious that it was much funnier if Wanda blew it for her purposes, because my astonishment would play off her mercenary and manipulative behavior better," explains Cleese.

"So, almost everything there took a lot of shaping before it all fitted. There were odd moments when you get an inspiration—the scene in which Michael Palin tried to kill the old lady and got the dogs instead—it was a week before I felt that was right, because I thought 'Will the idea of him trying to kill someone be bought by the audience, or is it just outside the limits of this movie?' And it was really only when I told Charlie about it, and he sat with the idea for two or three days and came back and said he thought it was fine, that I thought 'Yeah, I think it is fine.' So, even what might look like a moment of inspiration took a week before I decided whether it was right or not. It's a very slow process."

Even after he thought he had finished the film, Cleese says they

A Fish Called Wanda *became John Cleese's greatest post-Python film success.*

screened it for audiences and did a brief bit of reshooting. He says the original ending merely involved Archie and Wanda flying off on the jet, and didn't end the movie with the desired laugh.

"We changed the ending so that Otto survived and gave us a good joke by coming to the airplane window. We went out on Otto falling off the plane, which was much better than the original ending, which lacked a good laugh," he reveals.

"And then we made Jamie's character a little more sympathetic—I hadn't written it right, and it was a little cold at the end of the movie. We put in a different scene in the car, when I jump into the car with her outside the court, in which there's that little row, and suddenly the ice is broken.

"We put in a little bit of protest, which we shot inside the car, when Kevin jumps into the car to drive off with Jamie, after I've gone into the flat to see Ken. There's four seconds of argument—'Wait, wait, Otto!' 'Come on, baby, let's go!' That made a big difference. We also put in a shot of Jamie calling me from the airport, going 'Come on, Archie, pick up the phone' to indicate that, having got rid of Otto, she immediately tried to get back in touch with Archie.

"And at the end of the naked scene, Jamie had originally come down the stairs and said 'Oh, bad luck, Archie, third time lucky,' and left. She was dumping him too much, she was too unsympathetic, so we just cut that. It made a huge difference! And I think that was it, I don't think we shot anything else. There was about seventy-five seconds, but it changed it radically by warming up Jamie's character."

Cleese says the hardest filming for director Crichton involved the dog-killing scenes and the steamroller sequence, although he nearly had a problem breaking up on one take.

"I think it's when she says to me 'I want you,' and I say 'What?' [during the scene in Archie's office]—I said it so perfectly on that take that I just begin to break up. We shaved it as fine as possible. I can still see me just beginning to go—nobody else sees me—then we cut to a wider shot when we go to the phone," he says.

He also had to work with special effects supervisor George Gibbs in order to be hung out the window upside-down by Otto, he explains.

"I had a wire up each trouser leg, attached to a harness which I had on underneath my body, a full body harness made of canvas, which took the hooks and wires. But I was never dangled backwards and downwards outside the window, because they had a trolley thing on rails on the window underneath. So, I lay on that, facing outwards. They pushed that out horizontally so it stuck out, and then they fed the wires down from the window above.

"When they wanted to get me up, they just lifted me, very gently, so eventually my shoulders and head were just hanging on the trolley. Then they'd lift me up, move the trolley back in, and I'd be hanging there. When they wanted to get me back down again, they brought the trolley out, lowered me down from the window above onto the trolley, and I could get lying straight out again and take a break before I went up," he explains.

Cleese says compared to his Monty Python filming, he found *Wanda* much more interesting.

"There was a greater feeling of teamwork, in a funny kind of way. It was particularly more exciting at the rehearsal stage. With Python, once we'd done the writing, the real work was done—rehearsing was just completing the process. I felt with *Wanda,* we were contributing more with the acting," he relates.

"Also, of course, it was a much more interesting thing for me to play than another Python sketch character, because I was going into areas I'd never gone into before. I also learned far more from working with Kevin and Jamie, American styles of acting, than I would have learned working with these guys I've worked with for so long. Which isn't to say it isn't a pleasure to work with Michael, but as a learning experience, it's more intriguing to work with people from different backgrounds."

His fellow Python agrees that *Wanda* was a learning experience for them both.

"It was the first major film that John had really written on his own, post-Graham. In a sense, for both of us, it was a post-Python experience," notes Michael Palin. "He'd been very interested in having a character who stammered—this was ages ago, since 1985. He'd asked me about that character, knowing that my father had had a stammer, or a stutter, as they say in America. We discussed how the character would speak, and that's how it led to me doing the part, and he always had the part of Ken Pile there ready for me.

"John is very generous once he's decided he wants to use somebody, he's very generous with the time he spends with you, the chance he'll give you to rewrite the script if you want to. He also wanted to work with Jamie very much. Who wouldn't? And Kevin, he'd become friends with in the States, and that was our little team. John very single-mindedly and rather efficiently got it together."

Palin's character became the target of controversy after the movie was released, and some stutterers' groups claimed to take offense at the character of Ken. Despite protests from the filmmakers, ABC-TV edited out portions of Kevin Kline's insults that were directed at Ken when it

John Cleese, early 1990s. Photo copyright KHJ.

was broadcast in 1991. Despite such small-minded attacks, the film became phenomenally popular. Palin says the huge success of *Wanda* surprised them all, just as the success of Monty Python surprised the group many years before.

"I never had any idea it was going to be big. You really just don't know. We regarded Python as something that essentially worked amongst the group of us. We had *no idea* how it would work beyond that, just *no idea* how people would react to the silly things we were doing. Python's success

came very slowly, really, in fact, as each year goes by, more people begin to regard it as a more of a sort of distinguished show. So, we were brought up on surprises," explains Palin.

"*Wanda* felt good when we were doing it, but again, you never know who your audience is going to be. I think the degree of its success took all of us completely by surprise—in fact, it was a global, international success in every country except for Japan, massively popular."

Still, for John Cleese, the realization of *Wanda's* success came very gradually.

"It was a process of, first of all, showing it in New York and realizing that it was gonna be okay if I fixed certain things. And then, in L.A., having wonderfully expert criticism from Rob Reiner and Steve Martin and Harold Ramis, among others. Then coming back and reshooting the ending, and suddenly realizing that it was working, and doing all that publicity in the States for six weeks.

"And I remember, the crucial moment was getting the two thumbs up [from Siskel and Ebert]—that was when I *really* felt 'Now we've made it.' It was like we'd moved it up into a different league, when we got that," reveals Cleese. "My only criticism is that it's not about anything important.

"It went on for week after week, with good figures coming in. It isn't the money, it's an indication of how much people like it—it's measured by the number of people coming in, and that's measured by box office. Then there were great thrills, and I was very, very pleased when we ran it in Edinburgh to see that the Scottish audience loved it, and the biggest thrill of all in some ways was watching it at the Venice Film Festival, and seeing an Italian audience laughing in exactly the same places as the British and American audiences. So, that was an exciting moment, very rewarding!"

The origins of *Fierce Creatures* were actually in a pre-Python sketch written by Terry Jones and Michael Palin.

"Terry and Michael wrote a half-hour sitcom script a long time ago in which the main idea was a guy who ran the zoo who thought that no one was interested in any animals that weren't fierce," says Cleese. "It always struck me as being a very funny idea. I never saw their script. I think I asked Terry to send it to me, but I never read it, because I didn't want to be influenced. But I asked him some years ago at lunch if he would have any objection to me

pinching the idea, and he said 'No,' that was fine. I did a completely free day on *Wind in the Willows* for Terry. I knew Michael wouldn't mind, because obviously, he was getting another good part out of it!"

Fierce Creatures experienced extensive reshoots shortly before its release and there were rumors about problems with the film, but test screenings just before the release were very encouraging, as were many of the reviews, making the disappointing box office showing harder to explain.

Palin's role in *Fierce Creatures* was actually wrapped around his schedule for *Full Circle,* he notes. "I remember a lot of waiting around and some wonderfully funny scenes involving lions and tigers and leopards, enormous predators which I have not seen in comedy sketches since Python—we had a tiger in one of the Python sketches, which Graham's character had been giving drugs to, and it was completely inert in a kitchen set! But these were real animals prowling around, hadn't been fed for two days so they'd stand up in the back of the scene. That was really quite remarkable to do. It was great to see John in form again, doing some wonderful, wonderful comedy. There were some amazing scenes involving me in tiger skins that were removed from the movie, I think quite rightly, because the ending was not working.

"I was relieved at seeing the two sections of the film separated by a year, stitched together and felt that they worked really well, and generally feeling that people were happy with the movie— some good reviews, some not so good reviews— but there were generally good reviews, as good as the ones we had for *Wanda,*" says Palin. "I was somewhat bewildered at the lack of success of the film in the States, which just doesn't quite equate with the enthusiasm we were getting from press and interviewers when we were doing our press, the enthusiasm of the reviews and all that. But it didn't perform as we hoped it would, and one wonders why."

"I'm puzzled by the reaction to *Fierce Creatures,* because we kept getting very good indicators," says Cleese. "We were honestly amazed by the enthusiasm of all the people interviewing us during the press junket. Jamie, who didn't feel optimistic about the movie, came up to me at the end of the first day's publicity and said 'They love it, John,

1997's **Fierce Creatures** *reteamed John Cleese and Michael Palin, along with Jamie Lee Curtis and Kevin Kline. Universal Pictures, from the collection of John Cleese.*

we're going to have a hit!' We got a marvelous review in *Variety,* and very good reviews from the radio and TV stations. In the same day, I read great reviews from Janet Maslin, Michael Medved, and Gene Siskel, whom I've always liked. There were a couple of perfectly friendly ones in *Time* and *Los Angeles Times* and *People* magazine, which said something like 'In every way an equal.' But I heard that it wasn't tracking well—they were polling people to find out their awareness of the film, and they just don't know it was on. I found this very puzzling, because I thought Universal did a very good job on the advertisements, but when the movie came out, people just didn't go. They did go in more sophisticated cities. For example, it was number one in San Francisco opening weekend, but when we got down to places like Denver and Cleveland and Detroit and Miami, I don't think they even knew we were on. Also, we got quite a few negative reviews in those cities.

"*Wanda* was killed by the *New York Times* and Gene Shalit hated it, but then the good reviews started to come in. With *Fierce Creatures,* it was quite the other way around—we started out with rather good reviews and kept hearing of rather negative ones. It's confusing if you're in the center. If you read Gene Siskel and his very complimen-

tary review, and then you read a very negative review, you think 'What's the reality?' Well, the reality is, it didn't do well at the box office. The second week, we were killed by *Star Wars,* and then *Dante's Peak* came in, so we were crushed by the juggernauts!"

"It's a funny movie," says Palin. "There's plenty of funny material in there. I think what distinguishes a movie nowadays, especially with big releases, is a 'must-see' quality, otherwise you're trampled underfoot by big advertising campaigns. From all I can tell, it had an average first weekend in the States and everyone was fairly happy, and then along comes *Star Wars* rereleased and tramples over all opposition, and suddenly everyone's talking about all of that, and those films that haven't performed as well just get forgotten. Maybe that's what's happened. *Wanda* became very big and became the movie everybody was talking about. *Fierce Creatures* is *one* of the films people were talking about, not *the* one. Seeing how everyone flocked to *Star Wars,* maybe we should have rereleased *Holy Grail* with an extra eight minutes and put it on 5,000 screens, and maybe we'd have been all right!" Palin laughs.

John Cleese as the lawyer in **Mr. Toad's Wild Ride.** *From the collection of Terry Jones, used by permission.*

"I think it was a good idea to get together and do a different story with different characters, and it left *Wanda* sort of untouched," says Palin. "So oddly enough, it may have done more to increase *Wanda*'s legend than its own performance. It's certainly done nothing to decrease *Wanda.*"

In addition to working with Michael Palin in *Wanda* and *Fierce Creatures,* Cleese joined with other individual Pythons over the years for several projects, including smaller roles in Terry Gilliam's *Time Bandits,* Eric Idle's *Splitting Heirs,* Graham Chapman's *Yellowbeard,* and Terry Jones's *Erik the Viking* and *Wind in the Willows.*

Following *Fierce Creatures,* Cleese had been set to star, along with Robin Williams, in a new production of *Don Quixote,* but the project fell through when the script could not be perfected.

Cleese appeared in *Wind in the Willows* as a favor to Terry Jones for giving him one of the ideas for *Fierce Creatures.*

"I don't think he or I ever knew what was appropriate as a way of letting me borrow or steal the idea about the fierce creatures at the zoo. We informally arranged that I do a completely free day on *Wind in the Willows,* my acting rate being quite sizable these days, that was felt to be a reasonable recompense for borrowing a decent idea," says Cleese. "I read the script and it was a very good little part. I very much enjoyed my day, although I was a bit flu-ey, and it was a little bit of a struggle to get through it. But as you get older, you know how to marshal your energy at crucial moments, and I was very pleased when I saw the scene—it seemed to get shown a lot on television."

He doesn't have current plans to write an autobiography, and is less than thrilled with *Cleese Encounters,* an unauthorized volume by Jonathan Margolis.

"I'd told this guy that if I was ever going to do a book of this kind, I would do it with George Perry," says Cleese. "That had usually been enough to persuade people to back off. But Margolis went ahead. I had already circulated to something like fifty friends with a letter that someone else whom I had been very much warned against was sniffing around. Basically Margolis did a little digging into my family history and came up with one interesting fact about my father's family. Otherwise, it was simply a press cutting job. When I received the book, I had a very uneasy feeling about it.

When I opened it at random and read a page, there were nine errors on the page. I then opened another page at random, and there were seven errors on that. I then opened a third page and there were three errors, but one was quite a major one. So after those three pages, I never bothered to open it again. It wasn't an unpleasant book and he didn't include anything malicious, it was just a chance to make a little money out of me. It is riddled with mistakes."

Cleese feels the Python TV shows remain funnier than most TV comedies, despite some tabloid reports to the contrary, though he does believe many of them have some slow sketches.

"When I watch the television shows now, most of them seem to me to be very uneven," says Cleese. "The really good thing about them is that they always have at least three sketches which are quite outstandingly funny, much funnier than most of the stuff that you see on television. They usually contain a certain amount of stuff that's fine, but all of them that I've watched in recent years also seem to contain stuff that really doesn't seem to be very good at all and seems a bit pointless. I find myself looking at 20 percent of the material and thinking, 'What on Earth was this supposed to achieve? Why did we ever put it in the show?' Maybe in 1969, one of those sketches was much funnier because nobody had ever done a sketch like that before and it had the virtue of being completely original, even if it wasn't that funny. But, you just can't remember, so you shrug your shoulders and say, 'I certainly wouldn't put it in a show these days!'

"Similarly, I always felt that our films were uneven. I always felt *Life of Brian* was the best, and I was just a *little* bit disappointed when I watched it in mid-'95. We had a charity showing of it in California to raise some money for a theater in Santa Barbara. I hadn't seen it for a long time, and I had the same reaction. I thought some of it was absolutely *wonderful*. I thought some of it was breathtakingly original, brightly colored and very, *very* funny. But other bits of it, I thought we just didn't do very well. The way in which Graham falls from his hiding place and lands on a ledge where a number of people are delivering religious messages so that he is forced to join in is badly done. You just don't buy it. I'd always thought of *Life of Brian* as very much our best film, so I was disappointed to find that bits of it—not large bits, but noticeable bits—weren't as good as I'd hoped they were going to be. Our weakness was always in telling stories well. We just didn't have much experience in it. I'd always hoped that *Life of Brian* had rather overcome our weaknesses in that department, but I realized there were moments where our weakness in storytelling showed through. At the same time, there are some bits that are just as good as anything I've ever seen!"

Cleese has taken a much more relaxed attitude about future projects.

"I've reached the stage of my life when I'm happy to let things unfold without having a clear sense of where they're going to take me," says Cleese. "My present feeling is that I enjoy small quantities of acting, but not large quantities of acting. If somebody says to me, 'Come to somewhere interesting and do three or four weeks on a movie, but you'll only be shooting three days a week,' and I like the sound of these people and the look of the script, then I'd be interested. If somebody says to me, 'Come and do fourteen weeks in a studio in Burbank, it's a very funny middle-of-the-road comedy,' I would think, 'Do I really need this money?' I don't particularly love Los Angeles. How exciting are the people involved? Is it Steve Martin? In which case, probably yes. Is it someone who is perfectly nice and a fairly funny person, but someone that does not cause the adrenaline to run? In which case, probably no. So, I'm looking at movies as life experiences, rather than as the next piece of work that I do."

In the wake of *Fierce Creatures,* Cleese says he is undecided about writing another film.

"Whether I'd want to do another movie of my own, I don't know," he explains. "The great problem with *Fierce Creatures,* as with the second series of *Fawlty Towers,* was how do you match the almost unreal expectations created by the first work? And doing that is pretty exhausting, because no matter how good it is, people will always say 'It's very funny, but it's not quite as good.' In which case, if they're going to say 'It's not quite as good,' then why are you doing it? The only reason to do it now would be because the subject matter was of overwhelmingly powerful interest. I don't think that I would be prepared to put another two years of my life into a movie if it was just a good, funny, middle-of-the-road comedy. I think it would have

John Cleese, 1997. Photographed by Terry O'Neal for John Cleese, used by permission.

to be about something I cared about more than that."

Approaching sixty, Cleese says he is much more selective in his use of time.

"At my age, you're very aware of the limited amount of time you have left, particularly the amount of professional time you have left, and the question is 'Is what I could be doing more interesting than anything else I could be doing?'" says Cleese. "There is so much that I want to do in terms of reading, getting to know some people better, traveling, understanding some cultures, generally finding out more about different aspects of the world—aspects I've always been fascinated by, but never been able to pursue with a sufficient degree of focus because work intervenes. When I'm working on something, I have a perfectionist streak, because I can't stand the thought that people are going to say 'Well, that was rotten, wasn't it?' So I tend to be occupied with almost anything that I'm doing until I've done it to my satisfaction. And during work on a project therefore, I find it difficult to give my full attention to anything else.

"There are a number of areas that I want to explore and understand much better to allow my more academic side to emerge and also my more contemplative side. These are quite strong forces within me that always tended to get squeezed out in the past because I didn't really feel I was entitled to do that. Plus, there was always this necessity to make sure that the income was sufficient to match the expenditure.

"I'm not sure how much I will want to become a writer, which has always mattered to me more than acting, or the extent to which I simply want to explore the world. I may do a certain amount of exploration and then find I need to turn that into a script or even a film, but I don't know. I'm very happy for it to be decided more spontaneously than by any plan hatched in the intellectual part of my mind. Studying something simply because it gives me a greater understanding of what's going on in the world around me might be sufficient or I might find I have to make that information into a book, play, or film. But I don't know how I will react, and I can't even guess."

When future generations look back on him, Cleese knows how he wants to be remembered.

"I'd like to be remembered as the first man to live two and a half thousand years without losing his looks."

Fawlty Towers

By far, Cleese's most successful non-Python TV project has been his portrayal of Basil Fawlty in *Fawlty Towers*. Written with and costarring Connie Booth, Cleese says the series actually came about because the two of them, married at the time, had wanted to work together when Cleese left Python. After the couple had written a sketch for one of the German Python shows, and scripted and performed a short film, *Romance With a Double Bass*, they briefly considered doing some man-woman sketches. But when the BBC approached Cleese about doing something else, it took them only one hour to hit on the idea of a hotel.

"It was based on a hotel I'd stayed at back when I was filming Python—the manager was just

wonderfully rude," Cleese recalls. "He was like Basil, but much smaller, a skinny little guy about five-foot four-inches, with a large wife who dominated him. We reversed the sizes.

"I had written some *Doctor in the House* TV shows, and had set one of the episodes at a hotel that had been based on this one. An old friend of mine said to me, 'There's a series in that hotel.' I thought 'Bloody television producer, can't see a program without thinking about a series.' The extraordinary thing was, he was absolutely right. When Connie and I sat down three years later, it was the second or third idea that came into our minds."

There are several advantages to setting a series in a hotel, according to Cleese. "We could have almost anyone we wanted walk in, without trying to find an explanation. Plus, we had our basic regulars. It's a situation which almost everyone understands. Everyone knows what it's like to walk up to a front desk, what it's like if someone's casual, rude, or inattentive. We didn't have to explain or set anything up. It's all very straightforward and conventional, so we could start right away with the jokes."

Michael Palin, who has kept a journal for many years, confirmed Cleese's account of that legendary hotel in Torquay with his notes:

Tuesday, 12th of May. Our hotel, the Gleneagles, was a little out of Torquay, overlooking a beautiful little cove, plenty of trees around. Eric and John were already there, sitting beside the pool. Decor was clean, rooms nice. However, Mr. Sinclair, the proprietor, seemed to view us from the start as a colossal inconvenience. When we arrived back at 12:30 a.m., having watched the night's filming, he just stood and looked at us with the same look of self-righteous resentment and tacit accusation that I've not seen since my father waited up for me fifteen years ago. Graham tentatively asked for a brandy; the idea was dismissed out-of-hand. And that night, our first in Torquay, we decided to move out of the Gleneagles.

Back at Gleneagles, avoided breakfast. Graham, Terry and I have been fixed for one night at the Osborne, from then on at the Imperial. Asked Mr. Sinclair for the bill. He didn't seem unduly ruffled, but Mrs. Sinclair made our stay even more memorable by threatening us with a bill for two weeks, even though we hadn't stayed. But off we went, with lighter hearts . . .

In **Meetings, Bloody Meetings,** *Cleese plays a manager who has nightmares over his ineptitude in conducting meetings. Photo copyright Video Arts.*

The acclaim that the shows received surprised Cleese; especially gratifying was their success around the world. "Connie and I did something we thought would get a smallish but friendly audience on BBC 2, and we finished out with about three times the audience we had originally guessed," says Cleese. "We thought it was almost a private little joke, and I'm still astounded to find that it plays in Hong Kong in Cantonese! I don't understand it—Basil must be some kind of archetype."

Strangely enough, there were two separate attempts to adapt *Fawlty Towers* to American television. The first was a pilot titled *Snavely* starring Harvey Korman, while the second, titled *Amanda's* (which actually ran briefly on ABC), starred Bea

A typical pose for Basil and Manuel: John Cleese and Andrew Sachs in **Fawlty Towers.** *Photo copyright BBC.*

Arthur. Both attempts were quickly, and rightfully, forgotten. "I asked the American company how the adaptation was looking, and they told me 'It's looking good. We've only made one change.' They wrote out Basil Fawlty! Incomprehensible." In 1998, CBS-TV announced plans to develop a third American version of *Fawlty Towers,* to star John Larroquette.

"Balance Sheet Barrier," which co-stars Ronnie Corbett, sees Cleese as a "sophisticated" manager who is taught the basics of business finance by a crude, but knowledgeable, small businessman (Corbett). Photo copyright Video Arts.

 **Fawlty Towers Index**

The first series was aired in Britain beginning September 19, 1975, while the second series began February 19, 1979. Both season featured the same cast of regulars:

Basil Fawlty . . . . John Cleese
Sybil Fawlty . . . . Prunella Scales
Manuel . . . . Andrew Sachs
Polly . . . . Connie Booth
Major Gowen. . . . . Ballard Berkeley
Miss Tibbs . . . . Gilly Flower
Miss Gatsby . . . . Renee Roberts

First Series

Show 1: "A Touch of Class" Basil tries to attract a higher class of clientele to Fawlty Towers by advertising in upper-class publications. Thus, when a "Lord Malbury" checks in, Basil gives him royal treatment.

Show 2: "The Builders" The Fawltys go away for the weekend, leaving Manuel and Polly in charge. Against Sybil's strict orders, Basil hires a cheap builder to do repairs at the hotel while they are gone.

Show 3: "The Wedding Party" Sybil rents a room to an unmarried couple. Basil is outraged, and tries to have them thrown out.

Show 4: "The Hotel Inspectors" Basil hears that three hotel inspectors are in the area, and rolls out the red carpet to a likely looking trio.

Show 5: "Gourmet Night" Basil attempts to host a gourmet night at the hotel, which goes awry when his chef gets drunk and Basil must take charge.

Show 6: "The Germans" While Sybil is in the hospital, Basil attempts to hang a moose head, run a fire drill, and host some German guests.

Second Series

Show 7: "Communication Problems/Mrs. Richards" A troublesome elderly guest accuses the staff of stealing her money.

Show 8: "The Psychiatrist" While trying to prove a young bachelor has smuggled a girl into his room, Basil finds himself in a variety of compromising positions.

Show 9: "Waldorf Salad/The Americans" Basil must contend with an overbearing, obnoxious American guest who challenges his limited abilities as a host.

Show 10: "The Kipper and the Corpse/Death" After a guest dies overnight, Basil and the staff try to remove the body without being detected by the other guests and a health inspector.

Show 11: "The Anniversary" When Sybil walks out after an argument with Basil just before an anniversary party, he recruits Polly to impersonate his wife.

Show 12: "Basil the Rat" Manuel's pet rat, named "Basil," escapes while a health inspector is expected, and the real Basil deals with a poisoning scare.

Books and Records

Two books of scripts were released; *Fawlty Towers* in 1977, and *Fawlty Towers 2* two years later. Both trade paperbacks are fully illustrated with stills from the TV shows, and contain all the text of the first series of shows.

Finally, *The Complete Fawlty Towers* was released in 1988, containing the scripts from all twelve shows, but with a limited number of photos in the volume.

Three soundtrack albums were released by BBC Records: 1979's *Fawlty Towers* contains "The Hotel Inspectors" and "Mrs. Richards." *Second Sitting,* released in 1981, includes "The Builders" and "The Rat." Finally, *At Your Service,* recorded in 1982, features "Death" and "The Germans."

Terry Gilliam

Terry Vance Gilliam was born in Minneapolis, Minnesota, on November 22, 1940. Before moving to Los Angeles eleven years later, he was influenced by the cartoons and films that would play such a big part in his later life.

"I loved Disney cartoons and animated films, I really loved them all," he says. "*Thief of Bagdad* had an incredible effect on me—I think it was just the scale of the genie, things like that—playing with scale, and not in cartoon form, with live action. That's something that's always stuck with me. I always used to really like musicals. My interest in films is really eclectic, because most of it was just watching fairly popular films and enjoying them. I liked Jerry Lewis films—I was pretty nondiscrimi-natory. It was only when I got to be about sixteen or seventeen that I began to realize that there was more to films than entertainment. The first one that really struck me that way was Stanley Kubrick's *Paths of Glory.* I saw it at a Saturday afternoon matinee for kids, and I thought 'Jesus! You can make films like that?!' It actually said something about life and justice. It was also the first time, I think, where I was aware of camera moves, because of these incredible tracking shots in the trenches. I thought, 'Wow!' I'd never recognized anything like that before. It kicked me into another plane of film appreciation."

Growing up in the late '40s and '50s, Gilliam also admits to a soft spot for the science fiction

A twelve-year-old Gilliam has nothing up his sleeves on Christmas Day, 1952. Photo copyright Terry Gilliam.

films that flourished during that era. "All of the sci-fi movies—*War of the Worlds, Them!*—I loved 'em all!" Gilliam explains. "I suppose that's the fantasy side of it—kids escaping into a more extraordinary world than the one they were living in. I think it's quite clear that my life has been about that. Even going to Europe was getting away from what seemed to me to be the ordinary, uninteresting world of the San Fernando Valley. And I've always been doing that. The idea of castles on hills that people really lived in five hundred years ago still gets me excited."

Gilliam always cites the influence of Harvey Kurtzman's *Mad* comic book-turned-magazine, but points out other comic influences when he was young.

"I was always a comic book fan. I loved *Mad* and *Tales from the Crypt* when they started up," he says. "There were *Donald Duck* comics, and there was *Classics Illustrated,* which I really liked. There you could get Daniel Defoe, Victor Hugo, James Fenimore Cooper, all in comic book form."

Although films, TV and comics played a part in influencing Gilliam, he says his greatest influence of all may have been radio.

"Radio was alive and well in the late '40s and early '50s," he says. "The great thing about radio is that there are no images, so we have to invent them. It's an incredibly good exercise at imagining images! All you get is the voice—you have to dress these people and put them in the room. The demise of radio actually weakened people's imaginative

skills. And I read a lot. Again, it was books—*without pictures*—words, and I had to make the leap. I think that really strengthened my visual imagination, so that when I did start seeing movies and comic books, it was like 'Oh! There's the world, and the things I imagined!' Then I could leapfrog from that, and go even further. It was like all of the muscles in my brain had been exercising at a very early age, imagining things."

The Python star ironically says television may be stilting the imaginations of the current generation. "The problem is, television does all of the work for you, so you don't have to bring anything to it. You just sit there, and it does everything. It shows you the pictures and gives you the answers, it does the laughing for you. And I think that's the problem. It doesn't engage you in a really healthy, exercising way."

He notes that only one TV performer had a major influence on his style.

"We lived in Minnesota, and I remember having to go to a neighbor's house to watch television," he says. "The one thing that jumped out of the television at me, the one thing I remember most strongly, was the Ernie Kovacs show. Nobody was doing anything like this surrealist humor on television. I also remember the Milton Berle show, but Ernie Kovacs was the one. Here was a guy who had, in effect, brought European surrealist humor to American television. Nobody was even playing in that world in the mass media then—that was a big leap for me."

In 1958 he enrolled in Occidental College, where he edited *Fang,* the school humor magazine. After graduating in 1962, he headed for New York City in hopes of meeting his other hero Kurtzman. As luck would have it, associate editor Charles Alverson had just resigned from Kurtzman's *Help!* magazine at that time, and Gilliam found himself employed (his most notable work for the magazine turned out to be a fumetti strip which featured a man who fell in love with his daughter's Barbie doll).

"I went rushing off to New York to go off on my big life adventure, just like in fairy tales, I ended up as the apprentice to the master!" he says. "At first it was exhilarating, I couldn't believe it. I didn't say 'Wow!' but in retrospect, I can't believe I was lucky enough to get into that.

"There was Harvey, surrounded by Will Elder,

Arnold Roth, Jack Davis, all of these cartoonists. Just working around these people was exciting, because I learned bits and pieces when I saw them at work. Harvey worked nonstop, he seemed to have an endless amount of energy. He set his standards very high, and I think that was important. That's what he taught me more than anything. If you're doing parodies and comedies, the more realistic or truthful or elaborate you are in your depiction of the world you're parodying, the funnier and more effective it is. That really carries over. When you look at *Holy Grail* or *Jabberwocky,* when we were taking the piss out of a certain time and place, we were doing it as beautifully and seriously as Visconti would in doing *The Leopard.* Our approach in creating those worlds was just as serious, and we tried to do it right, but for a comic effect, as opposed to serious effects."

After *Help!* folded in 1965, Gilliam traveled around Europe, and returned to Los Angeles the next year where he illustrated children's books, failed as a freelancer, and went to work as a copywriter and art director for an advertising agency. He soon discovered that this attempt at a respectable job was boring, and moved to London in 1967, where he found work doing freelance illustration for *The Sunday Times Magazine* and other publications. During this time, he also drew for some American comic magazines like *Car-Toons* and *Surf-Toons* as a freelancer. He became artistic director of *The Londoner* magazine, which also went under not long after he joined it.

Finding himself jobless once again, he turned to John Cleese, who introduced him to producer Humphrey Barclay. He sold two sketches to *Do Not Adjust Your Set,* and was befriended by Eric Idle, becoming the resident cartoonist for *We Have Ways of Making You Laugh,* which occurred between the two series of *Do Not Adjust Your Set.* It was for this show that Gilliam did his very first piece of animation, to help them deal with a tricky spot. Although given only two weeks and four hundred pounds, he impressed them enough to be asked to do more, and ended up doing three animated films for the second series of *Do Not Adjust Your Set.* He became more friendly with Michael Palin and Terry Jones, and the following year was asked to join a new project called *Monty Python's Flying Circus.*

Gilliam's cutout animation for Python integrated itself perfectly with the live-action comedy produced by the other five members of the group, and Gilliam confirms that many of their attitudes were remarkably similar to his own.

"When I first met the others, I was surprised that, having come from a place 6,000 miles away, I seemed to see the world in the same way they did, with the same kind of irony and intelligence and silliness and madness. And that, to me, was the magical moment," says Gilliam. "I realized that we had completely different backgrounds, completely different education systems, and yet we seemed to look at the world in the same way. They were able to portray it with dialogue and performance, while I dealt with it in my cartoons."

Working chiefly as the animator, he would seldom appear onscreen, although as the series progressed, he began performing more often. But it was in his new-found career as an animator that he made his mark on Python, influencing the feel, shape, and flow of the shows, giving Python a look unlike any other program.

Even while working on Python, he pursued outside projects as an animator. In 1970, he created the title sequence for the film *Cry of the Banshee,* and the following year animated twenty-five minutes worth of material for ABC's *The Marty Feldman Comedy Machine.* He shot his first commercial in 1972, part of a campaign for the British Gas Board, and also designed the title sequence for *William,* a CBS special on Shakespeare.

When *Monty Python and the Holy Grail* was conceived in 1974, the group wanted to maintain as much control over their material as possible, so Gilliam and Terry Jones codirected the film, whetting Gilliam's appetite for the big screen. He has, of course, maintained his Python relationship—although Terry Jones directed *Life of Brian* and *Meaning of Life* on his own, Gilliam designed *Brian,* conceived and directed "The Crimson Permanent Assurance" sequence for *Meaning of Life,* and acted in both.

Gilliam gives Monty Python all of the credit for his current career as a director.

"I owe everything to Python because it put me in the right thing," says Gilliam. "To be able to direct films, to be put in the position in Python where one could direct a film without having done it before—it doesn't happen to many people! That's why it's so unbelievably lucky. I wanted to

be a film director, but didn't want to work myself up from tea-boy. So, I went down this path that eventually got me where I wanted to go. I'm no good at working my way up through organizations and systems. So coming out of college and cartooning, I was doing what I *could* do, and having control over what I was doing. Falling into the animation just before Python was, again, one of those things I didn't set out to do, I was just at the right place when they needed something, and I had a certain skill, so I became an animator overnight. Everything I did, I did overnight. I don't work my way up! Then to be in the position to direct *Holy Grail* was great! Once your name's up there on the screen saying 'Film directed by———', people believe that, and they hire you and give you money!"

Terry Gilliam has said that the filming of *Holy Grail* often pitted the two directing Terrys against the other four, but he admits that there were intradirectoral squabbles between Jones and himself, too.

"Even though we saw the film the same way, I think our work habits were different," he explains. "Early on, it was quite clear that there were two different voices speaking. The way we resolved it was that I retreated back to the camera and concentrated on what the camera was doing and the look of the thing. Terry concentrated on telling the others what to do. That kind of worked, and there

Dennis (Michael Palin) woos Griselda in this tender scene from **Jabberwocky**, *Terry Gilliam's first non-Python directing effort.* **Handmade Films/Jabberwocky.**

was a lot of times even within that when there were a lot of disagreements.

"Basically, we got through it fairly easily. Terry seemed to get on with the others better than I, because there were certain sketches which, say, John and Graham had written, that demanded a certain thing. If you want cows and animals thrown over a battlement, you've got to do a special-effects shot. You need a matte shot, and the only way we could do it with the money and skills we had then was to make sure their heads were below the line of the parapet of the castle. To do that, it meant that they had to kneel down, and they didn't like that, and they couldn't understand why they had to be kneeling down!" he laughs. "I said, 'To make this work!' and I wasn't particularly good or patient at explaining why it was necessary. 'You fucking wrote this script, I'm just trying to put it on film for you!' Moments like that tried everybody's patience."

Following *Holy Grail*, Gilliam was approached by producer Sandy Lieberson to direct a World War II documentary feature called *All This and World War II*, with a soundtrack made up entirely of Beatle songs. Gilliam had been keen to do a short film for the BBC based on Lewis Carroll's *Jabberwocky*, however, and turned him down. Lieberson then asked Gilliam to do *Jabberwocky* as a feature for him.

In 1977, Gilliam's *Jabberwocky* was released,

Terry Gilliam, mid-'70s. Photographed by John Sims for Python Productions, used by permission.

starring Michael Palin, with brief appearances by Terry Jones, Gilliam, and Neil Innes. The script was cowritten by Charles Alverson and Gilliam. The dark medieval comedy/fantasy followed young Dennis (Palin), a cooper's son who goes to the city to make his fortune and ends up confronting the feared Jabberwocky. Unfortunately, the film was promoted in some areas as "Monty Python's Jabberwocky" and even "Jabberwocky and the Holy Grail," which, understandably, made Gilliam furious. It would not be his last battle with the film establishment.

"Python was still the dominant force in my life then, and things like *Jabberwocky* were really attempts to do what I didn't think we'd achieved in *Monty Python and the Holy Grail.* I thought we'd lost out on a lot of atmosphere and detail, and that's what I definitely tried to get in there," he says. "But to me, it's a film that's still tied in with a Monty Python comic approach to things. Even though the visuals are really beautiful and I spent a lot more time on creating the world, I'm still doing cheap, silly Python jokes. Yet at the same time, I was trying to tell a story and be more narrative than Python was, trying to deal with adventure and suspense in a more movielike way.

"I think it's a real transitional film, that one. It was also a chance to work with actors, and discover that, in a strange way, I could. When we were doing *Holy Grail,* it was very difficult working with the others, because I had just come out of my garret, where I had been working on my own for all those years, and not having to communicate properly. Suddenly I was on a set, trying to tell people what to do. I was not as good at it as I should have been, and I got really pissed off at myself *and* them, so when I started doing *Jabberwocky,* it was really amazing to see how actors, no matter how old and experienced and wonderful they are, would sit and listen to the director—which was *me,* because I had the director's chair, and they would do what I wanted them to do without bitching and moaning like the Pythons were!"

As Michael Palin recalls, *Jabberwocky* was "six weeks of shit and toothblacking."

Jabberwocky was the first solo feature film created by any of the Pythons. Terry Gilliam had wanted to make a live-action feature based on the Lewis Carroll poem; he planned to direct it himself, and enlisted Charles Alverson to cowrite it with him.

The two of them had worked together, but never written until they reconnected at a party at Terry Jones's house in the summer of 1975. After Alverson moved to Cambridge in September of that year, Gilliam asked if he'd be interested in writing *Jabberwocky* with him. The screenplay was completed in early 1976. (Gilliam had originally planned to do the project as a short for the BBC).

The original poem had very little to do with *Jabberwocky;* it served merely as a jumping-off point for their imaginations; Alverson says Gilliam did not have the story plotted out when he suggested they collaborate.

"Terry had the beginning scene, in which Terry Jones gets killed, and he had the end scene, and he had a few points he wanted to make en route, and that's all. We started from the beginning of the story in which Terry Jones gets killed and worked it out. It was a process of saying 'Who's our hero? What's he doing? What does he want to do? Why does he do this?'

"It was worked out scene by scene, arguing and fighting about the socioeconomic premises," Alverson states. "Terry used to come up to Cambridge. I was working in my garage then. I was be-

hind the typewriter and Terry would sit in front of me reading a magazine until I got pissed off at him and made him do some writing.

"See, Terry had never been a writer. He'd written captions for his animation, but he'd never written any continuity, and so we'd say 'What about this? How about that?' And then Terry would go back to London, and I'd work by myself up in Cambridge on three or four more scenes. I'd take them down to London and we'd work on them up in his studio, and he'd rewrite me. Eventually, from just sitting there throwing ideas, he'd sit face

This cast shot includes Neil Innes (second from left in background) and Max Wall (as king on the throne), in addition to Michael Palin and the rest of the **Jabberwocky** *cast. Handmade Films/Jabberwocky.*

to face with the typewriter and we'd hand things back and forth for rewriting. Terry's a much better rewriter than a writer.

"When Terry gets an idea, once you put that idea down and give it some decent clothes, he can shift it around and make it work—that's his real strong point," Alverson said in a 1978 conversation. "The more he writes, the better he'll write. I'd never written a screenplay before either, and we both learned as we went along. I taught him what I knew about writing—which isn't much—but most of it was me laying down a basic scene and him

suggesting or improving it, or saying 'how the hell can we get over this point?' Of course, neither of us knew what we were doing. We didn't have a clue, but we learned a bit."

"I really enjoyed directing *Jabberwocky,*" Gilliam recalls with a smile. "It was awful, but I enjoyed it, because it wasn't the same sort of thing as Python. In *Jabberwocky,* the actors added a lot—they changed lines and everything—but they were still willing to let it be the thing that I started. They were helping me get it done, whereas with Python, all of our ideas are in there, and when you start doing a scene, everybody has a different way of doing it."

Gilliam says some of the negative aspects of the film were still lingering more than a decade later.

"I think the smells were the worst thing. I've still got a sweater that smells of burning tires, because that's how we created most of that smoke—it just becomes burnt rubber, which sticks to everything. It gets in your nose, your ears—inside the castle we were using Fuller's earth* all the time, and we'd come out of there with it just stuffed in every orifice! It was pretty foul, and there was oil-based smoke going all the time, so it always smelled like a church," he recalls.

"The thing I remember most, though, was that there was this other film being made at the same time at Elstree, which everybody was pooh-poohing. Everybody thought ours was a wonderful film to be on, and I really knew what I was doing, and it was going to be a big success. This other film was being made by somebody who clearly knew nothing about directing and it was just disastrous, until the film came out. The film was *Star Wars.* And the minute the film was a success, they all started wearing their *Star Wars* T-shirts, which they had refused to wear up until that moment!"

*A "cleaner" type of dirt scattered around the sets to provide a more authentic "look."

 2 8 2

Gilliam says that since they were on a budget with *Jabberwocky,* they had to recycle materials.

"We used the old *Oliver!* sets from the film musical. They were still standing, so we just adapted them," he explains. "We had very little money, and to try and do something as ambitious as a medieval film, we were stealing all the time! Anything that wasn't nailed down, our boys went out there and took it! The *Oliver!* set we redressed, and we bought some sets off a German company which had just done the *Marriage of Figaro*—they were five thousand pounds, and we converted them to interiors.

"At the time, Blake Edwards was making one of the *Pink Panther* films, and he had just built a castle out at the back lot of the studio at Shepperton. Amongst other things, he had a wonderful sewer set which I saw, and then wrote a scene for, and he also had a catapult, which we needed for our film.

"Rather than let us have any of these things, or even let us pay for and redress them, he smashed them all up. That was just mean-spiritedness. People were so obsessed by the fact that they thought our film would get out first, and we would have used their things—they didn't realize that there was no intention of that. The whole point was to disguise anything else we got, but he literally burned his catapult and smashed his sewer set. We still managed to scrape through."

Because of the demolition, however, the sewer scene was never shot for the film.

"The scene wasn't in the original script, it was only when I saw this great thing—it was going to be a great way of getting into the castle, it was going to be up through the toilet system, so that Dennis came in completely covered with shit. I think in the end, we probably did the best thing, which is our peeing dawn chorus—the guys on the battlements taking their morning piss on him. Scatology was the order of the day. Anything that was shitty or dirty or anal, we went for!" he laughs.

Despite the lack of the sewer scene, Gilliam says he didn't have to edit any scenes out of the final print.

"I think everything got in there. There was really no fat. The scene that I'm in, playing the guy with the rock, Dudley Moore was originally supposed to do that part, but he went on to bigger things, and I had to stand in for him."

Ever aware of his directorial responsibilities, Gilliam made sure he didn't ask any of his unit to do anything he wouldn't do himself.

"I recall going to an abattoir to get guts from cows to use for the skin of the monster." He laughs. "We took tripe and stomach linings and lungs. I felt I had to do this myself . . ."

Jabberwocky was also Michael Palin's first lead in a feature film; he would later go on to work with his Python teammate in *Time Bandits* and *Brazil.* Although he loved working with Gilliam, he did note what he refers to as the director's natural propensity toward filth in *Jabberwocky.*

"There was dirt . . . mud . . . soil . . . dust everywhere. It was Terry's view of the Middle Ages. No one could see a thing, they all had rotting teeth, and it was all generally falling apart," Palin laughs. "Which is a nice conceit, but it obviously wasn't all like that. It made for a nice theme to the film—whatever you touched crumbled slightly. And it's brilliant—visually it's absolutely stunning—it has a freshness and power that very few other films have. I was very pleased to do it, and it was actually a very happy film, very enjoyable. But dirty. God, it was dirty!"

His first post-Python collaboration with Gilliam cemented a cinematic relationship that would continue through the years.

"I enjoy working with Terry—it's rather bracing. It's not easy, but at the same time, it's not difficult. I find the difficulty is when you find you're doing something you're not enjoying, or you're being asked to do things you may not especially like. It wasn't difficult like that—Terry knew what he was doing. It was just physically hard work, and there was quite a lot of argument and dialectic going on to get the thing done. But that was fine—it just means you worked hard," he explains.

Palin also remembers *Jabberwocky* for another reason, one that involved a scene outside the castle.

"It's the first time I exposed my bottom to the camera," reveals Palin. "Terry Jones, of course, had done that in several Python episodes, and it was my first moment, outside the castle. I presumed they were going to give me some sort of underpants, and they said 'No, no, there were no underpants in the Middle Ages—when you take your trousers down, that's it.' So I just did it in the end.

"The castle was open to the general public at

the time. They hadn't been able to get it closed, so there was a whole line of tourists. We did three takes, and they edged closer each take, so by the third take they were practically inches away from my buttocks, old ladies with their cameras clicking away. Somewhere, in yellowing photo albums in the country, are pictures of my bum!"

Alverson says one of the least convincing scenes for him, and one he wished they could have done over, was the climactic fight with the Jabberwock. The monster was actually a man inside a suit; Gilliam had him backward in the costume, so that his leg movement would appear different, walking almost like a chicken. To make the creature appear larger, the filmmaker actually shrank the knight by shooting a child in the armor for a few shots.

"I wasn't really convinced by the fight. I felt Terry went in too much for static shots, where we see the whole of the character, we see what he's doing," said Alverson. "There were three knights, three different sizes, and the kid in the final one was just running at empty air. I would have done it with a bunch of random detail shots and put it together as a composite, rather than show the whole thing—I thought it was a boring fight. I didn't believe he was in danger. I don't know how it looks to somebody who doesn't know the film, but I'd liked to have seen a better film—it should have been a lot better written, because we didn't know what played and what didn't. I think the next one, if there is a next one, will be much better."

There would indeed be a next one—and one after that, and more after that—for Terry Gilliam, even though the release of *Jabberwocky* proved to be a nightmare for the director. Fans of Gilliam are familiar with his battles with Universal over the ending to *Brazil* and the financial fights over *Baron Munchausen,* but not many remember the problems he experienced when his first movie was released.

Against his strict instructions, *Jabberwocky* was identified as a Monty Python film, even though it clearly wasn't, so when ads for *Monty Python's Jabberwocky* began appearing in newspapers across America, Gilliam hit the ceiling.

"It's a sore subject, it really drove me out of my mind," says Gilliam. "It had always been agreed all the way through the thing that it wasn't a Python film. We argued about this, because from their point of view, it was obviously the easiest way of selling this thing. And I said 'Well, whatever it is, you can't sell it this way!' The interesting thing was that in some of the early screenings, the audience understood my point. They gave out brochures to some screenings that gave people the impression that they were seeing the new Python film, and they came out very confused. I said 'If people come to this film thinking it's a Python film, they're going to be disappointed, because it isn't.'

"We actually had meetings, and they agreed 'Yes, the one thing we must not do is sell this as a Python film. It's got to be sold on its own merit.' I thought we'd finally cracked it, I thought 'That's it, fine.' And then it came out: *Monty Python's Jabberwocky*. We sent letters off and stopped it, but our lawyers buggered it up a bit and let them off the hook—I was really angry, I wanted to sue them.

"I was very confused personally on how they should sell the film, but the one thing I knew was that I didn't want it to be sold as a Python film. That was the only thing I knew, and that was the one thing they did. Somebody saw it in California as *Jabberwocky and the Holy Grail!"*

Gilliam decided to leave the direction of *Life of Brian* in 1978 to Terry Jones (and served as art director instead), partly because of his *Holy Grail* experiences, and also because he had developed a taste for solo direction with *Jabberwocky* the year before.

"I really enjoyed directing *Jabberwocky* on my own, not having to get into the same kinds of arguments that we did on Python. By the end of *Holy Grail,* I really felt having two directors wasn't the best way to work. By the editing, Terry and I were disagreeing on a lot of things, and I thought it was a frustrating way to work. Terry didn't feel that, but I did, so I thought I would just concentrate on the look of the film again, but not deal with the shooting of it—I'd design it. But that also became frustrating, because we would design something and plan it carefully and storyboard it, and when Terry got out onto the floor, he wouldn't shoot it the way we'd planned. We'd end up having built sets and spent money that wasn't on film, and that sort of waste always irritates me. If we were going to shoot it the way Terry ended up shooting it, then we wouldn't have had to build all this other

stuff—and we wouldn't have. That's just my side of trying to be a responsible, efficient, effective filmmaker.

"Also, the other side of designing something ultimately—I know that no matter how you design it, it's where you put the camera and what you do in it. There were a lot of times where Terry wasn't putting it where it should go to make the most of what we had there. There are certain sequences where I ended up getting in there and saying 'Stick the camera there,' especially when Terry was acting—he was usually away from the camera, so that was good. I could get it in the right place!" he laughs.

His first book was released in 1978 (although he did illustrate a volume called *Sporting Relations* two years before). *Animations of Mortality* was conceived as a "how-to" book on animation, using a great deal of Gilliam's old artwork. He created Brian the Badger to take the reader through the whole process. Throughout the book Gilliam tells the story mostly with pictures—at least until Brian is killed by the Black Spot . . .

"The reason I did the book was because, basically, I thought it would be quite easy to just get my old artwork out to put in the book. In fact, we had to redo most of the artwork—it works in the animation because it's moving and everything, and you can get away with it looking less good. When it's still, you can see all the flaws in it.

"So, I had to redo all the artwork, and it turned out to be a lot more work than we had planned on," Gilliam relates. "Then I did a lot of original stuff because I'd get bored with the old stuff. We're also using a lot of the old stuff in different ways. There are a lot of things in there on how to be an animator and how to do animation—or how to avoid doing animation. *Animations of Mortality* is a slightly pretentious title. . . ."

Like so much of Gilliam's work, it isn't easy to attach a short, convenient description to his book. "I told the publisher to advertise it differently to each market. They could advertise it in proper serious art review books as a serious art book, then they could advertise it in lighter fiction books as a light comedy book. They could advertise it in financial sort of magazines as a serious study of business methods in animation. It's a lie, totally, because it's a bit of all those things. It's a rather silly book, but it's what I wanted to do, rather than a collection of artwork, which is a bit dull," notes Gilliam. "I decided to do a book with a shape to it, with a character. Brian the Badger comes in and tries to explain how animation is done, and he's totally obsessed with good business practices. He's a terrible, greedy, money-hungry little creep, and he actually gets killed in the book by the Black Spot. It's very hard to do a fiction book that you actually have to read from beginning to end to actually get the sense of it, because there's a flow to it like a novel. But basically, it's all pictures."

Gilliam also made a few peculiar solo appearances following Python. During the City Center shows, he appeared on the game show *To Tell the Truth.* Two of the panelists had seen the show and disqualified themselves, while the other two voted correctly for Gilliam.

He also made a brief cameo appearance as an actor a few years later in the Chevy Chase/Dan Ackroyd film *Spies Like Us.* But Gilliam's future was clearly on the other side of the camera.

After the success of *Brian,* Handmade Films was eager to work with Gilliam on his next film. When they rejected what would eventually become *Brazil,* he came up with the basic story for *Time Bandits* over one weekend.

It was 1981's *Time Bandits* that made him an individual to be reckoned with inside the film industry. A bigger money-maker than any of the Python films, Gilliam cowrote and directed the story of a boy who encounters six dwarves who have stolen the map of the Holes in Time and Space from the Supreme Being. He accompanies them through history, where they meet real-life and fantasy legends, including King Agamemnon (Sean Connery), Napoleon (Ian Holm), and Robin Hood (John Cleese). Michael Palin, who cowrote the script with him, plays a dual role with Shelley Duvall, as star-crossed lovers in Sherwood Forest, and on the *Titanic.*

"I thought—Let's go commercial, write a film for kids. Let's do something that *might* get made. Out of desperation, one weekend I just sat down, and *Time Bandits* poured out of me very quickly.

"The project got interest right away from Denis O'Brien, who, with George Harrison, put up the money for *Brian.* He just said 'Go ahead.' Michael Palin started writing dialogue with me,

and we finished the script in February. By May [1980], we were filming in Morocco with Sean Connery."

His first day of filming on the big-budget project saw him jumping in headfirst.

"We began by not doing the easy stuff first but the most difficult," Gilliam explains. "Which meant flying off to Morocco and doing the fight with the Greek warrior and the bull-headed warrior. I hadn't directed a film in four years, so I was a bit rusty. We were up on this hill in 130-degree heat, and everything was going wrong on Day One. I've got twenty-five setups on my storyboards to do, and they're all elaborate, and it's a fight, and we've got these cumbersome costumes.

"Craig Warnock, the boy, was so nervous dealing with Sean Connery that he completely froze up. Everything was going as badly as it could go, and we started sliding behind very quickly," he reveals.

Terry Gilliam (right) directs Katherine Helmond and Peter Vaughan, playing Mr. and Mrs. Ogre in Time Bandits. *Photo copyright Handmade Films/Time Bandits.*

Gilliam claims that Sean Connery came to their rescue on that crucial first day.

"Connery was just great. He sensed immediately that we had overreached ourselves and said 'Listen, all you've got to do is shoot my stuff first, get it out of the way, I'll do it in one take and we can be out of it. Then you can spend time after-

wards with the boy.' And that's exactly what we did. Sean, in a strange way, got me through that film on the first day—he said 'Just cut out all this fancy stuff, just do the basics and get it on film!'

"It was nice too, because I think he could see immediately that I'd bitten off more than I could chew, and I was doggedly pursuing my own little storyboard. Sean is incredibly efficient, and he's had a lot of experience. He wouldn't allow me to film him getting on his horse, because he said 'I'm not going to be good at this, I'm getting too old for this.' Some stars trust the director, other stars won't give the director anything that could make them look bad. Sean is a bit like that, he creates situations that you've got to get around—they're all do-able, they just take a little bit of fiddling. But we were sitting in these dusty hovels, and he's got his box lunch like everybody else, because we had no trailers, nothing. I think he really enjoyed it—it was like going back to basics for him."

Although they were minuscule compared to the difficulties he would have on his subsequent movies, Gilliam had some other troubles filming *Time Bandits.*

"The real problem was we were rushed, and didn't have enough time for preproduction. We could only get Sean Connery for two weeks before he began *Outland.* We had to start in May, which didn't give us enough time. Halfway through shooting, we really ran into trouble. That was when we realized we hadn't planned an *ending* for the film," Gilliam revealed.

"So, we did a big battle scene—a Sherman tank, Greek archers, American cowboys, medieval knights, laser guns, and giant toys, all fighting in the Land of Legends. It was supposed to take five days to film; it took *weeks,* because we were in such a state of confusion.

"The weather was consistently against us. I've never seen anything so appalling. Every time we went outside, it pissed down. Every time we went inside, closed the studio doors and started pumping smoke and Fuller's earth into the air to create a dust storm, it would be blistering hot outside and suffocating inside. It was awful. We were filming in Morocco on a mountain; we were sweeping up all the dust on this mountaintop and putting it into plastic bags, which we then threw into the air. The locals thought we were quite mad!"

It was a mostly successful shoot, and Gilliam

was able to bring the movie in on a surprisingly small budget, the final product looking as if it had cost much more than it actually had.

Not everything shot for *Time Bandits* made it into the final cut, however, to Gilliam's regret.

"There's one really good scene, a wonderful scene with the Spider Women, which takes place after they escape from the Giant. It's two ancient, old ladies, Edwardian ladies sitting in their parlor with lace everywhere. The lace is part of what they're weaving, and they're weaving webs. Each of the Spider Ladies has eight legs under these great broad skirts—you look down and see all these tiny little feet.

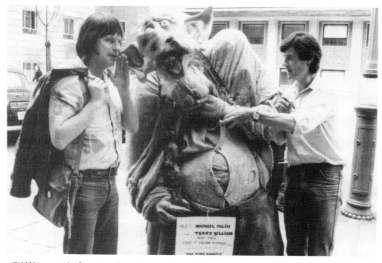

Gilliam (left), Palin (right) and unidentified friend (center) promote the Time Bandits *book at a London bookstore. Photo copyright Tara Heinemann.*

"And they're basically these lonely women looking for knights in shining armor, beautiful young men, and they trap Og in one of their web-snares and drag him into their cave, and hanging in the webs above them are these knights in shining armor.

"It's a nice, spooky, funny scene. The problem was, we had run out of money, and it required a scene on either side of it to connect with everything that was happening, and we just ran out of money and time. We couldn't afford to shoot the scenes that we had written for either side," he explains.

"A couple of months after we had finished shooting, out of desperation, I came up with the idea that if we lost that scene, we'd have to get from the Giant to the Fortress of Ultimate Darkness, and we had to do it as quickly and economically as possible. I came up with the idea of having an invisible barrier—they were actually there already, but they just couldn't see it. So that's what we shot to replace the three scenes that would have been required instead."

The cast of *Time Bandits* included a variety of major international stars, actors who weren't always known for their work in comedy; Gilliam said this was an attempt to expand the appeal of the movie beyond just Python fans.

"It's an insurance policy to make sure the audience didn't consider it another Python flick. Frankly, we didn't expect to get the actors we wanted. In the script, we had King Agamemnon pulling off his helmet to reveal himself as none other than Sean Connery, or someone of equal but cheaper stature. Our little joke, it was. Denis said 'Well, let's find out if Sean Connery wants to do it.' We were stunned when he said 'Yes.' Everybody we showed the script to wanted to do it!"

For the still-unseasoned director, it was an incredible way to do a film. "It was an amazing experience. We had these expensive, big-name stars turning up every week or two, and only a few days to work with each of them. We had to develop a relationship to convince them—unless they could convince me—of a way of doing a scene. But we did it, and then they were gone. There's not much margin for error, and that makes it very difficult. The pressures are awful; it's hard to enjoy anything, because you're so worried all the time," Gilliam explained shortly after wrapping the production.

Although he had to work with very experienced stars like Sean Connery and Ralph Richardson, Gilliam also cast some more familiar faces, like Palin and Cleese.

"I was sent the script, pointed at Robin Hood, and read the stage directions—'to be played like the Duke of Kent'—I thought it was very funny, and said I would love to do it," Cleese notes. "I enjoyed doing *Time Bandits* enormously, despite the

fact that Terry made me shave my beard off—I did it the morning of the shooting, seven A.M. in the forest!"

Aside from the loss of beard, there were not too many mishaps on the production, although one of the most interesting was actually caused by the director.

"The gang tends to plummet out of the sky a lot, since the Time Holes' exit points are usually up in the sky. They tend to land on Michael Palin and Shelley Duvall most of the time. Mike and Shelley play two young lovers in various historical periods. Each time they're about to get it together at last, bang, they're interrupted by the gang.

"I was on top of a ladder, trying to convince them that it's perfectly safe to jump onto this couch where Mike and Shelley are sitting, showing them how to do it; I fell directly onto Shelley and nearly broke her neck. There was a terrible note from the doctor—he had to report each day's injuries, like 'Someone got scratched—right hand,' or 'Someone got punched in the eye.' This day it said 'Miss Duvall treated for neck injuries because director fell on her.'"

The neck incident failed to ruin the director's career.

The success of *Time Bandits* allowed him to virtually write his own ticket. He was besieged by offers to direct such projects as *Enemy Mine* and *The Princess Bride.* Gilliam stuck to his guns, however, and insisted on directing an original film, his beloved *Brazil.* Written along with Charles McKeown and Tom Stoppard, Gilliam created his own world to tell the story of Sam Lowry, a lowly clerk in the Ministry of Information Retrieval.

In a story often compared to *1984,* Lowry challenges the repressive bureaucracy when he falls in love with a beautiful revolutionary (Kim Griest); his best friend (Michael Palin) becomes his torturer, and an air-conditioner repairman (in a hilarious cameo by Robert DeNiro) becomes their greatest hope. The true star of *Brazil,* however, is the world designed by Gilliam, which incorporates elements of the past, present, and future existing simultaneously with Lowry's flights into fantasy.

The inspiration for the movie actually occurred while scouting locations for *Jabberwocky.* "We were at this steelmaking town in Wales, on the beach at sunset," Gilliam relates. "There were these great

bays where the ships come in bringing the coal, and the coal is transported by conveyor belts over the beach to the steel plant. The beach was covered with coal dust, so it's a pitch-black beach. The sun was going down out there on the sea, and I had the image of someone sitting with a portable radio picking up strange Latin American music in this desolate world—that's where the movie started. None of that is in the film, but that's how it began—and we went from there."

Raising the money for the film proved more difficult than he had anticipated. *Brazil* had to be put on hold for several years, and it was not until *Time Bandits* proved to be a success and Gilliam could not be interested in any other project that studios finally took him seriously about his pet project.

"The problem was that I did *Meaning of Life* right after *Time Bandits,* so as far as Hollywood was concerned, I was out of circulation. By the time I was back to trying to get the money, I had gone cold. It was hard to get any interest until I turned down another project they were very excited about. They decided if I was turning it down, I must have a really good reason—and that was *Brazil.* They started looking at it more seriously."

Gilliam brought in playwright Tom Stoppard and actor-writer Charles McKeown to collaborate on the script. "It seemed a good idea to get somebody who's as clever verbally as the pictures were going to be—that's really why [Stoppard] was involved. It was a tidying-up operation—Tom was trying to make sense out of many jumbled thoughts, which he did. We tightened up much of it," Gilliam reveals.

"After Tom had done a few drafts, I started working with Charles McKeown to finish it off in its present form. Even the screenplay that the three of us ended up with isn't what's actually in the film—that has all changed during the filming and editing. In that sense, it's very organic.

"Little things were added all the time. Jonathan Pryce was always coming up with new and interesting ways of doing things. When we got on the set with all these objects, things began changing, and we really had to use them. I have a preconceived idea that I'm working toward, and I still storyboard it all, but things can change on the set, and I must go with it. It's a process where I know

where I'm going, and I'll go off on tangents. In the editing stages, I try to bring it back to where I was originally going—but it has altered in the process."

The final result is a dazzling, depressing, completely original film that has been described as "Walter Mitty Meets Franz Kafka," a label Gilliam agrees is accurate.

"We've got another catchphrase which is rather boring—'a post-Orwellian view of a pre-Orwellian world'—it's really tedious-sounding, and I think Mitty and Kafka are the truth of the matter. It's really about someone who doesn't take reality seriously enough, and spends too much time day-dreaming. It can be a dangerous thing—one has to keep one's eyes peeled. It creeps up from behind when one isn't looking," Gilliam noted shortly after completing the production.

"The film takes place everywhere in the twentieth century—that was the original idea. We're surrounded by things from another technology, items out of date from another era, and we always seem to accept it as normal—so, we tried to push that idea almost to the cartoon level," explains the former Python animator.

Shooting the picture involved its own nightmares, he notes. "We had some terrible troubles. We were out at this British offshore petroleum refinery which had been shut down. We were filming in the middle of winter and the cold was unbearable. We had to fill the place with black smoke and huge explosions. Physically, that was the worst day we ever experienced—by day's end, everybody was pitch black. One couldn't see anything but the whites of eyes.

Python-as-director: Terry Gilliam takes charge. Photo from the Collection of Terry Gilliam, used by permission.

There were these terrible underworld terrorist figures all creeping around, trying to stay warm and alive," relates Gilliam.

"We shot for nine months, and it was *extremely* painful. Each film gets harder and harder. I don't know how to judge them anymore—they all become nightmarish, and *Brazil* puts all the others to shame. *Everything* at every stage was difficult.

"There are some FX which are done with live-action and are full-size, but the rest is all models—there's a truck chase, ministry buildings slowing up—all standard model work. They were just more complicated because to have a man in a silver suit of armor, flying with an eighteen-foot pair of wings, is tricky. Most people don't even realize it's a model, they just assume we've somehow flown him. It really works."

Gilliam says he was very pleased with his cast as well, starting with Jonathan Pryce. "Jonathan is brilliant, he's the best I've ever worked with—even more than the Pythons. He's not only extremely funny and inventive, he's a great serious actor as well, and the combination is extraordinary."

Fellow Python Michael Palin appeared in his third film for Gilliam with *Brazil*. "Michael plays Jonathan's best friend. Who would you rather have for your torturer than your best friend? Mike is ambitious, he's the image of success and does everything right."

Working with Robert DeNiro in such a small role was very interesting, according to Gilliam. He says DeNiro originally wanted to play the role of Jack, but it had already been promised to Palin.

"I met Robert DeNiro through our producer [Arnon Milchan]. He said Bobby was interested in the things we were doing and got us together, which eventually led to him doing the movie. It's the first time he has ever done a bit part in a film. In many ways, his character does the same job that Sean Connery's did in *Time Bandits*—he's there for a brief time and then gone, but his character is absolutely crucial. It was a new experience for him to come and do a week-and-a-half's worth of shooting and then leave. Normally, he's in the center of it all from the word 'Go!'

"DeNiro works in a slightly different way than we do. We tend to get things done in one or two takes, where he works in a much more American way, rehearsing on film. But he's very intelligent

and intense. Once he gets involved with something, he thinks about it nonstop—he just won't let it go, even if he's only on screen for five minutes. I'm sure he spent as much time thinking about it as he does for a lead role in a film."

Although he had plenty of offers to do a sequel to *Time Bandits,* Gilliam says there was no question about it when he got the chance to make *Brazil.* "Actually, I think *Brazil* is the sequel. It's a strange thing, but I think the character Jonathan Pryce plays in *Brazil* is like the boy in *Time Bandits* fifteen years later. He has the same problems, he still dreams, but he's a bit older and things have changed. If I were making a trilogy, this would be part of it. Actually, I think I'm going to call this the fourth part of my trilogy," he laughs.

Twentieth Century-Fox had the rights to *Brazil* everywhere but in the U.S., and released Gilliam's version. But Universal refused to release the director's cut in the States when he turned it in, even though American critics—who had to be flown out of the country to see it—lavishly praised the picture.

There was originally talk of releasing *Brazil* for Christmas 1984, and an Easter 1985 release was finally agreed upon. The release was then pushed back to fall, and it was only after a massive effort by Gilliam and Milchan, assisted by many of the nation's top critics, that it was released for a week on December 18, 1985, in New York (and a week later in L.A.) to make it eligible for the Oscars. Prior to that, the L.A. Film Critics voted it Best Picture—even though it still hadn't been released!

Brazil's troubles began in January of 1985, when Gilliam turned in his cut to Universal, which insisted it was seventeen minutes longer than they had contractually agreed upon. They compromised, and Gilliam agreed to cut seventeen minutes from the film. He delivered his 131-minute version on time a month later.

"It took me more than a month to recut it," says Gilliam. "Normally, when people reedit a film for the States, they just chop out scenes to save time. To shorten it without actually losing anything, I did cuts within scenes—we redubbed the film, put in some new opticals, and made the ending appear less pessimistic. It makes my viewpoint very clear, but still has the same impact as the original ending, with one more element—it almost becomes religious!

"We turned in the shorter version that didn't change the film's content or shock in any way, and Universal told me 'Oh, yeah, terrific, works a lot better, it's wonderful. We think actually, though, it needs a major rethink.' Universal insisted they wanted to *keep* cutting it—their whole argument was over the length, not the content, but I think they felt the ending was too strong for the American public. The 'up' happy ending that they wanted would be a complete and utter travesty of the film. Everybody agrees that the ending really emblazons *Brazil* into one's brain. Universal wanted to try a happy ending at some preview showings to convince me, but there's no way we could change the ending, it's the one thing that's totally nonnegotiable. It's the essence of the film, as far as I'm concerned. There are no surprises in what I did—it's exactly what was scripted, so if they didn't like the ending, they should have told us and not given us the money."

Gilliam's shocking, downbeat ending of the film upset studio executives and actually caused most of the problems with its release.

"There are several endings to *Brazil,* and the penultimate ending is a happy, fairy-tale ending, and the audience cheers. *Then* comes the *real* ending, and the audience goes out quietly thinking. The studio executives hear the cheering three minutes before the film ends, and would *love* to end the movie that way and have the audience go out dancing in the street. Unfortunately, that's not the ending we set out to have—it has always been very crucial to the whole idea of *Brazil,*" says Gilliam.

Frustrated, Gilliam and Milchan began doing interviews of their own, and in October 1985 they placed a full-page ad in *Daily Variety* reading "Dear Sid Sheinberg: When are you going to release my film, *Brazil?* Terry Gilliam." They flew journalists out of the country so that they could legally see the movie.

"We tried to warn Universal that we were very serious," says Gilliam. "*Brazil* is a very special film—it's not infinitely malleable. They just kept plodding on, using the 'scientifically proven' process of previews to determine the best film to release, which really forced our hands."

The movie was shown at the Deauville Film Festival in France, to an enthusiastic response. "It's such an obvious, simple story—struggling artist

against huge established filmmaking machinery. Judith Crist, Joel Siegel, and others were raving about *Brazil,* and it isn't often that people get so excited about a film that they're willing to go public and commit themselves," he says.

Universal eventually took his reedited film away from him. "Universal started fiddling with it—I had no involvement. In one cut, I heard they were trying to end it by turning it into a revenge film like *Rambo!* They don't think the American public is ready for an antiauthoritarian film like *Brazil.* Anybody with any intelligence who has seen the movie understands what it's about, and either likes or dislikes it on that basis."

Gilliam likes to use a culinary analogy.

"The difference is between McDonald's hamburgers and Cordon Bleu cooking. McDonald's hamburgers are a safe, neither good nor bad, meal. It's quick, it's easy, it's almost predigested. A Cordon Bleu meal is a spectacular affair, with lots of ideas, changes, and surprises. That's what *Brazil* is about—it's constantly surprising. One minute we're zipping along in a sort of Steven Spielberg truck chase, and the next, there are several disturbing images that make one think 'Wait a minute! That wasn't all just fun.' It really jerks the audience around. Sometimes the story is in the background instead of the foreground.

"It switches between very comic things and very tragic things, and people aren't used to that—it's bled out of the cinematic experience. Cinema today can either be fun, frolicky escape, or serious artistic statement—the two are seldom blended together in one film. I hate great successful films like *Gremlins* and *Ghostbusters,* because most of them are only on one level—they're McDonald's hamburgers. I miss the chance to see movies that give you those same sort of spills and thrills, but also let your brain come along for the ride."

Universal, finally forced to relent under the pressure, released *Brazil* nationally in early 1986; not surprisingly, the studio failed to promote it adequately and it proved to be a box-office disappointment. Nominated for Academy Awards for Best Original Screenplay and Best Art Direction, it didn't win any.

And Universal still didn't give up—when *Brazil* was shown on broadcast TV, it was so severely edited (the studio restored the happy ending it so loved) that Gilliam threatened a lawsuit.

Perhaps the greatest irony of *Brazil,* however, was the way Gilliam's battle with the huge corporation was reflected in his movie.

For Gilliam, the strangest, most exciting time of his filmmaking career may have been the battle over *Brazil.* It was also, ironically, a perfect example of life imitating art, as Gilliam, the fantasist, took on Universal, the realists.

"At the time it was a nightmare, but in many ways, it was the high point," he says. "I knew we had done an extraordinary film. I didn't know how good or bad it was, but I knew it was extraordinary. It was a chance to take on the studio system that I hated so deeply, from having lived in California, wanting to get into films, not liking the rules of the game and refusing to follow them. To come back with this film and be in battle with Universal Studios—my last job in America, before I left in 1967, was an advertising copy writer and art director doing ads for Universal Pictures, which were real shit pictures then! I found myself up against the most conservative of all Hollywood organizations as this little David against Goliath. It was depressing for most of the time, but it was also wonderfully exhilarating!

"In many ways, it's created a reputation that makes my life a lot more interesting now," he says. "People think I'm much more dangerous, much more crazy, and it tends to frighten a lot of people away from me. But, it's usually the people I don't want to work with anyway, so it's handy!"

Controversy seemed to dog Gilliam's efforts, but the problems on his next film nearly overshadowed all of his previous troubles. Shooting on *The Adventures of Baron Munchausen* was behind almost before he began, with the movie rushed into production long before Gilliam was prepared. The project ran over budget, and the studio threatened to take the picture away from Gilliam in the middle of the shoot. He found himself battling the studio to retain control of his film, and also fighting to complete the shooting. His efforts were not in vain, however, and *Munchausen,* with Eric Idle and John Neville in the title role, was completed as Gilliam had hoped.

"The idea of *Munchausen* had been around for some time, because I liked the (1962) Czechoslovakian film, in particular. I liked the stories. When we were doing *Brazil,* and I was convinced *Brazil* would be the biggest disaster of all time, Arnon

Milchan and I were saying 'Look, we'd better have something planned for next.' When he asked what I wanted to do, I told him I'd been thinking about Baron Munchausen, and he turned out to be a big fan.

"So, we went to Twentieth Century-Fox and he said 'Terry and I want to do *Baron Munchausen.*' And he said 'Wow! We're all Munchausen people here!' And they did a deal. We actually had a deal to make the film with Twentieth Century-Fox.

"After *Brazil,* Arnon and I went separate ways, and Fox ultimately turned it down, because the people who had made the deal were no longer there—there were new people at Fox. But I had nothing else happening, and momentum on the *Baron* just kept going. Occasionally, art overtakes life," he laughs.

"At one point, I was being pretentious, and pretending I was making a trilogy with *Time Bandits, Brazil,* and *Munchausen*—the young boy as fantasist, the man as fantasist, and the old man as fantasist—there are connections for this.

"The book is really just a series of tales that don't have any narrative connection, so Charles McKeown and I invented a tale about a town under siege, the group of actors trapped in it, trying to perform *The Adventures of Baron Munchausen,* when the real Baron turns up and starts doing all the things that only happen in fantasy."

The most difficult character for the director to cast was the title character, as the Baron is also the most important role of the film. "I did a lot of screen tests with a lot of different people in mind, it went on and on and on. But the extraordinary thing was that one name kept popping up—John Neville. It kept popping up every month or so—somebody would pop in and say 'I've got just the guy for you—his name is John Neville,' and I'd say 'I *know* that, but . . .'

"John Neville was the director of the Stratford Ontario Shakespeare Festival, he did fifteen productions a season. We had approached his agent and been told he had no time for films. So, I kept looking for somebody else.

"Then one day when we were in Rome working, I was telling the lady doing the makeup about the problems in casting the Baron, and I said the person I kept thinking about is John Neville. She said 'Well, I know him, I grew up with his daughter. I have his phone number, I'll call him.' She

called him in Canada and said 'Terry Gilliam's making a film, and he'd like to meet you.' He turned out to be a Python fan! I met him and said 'Bingo! Baron Munchausen!'

"What I had been looking for was a star, a great actor who had faded or disappeared, and that's what John was. In the sixties in England, he, Burton, O'Toole, they were all just the top—he was equal to all those guys. Then he left the West End stage and went into provincial theater, then emigrated to Canada. In effect, he disappeared from the world as most of us know it! He was doing incredible work all through Canada, setting up theaters and all. So, he fitted the bill," Gilliam smiles.

Gilliam is no stranger to controversy, both in his Monty Python years and in film, particularly his previous movie, *Brazil.* And *Baron Munchausen* faced problems that would have broken most directors. Forced to begin production before he was ready, the project soon ran into budget problems that caused the studio to threaten to replace him. Still, Gilliam retained his sense of humor through it all.

"I just grow thicker and thicker skin. I'm a walking callus," he says with a laugh. "This film was terrifyingly difficult, even before those other pressures from the studio began. The fact that the film was falling apart at the seams was bad enough—the organization was terrible. It was a very foolhardy thing to go to a foreign country—in this case, Italy—that isn't particularly equipped to do SFX films, mixing English and Italian crews. At one point, the crew was English, Italian, German, and Spanish. They were speaking in four different languages, which in this kind of film was a very silly thing to do.

"On the other hand, this film was about the impossible and going on impossible adventures—and that's what the making of the film is also about," Gilliam laughs, "Life imitates art again!"

Fortunately, Gilliam had the strong support of his cast—including fellow Monty Python member and old friend Eric Idle—even though the director required him to make sacrifices.

"Eric was great, because I think he enjoyed the process. He was constantly supportive, and once he shaved his head, he was a good person—it just took a little while to get him to shave his head. That altered his personality to no end, and im-

proved him as a human being," Gilliam jokes. "Now that his hair's growing back, I'm frankly less fond of him!

"At one point, we were out in Spain, and things were at their very, very worst. I was ready to quit. I knew there was no way we'd get through the film. Eric really came in there, saying 'You've *got* to, if for no other reason, you must make this film *to spite John Cleese,*" he laughs. "That got me going!"

And that's why Eric Idle says he made the comment. "I had to motivate Terry to keep going. I didn't want the film to go under, because I'd already gotten my head shaved, and I wanted to be sure I got paid!" he recalls with a chuckle.

Idle agrees that an ordeal like *Munchausen* was easier to face with a friend; he says that Gilliam was under tremendous pressure during the shoot but managed to handle it all wonderfully.

"Terry's very good at dealing with pressure, which is why he's a very good director," Idle explains. "What he does, basically, is take a pure artistic line, saying 'This is not my responsibility. Here I am this morning. I want to shoot this shot. Money is a producer's job.' I think that's absolutely the only possible way to deal with a situation like that. The moment I would think about taking on vast responsibilities, I wouldn't be able to do anything—I would just stay in bed and have a nervous breakdown."

Following Michael Palin's roles in *Time Bandits* and *Brazil,* Idle says he's happy to take over the Python role here.

"It's important and very useful to have old friends around. Michael always played the role of the old chap you used to do comedy with, who you can talk to—because filming is madness. It's good to have an old colleague like that, so he can't pull any 'I'm the director' shit. Still, when there's a crisis, I'll take him off and have a coffee and say 'Don't worry.' I really enjoyed playing that role. It's tough directing. One needs supporters and pals, and it's best if they're on the set too, because they're up to their necks in water when you're asking."

He says he was happy to work with Gilliam here, despite such unpleasant moments.

"I felt it was unlikely that I'd work with Gilliam again, and I've always respected him—he's a wonderful director," Idle notes. "I was thinking that I'd be too old to work with Gilliam next time

around—he'd kill me in another few years, so I'd better go do my stint now.

"I had my head shaved for six months. That bastard Gilliam," he laughs. "Pure sexual jealousy. . . . I also had false teeth made, horrible ugly false teeth. I look a real wreck in that film. Didn't get laid from that one, that's for sure!"

One of the further complications of *Munchausen* resulted from Gilliam's rejecting the traditional show business axiom of not working with animals, children, or water.

"We were smart when we did *Monty Python and the Holy Grail* and used coconut shells for our horses. This had everything. Animals, small children, water FX—everything you should never do in a film, they're all in this one. Hopefully, I've gotten it out of my system now. The elephants were difficult. We trained the horses for months, and just before we went to Spain to shoot, there was an outbreak of horse fever in Spain, and the place was closed. We couldn't bring in the horses that we had trained to do all these things. . . .

"There were two dogs used for the Baron's dog, and they both came down with a liver complaint the same week the horses weren't allowed into Spain. A couple weeks before we would start, the horses couldn't go to Spain, the dogs came down with some disease, and David Puttnam [of Columbia] got the sack—all in three days. What a week!" Gilliam laughs.

The director says he had better luck with the eight-year-old newcomer, Sarah Polley, who plays one of the Baron's companions, and had to hold her own on the screen with John Neville, Eric Idle, Oliver Reed, and Robin Williams.

"She was fantastic, and professional. I treated her no differently than any of the others, and she was there all the time. She was amazing—quite frankly, we couldn't have done the film without her being as good as she is. The cast is brilliant."

Baron Munchausen contains elements of swashbuckling fantasy movies of the past, Gilliam explains, almost excessively so. "If this film suffers from anything, it's too much of everything. "Americans are desperate for more and more and more, and this has got more than anything. On the one hand, it's like all the films that used to be made, all the great SFX-fantasy movies like *Sea Hawk* and *Thief of Bagdad*—it's like all of those films, and yet it's totally different," he explains.

"When we were making it, I kept going 'Wow!' because there was black-and-white video all the time we were shooting. I kept looking at the images, and it just kept reminding me of picture after picture that I'd grown up with."

In addition to the many SFX shots, Gilliam's project also involved extensive makeup.

"The makeup was the worst part about it for someone like John Neville, who was sixty-three—he had to play the Baron at thirty-five, at sixty-five, and at eighty, so he had to go through all these different aging makeups. He was spending three to four hours a day in the makeup chair, which is murderous.

"We tried to make Robin Williams a floating head out of marble. The Queen of the Moon has got three violin necks sticking out the top of her head," he reveals.

"All the characters had to age and get young, and they're wearing false teeth. We shaved everybody's head, because they had to be old—rather than wearing bald caps all the time, which are very sweaty, and stain with makeup. Audiences can always see the joint. So, I convinced them all to shave their heads. They'd wear wigs when they were young and be naturally bald when they were old. There were a lot of sacrifices on people's parts."

Gilliam says making the film was not much fun and, in retrospect, claims that each scene was a nightmare to film; in addition to problems with the budget, pressures from the studios, and lack of pre-production time, he was forced to shoot under less than state-of-the-art conditions on location in Spain, and at Rome's Cinecittà Studios, where Fellini was based.

"I really didn't enjoy making this film, I hated it all the time when we were shooting it—I was just trying to survive. It wasn't about making the film, it was all about surviving! So, I have a strange lack of memory about the experience. . . ."

One day that Gilliam does remember is the sequence with the huge balloon, with a gas bag consisting of women's underpants sewn together, used to escape from the besieged city. In fact, the director says that day was the turning point of the entire film.

"Our finest day was the day the balloon flew in Spain. They were pulling us out of the country before we were finished and threatening to fire me.

Everything was going wrong, the whole production. The day before, we had shot the death of the Baron, and I thought that was it—it was all over, because just like *Brazil,* the making of the film followed the script itself," he recalls with a laugh. "We were shooting the Baron's death when the film was falling apart and we were closing it down.

"We then had to shoot the balloon going up. The balloon, which cost a fortune and had to be supported by a three-hundred-foot crane, could only fly if there was no wind. There we were, on this hilly bit of Spain, where there was *always* wind. We got up in the morning, and of course the wind was blowing, so they couldn't get the balloon up. The day was ticking by while we were doing this, that, and the other thing, and the balloon wouldn't fly. I had said the night before that if the balloon goes, the film will be all right, and if the balloon doesn't go, we're dead—it's very simple.

"The sun set at five-thirty P.M., and at four-thirty we still hadn't gotten close to getting the balloon up and across the battlements. The clouds would come in, and every time we'd start taking the balloon across the battlements, it would turn in the wrong direction.

"The little gondola underneath would be pointing backwards and every which way. To get it the right way, we had to disconnect wires, turn the boat around, stick the wires back on and put it up—then it'd go the wrong way again!

"At five, everything was still going on, though luckily the wind had dropped. The line producer was saying 'What are we going to do?' I said I didn't know, and we couldn't decide which way to turn the balloon for the last time. I finally said 'I think it ought to go that way—turn the wires that way.' He said 'Are you sure? Then let's do it that way—it's got to work that way.'

"We pulled the balloon up, and it was pointing the wrong way. Then it started to move. It turned. The sun came out in the late afternoon, and *the balloon flew!* It was stunning. Off across this battle below, and walls filled with people, the Turks going on and the cannons firing, and it went! It was just so amazing—everybody went crazy and started grabbing shots madly. The last shot we got is the flag flying over the town, with the last bit of sun catching the flag—it was a perfect day.

"I don't know if that was the turning point, I

just knew the film would get finished," he says, laughing. "The filming got worse after that, but at least I knew secretly that it would get done."

Gilliam received most of the blame for widely reported cost overruns on *The Adventures of Baron Munchausen,* but he says he is actually a very economical filmmaker.

Terry Gilliam poses with a friend—the model used for Robin Williams as the Moon King in **The Adventures of Baron Munchausen.** *Photo copyright KHJ.*

"Even on *Munchausen,* I was efficient," he says. "What we did there was efficient—it just happened that the production was completely out of control. What we set out to make was not being provided for, and when that starts going wrong, you get into a situation where this juggernaut of a film is marching forward, and there's nothing you can do about it except spend more money and try to keep going. It's one of those situations where you either stop it and you lose whatever you put into it, or you carry on. The choice was made to carry on. If we'd stopped it, the money would have been lost totally. There wouldn't have been any film to have a chance of recouping the money.

"A case in point on *Munchausen* was that the Turkish Army was originally going to be 800 soldiers. I cut it down to 400, so immediately there was a huge savings in cost of numbers of extras. However, when we got to Spain, the main costumes had been left behind in Italy, and they got caught up in a customs strike in Barcelona, and they arrived a week late. We were down on a beach in Spain where we were supposed to be shooting one set of scenes, and the only set of costumes we had were for the Turkish Army, which was supposed to be shot a couple of weeks later in a different part of Spain!

"We ended up getting some extras and shooting the army, but we had to fake everything—we didn't even have a set. What you see there *looks* like a set, because I had one bit of parapet for the town wall that was built up on this cliff that was only about 15 feet across—it was designed to be used as a foreground piece that we would shoot over the parapet, toward the Turkish camp. So it was a small little piece, it was for one specific shot, and that's all we had down there. I was able to still get shots by taking battle towers and sticking them so that they filled up nine-tenths of the screen, and yet several hundred yards away in the distance, you see this wall with these troops on top firing down. All you see of the wall is literally 15 feet—one inch of the screen is cropping it, and the battle tower is cropping the other, and yet there's this sense of this huge wall, and it was made with that. You can always do things like that. But, when you get into a situation like that where all the planning goes awry, then it's not efficient—it's just struggling through, trying to keep shots going. We made tons of mistakes, and the thing just got worse and worse."

The Adventures of Baron Munchausen was a success with critics, but very few people had the chance to see it, and Terry Gilliam is still angry that the movie fell victim to studio politics.

"I was disappointed that the studio didn't release the film," he explains. "They didn't distribute it. There aren't many films—especially films that big—that have been dumped so successfully by a studio. The did 115 prints—that's all that were made of that film. My mother lives out in the San Fernando Valley, and it never got out there. They spent on promoting it less than half of what we spent on *Time Bandits,* and that was ten years ago.

"The studio was basically being run by the ac-

countants at that point, and they were trying to tidy it up for a sale to Sony. They made the books look good by spending absolutely no money on promoting, marketing, and distributing the films. I found out they spent more time trying to justify why they weren't putting money into the film than actually doing it. The actual distribution of that film was so terrible—in places like France and Australia and Spain, where the foreign guys actually got to work on it, it did fantastically well. I don't know if I'll ever get over that one, because it's a film that was really meant to be seen by the public. Columbia had convinced themselves that it would only work in sophisticated urban centers, and only the big ones, at that, which is just rubbish—totally untrue. They could not understand that it was also mainly for kids.

"Basically, they just put no money into it. They probably spent $2 million on the release of that film. The problem when you do that, when you've got a big film that has to be sold like an epic and you don't put money behind it, is that I think the public smells a rat. 'Something's wrong here, this one has to be a stinker.'"

Munchausen got very respectable notices, but it wasn't enough to get Columbia to save the film.

"They had gotten the best notices they had gotten since *The Last Emperor;* they did the best business they had done since then too on the opening week. It did fantastic, it was great. Dawn Steel was on the phone to me, so excited about how well it had opened. The whole plan was that it would open as it did, and a couple of weeks later, go to five hundred prints, and on and on. They didn't do any of it. They just pulled the plug on it. It makes me angry, because as far as I'm concerned, it was just a total act of betrayal. We'd been told that if the film opened well, they'd be right in there. The problem was that Dawn Steel was, at the time, pretending to be president of the place. I foolishly believed she actually had some power, and she didn't. It was Victor Kaufman, the money man, who was really calling the shots at that point. That's the part that angers me—not that it didn't do well, but that the people didn't get a chance to go see it."

He admits that he inadvertently helped Columbia to sink the film by discussing the problems involved during the shoot, so that most of the press received by *Munchausen* concentrated on the problems attached to it rather than the movie itself.

"I should have kept my mouth shut. I was so brain-damaged by then that I couldn't *not* talk about the awfulness of making the thing, and again, people in this day and age are terrified of things that sound like they have problems attached to them. Twenty years ago that wasn't the case—people would rush out to see what it was about, but unfortunately, that's not the world we're living in now. I would get trapped by most of the interviews, because they would just want to talk about it going over budget and all those things, which is really beside the point. Nobody was talking about how good the film was, or how fantastic or whatever."

After it was too late to do anything about it, Gilliam discovered that the film had indeed been made a victim of studio infighting.

"It partly had to do with the backlash toward David Puttnam, because there were a lot of people who perceived this as a Puttnam film. They were really out to get him. There were so many reports coming in about this film in *Variety* when we were shooting in Rome, I couldn't work out where they were getting this information, because number one, a lot of it wasn't true, and number two, where were they getting it? It was being fed to them—I actually know how it got to them, but it was a way of beating Puttnam as well as me.

"I had a talk with Warren Beatty before I left L.A. after shooting the film, and I got a clearer picture of what was going on. He really felt it had been a way of getting at Puttnam."

For as long as Terry Gilliam has been making movies, he always said he would never do a project like *The Fisher King,* but after his battles over *Brazil* and *Baron Munchausen,* he admits he was tired of fighting studios. The script for *The Fisher King* arrived at a time when he was finally willing to shoot a movie in Hollywood and direct someone else's screenplay.

"It's funny that this particular script turned up when I was feeling rather shagged out after *The Adventures of Baron Munchausen,* and pretty depressed. It was just a funny script, and easy reading. It was one of those scripts that I wished I had written, because I understood the attitudes and the characters totally.

"The fact is, it really involved four characters,

and it didn't involve special effects. I'd really been thinking after *Munchausen* that I wanted to do something small, so there it was."

At the time, Gilliam was going to make another attempt to write a project with Michael Palin, but schedule conflicts and other problems prohibited that work.

"The project that I'd been working on at the time, which was *The Minotaur,* was going rather slowly, and the actual script really wasn't coming together properly. This thing popped up and I thought I'd better think about it. Then the producers and a studio executive flew over here and I talked to them, I said 'Why not do the very thing I said I would never do?' The important thing about making rules is to then break them, it seems!" he says, laughing. "So, there we did it!

"I always said I wouldn't work in the States, I said I wouldn't do somebody else's script, and I said I wouldn't work for a studio, *especially* I wouldn't work in Los Angeles—and I did all of those things. The extraordinary thing is, it's actually proved to be the easiest film I've ever made."

Gilliam's imagination, which made studio accountants cringe on *Baron Munchausen,* was much easier to hold back on *The Fisher King,* he explains.

"Every time I started to elaborate or make things more complicated or fantastical, I kept checking with [screenwriter] Richard Lagravenese. I'd say 'What do you think? Am I pushing too far?' I kept him around the whole time, because it's his script—as far as I was concerned, it's his film, and I wanted to make sure I wasn't violating it. I kept him there as my conscience. . . .

"There are certain things that weren't in the original script that I now have in there, like a thousand commuters during rush hour at Grand Central Station, all waltzing. That was never in the original script," Gilliam reveals. "Things like that were my additions, just because it seemed like a good idea at the time. That was the thing that just worried me the whole time, though—I didn't want the characters to get lost or pushed into the background by big ideas. The Knight is pretty spectacular, and that was one of the things I was worried about.

"First of all, to get a horse painted red is harder than you'd think. And to get a Knight with smoke pouring out of its armor everywhere, and flames shooting out of its helmet—this proved to be a bit

more difficult than we had envisaged, because it all had to be able to work in New York City, not out in the protected environment of a studio. We were right in the heart of the city! That ended up consuming so much time and energy, I was beginning to think the film was about the Red Knight. Once you've expended that kind of energy, you want to shoot it for all it's worth. And I thought 'Uh, oh, I'm getting in trouble here . . .' But in the end, I don't think it overbalanced the original material."

The only actor Gilliam had worked with before was Robin Williams, who played the King of the Moon in *Baron Munchausen;* Gilliam says he and his star are alike in many ways.

"Robin, in a way, suffers from the same problems I do. One always goes straight for the over-the-top, biggest, most spectacular, and feels comfortable doing funny things. When we first met and talked about it, I said that everything about the part of Parry, no matter how funny it is, has really got to be based on the pain of his particular tragedy—the loss of his wife. If that's solid, we can be as silly as we want, but it's got to come from that.

"One of the reasons I wanted Jeff Bridges was because I knew Jeff would ground both of us, and stop us from going the cheap and easy routes that we were comfortable with," he explains.

"Like any comedian, Robin is more nervous about really exposing himself than most actors, because almost every comedian uses comedy as a defense mechanism, so they can avoid revealing what they really are and what they're really feeling. I just had to keep making sure Robin was feeling confident and secure so that he could actually open up the wounds as much as they needed to be opened up for this thing. He's nonstop inventive, and in a sense I was always pulling him back, trying to stop him from doing that, because he doesn't need to. He does it because he feels comfortable doing it."

Still, Gilliam says he allowed for Williams's input in *The Fisher King,* largely because he would have been foolish not to.

"There would always be at least one take that was just for him to ad lib whatever he wanted to, to come up with anything that might happen. He never felt comfortable unless he was given that opportunity to go at it. I didn't use many of those takes, though—we pretty much stuck to the origi-

nal script. But there are several ad-libbed moments that are wonderful, and you gain, so it's silly not to use Robin for that."

Williams was actually involved with *The Fisher King* before Gilliam, and indirectly led to the director getting the job.

"The whole thing was a bit weird, a bit chicken-and-eggy, because Robin was interested in it, and the studio was interested in him," reveals Gilliam. "Apparently, there were only a handful of directors that he was interested in working with, and I was on that list, so I think the studio then approached me as a way of securing Robin. So, once I said yes, I had to go through it with Robin and convince him. I did actually have to spend a fair amount of time with him and his managers and agents to secure the whole thing."

Gilliam says their work on *Munchausen* was one of the things that led to their collaboration.

"We had a really good time on that one. We got on really well and it was great fun, so he felt comfortable," he explains.

He says he cast Jeff Bridges in part because audiences like him so much.

"That was definitely one of the reasons. I knew we could make him a real asshole and the audience would still stay with us, because Jeff is likable—they just go for him. It's a strange bit of casting for the part of a New York, smart-ass D.J. The first person you would think of is not Jeff Bridges. It was the thing that excited me the most, because it was the scariest part of the casting. It was so much of a leap into areas that Jeff had never really dealt with. I got a glimpse of it in *Baker Boys,* enough to get me excited.

"In a strange way, I also like Jeff doing it because it's really a fairy tale, and Jeff is the representative of America, and where it's got to. It starts out with this D.J., and his smart-ass, sarcastic attitude—he's got everything in the world, it's like a dream come true. He's clever, rich, and successful, and it's totally empty. It's more interesting than taking some street-smart New York guy and turning him into this kind of D.J.—if you take a guy from the heart of America and turn him into that, he's got further to fall than another guy who's already started that way. I quite liked the idea of coming out of the heart of America and aspiring to being this kind of person. I don't know if any of that's in there. . . ."

The part of the fast-talking disc jockey sounds, on the surface, like Williams's role in *Good Morning, Vietnam;* when the project was first announced, Gilliam says many people thought Williams would play the D.J., but he's happy with his decision.

"I actually think it works best this way. The thing about Robin and Parry is that Parry is totally vulnerable and crazy, and Robin is that. Robin is so vulnerable—and it shows—that you get much more out of him being Parry. I didn't know if Jeff would make a good Parry, frankly. I think the way we did it was right. When we were getting together a list of people to play the part of Jack, a page-and-a-half list that the casting director came up with, strangely enough, all the names were there in capital letters and lower casing, except for one name that was in all lower casing, and it was Jeff Bridges. Which is wonderfully odd," he recalls with a smile.

A crucial bit of filmmaking improvisation that Gilliam is proud of occurred during the shooting of *The Fisher King.*

"It was during the Chinese restaurant scene, when they were all sitting around the table eating, and the Amanda Plummer character is making a mess," he says. "We were in New York on a five-week shoot, and the studio didn't give me any weather cover. So, we shot through everything, until finally one night when we were out in Central Park, it began raining so badly that we just couldn't shoot. So I said 'All right, we'll go do the Chinese restaurant.' There was a place I had seen and said we could use it if we got in trouble—it was this restaurant with a beautiful back wall with Chinese dragons on it. We rushed down, hung some paper lanterns, and shot the scene. We had no rehearsal time, so we just shot it. I said 'We'll push the camera in and lock it off, and do lots of takes—just keep bringing the food in. It'll all be improvised, and I'll work it out later.' So, that's what we did. We did wipes across the screen, and just used the good bits. That was not the way the scene was written or planned, but that's what I did, and it worked better than if I'd done it in a normal way. I was forced into that situation, but I really liked it. Then we didn't have an end for the scene. I saw these reflections on the tabletop, so I said 'Let's see if we can do a pull back.' The crew had to rig up a whole crane dolly setup, just with two-by-fours. It was one of those nights where

everybody was just improvising everything, and we ended up with some really nice shots and a good sequence."

The Fisher King didn't disappoint his fans, critics, or the public in general, and it proved to be the award-winner many thought it might. Mercedes Ruehl won the Best Actress Oscar, and the same award from the L.A. Film Critics. Robin Williams was nominated for the Best Actor Oscar (and won the Golden Globe), while *The Fisher King* won the highest award at the Toronto Festival of Festivals. Gilliam's response to the latter: "Thank you for justifying my decision to sell out."

Despite its accolades, the director says he still isn't sure if *The Fisher King* is a "Gilliam film."

"I don't know what it is," he laughs. "It's 'Gilliam Sells His Soul and Goes to Hollywood.' In a strange way, it's clearly my film somehow, and yet it isn't my film. That's the odd thing. I think you can actually say it's a Gilliam film, and yet there's nothing in there that makes it a Gilliam film—it's written by somebody else, it was somebody else's idea.

"It's kind of intriguing, that one. . . . I suppose this is what happens with directors. 'Is this an Oliver Stone film?' I mean, it's what you choose

Terry Gilliam, early 1990s. Photo copyright KHJ.

to do as director. You're still always the filter. Whether it's the script, originally, that you're choosing to do, because it's what you're about—it works that way, I think. You don't *have* to write the stuff. When you're making the film, the actors are doing things all the time. I'm not doing them, they're not my ideas—all I do is be the filter, I say 'That stays' or 'That goes.' In that sense, you always make the choice toward what your own sensibilities are."

Prior to *The Fisher King,* Gilliam admits that he felt he had to write the script in order for a film to really be his, but says this film changed his mind.

"I just wanted to make the other films totally mine. It's like a painting—it's having an idea and carrying it through all the stages. You may hire a lot of assistants along the way who can paint grass or trees better than you can paint them. To me, the reason for making films was always that I had an original thought, and I wanted to carry it through. It's a great relief not to have to do it all," he says with a giggle. "I quite liked this way of making films."

Gilliam has always talked about his three previous films as constituting a fantasy trilogy, with *Time Bandits* portraying the fantasist as a boy, *Brazil* showing the fantasist as a young man, and *Munchausen* viewing the fantasist as an old man. *The Fisher King* doesn't have a place in that trilogy, he explains.

"I think it's my 'Mature Film,' is what it is— 'the one where he at last comes of age,'" he laughs. "I think we can safely say it's my Hollywood Film, since I did make it there, and it's for a studio, and all that stuff. . . . What's nice about it is because I was more relaxed and less frenetic about all this, I think it actually does have a certain 're- laxed maturity' about it, or 'confident maturity.' I've maintained a much cooler attitude toward this film through all the stages, and it's interesting to see how it works.

"The themes are similar—there's still the elements of fantasy and reality, and madness and sanity, materialism and romance—they're all there. And there's definitely the search for the Holy Grail in there! It fits in the same themes. I want to think of *Jabberwocky,* I see some similarities there. . . ."

The Fisher King is actually different from all of his prior movies, he feels. "It's not really like any of them—that's what's intriguing. I actually don't

know how to compare it to anything—I don't even know how to describe the film very well. I was looking at it yesterday, and it's like three films all put together—it shifts gears and styles, and somehow it all holds together and seems to work. It's the most eclectic film I've done. It's like several different ones all strung together somehow."

Although it couldn't compare to *Baron Munchausen,* Gilliam says *The Fisher King* still had some tough scenes to shoot. "Physically, the most difficult scene was climbing this tower, because we were working on Madison Avenue, and we had to bring in all these cranes to put the camera on. That was a slow and tedious process."

"The one that came closest to almost not working was the big waltz at Grand Central Station, where we had a thousand extras trying to learn to waltz. We had supposedly gone to all these dancing schools for people who would know how to waltz, and we got 'em down there, and most of 'em didn't know how to waltz. We were sitting in Grand Central Station with a thousand extras and a choreographer trying to train them, and we've got to be out of there by dawn, when the trains start arriving. The camera finally started turning about four-thirty in the morning, and we had to be out of there at six! That was a close one. We just started rolling cameras, we were pushing and shoving. . . .

"There's shots at the end of it where people are getting off the first trains, and we're still shooting. I said 'Robin, just go in there,' and we had everybody walking back and forth in circles, I had the crew going in there just to make the scene look busy as the first commuters were coming off the train. We were not very popular at Grand Central Station!"

Gilliam compares the waltz sequence here to the raising of the hot-air balloon in *Munchausen,* in that both of them were do-or-die attempts at grabbing shots. Fortunately, he says there were very few problems compared to his previous experience.

"That's what was nice about this film. Whatever problems we had, they were *nothing* to what I had been through in the past. I was able to float rather balloonlike through the whole thing."

Despite Gilliam's impressive body of work thus far, none of his films comes close to exemplifying his rich vision of fantasy.

"I hate all my films," he jokes. "I think the Grand Central Station waltz sequence in *Fisher King* is as good as anything I've ever done. Being my only real contemporary film, that's an amazing way of expressing what fantasy can mean. The flying sequences in *Brazil* are still phenomenal. I'm the worst judge of this. None of my stuff is what I set out to do—some of it is better than what I set out to do, and most of it isn't. Individual bits within films I think achieve what I want to achieve—I don't think any film in total has achieved it."

Terry Gilliam at the desk of his north London office. Photo copyright KHJ.

Gilliam directed *12 Monkeys* in 1995, which saw Brad Pitt nominated for Best Supporting Actor. The film stars Bruce Willis, who is sent back to 1996 to prevent a deadly virus that nearly wiped out the Earth in the future. "That was even more complicated than my other films in some ways," he says. "Somebody's gotta do this shit! Somebody's gotta keep breaking down the boundaries of generic filmmaking!"

As he previously did in *Brazil,* Gilliam admits he's created another dark vision of the future here.

"It's not a very happy future," he says. "It's certainly a Spartan, pretty severe kind of future, because if you're living underground, it's not going to

be all sunshine and roses. Strangely enough, the future part was the *least* interesting part of the film for me. It was territory I've played with before. The point of this future is that it may be real and it may not be real—it may be the product of a deranged mind. This character *may* be a time traveler coming back to find the virus, or he may just be an apocalyptic madman."

12 Monkeys utilizes plenty of SFX, particularly in its depiction of the future.

"This is an underground world, which has been done," says Gilliam. "We built sets, we worked inside disused power stations, like *Brazil.* We tried to make them look *different* than *Brazil,* and we actually used computer-generated backgrounds. We had to make an aboveground world of the future that's just populated by animals, and we had to make it winter. So, we've got Philadelphia, overgrown with vines, with snow everywhere, and buildings decayed and abandoned. There are lions, bears, and other animals roaming around."

Unlike some directors, Gilliam says he isn't afraid to work with real animals.

"Even though later on we've got some computer-generated giraffes, we had lions and a real bear when we were shooting in Philadelphia," says Gilliam. "It was outside City Hall, and we had a Kodiak bear called Doc."

Unfortunately, Doc was not a bear who took his direction well, he notes.

"At the end of the day, we were running late, and the sun was disappearing," says Gilliam. "He was brought out of his box, which was some ways down this arcade. Then, he decided to take about twenty minutes to walk up to the camera, as the sun was sinking rapidly. All we actually had to get him to do was rear up and roar at one point, and he *finally* did that! Animals are a pain in the ass, basically."

The director explains that Bruce Willis did not become involved with the film until after Gilliam had agreed to film it.

"To start with, they just had a script and me," says Gilliam. "The script was languishing. The studio was fairly nervously about it because of its different nature. I don't know exactly how Bruce got wind of it, but I heard that he was really keen. We had met on *Fisher King,* and I was quite intrigued with him, but he went off and did *Hudson Hawk*

instead. So, when he showed interest in this, we met and talked, and it was a go!"

In a scene reminiscent of Python, he required Christopher Plummer to act inside a body bag.

"I told him he could put that on his resume, 'Can act in a bag.' " He laughs. "His final shots are lying tied-up in a body bag, with a biohazard sticker across his eyes. When I looked at him there at the end in his last shot, he looked like he was having some sort of epiphany! Suddenly everything vanished, and he was very calm and happy lying there bound and blindfolded in a ody bag. I think all actors should have to do this at least some time in their lives!"

The *12 Monkeys* shooting process was rather challenging, even for the director of the beleaguered *The Adventures of Baron Munchausen.*

"This was a more complicated mixture," he says. "We had major superstars in the film and very difficult conditions to work in. It's a strangely imbalanced kind of film. Our budget was less than $30 million, so on one hand there were restrictions on what we were doing because we didn't have the money to do it the way one might with a bigger budget. On the other hand, we had some big stars who had to be treated a certain way, so it's very confusing sometimes for the crew to know what kind of film they're making.

"There were a lot of physical problems. We had to do all of these scenes in the winter in Philadelphia, and it *didn't* snow. We had to keep grinding up blocks of ice and spreading snow around the place, which became irritating beyond belief. It wasn't great, breathtaking visual effects, it was just trying to maintain continuity in the face of nature, which was refusing to cooperate!"

He admits that most of his movies manage to convey a deeper message.

"It's hard not to take advantage of the podium that a movie is, because I feel that there's a responsibility to not just entertain people, but to actually inform them and make them think, make them perceive things differently," he says. "It's not so much always a message, but at least it's trying to make people look at life and the world with fresh eyes."

12 Monkeys doesn't have a simple message that can be easily conveyed, he notes.

"It's not that kind of a movie," he says. "It's complex. It says a lot of different things, some of

them conflicting, but at least it demands that people become involved in it, and made to think. Those that don't want to work a bit are probably going to be disappointed. It's trying to *not* do what television does. It doesn't try to spoon-feed anybody. So maybe, the message is the medium, and the medium is a complex film that you've got to work at!"

12 Monkeys did well on video, in addition to its theatrical success.

"We made a video hit! When it came out in England, it was in the top ten for more than four months!" says Gilliam. "There was an article in *USA Today* about this extraordinary phenomenon, the fact that this thing was number three, then dropped down to number seven, then it would go up to number five, and it was just staying in there. It had turned out that because people seemed to love watching it again and again, and arguing over what it means or what it doesn't mean, or trying to catch us and find all the flaws in our logic—there have been Web sites developed around it. It did about $165 million around the world, and I think it was the seventeenth most successful film of 1995. So all in all, it's been a failure, because we wanted to make this little arty film that no one would see, and it was pure and unsullied by audiences—and we failed."

In recent years, Gilliam's name has been connected with a number of film projects which, for various reasons, have never gotten off the ground, everything from the film version of Alan Moore's comic book epic *Watchmen* ("I didn't think we were capable of solving the problem of how to reduce *Watchmen* to two hours, so I think I was actually *relieved* that we didn't have to do it!") to an adaptation of Mark Twain's *Connecticut Yankee in King Arthur's Court* ("It was one of those doors that open at a certain time, and I thought was interesting—I felt it had to do with American arrogance and its belief that technology can solve everybody's problems"). He even cowrote an adaptation of *Don Quixote* with Charles (*Brazil*) McKeown long before a similar film was offered to John Cleese ("For a script that was thrown together in about a month, it's brilliant!"); in recent years he began developing a script retelling the Minotaur legend.

Gilliam fought an uphill battle with U.S. film studios to fund *The Defective Detective,* his second collaboration with Richard (*Fisher King*) Lagravenese.

"It's about a middle-aged, cynical New York cop effective having a nervous breakdown and ending up in a children's fantasy world, where the rules are children's rules, not New York street rules," says Gilliam. "And he has to deal with this new world. But he has to sacrifice himself at the end for something that may be a better future—or it may not, and that really sticks in their craw."

Gilliam is taking an executive role in a sequel to *Time Bandits.*

"I'm the executive producer, the quality-control man," says Gilliam. "Our choice of director, David Garfath, was the operator on *Brazil* and *Time Bandits;* he's been doing commercials for several years and it's about time he got into features. Charles McKeown is writing it, Charles and I have been working on the script. Universal agreed to go the next stage on the development, so we'll see."

Among other potential future projects is *The Minotaur,* which he originally began with Michael

Terry Gilliam circa 1997. Comicitta photo from the Collection of Terry Gilliam, used by permission.

Palin (though Palin has since dropped out), and a Western!

"Larry McMurtry is writing a script based on his book *Anything for Billy,* which is about Billy the Kid, and I've been working on that as well," says Gilliam. "That would be an interesting one. It'd be a real change to do something like a Western. There's one side of me that wants to perfect the things I'm really good at, and there's another side of me that just wants to do something totally different and see where that leads."

Nowadays, Gilliam is probably as well known for his own movies as he is for his work with Python.

Gilliam says he doesn't really view himself as a fantasy director, despite the fantastic elements of his feature films, and is more interested in the juxtaposition of fantasy and the real world.

"I'm always playing with the borderline between what's perceived as fantasy and reality, and that's what intrigues me," says Gilliam. "Fantasy per se, and the way it's normally done, *doesn't.* Fantasy seems so often to be about escape, and I like the idea of dealing with how you maintain a fantasy life and still live in the real world. Both are equally necessary, and each can be as real as the other. Reality often seems more fantastic than what is considered fantasy, and vice versa. I tend to think in terms of imagination—not just what's immediately in front of you, but expanding upon that, either forwards, backwards, up, down, or in any direction. That's where the interesting area lies. I'm probably trying to define the line between fantasy and reality in what I do, or I'm trying to keep a balance between the two things."

He notes he isn't interested in most contemporary films.

"Everybody else is doing the twentieth century," Gilliam laughs. "I've always gone in the opposite way. If everybody's marching in one direction, I'll march in the opposite direction, just to see what's there. I think most contemporary films at the moment don't leap beyond cops and people shooting and car chases, but they're based in the limitations of the existing world. Leaping into another period is a way of abstracting. I'm trying to use the look and the feel and some of the ideas of another period as a way of looking at the contemporary world. That's why I've always en-joyed cartoons and puppet shows—they're forms of abstraction of the real world. They're not tied down by the world as seen and lived by most people, yet they can still comment on the real world."

Gilliam's primary interest remains with film directing, and he doesn't know whether he will remain in the Hollywood system or not.

"I'm just trying to make films," says Gilliam. "The thing I find interesting at the moment is that with *Defective Detective,* I kept saying that if I couldn't get that one off the ground, I'm going to turn my back on Hollywood and just work on smaller-budgeted things. It's pretty painful to even consider, because there's one side of me that just wants to put on screen extraordinary visuals that no one else can do, but they cost money, and with the kind of stories that I want to tell, I'm not certain how much I can get away with like this. *Brazil* was a rare thing—even *Munchausen* was rare. Hollywood is getting more and more timid right now, and what I find so frustrating is that having done two films within that system and made them a lot of money, that I'm still not able to get off the ground the things that I want to do . . . So, the other way of thinking about it then is reverting back and just working on lower budgeted things and staying away from Hollywood, because I find that I'm wasting a lot of my life trying to overcome that system."

The Python-turned-director knows how he wants to be remembered.

"As a guy who lived as long as he possibly could," laughs Gilliam. "I know what I'm going to put on my tombstone. 'He giggled in awe.' I was promoting *Munchausen* in Dallas on a radio call-in show. Some guy with a thick Texas accent said, 'I just gotta say, I saw that film and I giggled in awe!' And I thought, 'There's the perfect epitaph.' "

The Ministry?

Although *Brazil* was not released until 1985, Terry Gilliam had been planning it for many years. He had hoped to film it shortly after *Life of Brian* in 1978, but that was not to be. Unable to raise the money for such an ambitious project, he was instead forced to come up with a more commercial

movie. It was the enormous financial success of *Time Bandits* that gave him the power, influence, and reputation to write and direct 1985's *Brazil*.

It was seven years prior to that, however, that Gilliam first sat down to describe his plans for the film. In the top-floor studio of his home in Hampstead (on August 19, 1978), while preparing to leave in a month to shoot *Brian*, Gilliam talked about his dream project.

"At one point, I was going to call it *Brazil*, just because I like the song. We're going to use a lot of Latin American music, terrible 1940s Carmen Miranda stuff all through it, so it's all lush and romantic, even though it's very gray and grim. It was going to be called *Brazil*, but getting into the Ministry of Torture, we might just call it *The Ministry* and let it go at that," Gilliam explains.

At the time, he said, he was working on the story with Charles Alverson, his collaborator on *Jabberwocky*. Interestingly, his basic concepts seem to have remained much the same in the years from conception to final edit.

"I've been working off and on for the past year. It's a thing that floats around," Gilliam explains, "After I wrote it, I decided to get someone who is better at dialogue than I am—I'm terrible at dialogue and Chuck's very good, and we work well together. After I got Chuck in, we went through it and fiddled around, and we're ready to hand the treatment over and see if someone will give us the money to get on with it.

"At one point, I was going to say it takes place everywhere in the twentieth century—I'm not sure what that means, but it sounds right. It's a very odd film about someone who works at the Ministry of Torture, and leads an incredibly elaborate fantasy life at night. He blindly goes through his job all day long, without thinking of the consequences of being a small cog in this great machine, what it's all about; he maintains a job for eight hours a day, then goes home and lives his real life, which is amazingly adventurous in his dreams.

"He suddenly changes from being a cog in the system to one of the victims. He has to make a choice between living in reality, in fantasy, or in madness, and I won't say which choice he makes, because it's very odd. In the fantasy sequences, I'm trying to do what I did in the animation, but with live action—real mind-blowing stuff, really amazing things.

"I'm not sure how I'm going to do it yet, but I'll probably combine models, animation, and live action to produce the fantasy images. The real world where these horrible things are happening is a very gray place, and most of the horrifying aspects of it all, like the torture, are never seen—we see or hear the results, but never any of the nastiness. People's attitudes in the film are like the attitudes now: if they don't see it, it's not happening; everyone's getting along with shopping."

The sound effects employed many of the same methods Gilliam had originally considered. In 1977, Gilliam, as a director, was more worried about maintaining the proper balance between fantasy and reality (in fact, early drafts contain longer, more elaborate flights into fantasy, but those were trimmed significantly for budgetary reasons).

"When we got done working one day, Chuck said 'I think we've got a horror film on our hands here.' On one hand, the fantasies are really a good adventure, but the other stuff is fairly strong. I don't know whether I can pull off this odd balance. People are going to come to see the fantasy sequences, and they're going to be surprised by all this other stuff, because it's probably more serious than they expected. It's going to be a fine line. I still haven't worked out where to draw the line between a film that's saying something, and a film that's entertaining."

The basic concept for the film arose when Gilliam watched an oil refinery spewing forth fire and smoke near the seaside, and the image clicked in his mind. "The city will look just like an oil refinery at night, all metal and hard and gray. We might just move into a steel refinery and turn it into a city! We're going to re-create the whole world—it's almost like a science fiction film, in a way.

"The public transportation is like a series of cages, and people are shuffled around like animals. Nobody minds it, because that's just how things are," Gilliam explains, and says his hero's home is automated. "His flat is ultra-efficient—he pushes buttons, and his breakfast comes up. It's all mechanized."

Although some concepts were changed—the public transport in cages didn't survive, for example—most of the images Gilliam developed made it into *Brazil* in one form or another, including the memorable sequences involving the repairmen played by Bob Hoskins and Robert DeNiro.

"The room is very barren-looking, but when things start going wrong, the repairmen come and start pulling wall panels off. It looks like guts behind the wall, except it's all mechanical. It's like taking a car apart, and the whole room gets taken over by all the tubes and stuff behind the walls. It would be amazing if we could do it, but I'm not sure if anyone's actually going to give me any money."

The battle for the money took almost seven years, and then Gilliam had to fight another battle with Universal to release the film his way. But the *Brazil* he ended up with was remarkably similar to the story he visualized long before.

Eric Idle

Born at Harton Hospital, South Shields, on March 29, 1943, Eric Idle lived in Oldham and Wallasey, before being sent to boarding school (Royal School Wolverhampton) in 1952. Deciding to major in English, he went to Pembroke College, Cambridge, in 1962, and was voted into the Footlights the following March, where he met upper-classmen John Cleese and Graham Chapman. It was in September of that year, while performing in the Footlights Review at the Edinburgh Festival, that he met Terry Jones and Michael Palin, who were performing in the rival Oxford Review.

Elected president of the Footlights in 1964 (his first act was to initiate a bill allowing women to join), he appeared in their revue *My Girl Herbert,* touring with it in 1965. After graduating that year, he performed some cabaret with John Cameron at the Blue Angel, was featured in the Richard Eyre production of *Oh, What a Lovely War* in Leicester, and

Receiving the last touches as King Otto, in a sequence all but removed from the final version of Brian; *Idle plays the leader of a crack suicide squad that pledges their support to an unwilling Brian. Photo copyright KHJ.*

spent part of the Christmas season in the farce *One For the Pot,* also in Leicester.

His writing career began to blossom in 1966. He wrote for many of his old Footlights colleagues on BBC Radio's *I'm Sorry, I'll Read That Again;* he was recruited by David Frost to pen "clever ad libs" for *The Frost Report,* and wrote for Ronnie Corbett's series *No, That's Me Over Here.*

In 1967, Idle joined Palin and Jones for two seasons of *Do Not Adjust Your Set,* where he met and befriended Terry Gilliam. Between the two series, he and Gilliam both appeared on *We Have Ways of Making You Laugh,* notable for Gilliam's very first animation. When Idle went back for the second series of *DNAYS,* he brought Gilliam back to do cartoons for them.

The year 1969 brought two very big changes to Idle's life with the advent of *Monty Python's Flying Circus,* and Idle's marriage to Lyn Ashley on July seventh (during the first week of Python filming).

He appeared in all the Python TV shows, films, and stage shows, and was also principally responsible for putting together the Python books as well.

As the TV series drifted to a close, he was eager to begin his own projects. Idle wrote his first novel, *Hello, Sailor,* which was published in 1975.

Although the writing itself came very quickly, it was several years before the results saw print.

"I wrote *Hello, Sailor* in 1970, and it was published in 1975. It took a long time to get out. A scurrilous book," he laughs. "I nearly got it published right away toward the beginning. There was this publisher that was really keen to publish it, and I went to their office, and they said 'We'd like to make you an offer, but we have to wait until the one o'clock from Chepstow' [the racetrack]. He said 'Do you mind coming across to the pub?' We went across to the pub, and we had a drink, and he's watching this race, knuckles gripped on the table, and he's going 'Aarghhh!'

"The horse came in, and he went 'Right, now, I'm prepared to make you an offer,' " Idle laughs. "I thought 'Hang on a minute—if their entire business was on this horse, tomorrow the offer could just as easily be rescinded.' I decided not to go with them."

When it was eventually published, it ended up doing well, Idle recalls happily. "It's always sweet when a book's published. It didn't do big in hardback, but it did over 20,000 in paperback, which in those days was quite a lot for a first novel."

In 1975 and 1976, BBC 2 broadcast two six-show series of *Rutland Weekend Television,* purporting to be Britain's smallest, cheapest independent TV station. It was written by Idle and included Neil Innes, who did much of the music. A comedy album, *The Rutland Weekend Songbook,* and *The Rutland Dirty Weekend Book* both resulted.

Idle had decided to bow out of Monty Python after the fourth series of six shows, and the others reluctantly agreed. He was ready to strike out on his own, and a radio project he had been working on during *Python* gave him an idea for a TV series.

"I'd done a radio show somewhere in the middle of *Python,*" says Idle. "There were four radio stations in England, so I did a show called *Radio Five.* Now there *is* a Radio Five, but in those days, that was a joke. I used to come on to Radio One, which was the pop music station, about as hip as Dick Clark, and do an hour's show a week. I had lots of different voices which I'd prerecord, with rock music playing in between. It would take me hours—it would take me ten hours to record one hour's worth of material, because I had to play all of the voices, and in those days the technology was really primitive, and we didn't have anything like dubbing. If you were doing both voices in a sketch, you had to lay all that voice down and time yourself back and forth.

"That was what sort of set me thinking about independent stations. So, *Rutland Weekend Television* seemed to be a good takeoff on it. *Rutland Weekend Television* was actually a title suggested by John Cleese. I paid him a pound for it. I'd been doing one or two appearances on what was called *Up Sunday,* a late-night Sunday satire show on BBC-2, which was put on not by the Light Entertainment Department but by Presentation, which would just make announcements and say 'Here on BBC-2 . . .' "

Rutland Weekend Television was done on an extremely tight budget, and Idle was forced to make do with what they had available. Although he wrote all the scripts himself, Neil Innes was along to perform original music in each show, most of it comedic, and both of them struggled with the budget offered them by the Presentation Department.

"We did the only comedy show Presentation's ever done, and we did it in a *tiny* little studio about the size of the weather forecast studio next door on the fourth floor of the BBC. We did a series for about 30,000 quid," Idle laughs. "It shows a bit, but it's really very ingenious if you know how little was spent on it. We'd run on tape, there was never an audience participating. [There are] some really very respectable sketches.

"The second series was slightly difficult, we went back and discovered that they'd put us in a studio in Bristol! Neil Innes would do a song or two a week, and he'd be in the sketches. It was pretending to be a TV station, and we had dramas and documentaries. It seems to have gotten quite a cult following now. I hear a lot about it more and more these days, but because there was no audience laughter, I never quite knew how funny it was, I could never tell, and now there's all these pressures to rerelease it."

Unlike *Fawlty Towers* and *Ripping Yarns, Rutland Weekend Television* was never shown on American television or available on videocassette.

Eric Idle, mid-'70s. Photographed by John Sims for Python Productions, used by permission.

wonderful moment where I keep trying to say 'Our special guest, George Harrison,' and he keeps saying no, he wants to sing a pirate song. 'No, no, we want you to be George Harrison, come on,' and so right at the end of the show 'And now, ladies and gentlemen, George Harrison,' and he comes on with his white things, his Bangla Desh robes, and plays [intro to *My Sweet Lord*] [sings] 'I want to be a pirate, a pirate's life for me, all my friends are pirates and we sail the BBC. I've got a Jolly Roger, it's black and wide and vast, so get out of your skull and crossbones and I'll run it up your mast,' and we go 'Stop, stop!'

"I'm glad to say that's an Idle-Harrison composition and it's actually in *Songs by George Harrison,* the illustrated book. 'The Pirate Song.' It's a very funny gag, because you just do not expect him to launch into—he looks *so good,* you know, he looks the same, with the full band and everything. It's a very good gag. . . ."

George Harrison's association with Monty Python dates back many years. He was a fan of the show almost from the start, and claims Python helped to get him through some rough times around the breakup of the Beatles.

Harrison hadn't actually met any of the Pythons until 1975, however, when Eric Idle and Terry Gilliam flew to Los Angeles to promote *Monty Python and the Holy Grail.*

"I met George backstage at the Directors Guild in L.A., when we screened *Holy Grail,*" recalls Idle. "Terry Gilliam and I came over to promote the film. That's when we met, and we became very, very friendly and palled around for months."

Before the days of MTV, many performers used to make short films to promote their singles and albums. Harrison was just finishing up his 33 1/3 album, and asked his new friend to film a couple of the songs.

"This was really long before people did videos. The Beatles always made films, so George said 'Come on, let's make a couple of films,' so I did. I organized and directed each—it was about three days' shooting. They're quite sweet, actually— *Crackerbox* is still a little manic, because we were on a tight budget. We brought all the *Rutland Weekend* people in and used everybody. I quite like *True Love*—it's very sweet," remarks Idle, who brought the films with him when he hosted *Saturday Night Live.*

"It's never run in the States because I always had the American rights," he explains. "They wouldn't pay me any money, so I insisted I had the American rights, and I wouldn't let them use it."

Between the two series, Idle did a *Christmas with Rutland Weekend Television* special that featured a friend he had made earlier in the year—George Harrison.

"There's a *terrific* gag in that Christmas special. We had a wonderful time, we'd never been so legless doing that show. We were pissed through most of it. It's not that funny a show, but there's a

Although the short films for George Harrison were technically his first directing credits, Idle explains that he essentially served as a director for *Rutland Weekend Television.*

"When I was doing *Rutland,* I directed virtually everything," he reveals. "I mean, I was in charge of everything. I'd say 'Put the camera over here,' and I used to have to edit it all. There were people helping in the studio and all that thing, but the responsibility of what's on was mine, and I had the pressure of all that."

The personal and professional relationship between the Beatle and the Python continued from that point, and Idle contributed Pepperpot voices for some of Harrison's music, most notably the hit single "This Song" (which deals with the lawsuit filed against Harrison over "My Sweet Lord") on the 33 1/3 album; between verses, Eric screeches "Could be 'Sugar Pie Honey Bunch' " "No, sounds like 'Rescue Me!' "

"I did a voice on *Extra Texture* too. That's when I met him, he was mixing *Extra Texture* in L.A. with Tom Scott," he recalls. "I can't remember what I did—some Pepperpot voice. I think I also did the radio ads for *Extra Texture* in England, because it was 'Onothimagain.' "

Harrison even turned up at the City Center in New York for the Python stage show; dressed as a Mountie, he joined the group onstage for "The Lumberjack Song" and was virtually unrecognized by the audience. Harrison appeared on the *Rutland Weekend Television* Christmas special, and in 1977, Idle filmed *The Rutles,* which included an appearance by Harrison.

Their collaboration continued throughout the years, most notably when Harrison helped organize Handmade Films in order to make *Life of Brian.* The first Traveling Wilburys album has liner notes written by Michael Palin, while Eric Idle wrote the notes for their second album (*Volume Three*).

Shortly after *The Rutles,* however, Idle did the last of his short music films. Idle and Rikki Fataar, as "Dirk and Stig" of the Rutles, released a single with "Ging Gang Goolie" and "Mr. Sheene." Although Harrison wasn't directly involved, the promo film was in the spirit of Idle's 33 1/3 films.

"We shot at Ringo's, which used to be Lennon's old house at Tittenhurst. We had everybody dressed up as Boy Scouts, and all the girls were wearing Brownie costumes with suspender belts—garter belts to you. Nowadays that would be sexism. Then it was just sex. It was great. The guys said it was the best day's filming they'd *ever had,*" Idle recalls with a laugh. "So there were three of those little films—that one was for Ringo Records."

Eric Idle was the first Python to appear on *Saturday Night Live,* and even though the show led to him meeting his wife, Tania, (whom he married in 1981) and the filming of *The Rutles: All You Need Is Cash,* he also found it frustrating at times.

The cast of *SNL* were Python fans even before *Saturday Night Live* had been created. "When we first saw Belushi doing a show and we came backstage, it was really creepy to Gilliam and I, because he practically sat at our feet." Idle laughs, recalling that it was probably around the time they were promoting *Monty Python and the Holy Grail,* in spring of 1975. "He was doing a show with—Bill Murray, I think, and Gilda was in it."

Since the *SNL* crew were fans of Python, it wasn't surprising that they wanted to work with the group members. Cleese had no interest in doing live TV at such a frantic pace, and for Eric Idle and Michael Palin, who each hosted several shows, it was an experience that was alternately rewarding and frustrating.

Idle's first show was at the beginning of the second series of *Saturday Night Live,* though he had actually met the group the previous spring. "I was a friend of Paul Simon and when we were in New York, he introduced me to all of the *Saturday Night Live* people," he explains. "We were doing the City Center, and they all came along to the opening party that Clive Davis threw somewhere or another. . . . I met Lorne there, and Chevy [Chase], and [John] Belushi, and [Dan] Ackroyd. And then after our show on Saturday night, I think I went and watched [their show] from the floor—I came in on them doing the show live. They still had the Muppets on in those days."

His first show may have been an adjustment for Eric, but he was very well received by the cast and the audience. "Chevy got injured the week before. I said we'd have to visit him once during the show, because he did a [Gerald] Ford fall and injured himself the week before I hosted, and Penny Marshall and I visited him in his apartment, lying in bed. I don't remember how he injured himself—

I think he did one of those terrific tumbles off a podium, I think. So, he was lying in bed, and I used to go to visit him."

It didn't take long for Idle to realize the level of priorities of *SNL,* as established by producer Lorne Michaels.

"The show is organized around Lorne's dinner schedule. When I used to do the series, Lorne said 'Here's how the show's going to be this week. Monday, we're having dinner with Meryl Streep. Tuesday, we're going to have dinner with—' and it was all names," he laughs.

"It's because he doesn't get up until two, and then they work late at night, after his dinner, so he likes to think he's contributing to the writing by going out to dinner with celebrities," Idle says with a laugh. "The show is actually based on a comfortable life-style for Lorne Michaels—that's the premise of the show."

Eric's second appearance on the show was as one of a number of guests on a special broadcast live from the Mardi Gras in New Orleans, and he says he was one of the few performers who truly enjoyed himself.

"That was fun. I was getting smarter on Lorne Michaels then, realizing that basically, he goes to dinner. We went down to Mardi Gras to try to do a live show, which is a brave thing—insane, but brave. He tried to get me to host the Mardi Gras Ball with all drag—the drag ball—and I thought 'No way am I going to stand here improvising under these circumstances!'

"So, I wrote myself a totally isolated sketch— one of my favorite sketches, one of the best things I ever did. I did it from a deserted street, saying 'Only minutes ago, there were thousands of people here, all dancing and singing and having a great time, only a few moments ago, just before you came here. . . .' It's about a guy desperately trying to fill in on TV. You would cut to the only part of the party that's not happening.

"And it was very strange, because when they did it, they had a live audience in a big building where Randy Newman and the orchestra were, and I had them in my ear. It was a fabulous way to do location filming, because I said the first line, and there was this terrific 'Wahhh' in my ear of the audience laughing, so I slowed the whole thing down. I could pace it, so where I normally would have done it as a sort of film piece, much faster, I could pace it to their laughs, which I could hear in my ear. That was good fun," Idle recalls.

"I was the only person who had a good time. They got Penny Marshall to do the thing I was asked to do. I've got it on video—it was a classic painful moment. She's sitting there—she was supposed to host it with Cindy Williams—and the camera comes up live. She's sitting there reading, and they tell her she's on. She's like 'I'm on? Now?' I mean, they did exactly my nightmare of what would happen, and it happened, and she was left desperate, without Cindy, trying to stumble through a piece—because it was a chaotic show.

"The whole point was, there was this parade, and Buck Henry and Jane Curtin were hosting it, and they always said 'Well, if anything happens, we'll just cut to the parade.' During the entire two hours of the show, the parade *didn't arrive.* The entire parade didn't show up!" he laughs. "So, that was chaos. But it was fun. The only way you could get to any location was by being on the back of police motorbikes, Harleys, so I just remember guys in drag, and these police getting everybody from set to set, all these actors in makeup and costumes. It was really bizarre."

By the time he did his last show in 1979, Idle says the show had become chaos. To make matters worse, he had fallen ill late that week, and by airtime he had a 102-degree fever.

"I'd lost my voice, I had to save my voice all the time. That was chaos. They'd got Dylan on— Dylan had recently become a Christian, so that freaked people out, ethnically. That show was always more hype than humor, in my opinion," he laughs. "They had Dylan on, and there was this huge attitude—you couldn't focus on writing comedy. I remember realizing I wasn't very well, and then I remember in the afternoon, about three o'clock, realizing that nobody was going to write the monologue—there was not going to be a monologue! So, I just grabbed a couple of people, and we just improvised stretcher impersonations. I had to go on there, and I had nothing—that's when I realized it wasn't as professional a show as one would have enjoyed."

It was a very different show from Python, different from the way they had been used to working in general. Although they were experienced in theater, performing on live television was another matter, particularly on a show that was put together in less than a week. The Pythons were very exacting in their scriptwriting, taking the time to perfect each line, whereas *SNL* was constantly changing sketches up until air time.

"There was a lot of hanging around at *Saturday Night Live,* and then chaos. It was just quite different," Idle relates. "They seemed to be proud of working very late hours, which of course was fun, you didn't have to get into the office [early].

"But Python worked office hours. By and large, it's more efficient to work nine till five, get some stuff done and rewrite it, and then look at it and look at it. They sort of pride themselves on doing a very bad dress and trying to pull together a very average show for air. It seemed like a triumph, but only because you'd just done a terrible dress [rehearsal]!"

Despite the circumstances under which it was created, Idle says that he was able to do some successful writing for the show.

"They never rewrote a word. I never understood the point in trying to write it late on Tuesday night, because it's not all that topical. I mean, some bits were good. I did a couple of films with Gary Weis. The first one we did was 'Drag Racing' which I wrote. That's the other thing—I wrote tons of their stuff, and I didn't even get a writing credit," Idle laughs.

" 'Drag Racing,' was me and Dan Ackroyd at Flatbush Airport, racing down in drag. The second one I did with Gary was 'Body Language,' which was another little film I wrote for them. So, I worked with him twice. And then Lorne suggested that he co-direct 'The Rutles' with me, which was a good move.

"There are some very good bits. There's no question that Ackroyd was brilliant, and Chevy, when he was on, was brilliant. Belushi was a phenomenal performer, and Murray too, and Gilda—I mean, they were great performers. But if you're talking about writing, they went about it in a very bizarre and difficult way. On the other hand, it is qualitatively different from the rest of American television."

Despite disappointments with certain aspects of the show, Idle has some favorite moments. "I liked Nixon/Ford, which I also wrote with Danny. And I thought 'Body Language' was a good film. It was very hard to get things very funny. It was always an uphill struggle, and there was always an underlying tension and chaos and the girls were upset because of this and that reason, they didn't have enough material—there was always a whole underlying subtext which I never got, coming from English show business," he laughs. " 'This is our show, you know.' And if you ever suggested 'Well, maybe we should do some new characters, instead of just sticking to the old ones,' they'd get very shirty. 'Well, we do it this way!' 'Oh, excuse me.' "

One of his greatest successes also stemmed from *SNL*. Idle and Neil Innes had parodied the Beatles in a brief film clip and song, and when Idle hosted *Saturday Night Live* on October 2, 1976, he showed the "Rutles" clip, and left to do a Canadian publicity tour for the book (he vowed at the time it would be his last publicity tour). He then spent Christmas in Barbados with *SNL* producer Lorne Michaels, who persuaded him to do a full-length Rutles TV film for NBC. Idle began writing in New York and, the following February, appeared on a *Saturday Night Live* prime-time special from the Mardi Gras in New Orleans. Idle hosted once again on April 23, with Innes as musical guest (performing the very Lennon-like "Cheese and Onions"). After great ratings, all was "go" for the Rutles.

Innes wrote nineteen "new" Rutles hits for the soundtrack album, Mick Jagger and Paul Simon were interviewed on the influence of the Rutles, and Idle had his appendix removed at Arab Hospital in St. John's Wood, London. The final script was completed in July, and filming began later that month in London, Liverpool, and New York. Innes recorded his songs in two weeks, while the editing took three months.

The result was an incredibly accurate parody of the Beatles, with Innes's uncanny music echoing all the phases of their careers. The cast included Dan Ackroyd, John Belushi, Bianca Jagger, Bill Murray, Michael Palin, Gilda Radner, and George Harrison as an interviewer. First broadcast on NBC on March 22, 1978, ratings for *All You Need Is Cash* were disappointing, but it was roundly praised as an artistic triumph.

Idles's talents are spread among film, books, and records, but his strongest interest has been in writing. He has been quite prolific, but admits a reluctance to go through the politicking necessary to get his scripts produced.

Idle even wrote a stage play that was produced in London's West End, which he recalls as a mostly

enjoyable experience. He notes, however, that although he had always wanted to write a play, *Pass the Butler* wasn't necessarily intended for that form; he says he came up with the story and wrote it in France in 1979 after determining that it worked best as a play.

"All I attempt to do is have ideas, and then I try to slot them into what is the best format for the idea. Some things are film ideas, some things are play ideas, and this was clearly a play idea," he explains.

"I wrote it when I was in a little tin shack in the woods. We were just going away for two weeks, and my wife said 'Well, why don't you read me the play, as far as you've gotten?' So I brought it down and I read it to her. The tin shack burned down three days later, there was a tremendous fire that totally destroyed everything," he laughs. "So, she saved it!"

He says he loved the whole experience, even though he wasn't as closely involved with the production as he would have liked to be when it ran in London.

"Well, I was not involved very much in the West End production, because we were in the West Indies writing *Meaning of Life* at that stage, but I certainly was on the [initial] tour. We started in Warwick, and went into Cambridge, and each place I went I would tape it, and come back and study it and listen to what the audiences were doing, and cut things and move them around. It played very well with an audience.

"I came back in time for the first night [of the West End production], and it was a very strange first night. I mean, they tensed up for the first time, and it shows how artificial the first night is. You take what is really going well in front of an audience, and then you take half the seats and stalls out and give them to critics and their dates. You've got all the tension, and put all of the friends and relatives and aunts and uncles in the dress circle, and you have a really strange experience. They tensed up.

"Funny play. It goes on all the time, I get royalties from all over the world. It's the longest-running play in Sweden, and Oslo had two productions of it on in three years, or something strange like that. It's very big in Scandinavia."

Idle also appeared on stage, to very good reviews, in a London production of *The Mikado* in 1986, directed by Jonathan Miller; it was so successful it was even brought to Houston for a short run.

Jonathan Miller, of *Beyond the Fringe* fame, transferred his acclaimed, highly successful production of *The Mikado* from Japan to 1920s England. After a successful run in the fall, it was revived again the following spring in London, and the production was also presented in Los Angeles (with Dudley Moore as Ko-Ko) and in Houston (with Idle as Ko-Ko again).

Eric Idle says his involvement began when he got a phone call from Miller. "He called me up in France and said 'I want you to be in *The Mikado*.' I said 'What are you going to do?' and he said 'I'm going to get rid of all that Japanese nonsense, for a start.' I said 'I've got to see this, I want to be a part of this.'

"I love Jonathan. When I first went to London in 1962, I went to see *Beyond the Fringe*. I rolled around and nearly died. I had never seen anything so funny. Still really haven't laughed as much in the theater. Jonathan Miller, Alan Bennett, Peter Cook and Dudley Moore—I decided that I wanted to do comedy after that. I bought the record and learned all their routines. They were GREAT," enthuses Idle.

The Mikado was not the first time he had worked with Miller, however.

"I was in Jonathan's *Alice in Wonderland* in 1966—it was like the second gig I did. The first was a Ken Russell film called *Isadora,* where I played the part of Death's chauffeur and drowned the children in the Seine, accidentally. A true story—that was the Ken Russell film. Then I was in *Alice*. Peter Sellers was in it, every theatrical knight in the world was in it, that was the BBC's classic little black-and-white piece. So, I always wanted to work with Jonathan, I always loved him, and the experience was great. I mean, he's such fun, and he's so interesting and entertaining."

One of Idle's biggest worries was the singing involved with the part. "Jonathan said 'Would you mind coming and singing, so you can prove to us you can sing, because we were a little bit nervous offering you a part in this opera . . .' So, I flew in and stood on the stage of the Coliseum, which is the largest theater in London, I think a two-thousand seater, and they ran me through a few of the songs. Of course, it was a doddle," he laughs.

"It was really fun, because I clearly wasn't an opera singer. I had to rehearse the whole show with the opera company, but they were very supportive. It was interesting, because I was always a bit scared of singing publicly, or at least apprehensive, but I realized quite early on that they were far more apprehensive about speaking, because they would 'Tend To Speak Like This [loud, overenunciated], If You're Not Careful, Singers!' So, when I realized that, it was fun. Then it just got more and more fun, and progressively sillier, and it was a terrific production. It looked great."

Before getting involved with the production, Idle says he was "sort of" a Gilbert and Sullivan fan, and had even tried to film his own Gilbert and Sullivan operetta in the early 1980s. "I like a lot of what they do. I like a lot of Gilbert's writing, he's very clever, and I love Sullivan's tunes, like everybody else. I tried to do a film of *The Pirates of Penzance*. I did a screenplay at one stage, after *The Rutles,* and I wanted to do it very much live action. I went down to Penzance—there's a beautiful castle there that he'd obviously written it for, and I wanted to make a sort of Victorian film of it. I tried to get that going and nobody wanted to do that.

"Of course, suddenly there was the Joe Papp production [on Broadway], suddenly I had the screenplay. [Producer] Ed Pressman bought it. He loved it and wanted to make it, and then he decided he wanted Papp. He was in a terrible, silly bind because he couldn't shoot anything on location, because I'd gotten all the locations. He shot the stage version on a sound stage, which is the worst of all possible worlds. He made a big mistake, it was a big error.

"He should have done my screenplay and their cast, because I loved Kevin Kline playing the Pirate King, he's terrific—I'd wanted Albert Finney or Michael Caine to play this part; in my version, Bette Midler was to be the Pirate Queen. I went to the very Victorian, because Victorian paintings are Cinemascope—they take that shape, all big and wide, and I wanted to do that, like it was done by the pre-Raphaelites and various Victorian painters, and the beginnings of photography. So, I'd gone into it quite in depth, and I think Pressman made a mistake—he admitted to me afterward that he did, anyway. It was very nice of him to say. Well, you never know—mine might have been a flop, too."

One of his more interesting diversions—not unlike Palin's and Jones's children's books—was the result of his friendship with Shelley Duvall, the producer of Showtime's *Fairy Tale Theatre.* For her, Idle directed Robin Williams and Teri Garr in his version of "The Frog Prince" in 1983, and three years later starred in the title role of "The Pied Piper of Hamelin."

When Shelley Duvall was organizing her *Faerie Tale Theatre,* she phoned her friend Eric Idle to write and direct the very first program, *The Frog Prince.*

"Well, Shelley came to me and said 'I'm doing *Faerie Tale Theatre'*—it was the very first one," notes Idle. "She said 'Would you write it and direct it?' The cast was Robin Williams and Teri Garr, and that was such a lovely cast that I wrote it quite effortlessly. It was quite easy to write. Then I went over and directed it.

"And it was fun, really, putting Robin in a mask and making him use body language. I think he often has problems with what to do with his face—men who are very verbal and physical often have trouble with the face. We put Robin in a mask and he was wonderful as the Frog, he was really great. And Teri Garr was just very funny.

"It was one of those things I just had to roll up my sleeves and get on with—it was a bit like doing *Rutland Weekend Television,* you know—suddenly everything's at a standstill, and I'm watching, trying to get this thing together, and I went [clap!] 'Come on, let's go!' and I got cameras and grabbed people—it's television, and I know about television from about fifteen or twenty years. It was fun. And really, I ought to be receiving royalties ever since, because *I did the pilot,"* he laughs. "*The Frog Prince* won an Ace Award for me and the first of a million for Shelley Duvall."

Despite the Ace Award, Idle didn't appear on-camera in a *Faerie Tale Theatre* production until three years later, in *The Pied Piper.* David Bowie was slated to star in the title role for Duvall, when fate stepped in.

"Shelley called me up—it was very funny, an odd experience. I was having dinner with Bowie, and I said 'So you're about to go and do *The Pied Piper* with Shelley,' and he said 'No, I'm not going to do it, I've got some songs to write.' I got home that night, and there was a weepy message on the answering machine from Shelley saying 'Can you come over? There's been a disaster! David's can-

celed! Can you please come and be the Pied Piper?' I always used to be a sucker for show business, help 'em out in a crisis—I've learned better now. So, I flew, almost within twenty-four hours, because it was all set in Toronto—they'd set it all up there for David's tax purposes," explains Idle.

"I remember the dressers being terribly disappointed, because they'd designed this special jock strap for David that they were hoping to lace him into. I said [deep voice] 'I'll put that on, thank you very much,' " he laughs. "Anyway, it was fun. It was directed by Nicholas Meyer, we became good friends. In performances, I thought it my Richard IVth!"

Eric has been much in demand as an actor for a variety of films, from Terry Gilliam's *Adventures of Baron Munchausen* and Graham Chapman's *Yellowbeard* to Steven Spielberg's *Casper the Friendly Ghost.*

He appeared as a hapless, ever-polite English tourist in *National Lampoon's European Vacation.*

Although the sequel to *National Lampoon's Vacation* was generally considered disappointing, Eric Idle has a few nice moments with his role. The filming itself proved to be even more memorable, however, and directly contributed to his lack of dialogue during his final scene.

"I'd met Chevy when he'd injured himself way back. I did a day in London right at the beginning of the film and it went quite well, and then I went to Rome for a two- or three-day shoot, and we actually did a whole fountain scene in Frascati. Actually, Frascati doesn't have a fountain in the main square—the film built one," explains Idle.

"I eventually ended up living in that town during *Munchausen.* I just remember one memorable party with Keith Richard in Rome. I was trying to be very good, because I was filming the next day, and he said 'Come on, sing, Eric, come and sing.' I sang *all night,* 'cause I had finished my talking part. Chevy comes to me the next day—I think it was the day after, actually, because I'd lost my voice totally, because we'd sang all night," he laughs. "A real good ding-dong! And then Chevy comes up and says 'All right, I've rewritten the scene, and this is what you say—' And I went '[raspy, inaudible sound]' So, I don't speak in the last scene there, I just flounder about in the water."

After *European Vacation,* Idle did some work on another possible sequel to be set in Australia, though it was never filmed. "It's a little-known fact that I wrote a *Vacation* for Chevy—*Vacation Down Under,*" reveals Idle. "We spent some time working together on it. It had some nice shark gags, but I can't pretend it was in any way finished...."

One of his finest starring roles was in a 1989 production for Handmade Films. *Nuns on the Run* was strictly an acting job for Eric Idle, but proved to be his biggest film success in many years. He became involved with it through old friend Jonathan Lynn, and even though the Pythons' own film company, Prominent Features, didn't produce it, Idle still quickly agreed to be in it.

"Johnny Lynn came to me with it and asked me to produce it through Prominent. I tried to get it done through Prominent, but we didn't have our deal in place. So then Handmade picked it up while I was in Cannes. I was walking down the Croisette and I came face to face with Denis O'Brien, and he said 'I really want to do *Nuns on the Run*—what do you think?' He took me out to dinner, and we had a three-minute business meeting, and he said 'Will you do it? Will you be in it?' and I said 'Yes.' He said 'In that case, it's a movie.' So we did it, and that is truly the magic of cinema, *Nuns on the Run,* and the magic is that we took [in] three-and-a-half million pounds, and not a single penny went into my pocket! And that was just in England," declares Idle.

Although dissatisfied with the financial aspects, Idle says he enjoyed everything else about *Nuns on the Run.*

"A wonderful experience. I know Johnny Lynn, he directed my play, we were lads at Cambridge together, and we auditioned for the Footlights together with a script I wrote in 1963. He did *Yes, Minister!* and all that—he's wonderful," Idle notes, and says Lynn's intended cast was slightly different from the final result.

"He wanted me and Mike [Palin] to play it, and Mike was still trying to do *American Friends* at that time. So, I suggested Robbie Coltrane. We got Robbie, and Robbie's wonderful. He's fabulous—it was one of those great experiences, like 'The Rutles' was a great experience. I really had a great time. It was the right team, all together, no shitty people intervening and trying to say 'This is the way it should be done.'

"So, it was good fun. Then it went to Fox, and a very good man runs Fox, whose name escapes me—I must have show business Alzheimer's dis-

ease, I can't think of his name. Joe Roth. He loved it—still in love with it. He said it just needed a new ending, so he gave us another $500,000 to shoot a new ending and tighten it up, which was what it needed. They were really hoping for big things in America, and it didn't happen, and I felt rather sorry for him. But it did happen everywhere else—it happened in Europe, it was big in England, the video was big. It was nice, but they didn't make a killing in the States like they wanted to do."

The original ending for *Nuns on the Run* was actually more quiet and unexciting, notes Idle, before they were able to reshoot it. "We just left on a boat, and stood on the deck, and it was just like a nothing end. So, Jonathan Lynn, the writer, wrote much funnier stuff. I mean, it's nice to come back and write new stuff for a film when you get to do it. It's a good idea, it helps you a lot. 'I wish I'd done that scene.' And we did another of the love scenes, we retook, we did about three or four days more filming, and it really helped it."

Although they meant to promote *Nuns on the Run* well, Idle says they made mistakes in America.

"It was on the back of every bus, and they did a big television campaign, and they didn't open it wide until three weeks later. The American attention span is twenty minutes, and you've got to be on in the cinema if you're going to promote wide and spend all that money—it has to be there the next day. Otherwise, there's so much else intervening. So, I thought they didn't promote it very well, I thought they got it confused.

"They kept saying they wanted to do it like *Wanda,* put it in small theaters and build word of mouth—and then they didn't," he laughs. "They got confused and caught between two marketing plans. But, that being said, I think they never totally achieved it with that film, because Americans ultimately only want to see Americans in films—how can you blame them? So, you've got to have Americans in comedies. Python is only cult over there. You've got to make American films to be successful in America.

"It's a sweet film," sums up Idle. "One day I hope to get paid for it!"

Another lead role was shot for the father-son team of Robert Downey Jr. and Sr. Although the film was unreleased for over two years—and eventually premiered on Cinemax in America—Eric Idle is rather proud of his work in *Too Much Sun.*

"I like my character, who is a gay guy who has to jump on women. That, essentially, is a comedy idea. What you need is to bring the ideas into collision, but not extend it and go off into other little areas that he tended to ramble off in. You've got to face all the problems, and bring them in and try to address them honestly, and address them in the comedic fashion—which is essentially funny. I mean, how do two gay couples have a baby? It's almost a Shakespearean idea, but it needs far more skill on the text, and that, ultimately, is where it was just a drag. I made that film for nothing—we ended up shooting eighteen-hour days," Idle remarks.

Too Much Sun appealed to him initially because of the opportunity to play an American and to work with his friend Jon Lovitz.

"I quite liked Sonny, the character I chose, and I also wanted to play an American. That, for me, was the key thing—I wanted to see if I could play an American. It's easier to play a gay American, because they're more stereotyped in the gay roles, because they're sort of playing a role anyway, which is forced on them by society or whatever," he says. "It's easier to latch onto as an actor, because it's a slight parody of behavior anyway, so it's easier to act. It's much more extravagant and outrageous, and therefore interesting as an acting attempt.

"So, I enjoyed the moments of acting Sonny—it was interesting to me. I don't think it was entirely wasted from my point of life. It was certainly wasted financially," he laughs. "And frustrating in a comedy sense. It was typical Hollywood. They call up and say 'Will you be in this film with Jon Lovitz and Alan Arkin?' Okay, yeah, that sounds like a fun cast. You get there, and it's not Jon Lovitz, because he backs out, and it's not Alan Arkin, because he hasn't finished his other movie.

"The producers sued Lovitz—I'm glad to say I defended him in court. I had to sit here, and they phoned me up, and they were saying 'You are now in the Court of California, your voice is now coming from a box in the court. Do you swear to tell the truth, the whole truth, and nothing but the truth?' and I'm sitting in my living room. Cleese is arriving for dinner, and I'm giving evidence! They were trying to blame Lovitz for all the overspends," explains Idle.

"Silly piece of shit . . . and you can quote me!

I'll never work for that bunch of no-paying [inaudible expletives]. I worked for scale, and my expenses were more than my salary."

Idle looks at *Too Much Sun* as a great story for a film with enormous potential, which was ultimately wasted.

Eric Idle, early 1990s. Photo copyright KHJ.

"The people that are best in comedy have no certainty about it, and are open to anything that is said. Whereas I find more and more that people who do not have any idea about comedy are very dogmatic about it," he notes. "That was a sort of sad film, because it could have been good, or at least interesting, because it was on that dangerous nerve area. But ultimately, it became about nothing. It just waltzed out of control. It was a nice idea—two gay couples had to produce this child. A simple, classic problem."

Idle says he overheard one exchange between Robert Downey, Jr., and his father that almost summed up his attitude on the filming. "I heard his father say to him 'When do you learn your lines?' Junior says 'Usually about the third take!' "

He had a smaller part in the sci-fi comedy *Mom and Dad Save the World.* Although he didn't spend a great deal of time on the set, Eric Idle says he enjoyed filming his dungeon scenes.

"It was nice. I knew some of the people, like Teri Garr and Jon Lovitz and Wallace Shawn, so it was a very pleasant day's shooting with them.

And a very pleasant day being chained by the throat filming with Jeffrey Jones, who is very funny—I liked him a lot.

"But the best thing about the main day was that I fell totally in love with Kathy Ireland's legs," he laughs. "She does have, outside of my wife, the best legs in America. It was the high point of my career, really, and I hope she felt the same way about my legs, although mine were not so exposed as hers. The great thing about all planets, as we know, is that all girls with lovely bodies tend to wear little fur bikinis. . . .

"It is odd, isn't it? Because you look at the space programs, and they tend to be wearing a lot of clothes. But, when the girls get up there, little fur bikinis are the order of the day. . . . I don't know why this is Hollywood's view of the future."

His own role in *Mom and Dad*—also known as *Dick and Marge Save the World*—was rather limited, Idle notes. "My perspective is, I was king of this planet, who was deposed and put in jail by Jon Lovitz, whose film it is—I spend most of the film in jail. The people in the film who are funny are Lovitz, Teri Garr, and Jeffrey Jones—my take on it is very limited, which is why I talk about Kathy Ireland's legs," he jokes.

"The basic scene that I'm in is that Jeffrey Jones is on this planet, in the midst of rebellion, and he finds me chained to the wall of a dungeon. He finds this strange creature covered with cobwebs just going 'Waugghhh. . . .' He keeps telling him something very important, but keeps forgetting it. . . ."

In a welcome contrast to his work with Terry Gilliam on *Baron Munchausen,* Idle notes that his part was relatively free of special effects. "I have done my days with SFX. No actor likes working with SFX, no actor in the world. It's just the pits—it's just there to annoy you and make you suffer.

"My particular part was not full of SFX—it was very Python. It was chained to the wall of a dungeon, a lot of facial hair, and smoke blowing in your face. Instead of Graham Chapman, it was Jeffrey Jones. Normally, it would have been Graham going 'What?!' and doing all those reactions. I had to go 'Now, this is very important. . . . Did I say

we are idiots?' It wasn't different or difficult for me to play that part! Then at the end, I'm freed from prison and brought out, because Mom and Dad save the planet, or the universe, or whatever it's called."

Although he isn't certain why he was approached about the project, Idle has his suspicions.

"I think Lovitz got me into it, but I'm not sure entirely. Michael Phillips, who's the producer, just asked me. It was a nice role, they sent it along, and it fit in nicely with my schedule. It was fun to do, really," he recalls.

He notes that his character was not too great of a departure from characters he has played in the past.

"It was very Pythonic, really—it was a character that could easily have been in a Python movie. So, it was kind of not hard to play. He was just a guy who keeps forgetting things—he just constantly has amnesia, which I'm getting very close to having myself lately," he laughs.

"So, it was fun, really except for one line which I had to say. Teri Garr ripped me unmercifully afterwards when she saw me at a party: 'I have reversed the polarity on the magno-beam, you are now safe to return.' A very hard line to have to deliver, because you haven't got any idea what you're talking about," he says, laughing. "I hope I managed to pull that line off, or else they cut it—one way or another!"

Idle, who wrote his own science fiction musical called *Outta' Space* (formerly *The Road to Mars*), says *Mom and Dad Save the World* is quite different from his movie, even though they both involve outer space.

"This is a SFX movie. They have enormous, clever, complicated creatures with heads that move and eyes that roll—it's that kind of space, as opposed to *Road to Mars*," he says.

"I was trying to make a thirties film of the future—nostalgia for the future is my key. I personally believe the future will be much more about human beings than about little furry creatures. I was trying to go for a non–*Star Wars* look of the future, reality from a show business perspective. It's like a Bob and Bing *Road* picture, it's two comedians in the future. The only thing you can be certain of about the future is, there *will* be show business in it. And we'll be the same kind of assholes!" he laughs.

Working on an American film like *Mom and Dad* doesn't require much adjustment for English actors, noted Idle.

"The difference is in the script. I think that Brits tend to rewrite more deeply into the script, and the Americans tend to just put alternatives in. Something like *A Fish Called Wanda* had four drafts by the same author, whereas in America you'd have had eight drafts by twelve different authors. The advantage is that themes and characters emerge better. Of course, the advantage of the American way is that they still have a film industry.

"I was having tea with somebody who observed that American humor was getting tougher, and he observed conversely that English humor was much tougher, but was now getting weaker," he comments. "I think that's true. By weaker, I mean more sentimental, much more television-type humor, blander, and much less sure. I think you have to be sure of where you are in the world to be tough about things. American humor is actually getting tougher, I think. People are no longer content with bland sitcoms all the time."

Idle wrote and starred, along with Rick Moranis and Barbara Hershey, in his own *Splitting Heirs,* which even featured an appearance by John Cleese. He has not necessarily avoided television roles, and was featured with Pierce Brosnan in NBC's 1989 remake of *Around the World in Eighty Days.*

The six-hour adaptation of *Around the World in Eighty Days,* starring Eric Idle, was aired over three successive nights on American television. Strangely enough, Michael Palin set off to attempt a real-life version of the Jules Verne novel at about the same time Idle was filming. Idle says it was especially confusing to the viewers who often mistake him for Palin.

"It was just one of those strange coincidences that happens—'Is it Mike or Eric?' Now, we get totally mistaken for each other, so it doesn't really matter . . ." jokes Idle.

The film was actually shot in London and on location in Macau, Hong Kong, Thailand, and Yugoslavia, which was one aspect of the project that appealed to Idle.

"It was fun—again, it was a nice part. I loved Passepartout," notes Idle. "It was lovely locations, we went shooting all over. I love Pierce, I thought he was good, and Ustinov. It was a great acting part

for me, because it wasn't entirely just silliness. It was a through part, and I played the same person. But it didn't quite work out. Pierce didn't quite make it, he didn't quite pitch his performance in the right way, I think he should have been funnier all the way through. I think they threw out a lot of comedy. It's the hit-and-miss stuff."

It was NBC's confidence in Eric Idle and his work on *Around the World in Eighty Days* that led them to offer him a regular TV series of his own, which turned out to be *Nearly Departed.*

"NBC was very hot on me because I was in *Around the World,* and I was being cute as Passepartout, so they picked up the series," explains Idle. "Well, they didn't actually pick it up, they asked us to reshoot the pilot, because it was fairly lame. We got a very good director called John Rich, who is fabulous, and we went very well. That show started, and they said 'Okay, we'll do six,' and they ordered six. It was the classic American way—it took a year and a half on one script, the pilot, and then you've got three weeks to produce the next five scripts! It's a classic waste . . . ," he laughs.

"So, we did pretty well, and it started to get good. We recast—we put in that very funny guy, Stuart Pankin, and the show was really starting to go. It was really getting together by the end. In fact, the last two are terrific. I did one where I played my own aunt. You never saw that one [in the U.S.]. The last two were very funny, and they should have put them on first. It got better and better, and we were nearly about to do a whole series, and then they just canceled us just before they were about to order another eighteen."

The experience left Idle frustrated with American network television.

"It would have been good, that series," he says regretfully. "I mean, it was getting to be quite good, on everyone's terms, but they didn't allow it to grow. John Rich is still furious. He did *Dick Van Dyke* and *All in the Family* and he said both of them started the same way. Nowadays they don't develop, they won't go with a show and let it grow. So, you're straight on, and get results right away. And it didn't get bad results—it was like twenty-five, twenty-three, nineteen, twenty-two Nielsen ratings—it was up and down. I blame Lorne Michaels—he must have had a word with them. . . ." he laughs.

The first four *Nearly Departed*s aired in America, but Idle says he wasn't disappointed months later when the final two shows weren't aired in America, even though they were the best two of the series, because he had moved on to new projects.

"They pulled it off the air just like that. It was pointless—it wasn't like we were canceled, because we did them in January, and they aired in May, so it wasn't like it was any disappointment— I was in France at the time. I mean, why not just put out the next two—they were the funniest two. They aired here in England.

"As I say, we got better. That's what happens with comedy. But then they're mad, I mean, it's really impossible to do sitcom properly. We'd get notes from these twenty-three-year-old network people and they'd say 'Wear more green. Our research shows that people like people who wear green.' Really useful note, thanks a lot! I said 'Where's the exit?' "

Eric Idle has continued his acting success with the lead in *Burn, Hollywood, Burn: An Alan Smithee Film,* and furnished the voice for a two-headed dragon in the Warner Bros. animated feature *Quest for Camelot* (the other head was voiced by Don Rickles). He also wrote and starred in *Pirates,* which also stars Leslie Neilsen, as a short film developed exclusively for Seaworld of Ohio.

In addition to his acting, he wrote the children's book (and accompanying cassette of original songs) *The Curious Adventures of the Owl and the Pussycat,* which was nominated for a Grammy award in 1998. His most ambitious recent project is a novel, with anticipated release in late 1998. In addition to all of his writing and performing, he still holds Python dear, and was the main force in developing PythOnline.

The Rutles

The greatest group never in the history of rock music, the Rutles' career actually began with a clip of them performing "I Must Be in Love" on *Rutland Weekend Television,* later shown on *Saturday Night Live.*

All You Need Is Cash, the ninety-minute "docudrama," was first aired on NBC on March 22, 1978,

and chronicled the career of the Pre-Fab Four: Dirk McQuickly (Idle), Ron Nasty (Neil Innes), Stig O'Hara (Rikki Fataar), and Barry Wom (John Halsey). The rest of the cast included Mick Jagger, Paul Simon, Dan Ackroyd, Terrence Baylor, John Belushi, George Harrison, Bianca Jagger, Bill Murray, Michael Palin, Gilda Radner, Gwen Taylor, and Ron Wood. Scripted by Idle and codirected by Idle and Gary Weis, Lorne Michaels served as executive producer; in addition to America and Britain, the show was also sold to Canada, New Zealand, Japan, Belgium, Denmark, Iceland, the Netherlands, Sweden, Austria, Norway, and Finland.

Shot on location in London, Liverpool, New York, and New Orleans, the production values are superb, expertly re-creating the feel of the time period covered. For the few not familiar with the Beatles, it holds up on its own as simply a very funny documentary parody; for the rest of us, it is a near-perfect parody as timeless as its targets. It demolishes all of the old Beatle myths, and at the same time elevates them to even loftier heights.

As Neil Innes recalls, they had help in getting it all started. "George Harrison showed Eric and me the film Neil Aspinall had made of the real Beatles. We watched this, and it got depressing, because it was real. When they broke up, it really was a downer. When Brian Epstein died, it just became a bit too real, and the fun definitely stopped. The general feeling was, we could probably tell the story as accurately with the Rutles, but in a more palatable way, because it wasn't really them—it was the Pre-Fab Four, not the Fab Four," says Innes.

"George Harrison was in it up to his neck. Michael Palin played Derek Taylor, and George played Mike!"

All You Need Is Cash effectively touches on all of the high points of the Rutles' careers: their beginnings at the Rat Keller in Hamburg, the fifth Rutle, Leppo, their trousers, Rutlemania, the concert in Che Stadium, *A Hard Day's Rut* and *Ouch!*, Sgt. Rutter, The Rutle Corp., their breakup, and the lawsuits.

At the same time the film was

aired, Warner Brothers released the soundtrack, *The Rutles,* containing fourteen all-new Rutles classics written and performed by Neil Innes. It was packaged as a retrospective of the group's greatest hits, including "Hold My Hand," "Doubleback Alley," and "Love Life." Innes uncannily captured the Beatle sound while writing completely original songs, although one song heard in the film, "Get Up and Go," was reportedly not included on the album because of a too-close resemblance to "Get Back." The album was packaged with a twenty-page booklet highlighting the Rutle years with excerpts and photos from the film. In England, the album received a silver disc for sales of over 150,000 pounds; in America, it was nominated for a Grammy Award as Best Comedy Recording of 1978.

"The songwriting wasn't easy, but it was a labor of love," says Innes. "I didn't listen to any Beatles stuff at all. The hardest songs to write were the early ones, when I had to remember what it was like to hold a girl's hand for the first time, and make it sound meaningful. Those early songs were the hardest to emulate—they're probably more exposed, and they had to be good in a simple way."

Innes assembled some musicians to record the songs, and decided to treat them as a real band. "The cleverest thing I did was to have everybody work together and live together at Hendon for two

The Pre-Fab four. Left to right: Ron Nasty (Neil Innes), Stig O'Hara (Ricky Fataar), Dirk McQuickly (Eric Idle) and Barry Wom (John Halsey). Photo copyright Python Productions.

weeks, rehearsing just like a group, and we made the album in two weeks because of that. And the feel of it was just wonderful. We've got the quarter-inch tapes of the Rutles Live at Hendon someplace. We really sounded like a group, because there was no overdubbing or anything," Innes says.

When asked about a Rutles follow-up project in the 1980s, Neil Innes turned to the show: "To quote Mick Jagger, 'I hope not!' " Nevertheless, the Rutles—or more precisely, Neil Innes—did return in the guise of "The New Rutles," with two sold-out performances at the Troubadour in L.A. in the fall of 1994, which tied in with the Python 25th anniversary retrospective at the Director's Guild. These proved so successful that Innes and the band recorded a new CD in 1996, *The Rutles Archaeology* after Eric Idle gave Innes permission (Idle did not participate). The Rutles—or part of them—were briefly revived, and served to make the legend of the original film and album even greater.

Terry Jones

Born February 1, 1942 at Colwyn Bay, North Wales, Terry Jones attended Royal Grammar School, Guilford in 1953. Studying history, he went to St. Edmund Hall, Oxford, in 1961, and eventually became attracted to the theater scene. He appeared in the Oxford Revue * * * * at the Edinburgh Festival and at the Phoenix Theatre in London in 1964. Jones also played the condemned man in *Hang Down Your Head and Die*, an anti–capital punishment revue presented at Oxford, Stratford, and London's Comedy Theatre. It was around this time that he met Michael Palin.

Graduating a year before Palin, he found himself working for the BBC Light Entertainment Script Department, as a script editor, producer's assistant, gag writer, and whatever else needed to be done. Joined by Palin, the two contributed to *Late Night Line Up, The Ken Dodd Show, The Billy Cotton Bandshow,* and *The Illustrated Weekly Hudd,* and did various kinds of writing for Lance Percival, Kathy Kirby, Marty Feldman, and *The Two Ronnies.* The pair made short films for *The Late Show,* and in 1967, became script editors for *A Series of Birds* and *Twice a Fortnight.* More significantly, the two began writing for *The Frost Report,* which included other future Pythons among its writers. The pair also collaborated on two pantomimes for the Palace Theatre, Watford: *Aladdin* in 1968, and *Beauty and the Beast* in 1969.

It was 1967 that saw the first of two series of *Do Not Adjust Your Set,* a children's show written by Jones, Palin, and Eric Idle, with animations by Terry Gilliam, as well as appearances by Neil Innes and the Bonzo Dog Doo Dah Band, all of which led into *Monty Python's Flying Circus* in 1969. During the second season of *DNAYS,* the pair wrote and performed in an acclaimed six-part series called *The Complete and Utter History of Britain* for London Weekend Television.

"Mike and I were doing the last season of *DNAYS* at the *same time* we were doing the *Complete and Utter Histories.* It was absolutely manic!" says Jones. "The basis of the *Complete and Utter Histories* was that it was history as if there had been television cameras there—things like William the Conqueror in the showers after the Battle of Hastings, all done with an ITN sports reporter asking what the battle had been like. It was like a football match, with a playback of the battle.

"They weren't very satisfactory in many ways, but they did have funny material in them. I think it was the *Complete and Utter Histories* that got John Cleese keen on doing something together . . ."

Jones and Palin wrote together for all the Python TV shows and films, both on their own as well as with the group. The pair had always tended to write longer pieces that would not fit into the half-hour Python format; one of those was a short play called *Secrets,* which aired on BBC 2 in August 1973. The story of a chocolate company that becomes successful overnight (after a body falls into the vat), was turned into the 1988 film *Consuming Passions* with Vanessa Redgrave, though Jones and Palin had little to do with the production. The Jones/Palin team also wrote two short plays for the Sheffield Crucible Theatre, under the single title *Their Finest Hours,* which were presented in 1976.

When the Python TV show came to an end, Jones and Palin set their sights on another series.

The pair wrote the pilot for *Ripping Yarns,* aired in January 1976; "Tomkinson's Schooldays" was successful enough for the BBC to authorize a series of six, broadcast in the fall of 1977, and a second series of three, aired two years later. The writing was first rate, as were the production values, but as well received as the shows were, they were too expensive for the BBC to continue. Jones cowrote all the shows with Palin, but appeared only in the first.

The shows were all very British, rooted in the stiff-upper-lip stories of English pluck, with a fine, ironic edge. Each story is separate, and the hero (played by Palin) escapes from prisoner-of-war camps, leads an expedition over the Andes, and prevents the Germans from starting World War I ahead of schedule.

The scripts for the shows were published in two volumes, the first six as *Ripping Yarns,* and the last three as *More Ripping Yarns.* The pair also collaborated in 1976 on *Dr. Fegg's Nasty Book of Knowledge,* published in the U.K. under the title *Bert Fegg's Nasty Book for Boys and Girls* (revised and reissued in America in 1985 as *Dr. Fegg's Encyclopedia of All World Knowledge*).

The money Jones earned from *Holy Grail* was in part invested in an old restaurant and brewery in the English countryside. Jones is a fierce proponent of CAMRA, the Campaign for Real Ale. He insists that his beer be brewed in line with the most traditional methods.

The *Grail* profits also allowed Jones the time and money to pursue another pet project that had been brewing for years. He wrote a book, *Chaucer's Knight: Portrait of a Medieval Mercenary,* the scholarly study of a few lines of the *Canterbury Tales,* "explaining some 700-year-old jokes" that he felt had been misinterpreted for too long. Terry Jones has long had an interest in things medieval, and *Chaucer's Knight* had long been a pet project for him. Although he knew the book would not be particularly commercial, he felt the need to correct what he saw as the misinterpretations of this part of Chaucer's work, even though it involved only about thirty lines from the general prologue. The book points out that the battles Chaucer attributes to his "veray, parfit gentil knight" were not the triumphs most literary interpreters assume them to be, and Jones provides a preponderance of evidence in its 300-plus pages.

Terry Jones, mid-'70s. Photograph by John Sims for Python Productions, used by permission.

"I really decided to do it because I'd gotten this feeling that there were these thirty lines of Chaucer that I just didn't understand. I started work on it when I was in university," explains Jones. "I wrote an essay on what it meant when Chaucer said the knight was at Alexandria, but all I turned up with there was when I read the literary critics, they said it was a great victory, and when I read the historians, they said it was a terrible massacre. I felt 'Well, there's some difference here.'

"To begin with, I went off on the wrong track, but it gradually became an obsession. All the time we were doing Python, for a period of about ten years, I spent time moonlighting at the British Museum, just reading everything I could that would illuminate what Chaucer meant in these particular lines about the knight," he relates.

"Eventually it took quite a while to realize that the history of the fourteenth century was quite different from what we'd been taught, and this movement from the old feudal hosts to the mercenary army, a paid standing army, was very significant in Chaucer's day. The idea that Chaucer could have written this description of a knight without actually mentioning that movement was just ridiculous."

Both the theory and the fact that it was being proposed by a Python drew a great deal of attention among scholars.

"It had quite an impact on the academic world. I think it took a lot of people by surprise, especially the line where Chaucer says he'd been on raids into Russia. Russia was a Christian country, and no English had ever pointed out that it was a Christian country. For Chaucer's knight to have gone on raids as this great Christian militarist fighting evil for Christianity was sort of negated by the fact that he was going on raids into Russia, which was Christian—it was Greek Orthodox, but it was still Christian."

Jones says he still isn't completely satisfied with his work, though it is convincing others of his theory.

"Eventually I think the academic world will come around to realizing that a lot of my thesis is right. I keep thinking that I'd really like to rewrite it. I can still find it very unreadable, because there are aspects of my first ideas and attitudes that are in the book and shouldn't be there.

"I'd revise quite a bit of it if I rewrote it now. I did rewrite when the paperback came out, especially the chapters on Prussia, because new material came up and I included that. The paperback is more accurate than the original!"

Terry Jones became a successful author of children's books with the publication of *Fairy Tales,* stories he wrote to tell his daughter Sally at bedtime, a sideline he says he came to love.

He followed this up in 1983 with *The Saga of Erik the Viking,* written for his son Bill. Yet another children's book, *Nicobobinus,* was issued the following year. Jones wrote screenplays based on the latter two, filming *Erik the Viking* for release in 1989. A book of children's poetry, *The Curse of the Vampire Socks,* was released late in 1988.

Jones's *Fairy Tales* was adapted for television, first as a series of seven shows, with another series to follow; titled *East of the Moon,* they were nominated for an Emmy Award.

"I think in some ways, my children's books are my favorite things. They're the most me. They don't do much over in the States, but over here, they're used in schools a lot. They've devoted assemblies to them, and I don't quite know why," Jones laughs. "That's terribly rewarding. It's lovely when people say 'Our kids just love them,' or 'We're reading *Erik the Viking* at the moment.' "

Writing a children's book is not that difficult, he says.

"Just write what you'd like to hear yourself, basically. That's also what I remember Chaucer saying—you don't write in a style, you just write as you talk. That's what I try and do. I don't know what the trick is, but I just try and write how I talk. I think it does help to actually read things out, because it's amazing—you can kid yourself until you read something out, but when you actually read something terrible to someone, you know. It's the same as performing—you know if you're embarrassed by it or not, and if you like it or not. At that moment of doing the lines, you can tell whether it's working or not."

His *Fantastic Stories* actually started out as another book of fairy tales, but his imagination took hold and stretched him even farther.

"Originally this was going to be another book of fairy tales, and a lot of them *are* fairy tales," Jones reveals.

"But even though most of them are really fairy tales, there are some bizarre elements in them, and they're a bit longer than the original tales. It's like a companion book to *Fairy Tales,* but it's just a bit different."

Fantastic Stories actually was written due to continued requests—from his publisher.

"I don't suppose [my children's books] are seen much in the States, but I get an awful lot of correspondence on them actually, and the first two have been published in three different forms and reprinted endlessly. They just keep going, really, so my publisher had been nagging me to do another book of them. Hence, *Fantastic Stories!*"

The year 1988 saw the publication of *Attacks of Opinion,* a collection of columns written by Jones for the *Young Guardian* "Input" column earlier in the year.

His interest in the Middle Ages also led him to

write a serious screenplay based on the Peasants' Revolt, called *1381*. "It's glossed over in most history books, and it was a most extraordinary, apocalyptic event. These people actually won, and took over London! They revolted not because they lived under such terrible oppression, but because they suddenly realized a much better, more equal life was in their grasp, and they could actually do something about it," Jones says.

Jones's reputation as one of Britain's leading children's authors resulted in his collaboration with Jim Henson on *Labyrinth*. He ended up writing the text for the Brian Froud illustrations done for the film, published as *Goblins of the Labyrinth* in 1986.

Although Terry Jones isn't sure how much of the completed film is actually his, he did receive credit for writing the screenplay. Having made a name for himself as a children's book author, in addition to his Monty Python work, he seemed a logical choice to pen the Jim Henson movie.

Actually it was his second children's book that led to his collaboration with the Muppet creator, he says. "I had been thinking about turning *Erik the Viking* into a film, and I thought it was something Jim Henson might be interested in," explains Jones. "I rang up his office, and they said 'That's funny— he was trying to reach you yesterday. So, Jim and I met up—he was setting up *Labyrinth* at that stage—and he wanted to know if I would like to write the screenplay.

"Jim's daughter Lisa had just read *Erik the Viking* and suggested that he try me as screenwriter—and that's how it came about. I hadn't really known Jim before our *Labyrinth* meeting. We had bumped into each other when the Pythons were first in the States. We were in the street, getting out of cars, when he called out 'Hi, I'm Jim Henson!' That was about 1975, but we hadn't met since then."

Although it was Jones's screenplay, the original idea belonged to Henson. "Jim had the basic story for *Labyrinth*," explains Jones, "but I really agreed to do it on the basis of the characters. I wanted to have a fairly free hand at the episodes. I just started fresh, using the same characters. I'd undertaken the thing in a rather cavalier fashion. I'd read their synopsis, and they'd had a novella of the film-to-be. It was about ninety pages of story, and I

thought it didn't work at all, so originally I said I wasn't really interested. Then after a couple of bottles of wine with Jim, I said 'All right, maybe I'll spend three weeks writing and see if something comes up.'

"That's what I did, and it was great. I had all of Brian Froud's drawings in a stack—he does the conceptual designs and drawings on which the models are based," he reveals. "I had this pile of drawings, so I sat there with this basic story outline and had all these characters. When I came to a new scene, I just picked out a character I liked and wrote a scene around it, like the old man with the hat with the duck's head, and the hat talks back— it just seemed obvious. It was there in the drawing.

"In some ways, *Labyrinth* was Brian Froud's project. I think he came up with the idea of doing something about a labyrinth. Whenever I got to a situation where I wanted to invent a character, I would flip through his creations until I came to one that I liked, and give it words—I was collaborating in a funny way with Brian Froud, because I was springing off his drawings."

The film was much like a fairy tale. Because there were only two human stars in *Labyrinth*, played by Jennifer Connelly as Sarah and David Bowie as Jareth, Jones was able to concentrate much of his attention on the creatures.

"I thought the first draft I wrote was pretty good, really. I thought it was fun, and everyone was excited about it. Then it disappeared for a month, and Jim came back and said 'We've got some problems.' The main problem was this labyrinth—the original idea was to do this thing about the labyrinth. They wrote this magical character, Jareth, who is all-powerful and does magic. I thought there was no contest. This girl goes into the labyrinth, and you've got this magic character, so she can't win.

"So, in my version, she goes into the labyrinth, and eventually she finds out there is no solution. She keeps thinking she's solved it, and then it keeps cheating on her. The idea in the end is that she finds out there's no solution, you've got to enjoy it. When she gets to the center, she finds out that the character who seemed all-powerful to begin with *isn't* all-powerful. In fact, he's someone who uses the labyrinth—which is basically the world—to keep people from getting to his heart.

She gets there and annihilates him in the end. So, it's about the world, and about people who are more interested in manipulating the world than actually baring themselves at all, having any kind of emotional honesty. Jim couldn't understand the story at all.

"The other thing I thought was, you mustn't get to the center of the labyrinth before the girl does, because that's your hook for the audience—what is at the center of the labyrinth? Jim had two problems. One was that Jim wanted Michael Jackson or David Bowie to play Jareth, so he wanted him to appear all the way through, and he wanted him to sing. That was a real shock. Then he also wanted to go to the center of the labyrinth before the girl does. Both were things I felt were wrong.

"But I wrote a second version which had Jareth singing. He went for David Bowie, and it all went away for about a year. When the script came back, I didn't recognize any of it. Jim said 'Can you do a bit more to it? David Bowie doesn't want to do it anymore because it isn't funny anymore.'

"It was more or less mine up to the part where Sarah goes down the Pit of Hands, which was mine. It's sort of mine up to the point where she eats this apple, which is something Jim wanted to put in and I didn't like at all—that's when I thought it was no longer mine, it was nothing I had much to do with."

Because of Henson's story and the changes made to his script, Jones says he doesn't feel very close to the movie.

"I didn't really feel that it was very much mine. I always felt it fell between the two stories. Jim wanted it to be about one thing, and I wanted it to be about something else. But Jim was great, really smashing to work with—he was the kind of person one wanted to do things for because he was so nice and so straight—even when we disagreed about things. He was always open to other ideas.

"The things I like most about *Labyrinth* are not necessarily things I contributed," notes Jones. "I had an idea to do this Shaft of Hands—she falls down this dark shaft with these hands sticking out, hands all talking to each other—and it actually works! They realized it much better than I imagined it when I wrote it down as an idea. In a way, my best contribution was just starting off something that the puppet makers have made much

better and improved. I just started the ball rolling, but I think it's the sequence that works best."

In addition to *Labyrinth,* Terry Jones also worked on another fantasy film, although his contributions weren't utilized in the final version of *Gremlins II.* "I hadn't meant to get involved with it, but I talked to Steven Spielberg and Joe Dante. I told them I didn't think I was the right person to do it, but I suddenly got an idea. My outline involved many of the same characters [as the first film] and a forgotten rule, but it all took place in America, so I didn't think I was necessarily the best person to actually write it down."

His varied interests also found an outlet on TV. He hosted a series of shows called *Paperbacks* in June and July, 1981, and directed a tribute to one of his boyhood favorites on Channel Four's *The Rupert Bear Story,* in December 1982.

Film appearances by Jones have become less frequent recently. One of his few non-Python roles had him fall victim to Gilliam's *Jabberwocky* in the first few minutes of that film.

Directing has occupied much of Jones's time as of late. Although he took an active interest in the direction and editing of the Python TV shows, he did not actually get involved until he and Terry Gilliam codirected *Holy Grail.* Jones then went on to tackle the same chores by himself on *Life of Brian* and *Meaning of Life.* Although he is chiefly interested in directing his own projects, he did win acclaim for his work at the helm of 1987's *Personal Services.*

Personal Services is the thinly disguised real-life story of English madam Cynthia Payne (here called Christine Painter), who ran the best little whorehouse in London, which catered to the rather kinky tastes of older government officials and military men. Jones says many aspects of the story appealed to him.

"I read the script and thought it was really good. It was just so honest, so raw, and I thought it was very funny and touching as well. One of the things that appealed to me most was the character of the Major, who was somebody who was anarchic. He was seventy-four years old, and he felt 'I'm going to die in a few years, and so I don't give a shit what I do—I'm going to do what I like. If I sound like a silly old fart, I don't care,' " Jones says with a laugh.

343

"There's a deep anarchy in old age which I thought was really interesting, so that was one reason I wanted to do it. Also, it was the only script I've ever picked up and thought 'I wouldn't change a word'—it's all there."

Although the film received good reviews, it wasn't promoted or distributed well enough in America for it to succeed.

"It's a film that I'm sure will be rediscovered in the States. It never had any life in the States. It was Vestron, and their entire personnel changed after they bought it, and the new lot didn't like it, and had a vested interest in it not working. I remember David [Leland] was over there, and he said 'What's happened to it? There's not a single advert for it,' " he recalls.

Still, Jones feels the film was worth the struggle; he notes that the main reason he decided to direct *Personal Services* was because of the screenplay written by Leland, an old friend.

"It was a terrific script. David and I codirected it, really. David worked all the time with Julie, and we kind of did it together. I would hope it's as near to what David wrote as he wanted."

Terry Jones took on his first solo non-Python feature in 1989 wearing three hats—writer, director, and actor—on *Erik the Viking*. The original drafts of *Erik the Viking* were actually based on Terry Jones's children's book *The Saga of Erik the Viking*, but the completed film has very little to do with the stories in his book.

"My book is actually twenty-eight separate stories about this Viking gang, and I sidetracked into a film. I saw a couple of sections of it and thought 'Hmm, good visuals there, going over the Edge of the World, and the Dragon of the North Sea. . . .' I started a script and got stuck about halfway through it.

"I thought it might help if I had somebody else involved, so I rang up Jim Henson. I asked him if he'd be interested in doing the monsters and things, and he said he was just about to ring me up, to ask if I'd be interested in writing a screenplay for this thing called *Labyrinth*. So instead of getting him involved in my film, I got involved in his!"

Subsequent attempts to redo the *Erik the Viking* screenplay, both alone and with others, proved unsuccessful. It wasn't until Jones found a Viking scene written by him and occasional partner Michael Palin (during a failed attempt to write another Monty Python film) that things began to click.

"I eventually decided I didn't want to make a film of the book. The book's the book, and I'd spend a year of my life setting up and making a movie of something I've already done—it's like retreading old material," relates Jones.

"I was about to chuck it all in, when I suddenly came across a scene that I had written, when Mike and I had been having a go at writing a Viking script. We had abandoned it—we actually produced a short screenplay, but neither of us liked it. I had written this scene for that. I suddenly thought 'Wait a minute, there's a story in this'—this Viking kills a girl and starts to think that maybe his way of life isn't right. So, I just started writing the script the way it is now. It wrote out very quickly, in three or four weeks, and I decided to drag in anything from the book that was useful. The Edge of the World and the Dragon of the North Sea came in there, but nothing else is from the book—everything else is new."

Erik's home—a Viking village on a Norwegian fjord—was constructed down to the smallest detail in a huge sound stage at London's Shepperton Studios. The village itself was built upon a five-foot-high platform that extended over nearly all of the massive stage. This, in part, was to accommodate the man-made lake at one end of the building, where the dragon-prowed Viking ship was docked. Campfires were burning, a small duck pond was constructed in the center of the village, and pigs, ducks, and chickens roamed free; snowy mountain ranges appeared to veer off in all directions.

"I originally wanted to do it on location in Norway, but the way the film worked out, we couldn't—there was no daylight there at that time. To get both daylight and snow, it would have meant starting out there in the spring, and we couldn't have put the whole thing off for six months," reveals Jones, who says they were able to do a little exterior filming in Norway after the main production shooting had wrapped.

Most of the water sequences were shot in Malta, Jones explains. "We used Malta for Hy-Brasil, which is the Celtic version of Atlantis. So, we started off shooting in the court of the king of Hy-Brasil and then flooded the stage to shoot the Hy-Brasil sinking. We then got rid of that set and

shot all of the water scenes—the battles, and things like that.

"In Malta, they've got this tank the size of a football pitch that we could flood up to four feet. It's built on the coast, so it looks out to sea, and has a spill wall on the sea side. So, when we chose the angle right, we were looking out to sea and an unbroken horizon. We could shoot our sea stuff in a tank, which is much more controllable. Actually shooting in the sea involves tides and weather conditions, and it gets a lot more tricky. Just shooting in a tank with four feet of water is much more controlled, and we could do it much quicker. We really wouldn't have been able to film it without that.

"Of course, we had snags. It's built right on the edge of Valletta Harbor, which must be one of the busiest harbors in the world!" he laughs. "We had a problem with boats on the horizon until we got it together. We eventually managed to reroute boats, but at first we'd sit there, waiting for the ships to go past."

Terry Jones at the helm of his epic **Erik the Viking.** *Photo copyright KHJ.*

The facilities at Malta allowed the crew to shoot some of their SFX there, including shots of the Viking ship going over the Edge of the World.

"They've actually got two tanks in Malta. They have their original tank, and then a deep tank, about thirty-five feet deep, which they built for the underwater sequences in *Raise the Titanic!* We used that as well.

"We built a ramp inside the deep tank and pumped up a huge quantity of water, to give us the Edge of the World waterfall. With various-sized models, it looked great. We actually did a lot of the model work out there," Jones says, explaining that a second unit directed by Julian (*Brazil*) Doyle was doing much of that filming.

"We had one go at the Edge of the World, but it didn't really work out the way we did it there. We shot it at night and lit it for day, so that when we crane up, we see it's daylight, with stars below—the stars didn't really work very well."

Another *Erik* effect shot in Malta was just as challenging for Jones the actor, in his role as the king of Hy-Brasil. When the last group of Hy-Brasilians are standing on the remaining roof as it sinks, the king is talking as he goes under.

"That was quite interesting to shoot. We were all sitting on this roof, and had these Maltese extras. It's quite tricky to stay underwater for that length of time, and the extras on the edge of the building were sinking underwater about thirty seconds sooner than me. They went under right at the beginning of this little speech, so they had to learn to hold their breath for quite a long time—and look unconcerned as they went down," he recalls with a laugh.

"It was quite tricky. I had been practicing it and thought I wouldn't have any problem. The one thing I'd forgotten when we did the shot was that because I was talking the whole time—and it was essential for me to be talking the whole time I was going down—when I actually got underwater, I realized suddenly that I didn't have any breath left at all.

"I only managed to keep down for a couple of seconds. Fortunately, it was long enough for the shot. I didn't want to redo the shot, because I only had one wig, and it would take about an hour to get it all ready again!"

Not all of the challenging SFX shots were saved for Malta, though, including the battle with

Tim Robbins, Terry Jones, and Mickey Rooney gather around a monitor to watch a playback on the set of Erik the Viking. *Photo copyright KHJ.*

the Dragon of the North Sea. Jones explains that the creature is so huge, the whole thing is never seen on the screen; most of it was shot with models, but the eyes and nose were built life-size.

"The dragon was huge, vast—he took up the whole sea stage, and that was just the quarter-sized model! We never really see the whole dragon on screen, we only see bits of it. We did do some life-sized sections—its nose and eyes were life-sized, but those are the only things that weren't done as smaller models," he explains.

"Everything else was model-sized. At one point, Erik leaps onto its nose and goes into its nostril, so we had to build that life-sized," he laughs. "It's very big!"

Jones explains that he had to work with water, smoke, snow, and animals—traditional banes of all film directors. "The water's obviously a tricky thing—it slows everything up," he notes, and indicates that the use of smoke was also intended to disguise the fact that they were actually shooting in a studio.

"It was a wonderful set, but sets are always sets. When we saw the first day's rushes, the way we shot it still looked very 'set-y' to me. So, we realized that we needed to keep it moving, keep it alive all the time. We always need wind and a bit of snow on everybody, and we had to break the

background up a bit to keep it real."

Despite the workload involved for the film, Jones says he likes his job.

"I really enjoy directing." Jones smiles. "I always find it easier than *not* directing."

Erik the Viking marked his first attempt to direct his own non-Python script, which caused him to plan carefully during preproduction.

"I find I have to think it all out beforehand, and I have to have a storyboard. Even still, that just helps me keep my ideas straight. There are always unforeseen things happening—actors have different ideas of how to do things, and so they can change. But I wouldn't be able to do it if I hadn't really got tight storyboards. Sometimes we get away from the storyboards, and I suddenly realize there was a reason for having it like that on the storyboards. Then again, sometimes a storyboard is overelaborate—I'd think I needed all these shots, and we could cover it in one."

Jones says his approach to directing has mellowed over the last fifteen years, something he realized while shooting *Erik the Viking*. "I'm a lot more relaxed about it now. There's much less pressure, and I feel I tend to let things go a bit more—I don't want *everything* to be absolutely right.

"When we had some chickens up on a roof, they would *never* stay in the same place—but it's much more important to get all the sharp performances than to get the chickens in the right place. I wasn't going to hold the whole shot up just so we could have the chickens in the background—I know it doesn't matter in the end! So, I get less worked up about things like that.

"I'm also terribly lucky in having technicians around me who I really trust, so I can ease up on that. It's just wonderful to let George Akers, our editor, go off and edit, although I want to get my hands on the film at some point. I love cutting, actually, but I just have total confidence in George's cut, and he can do it so much quicker than I can! All I have to say is 'I think we should do this with

that,' and George can do it—generally, he comes up with ideas that are always improvements," Jones says.

Fellow Python John Cleese was invited along to play the villainous Halfdan.

"Actually, Halfdan the Black was one of the great kings of Norway. He was always reckoned to be a good bloke—until now!" Jones laughs.

In addition to Cleese, Python colleague Neil Innes scored the film for Jones and even a did a bit of acting. "I wouldn't call it acting, though," he says, smiling. "Terry very kindly gave me some important parts with one or two lines, just because I happened to be in Malta. Supporting roles, like 'Citizen at the Back,' 'Man with Donkey,' and I think I'm 'Third Drowned Hy-Brasilian.' They're always doing something to me. I got drowned in this film, though I wasn't alone—a lot of others got drowned too."

The critical reaction to *Erik the Viking* was generally negative, which Jones says was largely due to audiences expecting a Python movie.

"I was very upset by the critics' reaction to it, especially over here [in Britain]—it got annihilated by most critics. I think it was partly perception, and people were expecting something else. I knew it was dangerous starting with the rape scene, and I think it kind of set up the expectation of a Python kind of thing, which it isn't—the whole thing is basically a fairy tale. It's amazing, because it appeals like mad to ten-, twelve-, thirteen-year-olds, which really is who it was aimed at. Kids just love it, and that's what it was meant to be. I hoped adults would like it as well, but if you approach it as a Python film, you'll just say 'What is this?'" he said, analyzing its reception from his London home.

"With Python, you're always telling people not to suspend their disbelief, but *Erik* was a fairy tale, so you *have* to suspend disbelief—if you don't, you don't get on to it. I should have done something else to get people to suspend their disbelief, whereas the first scene is actually more Pythonic, and you're led the wrong way."

Most upsetting to Jones was that his final cut of the film was not the one released in theaters in Britain and America.

"The worst thing for me was, both in the States and in England, was that the version that was released was not the final, best version. There was another one which was about ten minutes shorter, which I reedited with Julian Doyle, after it had been released over here, and I was wondering 'Why did they go so against it?' One of the things I thought was the first location shot, which was Tim running over the mountain. I'd put this boiling sky onto it, and it hadn't quite worked. It was one of those opticals that arrived at the last moment, and we had to decide whether to put it in or not. I thought 'I always wanted this boiling sky,' and what happened when I put this boiling sky on was, it made the mountains go flat. I don't know why, but they looked like they were cardboard. So, instead of being the first shot of actual location when he runs toward the mountains, it looked like he was in the studio again. And I thought, 'It

John Cleese calls Terry Jones "the most broad-based talent" of all the Pythons; here he wrote, directed, and co-starred in **Erik the Viking.** *Photo copyright KHJ.*

doesn't work. The first visual effect of the film, and it doesn't work.' So, I took that out and just put in the ordinary shot.

"We took out about ten minutes. The sinking's much better, and towards the end it goes a lot faster. Unfortunately, we weren't in time to get it cut for the American distribution, they'd already printed three hundred copies of the other one.

"But what *really* pissed me off was in the States, when they released it on video, despite everything we said and did, despite their assurances that they would release the right version on video, they released the same version. But in this country, the video is the proper version, the shorter one."

Still, Jones has hopes for the future of *Erik*.

"I think it's one of those things that will come back and be rediscovered someday. I got a card from Tim Robbins, and he said [reads] 'People tell me how much they love *Erik*. He lives on!' People stop him in the street and tell him how much they really like it, where he probably thought it was a bit of a write-off," Jones declares.

"I find it too, especially when it was released on video. It did quite well over here on video. But I still wish we'd done it on location, rather than in the studio."

Another of his more ambitious projects was his 1994 multipart documentary series on *The Crusades* which took him to Jordan, Syria, Turkey, and Israel. A longstanding interest in history attracted him to the project, though he quips that it was the best chance he had to read his own books on the subject.

"[BBC producer] Allan Ereira and I had done a short program together once, and he suggested doing *The Crusades*," says Jones. "I thought 'That sounds really interesting, it's a subject I know absolutely nothing about.' I'd gotten Stephen Runciman's three-volume history of the Crusades, it had been sitting on my shelf since 1964 or so. I thought, 'The only way I'm ever going to read these three volumes is if I say yes to this!' Now, instead of my pristine three volumes, I've got battered, dog-eared versions. That's really why I said yes, I thought I might learn something. Which I did!"

The location filming was like a trip through time, he notes. "One of the most amazing things is the feeling of going back in time, which you really feel in a place like Syria," says Jones. "I suppose it's a fascist government, really, with Assad, but it's a great place. Whatever you think of the government, the people seemed really happy to me. You go to certain places where you're in a really nice hotel in the middle of this wasteland right in the middle of this city. I think it was in '87 when they massacred huge numbers of people and razed the section of the city where they lived. This was the Syrian government that wiped out the Muslim Brotherhood."

Jones related the history of the Crusades, retracing the paths of the Crusaders in many cases, teaching viewers without being at all heavy-handed. Some of the highlights were anecdotal incidents, including one of interest to Python fans!

"What struck me most about the Crusades was how much they cribbed from Python," jokes Jones. "We were walking around the headquarters of the assassins. The assassins were the majority Muslim sect and believed in direct political action—killing people publicly. They were so against the other Muslim sect that they were happy to get in bed with the Crusaders in order to attack the other Muslims! So they would try to do deals. One of the Crusaders, a nephew of Richard II, had been invited to visit the old man of the mountains, who was the head of the assassins in Masyaf, where we were walking around. The story went that while he was there, the head of the assassins wanted to

Terry Jones, early 1990s. Photo copyright KHJ.

demonstrate how well trained his people were. He got them to jump off the battlements on the edge of the castle to show him how well trained they were. After two of them had jumped, they asked him if he wanted to see some more, and the Crusader said, 'No, no, no, that's quite enough, thank you very much!' Which was a terrible pinch from the 'Kamikaze Highlanders' sketch!"

One of Jones's more successful books was the result of what was initially a reluctant collaboration with illustrator Brian Froud, with whom he collaborated on *Labyrinth. Lady Cottington's Pressed Fairy Book* was allegedly a Victorian relic kept by a young girl who would hold the book open and snap it shut on any fairies that flew too close to her. The pair even wrote a sequel, *Strange Stains and Mysterious Smells: Quentin Cottington's Journal of Faery Research,* published in 1997. Jones reveals that he was initially reluctant to get involved with it all.

"Brian Froud had contacted me—the whole squashed fairy thing was his idea," says Jones. "Brian rang me up and said he had this idea for a book. I was a bit busy and couldn't do anything, but he said 'Couldn't we just meet up and talk about it?' I said, 'Couldn't you just tell me over the phone?' and he said 'No, I really have to tell you about it in person.' He lives in Devon, so he did a three-hour train journey into town, and we met for lunch. I was going to say no, and he told me that the basis for this book was, instead of collecting pressed flowers, you squash fairies. He did a demonstration, and I said, 'Yeah, I'll do it!'

"We immediately went around to my publisher, Colin Webb, whose offices were just around the corner from the restaurant where we were. We were extremely well-oiled with a couple of bottles of wine when we commandeered Colin and said 'Here, we've got a great idea for you!' We told him and Colin said 'Yes, I'll do it!' I said to Brian 'That is the quickest sale anybody's ever done with a book—you proposed it to me and we got the publisher to agree, all within an hour!' But it didn't work out like that. Brian had just got a new agent in New York who said, 'You can't do that—you can't set up a book that quickly, this is such a hot idea we've got to send it around a bit!' A year passed, in which Brian's agent in New York tried to hawk the book without any success. Finally, Brian fired him after the agent told him it was unsaleable. We went back to Colin, and Colin pub-

lished it with tremendous success! It was a huge hit in France, oddly enough, as is the *Goblin Companion,* which is basically the same book as *Goblins of the Labyrinth.* It got fantastic, rave reviews in France!"

Jones staged a mini-Python reunion with his filmed version of *The Wind in the Willows.* The children's classic, written and directed by Jones, featured four of the Pythons onscreen, though he explains it was because they were right for the roles and not because they were teammates.

"The parts just seemed to fit," says Jones. "I wrote the part of Mr. Toad's lawyer with John in mind, I really wanted John to do that. Mike just seemed like a very good Sun. It was just a question of casting, it wasn't because they are Pythons. And Eric is a superb Ratty, he's just wonderful—I think it's one of the best things he's ever done as an actor, actually."

The filming went very smoothly, and the result elicited strong responses from critics and audiences.

"We had a great time making it, and it's something I'm really pleased with," says Jones. "I think it's a really nice film. It seems to be exactly what it was meant to be, which is taking a gentle, tranquil book and turning it into an action/adventure film for kids, which I rather enjoyed! It's very odd, because the film *totally* splits the audience over here, a bit like Python did in a way—it certainly split the critics. There are hardly any halfhearted reviews— they either loved it or hated it!"

Cleese appeared in *Wind in the Willows* as a favor to Jones, and as a way of thanking him for the idea that led to *Fierce Creatures.*

"John rang me up about four or five years ago and said, 'You know that thing about the zoo?' " says Jones. "It was a half-hour thing that Michael and I wrote for ourselves in '68, before Python. Oddly enough, although we hadn't done Python yet, we cast John as the zookeeper who was only going to allow *fierce* animals in his zoo, animals above six feet that ate people. Mike was going to play the Small Mammal Keeper, and Graham we wanted to play Mr. Megapode, the Keeper of the Aviary. And that was before we ever worked together! We just wrote it as a half hour and nothing ever happened to it. So, when John said 'Are you doing anything with it?' I said no. He asked, 'Could I use it?' because he had an idea of where

329

to take it, and I said, 'Oh, yeah, fine.' I told Mike, and Mike said, 'Did you discuss money?' I hadn't, but in the end, he appeared in *Wind in the Willows* for nothing."

Terry Jones's version of **Mr. Toad's Wild Ride,** *featuring Eric Idle as Ratty, was enthusiastically received by young audiences. From the collection of Terry Jones, used by permision.*

When Terry Jones follows his own interests, they always seem to lead in several directions.

"I finished a children's book, a historical novel, that was released in Britain in 1997," says Jones. "It's called *The Knight and the Squire*. It's a little bit older than the other books I've written, and it's set during the Hundred Years' War in the middle of the fourteenth century—1359, in fact, and it's based on actual historical events, though it's just a fantasy. At the moment I'm finishing a film script called *Longitude* for Granada TV, based on the discovery of longitude in the eighteenth century. Then I've got a three-part TV series lined up for the Discovery Channel called *Ancient Inventions*. I'm getting very historical at the moment. I like to do what interests me, and what gets me going."

In addition, Jones also revived his *Mirrorman* screenplay in 1998, rewriting it with an eye on directing it as a feature film. He has written a pilot for an animated *Dr. Fegg* TV show, but his other projects slowed up any further development on the cartoon. He says his future will undoubtedly hold more children's books (his *Fairy Tales* and *Fantastic Stories* were released in 1997 as a double-sized book), but isn't pinning himself to anything specific.

Terry Jones isn't as concerned with the thought of long-term projects. "Long term? I don't know," he says. "I've never had long-term projects really—just to make things, really, that's all I've wanted to do."

His proudest achievements outside of Python are both related to young people, he notes. "I'm very pleased with my kid's books, really, and also with *Wind in the Willows*," says Jones. "It's had a very mixed reaction over here, but it's gotten a great reaction from kids and from adults who are not critics!"

The most satisfying projects for Jones seem to be films and books. "I suppose writing a book is one of the best things, because it's so direct and so 'there it is!' " says Jones. "What you write is there. I do enjoy making films—I just wish I could write them quicker! Films and books are really what I'm into at the moment."

Terry Jones in **Mr. Toad's Wild Ride.** *From the collection of Terry Jones, used by permission.*

Ripping Yarns

The first major post-Python project for Terry Jones and Michael Palin was the series *Ripping Yarns.* The first of them was "Tomkinson's Schooldays," the story of life at a very strange British public school. Beautifully photographed and with outstanding production values, the half-hour, broadcast early in 1976, impressed the BBC enough to authorize the next five.

Written by Jones and Palin, Jones only appeared on screen in *Tomkinson,* though Palin starred in all the episodes. "They all have a little hero figure, who really isn't a hero," Palin described them at the time. "In one, I play a boy of about eighteen, which is getting increasingly difficult; in another, I play a man of sixty, which is getting increasingly easier . . ."

The immediate forerunner to *Ripping Yarns* may have been one of the Python TV shows in the third series. Michael Palin and Terry Jones were, by that time, tending to write longer-form sketches. One day they came into a Python meeting with one long, episodic sketch called "Cycling Tour" that took up the entire half-hour show. Palin played Mr. Pither, who, while on his cycling tour of North Cornwall, has a variety of misadventures; he meets the peculiar Mr. Gullivar, and winds up at the USSR 42nd International Clambake.

Unlike the Python shows that came before, "Cycling Tour" had one linear story from start to finish. (The Python opening

Terry Jones circa 1997. Photographed by Sian Trenberth for Mayday Management, used by permission.

credits and music were never even included in the half hour.) The fourth season of Python, without John Cleese to balance the mix, saw Palin and Jones becoming more dominant, and several of those shows have a strong linear story thread throughout, including "The Golden Age of Ballooning," "Michael Ellis," and "Mr. Neutron."

By the time they were offered the chance to create a new TV show, the pair was getting accustomed to working in the half-hour format. Their series is based on the English stiff-upper-lip stories of the early 1900s.

"They're about school life, escaping from German prisoner-of-war camps, plucky stories of chaps doing their best, all with a fine edge of irony. They're all made on film, apart from one, beautifully shot—I'd love to see them in a theater rather than television," admits Palin.

Palin hadn't thought about creating the show until after Monty Python had ended its TV run.

"One of the people who liked my work in Python was a guy called Terry Hughes, who has now done shows like *Golden Girls* and all that," explains Palin, noting that Hughes also directed the film version of *Monty Python Live at the Hollywood Bowl.*

"He approached me to do a show on my own after Python, a sort of 'Michael Palin Variety Show,' and I just really didn't fancy putting on a suit, coming down stairs, singing with the Three Degrees, and introducing Des O'-Connor or whatever. So, I talked to Terry about it—we were working on stuff at the time, and we'd just done the Fegg book and all that.

"I just wasn't sure which way to

go, when Terry's brother had seen a book on Terry's shelf called *Ripping Tales* or something like that, and he said 'Why don't you do something about those sort of stories?' And that was a very good tip. I started something called 'Tomkinson's Schooldays,' which I wrote in about ten minutes at one go, and then Terry took over, and together we saw it through," he says.

The result was a very British show; nothing on American TV was comparable to *Ripping Yarns.*

"I've never seen anything in *England* that's comparable to the *Yarns!*" Palin laughs. "It was really trying to put a very, very British literary tradition, the Edwardian era, into the form of a TV comedy half hour. The stories that were around all had to do with the imperial or postimperial stage of Britain's history. They were about winning wars and fighting, pluck and courage, going out to all the far-flung corners of the world.

Ripping Yarns are nine delightfully quirky shows that marked the last work of Michael Palin and Terry Jones as a team, aside from Python collaborations.

Palin and Jones had been writing together for over ten years, and theirs was (and is) probably the closest friendship among the members of Python. After the TV shows ended, the Pythons tended to drift toward their own projects, all the while remaining good friends. Still, the Palin-Jones creative team continued working together.

When the offer came to Palin for his own show, he naturally called Jones. Although they wrote the scripts together, Jones found some friction working with the BBC crews. Throughout the Python years, Palin was nearly always genial and easy to work with, whereas Jones was more meticulous and determined, and strove for perfection in the editing process. As a result, Jones acted in "Tomkinson's Schooldays" but didn't feel comfortable performing in the series.

"I was in 'Tomkinson's Schooldays,' the first one, but I found it a bit awkward," explains Jones. "Generally, I think I had a very bad reputation at the BBC as being an awkward bugger, because I made life hell for poor Ian MacNaughton [who directed nearly all of the *Python* TV shows]! I was always insisting on editing the shows and going all over the locations, and keeping my sticky fingers all over everything, especially during the filming. I found it very uncomfortable doing 'Tomkinson's

Schooldays,' because Mike had been offered a series of his own, and I think there was a feeling amongst the crew of 'Why was I interfering?' and I was saying my usual thing of 'I think we could get some shots over there.'

"Finally, I said to Mike 'It's either got to be our joint show, or I'll just write it with you.' I think Mike quite liked the idea of doing his own show, anyway," he says, laughing. "I decided 'I'll just duck out here.'

"It was quite a difficult time, really. Up until then, Mike and I had been definitely working outright as a team; it was the first time we'd stopped. It was really because Mike wanted to do his own thing."

The first series of six *Ripping Yarns* were successful enough to warrant more. "We picked up an award from the Broadcasting Press Guild, an informal gathering of critics in England, for the best comedy show of the year," reveals Palin. The shows were expensive to produce, however, and so with BBC cutbacks, only three more shows were created for the second series. But the production values remain consistently high for all nine *Ripping Yarns.*

The pilot was aired in the U.K. on January 7, 1976, and the other five, broadcast from September 27 to October 25, 1977, completed the first series. The second series of three shows appeared October 10–24, 1979.

First Series

Show 1: "Tomkinson's Schooldays" A young boy at a very peculiar public school, where students must beat the headmaster and runaways are hunted down by the school leopard, rises through the ranks to become the new school bully.
Show 2: "The Testing of Eric Olthwaite" A young man so boring that his parents run away from home (all he can speak of is rainfall, shovels, and black pudding) is idolized when he becomes the leader of an outlaw gang.
Show 3: "Escape From Stalag Luft 112B" A British P.O.W. who holds the record for escaping from German camps is sent to the most impregnable camp of all, but his plans are thwarted by his fellow Englishmen.

Show 4: "Murder at Moorstones Manor" Trouble breaks out at a country estate when a family beset by murder finds there are more confessions than corpses.

Show 5: "Across the Andes by Frog" Capt. Snetterton leads the first High Altitude Amphibian Expedition across the Andes, but the natives and his crew are more interested in schoolgirls and listening to football.

Show 6: "The Curse of the Claw" An old man recounts the story of his youth, and the mysterious claw given to him by his Uncle Jack (who was totally unconcerned about contagious diseases).

Second Series

Show 7: "Whinfrey's Last Case" While on holiday, a British hero foils a German plot to begin World War I ahead of schedule.

Show 8: "Golden Gordon" The Barnestoneworth Football team's most fanatical supporter takes action when his team is sold.

Show 9: "Roger of the Raj" A wealthy young soldier-of-fortune stoops to the most despicable act known to the British Army.

Michael Palin

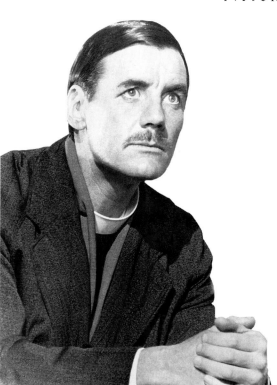

A fervent-looking Michael Palin (here in the title role of The Missionary*). Photo copyright Handmade Films/The Missionary.*

The son of an engineer, Michael Palin was born May 5, 1943, in Sheffield, Yorkshire. He began attending Birkdale Preparatory School in 1948, where he made his first dramatic appearance as Martha Cratchit in *A Christmas Carol,* and fell off the stage. He then attended Shrewsbury School in 1957.

Majoring in history, Palin began studying at Brasenose College, Oxford, in 1962, where he wrote and performed his first comedy material at the Oxford University Psychology Society Christmas Party. He began acting with the Oxford University Dramatic Society and the Experimental Theatre Company, where he first met future writing partner Terry Jones.

The two were featured in one of the Experimental Theatre Company's most notable productions, *Hang Down Your Head and Die,* a musical anthology which carried a strong anti–capital punishment message; the show was specifically designed around the talents of a few ETC members, including Palin and Jones, who both contributed material, as well. It was presented at Oxford during the winter term of 1964, and played forty-four performances at London's Comedy Theatre in March 1964. Later that year, Palin appeared with Jones and others in *The Oxford Revue* at the Edinburgh Festival, and also played McCann in the ETC production of Pinter's *Birthday Party.*

The following year, after Jones graduated, Palin wrote, directed and appeared in *The Oxford Line* revue at the Edinburgh Festival in 1965, and received a degree in Modern History. He appeared briefly as the co-compère of *Now!,* a TV pop show produced in Bristol for the now-defunct Television West Wales, and simultaneously resumed his partnership with Jones, rewriting a Jones script called

Palin at home in 1978, strangling one of his sons with the Claw used in the Ripping Yarn "Curse of the Claw." Photo copyright KHJ.

The Love Show, a documentary dealing with sex. In April of 1966, he married Helen Gibbins.

Palin and Jones began contributing to a number of TV shows around this time, including *The Billy Cotton Band Show, The Ken Dodd Show,* and *The Illustrated Weekly Hudd,* as well as writing for *The Two Ronnies* and Marty Feldman. The two of them also wrote and performed in short films for the BBC's *Late Show. The Frost Report* found them working with Cleese, Chapman, and Idle, while the pair of them were script editors on *A Series of Birds* and *Twice a Fortnight.* It was on the latter program, a late-night satirical show in 1967, that Palin and Jones got their first chance to perform. Palin and Jones also wrote pantomimes of *Aladdin* and *Beauty and the Beast* for the Watford Palace Theatre in 1967 and 1968, the latter of which Palin characterized as "fairly dreadful."

It was in 1967 that Palin teamed with Jones and Eric Idle to write and perform the first of two seasons of *Do Not Adjust Your Set,* a forerunner to Monty Python. Between the first and second series, Palin and Jones wrote their own six-part series, a historical comedy called *The Complete and Utter History of Britain,* for London Weekend Television. Palin also appeared in a TV special written by and starring Cleese and Chapman, called *How to Irritate People.* Cleese and Chapman, had written a

sketch for the show based on Palin's experiences with a defective car, which was later rewritten and turned into the "Dead Parrot" sketch for Python. Palin and Jones also appeared in *The Late Show,* and did more writing for Frost, the Two Ronnies, and Marty Feldman's series as Python got underway in 1969.

During the Monty Python years, Palin managed to keep busy with other activities outside the group. In 1973, he and Jones cowrote a BBC play, *Secrets,* an hour-long black comedy about a worker in a chocolate factory who falls into a vat; the play was later adapted into the 1988 film *Consuming Passions* starring Vanessa Redgrave. On New Year's Eve, 1975, Palin appeared in a Tom Stoppard adaptation of Jerome K. Jerome's *Three Men in a Boat,* directed by Stephen Frears and costarring Tim Curry.

Palin and Jones also wrote two short "Their Finest Hours" plays for the Crucible Theatre, Sheffield, the following year. *Underhill's Finest Hour* took place in a hospital delivery ward, where a woman giving birth finds that her doctor is more interested in listening to cricket; *Buchanan's Finest Hour* took place entirely inside a large box.

Charles McKeown, who went on to cowrite and appear in *Brazil,* appeared in both of them. Of the latter, he says, "It was about an international packaging organization that had been taken for a ride by an even bigger packaging organization, in which there were three of us inside a large crate. We never saw the audience, and the audience never saw us. We sat in this crate.

"There was a conservative M.P. and his agent, and a French escapologist who also turned out to be inside the box within about ten minutes of the start of the play. A little later, his decapitated wife was also found to be inside the box. We thought we had been delivered to a place where we were going to receive tremendous publicity in front of an audience, and it becomes clear to us that something has gone tremendously wrong, and there's nobody there at all. Later we hear a truck, and another box is brought in containing the Pope. He has also been duped by this even larger international marketing company to be part of their publicity campaign."

Contributing to the Python books, Palin and Jones also wrote *Dr. Fegg's Nasty Book of Knowledge* (released in the U.K. as *Bert Fegg's Nasty Book for*

Boys and Girls, and subsequently retitled in 1985 as *Dr. Fegg's Encyclopedia of All World Knowledge*) in 1974. Palin has also contributed articles to *Esquire* magazine, *The New York Times*, *The Sunday Telegraph Magazine*, and *Punch*.

Palin's writing following Python, however, tended to be more concerned with teleplays and screenplays. He and Jones wrote and performed "Tomkinson's Schooldays" for the BBC, a travesty on English schoolboy stories popular in comics and juvenile books in the '20s. The story of a young man who rises to the post of School Bully became the first in a series of six *Ripping Yarns*, which won a Broadcasting Press Guild award for Best Comedy Series of 1977. Three more shows were aired late in 1979. Although Jones only appeared in the first show, Palin starred in all nine of the *Yarns*. Two books of scripts were released containing all the scripts from both seasons, *Ripping Yarns* and *More Ripping Yarns*.

Perhaps inspired in part by Jones's success, Palin also tried his hand at writing chil-

Michael Palin with the un-Gwen Dibley-like Maggie Smith in **The Missionary;** *the pair subsequently teamed up again for Alan Bennett's* **A Private Function.** *Photo copyright Handmade Films/The Missionary.*

Here, Palin insisted that the above picture be taken, as proof that the director kept them on the **Life of Brian** *set until 6:45 P.M. Photo copyright KHJ.*

dren's books, beginning in 1982 with *Small Harry and the Toothache Pills.* He also wrote *The Mirrorstone,* a book illustrated with holograms, and penned two Cyril books, including *Cyril in the House of Commons.*

"I'm probably a lazy old sod, and wouldn't have done anything if I hadn't been pushed. I had three children growing up at that time, and I spent a lot of time reading them stories. I felt I knew what was a good story to read and what was a bad story to read," he declares.

"So, I felt 'I want to have a go at that,' because there's nothing better than the attention of a child, and they're really gripped by a story—it's wonderful, they're a great audience. So, I think I wanted to have a go at that and see if I could do that, and make it something that a parent would enjoy reading, and the children would also be involved with," notes Palin.

"It's a tough audience to write for, but I've found that it's very gratifying when it works."

Beginning with his lead role in Terry Gilliam's *Jabberwocky* in 1977, Palin also launched a successful solo film career following Python. He cowrote and played a dual role in 1981's *Time Bandits,* also written and directed by Terry Gilliam. The following year, Palin wrote, co-produced, and starred in *The Missionary* for Handmade Films, his first major solo film project. As the title character, returning from Africa, he is called to work among the fallen women of Victorian London. His subdued, low-key humor stood as a marked contrast to his Python work, and the film was generally received well by critics and audiences.

When Denis O'Brien and George Harrison of Handmade Films approached Palin, they essentially gave him a blank check to make whatever type of film he wanted.

"*The Missionary* was the first time I'd been given carte blanche to make a film of my own," Palin relates. "Denis and George said 'Come up with a script and have a go, come up with an idea and do it.' I think I needed, then, to try something on my own. You always feel yes, there's something you really want to say, but when you actually start thinking about it, of course, it's like being asked, given all the ice creams in the world, which flavor do you want? It's really difficult, you can't decide what to go for.

"I came up with the idea of a missionary who comes back a changed man, and what he was particularly good at in Africa makes him particularly susceptible to the hypocrisy back in this country. He suddenly finds himself the object of quite a lot of people's affections. He's really only trying to do his best, and he has to do that quite regularly!" he explains.

"The idea of *The Missionary* formed in my mind about March of 1981, after doing *Time Bandits,* and I put the script into Denis O'Brien and George Harrison's hands, knowing that George had always been quite keen on the *Ripping Yarns,*" notes Palin, but he says *The Missionary* is quite different.

"I suppose it's a bit similar to a *Ripping Yarn* in that it's a period tale and a comedy, but it's really quite a long advance on from *Ripping Yarns,* with the sort of casting we can do, and the quality, and the extent to which we can get locations and spend a bit more money on it.

"So, it was really about this area that I explored a little with Terry in *Ripping Yarns,* which was British hypocrisy and the different levels on which the British operate. I though this would be good ground. Richard Loncraine wanted to direct it and loved the script, and we suddenly started getting good actors, like Denholm Elliot and Maggie Smith.

"Throughout, I had the say on casting, but Maggie was actually Richard Loncraine's selection. I think she was marvelous. I wasn't quite sure who to suggest for that part, and she's absolutely perfect. Trevor Howard, we thought of together for the crusty old English reactionary, which he did very well. He liked Python, and that helped.

"A lot of these straight actors are bored stiff doing the straight roles all the time, playing Shakespeare and classical Greek tragedy, and they really

want to play a bit of comedy. The difficulty was, I wanted them to play themselves straight, and the comedy would come out of that—it's not a film for silly walks and people wearing goose costumes. It's a comedy that comes out of the look of the period, from realistic and authentic characters," he explains.

Some of the most interesting filming that took place involved the establishing shots at the beginning of the movie, where his title character is in Kenya.

"When we were filming in Africa, I had to do some scenes of me passing by wild animals. The ranger who was guarding us as we were doing the filming actually had to cover me with a gun as I walked past the elephants. I thought elephants in the zoo were really rather nice things, without guns and all that, but apparently in the wild they become the fiercest animals of them all! So, there I was, doing my jaunty comedy walk, being covered by a man with a gun behind a bush. I never discovered whether he was going to shoot me or the elephant. . . . "

Palin says that although it isn't perfect, he is happy he had the opportunity to make *The Missionary.*

"Although I think it had faults, especially toward the end, I was able to break out of the slightly restrictive world of Python, playing all the parts ourselves, into getting the best people around to do them—there's no doubt Maggie Smith introduces an enormous extra element to the work she does. The same with Denholm, and of course, Michael Hordern, who played the butler—I can't imagine anyone doing that as well," notes Palin.

"I was pleased that it was a departure from Python. It was more conventional, but a lot of the humor worked very well. Unfortunately, I don't think the drama worked quite as well as it should have done, but it's still a nice film, a beauty to watch."

In 1984 he was reunited with Maggie Smith, his *Missionary* costar, performing Alan Bennett's screenplay of *A Private Function,* the story of a social-climbing family and their pig in the heavily rationed days of post–World War II Britain.

Michael Palin recalls that he was hired onto *A Private Function* simply as an actor by one of the *Beyond the Fringe* creators, and given the opportunity to team again with his *Missionary* co-star.

"The phone call came from Alan Bennett, who is a very well-respected writer who I like very much indeed, a marvelous eye for detail. To be asked by him to be in a film is something you just sort of accept," explains Palin. "I worked with a tremendous cast—I got to work with Maggie again."

He says he didn't realize until later that one of the reasons they were asked to do the film was so that it could be made! "I was so pleased to have a chance to do it, and I suddenly realized that actually, they asked me and Maggie in the hope that we'd get Handmade Films to put money into it! I remember going to the first meeting with Alan and the producers, and I thought they were going to tell me when they were doing it, and the locations, and how big the caravan would be and all of this sort of stuff, when in fact they were asking me about where they might get the money. I said 'Hang on!' " he recalls, laughing.

"But we did give the script to Denis [O'Brien] and George [Harrison], and they have been wonderful supporters throughout the last ten years, and they supported this! I don't think Denis understood it at all, really. I don't think he knew quite why he was doing it, he just felt that if I wanted to do it, it was good enough for him! And I'm very grateful to him for that. I think that turned out into a pretty idiosyncratic and interesting movie, very different from anything else I've done, and will stand the test of time. It keeps getting repeated, and is noted with interest."

The film was well received by critics, and Palin notes he had agreed to star in it before there was even a script.

"I hadn't actually seen the script first, it was just Alan Bennett's reputation. He's a very fastidious writer, very careful and thorough, so he'd know the area he'd been involved in with intense personal detail, and he has a very good ear for dialogue. So, I was pretty well converted before he even began doing it. Then I read the script, and it had a lot of the qualities that I like to put in my own scripts. It's a slightly self-regarding way of talking about it, but I think I saw in Alan things I liked, and that was fine. . . . "

In 1985, Palin returned to yet another Gilliam project. In *Brazil,* he played Jack Lint, the hero's best friend who eventually becomes his torturer. 1988 saw Palin in a much lighter role in Cleese's *A Fish Called Wanda,* playing the stuttering animal

lover Ken, who inadvertently kills three dogs and runs over Kevin Kline with a steamroller.

And of course, in 1997 Palin reunited with the *Wanda* ensemble to portray the keeper of the Insect House of Marwood Zoo in *Fierce Creatures.*

"Four days after finishing *Fierce Creatures* and four days after leaving a cupboard in Pinewood where I was with John Cleese and Carey Lowell and a tarantula, I was in Alaska starting a full-circle trip around the Pacific. And four days after getting *back* to Alaska, to this island in the Bering Straits, I was in a bee costume a year later at Pinewood! I

As The Missionary, Rev. Charles Fortescue (Michael Palin) assists one of the fallen women (Tricia George) of his Ministry. Photo copyright Handmade Films/The Missionary.

wasn't really looking forward to it, but it was an excellent reshoot. I had more to do and I was more involved in the action. That was a very intense period, while the summer before was a bit laid-back time when we all sat outside animal cages, usually half dressed as bees or kangaroos, and waited to be called to do something."

Working with John Cleese again in *Fierce Creatures* also gave Palin the opportunity to work with another Terry again, as well—this time, however, it turned out to be a tarantula.

"It's a big spider, the tarantula," says Palin. "That's kind of reassuring, because you can see its eyes. It's those little ones, where you can't actually

see anything that I worry about—you can't tell where they're off to and what their intentions are! I could always see this tarantula smiling, which was very nice. It had been very well-bred and very well looked-after.

"We just had to do a sort of test to see if I could work with it or not. I had to go in there and put the tarantula on my outstretched palm, which took, I have to say, a certain amount of courage on the part of the tarantula. We bonded pretty quickly! It was called Terry. I think this was to help me get to like it more easily. Maybe it was being trained up as the next Python film director! We've been through two, now he's the third. . . .

"It was a great triumph of Terry the tarantula and our relationship that although they had an animatronic tarantula which was standing by for all the difficult scenes, Terry did most of the stunts himself. In fact, he actually did the scene where he goes across the desk to John and frightens him.

"The way you coax spiders to act is not by giving them large contracts and limousines and caravans of their own. You blow cold air at them from either side. If they feel the slightest bit of cold air, they go the opposite way, and you can get them to go in a straight line. So, in the scene where John sits at the desk and the tarantula's going across to him, if you had widened out six inches on either side of him, you would have seen two spider wranglers with plastic tubes blowing air at this spider, which I think was a lot funnier than what you actually saw on the screen!"

Like many other fans, Palin was disappointed in the weak box office showing of *Fierce Creatures.* "It was a bit like *American Friends.* So many people went to see it and really liked it, but it didn't have that 'must-see' quality, it wasn't the film everybody was going to see that week, and I think that affects how things work," says Palin. "It's so intriguing, that with all of the research and focus

groups and all that stuff in Hollywood that they can get it wrong!"

Palin wrote and starred in *American Friends* in 1991, the first time he wore both of those hats in a feature film since *The Missionary.*

American Friends was loosely based on the diaries of Michael Palin's great-grandfather, and it was a film he long attempted to make. Despite some lighter moments, it isn't a comedy, and is closer to a love story than any other genre, which may have made it difficult for him to raise the production costs. In fact, it took nearly five years from the first ideas to the final product, he says.

"It was the counterpoint to the last five years," notes Palin. "The initial idea came up in 1986, and I spoke to various people about it. Eric [Idle] encouraged me to have a go at writing it into a screenplay. It was different from what I'd usually done. It wasn't comedy; therefore, it was hard to know when it was right. In comedy, you read a page, and either it makes you laugh, or it doesn't. With this, it was very difficult to know what to put in, what not to put in, how serious to be, how comic to be. . . . "

There were numerous interruptions along the way, but Palin never gave up; he says he was very happy with the final result.

"I was continually doing other things—I started writing in 'eighty-six, and along came *Wanda,* and then came *Around the World in 80 Days,* and I was still going in and out with this thing, doing rewrites. Although I lost heart occasionally, others, especially Steve Abbott and Patrick Cassavetti, said 'Right, we're going to go ahead, we're going to do this,' and they kept me at it, and I was very, very pleased with the result."

Palin still enjoys writing as well as acting, and scripted *East of Ipswich* for the BBC in 1986. He also starred in *GBH,* a seven-part television drama aired in 1991, which saw him take on a more serious acting role.

Michael Palin was happy to play such a different role in *GBH,* which he said was unlike anything he'd ever done before. He was convinced by the Alan Bleasdale script, which ended up being much more than the standard good versus evil story it first appeared to be, and he got good critical notices for the dramatic part.

"Alan Bleasdale isn't known in the States, but he's one of the most respected and successful television dramatists we have here," explains Palin.

"He's also written stuff for the theatre. His work is very British and local, in a way, and deals with situations from a fairly critical and usually left-wing perspective.

"He got in touch with me and said he'd written this character of a charismatic council leader who's gone completely mad, and it's set up in the north of England. It's really an examination of what happened in political life in Liverpool in the last years of the Thatcher administration," he says, explaining that it was a drama with elements of comedy.

"It tells of this council leader trying to terrorize this schoolmaster into toeing the party line. The schoolmaster is a sort of a stroppy, independent-minded character who fights against this, and the two of them go through a lot of adventures, dragging themselves down as they go.

"He offered me the part of council leader. It was a huge work, ten hours of television. I was very flattered to be asked to do it and agreed. Then, for various reasons, he changed the casting around, and I played the stroppy schoolmaster, Jim Nelson, who is also cracking up! It was a seven-part series of ninety-minute films. There was a lot of comedy in it, and I suppose it was a meaty acting role—a chance to see if I could do some meaty acting."

Palin wasn't involved in any of the writing, and says he was glad to be able to limit his participation to acting in *GBH.*

"I was able to concentrate purely on acting. After doing *American Friends,* where I felt responsible for writing and many other aspects of the production, it was a relief to do a purely acting role."

His career as a travelogue host, which led to *Around the World in 80 Days, Pole to Pole,* and *Full Circle* actually began with a simple railway journey for the BBC several years earlier, in 1982.

Conceived as one of the *Great Railway Journeys of the World* for the BBC, a seven-part series that included trips by various travelers literally around the globe, Palin's journey across Great Britain was the fourth show of the series. Although he had loved trains and travel since he was a boy, the opportunity to do the program came from nowhere.

"A lot of things came from out of the blue," explains Palin. "I had been talking on the radio about my favorite form of transport, which happened to be the train. The next morning, a guy rang me up

and said 'I'm a director, I'm based in Manchester for the BBC, we've got one more in a series of *Great Railway Journeys* to do, a train journey around Britain. Would you be prepared to be our traveler?' Thank you, Ken Stephinson! I did that with him, and I think probably as a result of that, along came *80 Days* years later."

Confessions of a Train-Spotter established Palin as an amiable, friendly, entertaining traveler, and when the BBC decided to do a real-life *Around the World in 80 Days*, it was no wonder Michael Palin was their guide. His reputation was established even more firmly two years later when he went around the world again, this time from North Pole to South Pole.

The decision to do the initial, less grueling train trip was somewhat of a career change for Palin, but it was obviously an enjoyable experience.

"It was a different direction for me, because at that time, I was still just writing and performing for film or television. To be asked to do something like that was a nice change of direction," he states. "I remember Denis O'Brien of Handmade Films, who was sort of our Python manager for a while and doing my financial management, could not believe that I wanted to do a thing on railroads when I could have had any film I wanted! But I said 'I love railways,' and he said 'Don't worry, I'm going to get you a really big fee.' He was totally defeated by a lady called Barbara who worked in the basement at BBC-Manchester in a sort of soundproof box. He couldn't budge her. There's a man who can rock Hollywood, but he couldn't move this lady in Manchester.

"So, I got paid very, very little, but of course it's paid off enormously in the long run, which I knew it would. It's typical of the BBC. They don't pay you much the first time around, but they do tend to make the sort of programs that sustain, and keep getting repeated, so I can't complain."

One of the endearing traits of Michael Palin— and indeed, all of the Pythons—is that they have been less concerned with making huge sums of money and more concerned with doing a project that interests them. And railroads have always interested Michael.

"I thought a railway journey through England and Scotland not only will be beautiful, lovely scenery and all, but I get to ride on one of the old steam engines and all that—things I'd always wanted to do, things I'd have given my right arm to do twenty years before. So I said, why not now?" he says. "I didn't think about whether I should be doing it for career reasons, or money reasons or any other reasons, I just thought it would be a good thing to do, and a great experience, which is rather the way I approached *80 Days* in the end. And of course, I'm glad I did both!"

On September 25, 1988, Michael Palin left London with a five-man BBC crew to record his adventures on a round-the-world trip, a journey presented for a six-hour BBC documentary and in a full-length book that reprints Michael Palin's journal.

As it inspired him to go on a follow-up trip a few years later from North to South Pole, Palin says the first trip must have agreed with him.

"I can't have disliked it that much, because I'm off again!" he noted, shortly before embarking on the pole to pole trip. "It certainly didn't cure me of the travel bug—in fact, it stimulated me and made me more curious about what lies out there. Overall, you can't emulate the *Eighty Days* format, because a part of the fun of it was that it was a race against time, and I don't think you can do a travel series like that, with three days' break in eighty days of filming—you just can't do it. Physically, it's almost impossible. I was quite surprised that we got as much as we did out of it in the end.

"But when we hit somewhere like the dhow, it obviously struck a chord with people. A lot of people said that I made them feel as though they were on the journey with me, and they were very close to it all, and it made them want to travel the same areas. Also, the nicest thing of all, is I heard from people in the States who teach classes with kids, that it's not patronizing, and doesn't talk down, and doesn't try and seem that we're better than anyone else. That's high praise, and I'm flattered that people think that," notes Palin. "So, for all those reasons, I thought we ought to have a go at another one!"

Michael Palin's first global journey for the BBC, *Around the World in 80 Days*, was so successful that he was asked to make another trip; since he had already traveled west to east, the north-to-south route seemed appropriate.

The biggest reason Palin wanted to make the

polar journey, however, was the overwhelmingly positive response he received to the first shows.

"I thought we ought to have a go at another one, partly to satisfy my own curiosity, and partly because of the very, very different route, down through Finland and Russia, and right through Africa—from Cairo to the Cape, the historic route down the Nile. . . .

"My director, Clem Vallance, was looking at what journey, what *epic* journey we could do, and decided 'We've done across, let's go *down*.' The thirty-degree line of longitude goes through land almost all the way, and quite interesting, varied land."

A few weeks before he was set to depart, Palin discussed his preparations for the trip eagerly.

"I'm terrified!" he laughed. "Well, I am now. A couple of months ago, I was saying 'Oh, I'll be going from pole to pole, pretty cool, this is my next job,' blasé, blasé. Now I'm beginning to think of the realities of it and bringing back all the film, and it's quite terrifying. But it'll be great. Mentally, I think I'm ready for it now.

"*80 Days* was an unknown quantity, I just didn't know what it was going to be like, *how* it was going to be like, what *tone* we were going to adopt, how it would work. In the end, the people we met made the show—it just wrote itself as we went 'round. That was just a basic fear of the unknown," Palin recalls.

"This isn't quite so unknown. The technique we now know. Roughly, the sort of tone of it, we know. So, it's really just the places we go through that are going to be different—but they're *very* different, and there's less time for luxury. A lot of it will be much rougher."

His trip was actually begun in July of 1991 at the northern tip of Norway, and he spent the rest of the year traveling to the South Pole; due to climatic conditions, he had to complete the beginning of the journey in April of 1992.

"We hadn't completed it, because owing to the vagaries of climatic conditions in the north, we had to go to the North Pole at a time when it was safe to land there. That's only a short period of the year, late April and early May," he explains.

Palin explains that having done most of the trip and having to go back months later to do the "beginning" is a little frustrating.

"We went from the north of Norway, the first bit of land in Europe, to the South Pole. It took us about five months. We traveled overland and didn't catch any major diseases, though I cracked a rib white-water rafting in the Zambesi."

"Apart from that, there were no great problems as far as I was concerned. Some of the crew got sick, but we managed to film every day, despite the extremes of heat and cold, and the film all came out. It makes a pretty rich series, much different in content from *80 Days*."

The main difference from his trip *Around the World in 80 Days* is that the polar voyage involved very little sea travel.

"It was nearly all overland," he reveals. "Instead of going from city to city, which we tended to do in *80 Days,* we went across a lot of bare, difficult country terrain. We also went through a lot more different climatic extremes than we did in *80 Days.* It was even hotter than *80 Days,* and of course we also had extreme cold. I think that the overland journeys through the countries were more difficult, but in the end, more rewarding, because the scenery that we saw and the beauty of the countries was much greater than we really had time to see in *80 Days*."

There were some problems along the way, of course, but Palin says the trickiest area of the journey was traveling through the Sudan.

"It's not an easy country to work in, for many reasons," he notes. "It was very, very hot. It's largely desert, and its government is xenophobic in the sense that they're not very keen on the West. There's an Arab fundamentalist government and life is quite hard there for Westerners. Also, they are very bureaucratically obstructive, which again meant that just getting through it was difficult— you have to have papers and permissions, and lots of queuing up at offices.

"To compound all that, it is an *enormous* country," Palin says with a laugh, "so it takes a long time to get through anyway. The final section of that was to cross the border into Ethiopia along what appeared on the map was a road, but in fact turned out to be nothing but a track which had been heavily indented by trucks. We got stuck, and it took us hours longer than we intended to get across. It was undoubtedly the most difficult place."

Palin and his BBC crew actually avoided the turmoil in the Soviet Union during late 1991,

though he takes the credit for having instigated it all.

"We started it all. I think we finally precipitated the total collapse of the Soviet Union," he laughs. "Within forty-eight hours of our intensive, searching documentary, literally as we were crossing the Black Sea, the coup happened, and we heard a few days later that it had collapsed and Gorbachev was back. The major change happened about forty-eight hours after we left!"

By the time they arrived in Antarctica at the end of the trip, Palin says they were all rather tired.

"We were airlifted out from the southern part of Chile to the central part of the Antarctic plateau, looked after on a small base there, and then flown to the Pole. If you've got a fear of flying, it's a difficult place to be, because there's just this emptiness below, and even though it was summer, the temperatures were very low.

"But we were well looked after there. We got to the Pole, and there was an American base there. It was rather like going to a Python fan convention. The most remote part of the earth, and there are people there with copies of *Wanda* that they want you to sign. That didn't happen to Captain Scott!"

The most expansive, perhaps the most ambitious of his travelogues, *Full Circle* saw him circle the entire Pacific Rim.

Michael Palin, early 1990s. Photo copyright KHJ.

"It starts on what is the most remote island in Alaska, Diomede, which is in the Bering Strait in between the coast of Alaska and the coast of Russia," says Palin. "So, it's a sort of key place, right there at the northern end of the Pacific. We started deliberately in an area where you could see both Asia and America at one point, and then the Pacific widens to 11,000 miles at another point. The journey is around the countries that border the Pacific, through eighteen countries. We start on Diomede and end up on Diomede a year later.

"If people have seen any of the other travel series, they won't be disappointed by this, because it's longer, more exhausting adventure, it's probably richer than the other two in terms of the number of people we see, the countries we go through, and the number of adventures I have. There are some pretty unusual things in it.

"In Australia, there's a sequence with me trying to lasso wild camels, which looks like *Lawrence of Arabia* gone mad!" Palin laughs. "It's an amazing day spent with these cowboys—or camelboys—in Australia. The toughest day's filming I've ever done in my life was the camel-mustering. I actually get involved in a Lumberjack Festival in British Columbia. By that time I'm getting very weary, and I have to do things like run across a log over a river and not fall in—and of course I fall in. There are humiliations a-plenty! There are some beautiful things to see, we do go through some extraordinary volcanic areas around the Pacific, looking into actual live volcanoes where gas is still escaping from underneath the earth in Russia and in Java. Not a dull day in it, really, I just hope it comes across like that on film."

Michael Palin has been branching out into a number of areas beyond his films, children's books, and travelogues, with a full-length novel and a stage play to his credit.

Palin wrote the script for his first full-length play, *The Weekend,* and helped the director and cast shape it for the stage. *The Weekend* opened in May 1994 in London's West End Theatre District after tryouts and previews outside of London. As it turned out, however, audiences enjoyed it far more than the critics.

"It was heavily attacked in the press," says Palin. "That got very bad reviews in London. West End Theatre is a club and when someone from television comes into it, they look at you very,

very beadily. I had a major television star playing the central role, and I think there was a great deal of resentment among the theatre establishment that television had waltzed into the West End and taken over a theatre just like that. It was as if we hadn't paid our dues. We didn't do a great first night for some reason, it was one of the less good performances and because the knives were out already, it just made things worse. I had to go through what I describe as a mugging by the critics. There were some quite unpleasant things said about the play, which one had to deal with—and I have dealt with it.

"Still, it was a play I'd written some time ago, and it wouldn't have been chosen for the West End unless people had really liked it. We had a couple of experienced producers who encouraged me to get it cast—I wasn't rushing to get it out. Whenever we had a reading, it made people laugh a lot, and I think it remains very funny and quite a touching play at the end. I'm heartened by the fact we played to packed houses in six cities we went to before coming into London.

"It's not a play that I'm burying at all. It's had lots of amateur productions since, and I would very much like to be more closely involved next time in the production, but something did go awry and I'm not blaming the critics for its demise at all. It ran for its eleven weeks as booked and didn't lose anyone any money, so plays have done worse!"

His novel, *Hemingway's Chair,* was released in Britain in 1995. The story features Martin Sproale, an assistant postmaster in a quiet English town who is obsessed with Ernest Hemingway; when a new postmaster is brought in and begins modernizing the quaint old-fashioned post office, Martin decides to take a stand. A light, funny, sometimes touching read, *Hemingway's Chair* garnered many good reviews and convinced Palin to do another novel. Overall, Palin was pleased with it, though he notes he would have liked to spend just a little more time on it.

"I could have done with an extra six months on that—well, maybe three months," says Palin. "I was very happy writing it. It was a big effort. I had about three or four months to write the whole thing. It was a very intense period, I worked closely with an editor on the last section of the rewrites. I was 70 percent pleased with it; I would have reordered and reconsidered 30 percent of it if I'd had those extra months. I was very pleased with the characters in the book as a whole, I liked them all and I'd liked to have gotten along with some of them which I didn't have much chance to develop. I'd liked to have had a little more space at the ending, but these are things that happen with anything you do. I don't know of many people who say they've got a film or book or play exactly right. Bearing in mind that it was done fairly fast, I was really pleased with that, and the proof of that is that I'm already discussing the prospect of writing another one, bearing in mind what I've learned from doing *Hemingway's Chair.*"

A screenplay based on the book is also being written by another scripter with an eye on a possible BBC-TV film, he notes. Overall, Palin was quite pleased with the overall reception of *Hemingway's Chair.* "What I was most pleased about was that the very sniffy London literary press who are very difficult—they don't like outsiders coming in—they were pretty good on the whole," he says. "Outside London, we had some extremely good reviews in places like Ireland, which is a country I have great respect for in terms of producing writers—I think the best review of the book was in the *Irish Times.* It's also done extremely well on the Continent, with a lot of serious attention from Germany and Denmark, and in the press from Scandinavia. It's quite hard to do a novel and be taken seriously when you've been a Python and all that. The next one might be easier, having taken that turn and broken that ground, people will be perhaps more acceptive that I'm not just doing it as a joke idea."

After promoting *Full Circle,* Palin kept busy with several smaller projects, including *Palin on the Redpath,* a short documentary on Anne Redpath done for BBC Arts Scotland. Because he owned a painting of a small town in France which she had rendered in 1939, he retraced her steps to find out exactly where it was done. He also agreed to do a small role in *You've Got Mail* with Tom Hanks, as well as a three-part documentary on Ernest Hemingway.

Although an unauthorized biography by Jonathan Margolis (who also wrote the unauthorized *Cleese Encounters*) was released in 1997, an autobiography or memoir isn't likely anytime soon. Palin has kept his own journals for decades, but

says he hasn't seriously considered publishing them or writing an autobiography.

"I have no plans, but on the other hand, I've got a lot of material going right back to the very start of Python," says Palin. "I'm not quite sure whether to bequeath it to somebody or at some stage to use it. I think very probably I would write a memoir of a certain part of my life, Python or something else, from the diaries and the journals rather than do the whole lot. But I don't really envision myself doing that until I'm quite old—another ten years, possibly. It's like going back on ground you've been over and I'm not sure I want to do that at the moment. I just want to break new ground for a bit. I may well do it at sixty-three. Ask me then if I'm still around! I would be interested in some way evaluating the early years of Python, how it came to be, and I've got some good stories of Graham and all that, but I'm not in memoir-land yet. I've got this stuff here, but there are huge chunks missing, which is what's so wonderful. When Python was beginning, I was much more interested in my newborn son, whether he could crawl or stand up or say a word, than I was with newborn Python. Now, looking back, Python was important—but the diary was for me and my family as much as anything. It's quite interesting how things are left out. Over the years, I've kept a fairly good bead on Python, but I don't know whether everyone would appreciate my diaries, really."

Like the other Pythons, Palin is responsible for a wide variety of works in addition to his TV and film comedies, including novels, children's books, stage plays, travelogues, and much more. He says that Python actually provided the encouragement that inspired him to branch out.

"I have done a lot of different things," says Palin. "My modest talents—they're there, but they *are* modest—should show that other people can do these things, as well. One other factor that I think is important, and which Python taught me, was to be steadfast in your purpose, to make up your own mind in the end. While it may not seem like the easiest thing in the world, to go where your own sort of feelings take you and not be dictated to by others for short-term reasons—you've got to speak up for yourself at a certain point. Python taught me this—healthy independence. It may be a risk, a lot of people will say it's rubbish, and try to prevent

Michael Palin circa 1997. Photographed by Jane Brown for Mayday Management, used by permission.

you from doing what you want to do, especially if it's something new. But if you believe in it, you've got to do it."

His long-range projects are rather flexible, and that suits Michael Palin very well.

"Anything that's new and fresh and gets my enthusiasm going—I don't care what direction it's in particularly," says Palin. "I would like to do some comedy again, because that's one of the few things I can do. I'd also like to travel again, though I'm not intending to do anything on the epic scale of the journeys I've done before. I enjoy writing very much, and that seems to point toward having a go at another novel—I certainly will at some point. So, after spending a year writing and publicizing the Pacific series, spending a quieter year doing something like a new novel appeals to me. But I look at the morning post or get a phone or a fax, and life can completely change! I don't know what's going to be happening, to be honest, but it'll have to be something new, because I get bored very easily."

When future generations look back on his life,

Palin would like to be remembered as someone who entertained and perhaps inspired others.

"We're entertainers in the end, so I suppose I want to be thought of as someone who entertained people, diverted them, brightened a few lives, made people try to do things they wouldn't normally have done, and broadened some imaginations," says Palin. "That's really it. That'll do for me.

"I still am a comedy writer, really. Even though I'm doing these documentaries, and working on commentary on *Full Circle,* I look for opportunities to put jokes in there. Comedy, or an awareness of the absurdity of life, forms everything that I do. I'd like to be remembered for that, really. 'He saw through it!' "

Though he is unlikely to be bored in the future, Palin is quick to cite his only long term plan: "Survival."

The Last Sketch

In September of 1989, the six members of Monty Python got together for the last time at the Python offices and adjacent studio to film a few moments for a twentieth anniversary special, aired in America on the Showtime cable channel in two segments: a greatest-hits compilation of sketches titled *Parrot Sketch Not Included* and a documentary on the group titled *Life of Python.* Steve Martin flew in from America to host the latter show.

Graham Chapman was determined to make it to this Python reunion. At that time, he seemed to be winning in his battle with cancer, or at least told friends and colleagues that he had beaten the disease, appearances to the contrary. He arrived in a wheelchair looking frail and thin, but his mind was alert; no one could have hoped for a better morale-booster for Graham than the get-together, and some informal talk of another group project lifted his spirits that much more.

One of the highlights of the special was to be an original sketch in which Martin appeared with all the Pythons as schoolboys. The origin and fate of that sketch remains one of the unsolved mysteries of Python. In fact, none of the Pythons themselves are completely sure who conceived of it or wrote it, nor can they agree on the quality of the finished product. And to add to the mystery, it was cut out of the program and never aired in America, which bothered some of the Pythons more than others.

"We shot it during a time when Graham was seriously ill, and that I think occupied me," says Cleese. "But it was fine, I was not bothered by it and I was astonished when I heard it had been cut out. I wasn't consulted and I would not have agreed to it, but it was presented to me as a fait accompli."

While Graham Chapman was too ill to participate; the other Pythons joined Steve Martin in a sketch for a 20th anniversary retrospective. Photo from the Collection of Terry Jones and copyright Python Productions.

Terry Jones said he never saw the script until just prior to the filming, and even speculated that it may have even been written by someone outside the group, but John Cleese disagrees.

"I vaguely remember having some hand in the writing of it," says Cleese. "My recollection is that I was associated in some way with the writing, and perfectly happy with the production of it, and that it was a complete surprise when I was told a long time later that it had all been cut out. I was told after it had been transmitted, so there was nothing I could do. I was very embarrassed. This was a big surprise. I thought while we were doing it that it felt funny, so I had no worries about doing it."

Jones says that he had nothing to do with the decision to cut it from the show, though he was annoyed in the way that the sketch was presented to them as a done deal.

"I'm a bit vague, but I remember getting very angry about it, saying it was presented as a fait accompli. I don't know who'd come up with it or written it," says Jones. "Maybe it *was* John who had written it. Certainly *I* wasn't involved in the writing of it and I thought it was terrible. I'd had to come back from France or somewhere, and it had all been organized, sort of out of our control, and it was the first time we'd all agreed to come along and do something that we hadn't written, hadn't actually all sat around together—and it just didn't work. I was a bit pissed-off with it, really. I don't think we should have been put in that position, because it wasn't a funny piece. I don't know where it came from . . . I've got a feeling that whoever wrote it had written it very quickly as a basis for something, hoping that somebody else would write it out properly, but nobody had—there we were, all flying back with Steve Martin coming over to do something that wasn't worth doing, really."

Terry Gilliam was likewise unimpressed with the sketch and with the whole event in general, noting that it probably didn't air for good reason.

"I don't think it was very good," says Gilliam. "It certainly didn't feel good at the time. I don't know who wrote it. It involved dragging everybody in for this day to do something. The awful thing is that it was the Python office, yet it was turning into some kind of holy event—'the gathering, everybody for the first time in blah, blah, blah, there was greatness in the air!' There was this fuss going on. It was the sort of thing that we always avoided, the stuff that we always took the piss out of, and suddenly it was happening to us. It was nice to see everybody together in one room in silly costumes, but the sanctimoniousness that was surrounding the whole thing—and it wasn't coming from us, it was coming from our keepers—I didn't like it at all."

And so, the writing and the fate of the final Python sketch with Graham Chapman appears to remain a mystery.

"It's an *extremely* good question!" says Michael Palin. "It must have been a sort of committee thing, but I really don't know! That's a real mystery . . . The idea of us all dressing up as schoolboys was—well, someone must have suggested that, because we were rather fond of doing schoolboy sketches as Python, little lads with caps on. Who actually put it together, I don't really know . . . I'm surprised that Terry J. denies it, because usually it was Terry who managed to get these things together. Everyone else would sort of opt out, dear old Terry and very often I would end up having to cobble them all together. Maybe we chose to forget it. I don't know. One of the great mysteries of Python."

Anniversaries

Monty Python has been the subject of several retrospectives and anniversaries in recent years, with varying results. One of the first major tributes was held at the Museum of Broadcasting in New York, which assembled a great deal of existing pre-Python TV footage.

Plans for a twenty-year celebration to be held on the anniversary of the first broadcast on October 5, 1989, were postponed due to Graham Chapman's death the night before. But two months later, friends and colleagues gathered in London one afternoon for a celebration of Graham's life. It was followed by a party that evening, ironically held in the hall where the Mr. Creosote scene in

Meaning of Life was filmed. Among those attending were friends and co-workers dating back to the early days of Python, and a jolly time was had by all.

"It's very important when you do those things that you really organize it yourself, because you have to think, 'What do I want out of this?' " says Cleese. "You're always prepared to chat to people for a bit, but you also want to spend some time with your old friends. Otherwise, really, what's the point of it? You're not doing it for total strangers, you know. At the Python twentieth anniversary party, I was familiar with most of the faces there, and they were people I felt very fond of. On those occasions, you want to enjoy the memories of those friendships and professional relationships that you enjoyed for long periods of time. If it's put together by some producer, it becomes some other kind of event, and it's too late to do anything about it."

Five years later, the twenty-fifth anniversary was commemorated by a screening at the Museum of the Moving Image in London, and a retrospective in Los Angeles at the Director's Guild of America from September 9–13, 1994, both of which were organized without them. For Terry Jones, the former was a less than enjoyable experience.

"I was absolutely floored, because I thought it was just a party, and when we got there, it was all press," says Jones. "It was a press thing. I hadn't realized how much I actually prepare myself subconsciously when I'm talking to the press, and I just wasn't ready for it at all. I felt really put out."

The Los Angeles retrospective was attended by Terry Gilliam, Eric Idle, Terry Jones, Carol Cleveland, and Neil Innes, with programs devoted to each of the individual Pythons.

Also attending the opening night ceremonies, dedicated to Graham, was David Sherlock, Graham's long-time companion—or as he preferred to be called, "the widow Chapman." Sherlock—and Graham—were responsible for the most outrageous Python moment of the week, and probably of the decade.

Prior to the screening of *Life of Brian* that would kick off the retrospective, Sherlock was asked to address the crowd. He spoke briefly about Chapman, and concluded his comments by saying ". . . and I've brought a little bit of Graham with me here tonight."

The audience felt a bit sentimental by David's moving comments. Then, before the assembled group, he reached in his pocket, pulled out an envelope, reached inside and sprinkled a few ashes into the crowd. The reaction from everyone was bewilderment, which quickly changed to shock and gasps of disbelief, and finally, wonderful laughter and applause. It was one of the all-time greatest moments in Python.

"It's the first time I've ever seen Eric, Terry and Terry so completely speechless!" laughed Carol Cleveland. "Terry asked me if they were really Graham's ashes, and I just thought 'Who *else's* ashes would David Sherlock be carrying around in his pocket?!' "

Sherlock confirmed afterward that he had indeed brought some of Graham's ashes with him to the celebration. With David's help, Graham had managed to shock everybody one last time.

The rest of the L.A. celebration was not as much fun, notes Terry Gilliam, because it developed into a respectful, almost reverential observance.

"The twenty-fifth anniversary was quite jolly. Of course, the best thing was David sprinkling Graham on the crowd. That was one of the finest moments in Python history," says Gilliam. "That was fine. But then Carol and I end up on a television show! I guess we were there promoting something. But we get dragged in doing these awful things, and I hate it all. There's such an expectation that we're these demigods, and I don't feel like that. I still like saying things that irritate and shock, because I hate most of the television shows we end up on—they're lightweight, foolish, pathetic shows, and everybody's so cautious. I said some awful thing; it was the day somebody had tried to fly a plane into the White House, and I made some really tasteless joke about it which shut everybody up. But I don't like being there and I don't like doing it."

Programming did include a number of highlights. Rare early material included excerpts from *The Frost Report, At Last the 1948 Show,* the recently discovered first episode of *The Complete and Utter History of Britain, "From the Dawn of History to the Norman Conquest," Twice a Fortnight, The Late Show, Do Not Adjust Your Set,* and extremely rare industrial films that the group wrote and shot for Bird's Eye Peas, Harmony Hair Spray, and Gibbs Sr.

While the media watches, Terry Jones, Terry Gilliam, Carol Cleveland and Neil Innes sample the Crunchy Frog, Anthrax Ripple and Cockroach Clusters at the 25th Anniversary celebration in L.A. Photos by Laurie Bradach.

and Spam, Prawn Salad, Ltd., and Crunchy Frog, Anthrax Ripple, and Cockroach Cluster desserts.

John Cleese and Michael Palin were not in attendance in Los Angeles, Cleese being particularly unenthusiastic.

"It seemed to me to be more of a PR event, with a few people very aware that they could make a bit of money out of it," says Cleese. "That was the impression that I got of it. I didn't have any sense that I wanted to go, and from what I heard afterward, I was extremely glad that I hadn't gotten involved. It didn't seem to me to be an intrinsically Pythonic event. I felt that it was one or two people—one of them was obviously Martin Lewis—trying to cash in on the Python name, with which they had no genuine connection whatsoever. From all reports, what came out of it was a not very satisfactory event, which I think was eminently predictable. The whole point about any kind of Python endeavor over the years is that it is fundamentally originated because the Pythons felt enthusiastic about it, and because they were prepared therefore to play a central part in the organization of it. Neither of those conditions were true for this anniversary."

The five surviving Pythons did reunite on March 7, 1998 at the U.S. Comedy Arts Festival in Aspen, Colorado (perhaps a 28½ year anniversary celebration). Although it was a question-and-answer session, it was taped and presented later that month on HBO, and included clips of favorite moments.

Aspen aside, Michael Palin is generally unenthusiastic about such anniversaries and celebrations in general, and likes the programs to speak for themselves.

"It's all part of remembering Python," says Palin. "I'm not particularly keen on anniversaries, gala premieres, awards, that sort of thing. These

There were also directors' cuts of *Brazil* and *Erik the Viking,* marathon screenings of *Flying Circus* and *Fawlty Towers,* as well as rare outtakes from the Python films. The chef at the Sunset Marquis Hotel in West Hollywood devised a Python menu featuring, among other items, Spam, Spam, Spam, Eggs

seem to be things that are organized by people who love Python and that's absolutely fine. I have no great wish to be involved. What I feel is that we made the programs, we made the films, and they're there. People can celebrate them as and when they want, but anniversaries don't mean a huge amount to me. I accept that they do to a lot of other people and I think one cannot just ignore the fact that enthusiasm for Python involves people wanting to organize anniversaries or festival screenings or whatever. But I'm not so keen on that. Actually screening seasons of Python material, when the material itself is actually being shown again, perhaps in a different way to a different audience, that does interest me. But the dates that go by only remind you that you've gotten older!"

Eric Idle in 1996 for **Mr. Toad's Wild Ride.** *From the collection of Terry Jones, used by permission.*

Monty Python Returns: Once More, with Fooling?

The death of Graham Chapman in 1989 ended—at least temporarily—talk of another Python film, and the group was widely believed to be as defunct as the Norwegian Blue. But eventually, there were a few rumblings and rumors that began while John Cleese was doing publicity for *Fierce Creatures,* talk that the remaining members would reunite for a show in Las Vegas.

"It's been around for the last ten years or so, usually suggested as a bit of a joke," says Palin. "We'd all roar with laughter, and then at the end someone would say, 'But seriously . . . ' That's how some of the best Python ideas came up, things that obviously couldn't be done were derided by us all, and then suddenly someone would say, 'Oh, yes, that sounds quite good' and we'd do it! The Hollywood Bowl was a little like that, and we all thoroughly enjoyed doing the Hollywood Bowl."

A Python in Vegas show was a different matter, however, especially in light of the fact that only five-sixths of the group could actively participate. Eric Idle seemed to be a leading proponent of

the reunion when it first arose, and by the time of his *Fierce Creatures* publicity tour in early 1997, John Cleese was actively talking up the idea.

"Eric was very keen at one point, and was disappointed that others did not respond as enthusiastically," says Cleese. "My own response was enthusiastic to the project but not to the date."

While it might not be lucrative financially, that would not be the primary goal, says Cleese. "When you make a film of your own, you get paid a lot more money than if you have to split it six ways. I guess we would be doing it for love rather than money. There would be difficulty getting people together, but it's a project that I think could be very amusing and entertaining, and we might have a lot of fun."

Cleese speculated that the loss of Graham Chapman could be addressed with a plentiful supply of film and video clips of vintage Chapman, as well as some good old-fashioned Pythonic bad taste. "I love the idea of the bad taste of bringing Graham on stage, or apparently bringing him on stage in a coffin as part of a dance routine," says

Cleese. "If we put our minds to it, it could be very entertaining. We would constantly remind the audience of Graham's presence in all of the extremely bad taste methods that we could conjure up, like having a coffin by the side of the stage."

Reaction among the other Pythons to such a reunion was mixed, with Cleese, Idle and Jones generally in favor of it and Gilliam and Palin less enthused.

"Graham's dead, and we always said we weren't going to do it," says Gilliam. "I don't know who it's for, and what we would achieve by doing it. Do we need the money? Like Eric says, maybe Graham was the smartest of all of us—he died while he was still considered funny!"

Michael Palin's attitude is similar to Gilliam's, though he is more thoughtful and reflective about a reunion of the surviving Pythons.

"We are all now seventeen years on, and we have lost a vital, important member of the team, so I have misgivings over our ability to sell Python and old Python sketches without one of the team," says Palin. "Who plays Graham's roles? Do we do sketches which Graham was in with someone else being Graham? Or do we avoid sketches with Graham? If I were a real fan, I think that although I would love to see my team together again, I think I would very much miss the fact that one of the stalwarts was not there.

"Having said that, I also think we're kind of older, and Python always had a vitality and an energy which I'm not sure you can just immediately switch on. I may be wrong and I don't want to sound like I'm senile—I'm not at all, you have to just think very carefully about whether it would be as good. The magic of the sketches as people remember them may be lost. Python occasionally did stage shows, but it wasn't like the Rolling Stones, where they've done one every two or three years and have worked on them with amazing stagecraft and so on. People have gotten used to

seeing the Rolling Stones every two years or so. We haven't done a stage show since 1980, and that's a long time. Python is remembered from television and records and films, and I think there could be quite a danger in just trying to recapture these sketches and not doing them quite well enough, and therefore being a slight disappointment."

As talk about a Vegas stage show died down, the possibility of another Python movie suddenly sprang up when the *London Daily Express* published a fictitious interview with John Cleese in March 1997. The article claimed he was getting the group together again for a new film. However, Cleese says he was never interviewed by the newspaper and all of the quotes were completely made up—a practice not unheard-of by Fleet Street tabloids.

Unlike most such stories, however, there happened to be some substance to the main assertion. Eric Idle had indeed come up with a possible idea for a new film, and the news was even confirmed on PythOnline. In fact, the idea appeared to interest the other group members, even Michael Palin, and the discussions continue.

"We probably remain as undecided as we've ever been," says Palin. "But we're always talking. We do talk, and there are always plans under consideration, but to say that one plan now is better than another is not true, because there are some who would still rather do a Las Vegas show. There's a likelihood that we'll do something together, but what that will be is very much up to us to decide and get together about."

Whether the surviving members of Python will reunite as Monty Python remains to be seen. Attitudes among some of the group members seem to have had a history of shifting through the years, so there doesn't seem to be a way to predict the future of any possible project. And so, fans and the Pythons themselves are left to speculate: Would they? Could they? Should they? . . .

Pythons for Sale:
Licensing and Merchandising

For many years, Monty Python resisted any attempts to license the Python name for T-shirts, calendars, and any other merchandise. In the original Python spirit, they tried to keep the name as pure and commercial-free as possible, to the point where they would not even allow the TV shows to be broadcast on commercial TV because they would be edited and commercial breaks inserted. Their experience with ABC-TV, in which they successfully sued the network for heavily editing the fourth season shows, taught them a lesson, as did the television debut of *Monty Python and the Holy Grail* by CBS, which was thoroughly edited despite a late-night time slot (the group subsequently awarded the rights to PBS, which would air the film without cuts, even though it would earn the group less money).

For years, the closest they would get to cashing in on the Python name would be the Python books and records, for which they oversaw production and wrote

The Monty Python and the Holy Grail Collectible Card Game, *produced by Kenzer and Company, allows player to join King Arthur and his quest for the Grail (call 1-847-397-2404 for more information).*

new material themselves in addition to reworking previously existing sketches.

"I don't think we ever had any basic objection to the idea of merchandising, provided that the merchandise was actually rather good, and that it was sold in a rather honest and non-ripoff way," says John Cleese. "I think our first revelation was when we did the books with Methuen. We were terribly impressed with some of the work they did on the books and also some of their marketing ideas and campaigns were genuinely funny and so Pythonic that we could have thought of them ourselves. That gave us the feeling that there were a few good people out there."

Attitudes began to change, very slowly at first, with products like T-shirts and poster/programs sold to theatergoers at *Monty Python Live at City Center* and other such productions. A Python T-shirt was also produced and sold through the unofficial fan club mailings sent out by the American Python office.

"Times changed, and a very gradual process occurred during the life of Python in which we released our grip on the shows to a certain extent," says Michael Palin. "Early on, the battles were fought over censorship, especially over the ABC case in 1976, over whether the programs could be edited. Then we fought battles with film distributors over whether they should be dubbed or subtitled—we were very keen on subtitles. And all the way along the line, we were fighting just to make sure that people saw Python just as close to the way it was made as possible, and that anything that had the Python name on it was the product of the work of all six of us, whether it be records or books or whatever. And it was extremely important to us in those first ten or fifteen years, that everything that bore the Python imprint was our invention, and we had control over it, and it maintained the high standard that we required."

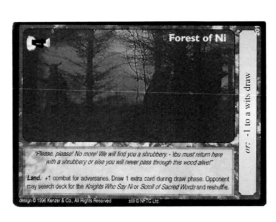

Videotapes of films and the Python TV shows were released in the 1980s. Eventually, a Terry Gilliam–designed T-shirt was licensed and sold in Britain. As time went on, the *Flying Circus* TV shows were sold to Comedy Central, which began airing them with commercials (if not completely unedited) after which the shows

returned once again to their old home at PBS. Part of the reason for the slow growth in merchandising was a concern for quality, as well as finding the people who would do the best job.

"I think we slowly learned that there were a few people around who were capable of doing it for us and doing it really well," says Cleese. "Then, more and more, people like Eric and myself thought, 'Why not have a few good T-shirts, provided Terry Gilliam is able to kind of supervise the design?' That seemed to be all right. Then we thought we could have a silly Python diary, and as each thing was done and seemed to be okay, we would hang around a bit and then move on to the next thing. We slowly got more confident that the merchandise could be done well. I think it's good quality and I don't think it's ripoff prices, and I don't think anybody feels that there's too much avarice at work."

Nevertheless, there were still fears before the licenses were given out.

"There was a lot of doubt at the start," says Cleese. "I think also there were one or two people—probably Terry Jones in particular, who is probably the most left-wing of us politically—who felt for quite a long time that there was something wrong with

making profit out of this kind of merchandise. I don't think I was ever bothered by it, provided the quality was good and the prices were fair. Michael may have been slightly more resistant to the idea, Eric and Graham and I didn't see anything wrong with it. I think Terry Gilliam was more worried about the quality of what was to be done, but once he was prepared to supervise things like T-shirts, the problems disappeared. I think Terry Jones got a little easier with the whole idea of it, and it slowly gathered speed."

"We didn't want to have any merchandising or commercialism, but I think by about the twenty-fifth anniversary, we all felt that 'Everybody knows what Python is now—why not?' I certainly felt like it didn't matter, so I said yeah, go ahead. We didn't feel quite so precious about our baby," confirms Terry Jones.

With the twenty-fifth anniversary came the largest assortment of licensed items to date. These included greeting cards, date books and calendars, as well as a set of coffee mugs by the Ink Group; Cornerstone Communications in Tucson, Arizona, issued Python trading cards and a half dozen different T-shirts; a *Monty Python and the Holy Grail Collectible Card Game* from Kenzer and Company in Palatine, Illinois; and PythOnline has of-

Catapult

"Twong"

Item. Place *Catapult* and a knight in the dead cart for entire Round Table to leap over any area. This counts as movement.

or: *"Run Away! Run Away!"* -3 to a combat draw

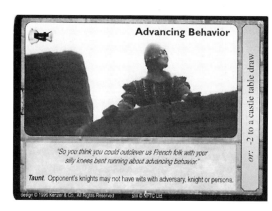

Advancing Behavior

"So you think you could outclever us French folk with your silly knees bent running about advancing behavior."

Taunt. Opponent's knights may not have wits with adversary, knight or persona.

or: -2 to a castle table draw

fered such items as original T-shirts. With typical humor, Gilliam describes it all as "recycled comedy."

"We were basically trying to get the Python office to justify its existence," jokes Gilliam. "It's recycling. It's green comedy, is what it is. It's recycling old comedy paper pulp and rain forest materials—we go to the comic forest, and rather than cutting down acres of that, we just recycle the old stuff. Ecologically sound comedy is what we're doing. Obviously, there are enough people out there who want the stuff and are willing to pay for it. I really don't pay much attention to it."

Of course, the greatest achievement in licensed products may be the Monty Python CD-ROMs, *Monty Python's Complete Waste of Time, Monty Python and the Quest for the Holy Grail,* and the *Meaning of Life,* which even excites Gilliam.

"I'm proud of the CD-ROMs," says Gilliam. "They're fresh and good and terrific, reusing the old stuff in a really fresh and inventive way. When you start licensing stuff, it depends who you're working with. We started doing the first one with 7th Level and that worked, and the second one worked even better."

Gilliam says he was one of the instigators on

Flesh Wound

"You are indeed brave, Sir Knight, but the fight is mine. - Oh, had enough,eh? - Look, you stupid bastard. You've got no arms left. - Yes I have. - Look! - Just a flesh wound."

Event. Permanently lower combat value of target knight by 2. May be played with a *Scratch*.

or: save a knight from death but with a permanent -2 penalty to combat

The Land of Logres

"Now listen, lad. In twenty minutes you're getting married to a girl whose father owns the biggest tracts of open land in Britain."

Land. +2 combat for adversaries. Draw 1 extra card during draw phase.

or: -2 to a combat draw against knights

the first CD-ROM, *Complete Waste of Time,* as well as the third, *Meaning of Life,* while Eric Idle was largely responsible for *Holy Grail.* Much of the content is constructed out of preexisting Python material for the award-winning Python CD-ROMs, admits Gilliam.

"They do most of the work," explains Gilliam. "We just throw around ideas, they get to work on it, and then we look at it and say, 'Couldn't we do this?' It works that way. See, the difference is, we're involved, but we're working with a really talented group of people who are on the right wave-length. So they're doing the bulk of the work. I throw ideas around to see what form it should take, and then keep an eye on it—improve it here, do this better there, be funnier there."

Advances in technology have allowed the group to do something that would have been unlikely a short time ago. A sketch that had been written for *Holy Grail* but never filmed was recorded and included on that CD-ROM.

"The King Brian the Wild sketch on *Holy Grail* was a sequence that was part of the film that never got shot," says Gilliam. "We recorded it like a radio show and we took a lot of my artwork, sketches in my *Holy Grail* sketchbooks, and we animated them! So it became an animated sequence."

"I think 7th Level did a very, very good job on the CD-ROM, and I had nothing to do with that at all," says Cleese. "I don't understand computers well enough to play it myself, but I've watched people play it. It's a wonderful piece of work. And that's marvelous, because every time you find someone out there who's really good, you just do a little cheer!"

The group is now much more open to licensing proposals than before, admits Palin.

"As time went on and we all got involved in other projects, it became very hard to get all the Pythons together to agree on anything," says Palin. "Decisions tended to be made by fax—someone wants to make some mugs, someone wants to make a calendar, there was no great problem with

that. We saw the quality of the work that was being done by, say, the Ink Group and others, and were quite happy with it, because it was really using what we had produced. It wasn't someone else creating a sort of false Python, which they could then mine at will. We're already on the slope for releasing more Python material for various other media, and I don't think that was anything that there was a very great battle over at all. The numbers were not enormous, it wasn't a huge amount of money involved, they were going to people who were confirmed fans anyway.

"Terry Gilliam had control over the T-shirt design and the design of the mugs. There have been various things coming out like Python cards—I don't know quite why they're coming out and who's buying them, but people evidently are. We're getting on now to things like Python plates, which frankly, I think we have minimal control over at the moment. If we ever had an agreed-on policy, we should probably control that in some way.

"The interesting new area is Python on the Internet, which is very much Eric's initiative. On the Internet, there is false Python material around—not false, but in the spirit of Python, there just has to be, because not everybody can spend the time writing new stuff. Similarly with the CD-ROM games—they are basically using Python material with a few additions here and there, inventing their own ideas for the games in the same way that the Internet invents little sort of Spam pages or whatever Eric comes up with. I think the crucial thing is that we do have, at some point, control over the design and the concept of these marketing ideas. Eric is keeping an eye on the Internet, Terry Gilliam and Eric are keeping an eye on the CD-ROM games, and that's great! The only thing is, when we move into areas—which possibly the plates typify, which no one is quite sure why we're doing it and for what reason," Palin laughs.

"The Python fans are out there, and I think if there's a demand for Python potato peelers, they would probably be very happy that we produced

Cornerstone Communications *produces the* Monty Python's Flying Circus *and* Monty Python and the Holy Grail *trading cards as well as Python T-shirts (contact Cornerstone at 520-722-1304 for more information).*

them," jokes Palin. "But I feel so long as there is a Python or Pythons involved in the conception of any new marketing concept then we're probably all right, because I trust the others, and I think we still do have an eye on for quality."

Apart from Python, Terry Gilliam supervised production of his very first signed, numbered full-color fine art lithograph in 1997. (Copyright Terry Gilliam, information available from 137 Inc., phone 1-815-434-9534).

Python in Cyberspace: PythOnline

One of the most successful—if unlikely—new venues for Monty Python was launched on "June 36, 1996." In an effort spearheaded by Eric Idle, Monty Python teamed up with 7th Level for PythOnline (located at www.pythonline.com). Suddenly, Python was active again.

The Web site was a treasure trove for Python fans, with games to download, news and updates from the individual members, cartoons by Terry Gilliam, and a shopping page with everything from exclusive T-shirts, calendars and diaries to CDs and books. Best of all for many was a chance to post messages and questions which the Pythons often answer themselves.

"Eric was very keen on it in the beginning. It was something he was really intrigued by and was prepared to put a lot of work into, which was good, because it meant there was a Python supervising it," says Cleese. "Secondly, it was an idea very much in tune with the times. My attitude was

always, provided Eric's keeping an eye on it, let's try it. I bought a computer at Christmas, so I am starting to log onto it myself."

Terry Jones says he wasn't really interested when Idle originally approached him with the idea. "I didn't know what he was talking about to begin with! Now, I tune in every third day or so, when I can get my Netscape working," says Jones.

"I quite enjoy tuning into it and hearing silly questions. There was a wonderfully silly sequence of questions and answers going on about "Is Terry Jones obsessed by sex?' It went on and on and on! I was just amazed by this piece of correspondence. It's very nice having this way of talking directly to people."

Many fans have been surprised by the large amount of original or rarely seen material that the individual Pythons have posted on their Web site.

"They needed stuff, so I went through sketchbooks and dug up what I had and occasionally draw something new," says Gilliam. "It's great—I send it in and the next minute, they've got it on! PythOnline's quite nice, because again, it's 7th Level involved in it. I think PythOnline's pretty classy...all we've got to do now is work out how we can pay for it!"

The last of the Pythons to go online also has a very good excuse.

"I'm not on the Internet yet," admits Palin. "It all happened in the last year, and I've been away circling the Pacific, doing the TV series. I've been so busy, and I'm slow working out these technologies, and I need a week clear to get myself connected up and work on it. That's part of it. I've got a lot to do at the moment without spending days on the Internet, so when I need to send Eric bits and pieces for PythOnline, I use the very old-fashioned Stone-Age technology of the fax!"

This way down

Copyright Python Productions/7th Level.

Highlights

Asked to choose a highlight of the Python years, most of the group were hard-pressed to select their single proudest achievement.

"I don't think there is *one,*" says John Cleese. "I think there's just the feeling that we did some very, very funny material in with some other material that isn't quite so good, and that we did it over quite a long period of time, with the result that we did create some rather famously funny moments."

"The script meetings for the first series and a half were a highlight," says Cleese. "I thoroughly enjoyed some of the filming sessions where we would all go off and film together for a couple of weeks, because it was a change of scenery, it was fun, sometimes we would be making things up as we went along. I can remember a very entertaining period when we stayed on the island of Jersey when we had wonderful weather and went out and ate every night, got a bit drunk and laughed a lot.

"Shooting of *Life of Brian* was a very happy pe-

riod, up until the last two weeks when I got a very nasty chest infection—it wasn't much fun up on the cross when you've got some quite virulent form of chest infection, even sitting on the bicycle seat!" he laughs. "I remember the Hollywood Bowl as being a good fun time. I liked the Canadian tour a lot, that was very good fun. I found the daily grind of Python, what I refer to as the 'sausage machine,' churning out show after show, week after week, a bit spiritually debilitating. When I start thinking of the best Python times, apart from the writing of the first series and a half, I notice that it was also connected with the fact that we were also somewhere a little unusual and in good weather."

Terry Jones agrees with Cleese on at least one of those counts, having directed or co-directed all of the original Python films. "For me, I suppose it was *Life of Brian* and 'Every Sperm Is Sacred' from *Meaning of Life,*" says Jones.

Michael Palin agrees that *Life of Brian* was probably their finest achievement as Python.

"I think that Python was really firing on all cylinders with *Life of Brian,*" says Palin. "I look back on both the writing and performing as sort of a peak. Intellectually, we were stretched to produce a script about the Bible story that wasn't just seen as a series of funny gags about people on donkeys riding into Jerusalem. I think we turned out a really good script which I'm very proud of to this day, about religion and the way religion is seen and interpreted by others and assumed by others, about those who use religious authority which they don't really deserve to oppress other people. Not only did it work intellectually, it worked in terms of comedy, and within that were some of my favorite Python performances.

"The sketch with the jailers processing people, where I'm sending them to be crucified, is probably one of my favorite performances—both of myself and certainly of Eric and Terry G.—in all of Python. It's a really nice moment, that, and it has some point to it. It's about a liberal dilemma. Here's this terribly nice man wanting to free these people, he hates being in this position, but in the end he's just sending them to their deaths because of his education and because he's Roman, it's given him the ability to do this. He's awfully sorry, but he's sending them to be crucified! I think it's an awfully good comment on evil, and how cruel de-

cisions and unpleasant acts are conceived and done, often by people trying to do their very best, not always by scar-faced monsters. I would say that was a high point."

Expatriate American Terry Gilliam is reluctant to choose one high point, but leans toward the day that Python conquered America.

"There's no one thing for me, it's just the whole thing of having gotten away with it," Gilliam giggles. "The experience was great. Nothing sticks out as the high point of it all, it doesn't feel that way to me. It's just a general feeling that we were plowing along doing good stuff. Maybe the most exciting moment—and maybe it is the proudest—is standing outside of Cinema One in New York when *Holy Grail* opened up, to see the queue all the way around the block, and they'd been waiting there for hours. That actually made us feel really good. I think that was it. I left, teamed up with a bunch of English losers, and I raised them to stardom! [laughs]. And to make it in cinema as well, because we had no idea what was going to happen. That was an amazing one."

Carol Cleveland looks upon the stage shows at the Hollywood Bowl as the highlight of her career.

"The Hollywood Bowl is probably the pinnacle of my career to date," says Cleveland. "It was wonderful, playing to 7,000 people a night. Nothing can beat that. The experience was just incredible, the fact that there were 7,000 people who knew every word to every sketch; we had this extraordinary sensation of going out on stage, but before we said anything, 7,000 people said the words for us. Quite extraordinary.

"The loveliest moment was the second night. They recognized the sketch as soon as the lights went up and they saw it was the Travel Agent sketch when they saw me sitting there at the desk filing my nails, and Terry behind the counter with his travel posters. They immediately let out this whoop of recognition. The second night, Eric and I were in the wings waiting to go out to take our places, when Eric said, 'Carol, don't say that,' meaning 'Do you want to come upstairs?'; say 'Such and such.' So I go out, lights up, big recognition, Eric walks over to me, I look up and say, 'Would you like a blow job?' And there was this stunned silence. Seven thousand people silent. And then I suddenly heard this whispering all over the

359

place, saying 'Did she say what I thought she said?' And the whole place went up in a great roar of laughter. It was moments like that which were so wonderful."

Performing the stage shows in America put them in close proximity of their frenzied fans.

"We got this whole wonderful pop star treatment," says Cleveland. "That was the amazing thing. At that time, we were on a par with the Beatles. The treatment we got when we first did the show in New York at City Center—the first time that we came out of the stage door opening night, there were hundreds and hundreds of screaming fans outside the door. And none of us were prepared for this. I mean, no way prepared for anything like that. I remember Michael and I came out the door first that night, and they all started screaming. And dear Michael, a painfully shy, gentle creature, two girls came rushing up and one of them threw herself at Michael and promptly fainted in his arms. I'll never forget Michael's face as he was holding onto this woman, looking for help!

"We had to make secret getaways after that. We couldn't go out the stage door. Starting the next night, they arranged for our limo to be driven to another entrance, and we'd get in the limo and the gate would go up and we'd zoom out, and these hundreds of fans would see the cars and go tearing up Fifth Avenue after this car. And when we got to Hollywood, it was even more-so, being treated like pop stars. It was wonderful! We'd be down in the VIP room a good ten minutes after the show, we'd

be down there having our drink, and they'd still be up there shouting and screaming for us. They'd throw flowers and knickers and homemade cookies. And as I've said before, unfortunately, nobody ever threw a jock strap on the stage toward me . . . The whole experience was wonderful."

Rather than singling out a few memories, Carol Cleveland says she is thrilled about every part of Python.

"I was proud to be a part of all of it," recalls Cleveland. "There was never a moment I wasn't proud to be a part of, there were so many sketches that I enjoyed tremendously. I'm just proud to be a part of Python. I'm very proud that I was there, and delighted and eternally grateful. My only disappointment is that I have not worked with or for any of the Pythons since *Meaning of Life,* and I would love to. I hope that one day they will do, because I do miss working with them. They certainly don't owe me anything, because they've done a great deal for me, and unfortunately I haven't gone on to do greater things, as they have. I think Python was my peak. I continue to work in this business because of Python. I often think if it weren't for Python, I may have chucked it in a long time ago. For instance, I just finished doing pantomime, and the showbill says 'Carol Cleveland from Monty Python.' I still get a lot of work because of my association with Monty Python, so in that respect, I'm eternally grateful. But I miss them and I want to work with them again. And I hope I do one day."

Looking Back in Laughter

While some aspects of Monty Python, most notably PythOnline and the CD-ROM games, are alive and well, it's now possible to put the films and TV shows into a historical context. And despite talk of possible future films, for at least some of the group, Python is essentially a chapter in their lives that ended when Graham Chapman died in 1989.

"In a way, it doesn't seem like Python has been that long ago," says Terry Jones. "It seems like part of us, part of our life. But I do feel it died with Graham. Although we did that [fourth TV] series without John, it died with Graham. To me, it *really*

died in the writing on the *Meaning of Life.* I felt that we weren't together as a group anymore when we were writing that. We couldn't get everybody together for any length of time. There was far more of my material in it than I thought there should have been—everybody wasn't clicking in the same way as they had done. And I can't imagine us all writing together again."

Terry Gilliam acknowledges that he misses many aspects of working with the others, and admits that he owes his directing career to Python.

"In the odd nostalgic moment, I think, 'Wasn't it nice, the six of us getting away with murder and

having a good time?' " says Terry Gilliam. "I miss that free and easy ability to work like that—an idea came and we had an outlet to deal with that idea. We could put a sketch together, draw a cartoon, and it would be on the air before you knew it. And that's really nice, because today we make films, and every project seems to go on for years—they're cumbersome, heavy things. On the other hand, if I hadn't been a part of Python, I don't know what I would have been doing now. I can't even imagine where I would have been."

Michael Palin says that while Python is no longer an active, creative force, its legacy and influence will continue.

"In one way it has ended, because with Graham's death, we are deprived of one of the six," says Palin. "Python was very much a combination and a communal effort and a work of cooperation between six people as writers and performers. It's like a six-legged table—once you take one leg away, it's still there, but the table is not as steady. I did find that with Graham's death, Python ceased to be what it was. One has to remember that it al-

ways was the six of us, we never extended it. We had sort of honorary Python members like Neil Innes and Carol Cleveland, but basically, the core of Python was controlled by the six of us. That's where it got its energy and that's where the material was generated from, and Graham was part of that. So, once he was gone, it wasn't the same unit capable of doing the same things.

"However, the great thing is that Python still exists, because we made the shows in such a rich fashion, with so much material and so many different side jokes thrown in, that it has survived pretty well. Which is a fine memorial to Graham, really—not that he was into memorials or things like that, but he would like nothing more than to feel that people were still chuckling at the Colonel or any of the daft characters he played. Still!"

Python conjures up different memories for each of the surviving members. In recent years, John Cleese says he has been most interested in his friendships with the others.

"I'm so much more interested in my continuing relationships and friendships with the Python

guys that I don't find myself looking back on Python a great deal," says Cleese. "Michael Palin is someone I've become more and more fond of and I see a great deal. Eric and I have become a lot closer emotionally over the years, too, although I don't see much of him. I've always distinctly admired Terry Jones for the sheer variety of the things he does, and I get on well with Terry, but we've never tended to socialize that much over the years—we get on well when we do, but our lives never seem to bring us together. Although I feel very warmly about him and always enjoy appearing in his films because he creates such a nice atmosphere on the set and he's so well organized, I don't suppose I'm really any closer to Terry than I was when we were making Python—but that's still pretty friendly! And when I look back on the Pythons, I look back on the relationship with Graham with a lot of affection."

Although Cleese says he felt his relationship with Terry Gilliam became somewhat strained around the time of *A Fish Called Wanda* and *The Adventures of Baron Munchausen,* he feels any rifts have long since been repaired. "We got together for a lunch in late 1995 and got on just as well as we used to in the old days," says Cleese. "We've seen each other a few more times since then, and whenever we're in the room it's always perfectly friendly. I haven't been in touch with him since, which is hardly surprising, because I've been so busy, and Terry is a full-time filmmaker. This means that he is constantly on the move, leading the kind of life that filmmakers have to do if they're going to set movies up. So, I don't see a great deal of him, but I have a sense that the friendship is restored now."

Many of Cleese's feelings about Python are somewhat mixed.

"I look back on the days of making Python as falling very much into two categories—the first series and a half, when I felt very happy, very motivated, and enjoyed very much what we were doing and felt that it was fresh and, to use that dreadful cliché, 'exciting' in quotes," says Cleese.

"Then, as I felt we were beginning to repeat ourselves more and more, that enjoyment waned and was diluted by a feeling of disappointment and growing irritation. I felt that the other Pythons didn't seem to be paying any attention to my feelings of disquiet, that we were repeating ourselves

too much and we were no longer fresh and original, as we had been, and I felt that we were working together for the sake of it, rather than out of any wellspring of shared creativity. I felt that the other Pythons didn't listen to me on this, and they just took the attitude that 'John will fall into line.' Then, on the plane to Canada in 1973 to do the stage tour, I eventually said that I didn't want to do the next television series because I felt we weren't going anywhere."

Not all of the Pythons were particularly happy with Cleese's decision to leave the group, he notes, but it probably turned out for the best.

"I don't think that Michael or Eric were very bothered by that, but Graham and Terry Jones were," says Cleese. "For example, in one newspaper article, Terry Jones accused me of disloyalty, which made no sense at all to me. As I'd said, I got together with them to make television programs, I didn't want to marry them! I felt it was quite appropriate that we should all go off and do our own projects, and still occasionally get together again. I like to think that in a sense I was proved right. That was why the group continued to be fairly fertile—we allowed each other space to go off and do our own projects, and that's the way it turned out.

"Graham and Terry were anxious at the time because they felt insecure about operating as successfully as they did as a part of Python. I think in Graham's case, that was a genuinely valid point of view. I don't think Graham ever did anything as good as Python once he left the group, so his annoyance with me was in a sense justified, because I think it made him feel very insecure. He was on to a very good thing with Python. Terry, on the other hand, is in some ways the most talented of us all. He's done a wider variety of things than the rest of us with the possible exception of Michael. I always felt that his fear that he wouldn't operate without Python was sheer lack of confidence, and experience subsequently showed that I was right. He's functioned extraordinarily well outside Python."

Ultimately, if the team had continued to do TV shows, it might never have had the opportunity to move into films, which restored the motivation and excitement of the earlier TV shows.

"I was sorry the group broke up with a certain amount of bad feelings, but by the time we got together in 1974 to do *Holy Grail,* as far as I remember, things were pretty friendly at that point," says

Cleese. "Certainly *Life of Brian* was an extraordinarily successful and enjoyable project—I can't imagine anything that could have gone much more smoothly or more enjoyably or in some ways had a much better result."

The writing of *Meaning of Life* was enormously frustrating for them all, and in fact it proved to be the final major group project of all six members.

"We made the mistake of starting work on *Meaning of Life* before any of us deep-down wanted to," says Cleese. "Denis O'Brien had said that if we made another film quickly, we would never have to work again in our lives, which turned out to be complete nonsense. But Denis was so smart business-wise and we knew so little about financial matters that we took him seriously, and that project never quite lifted off. We spent an enormous amount of time just writing. It wasn't all bad, it was just a bit aimless. We never had a central idea. It had an enormously long gestation time, and it was conceived at a time when no one really deep-down wanted it. If we'd simply waited a couple of years until we had an idea that ignited us all, it might have turned out quite differently. As it was, we pushed ahead. We never found a central notion that excited everyone. I realize in retrospect that the degree that we had been at one during the writing of *Life of Brian* was not what we thought at the time was a kind of norm, it was a little bit of a freak. We were so lucky to have discovered an idea to which we all had similar attitudes. That never happened again, and I don't think that the experience of *Meaning of Life* was as positive for several of us as the other films had been."

After the frustration that was *Meaning of Life,* Cleese decided he was tired of doing major projects within a large group.

"As I have said many times, at the age of forty-five, I had the feeling I did not want to be in the position where material that I thought was really interesting and risky was being voted out of films because I couldn't get enough votes together," says Cleese. "That's why I felt I needed to move on and set up projects of the kind that, for example, Terry Gilliam had already set up, where I was much more in charge. There was never a period when Python wasn't happening between 1969 and 1982. That's a long period of time. After that, I think we all knew that Python was basically over but there was no reason we couldn't get together occa-

sionally and have some ideas for things like CD-ROMs. But I think we knew from then on that the way to go was through individual projects, but that we would continue to appear in each others' films."

Terry Gilliam says Python happened to be the right people in the right place at the right time, and it proved to be a very lucky break for them all, despite occasional stereotyping.

"*Albatross!* It's become our *albatross!*" jokes Gilliam. "I actually think it was an amazing bit of luck. We got away with something that nobody's really pulled off since. The luck of our particular bit of timing, to be doing what we were doing on television at that point. It's kind of interesting, because the *Goon Show* had been around, there had been a lot of radio stuff around that had been brilliant, but the Goons had never translated into television. And we did! We were right there at the right time, and it was a particular time at the BBC when they were very laissez-faire and weren't interfering. Things happened because of all of these events."

Python has continued to be rediscovered by new generations and new societies, as was exemplified again when the Iron Curtain fell and Python cast its shadow across Eastern Europe.

"In the summer of 1996 I was in the Czech Republic, and they were just starting to get Python on television," says Gilliam. "It was having a huge effect. It's like this artifact! It's the product of a very specific time, and that time is gone. And I don't know if it's going to come around again. It seems to have a spirit of six people going crazy and getting away with it, and it seems to linger on. You watch *Saturday Night Live* or any of the other comedy things, and they don't seem to have quite the same longevity, because I don't think they were as pure of spirit as what was going on with Python, as mad and free and unrestrained by commercial concerns or involvement of producers or anything."

Perhaps one secret to the success of Python was that they didn't create the show to the specifications of network executives, audience research, or test screenings—the six of them created it to make each other laugh.

"That's why it was particularly unique, because we were doing that, and getting it on television. I think that is a rare thing," says Gilliam. "People had done it before in Britain, where you

could do it on radio and you could do it in small things, but never quite connected it all. We just happened to be in the right place at the right time. Others have said that the animation put it into a slightly different world. That combination had never been there before. All of these elements fell into place. I suppose it's why some chemical combinations work and others don't. Plastic works; I think we were that same type of combination. All of the molecules fell into place, and you got something that was useful and durable and long-lasting—it'll be around forever and you can't get rid of it! These things happen, and I think they're natural events, basically, the right mutation at the right time."

For Terry Jones, the biggest surprise about Python is that it's still around today.

"Things are different from one's own perception, different from what other people see," says Jones. "At the beginning, Mike, Terry, and I tried to stir up TV as a medium and use it as the Goons originally used radio. We always felt when we did it that it was going to be the funniest thing around, but I always thought 'Well, it's a pity it won't last, it won't have much of a shelf-life.' So I'm a bit surprised that it *has* lasted."

The highlight of the whole experience for Jones may have been the original creation of the material.

"The writing sessions were the most exciting part of Python in a way, because that's where it all happened, that moment where we all met," says Jones. "Maybe we'd all been writing for a couple of weeks separately, and then we'd all get together to read out the material, and we all knew, whoa! There was going to be some really funny stuff, and we'd have some good laughs. Those were the magic moments, when we were doing the writing."

For the First Lady of Python, nothing in her career before or since has come close to her work with Monty Python.

"I loved every moment of Python, and I look back on it with the fondest, happiest memories," says Carol Cleveland. "I look back on those years as being probably the happiest years of my life. Everything was going right for me in those days, and career-wise, I don't think I've done anything before or since that has given me so much pleasure or satisfaction, and such reward. I miss it terribly, I miss working with the Pythons. Obviously, it can get very boring hanging around film sets and television studios when they're setting up a shot, but I never got bored. I love all of the process of getting something together, so I would sit there fascinated by everything, so I don't recall ever, ever being bored or fed up."

Michael Palin looks on Python as the product of their youthful energy and eagerness to try everything.

"It's a mixture of memories," says Palin. "Some are of specific sketches which I always enjoyed playing, such as the Cheese Shop. Others are less specific, just a general impression of being young and out on the road and feeling that we were able to try anything—we only had ourselves to blame if it didn't work. That general feeling is my fondest feeling for Python. We would sit down to write or go off to film, and really wouldn't be at all sure what would come out the other end, but we knew it would be fresh and original, and would not have been done by anybody else making television comedy at the time. That didn't mean we thought it would be successful, but it did mean that it gave it all a marvelous spirit which ran through most of the early Pythons. About halfway through the second series it was clear that not everybody was as wedded to Python as everybody else, and once one got those slight clear indications of different empathies within the group as to what we should do, then I think the television series was all on a slippery slope."

Timeless

As exemplified by the emergence of Python in the Czech Republic, Monty Python seems likely to continue its appeal to new and different audiences through the years. Indeed, Python is already being discovered by the children of the first-generation Python fans in Britain and around the world, and in fact, a third generation has started to emerge. Perhaps because they were never created with longevity in mind (aside from a slight reluctance to use topical references, according to Graham Chap-

man, so that they would be rebroadcast by the BBC), the timeless aspect of Python is perhaps the most puzzling to the Pythons themselves.

"It's puzzling to me, because in a sense, what we were doing was making a great deal of fun of certain television conventions that were operating in England in the mid-'60s," says Cleese. "That was a great sense of liberation, to escape the shackles of a lot of those conventions. So, I'm not quite sure how the modern audience gets quite the same sense of delight from those. Perhaps it's a different sense. But one thing we did manage to do was to put up on the screen some archetypes that people seem to recognize no matter what their culture or generation. And I think people also like the basic attitudes of the shows, the refusal to take almost anything very seriously, and I think that's what's infectious."

Python never appealed to a mainstream audience in America when it first aired, tending to appeal to more esoteric and intelligent viewers, but three decades later it appears to be edging its way toward the mainstream, according to Terry Gilliam.

"One of the nicest things was when I was making *12 Monkeys* in Philadelphia," says Gilliam. "I kept getting recognized on the street far more than I'd ever expected, because the shows were on Comedy Central. At one of the power stations, these cops were all fans! It was like we permeated all sorts of levels of society that I didn't think we would ever reach, good working-class folks who found Python funny. And I thought that was great, to be recognized for the best possible reasons. I thought it was terrific that we had actually affected these kinds of people. And a nice thing happened at this film festival in the Czech Republic. They hadn't seen a lot of films from the West through the '70s and '80s, so I brought over a couple, and the thing that just went down a treat was *Life of Brian*. They couldn't believe what they were seeing. They loved it so much, they showed it a second time. They sent me a videotape which they'd made of the end of the film, and as 'Always Look on the Bright Side of Life' was sung, they brought the lights up in the cinema, and the entire audience was on its feet singing, in Czech, 'Always Look on the Bright Side of Life.' Now that's great, that it translates like that, and can continue to excite people—stuff that's twenty-five years old!

"There always seem to be a new generation coming along and finding it. In Germany, particularly in the east, the T-shirt concession was doing really well. I saw Python in my hotel room in Paris, and they were using it to teach English! It was all subtitled as a way of learning English! It got a bit complicated, because the subtitles had been done by a Belgian, so the references were specifically Belgian references, and this was playing in Paris to teach French kids how to speak English. They're on the right wavelength when things like that happen. I think that we rely on countri   that have been repressed and suppressed for a long time, because these are potential new audiences that we can keep alive with!"

It is inevitable that the TV shows will date, but as John Cleese points out, that really isn't important.

"They may date a bit, and there is a mysterious point at which films suddenly seem to date, but I don't think it matters," says Cleese. "Laurel and Hardy date, but there's no question they're very funny. I think that although we will date, people will be able to put the films in a frame of mind in which they'll be able to enjoy themselves almost as much as they did before they dated."

Terry Jones theorizes that because the TV shows were not tailored toward any specific audience but to the six members, they are not as likely to be passed by and forgotten as that particular audience tires of them.

"They seem to stand the test of time at the moment, but nobody knows what 'time' is with television," notes Jones. "I'm surprised in a way, because we didn't make them in the way of things that would last. The only thing I can think of is that they were just done for us. It was like they weren't done with any public in mind, so they hit a note that was not tailored to any section of the population."

Michael Palin believes that the basic attitude of Python makes them likely to stand the test of time.

"I think they have already," says Palin. "I don't think there are that many television comedy shows which jump a generation, which Python has now. The old farts who made it—it's now the grandchildren's generation which is almost coming to get to know Python, so it's almost jumped two generations already! And television doesn't usually have that sort of life. So in a sense, Python's al-

ready proved that the shows will stand the test of time, and I can't see, given the fact that they've lasted twenty-eight years, that they won't last another twenty-eight. I think that fashions change, and Python will probably come in and out of fashion, but I think we'll always be able to elicit the sort of response that there was to the first television shows from a certain type of person. It wasn't universal, but it was certainly very intense, just a delight in seeing something done in this absurd, mischievous, unreverential way. Unless society changes utterly, there's always going to be people wanting to see irreverence well-done and mischief made, and I think that's what keeps Python going."

A Legacy of Laughter

In recent years, Monty Python becomes less and less an ongoing entity and more and more of a comedic touchstone, leaving behind a legacy for generations yet to come. There seems little doubt that Python will be remembered for a long, long time, though even the group members can't agree on the way it will be remembered.

"I don't know how it will be remembered, and to try to guess feels futile, in some strange way," says John Cleese. "How I'd *like* it to be remembered— well, I would like people to think these guys were very, very funny, and I would like it to go on without our seeming to date much. We will date eventually, but I'd like people to think we were funny, some of the time in a very original and intelligent way."

Michael Palin says Python has helped people get through some difficult times, which makes it worthwhile for him.

"I'd like Python to be remembered as something which helped people to work out certain problems and difficulties in their own life through the comedy that we produced," says Palin. "I don't quite want to say anything like 'changed peoples' lives,' because that's far too pretentious, but I do get letters from people who say that it helped them through a bad time or a difficult period. That's the best you can hope, if Python has in some way helped people out of hard times."

Terry Jones says Python has proven to have a very positive effect on young people in some specific cases.

"Some teachers working at a tough inner-city school told me that Python had a big effect on their children," says Jones. "The teenaged boys tried to go around being very macho and bullying, and they now go around being very silly! If Python can have that effect on people, making them sillier, I think it's a very great achievement!"

Of course, Terry Gilliam is the most direct in his hope of a Python legacy.

"If it's remembered at *all,* that's enough. I don't want any more than that," says Gilliam. "Good, bad, indifferent, it doesn't really matter—as long as the name isn't totally rubbed out of the history books!"

Group portrait circa 1978. Photographed by John Sims for Python Productions, used by permission.

386

Too Silly, Too Silly—Graham Remembered

Graham Chapman: January 8, 1941–October 4, 1989

In the years that have elapsed since Graham Chapman's passing, he still looms large in the memories of his friends and fans. He left behind a body of work that will provide laughs to unborn generations. Those who were lucky enough to know the man know that out of the six Python members, Graham lived the most independent, outrageous, unrestrained, uninhibited—in some ways, perhaps the most Pythonic—life of them all. Graham loved to shock and the status quo was much too dull for him. Yet he was kind and generous almost to a fault; he would probably have been a bit uncomfortable with the notion that he was so beloved by so many. But he was, and is, and is very much missed.

Graham was a study in contradictions. He was a performer, yet he was almost painfully shy. He was a qualified medical doctor who kept up his license and his studies to the end, but he was also an alcoholic who had worked up to two bottles of gin a day before quitting cold turkey. He looked the very model of a proper upper-class English gentleman, yet he was openly gay at a time when it was considered forbidden to raise the subject. Of all the group, Graham probably best personified the spirit of Python. He was an accomplished mountaineer and a prolific writer, at one point working on three different TV series each day; a former Petula Clark writer who was launched from a catapult in central London by the Dangerous Sports Club. Graham, in short, could quite rightly be described as unforgettable.

Perhaps his greatest unrealized potential was as an actor, which he didn't truly begin to develop until after he had stopped drinking.

"He was a really fine actor," says John Cleese. "I don't think everybody realizes what a potentially wonderful actor he was, but he was very scared. Despite his extraordinary talent, once the drinking started, the fear that he always felt in front of an audience got worse instead of better."

Cleese and Palin each wrote tributes to Graham for London newspapers; Cleese's appeared in the October 6, 1989, *Independent* as follows:

Graham Chapman and I wrote together almost full time between 1966 and 1973, while producing sketches for The Frost Report, The 1948 Show, *and* Monty Python, *as well as several film scripts, none of which made their way intact to the silver screen.*

As a writing partner he had two rare gifts: the ability to get us un-stuck with some inspired off-the-wall conceit when I was enmeshed in very on-the-wall musings; and in addition, the priceless talent of knowing whether something was funny or not. I noticed this early and relied upon it shamelessly. In fact the Cheese Shop Skit—my all-time favorite—owes its life to him. Every dozen or so cheeses, I'd sigh and say "Gra, is this really funny?" and he'd puff on his pipe calmly and say "Yes, get on with it."

I wished he'd had the same confidence in front of audiences because he was probably the most talented actor of us all. But, he found the Python TV recordings a terrible strain, and some of his drinking was an attempt to dampen that fear. After he gave up the booze at Christmas 1977—for good—he gave us his splendid Brian, which is as clever and well-judged a piece of comic acting as you'll see.

Of course, he'd given up medicine to pursue comedy, but he was absolutely at his best when caring for others. He looked after the entire film unit practically single-handed while we were filming in Tunisia and I was reminded of this again in recent months when we visited him in hospital. I think he was just as keen to look after us then, and his optimism, cheerfulness and absolute lack of self-pity made me, for one, feel very, very small. We all bought his optimism, of course. We wanted to. But his elder brother John thinks that he knew better what the score was than he ever let on.

That his bravery was ended so abruptly and unexpectedly seems very cruel.

Michael Palin's lengthy tribute, which follows, first appeared October 6, 1989, in *The Guardian*:

I first heard of Graham Chapman as one of that pool of ex-Oxbridge revue talent that sloshed around the BBC in the mid-1960s.

I use the word *sloshed* advisedly, for many of our best times were had propping up the various bars of the Corporation. Graham was like a figure out of a Biggles story. Strong, finely-chiselled features, pipe at a jaunty angle in his mouth, pint in one hand and progger in the other. A progger was Graham's name for the flat-ended instrument which he used to bed down the tobacco in his pipe. I never knew whether it was a real name or not. Graham liked words and used them well, but if he felt the right one didn't exist he'd invent another one.

In the post-Cambridge days he was a journeyman writer, like us all. One day he would be working with John Cleese to produce a dazzling succession of successful sketches for The Frost Report, the next he would be writing filler jokes for the Petula Clark show.

He kept a low profile as a performer until At Last the 1948 Show *in which he revealed a talent for playing intense, rather serious characters hilariously. He was a charismatic performer, drawing the eye to himself, as much for the originality and un-showbizziness of his approach, as for the likely detectable hint of unpredictability. An audience was never quite sure what he would do next. Nor I think, as a performer, was Graham. During a singing court scene in one of the early Python shows he quite inadvertently substituted 'window dresser' for 'window cleaner' in his song. A Freudian slip at which we all fell about, especially Graham.

In 1969, when the mutual admiration society which became known as Monty Python assembled, Graham met David Sherlock and embarked on one of the many radical changes in his life, when they decided to live together. It was a courageous decision, which shocked some of his friends at the time but was borne out triumphantly by the fact that they shared the rest of their lives. David, together with their adopted son John Tomiczek, nursed and cared for him with stoic patience and quiet strength throughout his final illness.

Graham's need to relax himself with a dram or two took a disproportionate hold on his life as the pressures of a heavy Python schedule grew. Drink was not always the friend he thought it, affecting his performances and occasionally doing a great disservice to a much underrated natural acting talent.

His writing contributions to Python were of quality rather than quantity. Whilst all around were scratching their heads for inspiration. Graham would puff his pipe and glance sideways at the Times crossword and be quite silent for 30 minutes or so before coming out with a single shaft of inspiration that would transform a mundane sketch into something very mad and wonderful.

Such surreal flashes were the very essence of Python as were his memorable performances as the Colonel, as the Hostess in the Eurovision song contest, Raymond Luxury-Yacht and others.

His off-stage performances included collecting an award from the Sun *newspaper by leaping high in the air, emitting a loud squawk and crawling all the way back to his table with the award in his mouth, leaving Lord Mountbatten, who had given him the award, looking very confused.

But Graham's most memorable performances were sustained and demanding—as King Arthur in Monty Python and the Holy Grail *and Brian in the Life of Brian.

Around the time of the filming of Life of Brian, *Graham made a conscious effort to free himself from the dependence on the large G and Ts—after that "ice but no lemon please." His restless ever-inquisitive need to be freed from the boring and the conventional had led him to the brink, but his cautious disciplined rational side saved him at the last minute from toppling over. He gave up drinking and later, with immense difficulty also laid aside his pipe.

Perhaps Graham too easily overestimated the talents of others while underestimating his own and, as a result, his ventures outside Python—Out of the Trees *for the BBC and his two films, Odd Job *and Yellowbeard*—were full of good ideas badly resolved. The commercial failure of Yellowbeard depressed him.

His recent illness was another in a series of mountains which Graham had to climb. He always regarded death as highly overrated and could never understand why anybody made such a fuss about it. Despite great physical discomfort he remained alert, informed, articulate and humorous.

He hated to be bored which is why he joined the Dangerous Sports Club and once hurled himself into thin air attached to a length of rubber . . . "I was high for two weeks after that."

I suspect he would have enjoyed an old age of

increasing eccentricity, dispensing his considerable wisdom and hospitality, occasionally leaping in the air and shouting "Eeke!"

NOTE: Because he was openly gay and died relatively young, false rumors arose that Graham had died of an AIDS-related illness. This pervasive rumor has proven surprisingly difficult to squelch, but has absolutely no basis in fact.

The best proof of this is probably Graham himself. He was proud and quite vocal about his homosexuality—to the point of flaunting it, in some cases—and did everything he could to provide support and encouragement to young gays who were having problems adjusting to their situation. If Graham had suffered from AIDS, he would no doubt have been the first to publicly announce it, and use it to educate others.

No, the sad fact is that Graham died of cancer. As Graham explained it to me, he believed that decades of smoking a pipe took its toll. The stem of the pipe was aimed at a fragment of tonsil that remained in his throat, and every time he drew in on his pipe, it sent a concentrated stream of toxic gas at this vulnerable area. Apparently, that was where his cancer originated, though it ultimately spread through his spine and proved fatal.

Graham was a doctor himself and tended to value accuracy in such reportings, a good reason to set the record straight.

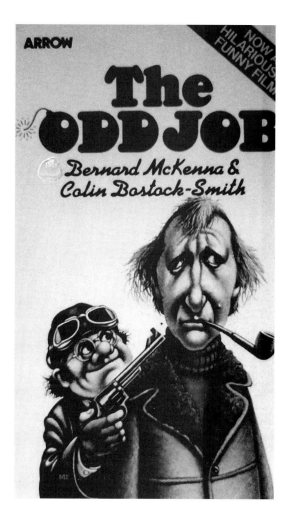

In His Own Words

During the course of preparing *Life Before and After Monty Python,* I uncovered a lengthy interview I had conducted with Graham in early 1983. Much of the discussion involved *Yellowbeard;* however, I was startled to discover that toward the end of that interview, Graham had talked for several minutes about his thoughts on life, death, and growing old, comments particularly poignant after his death five years later.

We began by briefly discussing his childhood, which he regarded as normal, "Apart from the Second World War. It didn't happen to everybody, but it happened to a lot of people. It was very normal, apart from people throwing bombs made in Germany outside our house," he said. "My father was a policeman; I suppose I did get to meet quite a va-

riety of odd characters because of that. But it was startlingly normal, really."

Graham said he occasionally liked to watch his old films and TV shows, though he was watching them more infrequently.

"I do for a short time. For instance, for about three or four years after the Python TV shows, I enjoyed watching them—not all of them, as there were some I was not so keen on. And I did enjoy that. I find I do that less and less, though," he noted in 1983. "Now, I suppose I feel a little more like once a thing is done, it's done. I'm probably a little more critical now before a thing happens than I was—of course, now there's more time to be so, because I'm dealing with movie scripts.

"I'm a little more tolerant of past errors now

than I was. I used to find them more irksome, and I wouldn't want to look at them again for that reason, things that I knew that weren't my best. No, that worries me less, I'm less easily embarrassed from that point of view. There are quite a few little moments like that, where one looks back on a history of alcoholism too," he said, laughing. "Moments that are actually recorded on tape when one was not at one's best. That, perhaps, makes me more tolerant than most."

Although he had many shaky moments during the Python TV shows as a result of his drinking, he was never surprised while watching the old shows by a sketch he had forgotten he had done.

"I can't think of anything offhand, but I'm sure there were moments. I have seen one or two old Python TV shows where I can definitely tell that I was a little more worse for wear than I should have been, the timing is a little slower. It's a very strange experience talking of this . . . " he said.

Graham said he had never planned out his life with long-term goals when he was starting his career.

"I don't think I did then—there were very vague ones. My progress toward medicine wasn't really with the set aim of doing that—it was sort of vaguely 'Oh, I'll do some research eventually that will be of immense benefit,' that sort of thought. But it was all really quite vague. I don't have any set goals as such, just as long as everything's going in the general direction of progress," he laughed.

In 1983, having made it through five years without alcohol, he could start looking forward in a way that he hadn't been able to before. He preferred not to think about what he'd be doing twenty-five years in the future, but remained optimistic.

"Up until five years ago I thought my future was more limited than that, but now it seems to stretch out more endlessly than I expected," he said with a laugh. "If someone could tell me what I'd be doing in twenty-five years, I wouldn't really want to know. I'd like it to be a surprise when it happens. I think that's one of the best things about life—it can be a complete surprise. I kind of like to think that by that age, I might have taken yet another switch in some strange direction—maybe ten years in movies, then a few years as a biochemist. Or becoming a beach bum! It's quite farfetched, but I don't know. . . . "

Without question, it was giving up alcohol that accounted for his positive feelings at the time. "The biggest change was the spirit of optimism that overcame me when I'd stopped drinking. It took time to emerge, really."

The one incident that made him decide to give up alcohol occurred in 1974.

"I've pinned it down rather accurately now. I think the precise moment of decision to really do something about it was on the first day of filming Holy Grail. That's when I resolved to do something about it as soon as I could.

"We were filming the Bridge of Death sequence over the Gorge of Eternal Peril. We happened to film it the first morning of the whole shoot up in Scotland. I hadn't gotten myself organized, and we were up on the mountainside at seven A.M., and of course I had taken no drink along with me at all. I hadn't gotten myself organized yet, and no one else had anything, either. I couldn't believe that out of an entire crew, no one there went without a little nip of scotch or anything. I was stuck and began to go through DTs on the mountainside during that sequence. Each time after we'd do a take, I'd go off and moan in the heather and the drizzle and have a good shake, and try to get myself back together again to go back and do it next time. That was really miserable!

"There is, in fact, a photograph of me in one of the Python books. I'm sitting down on the hillside with a white cap on, rather than the crown, and I'm looking fairly miserable. John Cleese assigned the total blame for that to the miseries of filming. In actual fact, it's quite a different story."

He explained that his shyness was one of the principal reasons for his alcohol abuse. "That was part of it, yes. I make a more ebullient, sociable person than an antisocial person because of it, I suppose. . . . "

Graham said he didn't fear death, although he planned to avoid it as long as possible.

"Like most people, I think it would be very pleasant not to have to go, but one accepts that. It's more or less inevitable. We try to do what we can to avoid the ravages and to keep your faculties about you, and if there is anything like an advance in health care, I'll be the first to take it.

"But it doesn't actually worry me a great deal, because I've been impressed by some wonderful

old people, and not just great ones like J. B. Priestley and Bertrand Russell and George Bernard Shaw.... So, I don't think there's any real fault that one should let one's brain give up easily. I have every intention of trying to remain as twinkly as I can until I feel like retiring, really. I think you could quite easily reach a point where people say to themselves 'Perhaps it's about time I turned a little off, you know, I've done just about everything I can think of—tried this, tried that—oh, I think I'll just retire and—oops, I'm dead!' I think it's important to go on living until something catches you.

"I don't really look back with regret on any feelings or problems I've had in the past. I think I'm more able to accept that kind of thing now as being part of the rough and tumble of life. There are bound to be ups and downs. In retrospect, when you've gotten past a rough period, it makes the good things that much better. Sort of a trite thing to say, but it doesn't seem to worry me that much!"

Besides keeping his regrets in check, Graham said he didn't attach too much importance to his successes, either.

"I'm a little more moderate on those now as well than I used to be. I don't get too elated—there's a more satisfying inner elation, and much less leaping up and down. From my own point of view, my life used to be very black and white in many ways. Now I appreciate tones of gray. That was really a coincidence with drinking too—I think my philosophy changed a little bit afterwards. Before, I had very little patience and had to do things *now,* and if someone annoyed me, I'd tell them. Now I can wait until they annoy themselves!"

The interview concluded with my asking Graham how he wanted to be remembered after he was gone. His words speak for themselves.

"I think I would like to achieve something lasting. Most people like to feel that they're a little unique—as everyone is—and I suppose that's it. If there's any vague ambition, it is that eventually, there will be something I've done which would be worth remembering, that I've done something that people can look back on and say 'Ah, he was good at that,' or 'At least he did *that.* That was good!' "

The Memories Linger

Bring up his name around his Python colleagues, and the stories soon start flying, many of them concerning boyfriends or outrageous antics while under the influence of gin and tonic.

"There are so many stories—they're just usually too rude to print!" Michael Palin laughs. "Graham was always doing wonderfully outrageous things, usually to do with drink or boyfriends. He was this classic Englishman, very well-read, doing the crossword puzzle, smoking the pipe. A very good doctor he was, too. All these sort of things that would just seem to be the classic upper-class Englishman in a way, and yet he had this raunchy side to his life which used to just crack us up. I learned an awful lot about just letting go from Graham!"

John Cleese had known Graham longer than any of the others, since his early days at Cambridge, and recalls that he was more shocked than almost anyone when Graham came out of the closet.

"When he announced to us all in 1967 that he was gay, it was such a surprise, because everything about him was so utterly butch—from the fact that he smoked a pipe and played rugby football and was a medical student and drank a lot of beer, through to the fact that he wore tweed jackets and heavy brogue shoes," says Cleese. "Every single bit of his personality was saying 'butch'! When he met and fell in love with David Sherlock on the island of Ibiza in 1966, Graham and I were writing a film script for David Frost that became *The Rise and Rise of Michael Rimmer.* He was particularly lazy on that holiday. He used to lie out on the balcony sunbathing while I would sit inside the room writing, and he would call suggestions out. I didn't realize at that time that he was beautifying himself for David's purposes!

"The next year, there were all these strange excuses—we'd finish rehearsing at half past ten, and we'd say 'Going to have a drink, Graham?' He'd look at his watch and say 'No, I have to go up to

Bart's [medical school] and cash a check.' Apparently if you were a medical student, you could cash a check at Bart's, but it was an awfully long way to go to cash a check! We thought he had a girl stashed away. And then he went away on holiday in '67 and he met a Swede called Stig. The Swede persuaded him that it was great to be gay, and what was he so ashamed of?

"So Graham came back from this holiday in '67 and had a sort of party in which he wanted to tell me that he was gay. Unfortunately, I was watching a very important football match on the television, so he told my girlfriend! She told me that evening, and I rang Marty [Feldman] up to tell him, and I remember Marty saying 'What is it, love, it's late?' I said, 'I just called you because Graham's decided he's gay. And I remember Marty saying 'Don't waste my time, love, it is late, what did you call me about?' He just didn't believe it. I said 'No, really, Graham's telling everyone he's gay.' And Marty said 'It's late! Why did you call me?' "

David Sherlock soon became one of the extended Python family, which resulted in some jolly times, recalls Cleese.

"Graham, Connie and I, and David were having dinner one evening. Afterward, I danced with Connie and Graham danced with David. Then after a time, Connie went and danced with David. Connie's 5' 1" and weighs about four and a half pounds—she is the slightest creature—and after she danced with David, she came back and said to me 'That was terrible.' When I asked her why, she said, 'Because he makes me feel like an elephant!' " Cleese laughs.

The other Pythons didn't see a great deal of Graham when they were filming on location or out on tour, notes Cleese. "We tended not to see much of him," he laughs. "He'd come down to the bar the first evening we arrived at the new location, and that was about the last we'd see of him. He was off on the chase!"

"I have all sorts of memories of Graham, and he is sadly missed," recalls Carol Cleveland. "I got on with all of the fellows, they were lovely and treated me like a little sister, really, they were all wonderful and very helpful. I had a bit of difficulty feeling relaxed with Graham in the very early days, I think because he was being so overtly gay and being an alcoholic, I had a bit of trouble relating to that in the very early days. But when I got to know him better, he was one of the sweetest men. I had a feeling that if I ever really needed help in any way, or if I was in any trouble, that I could call on Graham and he would be there for me. There was just always that feeling, that he'd be there. He was a lovely fellow.

"He could be tremendously outrageous, which sometimes was just great fun. I have to admit there were other times that his behavior embarrassed me, when he would really go right over the top. He was very keen to tell you all of the intimate details of his love life, to which I always said, 'Okay Graham, okay, okay, okay, thank you very much!' "

One incident that occurred during *Flying Circus* filming was recounted by Chapman in his *A Liar's Autobiography, Volume VI* and is fondly remembered by Terry Gilliam.

"We were at this huge hotel down in Torquay, and Graham was at the table in a cavernous dining room, very excited about his new date," says Gilliam. "He'd met this guy during the day, and was really excited, and kept describing him. There was a call for Graham, and clearly his date had arrived, and we were all buzzing, 'What's it going to be today? Is it going to be a seven-foot black guy? Is it going to be just another exotic type or what?'

"It was much more exotic than any of us had ever imagined. The door opened up and we heard this, 'Creak, creak!' It was a guy in a wheelchair—and that was his date. We all were just stunned. Graham came in and introduced him; he was a real gent, had a knowing smile on his face, and they went off into the night.

"We later discovered that Graham had met this guy during the day, and he also met this *other* guy. They both gave him their numbers, and Graham called what he thought was the good-looking, healthy one, but the numbers had been switched and he ended up with the paraplegic. Which was not the date he had in mind, but what was so great was he kept a straight face. He never let on, like a real gent, and went out with his cripple!

"It was a constant thing with Graham—what's he going to turn up with next? Who is he going to turn up with next? What trouble is he going to get himself into? I'm convinced he probably never had sex with anybody," jokes Gilliam. "He was probably leading a fantasy life for all of us!"

The record seems to show that Graham didn't need to fantasize much, however.

"There was a time when we were in Glencoe and Graham got thrown out of the hotel where we were filming," recalls Terry Jones. "Graham all of a sudden decided to kiss everybody in the hotel bar. A fight nearly started at one point when he tried to kiss some bloke, and I think it resulted in Graham being thrown out. Of course, those were the days when Graham was still drinking rather heavily."

Graham was not at all shy about his sexual orientation, which occasionally caused a few tense moments, recalls Carol Cleveland.

"We were on tour somewhere in Scotland, and Graham and I had gone off before the others to some little bar," says Cleveland. "We went in this pub where there were all of these big, rugged types. Graham was wearing this big badge proclaiming his being gay. It was a really big badge, you couldn't miss it, and these big, hairy butch guys were looking at this badge. I'm thinking 'Oh, oh, we're going to have trouble here . . .' They started picking on Graham, and I really thought there was going to be a punch-up. I kept saying 'Come on, Graham, come on, Graham, be quiet now, Graham, let's go over there and wait for the others.' I was thinking 'Oh, God, we're going to get beaten up.' But thank God the others arrived, and we went off.

"A similar occasion happened when we were doing the stage show in New York at City Center. We went on the air to do a live radio phone-in, and again, Graham and I arrived before the others. The female interviewer said, 'Let's start instead of waiting for the others to get here.' She threw the lines open, and it started off fine. Then this woman came on and asked a question about his homosexuality. Now, this was back in the early days, when being gay was not discussed quite so openly and freely as it is now—certainly not in New York. She asked him a question to which, of course, he gave a very straightforward answer, and this prompted all sorts of other phone calls. So many people didn't want to know about anything else, any questions regarding Python, it was all to do with Graham being gay. And some people were angry. We were getting some rather unpleasant phone calls.

"Instead of trying to steer away from all of this, Graham just made it so much worse! The phone calls stopped coming in and we had three minutes to go. She said, 'Well, the calls seem to have dried up,' and suddenly the phone rang. She said, 'We'll have one more phone call,' and this male voice came on the air. He said 'I just want to tell you guys, this is the Family callin', and we're gonna get you.' And put down the phone. That was it, the final call. I was terrified! I was thinking it was the Mafia, someone had taken offense! I remember going back to the theater and I told one of the stage crew about it. He said, 'The Family? Oh, no, that's not the Mafia, that's Charles Manson.' I went 'Aaaaahhhh!' Anyway, thank God we weren't got. But he did put us in some tricky situations!"

A possible preoccupation with window dressers—British slang for "someone who minces around in black outfits and little socks, dressing dummies in windows," according to Michael Palin—led to one of the funniest Python bloopers.

"There was a wonderful sketch, Cardinal Richelieu in court or something," recalls Palin. "A song had to be sung, 'If I were not inside this court, something else I'd like to be, If I were not inside this court'—and Graham's next line was 'A window cleaner me.' We got to the actual recording, and instead of saying 'window cleaner' Graham, his mind obviously being elsewhere, came up with the word 'window dresser.' And once he'd said 'a window dresser me,' I saw him stop for a moment, but he had to carry on, and unfortunately, he then carried on with the window cleaner business. So he went on 'a window dresser me, with a rub-a-dub here and a scrub-a-scrub there,' which was absolutely hilarious!"

Before he quit drinking, alcohol became an increasingly powerful force in his life. Although its effect was increasingly destructive, Palin says there were a few lighter moments as well.

"We were coming back from filming once, and he had a big old car driven by a guy called Andrew," says Palin. "Graham had him just pull over to the side of the road, with traffic flashing by us. I asked if everything was all right, if there was something wrong with the car, and he said, 'No, no, I think it's time for a G and T.' He went to the back, opened the trunk, and there was this wonderful set of glasses and bottles with gin, tonic and ice. We only had about another half hour to go to London, but Graham insisted on a sort of cocktail party en route!

"That all had its downside, because I can re-

member Graham not being able to finish a sketch when we were recording the shows. That was pitiful to watch, and very sad," says Palin. "Graham didn't like that at all, because he was always a great professional, but there were sketches which we never finished because he'd had a few."

When the other Pythons start talking about Graham, their stories inevitably get around to his lack of punctuality, which almost forced Michael Palin into moving at one point.

"Graham always used to drive Michael mad," says Terry Jones. "Michael always used to drive him to rehearsals and meetings because they lived quite close and Graham didn't have a car. When Michael arrived in front of Graham's flat, Graham would wave out of the window, and Mike would sit there, sometimes for up to half an hour, trying to imagine what on Earth Graham was doing."

Palin picks up the story:

"Graham lived about half a mile from where I lived, and it was really infuriating, because he was never ready," says Palin. "I would start at nine o'clock and be there at two minutes after. I'd honk my horn and wait down below. It would take ages. A tousled head and a bare torso would appear at the window, and he clearly wasn't ready at all. And sometimes two or three tousled heads and bare torsos. He would shout, 'Oh, Mikey, I won't be a minute!' I'd sometimes have to wait for twenty or twenty-five minutes, and then he would come down and we'd drive on. He wouldn't say very much—he was sort of recovering himself.

"Then, we'd get to rehearsal and everyone would be looking up from all around the table. I'm rather a punctual person and it used to irritate me that I was sort of held responsible. Graham was wonderful, he'd come in and rub the side of his sideburns with the tip of his left hand the way he did, and light his pipe and beam around at everyone, and just say 'Traffic!' After a bit, people got wise to this, and as soon as Graham entered there would be a chorus of 'Traffic!' from everybody! There certainly *was* traffic, but not of the normal kind! It was like I'd drawn the short straw. On occasions I would say to my wife, 'I think we'd ought to move house, so I won't have to collect Graham in the morning!' "

Carol Cleveland's fondest memory of Graham

Chapman, a revealing look at his lack of inhibitions, occurred during the Canadian Python tour.

"We'd all been out to have a meal one evening, and came back to the hotel after having a few drinks, all jolly," says Cleveland. "It was very late and there was no one around, so we decided we'd have a little midnight swim in the pool. So, we all just stripped off to our underwear, except for Graham, of course, who just stripped off entirely. We all got in the pool and swam about for about twenty minutes or so. Then we got out, but there were no towels! While one of the fellows went off to get some towels, Graham said, 'Oh, bugger this!' He went tearing out of the pool area and through the hotel, dripping wet and naked as a jaybird. He went tearing through this hotel, streaking around through the corridor and through the foyer. I have this wonderful picture of a couple that came in the front of this hotel just as Graham streaked past them like a flash of lightning, up the stairs and disappeared. They stopped, looked up the stairs, looked at each other and shook their heads as if to say, 'No, couldn't have been . . .' Wonderful. I have many, many happy memories of Graham. He was totally outrageous and wonderful with it."

The common attribute to most Graham Chapman stories is laughter, and that is ultimately, rightfully, how he is best remembered.

"I think I probably laughed in Graham's company more totally than I've ever laughed in anyone's company," says Palin. "Occasionally, we would have such a laugh that tears would roll from our eyes."

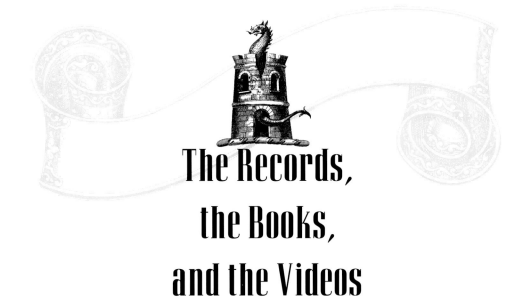

The Records,
the Books,
and the Videos

With the success of the TV series, it wasn't long before record companies and publishing houses took notice of Python. Although the group wasn't wildly enthusiastic about the ideas, they went on to success in both of those fields. The first books utilized some material from the TV shows, but with new twists and insights.

"It was Geoffrey Strachan at Methuen who actually proposed the idea of a book," explains Terry Jones, "and we'd all come to it rather half-heartedly. We always had somebody supervising our different projects, and it was Eric who edited the Python books. We were all quite surprised by how successful the *Big Red Book* was."

Their first album was a BBC recording of the soundtrack of the TV series, but they began incorporating new sketches and experimenting with the possibilities of audio scenes with their first independent record.

"Mike and I supervised the first record album, *Another Monty Python Record,* with the Beethoven sleeve crossed out," says Jones. "We had been approached by a record company—Mike and I handled that first one, and then Mike took over. We had such a horrendous time doing the first record! It got terribly involved, and everything seemed to be crucial, recording and using the stereo effect. . . . We recorded in this studio where the guys were on marijuana most of the time, and it just took forever. They recorded piles and piles of tapes, and they never made any record of what was on what. It was so ridiculous—it took forever to record. I didn't enjoy that at all."

The music, print, and video entries in the following pages hopefully include all of the most significant available works by the Pythons, individually and collectively. My own records have been double-checked against those of the Pythons and their offices. There is also Douglas McCall's fine book *Monty Python,* published by McFarland & Co., and an exhaustingly comprehensive online bibliography assembled by Hans ten Cate, which can be accessed through a link to PythOnline (at pythonline.com). Not every item may

still be in print, but some may be found at used book or record stores. Note that more items are referenced in the "Pythons for Sale: Licensing and Merchandising" section. Python Trading Cards and the *Holy Grail* role-playing card game are noted there rather than in the "Python Press" listings, and the CD-ROM games are also in the "Pythons for Sale" section rather than the video listings. Happy hunting!

Monty Python: On the Record

There are numerous variations in both the packaging and the contents of Python albums that have surfaced over the years, but the following discography is intended as a representative guide. There are special banded, promotional copies released to radio stations that have been censored, and in fact, the Pythons themselves have had to delete certain material, mostly for legal reasons (such as the "Farewell to John Denver" on the first release of the *Contractual Obligation Album*).

The Pythons always tried to innovate, and their records are no exception. *Matching Tie* was, on its initial release, the first three-sided record album: one side played normally, while the other had two sets of grooves cut into it, each with different material—the sketch that was heard depended on which groove the needle dropped into. The album was also packaged with an inner sleeve decorated with a tie and handkerchief visible through a hole cut out of the outer jacket. Unfortunately, cost-cutting attempts on later pressings resulted in the two double-sets of grooves pressed as only one, and the Gilliam-designed inner sleeve replaced with plain white paper, completely ruining the joke.

Instant Record Collection fell victim to the same cost-cutting measures as well. Its original release in Britain saw it packaged in an elaborate, Gilliam-designed fold-out cover, that could be assembled into a box that looked exactly like a stack of record albums, providing the title. Unfortunately, the record packages reportedly kept breaking open and unfolding in store bins, and all subsequent pressings, including the American versions, were released in a much more ordinary album jacket. Likewise, later pressings of *Another Monty Python Record* are lacking the "Be a Great Actor" inserts, including the instructions, effects sheet, and two plays.

Monty Python Sings, their most recent CD, contains many of Python's most popular musical selections, as well as a couple of rarities.

"Medical Love Song" is presented with the complete lyrics, and marks Graham Chapman's final Python singing contribution.

The other is a rare John Cleese vocal number called "Oliver Cromwell" that he first wrote and performed for *I'm Sorry, I'll Read That Again* in the years before Python.

"I always liked that particular polonaise [No. 6 by Chopin], and I just did it for a giggle one day," says Cleese. "I decided to try and put words to it. I looked up a few facts on Oliver Cromwell and then started to play with it. I think I did it for fun, very much in the same way that I did 'I've Got a Ferret Sticking Up My Nose.' It wasn't done for a particular show or a particular occasion. Then once I'd done it and it more or less worked, I did it once on the radio show. Because I'm such a terrible singer and was really rather nervous, I had a slightly difficult entry, or difficult at least for someone as bad as me. I tried it in front of this radio audience and got the entry wrong about three times, losing confidence and self-esteem by the second. The fourth time I got it right, but the audience applauded and cheered, so that wasn't any good and I had to do it again! I think I screwed it up the next time and then finally got it right. And after that, I think it was never used again, until we started looking for some silly material for the Python record. But it was very, very old."

Another of Cleese's rare musical performances is a song that has been often referred to but remains virtually unavailable at the present time, a song that dates back to *At Last It's the 1948 Show,* called "I've Got a Ferret Sticking Up My Nose."

"I think I wrote that when I was on holiday in Ibiza. I had this tune of 'Rose of England' in my head, and I wrote the lyrics to that tune and it amused me," says Cleese. "I did several verses. I

did it on holiday without any intention of actually doing it at the time. Then, when we were doing the *1948 Show* a few months later, I suggested that we do it with a big production number by the standards of the *1948 Show,* which meant about eight people singing. The director put some silly footage on the back of big ceremonial occasions, like coronations and state funerals, and we all wore starched shirt fronts and old-fashioned evening dress, black tie, and sang it as the final item of the final show of that autumn. Everybody thought it was very funny, and it was actually put out briefly as an EP, and I think 'Oliver Cromwell' may have been on the other side. I eventually went into a sound studio and recorded it. It was just a little EP that was in the shops for five weeks and was never seen again. It amused me, and I think when I was with Babs I wrote one or two extra verses, but I don't think I ever performed them anywhere. It's still sitting around as something I could do in an Amnesty Show."

The Albums

MONTY PYTHON'S FLYING CIRCUS (1970) BBC Records REB 73M (U.K.)/Pye 12116 (U.S.)
   The contents here are taken from the soundtrack of the TV shows.

SIDE ONE
Flying Sheep
Television Interviews/Arthur Frampton
Trade Description Act/Whizzo Chocolates
Nudge, Nudge
The Mouse Problem
Buying a Bed
Interesting People
The Barber/Lumberjack Song
Interviews/Sir Edward Ross

SIDE TWO
More Television Interviews/Arthur "Two Sheds"
   Jackson
Children's Stories
The Visitors
The Cinema/Albatross
The North Minehead By-Election
Me Doctor
Pet Shop (Dead Parrot)
Self-Defense

ANOTHER MONTY PYTHON RECORD (1972) Charisma 1049 *ANOTHER MONTY PYTHON CD* (1989) CASCD 1049 (U.S.)
   Packaged as "Beethoven Symphony No. 2 in D Major" and defaced by the Pythons to serve as their own record jacket. Most of the material is rerecorded versions of TV sketches, although some have been altered slightly; there are also a few new sketches and new linking material.

SIDE ONE
Apologies*
Spanish Inquisition
World Forum
Gumby Theatre, etc.*
The Architect
The Piranha Brothers

SIDE TWO
Death of Mary, Queen of Scots
Penguin on the TV
Comfy Chair/Sound Quiz*
Be a Great Actor*/Theatre Quiz*
Royal Festival Hall Concert*
Spam
The Judges/Stake Your Claim*
Still No Sign of Land/Undertaker

*Denotes sketches not in the original TV shows or film soundtracks, or at least significantly different from the TV and film versions.

MONTY PYTHON'S PREVIOUS RECORD (1972) Charisma 1063 (U.K.)/Charisma 0598 (U.S.)/Virgin Records (1989) CASCD 1063 (U.K.)

Contains a mixture of material from the TV shows, largely the third series, as well as new material. "A Fairy Tale" is a shortened version of a sketch done by John Cleese and Connie Booth for one of the German Python shows. Some versions of this came with the "Teach Yourself Heath" flexidisc.

SIDE ONE

Embarrassment/A Bed-Time Book*
England 1747—Dennis Moore
Money Programme
Dennis Moore Continues
Australian Table Wines*
Argument Clinic
Putting Budgies Down
Eric the Half a Bee*
Travel Agency

SIDE TWO

Radio Quiz Game*
A Massage/City Noises Quiz*
Miss Anne Elk
We Love the Yangtse*
How-to-do-it Lessons
A Minute Passed*
Eclipse of the Sun*/Alistair Cooke*
Wonderful World of Sounds*
A Fairy Tale*

THE MONTY PYTHON MATCHING TIE AND HANDKERCHIEF (1973)

Released as the world's first three-sided record, one side actually contains a pair of grooves cut into it, each containing different material; the tracks that played depended on where the needle dropped (see notes at "Monty Python: On the Record"). Later reissues eliminated the double groove. Most of the early versions of Python LPs featured more elaborate presentations and extras that were eliminated or modified over the years. *Matching Tie and Handkerchief* is a good example of these variations: the U.K. version featured a square die-cut window in the album jacket versus a round window in the U.S., and the "tie and handkerchief" is a part of the inner sleeve art. Cassettes rarely featured as many "extras"; and the release of CD versions even required some retitling: *Another Monty Python Record* became *Another Monty Python CD* and *Instant Record Collection* became *Instant CD Collection*.

Charisma CAS 1080 (U.K.)(Sleeve is drawn and shaped like a box with a square cut-out window; a matching tie and handkerchief are visible through the window. The tie and handkerchief are actually attached to a Gilliam rendering of a man hanging from a gallows and is also on a separate pull-out paper; there is also another insert with information about the record as well as "The Background to History.")

Arista AL 4039 (U.S.)(This is a promo version with bands for airplay and just one groove; it has a different cover design and an oval window instead of a square; the Gilliam hanging man and "Background to History" are part of the inner sleeve.)

CD: (1985, 1989) Virgin Records Ltd. CASCD 1080 (U.K.)

SIDE TWO

Dead Bishop on the Landing/The Church Police
Who Cares/The Surgeon and the Elephant Mr.
   Humphries*
Thomas Hardy/Novel Writing*
Word Association*
Bruces/Philosophers' Song*
Nothing Happened/Eating Dog*
Cheese Shop
Thomas Hardy*
Tiger Club*
Great Actors*

SIDE TWO

Infant Minister for Overseas Development
Oscar Wilde's Party
Pet Shop Conversions
Phone-in*

SIDE TWO

Background to History*/Medieval Open Field Farming
   Songs*
World War I Soldier/Stuck Record*
Boxing Tonight with Kenneth Clark

MONTY PYTHON LIVE AT THE THEATRE ROYAL DRURY LANE (1974) Charisma Class 4 (U.K. only)/VIP Records (1989) VVIPD 104 (U.K.)(CD release)

SIDE ONE
Introduction*/Llamas
Gumby Flower Arranging
Secret Service*
Wrestling*
Communist Quiz
Idiot Song (Neil Innes)*
Albatross/The Colonel
Nudge, Nudge/Cocktail Bar*
Travel Agent

SIDE TWO
Spot the Brain Cell
Bruces
Argument
Four Yorkshiremen*
Election Special
Lumberjack Song
Parrot

THE ALBUM OF THE SOUNDTRACK OF THE TRAILER OF THE FILM OF MONTY PYTHON AND THE HOLY GRAIL (1975) Charisma 1103 (U.K.)/Arista AL 4050 (U.S.)/Virgin CASCD1103 (U.K.)(C.D. Release)
    Contains excerpts from the film soundtrack, plus other film-related linking material.

SIDE ONE
Congratulations/Welcome to the Cinema*
Opening/Coconuts
Bring Out Your Dead
King Arthur Meets Dennis/Class Struggle
Witch Test
Professional Logician*
Camelot/The Quest
The Silbury Hill Car Park*
Frenchmen of the Castle
Bomb Threat*/Executive Announcement*

SIDE TWO
Story of the Film So Far*
The Tale of Sir Robin
The Knights of Ni
Interview/Director Carl French*
Swamp Castle/The Guards/Tim the Enchanter
Great Performances/Angry Crowd*
Holy Hand Grenade
Announcement—Sir Kenneth Clark*
French Castle Again
Close*

THE WORST OF MONTY PYTHON (1976) Kama Sutra KSBS2611-2
    This is actually a repackaging of *Another Monty Python Record* (CAS 1049) and *Monty Python's Previous Record* (CAS 1063), with a new album jacket. The two records were also packaged as a double-album set with their original covers, and sold as a two-record set.

MONTY PYTHON LIVE AT CITY CENTER (1976) Arista AL 4073 (U.S. only)

SIDE ONE
Introduction*/Llama
Gumby Flower Arranging
Short Blues (Neil Innes)*
Wrestling*
World Forum
Albatross/Colonel Stopping It
Nudge, Nudge/Crunchy Frog
Bruces Song*
Travel Agent

SIDE TWO
Camp Judges/Blackmail
Protest Song (Neil Innes)*
Pet Shop
Four Yorkshiremen*
Argument Clinic
Death of Mary, Queen of Scots
Salvation Fuzz/Church Police
Lumberjack Song

THE MONTY PYTHON INSTANT RECORD COLLECTION (1977) Charisma 1134 (U.K.)/Virgin Records (1989) CASCD1134 (U.K.)(CD release retitled *The Monty Python Instant CD Collection*)

Originally designed by Terry Gilliam and packaged to fold out into a cardboard box resembling a large stack of record albums, and now released in a normal record sleeve because the package kept breaking open in stores, this is essentially a "greatest hits" album, or, as it is billed, "The pick of the best of some recently repeated Python hits again, Vol. II." Most of the material here has been on previous albums.

SIDE ONE
Introductions
Alistair Cooke
Nudge, Nudge
Mrs. Nigger-Baiter
Constitutional Peasants
Fish License
Eric the Half a Bee
Australian Table Wines
Silly Noises
Novel Writing
Elephantoplasty
How to Do it
Gumby Cherry Orchard
Oscar Wilde

SIDE TWO
Introduction
Argument
French Taunter
Summarized Proust Competition
Cheese Emporium
Funerals at Prestatyn
Camelot
Word Association
Bruces
Parrot
Monty Python Theme

NOTE: The U.S. version of this album (Arista Records [1981] AL 9580 [U.S.]/Arista [1990] ARCD-8296 [U.S.] [CD release]) has many different cuts than the U.K. version, including tracks from *Matching Tie and Handkerchief, The Album of the Soundtrack of the Film of Monty Python and the Holy Grail, Live at City Center,* and *Contractual Obligation Album* as listed.

SIDE ONE
The Executive Intro
Pet Shop
Nudge, Nudge
Live Broadcast from London
Premiere of Film
Bring Out Your Dead
How Do You Tell A Witch
Camelot
Argument Clinic
Crunchy Frog
The Cheese Shop
The Phone-In
Sit On My Face

SIDE TWO
Another Executive Announcement
Bishop On The Landing
Elephantoplasty
The Lumberjack Song
Bookshop
Blackmail
Farewell to John Denver
World Forum
String
Wide World of Novel Writing
Death of Mary, Queen of Scots
Never Be Rude to an Arab

MONTY PYTHON'S LIFE OF BRIAN (1979) Warner Bros. K 56751 (U.K.)/BSK 3396 (U.S.)/Virgin Chattering Classics (1994) VCCD 009 (U.K.)(CD release)
Contains excerpts from the film, with brief linking material by Eric Idle and Graham Chapman.

SIDE ONE
Introduction*
Three Wise Men
Brian Song
Big Nose
The Stoning
Ex-Leper
Bloody Romans
Link*
People's Front of Judea
Short Link*
Latin Lesson
Missing Link*
Revolutionary Meeting
Very Good Link*
Ben
Audience with Pilate
Meanwhile*

SIDE TWO
The Prophets
Haggling
Lobster*
Sermon on the Wall
Lobster Link*
Simon the Holy Man
Sex Link*
The Morning After
Lighter Link*
Pilate and Biggus/Welease Bwian/Nisus Wettus
Crucifixion
Always Look on the Bright Side of Life
Close*

THE WARNER BROTHERS MUSIC SHOW: MONTY PYTHON EXAMINES "THE LIFE OF BRIAN" (1979) WBMS 110
A promotional album released to radio stations as part of the Warners series and never sold. It consists of an hour-long interview with the Pythons conducted by Dave Herman, along with excerpts from the soundtrack.

MONTY PYTHON'S CONTRACTUAL OBLIGATION ALBUM (1980) Charisma 1152 (U.K.)/Arista AL 9536 (U.S.)/Virgin Records-Kay Gee Bee Music (1989) CASCD 1152 (U.K.)(CD release)
Exactly what the title claims it is, this record contains all-new material, except for "String" and "Bookshop," both of which predate Python. "Farewell to John Denver" was deleted from later pressings for legal reasons, while "Sit on My Face," reportedly faced legal threats, as it is sung to the tune of "Sing as We Go," an old Gracie Fields tune. This is second only to *Monty Python Sings* as the most musical Python album, with over half of the twenty-four tracks consisting of songs.

SIDE ONE
Sit on My Face*
Announcement*
Henry Kissinger*
String*
Never Be Rude to an Arab*

I Like Chinese*
Bishop*
Medical Love Song*
Farewell to John Denver*
Finland*
I'm So Worried*

SIDE TWO
I Bet You They Won't Play This Song on the Radio*
Martyrdom of St. Victor*
Here Come Another One*
Bookshop*
Do What John*
Rock Notes*

Muddy Knees*
Crocodile*
Decomposing Composers*
Bells*
Traffic Lights*
All Things Dull and Ugly*
A Scottish Farewell*

MONTY PYTHON'S THE MEANING OF LIFE (1983) MCA Records MCA 6121/Virgin Chattering Classics (1994) VCCD 010 (U.K.)(CD release)
Contains excerpts from the film, with new linking material.

SIDE ONE
Introduction*
Fish Introduction
The Meaning of Life Theme
Birth
Birth Link/Frying Eggs*
Every Sperm is Sacred
Protestant Couple
Adventures of Martin Luther*
Sex Education
Trench Warfare
The Great Tea of 1914—18*
Fish Link*

SIDE TWO
Terry Gilliam's Intro*
Accountancy Shanty
Zulu Wars
Link*
The Dungeon Restaurant
Link/Live Organ Transplants
The Galaxy Song
The Not Noel Coward (Penis) Song
Mr. Creosote
The Grim Reaper
Christmas in Heaven
Dedication (to Fish)*

MONTY PYTHON'S THE FINAL RIPOFF (1987) Virgin Records Virgin 7-90865-1/Virgin Records (1987) 2-90865 (U.K.), 7-86034-29 (U.S.)(CD release)
Another "greatest hits" compilation, released when Virgin took over the Monty Python catalogue. This represents their first double-record set. All material here has been performed on previous records, except for some brief links by Michael Palin.

SIDE ONE
Introduction
Constitutional Peasants
Fish License
Eric the Half a Bee
Finland Song
Travel Agent
Are You Embarrassed Easily?
Australian Table Wines
Argument
Henry Kissinger Song
Parrot (Oh, Not Again!)

SIDE TWO
Sit on My Face
Undertaker
Novel Writing (Live From Wessex)
String
Bells
Traffic Lights
Cocktail Bar
Four Yorkshiremen
Election Special
Lumberjack Song

<table>
<tr><td>

SIDE THREE

I Like Chinese
Spanish Inquisition Part 1
Cheese Shop
Cherry Orchard
Architects' Sketch
Spanish Inquisition Part 2
Spam
Spanish Inquisition Part 3
Comfy Chair
Famous Person Quiz
You Be the Actor
Nudge, Nudge
Cannibalism
Spanish Inquisition Revisited

</td><td>

SIDE FOUR

I Bet You They Won't Play This Song on the Radio
Bruces
Bookshop
Do Wot John
Rock Notes
I'm So Worried
Crocodile
French Taunter Part 1
Marilyn Monroe
Swamp Castle
French Taunter Part 2
Last Word

</td></tr>
</table>

MONTY PYTHON SINGS (1989) Virgin Records MONT 1 (U.K.)(L.P.)/Virgin Records/Kay Gee Bee Music Ltd. CDV 3133 (U.S.)/Virgin Records, Ltd., MONTD 1 (U.K.)
　　Includes all of the best-known Python songs (see comments at the beginning of this section).

<table>
<tr><td>

SIDE ONE

Always Look on the Bright Side of Life
Sit on My Face
Lumberjack Song
Penis Song (Not the Noel Coward Song)
Oliver Cromwell
Money Song
Accountancy Shanty
Finland
Medical Love Song
I'm So Worried

</td><td>

SIDE TWO

Every Sperm Is Sacred
Never Be Rude to an Arab
I Like Chinese
Eric the Half a Bee
Brian Song
Bruces' Philosophers Song (Bruces' Song)
Meaning of Life
Knights of the Round Table
All Things Dull and Ugly
Decomposing Composers
Henry Kissinger
I've Got Two Legs
Christmas in Heaven
Galaxy Song
Spam Song

</td></tr>
</table>

THE INSTANT MONTY PYTHON CD COLLECTION (1994) Virgin Records CD BOX 3, ISBN 1-885381-04-2 (U.S.)
(Six-CD volume set; includes *Another Monty Python Record, Monty Python's Previous Record, Matching Tie and Handkerchief, Live at Drury Lane, Monty Python and the Holy Grail, Contractual Obligation Album, Life of Brian,* and *Meaning of Life.* Includes a forty-page booklet with material from the *Brand New Monty Python Book* and *Monty Python's Big Red Book.*

THE LUMBERJACK SONG/SPAM SONG Charisma CB 268

ERIC THE HALF A BEE (1972) Charisma CB 200

SPAM SONG /THE CONCERT Charisma CB 192

TEACH YOURSELF HEALTH contains original material, with an introduction by Michael Palin, lesson by Eric Idle, and examples by Edward Heath; included in the December 1972 *Zigzag.*

MONTY PYTHON'S TINY BLACK ROUND THING Election '74/Lumberjack Song, taken from *Drury Lane,* with a new introduction by Michael Palin; included with the May 1974 *New Musical Express.*

THE SINGLE (1975) Arista AS 0130 (U.S.)
   This is a promotional single for the *Matching Tie* album, containing shortened versions of: Who Cares/The Elephant Mr. Humphries; Infant Minister for Overseas Development; Pet Shop Conversions

PYTHON ON SONG (1976) Charisma MP 001
   A two-record set released in the U.K.
RECORD 1, Side A: Lumberjack Song (Produced by George Harrison) Side B: Spam Song
RECORD 2: Side A: Bruces' Song (with Neil Innes, from *Drury Lane*) Side B: Eric the Half a Bee

ALWAYS LOOK ON THE BRIGHT SIDE OF LIFE/BRIAN (1978) Warner Bros. K 56751 (U.K.)

I LIKE CHINESE/FINLAND/I'LL BET YOU THEY WON'T PLAY THIS SONG ON THE RADIO (1980) Charisma CB 374

THE GALAXY SONG/EVERY SPERM IS SACRED (1983) CBS Records WA 3495
   This is an over-sized picture disc released with *Meaning of Life,* shaped like a fishbowl and with a photo of the Python fish from the film.

   Python also released flexi-discs inserted into various British music magazines, some containing new material.

Always Look on the Bright Side of Life/I'm So Worried/I Bet You They Won't Play This Song on the Radio/Holzfaller Song (1991) Virgin Records Ltd., PYTHD 1 664740 (U.K.)(CD single)
   After being revived by English football fans who sang it in the stands when their teams were losing, "Bright Side" reached Number Three on the U.K. charts.

Spam Song/Lumberjack Song (1994) Virgin Records Ltd./Kay Gee Bee Music Ltd., Spammy 1 (U.K.)(CD single)
  (Included with *The Fairy Incomplete and Rather Badly Illustrated Monty Python Songbook* in Britain.)

Python is also represented on several compilation/sampler albums:
ONE MORE CHANCE Charisma Class 3 (U.K.) "Eric the Half a Bee"
SUPERTRACKS Vertigo Sport 1 (U.K.) "The Money Song"
25 YEARS OF RECORDED COMEDY (1978) Warner Bros. "Argument Clinic"

THE CHARISMA POSER: 25 YEARS OF THE CHARISMA RECORD LABEL (1993) Virgin POSER 1 "Eric the Half a Bee."

Records Featuring Members of Python

THAT WAS THE WEEK THAT WAS (1963) Odeon PMC 1197 PCS 3040 (U.K.)
  Includes recordings from the David Frost series, John Cleese's only written contribution to the album is the track "Regella."

SEVEN-A-SIDE (1965) MJB Recording and Transcription Service
Oxford University Experimental Theatre Club and Oxford Theatre Group
  Features Michael Palin and Terry Jones
  Recorded at Oxford in November 1964, this was apparently a private recording made for cast members, families, and friends, and contains material from the 1964 Oxford cabaret and theater shows *Hang Down Your Head and Die*, the Edinburgh *Oxford Revue*, and *Keep This to Yourself.*
Palin/Jones compositions and performances include:
"Grin" (Palin/Gould), performed by Palin
"Song About a Toad" (Jones/Gould)
"Forgive Me" (Jones/Gould)
"Song of British Nosh" (Palin/Gould), performed by Palin, David Wood, and Bob Scott
"I've Invented a Long-Range Telescope" (Palin/Gould) Palin
"Last One Home's a Custard" (Fisher/Palin/Jones/Gould), performed by Solomon, Sommerville, Sadler, Palin, Wood, Weston, and Scott

CAMBRIDGE CIRCUS (1965) Odeon PCS 3046 Original Broadway Cast
  Features John Cleese
  The soundtrack album from the show as it ran on Broadway.

THE FROST REPORT ON BRITAIN (1966) Parlophone PMC 7005
  Features John Cleese and Jean Hart
  Produced by James Gilbert; writing credits: David Frost and John Cleese, with Tim Brooke-Taylor, Graham Chapman, Barry Cryer, Tony Hendra, Terry Jones, Herbert Kretzner, Peter Lewis and Peter Dobereiner, David Nobbs, Bill Oddie, and Ludwig Van Beethoven.

SIDE ONE
Matter of Taste (Cleese)
Schoolmaster (Cleese)
Just Four Just Men (Cleese)
Internal Combustion
Deck of Cards
Top of the Form (Cleese)
Unknown Soldier (Cleese)

SIDE TWO
Scrapbook (Cleese)
Adventure (Cleese)
Numbers
Bulletin
Hilton
Zookeeper (Cleese)

THE FROST REPORT ON EVERYTHING (1967) Janus JLS-3005
   Features David Frost, Ronnie Barker, John Cleese, Ronnie Corbett, and Sheila Steafel
   Writing credits include Frost, Terry Jones, Michael Palin, Eric Idle, Graham Chapman, and John Cleese
(misspelled "Clease")

SIDE ONE
The State of England
Theatre Critic (Cleese)
Frost, What People Really Mean
Three Classes of People (Cleese)
Narcissus Complex (Cleese)

SIDE TWO
Frost on Agriculture, Speech
The Secretary (Cleese)
Frost on Commercials
Selling String
Executive and the Teaman
Three Classes (Cleese)

I'M SORRY, I'LL READ THAT AGAIN (1967) EMI M-11634
   Features John Cleese, Tim Brooke-Taylor, Graeme Garden, David Hatch, Jo Kendall, and Bill Oddie
   Among other roles, Cleese plays the Doctor, Mary's John, Little John, Sir Angus of the Prune, the MC,
Baby Rupert, Captain Cleese, and Wong Tu

SIDE ONE
The Auctioneer
The Day After Tomorrow's World
The Doctor (written by Oddie/Cleese)
Blimpht
John and Mary (Cleese/Oddie)
Robin Hood (Garden/Cleese)

SIDE TWO
Identikit Gal
Baby Talk
Family Favorites
The Curse of the Flying Wombat
Closing/Angus Prune Tune

I'M SORRY, I'LL READ THAT AGAIN (1967) BBC Records REH 342

FUNNY GAME, FOOTBALL (1972) EP from "The Group" from *Funny Game, Football* Charisma CB 197
Music by Neil Innes
   Features Michael Palin, Terry Jones, Arthur Mullard, Bryan Pringle, Bill Tidy, Joe Steeples, Michael Wale
   Written by Joe Steeples, Bill Tidy, Michael Wale

SIDE ONE
Piraeus Football Club
Crunch!
Rangers Abroad
An Open Letter to George Best
The Missionary

Sir Alf Speaks
World War III
Newsnight with Coleman
Soccer Laureate
Bovver Boys

SIDE TWO
Scilly Season
Government Policies
I Remember It Well

Floor's the Limit*
Director's Song
Blackbury Town
A Joke

THE RUTLAND WEEKEND SONGBOOK (1975) BBC Records REB 233 (U.K.)/(1976) ABC/Passport Records PPSD-98018 (U.S.)/Music Scene (1995) MSI 10079 (U.K.)(CD release)
    Features Eric Idle and Neil Innes, containing material from the BBC series

SIDE ONE
L'Amour Perdue
Gibberish
Wash with Mother/Front Loader
Say Sorry Again
The Rutles in "Rutles for Sale" ("I Must Be in Love")
24 Hours in Tunbridge Wells
The Fabulous Bingo Brothers
In Concrete—Concrete Jungle Boy
The Children of Rock and Roll
Startime—Stoop Solo
Song O' the Insurance Men
Closedown

SIDE TWO
I Give Myself to You
Communist Cooking/Johnny Cash Live at Mrs. Fletchers
The Old Gay Whistle Test
Accountancy Shanty
Football/Boring
Good Afternoon/L'Amour Perdue Cha Cha Cha
Disco—the Hard to Get
Closedown—the Song O' the Continuity Announcers

A POKE IN THE EYE WITH A SHARP STICK (1976) Transatlantic TRA 331 (U.K. only)
    Recording of the 1976 Amnesty International Benefit
    Features John Cleese, Graham Chapman, Terry Gilliam, Terry Jones, Michael Palin, Carol Cleveland, Neil Innes, Alan Bennett, John Bird, Eleanor Bron, Tim Brooke-Taylor, Peter Cook, John Fortune, Jonathan Miller, Jonathan Lynn, Graeme Garden, Bill Oddie

SIDE ONE
A Brief Introduction (Cleese)
Asp (Cook, Fortune)
Happy, Darling? (Bron, Fortune)
The Last Supper (Cleese, Lynn)
Telegram (Bennett)
Funky Gibbon (The Goodies—Brooke-Taylor, Garden, Oddie)
Appeal (Bron)

SIDE TWO
Courtroom (Chapman, Cleese, Cleveland, Gilliam, Jones, Palin, with Cook)
Portraits from Memory (Miller)
You Say Potato (Bird, Fortune)
Baby Talk (Bron, Fortune)
So That's The Way You Like It—Beyond the Fringe (Miller, Bennett, Cook with Jones)
Lumberjack Song (All)

THE MERMAID FROLICS (1977) Polydor Special 2384101
    Recording of the second Amnesty International Benefit, recorded May 8, 1977
    Features John Cleese, Terry Jones, Connie Booth, Jonathan Miller, and Peter Ustinov
    The first side is all music; the comedy side contains skits by Cleese, and Jones performs a song.

*A Python-ish quiz show with Palin as host, and Jones the unfortunate contestant.

THE RUTLES: ALL YOU NEED IS CASH (1978) Warner Bros. HS 3151 (U.S.) Warners K 56459 (U.K.)/Rhino Records (1990) R2 75760 (U.S.)(CD release)

>Features Eric Idle
>
>Soundtrack of the NBC/BBC 2 film with songs by Neil Innes, and a twenty-page booklet enclosed

SIDE ONE 1962–67

Hold My Hand
Number One
With a Girl Like You
I Must Be in Love
Ouch!
Living in Hope
Love Life
Nevertheless

SIDE TWO 1967–70

Good Times Roll
Doubleback Alley
Cheese and Onions
Another Day
Piggy in the Middle
Let's Be Natural

THE RUTLES (CD release)(1990) Rhino Records R2 75760 (U.S.)

>(The CD release contains six bonus tracks in addition to all of the original material from the LP, as well as a fold-out mini-poster, which has much of the material of the original twenty-four page picture book.)
>
>BONUS CD TRACKS: "Goose-Step Mama," "Baby Let Me Be," "Blue Suede Schubert," "Between Us," "It's Looking Good," "Get Up and Go"

THE RUTLES (1978) Warner Bros. Pro. E723

>A five-song promotional EP, released on yellow vinyl

I Must Be in Love
Doubleback Alley
With A Girl Like You
Another Day
Let's Be Natural

I'M SORRY, I'LL READ THAT AGAIN (1978) BBC Records REH 342 (U.K.)

SIDE ONE

Opening credits
Full Frontal Radio, Prune Manifesto, Buffers
Critics, Motoring Flash
Quickie (Cleese, Hatch)
Honours List, News in Welsh, Minority Programmes
Home This Afternoon a Go Go (Cleese, Garden,
    Hatch, Oddie, David Lee Group)
News Flash
Listening to the Flowers

SIDE TWO

Opening (Cleese, Hatch, the David Lee Group)
Talent Contest
Eddie Wang Impersonation
Sickman's Blues
Taming of the Shrew
Closing Credits

THE SECRET POLICEMAN'S BALL (1979) Island ILPS 9601

A recording of the 1979 Amnesty International Benefit, released on two records in the U.K., one containing the comedy portion of the show, the other with the music, including Pete Townshend

Features John Cleese, Terry Jones, Michael Palin, Rowan Atkinson, and Peter Cook. Python-related tracks include the following:

SIDE ONE
Interesting Facts (Cleese, Cook)
How Do You Do It? (Jones, Palin)
The Names of the Game (Cleese, Jones)
Stake Your Claim (Palin, Atkinson)

SIDE TWO
Cheese Shop (Cleese, Palin)
Four Yorkshiremen (Cleese, Jones, Palin, Atkinson)
The End of the World (Cook and cast)

FAWLTY TOWERS (1979) BBC Records REB 377

Features John Cleese and Connie Booth
The soundtrack to the TV shows "The Hotel Inspectors" and "Mrs. Richards"

FAWLTY TOWERS: SECOND SITTING (1981) BBC Records REB 405

Features John Cleese and Connie Booth
The soundtrack to the TV shows "The Builders" and "The Rats"

THE SECRET POLICEMAN'S OTHER BALL (1981) Island HAHA 6003/Castle Communications (1991) ESDCD 152 (U.K.)(CD release)

A recording of the 1981 Amnesty International Benefit, also released as a comedy record, and as a separate music album, which included Eric Clapton and Jeff Beck, Phil Collins, and Sting

Features John Cleese, Graham Chapman, with Rowan Atkinson, Alan Bennett, Billy Connolly, John Fortune, Alexei Sayle, and Pamela Stephenson

Python-related tracks include:

SIDE ONE
A Word of Thanks (Cleese and the cast)
Clothes Off (Cleese, Stephenson, Chapman)

SIDE TWO
Beekeeping (Cleese, Atkinson)
Song in a French Accent (Innes)
Top of the Form (Cleese, Chapman, Brooke-Taylor,
   Bird, Rhys Jones, Fortune, Atkinson)

FAWLTY TOWERS: AT YOUR SERVICE (1982) BBC Records REB 449

Features John Cleese and Connie Booth
The soundtrack to the TV shows "The Germans" and "The Kipper and the Corpse"

FAIRY TALES (1982) A recording of several stories from Terry Jones's children's book, read by a cast including Bob Hoskins and Helen Mirren

FAWLTY TOWERS: A LA CARTE BBC Records REB 484 (U.K.)

Includes "Waldorf Salad" and "Gourmet Night"

BRAZIL (1993) Milan Entertainment, Inc., 7 3138-35636-2 (U.S.)
Music from the original motion picture soundtrack.

THE MIKADO (1987) MCA Classics MCAD-6215
Highlights from the English National Opera production starring Eric Idle (as Koko), and directed by Jonathan Miller. Additional lyrics to "I've Got a Little List" are apparently by Eric.

THE SCREWTAPE LETTERS (1988) Audio Literature, Inc. ISBN 0-944993-15-X
Available on tape only, this is a three-hour, two-cassette version of the C. S. Lewis book as read by John Cleese.

THE ADVENTURES OF BARON MUNCHAUSEN (1989) Warner Brothers Records 9 25826-2
Instrumental soundtrack from the film; most songs are instrumentals except for "What Will Become of the Baron?" and "The Torturer's Apprentice" medley (the latter is cowritten by Eric Idle).

I'M SORRY, I'LL READ THAT AGAIN (1989) BBC Radio Collection ZBBC 1100 (ISBN 0-563-22717-6)(U.K.)
A two-cassette collection of some of the original radio shows.

SIDE ONE (Broadcast June 9, 1968)
Postal Announcement
The Kevin Mousetrap Show (David Frost parody)
Wonderful World (Scratchy Throat)
Doctor's Office
Melody Farm (song)
Favorite Stories from Shakespeare/MacBeth

SIDE TWO (Broadcast March 22, 1970—without Cleese)
Offensive Announcement
Full Frontal Prune Radio
The Rolf Harris Dirty Songbook
Babies
Is This Your Life?
Stuffing the Gibbon (song)
Prune Play of the Week (James Bond parody)

SIDE THREE (Broadcast April 5, 1970)
Show Tune Medley
Common Market/Radio Prune Goes International
Censored Tom Jones
It's a Washout
Thud Bang Bang (song)
Prune Play of the Week

SIDE FOUR (Broadcast December 23, 1973)
Ministerial Broadcast to the Nation
Radio Terrapin
Childhood Remembered
Just My Bill (Eddie Waring)
Brian Clough (song)
The Colditz Story

A LIAR'S AUTOBIOGRAPHY (1989) Dove Books on Tape ISBN 1-55800-120-4 (U.S.)
A book on tape featuring Graham Chapman reading from his autobiography on two cassette tapes, unabridged, 182 minutes. One of the last projects completed by Graham before his death.

JACK AND THE BEANSTALK (1991) Rabbit Ears Productions Inc./BMG KIDZ/Rincon Children's Entertainment RCE 74041 70760-2 (U.S.)(CD release)
Michael Palin reads the fairy tale, with music by Dave Stewart; also released on video.

FAMILIES AND HOW TO SURVIVE THEM (1991) BBC Radio Collection/BBC Enterprises Ltd. ZBBC 1244 (ISBN 0563-365196)(U.K.)

John Cleese and Robin Skynner discuss topics from their book for BBC Radio, 175 minutes; includes extracts from John Cleese's performances in *Fawlty Towers, Monty Python's Flying Circus,* and *Taming of the Shrew.*

THE FISHER KING (1991) MCA Records, Inc. MCAD 10249 (U.S.)

Original motion picture soundtrack; includes clip from Jack Lucas's radio show with Jeff Bridges; Harry Nilsson also sings "How About You."

A POKE IN THE EYE (WITH A SHARP STICK), VOL. II [or *THE COMPLETE A POKE IN THE EYE (WITH A SHARP STICK)*] (1991) Castle Communications ESDCD 153 (U.K.)(CD release)

A reissue of the original album with a large amount of unreleased material from those 1976 shows.

I'M SORRY I'LL READ THAT AGAIN 2 (1992) BBC Radio Collection ZBBC 1329 (ISBN 0-563-36657-5)(U.K.)

This collection of ISIRTA sketches includes the first episode of the series from 1964, and the twenty-fifth anniversary episode performed in 1989, with written contributions by Eric Idle.

SIDE ONE (Broadcast April 3, 1964)
Top of the Form
Jack and the Beanstalk
Inward Bound
Cricket Commentary
Time for Romance/Just My Jim (song)
Here Are the News/The Weather
Fritz & His Performing Hamsters
Sports Report/Wine Tasting
More Than Meets the Aye
Horrible Hairy Spiders
Trip to the Bank
Taxi Cab (song)

SIDE TWO (Broadcast May 9, 1966)
Rat Catcher Strike
Angus Prune Tune
Mrs. Glasshouse
Traffic Wardens
Promenade Concert/There Was a Ship That Put to Sea
    All in the Month of May (song)
Dr. Cleese
Somerset, Greatest Lawman of Them All (song)
Harmony Hearts Marriage Guidance Bureau
I'm Sorry Read-Out/Caesar
Angus Prune Tune

SIDE THREE (Broadcast December 25, 1989)
David Hatch
Angus Prune Tune
How It All Started
The Today Program/Green Party Conference
Spring, Spring, Spring (song)
Recycled Programming
John Cleese and Robin Onboard the Ferret 1
John and Mary; Tim Brooke-Taylor
Prune Playhouse: Jack the Ripper (Part 1)

SIDE FOUR (Broadcast December 25, 1989)
Prune Playhouse: Jack the Ripper (Part 2)
Listener's Letters
Meeting of the ISIRTA Cast/John Cleese's Silly Walk
    for Radio
BBC Broadcasting in the 90s White Paper
John Cleese, the Richest Man in the World
John Cleese's Training Film
John Cleese Buys BBC Radio
Late Arrivals at the Bar-B-Que
The Ferret Song
Angus Prune Tune

AROUND THE WORLD IN 80 DAYS (1993) BBC Audio Collection, ZBBC 6002 (ISBN 0-563-40141-9)(U.K.)
   A complete and unabridged account of Michael Palin's journey, written and read by Michael. On six cassettes, 455 minutes long.

DEAD PARROT SOCIETY: THE BEST OF BRITISH COMEDY (1993) Rhino Records R2 71049 (U.S.)(CD release)
   With material from the Amnesty International benefits "A Poke in the Eye (With a Sharp Stick)," "A Poke in the Eye (With a Sharp Stick), Vol. II," and "The Secret Policeman's Other Ball."
   Python-related tracks include:

The Dead Parrot (Monty Python)
The Courtroom—Scene I: "The Charges" (Monty Python)
Protest Song (Neil Innes)
Happy, Darling?
The Courtroom—Scene II: "Counsel for the Defence" (Monty Python)
Crunchy Frog (Monty Python)
The Oral Majority!—Part I (Graham Chapman)
The Courtroom—Scene III: "Police Constable Pan Am" (Monty Python)
Top of the Form (John Cleese, Graham Chapman, and company)
The Courtroom—Scene IV: "Counsel for the Prosecution" (Monty Python)
The Penultimate Supper?! (John Cleese, Jonathan Lynn)
The Courtroom—Scene V: "Very Expensive Gaiters" (Monty Python)
The Oral Majority—Part II (Graham Chapman)
The Courtroom—Scene VI: "There Goes the Judge" (Monty Python)
The Argument Clinic (Monty Python)
The Lumberjack Song (Monty Python and cast)

DID I EVER TELL YOU HOW LUCKY YOU ARE? (1993) Random House, Inc. ISBN 0-679-84993-9 (U.S.)
   John Cleese narrates this Dr. Seuss short story for children, which comes with a book and is also available as a videotape.

A LIAR LIVE (1994) Virgin 4PRO 14230 (cassette promo only)
   Virgin America Records reportedly put together a promotional cassette recording of the best of Graham Chapman's college lecture tours; the full-length lecture was eventually released in 1997 (see below).

HEMINGWAY'S CHAIR (1995) Reed Audio, REED 134 (ISBN 1-86021-944-6) (U.K.)
   A two-cassette version of Michael Palin reading from his first novel.

I'M SORRY I'LL READ THAT AGAIN 3 (1995) BBC Radio Collection ZBBC 1723 (ISBN 0-563-39084-0) (U.K.)
   More material from the radio show continues to be released.

THE QUITE REMARKABLE ADVENTURES OF THE OWL AND THE PUSSYCAT (1996) Dove Audio 43730 (ISBN 0-7871-1006-X)

The story and original songs cowritten (with John DuPrez) and performed by Eric Idle, tying in with his children's book of the same title.

A SIX PACK OF LIES (1997) Magnum Music CDVB 001 (U.K.)
    One of Graham Chapman's final lectures, recorded April 25, 1988 at Georgia Tech in Atlanta, GA.

CONTENTS
30 Seconds of Abuse
The Dangerous Sports Club
"Shitties"
The Even More Dangerous Keith Moon
Monty Python Fliegende Zirkus
Two Films and Six Snakes
Paralyzed at the Polo Lounge
The (Non-Inflatable) History of Monty Python
Who Wrote That and Who Didn't
A Horse, A Bucket and a Spoon?
Python's Progress (Circa 1988)
And Then There Was. . . Spam!!!
The Magic Christian
The Liar's Autobiography

DOUGLAS ADAMS'S STARSHIP TITANIC (1997) Simon & Schuster Audioworks 57745-X (ISBN 0-671-57745-X) The complete book by Terry Jones on four cassettes, read by the author.

 ## Additional Singles

SUPERSPIKE, PARTS 1 and 2 Bradley 7606
    "The Superspike Squad" with John Cleese and Bill Oddie
    All profits were donated to the International Athlete's Club's fundraising campaign.

I MUST BE IN LOVE/DOUBLEBACK ALLEY Warner Bros. WBS 8560
    The Rutles (the single from the soundtrack album)
    Features Eric Idle and Neil Innes

GING GANG GOOLIE/MR. SHEENE EMI 2852 (U.K. only)
    Dirk and Stig (Eric Idle and Rikki Fataar) of the Rutles

George Harrison's *33 1/3* album includes Eric Idle on "The Song," in which he delivers a few spoken lines during a bridge in a Pepperpot voice.

The Beatle bootleg *Indian Rope Trick* contains "Cheese and Onions," as performed by Neil Innes on *Saturday Night Live*, and credits it as a Beatle song; also on the bootleg is "The Pirate Song," cowritten by Eric Idle and George Harrison, and performed on *Rutland Weekend Television*.

A bootleg anthology album on the Kornyfone label, *T'anks for the Mammaries*, includes "Get Up and Go," featured on *All You Need is Cash*, but not included on the soundtrack album.

Python Press

After the first season of Python proved a success, the group was approached by Methuen Books about doing a tie-in with the television show. Eric Idle, in particular, was quite keen on assembling a book consisting of material from the TV series, but by the time he had finished, it looked much more like an original collection of humor. Most of the material used the Python sketches as a starting point, with Idle and the others extrapolating from them to develop new premises.

Lavishly illustrated with photo stills, original art, and Gilliam animation, *The Big Red Book* (with, naturally, a bright blue cover) was successful enough to warrant a followup. *The Brand New Monty Python Bok* (accompanied later by, of course, *The Brand New Monty Python Papperbok* edition) was even more elaborate, original, and innovative, with cutout pages and inserts to delight fans looking for more than just an ordinary book. Idle again assembled the material for the followup, which actually contained even more new material than the first volume. The hardcover edition included a white dust jacket (with smudged fingerprints on the back) over a cover that announced "Tits and Bums: A Weekly Look at Church Architecture," which the paperback did not have.

The books have always been steady, consistent sellers, but the group didn't decide to do another volume until *Monty Python and the Holy Grail (Book)*, as the group itself was moving on from television to film. In addition to the final draft of the screenplay, the edition also includes the first draft, which enables the reader to view the process the story went through (with much of the first draft material ending up in *Monty Python* Series 4). The book is loaded with photos and sketches, as well as the Cost of Production Statement. Appropriately enough, it was even designed to look like a script, and was edited by Terry Jones, the codirector.

It took another film for another book to result, although in the Python spirit of innovation—or simply trying to stir things up—it was packaged *Monty Python's Life of Brian/Montypythonscrapbook* as two books under one cover. The back cover of one book is actually the front cover of the other when it is flipped over. One is the reproduction of the script, illustrated with stills throughout. It is very nearly the final version, but a few items removed from the film at the last moment, including the scene with Eric Idle as Otto, leader of a suicide squad, remain in the book. The other portion of the book is indeed a scrapbook, with deleted scenes from various stages of the movie, excerpts from diaries, bits of animation, and a variety of other material (including the Bruces' "Philosophers' Song") not necessarily related to the film.

The *Meaning of Life* trade paperback reprints the script of the film with plenty of color photos, and includes scenes deleted from the final version in 1983.

The next Python book was not released until 1994. *The Fairly Incomplete and Rather Badly Illustrated Monty Python Songbook* features all the favorite Python songs and a few obscure treats, beautifully illustrated by Terry Gilliam and friends.

Each member of the group has been responsible for original books of a surprising variety, ranging from psychology to autobiography, literature, fiction, and children's books, in addition to all their movie tie-ins, and there is the bright prospect of many more to come.

MONTY PYTHON'S BIG RED BOOK Methuen, 1971 (U.K.)/Warner Books, 1975 (U.S.) ISBN 0-446-87077-3

Letter of Endorsement from Television Newscasters

"Juliette," featuring Ken Shabby and Rosemary

Why Accountancy is Not Boring, by A. Putey

Campaign Literature for the Silly Party

Batley Ladies' Townswomen's Guild

Sports Page, with Jimmy Buzzard and Ken Clean-Air System

The Importance of Being Earnest—a new version by Billy Bremner

Sir Kenneth Clarke—Are You Civilized?

The Greatest Upper-Class (Twit) Race in the World

Goat's Page

Johnson's Novelties ("Guaranteed to break the ice at parties")

Letter Retracting the Endorsement of the Book

Lumberjack Song

Whizzo Chocolate Assortment

How to Walk Silly

Poems of Ewan McTeagle

Piranha Brothers

THE BRAND NEW MONTY PYTHON BOK (hardcover) Methuen, 1973 (U.K.)/Henry Regnery, 1976 (U.S.) ISBN 0-8092-8046-9

Contents are identical to the paperback, except for the "Tits and Bums" cover under the dust jacket of this edition.

THE BRAND NEW MONTY PYTHON PAPPERBOK Methuen, 1974 (U.K.)/Warner Books, 1976 (U.S.) ISBN 0-446-87-078-1

Biggles is Extremely Silly (1938)

Notice of the Availability of Film Rights to Page Six

The Bigot (a newsletter)

The London Casebook of Detective René Descartes

The Adventures of Walter Wallabee (comic strip)

Film Review with Phillip Jenkinson

Rat Recipes and Chez Rat (menu)

The British Apathy League

Let's Talk About Bottoms

Page 71

Ferndean School Report for God

Cheeseshop (The Word Game)

The Official Medallic Commemoration of the History of Mankind

The Anagrams Gape (4) and the Anagram-Haters Page

Teach Yourself Surgery

THE COMPLETE WORKS OF SHAKESPEARE AND MONTY PYTHON: VOLUME ONE—MONTY PYTHON Methuen, 1981, ISBN 0-413-49450-0

A British compilation of *Big Red Book* and *Brand New Monty Python Bok*.

THE MONTY PYTHON GIFT BOKS Methuen, 1988, ISBN 0-413-14520-4
   A repackaging of the first two books, with an additional poster.

MONTY PYTHON AND THE HOLY GRAIL (BOOK) Methuen, 1977, ISBN 0-458-92970-0/Eyre Methuen, 1977 (U.K.) ISBN 0-413-38520-5
   Contains the first draft, final draft, production notes, sketches, and both production and candid photos; early editions were packaged to look like an actual script.

MONTY PYTHON'S THE LIFE OF BRIAN/MONTYPYTHONSCRAPBOOK Methuen, 1979 (U.K./Fred Jordan Books/Grosset & Dunlap, 1979 (U.S.) ISBN 0-448-16568-6 (oversized trade paperback)
   One half of the book contains the final script of the film, profusely illustrated with photos from the movie; while the other half contains the following assortment:
How It All Began: a comic strip featuring three shepherds
Diaries of Terry Jones and Michael Palin
What to Take on Filming
Python Cinema Quiz
Brian Feeds the Multitude
"Sharing" Magazine with "Sharing a Caravan with John Cleese"
The Gilliam Collection of Famous Film Titles
Cleese vs. The Evening Standard
Doc. Chapman's Medical Page

MONTY PYTHON'S LIFE OF BRIAN Ace Books, 1979, ISBN 0-441-48240-6
   The small paperback version of the script originally printed in the oversized Grosset & Dunlap edition, including all the photos, but without any *Montypythonscrapbook* material

MONTY PYTHON'S THE MEANING OF LIFE Methuen (U.K.) ISBN 0-413-53380-8/Grove Press (U.S.) 1983, ISBN 0-394-62474-2
   This trade paperback reproduces, in full color, the entire script; a great number of stills accompany it. Also includes material cut from the final release, including "The Adventures of Martin Luthor."

MONTY PYTHON'S FLYING CIRCUS: JUST THE WORDS, VOLUME ONE Methuen, 1989 (U.K.) ISBN 0-413-62540-0 (hardcover)/Pantheon, 1989 (U.S.) ISBN 0-679-72647-0 (paperback)

MONTY PYTHON'S FLYING CIRCUS: JUST THE WORDS, VOLUME TWO Methuen, 1989 (U.K.) ISBN 0-413-62550-8 (hardcover)/Pantheon, 1989 (U.S.) ISBN 0-679-72648-9 (paperback)

MONTY PYTHON'S FLYING CIRCUS: JUST THE WORDS Methuen, 1989 (U.K.) ISBN 0-413-62850-7 (both paperbacks shrinkwrapped together)/Mandarin, 1990 (U.K.) ISBN 0-7493-0226-7 (one very thick paperback incorporating both volumes)
   Complete scripts of the *Monty Python's Flying Circus* television series. Volume One includes episodes 1 through 23, while Volume Two features episodes 24 through 45. Both volumes include an index of sketches, and the original production and air dates. The U.S. editions were published as *Monty Python's Flying Circus: All the Words*. Both paperback volumes were also shrinkwrapped together in Britain in 1989 and sold with a thin paper wraparound and was labeled *Monty Python's Flying Circus: Just the Words* without reference to volumes. And both volumes were published under one cover in Britain in a paperback flip-book format, which includes black-and-white photos from the TV shows.

THE FAIRLY INCOMPLETE AND RATHER BADLY ILLUSTRATED MONTY PYTHON SONG BOOK

Methuen London, Ltd., 1994 (U.K.) ISBN 0-413-69000-8 (hardcover that includes a free CD single of the "Spam Song"/"Lumberjack Song")/HarperPerennial, 1995 (U.S.) ISBN 0-06-095116-8 (paperback)

Features the music and lyrics to virtually all the best-known Monty Python songs, including the "Spam Song," "Always Look on the Bright Side of Life," "Lumberjack Song" (including the Holzfallerliederhosen version from the German episodes), even including songs never before performed in Python, such as the "Rhubarb Tart Song" and "I've Got a Ferret Sticking Up My Nose." Includes photos and original artwork by Terry Gilliam.

MONTY PYTHON'S FLYING CIRCUS: THE 1995 MONTY PYTHON DATEBOOK, by the Ink Group, 1995 (U.K.) ISBN 1-875842-06-3 (hardcover)

A 1995 datebook with photos from the TV shows, material from the first Python books and Terry Gilliam art.

MONTY PYTHON'S FLYING CIRCUS: 1995 CALENDAR, by the Ink Group 1995 (U.K.) ISBN 1-875842-05-5 (paperback)

A wall calendar for 1995; incorporates many of the same features as the datebook.

THE NEARLY NEW MONTY PYTHON DATEBOK: 1996, by the Ink Group 1995 (U.K.) ISBN 1-875842-05-5 (paperback)

A new version of the datebook for 1996, drawing on classic Python book material, photos, and art from Terry Gilliam.

MONTY PYTHON AND THE HOLY GRAIL: CALENDAR 1996 A.D., by the Ink Group (U.K.) ISBN 1-875842-05-5

The 1996 wall calendar focuses on "Monty Python and the Holy Grail," with stills, artwork, and other material from the *Holy Grail* book.

MONTY PYTHON'S LIFE OF BRIAN: CALENDAR FOR THE YEAR OF BRIAN THE MESSIAH 1997, by the Ink Group (U.K.) ISBN 1-875842-05-5

This 1997 wall calendar is based on *Monty Python's Life of Brian,* featuring stills, artwork and dialogue from the film.

THE TOTALLY IRRELEVANT MONTY PYTHON 1998 CALENDAR, by the Ink Group (U.K.) ISBN 1-876129-14-X

This colorful 1998 wall calendar uses photos, dialogue, Terry Gilliam's artwork and material from the Python books.

 ## Books about Monty Python

THE LAUGHTERMAKERS, by David Nathan, Peter Owen Ltd., 1971 ISBN 0-720-60361-7
Published in the U.K., Chapter 10 is devoted to "Monty Python's Flying Breakthrough."

FROM FRINGE TO FLYING CIRCUS, by Roger Wilmut; Eyre Methuen, 1980, ISBN 0-413-46950-6
Another U.K. book, a significant portion of it is devoted to Python and its place in modern British humor.

MONTY PYTHON'S COMPLETE AND UTTER THEORY OF THE GROTESQUE, edited by John O. Thompson, British Film Institute, ISBN 0-85170-119-1
A series of forty-eight essays on various facets of Python, with an index.

MONTY PYTHON: THE CASE AGAINST, by Robert Hewison, Eyre Methuen, 1981, ISBN 0-413-48660-5 (paperback)/ISBN 0-413-48650-8 (hardcover)

A thorough study of the Pythons' battles against censorship, from the TV shows to the ABC lawsuit to the *Life of Brian* controversy, including script excerpts from the material in question.

LIFE OF PYTHON, by George Perry, Pavilion Books, 1983, ISBN 1-85145-057-2/Pavilion Books, 1994 (U.K.) ISBN 1-857-93441-5/Running Press Book Publishers, 1995 (U.S.) ISBN 1-56138-568-9)

A biography of the group, with individual chapters devoted to each of the six members, with an index. An updated edition was published in 1995.

FOOTLIGHTS!: A HUNDRED YEARS OF CAMBRIDGE COMEDY, by Robert Hewison, Methuen London, 1984 (U.K.) ISBN 0-413-56050-3 (paperback)

The story of the first hundred years of Cambridge University's Footlights Club, founded in 1883, including the years in which Graham Chapman, John Cleese, and Eric Idle were members. Preface is written by Eric Idle.

THE FIRST 200 YEARS OF MONTY PYTHON, by Kim "Howard" Johnson, St. Martin's Press, 1989 ISBN 0-312-03309-5 (trade paperback)

A complete look at the stage, screen and literary works of the Pythons, with extensive interviews, biographies and index.

AND NOW FOR SOMETHING COMPLETELY TRIVIAL, by Kim "Howard" Johnson, St. Martin's Press, 1991 ISBN 0-312-06289-3 (oversized paperback)

Python trivia and quizes, including individual projects but concentrating on the Python TV shows and films.

LIFE (BEFORE AND) AFTER MONTY PYTHON, by Kim "Howard" Johnson, St. Martin's Press, 1992 ISBN 0-312-08695-4 (trade paperback)

Comprehensive looks at the pre-Python and post-Python works of the six individual members, with extensive interviews.

MONTY PYTHON: A CHRONOLOGICAL LISTING OF THE TROUPE'S CREATIVE OUTPUT, AND ARTICLES AND REVIEWS ABOUT THEM, 1969–1989, by Douglas L. McCall, McFarland & Company, 1992 (U.S.) ISBN 0-89950-559-7 (hardcover)

An extremely detailed chronological listing of the group and individual achievements of the Pythons, including published interviews, features, etc.

CLEESE ENCOUNTERS, by Jonathan Margolis, Chapmans Publishers, 1992 (U.K.) ISBN 1-855-92551-6/ St. Martin's Press, 1992 (U.S.) ISBN 0-312-08162-6 (paperback)

A disappointing, unauthorized biography of John Cleese that depends greatly on press clippings; filled with numerous inaccuracies.

MONTY PYTHON'S COMPLETE WASTE OF TIME: AN OFFICIAL COMPENDIUM OF ANSWERS TO RUDDY QUESTIONS NOT NORMALLY CONSIDERED RELEVANT TO MOUNTIES! by Rusel DeMaria and Alex Uttermann, Prima Publishing, 1995 (U.S.) ISBN 0-7615-0139-8 (paperback)

A great way to win at the "Monty Python's Complete Waste of Time" CD-ROM game, filled with hints, instructions and strategies. Illustrated with maps and illustrations from the game.

FUN AND GAMES, by Harvey Kurtzman, assisted by Terry Gilliam, 1965, Gold Medal Books
   A book of brain-teasers assembled from Kurtzman's *Help!* magazine, assisted by Terry Gilliam.

THE COCKTAIL PEOPLE, by Terry Gilliam and Joel Siegel, Pisani Press, 1966 (U.S.).
   Terry Gilliam's first book, co-created by Joel Siegel, who would later become film critic on ABC-TV's *Good Morning, America.*

BERT FEGG'S NASTY BOOK FOR BOYS AND GIRLS, by Terry Jones and Michael Palin, Methuen, 1974 (U.K.) ISBN 0-413-32740-X (hardcover) ISBN 0-413-56430-4 (paperback); retitled *Dr. Fegg's Nasty Book of Knowledge* for its American release in 1976, and republished as *Dr. Fegg's Encyclopedia of All World Knowledge* in 1985; ISBN 0-87226-005-4
Natural History—Across the Andes by Frog
Fashion—Items from the House of Fegg
Sports—Soccer My Way, by the Supremes
Magic—Conjuring by Feggo!
Sex—All You Need to Know About Sex Education (with a revised version by a proper doctor)
Theatre—Aladdin and his Terrible Problem: a new pantomime
Religion—I Fought the Mighty Anaconda and Lived

SPORTING RELATIONS, by Roger McGough, with drawings by Terry Gilliam, Eyre Methuen, 1974 (U.K.) ISBN 0-413-32750-7 (hardcover)/ISBN 0-413-32760-4 (paperback)
   A collection of poems by Roger McGough, with eighteen illustrations by Terry Gilliam.

HELLO, SAILOR, by Eric Idle, Futura Publications, 1975 (paperback), ISBN 0-8600-7235-5 (U.K. only)
   The first novel-length fiction by a Python, Idle's novel features the Prime Minister's secret, the seduction of the daughters of every Minister in the Cabinet, astronaut Sickert's "space first," and much, much more.

THE RUTLAND DIRTY WEEKEND BOOK, by Eric Idle, Methuen/Two Continents, 1976 (U.S.) ISBN 0-846-70185-5/(U.K.) ISBN 0-413-36570-0/(Canada) ISBN 0-458-92100-9
   Contains material inspired by *Rutland Weekend Television,* with Neil Innes, and a guest page by Michael Palin.
The Vatican Sex Manual
A History of *Rutland Weekend Television* from 1300
The Rutland TV Times
Saturday RWT World of Sport Listings
Sunday Listings—Misprint Theatre presents The Wife of Christ
Rutland Stone
The Wonderful World of Sex
New Publications from Rutland University Press

THE STRANGE CASE OF THE END OF CIVILISATION AS WE KNOW IT, by John Cleese, Jack Hobbs, and Joe McGrath, Star Book, 1977 (U.K.), ISBN 0-351-30109-0
   Contains the script and stills of the London Weekend Television film. Two editions of the paperback were published: a TV tie-in with a photo cover, and a "humour" edition with a painted cover; contents of both are the same.

FAWLTY TOWERS, by John Cleese and Connie Booth, Futura/Contact Publications, 1977, ISBN 0-8600-7598-2 (paperback) (U.K.)
    Reprints the scripts of "The Builders," "The Hotel Inspectors," and "Gourmet Night" from the first series; illustrated with a generous portion of photos.

JABBERWOCKY, by Ralph Hoover, Pan Books, 1977 (U.K. only), ISBN 0-330-25012-4
    Paperback adaptation of the script by Charles Alverson and Terry Gilliam.

ANIMATIONS OF MORTALITY, by Terry Gilliam, with Lucinda Cowell, Methuen, 1978, (U.S.) ISBN 0-458-93810-6 (paperback)/Methuen, 1978 (U.K.) ISBN 0-413-39370-4 (Hardcover)/Methuen, 1978 (U.K.) ISBN 0-413-39380-1 (paperback)
    A delightful collection of Gilliam artwork loosely disguised as a guide to animation; includes pre- and post-Python works, as well as material from the TV shows, and Brian the Badger guides the reader through The Wonderful World of Animation.
Lesson 1 Creating Something Out of Nothing
Lesson 2 How to Ruin the Pleasure of a Painting Forever
Lesson 3 Discovering the Secret of Cut-Out Animation
Lesson 4 Where Ideas Come From
Lesson 5 Looking the Part
Lesson 6 Meaningless Political Statements

THE ODD JOB, by Bernard McKenna and Colin Bostock-Smith, Arrow Books, 1978, ISBN 0-09-918950-X (British paperback)
    The novelization of the Graham Chapman film.

RIPPING YARNS, by Terry Jones and Michael Palin, Methuen, 1978 (U.K.) ISBN 0-413-39390-9 (hardcover), 1980 ISBN 0-413-46250-1 (paperback)/Pantheon Books, 1979 (U.S.) ISBN 0-394-73678-8 (published as a hardcover and trade paperback in the U.K., and as a trade paperbook in the U.S.)
    Contains the scripts and photos from the six shows of the first series:
Tomkinson's Schooldays
Across the Andes by Frog
Murder at Moorstones Manor
The Testing of Eric Olthwaite
Escape from Stalag Luft 112B
The Curse of the Claw

FAWLTY TOWERS TWO, by John Cleese and Connie Booth, Weidenfeld and Nicolson, 1979, ISBN 0-7088-1547-2 (paperback)
    Contains these scripts, illustrated with photos throughout:
The Wedding
A Touch of Class
The Germans

TAMING OF THE SHREW: BBC-TV SHAKESPEARE, BRITISH BROADCASTING CORP., (1980) (U.K.) ISBN 0-563-17873-6 (paperback)
    A tie-in with the BBC/PBS production, with color photos from the production starring John Cleese as Petruchio.

MORE RIPPING YARNS, by Terry Jones and Michael Palin, Methuen, 1980 (U.K.) ISBN 0-413-47520-4 (hardcover) 1981, ISBN 0-413-47530-1 (paperback) Pantheon Books, 1980, ISBN 0-394-74810-7 (paperback)

Contains the scripts and stills from the three shows of the second series:
Whinfrey's Last Case
Golden Gordon
Roger of the Raj

CHAUCER'S KNIGHT: PORTRAIT OF A MEDIEVAL MERCENARY, by Terry Jones, Weidenfeld and Nicolson (U.K.) (hardback), Eyre Methuen, 1982 (U.K.) ISBN 0-413-49640-6 (paperback)/University of Louisiana Press (U.S.) 1980, ISBN 0-8071-0691-7

Long a pet project of Terry Jones, this scholarly volume illuminates a short section of *The Canterbury Tales,* which he feels has been misinterpreted throughout the years. Or, as Jones puts it, he's just "explaining a lot of 600-year-old jokes."

A LIAR'S AUTOBIOGRAPHY, by Graham Chapman, Eyre Methuen, 1980 (published in hardcover and paperback in the U.K., and in hardcover in the U.S.) ISBN 0-413-47570-0 (hardcover)/Magnum Books, 1981 (U.K.) ISBN 0-417-07200-7 (paperback) Methuen 1982 (U.S.) ISBN 0-416-00901-8 (hardcover)

The first Python autobiography, Chapman begins with lengthier fantasy passages, and eases into his own real-life story. He frankly discusses his battle with alcohol, his homosexuality, his medical studies, and of course, his involvement with Python.

FAIRY TALES, by Terry Jones, Pavilion Books, 1981 (hardcover) ISBN 0-907516-03-3/Penguin (paperback) (U.K.) ISBN 0-14-032262-0

An acclaimed collection of children's short stories, originally written for his daughter Sally and read to her each night at bedtime; a record album, radio, and TV adaptations have resulted. Several stories from the book were released in individual editions with watercolor artwork by Michael Foreman, including the following: *THE BEAST WITH A THOUSAND TEETH,* Peter Bedrick Books, 1981 (U.S.) ISBN 0-87226-374-6 (hardcover)/Pavilion Books, 1993 (U.K.) ISBN 1-857-930703. *THE FLY-BY-NIGHT,* Peter Bedrick Books, 1981 (U.S.) ISBN 0-87226-379-7 (hardcover)/Pavilion Books, 1994 (U.K.) ISBN 1-857-93090-8. *THE SEA TIGER,* Peter Bedrick Books, 1981 (U.S.) ISBN 0-87226-378-9 (hardcover)/Pavilion Books, 1994 (U.K.) ISBN 1-857-93085-1. *A FISH OF THE WORLD,* Peter Bedrick Books, 1981/1993 (U.S.) ISBN 0-87226-376-2 (hardcover)/Pavilion Books, 1993 (U.K.) ISBN 1-857-93075-4.

TIME BANDITS, by Michael Palin and Terry Gilliam, Hutchinson 1981 (U.K.) ISBN 0-09-145461-1/Doubleday 1981 (U.S.), ISBN 0-385-17732-1 (paperback)

Contains the illustrated script of the film.

TIME BANDITS, by Charles Alverson, Arrow Books, 1981 (U.K. only) (paperback) ISBN 0-09-926020-4

Contains the novelization of the film.

TIME BANDITS, Marvel Comics, February 1982

A one-shot comic book adaptation of the film, script adapted by S. J. Parkhouse, art by David Lloyd and John Stokes.

THE SECRET POLICEMAN'S OTHER BALL, Methuen, 1981 (U.K. only) (paperback) ISBN 0-413-50080-2

Proceeds donated to Amnesty International

This book of the Amnesty Stage show contains scripts and photos, with program notes throughout by Terry Jones and Michael Palin. The book includes "Introduction," by John Cleese and the cast; "Beekeeping," an interview sketch with Cleese and Rowan Atkinson; "Top of the Form," with Cleese, Graham Chapman, and others; and "Clothes Off," with Cleese, Chapman, and Pamela Stephenson; several backstage photos are included, as well.

NO MORE CURRIED EGGS FOR ME, edited by Roger Wilmut, Methuen, 1982 (U.K. only) ISBN 0-413-53680-7
A collection of scripts from comedy sketches and scenes going back to the Marx Brothers; Python-related material includes "Bookshop" (from . . . *the 1948 Show*), an excerpt from *Fawlty Towers* and "The Germans," and of course, the "Parrot."

THE MISSIONARY, by Michael Palin, Methuen, 1982 (paperback) ISBN 0-413-53680-7 (U.K.), 1983 (hardback) ISBN 0-413-51010-7 (U.K.)
Contains the script and photos of the film, with an original prologue and an "After the Story" follow-up section.

PASS THE BUTLER, by Eric Idle, Methuen, 1982, ISBN 0-413-49990-1
The script of Idle's play, which ran in London's West End, presented in 1981 by the Cambridge Theatre Company and later produced at the Globe Theatre.

SMALL HARRY AND THE TOOTHACHE PILLS, by Michael Palin, Methuen/Magnet Books, 1982, ISBN 0-416-21760-5 (hardcover)/ISBN 0-416-23690-1 (paperback)
The first of Palin's children's books, this is illustrated by Caroline Holden.

FAMILIES AND HOW TO SURVIVE THEM, by John Cleese and Robin Skynner, Methuen, 1983 (hardcover) ISBN 0-413-52640-2 (paperback) ISBN 0-413-56520-3
A series of dialogues between Cleese and his former therapist dealing with the variety of human relationships, from love and marriage to children.

GREAT RAILWAY JOURNEYS OF THE WORLD, with one chapter written by Michael Palin; E. P. Dutton, 1981 (U.S.) ISBN 0-525-24152-3 (hardcover) "Confessions of a Train-Spotter" is based on this journey, which involved his rail trip across Britain in 1983. A long-time train afficionado, Palin had an opportunity to travel across Britain for this BBC 2 series, which included railway routes all over the world. The text of his program is printed here, along with photos.

THE SAGA OF ERIK THE VIKING, by Terry Jones, Pavilion Books, 1983, ISBN 0-907-51623-8 (hardback), ISBN 0-14-031713-9, (trade paperback) (U.K.) Penguin ISBN 0-14-032261-2 (paperback)/Schocken Books, 1983 (U.S.) ISBN 0-805-23876-X (paperback)
This followup to *Fairy Tales* is a book of stories Jones wrote for his young son, Bill; actually one long story broken up into shorter episodes, it served as the rough outline for the 1989 film.

A PRIVATE FUNCTION, by Alan Bennett, Faber and Faber, 1984, ISBN 0-571-13571-4
The novelization of the film starring Michael Palin.

THE GOLDEN SKITS OF WING COMMANDER MURIEL VOLESTRANGLER FRHS & BAR, by Muriel Volestrangler, Methuen, 1984 ISBN 0-413-41560-0 (paperback)

 A collection of sketches written and cowritten by John Cleese ranging back to Cambridge.

Architect Skit*
Shirt Shop Skit
Goat Skit
Sheep Skit*
Top of the Form
Word Association Football**
Bookshop Skit
Arthur "Two Sheds" Jackson*
The Last Supper Skit
Merchant Banker Skit*
Cricket Commentators Skit
Fairly Silly Court Skit*
Crunchy Frog Skit*
Regella Skit
Hearing Aid Skit
Argument Skit*
The Good Old Days Skit
Lucky Gypsy Skit

Mrs. Beulah Premise & Mrs. Wanda Conclusion
 Visit Mr. & Mrs. J. P. Sartre*
Undertaker Skit*
Railway Carriage Skit
Cheese Shop Skit*
String Skit
Chapel Skit***
"Ones" Skit
Army Protection Racket Skit*
Slightly Less Silly Than the Other Court Skit Court
 Skit
Courier Skit
Ethel the Frog Skit*
Dead Parrot*

* Performed in the Python TV show
** From the *Matching Tie and Handkerchief* album
*** From *The Meaning of Life*

THE COURAGE TO CHANGE, by Dennis Wholey, Houghton Mifflin, 1984, ISBN 0-395-35977-5

 A collection of interviews with well-known alcoholics and their families, in which they discuss their battles with alcohol; included is a chapter on Graham Chapman.

THE LIMERICK BOOK, by Michael Palin, illustrations by Tony Ross, Hutchinson Publishing, 1985, ISBN 0-09-161540-2

 A children's book of original limericks.

NICOBOBINUS, by Terry Jones, Pavilion Books (U.K.) 1985, ISBN 1-851-45000-9 (hardcover); paperback ISBN 0-14-032091-1 (U.K.)/Peter Bedrick Books (U.S.) 1985, ISBN 0-87226-065-8 (hardcover)

 Jones's third children's book is the story of the title character, who sets off to discover the Land of Dragons (Jones has also written a screenplay based on this story).

THE GOBLINS OF LABYRINTH, by Brian Froud and Terry Jones, Pavilion, 1986 (U.K.) (hardcover) ISBN 0-85145-058-0/Henry Holt & Co., 1986 (U.S.) ISBN 0-03-008499-7 (hardcover)

 After writing the script of the film for Jim Henson (although his version was changed significantly), Jones also wrote the text for this tie-in, based on Froud's drawings.

CYRIL AND THE HOUSE OF COMMONS, by Michael Palin, Pavilion, 1986 (U.K. only) ISBN 0-85145-078-5

 A Palin children's book.

CYRIL AND THE DINNER PARTY, by Michael Palin, Pavilion, 1986 (U.K. only) ISBN 1-85145-069-6

 Another Palin children's book.

THE MIRRORSTONE, by Michael Palin, Alan Lee, and Richard Seymour, Jonathan Cape, 1986 (hardback) ISBN 0-224-02408-6
   This children's book is thoroughly illustrated and contains several holograms as part of the story.

THE UTTERLY, UTTERLY MERRY COMIC RELIEF CHRISTMAS BOOK, Fontana Trade Paperback, 1986 ISBN 0-00-637-128-0; proceeds donated to charity
   Contains "Biggles and Groupies," by Michael Palin (with an introduction by George Harrison), "A Christmas Fairly Story," by Terry Jones and Douglas Adams, and "The Private Life of Genghis Kahn," from a sketch by Graham Chapman and Douglas Adams.

CLOCKWISE: A SCREENPLAY, by Michael Frayn, Methuen, 1986 (U.K.) ISBN 0-413-60290-7
   Frayn's screenplay of the film featuring John Cheese as headmaster and efficiency expert Brian Stimpson.

LABYRINTH, by A. C. H. Smith, Henry Holt and Company, 1986 (U.S.) ISBN 0-03-007322-7 (paperback)
   The novelization of the film originally written by Terry Jones.

HAPPY HOLIDAYS: THE GOLDEN AGE OF RAILWAY POSTERS, by Michael Palin, Pavilion Books, 1987 (U.K.) ISBN 1-85145-192-7 (hardcover)/ISBN 1-85145-130-7 (paperback)
   Collection of railway posters of popular British resort towns from the 1930s through the 1950s, introduction is written by Michael Palin.

PERSONAL SERVICES, by David Leland, Pavilion Books, 1987 (U.K.) ISBN 1-85145-146-3 (paperback)
   The screenplay of the film directed by Terry Jones with an introduction by Jones.

THE SECRET POLICEMAN'S THIRD BALL, Sidgwick and Jackson, 1987 (paperback) ISBN 0-283-99530-0
   Contains the script of the Amnesty International show, as well as portraits of the cast; includes a brief appearance by John Cleese accepting an award.

THE BATTLE OF BRAZIL, by Jack Mathews, Crown Books, 1987 (hardback) ISBN 0-517-56538-2
   The chronicle of Terry Gilliam's battle with Universal to release his own *Brazil,* rather than the less-disturbing version; ultimately, it comes across as the David vs. Goliath story of the maverick director fighting against the giant studio for the integrity of his work.

THE COMPLETE (U.K.) FAWLTY TOWERS, by John Cleese and Connie Booth, Methuen, 1988 (hardback) ISBN 0-413-18390-4; Pantheon Books, 1989 (U.S.) (paperback) ISBN 0-679-72127-4
   The scripts from all twelve shows, with a brief photo section.

A FISH CALLED WANDA, by John Cleese and Charles Crichton, Methuen (U.K.)/Applause Theatre Book Publishers (U.S.) 1988 (paperback) ISBN 0-413-19550-3 (U.K.)/1-55783-033-9 (U.S.)
   Contains the final script of the film, and is illustrated with stills of the cast.

CURSE OF THE VAMPIRE SOCKS, by Terry Jones, Pavilion Books, 1988 (hardback) (U.K.) ISBN 1-85145-233-8/Penguin, 1990 (U.K.) ISBN 0-14-032733-9 (paperback)
   An original collection of children's poetry, including poems that first appeared in the "Dr. Fegg" and "Monty Python's Big Red Book."

ATTACKS OF OPINION, by Terry Jones, Penguin Books (U.K.), 1988 (paperback) ISBN 0-14-032895-5
   A collection of columns for the *Young Guardian* "Input" column, with Jones giving his opinion on a variety of timely, controversial subjects.

BRAZIL DE TERRY GILLIAM, by Louis Danvers, Crisnee, Belgique: Editions Yellow Now, 1988 (Belgium)
    Another retelling of the battle of *Brazil* and Terry Gilliam, with text in French.

AROUND THE WORLD IN 80 DAYS, by Michael Palin, BBC Books, 1989 (U.K.) ISBN 0-563-20826-0 (hardcover); ISBN 0-563-36213-8 (paperback)/BBC Books-Park West Publications, 1989 (U.S.) ISBN 0-563-20826-0 (hardcover)
    Michael Palin's journal kept while traveling around the world with a BBC film crew and illustrated with many of the photographs taken along the way.

THE ADVENTURES OF BRYON MUNCHAUSEN, by Terry Gilliam and Charles McKeown, Methuen (U.K.) ISBN 0-7493-0017-5/Applause Theatre Book Publishers (U.S.) 1989 (trade paperback) ISBN 1-55783-039-8
    The novelization of the Gilliam film by its cowriters, with line drawings.

THE ADVENTURES OF BARON MUNCHAUSEN, by Terry Gilliam and Charles McKeown, Methuen (U.K.)/Applause Theatre Book Publishers (U.S.) 1989 (paperback) ISBN 1-557-83-041-X
    The script of the film, complete with photos, all of the credits, plus twenty-five additional pages of material deleted from the final cut of the movie.

TERRY GILLIAM'S THE ADVENTURES OF BARON MUNCHAUSEN Now Comics, 1989 (U.S.) Vol 1, No. 1–4, July–October 1989
    A four issue miniseries adapting the film.

ERIK THE VIKING, by Terry Jones, illustrated by Graham Thompson, Robson Books, 1989, ISBN 0-86051-631-8 (paperback)
    The comic book adaptation of the film in a trade paperback format.

ERIK THE VIKING: THE BOOK OF THE FILM OF THE BOOK, by Terry Jones, Methuen, 1989 (U.K.) ISBN 0-413-62680-6 (paperback)
    The screenplay of the film, illustrated with plenty of stills.

ERIK THE VIKING, by Terry Jones, Applause Theatre Books/Grove Press, 1990 (U.S.) ISBN 1-55783-054-1 (paperback)
    The screenplay of the film, including credits and illustrated with a great number of stills (the American version of the previously listed book).

THE COMPLETE RIPPING YARNS, by Terry Jones and Michael Palin, Methuen London, 1990 (U.K.) ISBN 0-413-63820-0 (hardcover)/ISBN 0-413-63980-0 (paperback)
    The original two "Yarns" books published under one cover, with all the scripts and photos from the nine episodes.

LOSING THE LIGHT: TERRY GILLIAM AND THE MUNCHAUSEN SAGA, by Andrew Yule, Applause Theatre Books, 1991 (U.S.) ISBN 1-55783-060-6 (paperback)
    The chronicling of Terry Gilliam's fight to film *The Adventures of Baron Munchausen,* and of the subsequent release.

THE FISHER KING, by Richard LaGravenese, Applause Theatre Books, 1991 (U.S.) ISBN 1-8362-4213-0 (paperback)
    The complete screenplay of the Terry Gilliam film based on the LaGravenese screenplay, with an in-

troduction by Gilliam, a series of interviews with Gilliam by David Morgan, and unfilmed or deleted scenes.

THE FISHER KING, by Leonore Fleischer, Signet (AE 7222), 1991 (U.S.) ISBN 0-451-17222-1 (paperback)
   The novelization of the Richard LaGravenese screenplay.

FANTASTIC STORIES, by Terry Jones, Pavilion Books, 1992 (U.K.) ISBN 1-851-45957-X/Puffin Books, 1995 (U.K.) ISBN 0-140-36279-7/Viking, 1993 (U.S.) ISBN 0-670-84899-9 (hardcover)
   Another collection of short children's stories written by Terry Jones, requested by his publisher due to the continued popularity of his other children's books. These are similar to Jones's original *Fairy Tales* and includes a sequel of sorts to *Nicobobinus.*

POLE TO POLE, by Michael Palin, BBC Books, 1992 (U.K.) ISBN 0-563-36283-9 (hardcover)
   Michael Palin's journal kept while traveling for the BBC television series along the 30° east of longitude, through seventeen countries; generously illustrated with photographs taken on the journey.

LIFE AND HOW TO SURVIVE IT, by A. Robin Skynner and John Cleese, Methuen London, 1993 (U.K.) ISBN 0-413-66030-3 (hardcover)/Mandarin, 1994 (U.K.) ISBN 0-749-31108-8 (paperback)/W. W. Norton & Company, 1995 (U.S.) ISBN 0-393-03742-8 (hardcover)
   The follow-up to Skynner and Cleese's *Families* book, featuring a series of dialogues between the therapist and his former patient Cleese on what constitutes healthy behavior across a wide spectrum of life experiences.

DID I EVER TELL YOU HOW LUCKY YOU ARE¿, by Theodore S. Geisel (Dr. Seuss) Random House, Inc., 1993 (U.S.) ISBN 0-679-84993-9 (paperback with cardboard sleeve)
   This book comes with an audio cassette in which John Cleese narrates this Dr. Seuss short story for children.

MARY SHELLEY'S FRANKENSTEIN: THE CLASSIC TALE OF TERROR REBORN ON FILM, by Kenneth Branagh, Newmarket Press, 1994 (U.S.) ISBN 1-55704-208-X (paperback)
   This screenplay of the film includes director's notes and a behind-the-scenes look at the making of the film, which features John Cleese as Dr. Waldman, Dr. Frankenstein's teacher.

MAKING OF MARY SHELLEY'S "FRANKENSTEIN," by Kenneth Branagh, Pan Books, 1994 (U.K.) ISBN 0-330-33706-8
   The book of the film, which features John Cleese as Dr. Waldman.

POLE TO POLE: THE PHOTOGRAPHS, by Basil Pao, text by Michael Palin, BBC Books, 1994 (U.K.) ISBN 0-563-37018-1 (hardcover)
   Michael Palin wrote the text for this collection of photographs taken while journeying from Pole to Pole.

THE WEEKEND, by Michael Palin, Methuen Drama, 1994 (U.K.) ISBN 0-413-68940-9 (paperback)
   The script of Michael Palin's first stage play. Richard Wilson starred as Stephen Febble, an elderly gentleman who must endure a weekend with his daughter, her boring husband, and their child. Produced at the Strand Theatre in early 1994.

THE JUNGLE BOOK, by Rudyard Kipling, HarperCollins Publishers, 1994 (U.S.) ISBN 0-06-106286-3 (paperback)

This edition ties in with the Disney film, which features John Cleese as Dr. Plumford, Mowgli's teacher.

LADY COTTINGTON'S PRESSED FAIRY BOOK, by Terry Jones, illustrated by Brian Froud, Turner Publishing, Inc., 1994 (U.S.) ISBN 1-57036-062-6 (hardcover)
Designed and packaged to resemble a Victorian journal, allegedly written by Lady Angelica Cottington, who has been collecting fairies by squashing them in the journal's pages ever since she was a little girl.

CRUSADES, by Terry Jones and Alan Ereira, BBC Books, 1994 (U.K.) ISBN 0-563-37007-6 (hardcover)/Facts on File, 1995 (U.S.) ISBN 0-8160-3275-0 (hardcover)
This is a tie-in to the BBC series which also aired on A&E and the History Channel in America; the series was co-written and presented by Terry Jones.

GREAT RAILWAY JOURNEYS, with one chapter by Michael Palin, BBC Books, 1994 (U.K.) ISBN 0-563-36944-2 (hardcover)
The book that ties in with the BBC television series, including photos; Michael Palin wrote the thirty-five-page "From Derry to Kerry" about his journey for the series.

HEMINGWAY'S CHAIR, by Michael Palin, Methuen London, 1995 (U.K.) ISBN 0-413-68930-1 (hardcover)
Michael Palin's first novel stars meek postal assistant clerk Martin Sproale, who is obsessed with Ernest Hemingway. When an ambitious outsider passes Martin up for a promotion, he begins modernizing the quiet, old-fashioned facility, and Martin must decide whether to fight for his beliefs.

12 MONKEYS, by Elizabeth Hand, Harper Prism, 1995 (U.S.) ISBN 0-06-105658-8 (paperback)
The paperback novelization of the Terry Gilliam film, written by David and Janet Peoples.

CASPER: THE MOVIE STORYBOOK, by Leslie McGuire, Price Stern Sloan, Inc., 1995 (U.S.) ISBN 0-8431-3856-4 (paperback)
Children's storybook with many color photos from the film, including several of Eric Idle, who plays the villainous sidekick Dibs.

CASPER: JUNIOR NOVELIZATION, by Lisa Rojany, Price Stern Sloan, Inc., 1995 (U.S.) ISBN 0-8431-3854-8 (paperback)
Children's novelization of the film, with photos of Eric Idle.

CASPER, adapted by Laura M. Rossiter, Golden Book/Western Publishing Company, 1995 (U.S.) ISBN 0-307-12834-2 (paperback)
Photo-book with the story of the film for young children, with photos of Eric Idle.

CASPER EYE ILLUSIONS, by Jim Anderson, Honey Bear Books/Modern Publishing, 1995 (U.S.) ISBN 1-56144-679-3/ISBN 1-56144-680-7/ISBN 1-56144-681-5 ISBN/1-56144-682-3 (paperbacks)
Four books with "magic eye" pictures from the film, including photos of Eric Idle.

LADY COTTINGTON'S PRESSED FAIRY CALENDAR 1996, by Terry Jones and Brian Froud, Turner Publishing, Inc., 1995 (U.S./Canada) ISBN 1-57036-218-1 (calendar)
Twelve of the Brian Froud illustrations and Terry Jones's descriptions and narrative from the original *Lady Cottington's Pressed Fairy Book,* adapted to a wall calendar format.

CASPER: A SIXTEEN MONTH 1996 CALENDAR, Day Dream Publishing Inc./K. C. Knox Distributors, 1996 (U.S.) ISBN 1-57081-441-4 (paperback)

A sixteen-month calendar for September 1995 through December 1996 that features thirteen stills from the film, including one that features Eric Idle with Cathy Moriarty.

THE QUITE REMARKABLE ADVENTURES OF THE OWL AND THE PUSSYCAT, by Eric Idle, illustrated by Wesla Weller, Dove Books (Juvenile), 1996 (U.S.) ISBN 0-787-11042-6 (hardcover)

Children's book that draws on the poem and other writings and drawings of Edward Lear, which Eric Idle expanded into a full-length story. Also available on audiotape with an original music score and ten songs.

STRANGE STAINS AND MYSTERIOUS SMELLS: QUENTIN COTTINGTON'S JOURNAL OF FAERY RESEARCH, by Terry Jones and Brian Froud, Simon and Schuster, 1996 (U.S.) ISBN 0-684-83206-2 (hardcover)

A follow-up to the highly successful *Lady Cottington's Pressed Fairy Book,* featuring manifestations of unpleasant stains and smells (which are prevalent throughout the volume), with descriptions by Jones and illustrations by Froud.

THE GOBLIN COMPANION: A FIELD GUIDE TO GOBLINS, by Brian Froud and Terry Jones, Turner Publishing, 1996 (U.S.) ISBN 1-57036-284-X (hardcover)

This re-release of *The Goblins of the Labyrinth* contains most of the material for the original, though in a smaller size.

LADY COTTINGTON'S PRESSED FAIRY CALENDAR 1997, by Terry Jones and Brian Froud, Andrews and McMeel, 1997 (U.S./Canada) ISBN 0-8362-1770-5 (calendar)

A second set of twelve Brian Froud illustrations with Terry Jones's narrative from the highly successful *Lady Cottington's Pressed Fairy Book,* again in calendar form.

FULL CIRCLE, by Michael Palin, BBC Books, 1997 (U.K.) ISBN 0-563-371218 (hardcover)/St. Martin's Press 1997 (U.S.)

Michael Palin's journal kept for the BBC-TV series in which he travels around the entire Pacific Rim (filmed from August 1995 to August 1996).

FULL CIRCLE: THE PHOTOGRAPHS, by Michael Palin, BBC Books, 1997 (U.K.) ISBN 0-563-371684

Photographs from the journey, with text by Michael Palin.

LADY COTTINGTON'S PRESSED FAIRY CALENDAR 1998, by Terry Jones and Brian Froud, Andrews and McMeel, 1998 (U.S./Canada) ISBN 0-8362-3182-1 (calendar)

Another set of Brian Froud illustrations with Terry Jones's text from *Lady Cottington's Pressed Fairy Book* in calendar form.

DOUGLAS ADAMS'S STARSHIP TITANIC, by Terry Jones, Harmony Books, 1997 (U.S./Canada) ISBN 0-609-60103-2

The novelization of Douglas Adams's *Starship Titanic* CD-ROM (for which Jones provides the voice of the parrot).

GRAHAM CRACKERS, by Graham Chapman, compiled by Jim Yoakum, Career Press, 1997 (U.S./Canada) ISBN 1-56414-334-1

Death proves no obstacle to Graham, as this compilation of unpublished writings, autobiography, and scripts proves. This never-completed followup to *A Liar's Autobiography* features a foreword by John Cleese, a backward by Eric Idle and a sideways by Terry Jones.

BABES IN CLOUDLAND (or *TITS AT 10,000 FEET*), lithograph by Terry Gilliam, produced by 137 Inc., 1997.

This full-color signed, limited edition lithograph is the first of a projected series featuring the art of the cartoonist-turned-animator-turned film director (for more information, phone 815-434-9535).

Monty Python's Flying Circus Videocassettes (The Original Forty-Five TV Shows)

Vol. 1 *THE FIRST MONTY PYTHON'S FLYING CIRCUS VIDEOCASSETTE* (1970) Paramount Home Video (1992), PAR 12543 (ISBN 0-7921-0642-3), 60 minutes
  Contains episode 14 "Dinsdale" and episode 17 "The Buzz Aldrin Show"

Vol. 2 *THE SECOND (IN SEQUENCE, NOT QUALITY) MONTY PYTHON'S FLYING CIRCUS VIDEO-CASSETTE* (1969/1970) Paramount Home Video (1992), PAR 12544 (ISBN 0-7921-0644-X), 59 minutes
  Contains episode 15 "The Spanish Inquisition" and episode 29 "The Money Programme"

Vol 3 *THE THIRD (BUT STILL DRASTICALLY IMPORTANT ABSOLUTELY NECESSARY TO HAVE) MONTY PYTHON'S FLYING CIRCUS VIDEOCASSETTE* (1970/1972) Paramount Home Video (1986), PAR 12545 (ISBN 0-7921-0646-6), 58 minutes
  Contains episode 20 "The Attila the Hun Show" and episode 31 "The All-England Summarize Proust Competition"

Vol. 4 *THE FOURTH (EAGERLY AWAITED, IMPATIENTLY ANTICIPATED, ARDENTLY SOUGHT AFTER, RARING-TO-GO AND REAL GOOD) MONTY PYTHON'S FLYING CIRCUS VIDEOTAPE* (1970/1972) Paramount Home Video (1992), PAR 125060 (ISBN 0-7921-0648-2), 60 minutes
  Contains episode 22 "How to Recognise Different Parts of the Body" and episode 28 "Mr. and Mrs. Brian Norris' Ford Popular"

Vol. 5 *MONTY PYTHON'S FIFTH VIDEOCASSETTE* (1970/1972) Paramount Home Video (1987), PAR 12561 (ISBN 0-7921-0722-5), 59 minutes
  Contains episode 25 "Spam" and episode 32 "The War Against Pornography"

Vol. 6 *VOLUME SIX AND VIOLENCE* (1970/1972) Paramount Home Video (1987), PAR 12582, 58 minutes
  Contains episode 24 "How Not to Be Seen" and episode 33 "Salad Days"

Vol. 7 *PIPE DREAMS* (1970/1972) Paramount Home Video (1987), PAR 12583, 60 minutes
  Contains episode 18 "Live from the Grillomat" and episode 35 "The Nude Man"

Vol. 8 *BEHIND THE EIGHT BALL* (1970/1972) Paramount Home Video (1988), PAR 12600 (ISBN 0-7921-0728-4), 58 minutes
  Contains episode 26 "Royal Episode 13" and episode 36 "E. Henry Thripshaw's Disease"

Vol. 9 *SILLY PARTY AND OTHER FAVORS* (1970/1972) Paramount Home Video (1988), PAR 12601 (ISBN 0-7921-0656-3), 60 minutes
  Contains episode 19 "School Prizes" and episode 27 "Whicker's World/Njorl's Saga"

Vol. 10 *BLOOD, DEVASTATION, DEATH, WAR, HORROR, AND OTHER HUMOROUS EVENTS* (1970/1972) Paramount Home Video (1988), PAR 12652 (ISBN 0-7921-0602-4), 60 minutes
    Contains episode 16 "Show 5" and episode 30 "Blood, Devastation, Death, War and Horror"

Vol. 11 *DIRTY VICARS, POOFY JUDGES, AND OSCAR WILDE, TOO!* (1970/1973) Paramount Home Video (1992), PAR 12653 (ISBN 0-7921-0604-0) 60 minutes
    Contains episode 21 "Archeology Today" and episode 39 "Grandstand/The British Royal Awards Programme"

Vol. 12 *KAMIKAZE HIGHLANDERS* (1973) Paramount Home Video (1988), PAR 12654 (ISBN 0-7921-0606-7), 60 minutes
    Contains episode 37 "Dennis Moore" and episode 38 "A Book at Bedtime"

Vol. 13 *I'M A LUMBERJACK* (1969) Paramount Home Video (1989), PAR 12736 (ISBN 0-7921-2363-8), 60 minutes
    Contains episode 1 "Whither Canada?" and episode 9 "The Ant—An Introduction"

Vol. 14 *CHOCOLATE FROGS, BAFFLED CATS, AND OTHER TASTY TREATS* (1969) Paramount Home Video (1989), PAR 12737 (ISBN 0-7921-1008-0), 60 minutes
    Contains episode 5 "Man's Crisis of Identity in the Latter Half of the Twentieth Century" and episode 6 "The BBC Entry for the Zinc Stoat of Budapest"

Vol. 15 *"DEAD PARROTS DON'T TALK" AND OTHER FOWL PLAYS* (1969) Paramount Home Video (1989), PAR 12738 (ISBN 0-7921-1010-2), 60 minutes
    Contains episode 7 "Oh, You're No Fun Anymore" and episode 8 "Full Frontal Nudity"

Vol. 16 *A MAN WITH THREE CHEEKS, OR BUTT NAUGHT FOR ME* (1969) Paramount Home Video (1989), PAR 12739 (ISBN 0-7921-1012-9), 60 minutes
    Contains episode 2 "Sex and Violence" and episode 11 "The Royal Philharmonic Orchestra Goes to the Bathroom"

Vol. 17 *THE UPPER-CLASS TWIT COMPETITION* (1970) Paramount Home Video (1989), PAR 12740 (ISBN 0-7921-1014-5), 60 minutes
    Contains episode 12 "The Naked Ant" and episode 13 "Intermission"

Vol. 18 *DESPICABLE FAMILIES, NAUGHTY COMPLAINTS, AND KILLER FRUIT* (1969/1974) Paramount Home Video (1990), PAR 12765 (ISBN 0-7921-1908-8), 60 minutes
    Contains episode 4 "Owl-stretching Time" and episode 45 "Party Political Broadcast"

Vol. 19 *NUDGE, NUDGE, WINK, WINK,* (1969/1974) Paramount Home Video (1990), PAR 12766 (ISBN 0-7921-1910-X), 60 minutes
    Contains episode 3 "How to Recognise Different Types of Trees from Quite a Long Ways Away" and episode 43 "Hamlet"

Vol. 20 *PET ANTS, DEAD POETS AND THE MYSTERIOUS MICHAEL ELLIS* (1969/1974) Paramount Home Video (1990), PAR 12767 (ISBN 0-7921-1912-6), 60 minutes
    Contains episode 10 "Untitled" and episode 41 "Michael Ellis"

Vol. 21 *SCOTT OF THE ANTARCTIC* (1970/1974) Paramount Home Video (1990), PAR 12768 (ISBN 0-7921-1914-2), 60 minutes

Contains episode 23 "Scott of the Antarctic" and episode 42 "The Light Entertainment War"

Vol. 22 *MR. NEUTRON'S BALLOONISH BICYCLE TOUR* (1972/1974) Paramount Home Video (1990), PAR 12770 (ISBN 0-7921-1916-9), 90 minutes

Contains episode 34 "The Cycling Tour," episode 40 "The Golden Age of Ballooning," and episode 44 "Mr. Neutron"

A Note on Monty Python's Flying Circus Laserdiscs

Many episodes of *Monty Python's Flying Circus* have also been released on laserdisc (at least thirteen releases have been confirmed, the first releases contain three shows per disc, the remainder feature two shows). Much of the artwork has been lifted from Paramount's videotape series, which was released at the same time. Video contents do not necessarily have any correlation with laserdisc contents, though the catalog numbers for the laserdiscs correlate directly to the videotape series, with the prefix *LV* replacing *PAR* (for example, the sixth videotape is PAR 12543, the sixth laserdisc is LV 12653. The sixth videotape features episode 24 "How Not to Be Seen" and episode 33 "Salad Days," while the sixth laserdisc features episode 21 "Archeology Today" and episode 39 "Grandstand/The British Royal Awards Programme"— which were featured on videotape number eleven. Confusing? You bet!).

The Python Films

NOTE: All Monty Python films are now readily available on videotape—for contents and more information, see the "Python On Film" section.

AND NOW FOR SOMETHING COMPLETELY DIFFERENT (1971) Columbia Pictures/Kettledrum-Python Productions Film, distributed by RCA/Columbia Pictures Home Video (1991), 43396 6013 (ISBN 0-8001-1171-0), 88 minutes

Laserdisc version is letterboxed with original aspect ratio; distributed by Columbia Tristar Home Video (1994), 76826 (ISBN 0-8001-3813-9)

MONTY PYTHON AND THE HOLY GRAIL (1975) Cinema 5/Python Pictures-Michael White Film, distributed by RCA/Columbia Pictures Home Video (1991), 43396 92253 (ISBN 0-8001-1329-2), 90 minutes

Widescreen videocassette version from the Columbia Tri-Star Home Video 22623 (ISBN 0-8001-3799-X)

RCA Videodisc, RCA/03040/1974

The Criterion Collection laserdisc version of the film includes an unreleased twenty-four second sequence from "The Tale of Sir Galahad," a "coming attraction" trailer, an analog track featuring audio commentary by Terry Gilliam and Terry Jones (as well as an analog track with Japanese dubbing), and bonus stills taken behind-the-scenes. National Film Trustee Company, Ltd., distributed by The Voyager Company and Columbia/Tristar Home Video (1992), "The Criterion Collection," CC 1311L (ISBN 1-55940-324-1)

MONTY PYTHON'S LIFE OF BRIAN (1979) Warner Brothers/Orion Pictures, Handmade Films, distributed by Paramount Home Video (1990), PAR 12871 (ISBN 0-7921-2048-5), 94 minutes

Laserdisc is Paramount Home Video (1991), LV 12871 (ISBN 0-7921-2048-5)

The Criterion Collection laserdisc version of the film includes the complete film in widescreen format, two commentary tracks (one with Michael Palin and John Cleese, the other with Terry Jones, Terry Gilliam, and Eric Idle), the original theatrical trailer and radio ads, deleted scenes with audio commentary, and the documentary film *The Pythons*. which was shot on location during the filming of *Life of Brian*. Distributed by The Voyager Company (1997), "The Criterion Collection," CC 15041 (ISBN 1-55940-849-9).

MONTY PYTHON LIVE AT THE HOLLYWOOD BOWL (1982) Handmade Films and Columbia Pictures, distributed by Paramount Home Video (1991), PAR 12872 (ISBN 0-7921-2049-3), 81 minutes
Laserdisc is Paramount Home Video (1982) LV 12872 (ISBN 0-7921-2049-3)

MONTY PYTHON'S THE MEANING OF LIFE (1983) distributed by MCA Universal Home Video (1991), 71016 (ISBN 1-55880-676-8), 107 minutes

---

Videos about Monty Python

LIFE OF PYTHON (1990) distributed by Paramount Home Video, PAR 12903 (ISBN 0-7921-2556-8), 56 minutes
Laserdisc LV 12903 (ISBN 0-7921-3007-3)
This documentary produced for the twentieth anniversary contains interviews with the Pythons (excluding Graham Chapman), Dan Ackroyd, Chevy Chase, Steve Martin, and others about the history, relationships, and continuing popularity of the group.

MONTY PYTHON'S PARROT SKETCH NOT INCLUDED (1990) distributed by Paramount Home Video, PAR 12904 (ISBN 0-7921-2562-2), 75 minutes
A collection of some of the classic Python sketches (including material from the German shows) introduced by Steve Martin; at the end of the show, Martin pulls open a cabinet in which all six members of the group are hiding—the final appearance of all of the Pythons together.

Other Python-Related Videos

THE BLISS OF MRS. BLOSSOM (1968) Distributed by Paramount Home Video & Movies Unlimited, PAR 6810V (ISBN 0-7921-2196-1), 93 minutes
Comedy film starring Shirley MacLaine as a brassiere manufacturer's wife who keeps a lover in the attic; features John Cleese in a brief appearance as a Post Office Clerk.

HOW TO IRRITATE PEOPLE (1968) David Paradine Productions, distributed by White Star, 1656 (ISBN 1-56127-656-1), 65 minutes
Sketch comedy TV special co-written by John Cleese and Graham Chapman and starring John Cleese, Graham Chapman, Michael Palin, and Connie Booth; an immediate precursor to Monty Python.

THE MAGIC CHRISTIAN (1969) Distributed by Republic Pictures Home Video (1991), VHS 2548
John Cleese and Graham Chapman wrote additional material for this film about the richest man in the world, played by Peter Sellers, who adopts a disheveled young man, played by Ringo Starr; includes appearances by John Cleese as a Director in Sothebys and Graham Chapman as an Oxford Team Member.

CRY OF THE BANSHEE (1970) distributed by Orion Home Video 7007, 92 minutes
Features animated titles by Terry Gilliam.

VIDEO ARTS TRAINING FILMS by Video Arts
John Cleese co-founded Video Arts in 1971 to produce and distribute management training films for businesses; though he later sold his interest in the company, he still works on occasional films, along with other prominent British stars. For a complete list of John Cleese's Video Arts Training Films, phone 1-800-533-0091.

THE STATUE (1971) Cinerama/Josef Shaftel Productions, distributed by Prism Entertainment, PRISM 2858
Comedy film about a professor whose wife sculpts an eighteen-foot statue of him; with appearances by Graham Chapman and John Cleese (as a psychiatrist, a role added later to help explain the plot).

ROMANCE WITH A DOUBLE BASS (1974) Anton Films, distributed by White Star 1664/distributed by Pacific Arts Video Records (1984), PAVR-559 (ISBN 1-5611-1027-2), 40 minutes
Based on a short story by Anton Chekhov about a musician and a princess who lose their clothes while swimming in a river and must both sneak back to the castle in the buff, where the princess is to be married.

FAWLTY TOWERS (1975/1979)
Distributed by CBS/Fox Video (1986), 3719 (ISBN 8616-23719-3), 90 minutes; includes "A Touch of Class," "The Hotel Inspectors," and "The Germans."

FAWLTY TOWERS (1975/1979)
Distributed by CBS/Fox Video (1986), 3720 (ISBN 8616-23720-3), 98 minutes; video includes "The Builders," "The Wedding Party," and "The Psychiatrist."

FAWLTY TOWERS (1975/1979)
Distributed by CBS/Fox Video (1986), 3721 (ISBN 8616-23721-3), 90 minutes; includes "Gourmet Night," "Waldorf Salad," and "The Kipper and the Corpse."

FAWLTY TOWERS (1979)
Distributed by CBS/Fox Video (1986), 3722 (ISBN 8616-23722-3), 94 minutes; includes "Communication Problems," "The Anniversary," and "Basil the Rat."

FAWLTY TOWERS: THE COMPLETE SET (1975/1979)
Distributed by CBS/Fox Video (1992), 5714 (ISBN 0-7939-5714-1); a boxed set that includes all twelve episodes listed above on four videotapes.
Laserdisc boxed set is distributed by CBS/Fox Video (1993), 5714-80, 368 minutes, includes all twelve episodes on four discs.

RIPPING YARNS (1976/79) CBS/Fox Video 3754 (ISBN 1816-23754-3), 90 minutes: "Tomkinson's School days," "Escape from Stalag Luft 112B," and "Golden Gordon."

MORE RIPPING YARNS (1976/79) CBS/Fox Video 3755 (ISBN 8616-23755-3), 90 minutes: "The Testing of Eric Olthwaite," "Whinfrey's Last Case," and "Curse of the Claw."

EVEN MORE RIPPING YARNS (1976/79) CBS/Fox Video 3756 (ISBN 8616-23756-3), 90 minutes: "Roger of the Raj," "Murder at Moorstones Manor," and "Across the Andes by Frog."

SATURDAY NIGHT LIVE, VOL.1 (1976) Warner Home Video 209030, 67 minutes
 Eric Idle hosts on Oct. 2, 1976, with the Rutles, Killer Bees, Designer Babies, and Dragnet

JABBERWOCKY (1977) Distributed by RCA Columbia Pictures Home Video, VCF 3116E, 104 minutes
 Terry Gilliam's non-Python directing debut, starring Michael Palin, with a guest appearance by Terry Jones.

THE STRANGE CASE OF THE END OF CIVILIZATION AS WE KNOW IT (1977) Shearwater Films, distributed by White Star, WSV 1663 (ISBN 56127-663-4), 55 minutes
 TV film co-written by John Cleese in which Cleese plays the inept grandson of Sherlock Homes and Connie Booth is the granddaughter of Moriarty, with Arthur Lowe as Watson.

THE ODD JOB (1978) Columbia Pictures, distributed by Vestron Video (1984), VA 4120, 86 minutes
 Graham Chapman produced, co-wrote, and stars as an English gentleman who hires an odd-job man to help him commit suicide after his wife leaves him.

THE RUTLES: ALL YOU NEED IS CASH (1978) Rhino Home Video, RE 2234 (ISBN 1-56605-259-9)/Pacific Arts-Broadway Video PAVR 540
 The classic Beatle-parody TV film, conceived, written by and co-starring Eric Idle with music by Neil Innes, featuring guest appearances and cameos by numerous stars, including Michael Palin and George Harrison.

SATURDAY NIGHT LIVE VOL. 2 (1978/79) Warner Home Video 29036. 110 minutes
 Eric Idle hosts the shows on Dec. 9, 1978 and Oct. 20, 1979, with the Tunisian monologue, Madrigal Quartet, Prince Charles, "What Do You . . . ," Candy Slice, and Shoe Salesman.

THE SECRET POLICEMAN'S BALL (1979) Distributed by Columbia Tristar Home Video/Sony Music Operations. (U.K.), CVR 16920, 92 minutes
 The Amnesty International concert starring John Cleese, Michael Palin, Terry Jones, and many others.

DR. WHO: CITY OF DEATH (1980/1981) Distributed by Fox Video, 8102 (ISBN 0-7939-8102-6), 100 minutes
 Tom Baker stars, while John Cleese makes a brief cameo appearance with Eleanor Bron as a critic in an art gallery where the TARDIS has materialized.

GREAT RAILWAY JOURNEYS OF THE WORLD: CONFESSIONS OF A TRAINSPOTTER (1980) Public Media Video/BBC Enterprise, RAI 03, 59 minutes (also from BBC Video, BBCV 5223)
 Michael Palin travels from Euston Station to Kyle of Lochalsh, Scotland in the first of what would grow to be several travelogues. Originally aired Nov. 27, 1980, on BBC-2, as the fourth of seven shows.

THE TAMING OF THE SHREW (1980) Distributed by Time-Life Video/Ambrose Video Publishing (U.S.), 127 minutes
 John Cleese stars as Petruchio in this Shakespearean presentation aired in 1980 on BBC-2's "BBC Television Shakespeare" series and in 1981 on PBS's "The Shakespeare Plays."

THE GREAT MUPPET CAPER (1981) Universal Pictures, distributed by CBS/Fox Video, Catalog No. 9035/Distributed by Jim Henson Video, 1603 (ISBN 1-55890-603-7), 98 minutes
 John Cleese has a cameo as an upper-class English gentleman whose house is appropriated by Miss Piggy to impress Kermit.

TIME BANDITS (1981) Distributed by Thorn EMI-Paramount Video 2310, 116 minutes
    Laserdisc version is letterboxed: distributed by Paramount on laserdisc (1995), LV 2310-WS
    Terry Gilliam directs John Cleese, Michael Palin, Sean Connery and an all-star cast in this fantasy adventure-comedy. A Criterion deluxe laserdisc with commentary by Terry Gilliam is scheduled for release in 1998.

WHOOPS APOCALYPSE (1981) Distributed by London Weekend Television / Pacific Arts Video Records (1983), PAVR 541, 137 minutes/Distributed by Edde Entertainment (1992) ED0210, 121 minutes
    John Cleese stars as Lacrobat, a terrorist, in this six-part comedy about World War III, which premiered March 1982 on London Weekend Television. Cleese has no connection with the 1986 film version of "Whoops Apocalypse" with Peter Cook and Loretta Switt.

FAERIE TALE THEATRE: THE TALE OF THE FROG PRINCE (1982) Platypus Productions, distributed by CBS/Fox-Playhouse Video, 6372 (ISBN 8616-26372-3), 53 minutes
    Eric Idle wrote, directed, and narrated the fairy tale, which stars Robin Williams and Teri Garr.

THE MISSIONARY (1982) Handmade Films/Columbia Pictures, distributed by Thorn EMI Video, TVB 1605/Handmade Films/Columbia Pictures, distributed by Paramount Home Video (1992), PAR 15100 (ISBN 0-7921-2554-1) 86 minutes
    Michael Palin wrote and stars as the Reverend Charles Fortescue, who returns from missionary work in Africa and is assigned to help "fallen women" in 1906 London.

PRIVATES ON PARADE (1982) Handmade Films, distributed by HBO Video, TVF 1628/distributed by Paramount Home Video (1992), PAR 12997 (ISBN 0-7921-2558-4), 93 minutes
    John Cleese stars as "Major Giles Flack," head of a British Song and Dance Unit, Southeast Asia just after World War II, in this comedy-drama.

THE SECRET POLICEMAN'S OTHER BALL (1982) Miramax Films, distributed by MGM/UA Home Video /Miramax Films, MV800175, 101 minutes
    Graham Chapman, John Cleese, Terry Jones, and Michael Palin are featured in the highlights from the first two Secret Policeman Amnesty International shows.

YELLOWBEARD (1983) Distributed by Video Treasures, SV 9138, 97 minutes; distributed by Orion Home Video (1996), 8304 (ISBN 1-56255-247-3), 97 minutes
    Pirate spoof is co-written, co-produced and stars Graham Chapman, also stars John Cleese as "Blind Pew," and Eric Idle as "Commander Clement," along with a host of comedy all-stars in the story of Yellowbeard, who escapes from prison and goes searching for his buried treasure.

THE SECRET POLICEMAN'S PRIVATE PARTS (1984) Distributed by Miramax Films/Media Home Entertainment, M295, 77 minutes
    Highlights from the first four Amnesty International benefits, featuring Graham Chapman, John Cleese, Terry Gilliam, Terry Jones, and Michael Palin, as well as Carol Cleveland, Neil Innes, and Connie Booth.

BRAZIL (U.S. version) (1985) Universal, distributed by MCA Home Video 80171 (ISBN 47897-80171) 131 minutes
BRAZIL (U.K. version) (1985) British version has seven minutes of scenes not in the U.S. version, including Sam and his mother entering the restaurant, Sam and Jill's arrest, and Sam's arrest and trial in the Ministry, as well as a slightly different ending. Universal, distributed by Parkfield Entertainment (U.K.), PES 38029, 137 minutes

BRAZIL: THE CRITERION COLLECTION (1985) MCA/Universal, distributed by the Voyager Company (1996), CC 1348L.

Five-disc set with complete 142-minute U.S. release plus seven hours of supplemental material; including an analog track by Terry Gilliam, a one-hour documentary, storyboards and designs, detailing of script development, over 2,000 stills, the 94-minute studio cut with analog track.

FAERIE TALE THEATRE: THE PIED PIPER OF HAMELIN (1985) Platypus Productions, distributed by CBS/Fox-Playhouse Video, 6792 (ISBN 8616-26792-3), 47 minutes

Eric Idle stars as the Pied Piper.

NATIONAL LAMPOON'S EUROPEAN VACATION (1985) Warner Brothers, released by Warner Home Video, 11521 (ISBN 0-7907-0547-8), 94 minutes.

Eric Idle is the Bicycle Man who has several unfortunate encounters with the Griswalds.

A PRIVATE FUNCTION (1985) Island Alive/Handmade Films, distributed by Thorn EMI HBO Video (1985), TVA 3010/distributed by Paramount Home Video (1992), PAR 12998, 93 minutes

Michael Palin stars in this Alan Bennett story of a meek chiropodist who steals a pig during the height of rationing in postwar Britain. Maggie Smith co-stars.

SILVERADO (1985) Columbia Pictures, distributed by RCA-Columbia Home Video, 60567 (ISBN 0-8001-0969-4), 132 minutes

Criterion Collection Laserdisc version features a letterboxed version of the film on three discs, including trailers and extra scenes: Columbia Pictures, distributed by the Voyager Company (1992), "The Criterion Collection," CC 1228L. Also available in a two-disc version: Columbia Pictures, distributed by The Voyager Company (1992), "The Criterion Collection," CC 1229L.

John Cleese is featured as the sheriff of Turley, a small western town in this all-star Lawrence Kasdan film.

SPIES LIKE US (1985) Warner Brothers, distributed by Warner Home Video 11533, 109 minutes

Laserdisc: Warner Brothers, distributed by Warner Home Video/Laser Videodisc 40171, 109 minutes

Terry Gilliam is Dr. Imhaus, a German doctor in Afghanistan, in this brief cameo with Dan Ackroyd and Chevy Chase.

CLOCKWISE (1986) Universal Pictures, distributed by Cannon—Thorn EMI Screen Entertainment, TVA 9962/Lumiere Pictures/Republic Pictures (1994), VHS 0729 (ISBN 0-7820-0289-7), 96 minutes

Laserdisc distributed by HBO Video/Weintraub Entertainment Group ID 8003HB

John Cleese stars as "Brian Stimpson," a headmaster obsessed with efficiency who must travel to a conference.

LABYRINTH (1986) Tri-Star Pictures/Henson Associates/Lucasfilm, distributed by Embassy Home Entertainment, 7666 (ISBN 1-55847-0107) 101 minutes

Fantasy scripted by Terry Jones.

INSIDE THE LABYRINTH (1986) Embassy Home Entertainment 7675, 57 minutes

This making of *Labyrinth* video includes an interview with Terry Jones.

TRANSFORMERS: THE MOVIE (1986) de Laurentis Entertainment Group, distributed by MCA Distribution Corporation, VFHE-26561 (ISBN 1-55658-106-8), 86 minutes

Eric is the voice of "Wreck Gar," leader of planet of junked robots with whom the Transformers seek refuge.

BRANCHLINE RAILWAY (1987) BBC Enterprises, distributed by Public Media Video (U.S.) BRA 01, 47 minutes

Michael introduces historic railroad footage from the BBC: "Branchline Railway," and newsreel sequences—"Britannia Under Her Own Steam" and "Atlanic Coast Express."

EAST OF THE MOON (1987) released by Virgin Video, VVC 533

Kids video based on "Fairy Tales" with four stories: "The Island of the Purple Fruit," "Some Day," "Boodle-Dum-Dee," and "The Fly-By-Night."

EAST OF THE MOON (1987) released by Virgin Video, VVC 534

Kids video based on "Fairy Tales" with four stories: "An Old-Fashioned Day in the Country," "Think Before You Speak," "The Witch and the Rainbow Cat," and "The Sea Tiger."

THE MIKADO (1987) Distributed by HBO Video/Thames Collection (1990), VHS 0339 (ISBN 1-55983-252-5), 131 minutes

Eric Idle is Ko-Ko, the Lord High Executioner; aired on PBS's Great Performances on Oct. 28, 1988, and on ITV in Britain on Dec. 30, 1987.

PERSONAL SERVICES (1987) Vestron Pictures—Zenith Productions, distributed by Vestron Video, 5221 (ISBN 0-8051-0436-4) 104 minutes

Sex comedy based on a true story, and directed by Terry Jones.

THE SECRET POLICEMAN'S THIRD BALL (1987) Amnesty International, distributed by Columbia Tristar Home Video/Sony Music Operations (U.K.), CVR21431, 92 minutes

John Cleese appears briefly in a sketch with Stephen Fry and Hugh Laurie in which he accepts the "Silver Dick" award, spoofing his refusal to participate in that year's Amnesty International benefit.

CONSUMING PASSIONS (1988) Samuel Golden Company/Euston Films, distributed by Virgin Vision, 70070 (ISBN 2089-70070-3), 98 minutes

Based on the play *Secrets* by Terry Jones and Michael Palin.

A FISH CALLED WANDA (1988) Prominent Features, distributed MGM/UA Home Video (1993), M201247 (ISBN 0-7928-1759-1)/Distributed by CBS/Fox Video, 4752, 108 minutes

Co-written by and starring John Cleese, with Michael Palin, Jamie Lee Curtis, and Kevin Kline (who won an Oscar for Best Supporting Actor) in this comedy about a bungled jewel heist.

ADVENTURES OF BARON MUNCHAUSEN (1989) Columbia Pictures, distributed by RCA-Columbia Home Video 50153 (ISBN 43396-50153) 126 minutes
ADVENTURES OF BARON MUNCHAUSEN: THE CRITERION COLLECTION (1989) Columbia Pictures, distributed by the Voyager Company (1992), CC 1281L (ISBN 1-55940-223-7) 126 minutes

Three-disc set with analog track by Terry Gilliam, four deleted sequences, SFX compositing, trailers, production sketches and materials, storyboards, interviews, and notes on the historical Munchausen.

AROUND THE WORLD IN 80 DAYS (OUTWARD BOUND) 1989 The first half of Michael Palin's surface journey around the globe. BBC Enterprises, distributed by Public Media Videos (1990) ARO 01, ISBN 0-7800-0436-1 Two tapes, 164 minutes
AROUND THE WORLD IN 80 DAYS (HOMEWARD BOUND) 1989 The second half of Michael Palin's surface journey around the globe. BBC Enterprises, distributed by Public Media Videos (1990) ARO 02, ISBN 0-7800-0437-X Two tapes, 172 minutes

AROUND THE WORLD IN 80 DAYS (Complete on two cassettes) (1989) Harmony Gold Productions, distributed by Best Film and Video, 918 (ISBN 1-56480-224-8), 267 minutes. Released in two parts in Britain: Part 1 distributed by Guild Home Video 8619, 139 minutes; Part 2 distributed by Guild Home Video 8620, 127 minutes

 The U.S. video release of the NBC-TV miniseries with Eric Idle as Passepartout and Timothy Dalton as Phineas Fogg, originally aired April 16, 17, and 18, 1989.

THE BIG PICTURE (1989) Columbia Pictures / Aspen Film Society, distributed by RCA-Columbia Home Video, 50263, 100 minutes

 John Cleese makes a cameo appearance as a bartender in a black-and-white sequence shot like a scene from "It's a Wonderful Life," and later appears in a quick real-life color scene.

ERIK THE VIKING (1989) Orion Pictures / John Goldstone—Prominent Features, distributed by Orion Video, 8748 (ISBN 23568-08748), 104 minutes

 Written, directed by and costarring Terry Jones. Tim Robbins plays the title role, and John Cleese appears as "Halfdan the Black."

HYSTERIA 2—THE SECOND COMING (1989) Tiger Television Productions, distributed by Palace Video/Parkfield Entertainment (U.K.), PVC 2173 A, 80 minutes

 AIDS benefit presented live at the Sadlers Wells Theatre on September 18, 1989, featuring John Cleese in a segment with Tina Turner, as well as Hugh Laurie, Stephen Fry, Rowan Atkinson, French and Saunders, and Lenny Henry. Graham Chapman had originally committed to appear but had to cancel due to ill health.

JOHN CLEESE'S FIRST FAREWELL PERFORMANCE—THE MAKING OF "A FISH CALLED WANDA" (1989) Park Field Entertainment/Kentel Productions (U.K.), distributed by MGM/United Artists Home Video, SMV 11684, 49 minutes

 Outtakes, clips and interviews from *Wanda,* aired October 18, 1988 on BBC-1.

THE SECRET POLICEMAN'S BIGGEST BALL (1989) ITV, distributed by Columbia Tristar Home Video/Sony Music Operations (U.K.), CVR16921, 92 minutes

 The fourth Secret Policeman's Ball Amnesty International benefit features John Cleese and Michael Palin in a twist on the Parrot Sketch.

BULLSEYE! (1990) Distributed by Columbia Tristar Home Video (1991), COL 77153 (ISBN 0-8001-0383-1), 95 minutes

 John Cleese makes a cameo appearance in this comedy starring Roger Moore and Michael Caine as two scientists pursued by two lookalike con men.

NUNS ON THE RUN (1990) 20th Century–Fox/Handmade Films, distributed by CBS/Fox Video 1830 (ISBN 0-7039-1830-8) 88 minutes

 Eric Idle and Robbie Coltrane star as they hide in a convent to escape angry mobsters.

TOO MUCH SUN (1990) Distributed by RCA/Columbia Tristar Home Video, COL 90823, (ISBN 0-8001-0627-X), 98 minutes

 Laserdisc release on RCA/Columbia/Tri-Star 90826 (ISBN 0-8001-0725-X)

 Eric Idle stars with Robert Downey Sr. and Robert Downey Jr.

AMERICAN FRIENDS (1991) Millenium/Mayday/Prominent Features, an MCEG Virgin Vision Release, distributed by Vidmark Entertainment and Facets Multimedia VM 5719 (ISBN 31398-5719-3), 95 minutes

Written by and starring Michael Palin as Reverend Francis Ashby, an Oxford college professor who falls in love with a young American woman while on holiday in Switzerland. With Connie Booth and Trini Alvarado.

AN AMERICAN TAIL 2: FIEVEL GOES WEST (1991) Universal Pictures / Amblin Entertainment, distributed by MCA Universal Home Video, (ISBN 1-5588-0966-X), 75 minutes
  John Cleese is the voice of Cat R. Wall, a cat who tricks the mice in New York into moving out West.

THE FISHER KING (1991) Tri-Star Pictures, distributed by Columbia Tri-Star Home Video 70613 (ISBN 0-8001-0805-1), 137 minutes
THE FISHER KING: THE CRITERION COLLECTION (1991) Tri-Star Pictures, distributed by Voyager Company (1992), CC 1288L (ISBN 1-55940-191-5), 137 minutes.
  This two-disc set with analog track by Terry Gilliam includes deleted scenes, trailers, scene analyses, costume tests, and an analog track with a running commentary by the director.

G.B.H. (1991) GBH Films Production/Channel Four TV, distributed by Vision Video (U.K.) VVD 854, 255 minutes
  Michael Palin plays headmaster Jim Nelson, who crosses paths with politically ambitious Michael Murray. Episodes 1–3 "It Couldn't Happen Here," "Only Here on a Message," "Send a Message to Michael?"

G.B.H. (1991) GBH Films Production/Channel Four TV, distributed by Vision Video (U.K.) VVD 855, 311 minutes
  Episodes 4–7 "Message Sent," "Message Received," "Message Understood," "Over and Out"

JACK AND THE BEANSTALK (1991) Rabbit Ears Productions/UNI Distribution Company REV 10260, 30 minutes
  Michael Palin reads the fairy tale, with music by Dave Stewart.

IRON MAIDEN: FROM THERE TO ETERNITY (1992) Sony Music Video (SMV) Enterprises, 19V-49132 (ISBN 1-56406-132-9), 95 minutes
  This collection of Iron Maiden music videos features Graham Chapman as an overly strict schoolmaster who has hallucinations in "Can I Play with Madness."

MOM AND DAD SAVE THE WORLD (1992) Warner Brothers, Warner Brothers HBO Video, 90743 (ISBN 0-7831-0114-7) 88 minutes
  Eric Idle is featured in this SF comedy, which stars Teri Garr, Jeffrey Jones, and Jon Lovitz.

POLE TO POLE (1992) BBC/Prominent Features, distributed by A&E Home Video, AAE-10800 (ISBN 1-56501-133-3)
  Also available separately in four volumes:
Vol. 1 AAE-10801 ISBN 1-56501-134-1 Includes "Cold Start" and "Russian Steps"
Vol. 2 AAE-10802 ISBN 1-56501-135-X Includes "Mediterranean Maze" and "Shifting Sands"
Vol. 3 AAE-10803 ISBN 1-56501-136-8 Includes "Crossing the Line" and "Planes and Boats and Trains"
Vol. 4 AAE-10804 ISBN 1-56501-137-6 Includes "Evil Shadow" and "Bitter End"

DID I EVER TELL YOU HOW LUCKY YOU ARE¿ (1993) Distributed by Random House Home Video, ISBN 0-679-84627-1, 30 minutes
  John Cleese reads this Dr. Seuss story, with animated pictures from the book.

LEON THE PIG FARMER (1993) Orion Home Video & Fox Lorber Home Video OHV 1132V (ISBN 1-879482-99-1) 98 minutes

Eric Idle is executive producer of this story of a young Jewish man who finds he is actually the son of a Yorkshire pig farmer. Connie Booth appears as Yvonne Chadwick, wife of a pig farmer.

MISSING PIECES (1993) The Rank Organization/Aaron Russo Entertainment, distributed by Rank Film Distributors (U.K.) VC 3046, 89 minutes

Eric Idle stars as aspiring novelist Wendel Murphy, who must solve a mysterious riddle to receive an inheritance from his Chinese foster father. Robert Wuhl co-stars.

THE SECRET POLICEMAN'S EARLY BITS (1993) Distributed by Columbia Tristar Home Video/Sony Music Operations (U.K.) CVR 21432, 78 minutes

Combines the first two Amnesty International benefits, "A Poke in the Eye with a Sharp Stick" (1976) and "Mermaid Frolics" (1977); Terry Jones directed the latter. Most of the Pythons appear.

SPLITTING HEIRS (1993) Universal Pictures/Prominent Features, MCA Universal Home Video, 81494 (ISBN 0-7832-0742-5), 87 minutes

Laserdisc is letterboxed and distributed by MCA Universal Home Video (1993) 41672 (ISBN 0-7832-0746-8)

Written by and starring Eric Idle as the son of the Duke of Bournemouth who is accidentally abandoned as an infant and raised by a poor Pakistani family. John Cleese plays the lawyer who tries to kill the Duke's only remaining children.

TRACY ULLMAN: A CLASS ACT (1993) Witzend Productions, distributed by VCI Distribution Limited (U.K.) VC 6295, 42 minutes

Featuring four sketches with Michael Palin.

CRUSADES (1994) Arts & Entertainment Home Video, AAE-13400 (ISBN 1-56501-505-3) 200 minutes

A boxed set of all four volumes, also available individually:

Vol. 1: Pilgrims in Arms, 1995, Arts & Entertainment Home Video, AAE-13401 (ISBN 1-56501-506-1) 50 minutes
Vol. 2: Jerusalem, 1995, Arts & Entertainment Home Video, AAE-13402 (ISBN 1-56501-507-X) 50 minutes
Vol. 3: Jihad, 1995, Arts & Entertainment Home Video, AAE-13403 (ISBN 1-56501-508-8) 55 minutes
Vol. 4: Destruction, 1995, Arts & Entertainment Home Video, AAE-13404 (ISBN 1-56501-509-6) 55 minutes

GREAT RAILWAY JOURNEYS (1994) complete series of 6 videos, BBC Television, distributed by Atlas Video 33498 (ISBN 1-56938-058-9) 318 minutes
MICHAEL PALIN'S GREAT RAILWAY JOURNEY: FROM DERRY TO KERRY (offered individually or as one of the set above) BBC Television, distributed by Acorn Media, ISBN 1-56938-041-4, 57 minutes; or distributed by BBC Video, BBCV 5223, 54 minutes 1993

Michael Palin retraces his great-grandmother's emigration route across Ireland by train.

THE JUNGLE BOOK (1994) Walt Disney Pictures, distributed by Walt Disney Home Video (1995) 4604 (ISBN 0-7888-0177-5), 111 minutes

Laserdisc version is in letterbox format: Walt Disney Pictures, distributed by Walt Disney Home Video (1995) 4604 AS

John Cleese plays Mowgli's tutor in this live-action Disney version of Rudyard Kipling's classic.

MARY SHELLEY'S FRANKENSTEIN (1994) Columbia/Tri-Star, distributed by Columbia/Tri-Star Home Video (1995) 78713 (ISBN 0-8001-3594-6), 123 minutes
   Laserdisc version is letterboxed: Columbia/Tri-Star, distributed by Columbia/Tri-Star Home Video (1995) 78716 (ISBN 0-8001-7747-9), 123 minutes
   John Cleese plays Dr. Waldman, Victor Frankenstein's teacher.

ONE FOOT IN THE GRAVE: WHO WILL BUY? (1994) BBC Television, distributed by CBS/Fox Video 5966, 89 minutes.

ONE FOOT IN THE GRAVE: IN LUTON AIRPORT, NO ONE CAN HEAR YOU SCREAM (1994) BBC Television, distributed by CBS/Fox Video 5965, 89 minutes
   Eric Idle wrote and performed the theme song for the series; each tape features 3 episodes of the BBC comedy series (the complete series is available on video in Britain, these are the only two in U.S. video release at present).

THE SWAN PRINCESS (1994) Nest Entertainment, Inc., distributed by Turner Home Entertainment 8021 (ISBN 0-7806-0793-7), 90 minutes
   John Cleese performs the voice of a French frog named Jean-Bob in this animated feature.

THE TRUE STORY OF FRANKENSTEIN (1994) A&E Television Networks, distributed by A&E Home Video (1994) AAE-10065 (ISBN 1-56501-456-1), 100 minutes
   A documentary on the book and subsequent film versions of the story, including interviews with John Cleese, Robert DeNiro, Kenneth Branagh, and more.

THE YOUNG ONES: BAMBI, NASTY, TIME (1994) BBC Video, BBCV 4426 (U.K.) 90 minutes
   Featuring three episodes of the comedy series; Terry Jones is a vicar in the "Nasty" show.

CASPER THE FRIENDLY GHOST (1995) Universal Pictures/Amblin Entertainment, distributed by MCA/Universal Home Video, 82316 (ISBN 0-7832-1588-6) 101 minutes
   Eric stars as Dibs, boyfriend of Carrigan Crittendon, owner of the haunted Whipstaff Manor.

12 MONKEYS (1995) Universal, distributed by MCA/Universal Home Video 82785 (ISBN 0-7832-2172-X), 130 minutes
12 MONKEYS (1995) MCA/Universal 42923 Boxed laserdisc set includes an analog track with Terry Gilliam's running commentary and a letterboxed version of the film, as well as a short "making of" film in this three-disc set.
   Available in regular and widescreen editions. This fantasy/adventure starring Bruce Willis, Madeline Stowe, and Brad Pitt won a Best Supporting Actor nomination for Pitt.

WIND IN THE WILLOWS (1996) TVC London, distributed by Good Times Home Video (1996), 05-77261 (ISBN 1-55511-892-5) 74 minutes
   Animated feature, with Michael Palin as the voice of Ratty.

THE WILLOWS IN WINTER (1997) TVC London, distributed by Good Times Home Video 05-77289 (ISBN 0-7662-0029-9), 74 minutes
   Followup to the animated feature, with Michael Palin as the voice of Ratty.

FIERCE CREATURES (1997) MCI Universal Home Video 82824 (ISBN 0-7832-2206-8) videocassette; MCI Universal Home Video 43228 (ISBN 0-7832-2207-6) on laserdisc 94 minutes

John Cleese wrote, produced and starred in this follow-up to *A Fish Called Wanda*, reuniting with Michael Palin, Kevin Kline, and Jamie Lee Curtis.

PIRATES (1997)
Eric Idle scripted and co-stars with Leslie Nielsen in this short comedy, filmed exclusively for Seaworld of Ohio.

GEORGE OF THE JUNGLE (1997) Buena Vista Home Video 11774 (ISBN 0-7888-0980-6) 92 minutes.
John Cleese provides the voice of George's friend Ape, and even sings the closing number in this Disney hit.

WIND IN THE WILLOWS (1997)
Written and directed by Terry Jones, starring Steve Coogan as Mole, Eric Idle as Ratty, Jones as Toad, John Cleese as Toad's lawyer, with Nicol Williamson, Antony Sher, Stephen Fry, Nigel Planer, and Michael Palin as the Sun.
Though the film received virtually no U.S. distribution—less than 75 screens—*Premiere* magazine called it the best kids' film of 1997.

BURN, HOLLYWOOD, BURN (AN ALAN SMITHEE FILM) (1998) Hollywood Pictures
Eric Idle stars in the title role of a director who fights back when his film is taken away from him; scripted by Joe Eszterhas.

QUEST FOR CAMELOT (1998) Warner Brothers
Eric Idle is featured as one of the voices of a two-headed dragon (Don Rickles is the other) in this animated feature.

FEAR AND LOATHING IN LAS VEGAS (1998)
Terry Gilliam directs Johnny Depp in this adaptation of the Hunter Thompson book.

THE OUT OF TOWNERS (1998)
John Cleese is featured in this remake, which stars Steve Martin and Goldie Hawn.

ANCIENT INVENTIONS (1998)
A three-part documentary series written and presented by Terry Jones for the Discovery Channel, focusing on inventions involving war, sex, and cities.

YOU'VE GOT MAIL (1998)
Michael Palin has a supporting role in this Tom Hanks–Meg Ryan feature.

LONGITUDE (1998–9) Grenada
Terry Jones wrote this feature, based on the real-life story of the discovery of longitude.

ISN'T SHE GREAT
John Cleese co-stars in this bio-pic starring Bette Middler as Jacqueline Susann.

HEMINGWAY'S TRAVELS
Michael Palin presents this three-part series developed for Ernest Hemingway's centennial year.

THE SEUSSICAL
Eric Idle cowrote the book for the Broadway musical planned on the works of Dr. Seuss.